THE REMINISCENCES OF
Rear Admiral Julian T. Burke, Jr. U.S. Navy (Retired)

INTERVIEWED BY
Paul Stillwell

U.S. Naval Institute • Annapolis, Maryland

Copyright © 2003

Preface

When I was serving in the crew of the tank landing ship Washoe County off the coast of Vietnam in 1967, the commander of Task Force 76 of the Seventh Fleet visited the ship. He was Rear Admiral Julian Burke, and he was the first admiral I had ever met. Nearly 30 years later, a friend of his, Admiral Hal Shear, recommended that I interview Burke to the Naval Institute's oral history collection. It turned out to be a splendid suggestion, because Admiral Burke had a naval career that was both varied and interesting. The account is especially useful because he was willing to be candid—even blunt at times—in describing his memories of service.

Those who have long known Admiral Burke describe him as both a true gentleman and a demanding boss. He grew up in the genteel Southern tradition, accustomed to treating people with respect and dignity. Because of his upbringing at Episcopal High School in Alexandria, Virginia, and at the Naval Academy, Burke gained a highly developed sense of right and wrong. He demanded hard work and excellence from those with whom he served—and of himself. These traits were reinforced when he served with Commander Glynn Donaho, skipper of the submarine Flying Fish in World War II. Donaho was a by-the-book naval officer but without the warmth of Burke. Burke expected those under his commands to do their jobs capably and, above all, to have a strong sense of integrity. When subordinates failed to measure up, he gave them low marks and, in some cases, removed them from their jobs. As he put it several times, he didn't believe in carrying weak performers.

Admiral Burke is proud of the number of commands he held and particularly their variety: two submarines, the President's yacht, a destroyer, a submarine division, an attack transport, an amphibious squadron, an amphibious group, U.S. Naval Forces Japan, and Service Force Atlantic Fleet. He also put in useful tours ashore, notably in the Bureau of Naval Personnel, on the staff of Commander in Chief Atlantic Fleet, as executive officer of Bancroft Hall at the Naval Academy, reorganizing the Naval Reserve to make it functional, on the OpNav staff, and as Commandant of the Sixth Naval District. After his retirement from active duty, he helped many members of the Navy and

Marine Corps by working as vice president of the Navy Relief Society. During the many years of his career, the two jobs that give him the greatest satisfaction in retrospect were supervising midshipmen at the Naval Academy and behind-the-scenes negotiations that led to an aircraft carrier task group being permanently homeported in Yokosuka, Japan.

In the volume that follows, Admiral Burke frequently mentions his mother and the positive influence she exerted on his life. He talks often of his wife Betty as well. He jokes that theirs was almost an arranged marriage. It is also one with a great deal of mutual affection, as demonstrated by how often he refers to Betty Burke in telling the story of his own life.

George Van, a former naval officer, did the initial transcription of the interview tapes. Both Admiral Burke and I have edited the transcript in the interests of accuracy, smoothness, and clarity. For the sake of continuity, some material has been moved to different interviews from that in which it originally appeared. Duplicated material has been deleted. In addition, I have inserted footnotes to provide further information for readers who use the volume.

Ms. Ann Hassinger of the Naval Institute's history division has made a significant contribution through her diligence in the overall process of printing, proofreading, and overseeing the binding of the completed volumes.

Finally, the Naval Institute expresses its gratitude to the McMullen Family Foundation of Secaucus, New Jersey, for its generous financial support to facilitate completion of this memoir. John J. McMullen and Julian Burke were classmates in the Naval Academy's class of 1940.

Paul Stillwell
Director, History Division
U.S. Naval Institute
March 2003

JULIAN THOMPSON BURKE
REAR ADMIRAL, U.S. NAVY (RETIRED)

Julian Thompson Burke, Jr., was been born in Alexandria, Virginia, on 24 April 1918, son of Julian T. Burke and Alice Anderton Burke. He attended Episcopal High School in Alexandria before entering the U.S. Naval Academy, Annapolis, Maryland, as a midshipman from his native state. Graduated and commissioned ensign on 6 June 1940, he subsequently advanced to the rank of rear admiral, to date from 1 July 1967.

After graduation in June 1940, he was assigned to the USS West Virginia (BB-48) and in April 1941 reported on board the USS North Carolina (BB-55). Ordered to the Submarine School, New London, Connecticut, he had submarine training from April to July 1943, after which he served as torpedo and executive officer of the USS Flying Fish (SS-229). For service on board that submarine, he was awarded the Bronze Star with combat V and the Silver Star Medal.

From July 1945 to May 1946 he commanded the USS Guardfish (SS-217), which was assigned to New Orleans, Louisiana, for the 1945 Navy Day celebration, the first following the cessation of hostilities. He was detached from that submarine in May 1946 and in July 1946 reported as engineer officer of the USS Howard W. Gilmore (AS-16). In December 1946 he was assigned to the Enlisted Personnel Division (Assignments) of the Bureau of Naval Personnel, Navy Department, Washington, D.C.

He reported in July 1949 as executive officer of the USS Dogfish (SS-350) and in June 1950 assumed command of the USS Sablefish (SS-303). In March 1952 he joined the USS Williamsburg (AGC-369), to serve as executive officer, later commanding officer, until July 1953. In October of that year he assumed command of the USS Harold J. Ellison (DD-864). Detached from that destroyer in July 1955, he next had duty as assistant chief of staff to the Commander in Chief Atlantic Fleet.

From August 1957 to June 1958 he attended the Naval War College, Newport, Rhode Island, after which he commanded Submarine Division 63. In August 1960 he reported as executive officer of Bancroft Hall at the Naval Academy, where he remained until July 1963. He then assumed command of the USS Fremont (APA-44), and in August 1964 was detached for duty as Commander Amphibious Squadron Six.

In August 1965 he became head of the Navy Plans Branch, Office of the Chief of Naval Operations. In that capacity, he was awarded the Navy Commendation Medal. He assumed command of Amphibious Group Three in June 1966 and in April 1967 transferred to command of Amphibious Group One/Commander Task Force 76. For Vietnam War operations in that billet he received the Legion of Merit with combat V.

In January 1968 Rear Admiral Burke reported as Assistant Deputy Chief of Naval Operations (Naval Reserve) and for that duty was awarded a gold star in lieu of a second Legion of Merit. In August 1970 he became Commander U.S. Naval Forces Japan; he was awarded a Distinguished Service Medal for his service in Japan. In January 1973 he was detached and reported for duty as Commander Service Force, U.S. Atlantic Fleet. From December 1974 until June 1976 he served as Commandant of the Sixth Naval District, with headquarters at Charleston, South Carolina. He officially retired from active duty on 1 July 1976 and was awarded a Distinguished Service Medal for his achievements.

In addition to the two awards of the Distinguished Service Medal; the Legion of Merit with gold star and combat V; the Bronze Star with combat V and gold star; and Meritorious Unit Commendation with gold star, Rear Admiral Burke earned the American Defense Service Medal; American Campaign Medal; Asiatic-Pacific Campaign Medal with six stars; the World War II Victory Medal; Navy Occupation Service Medal, Europe clasp; National Defense Service Medal with bronze star; Armed Forces Expeditionary Medal (Dominican Republic); and the Vietnam Service Medal with two bronze stars. He also has the Republic of Vietnam Campaign Medal with device and the National Order of Vietnam, First Class.

Married to the former Betty Stuart of New Orleans, he has three children: Elizabeth Anderton "Tina" Burke, Julian T Burke III, and Sally Stuart Burke Brierre. Their second son, Charles Stuart Sanders Burke, died in 1967.

Deed of Gift

The U.S. Naval Institute is hereby authorized to make available to individuals, libraries, and other repositories of its choosing the tapes and/or transcripts of 12 oral history interviews concerning the life and naval career of the undersigned. The Naval Institute may also, at its discretion, use the material in electronic/digital format, including posting on the Internet. The interviews were recorded on 29 January 1997, 5 March 1997, 14 March 1997, 20 March 1997, 16 April 1997, 21 April 1997, 30 April 1997, 10 February 1998, 26 February 1998, 17 March 1998, 25 March 1998, and 3 June 1998, in collaboration with Paul Stillwell for the U.S. Naval Institute.

The undersigned does hereby release and assign to the U.S. Naval Institute the rights and title to these interviews, with the exception that the undersigned retains the right to use the material for his own purposes, as he sees fit. The copyright in both the oral and transcribed versions shall be the sole property of the U.S. Naval Institute. The tape recordings of the interviews are and will remain the property of the U.S. Naval Institute.

Signed and sealed this 16th day of September 2000.

Julian T. Burke, Jr.
Rear Admiral, U.S. Navy (Retired)

Interview Number 1 with Rear Admiral Julian T. Burke, Jr., U.S. Navy (Retired)
Place: Admiral Burke's home in Alexandria, Virginia
Date: Wednesday, 29 January 1997
Interviewer: Paul Stillwell

Paul Stillwell: Well, Admiral, it's great to see you on this bright, sunny morning and to begin hearing the story of your life for the benefit of history. I wonder if you could start out, please, talking about your origins here in the Alexandria area and some of your memories of your parents and childhood?

Admiral Burke: I came from Alexandria. I was born in 1918, and I didn't realize it at the time, of course, but my family's one of the old families here. My great-grandfather came into Alexandria probably around 1840 and married into a family that had been here right from the start of the city. The earliest Alexandria was a very small town. In hindsight, my recollection growing up in the '20s is that it was still suffering from the post-Civil War depression, and people were still very resentful about the Civil War and the Yankees.

Paul Stillwell: How did that resentment manifest itself?

Admiral Burke: Well, it was reflected in the school system. We all hated Yankees. That's just the way it was. Alexandria had been an occupied city, and the family business was Burke & Herbert Bank. My great-grandfather stayed behind and kept the bank protected. His partner, Mr. Herbert, went off with the Confederate Army. More than once Great-grandfather Burke's house was searched, and there was good reason, because he had taken the assets and brought them home. I was told that he had dug them up and put them in his wife's closet.

This was his second wife. His first wife was my great-grandmother. She died in childbirth, and he later married the granddaughter or great-granddaughter of Thomas Jefferson. And, as a result of that connection, she had access to Washington, D.C., where he didn't. Eventually the Washington family deposited the assets from the sale of Mount

Vernon in Burke & Herbert, where they banked.* Mrs. Burke took the money in her carriage under her skirts through the federal lines and deposited it in the Riggs Bank for the duration of the war.

In the teaching of history that I had all the way through high school, it was with a very strong southern bias. The town was segregated. My earliest recollection in Alexandria was in the winter of '21 and '22, when the roof of the Knickerbocker Theater collapsed because of heavy snow. Many were killed. The snow in our yard was taller than my head at age three and a half.

The winter of '21-'22 we were living with my Burke grandmother, who lived a block from the Confederate Monument down there on Washington and Prince Street. In those days, most of the streets in Alexandria were cobblestone. I recall attending the Decoration Day ceremony, the Confederate Memorial Day, at that Confederate Monument. A large segment of town was there. I don't recall how many, but all the Boy and Girl Scout troops were there and the various fraternal organizations. We gathered there, and the heroes that were there were the surviving Confederate veterans. Those gentlemen were my age and younger, right now, and some of them were in their 80s, but some of them were in the mid-70s. But they were the town heroes, and there wasn't any question about it.

Paul Stillwell: Did you talk to any of them?

Admiral Burke: Well, the one that I really remember was Colonel Warfield, later a general. He had been discharged as a buck private and was subsequently promoted by the veterans. His grandson lived across the street here for years until he died. He was a good friend. The Warfields were a prominent family from Alexandria. He had a Warfield's Drugstore on King Street at Pitt. And in those days Alexandria had a family drugstore on every other corner all the way up King Street, and Warfield's was one of the more popular ones where people used to gather.

Probably the first person killed in the Civil War was killed in Alexandria, right across the street from Warfield's Drugstore. It was a man named Jackson. The occupying

---

* Mount Vernon, in northern Virginia, was the estate of George Washington, who served as President of the United States from 1789 to 1797.

forces marched up King Street after they'd come down from Washington on a ship. This hotel across the street had a Confederate flag on it, and the colonel, whose name was Ellsworth, went in there to haul it down. He was accompanied by a couple of enlisted men. Mr. Jackson shot the colonel, and they killed Mr. Jackson. Mr. Jackson is a Confederate hero. The colonel became a Federal national hero.

We had servants. We called them "colored." They were family members. My father and his brothers and sisters were raised by "Mammy." They were her children. She was about four feet ten and tough as nails but loving. The grandchildren of "her children," the children she raised, were not allowed to call her "Mammy." We called her "Nana." She attended my father's funeral during my plebe year at the Naval Academy.* She died a couple of years later, and there's a memorial stone for her in the Burke family plot over here about a half a mile at Ivy Hill Cemetery. We had a split in the family because a couple of ladies that married into the family didn't want to honor a colored person in the plot, and it was a big serious split at that time. People were really upset in the family about it.

Paul Stillwell: Was she in fact buried there?

Admiral Burke: She was not buried there, but the stone is there, and it has "Mammy" on it. Her name was Ann Page Gordon, and she was very close to the ladies, particularly the girls, and my dad. So I still drive by the house, where she and Morella lived. Morella was the family cook after Grandmother died. The family bought them a house where they could retire. That house is still standing on North Henry Street in the 500 block. I go by and deliver Meals on Wheels right next door to it, and it always pings my memory and sentiment.

Paul Stillwell: Interesting how these things tie together.

Admiral Burke: Well, this is a little vignette. Alexandria was a very small town. It was essentially isolated from Washington. We had a streetcar line that went from Washington

---

* Burke's first year as a Naval Academy midshipman was 1936-37. His father died in the autumn of 1936.

to Alexandria, and a spur went down to Mount Vernon. Once an hour a car would go there. Starting about 1924 or '23, the A, B & W bus line was established. The streetcar line came right down King Street, circled at Royal and Fairfax, came around in front of Burke & Herbert Bank, and then went back up King Street to Columbus, thence over to Cameron. In those days you knew who people were. You spoke to them, whether they were black or white. I could walk anywhere at a very young age in Alexandria or ride on a bicycle, which I did frequently, and there was no fear. People sort of looked out for each other.

Paul Stillwell: What do you recall of your parents?

Admiral Burke: Well, my father was the next to youngest of five siblings, and he attended Episcopal High School. When he was finished, he went into the bank, because that's what all the Burkes did. He was much the younger brother of two in the bank. He had another brother who was about three or four years older who ended up as an ophthalmologist in Washington. My father was the key employee in the bank not a partner.

I'm going to talk a lot about the bank, because it's interesting as to what happened. When I was a child, we had four banks on King Street.[*] Burke & Herbert operated on the shake of a hand until 1933, when the national bank crisis occurred. They had to incorporate for the first time, and my father was not taken in as a partner. He was much younger than the partners. He was the key employee. He knew everybody's job, including the three owners. Below him were about six employees, including a janitor. And as a measure of how things have happened, the other three banks in town have disappeared. They've been absorbed. Burke & Herbert is the only one left. It's now the largest independent bank in the state, which reflects the expansion into northern Virginia.

My mother had a sister who had married a naval officer. Mother used to read us the letters Aunt Rose sent from faraway places, including two tours in the Orient. I decided I wanted to travel. And, looking around, the only people in Alexandria who could

---

[*] The main branch of the Burke & Herbert Bank & Trust Company is at the intersection of King and Fairfax streets in Alexandria.

afford to travel in those days were people who had married into the Navy. I decided I wanted to be a rich naval officer instead of a poor banker.

Paul Stillwell: [Laughter] Had your father hoped for you to go into the banking business?

Admiral Burke: No, he encouraged me go in the Navy, and we were fortunate. Our congressman was Judge Howard Smith, who later became the chairman of the Ways and Means Committee.[*]

Paul Stillwell: He had a long career in the House.

Admiral Burke: Yes. He was a family friend, and I had no trouble getting an appointment.

Paul Stillwell: Well, before we get to that, I wonder if you could talk some about your education during your growing-up years.

Admiral Burke: I started off in public school in the second grade. I'd been tutored at home by a cousin, and when I was started off at six years old I was so far ahead as a result of this tutoring, particularly in arithmetic, I was on the third-grade level. So they put me in the second grade; I was big for my age. I started off in the public schools. There was one up there on the grounds of the present Masonic Temple, which was under construction. My parents were not pleased with the public school, so I went to St. Agnes School for two years—third and fourth grade. The school is nearby, about 300 or 400 yards from here. It is an Episcopal day school. Then the Depression caught up with us, so I went back into the public schools for three years.[†] We had no eighth grade in those schools. My seventh grade teacher was Miss Cora Kelly, who was a famous name in Alexandria. She would have made a first class boatswain's mate. She was tough.

---

[*] Howard W. Smith, a Democrat who had been a judge in northern Virginia from 1922 to 1930, served in the U.S. House of Representatives from 4 March 1931 to 3 January 1967.
[†] Following the crash of the New York Stock Exchange in late October 1929, the United States was plunged into the Great Depression, from which it did not recover until the nation geared up for World War II at the beginning of the 1940s. The Depression was marked by high unemployment and many business failures.

Paul Stillwell: And she talked like a boatswain's mate?

Admiral Burke: She had a voice like a cannon, and she spanked people with a paddle and didn't hesitate to. She spanked a couple of my friends for misbehaving. She was tough, and she scared me into making good grades, the best grades I ever made, I was so terrified. I was afraid not to please her. From there I was a day scholar for five years at Episcopal High School. I had an older brother, two and half years older, and my mother used to drive me and my brother up there. Episcopal was primarily a boarding school, and there were about 200 boarders and 20 day students. Practically all the students came from the South—around Virginia, North Carolina, Charleston, Savannah, Atlanta, and Jacksonville.

Being an Episcopal High School boy has always opened gates for me whenever I've been in those communities. The best example I can think of is at the very end of my career I ended up in Charleston, South Carolina, as the base commander, and there were at least a half a dozen Episcopal boys that I had gone to school with, and we again opened our acquaintance and friendship. I'm still on their Christmas card lists and so forth and vice versa, and we are always welcome there. It was an enormous help to me when I was in Charleston on a professional basis.

Paul Stillwell: Were you involved in sports in school?

Admiral Burke: Yes, I played football, baseball, and basketball. I made a letter in football. Because of the fact that I had been pushed ahead in my school and that we had no eighth grade, I started in high school at age 12. Most of the boys I was in the classroom with at Episcopal were at least two years older, and I didn't do well academically. I was struggling all the way. Towards the end of my fifth year, the headmaster told me he thought I ought to forget about going to college. In those days you didn't have to graduate from Episcopal to go to college. You acquired college credits, and I had more than enough to get into the University of Virginia, which was easy in those days, or any southern college. But the headmaster thought it would be best for me not to attend college. I was bound and determined to go to the Naval Academy. In those days the academy had entrance exams, and so I took a year at Bullis.* Much to the surprise of Episcopal High School, I passed and got very good marks in math.

Paul Stillwell: What do you remember about the experience at Bullis?

Admiral Burke: Well, you've got to realize that I came from what you call southern gentry, and for the first time in my life I was exposed on a day-to-day basis with people who were not gentry. I got along fine, and I made good friends with a lot of the people there that are still my friends if they're alive. One of my very best friends was Stuart Robertson, Robby Robertson, who was from Orange, Virginia.† He had gone to Woodberry Forest School, which was the chief rival of Episcopal. Our mothers had known each other in girls' school in Staunton, Virginia when they were growing up. So we had similar family backgrounds and we fit. Robby had the first alternate to my appointment, and he actually got into Annapolis, but he didn't like it. He actually flunked out, but he was a lot smarter than I was academically, and he left because he really wasn't happy with it.

Paul Stillwell: What do you recall about Bill Bullis's teaching methods?

Admiral Burke: We had a test in two subjects every Saturday, sort of an end-of-year test. As I recall, by the time we took the entrance exams in mid-April we had covered the text three times, the entire academic test, and we had been quizzed in how to take exams, so it wasn't too much of a strain. We were used to taking exams.

Paul Stillwell: It was like practicing for it.

---

* William F. Bullis resigned his commission upon graduation from the Naval Academy in June 1924. He served as a second lieutenant in the Army, 1924-26, and subsequently earned a master's degree from George Washington University. In 1930 he founded The Bullis School in Washington, D.C., as a preparatory school for the service academies. He served on active duty as a Naval Reservist from 1940 to 1945 and eventually retired as a commander.

† Alexander Stuart Robertson, Jr., entered the Naval Academy as a potential member of the class of 1940 but resigned prior to completion of the course.

Admiral Burke: We were practicing. Everybody there had finished high school, so you were going back through it. Did you ever know Pinkston at the academy? Do you know who I'm talking about? Roland Pinkston?

Paul Stillwell: No.

Admiral Burke: He was class of '32, and he was one of Bullis's teachers and later ended up at the Naval Academy teaching physics.* When I was the exec in Bancroft Hall back in the early '60s, he was over in the physics department.† He was one of our favorite teachers when we were mids.

Bullis was tough, but I'd say I was used to the gentry principles of Episcopal High School. The honor system is very important. I learned the honor system at home, and going into Episcopal was no problem. So I've had it all my life ingrained in me, and that's the way we operate in my family. I'd say Robby and I gave Captain Bullis a bad time, because we'd been to a prep school that he sort of envied. The teachers and Bullis himself used to say "damn" and "hell" in class. We'd never heard anything like that. This caused our respect for him not to be too high at certain times, but in hindsight and having gotten out into the real world over a period of time, I'd say he got me in, and he got a lot of people in, and that's what he was for.

Paul Stillwell: What other values can you ascribe to your parents' teachings?

Admiral Burke: Well, my mother came from around New Orleans, and her father was English, came over at age 22, something like that, and married an Alabama gal, and they ended up on a plantation. He had a sugar plantation not too far from New Orleans, and so they were gentry. Her mother was southern, and then they moved north, because they lost

---

* Earl Roland Pinkston resigned upon graduation from the Naval Academy in the class of 1932. As a lieutenant (junior grade) in the Naval Reserve he joined the academy's faculty in 1942 as an instructor. After he reverted to civilian status, he remained on the faculty until his retirement as a full professor of physics in 1980 and then became professor emeritus.

† Bancroft Hall is the large multi-wing dormitory that houses Naval Academy midshipmen. It also contains the offices of members of the executive department, including the commandant, executive officer, and battalion and company officers.

the plantation in a flood. I'd say our family were raised on sort of the principles of southern gentry: courtesy and lots and lots of unwritten social rules that you had to be careful to abide by.

Paul Stillwell: What were some of these rules?

Admiral Burke: Well, you spoke to people. When ladies come in the room, you stand up. You had to be courteous. I mean, we always had a cook-maid in our house up until I went to the Naval Academy, and so we had three meals a day served. My father used to come down in coat and tie all three meals. My brothers and I were expected to be in coat and tie at all meals except breakfast. We just did it. These were intuitive, and it was built into us. The way we were instructed on the use of the language, not to use slang. People who said "ain't" were crude. You could judge people by the language they used. My older brother went to the University of Virginia in Charlottesville. I can remember that when I came home on leave from the Naval Academy I brought a couple of classmates home with me. They spent a night or something like that, were around the house for a while, and then went on their way home. He let me know that these weren't the kind of people I should be associating with, because they weren't gentlemen like they had in Charlottesville.

Paul Stillwell: So you had to make some adjustments when you got to prep school and the academy.

Admiral Burke: Yes, but I wanted to be in the Navy.

When I was at Bullis, my father had a heart attack about a month before the exams. I discovered that he wasn't going to live more than six or eight months, and he died in the fall. To give you an idea of the change in times, his salary at Burke & Herbert Bank was $2,400 a year—the owner's salary was $3,000 a year—and so he did other things. He invested. He played the stock market. He had a real estate license. There's an area here called Belle Haven. I don't know whether you've ever heard of it or not.

Paul Stillwell: I have. Yes.

Admiral Burke: Well, he and about a half a dozen of his best friends developed that from nothing. He was a founding member of Belle Haven Country Club. There were ten of them. He bought his life membership for $500.00. Just to get in the damn club now it costs you $30,000. [Laughter] But I'd say the Episcopalians ran Virginia. That's an outgrowth of the initial colonization. We and our social friends were all Episcopalians. I had one Catholic friend, and he was a good friend, because his father was on the vestry at Christ Church. His mother was Catholic. On the Jefferson side of the family, one of the sons, my great uncle, married a Catholic, and that split the family. They hardly spoke to each other. I mean, they did it on a very formal basis. It wasn't until I got to the Naval Academy, where I had friends who were Catholics, that I began to think they were all right.

When I was at Episcopal occasionally we would play Gonzaga over in Washington, and they were not on a level with us socially. You could tell. The language that they were using was different. They were using street language. If we were to use that language, we would have been walking demerits, and that was just the kind of difference. It's a hand-me-down from colonial days; the Episcopalians were the Church of England and ran Virginia.

Paul Stillwell: How active was your family in the church?

Admiral Burke: Dad was on the vestry for 15 straight years and finally had a fight with the minister and resigned. They were active. They both sang in the choir when they were young. My mother's family came here and lived in a boarding house. When Dad started courting my mother, he would call on her in the living room, and the other people after dinner would be gathered around there. He had a good tenor voice. Somebody would play, and he would sing to Mother in front of all these people. Can you imagine?

Paul Stillwell: Much different from today.

Admiral Burke: Yes. My family didn't own an automobile until I was ten years old. We returned to the Rosemont section. After we left my grandmother's house that one winter, we moved out to Rosemont to a house we owned. Rosemont is down the hill from the Masonic Temple there. We had a maid, and at one time we had a full-time laundress. When we peeled her off she would pick up our laundry once a week. She would do the family laundry for $5.00 a week, and the maid was about $10.00 a week.

I started to tell you about my Catholic friend. He lived up the street. His name is Welby Beverley; his mother was Catholic. He wanted to go to the Naval Academy, couldn't get in, but he got an appointment to West Point. He ended up by going to West Point. He was under 17 when he entered. Very bright guy. Had to pay his way the first three months till he got to be 17, which was their minimum age. When he graduated he was under 21, and he had to wait till he was 21 to get his commission.[*] He married the only girl he'd ever dated, and he died about two years ago. He was a major general. He made colonel during World War II. He was about a year older than I.

We had no Jews in the country club. And the blacks weren't blacks; they were called "coloreds," and I still think that way. On the other hand, I'd say my life in the service has caused me to accommodate to whatever environment I was in, with the help of my wife, who came from an equally rigid background. Her family name is Stuart. After I married her, I discovered the depths of their Virginia ties; they're old Virginia too. She's a fifth-generation Alexandrian, but her family moved away when her father was eight years old. But she is extraordinarily adaptable too.

Paul Stillwell: How much of an interest did you have in the wider world, say, in the 1930s, the developments overseas with dictators and Japan's aggression and so forth?

Admiral Burke: Well, you're looking at a poor student, and the only subject I really liked was history. I had four years, remarkable years, of history at Episcopal High School, and I think history, unbeknownst to me, taught me about people. We studied ancient history, and by the time I got to Bullis, I had had ancient history, English, European, and American

---

[*] William Welby Beverley was born 28 August 1917. He graduated from the U.S. Military Academy in the class of 1938 and eventually retired in 1970 as a major general.

history, which were requirements for the entrance exams. Towards the end of the year our history teacher at Bullis went to graduate school at Catholic U., and I managed to teach a couple of his classes while he was doing that. So I had a feel for what was going on in Europe. I have always been interested in current events. I take three newspapers right now. I take three newsmagazines. I'm getting rid of one of them because they're so damn Democratic. [Laughter] But I scan three newspapers every day, and I keep up with what's going on. I was aware of what was happening in Europe.

Paul Stillwell: What sort of hobbies or entertainment did you have in your growing-up years?

Admiral Burke: I played golf. I grew up on Belle Haven Golf Course, and I was a pretty fair golfer. I couldn't putt, but I could do all the other stuff very well. But when I got to Annapolis I was a poor student. I tried to play plebe football but I couldn't handle it and academics. I was always on the verge of flunking out until first class year, but I was high in aptitude. I was always way up in aptitude. I gave up golf for my profession, both at the academy and afterwards, and it wasn't until I got to Japan in 1970, where it was a requirement to be able to deal with the people that you work with, I began to play again. Instead of eating lunch I practiced every day, and then I'd play golf about once a week and, strangely enough, after a while my game came back.

Paul Stillwell: That was a long layoff.

Admiral Burke: Yes, but I got my handicap down to a seven or eight while I was out there, and I was very pleased with it.

Paul Stillwell: What do you recall about the transition to Annapolis and plebe summer and so forth?

Admiral Burke: Plebe summer was demanding.* You're looking at a guy who hates the plebe system, and I think we ought to get rid of it. I felt that way as an underclassman. I felt that way as a first classman. I felt that way as executive officer of Bancroft Hall. And I wrote a letter to Chuck Larson here within the last year urging him to get rid of it.† Basic reason is—I've sort of changed—I feel that there are two things wrong. It's poor leadership, and the second thing is it fosters classmate loyalty excessively. We didn't have an honor system when I was a midshipman. Today my classmates don't realize it. They think we had one. We didn't have an honor system, and you get people who commit offenses, particularly in the plebe system, as upperclassmen. Their classmates are in this conflict of not telling on the guys who they know have abused the system, and I think this is wrong.

The plebe summer did a lot for me. I think we ought to have a tough plebe summer to get people motivated; I buy that. But what happens, and it happened when I was there and it happened when I was the executive officer of Bancroft Hall, you'd get these people at the end of the summer, they're motivated, the parents think it's the greatest place, and then the upper class come back and the disillusionment begins.

Paul Stillwell: What sort of disillusion do you mean?

Admiral Burke: Well, the plebes had been taught to be perfect, and then they see their upperclassmen who aren't being as perfect as they should be, and so it's the upper class as a group aren't following the rules. They're hedging on the rules, because they rate doing it, and this is poor leadership. Every now and then you'll see somebody screw up—or takes advantage of somebody and does something wrong—and for whatever reason he gets away with it. This fosters animosity and disrespect that you'll never forget.

I was mishandled by a company officer in October of 1936. He did something that for my money was inexcusable. My father was dying, and my mother hadn't had a chance

---

* A midshipman in his or her first year is called a plebe; second year, youngster or third classman; third year, second classman; fourth year, first classman.
† Rear Admiral Charles R. Larson, USN, served as superintendent of the Naval Academy from 31 August 1983 to 19 August 1986. As a four-star admiral he again served as superintendent, from 1994 to 1998, in the wake of a midshipman cheating scandal.

to get down. One day I came back from class about 3:30, and there was a note on the table that she was arriving at 4:30 to meet me at Tecumseh.* I had one hour of extra duty or two hours of extra duty for something like turning my head in ranks or raising my hand, and it was the only time plebe year I had extra duty. I went down to get my company officer to excuse me so I could see my mother, and he wasn't there, so I went to the next company officer. This was the third battalion, and there was another company officer right there, and so I told him. He berated me and wouldn't even listen to me and just chewed me out. I would have skipped it and taken the punishment, because I knew I had seen my father for the last time. I had gone home on emergency leave for a couple of days and then came back, and we'd decided that I wouldn't go home again. So I went and found another officer and told him what the problem was, and he said, "Sure," and he excused me. I've never forgotten that guy who turned me down. That guy, incidentally, died about three years ago, and somebody told me about it, and, frankly, I felt a little bit better.

Paul Stillwell: Who was he?

Admiral Burke: I'd rather not tell you, but I know that his group of peers thought he was a good guy.

In the early stage of the war, people got killed; everybody lost people at Pearl Harbor.† My class lost about ten. I saw write-ups in magazines where reserve officers heard Annapolis people talking about So-and-so got killed, and the comment was, "Well, the son of a bitch deserved what he got." Well, I'd say that is a fostering of a system that shouldn't be functioning. I've talked to my own classmates once or twice in the last year. They're not interested. I think it's pathetic. I think you need to foster a system where you respect the people above you, and I don't think that the plebe system does it. I can talk for hours on this.

---

* Tecumseh is the nickname of an American Indian pictured in a prominent bust near the entrance to Bancroft Hall. It is a prominent Naval Academy landmark, often decorated in different colors to celebrate sporting events.
† In late November 1941, the Imperial Japanese Navy dispatched from the Kurile Islands in the North Pacific a task force built around six aircraft carriers. A force of some 350 fighters, dive-bombers, and torpedo planes attacked U.S. military installations on the island of Oahu, Hawaii, on Sunday, 7 December 1941. The principal focus of attack was the collection of American warships at the naval base at Pearl Harbor. The U.S. Congress declared war on Japan the following day.

Paul Stillwell: Well, by the same token, there should be respect for those below you as well.

Admiral Burke: Well, you don't gain respect by imposing unwritten punishment. I can remember as a plebe one day I turned my head in ranks. A first classman had me sit on air in his room until I fell and couldn't get up. But I didn't have a tough plebe year. I had two great first classmen. One was Ralph Cousins, and the other was Red Hessel.* Hessel was a tackle on the football team, and he was a tough guy. For those days he was big; he weighed 185. He just said, "If anybody tells you to come around, don't come around. You tell them you're coming around to me."† So I had that as a shelter, and generally the second class were afraid of him. Cousins was a very no-strain guy and a very compassionate guy.

But I didn't have any kind of a plebe year compared to some of the plebe years, except down at the mess table. Well, why should you go down to the table where you get all this harassment where you're supposed to be taught how to be a gentleman? I had been taught how to be a gentleman at home and at Episcopal High School, but I had to go through all this crap down there at the table, which wasn't anything constructive. When I got to be exec of Bancroft Hall we had had investigation after investigation. They make the rules, and every time they made rules if it's not written in the rules "Thou Shalt Not," then it's okay. The midshipmen are much smarter than the rules writers, and they'll come up with something stupid, and it doesn't foster respect.

Paul Stillwell: What were some of the examples of the petty things at the table?

Admiral Burke: Oh, hell. Sitting on infinity, making guys get up and scream and holler and do things just for the amusement of the upper class. That's what we did then. I don't know what they do now, but I've seen in news things about midshipmen yelling at each other right in the face. I never had anybody yell at me. I think it's much, much tougher

---

* Midshipman Ralph W. Cousins, USN, and Midshipman Edward W. Hessel, USN, both members of the class of 1937. Cousins eventually became a four-star admiral and Hessel, a captain.
† "Come around" was a practice in which midshipmen reported to the dorm rooms of upper classmen to receive admonishment for misdeeds—both real and imagined.

now than it was when I was there, because they have so many "Thou Shalt Nots," if they let them do anything they carry it to the extreme.

Paul Stillwell: What do you remember specifically about Cousins from that period?

Admiral Burke: A very bright guy. He was nice, sincere. Tended to be non-reg a bit.

Paul Stillwell: Anything else about the plebe summer? How well did you adapt to the regimentation?

Admiral Burke: I'd say very well. I had the disruption of the fact that my father was going downhill. I knew this, and I got called home on two different occasions plebe summer because they thought he was going to die and didn't. But I adapted, and I had friends there in my company that I was making who were very helpful and supportive.

Paul Stillwell: Any names to mention in that regard?

Admiral Burke: Well, I had a roommate named Tommy Baume, who was a happy-go-lucky guy.[*] He was from Hollywood, California. He flunked out February of plebe year, but he was a very likable, nice guy and we got along fine. I had another guy named Tom Adams, who came from Texas, Corpus Christi.[†] He was somebody that flunked out on his eyes at the end of plebe year, but I liked him very much. He had brother in the class of '39 at West Point. Bill Howard, who was from Mount Hope, West Virginia.[‡] He had had two years at VPI, and we later roomed together for two years.[§] He was a very close friend, and was somebody who had been through all this. He had been through a "rat" year at VPI, and he knew how to handle it at the academy. He'd had all the academics, so he didn't have to study and got along fine. It was sort of an inspiration to see. On the other hand, I had to study and study and cram all the time to stay in. Walter Fuhr, Tate Preston, who

---

[*] Midshipman Thomas A. Baume, USN.
[†] Midshipman Lewis J. Adams, USN.
[‡] Midshipman William C. Howard, Jr., USN, left the Naval Academy prior to completion of the course.
[§] VPI—Virginia Polytechnic Institute, Blacksburg, Virginia.

later was a roommate for two years.* Tate was killed in the war by a kamikaze. He became a very close friend too. Howard was a guy who liked the girls and liked to drink. As he got to be an upper classman, he got too much, and eventually it caused him to get kicked out first class year. It was very unfortunate, because he did have the potential, I think, to be a good naval officer.

Paul Stillwell: What were the opportunities to drink in that context?

Admiral Burke: Well, Howard probably was a year or so older than I was, and he liked to drink, and he liked the girls. He didn't have to study, and academically he stood right in the middle. He could have stood at the top of the class, but he wasn't working, and so he used to go out in town. There were ways to get liquor, I suppose, and when he was a first classman, as I recall, we could ride in cars. He dated girls that would have a car, and that led to his downfall. They went up to Washington one weekend on a Saturday night and got back late and got caught. There was a speakeasy out there on King George Street, right outside the fence. It was a private home that was across the street and up towards Maryland Avenue a little bit, but it was a speakeasy there and it was a first class rate.

Paul Stillwell: What do you mean by a rate? A privilege?

Admiral Burke: It was a privilege. It was an unofficial rate for the first class who wanted to go in there, and I suppose the owner of the place had to allow that or had to recognize them or they had to be introduced. I never went there. I've only been to a speakeasy once in my life, and that was Honolulu, and I had to be introduced.

Paul Stillwell: By rate do you mean an unofficial sort of thing?

---

* Midshipman Walter E. Fuhr, USN, left the Naval Academy prior to completion of the course; Midshipman James Tate Preston, graduated from the academy in the class of 1940 and was subsequently killed 16 April 1945.

Admiral Burke: Oh, sure, it was unofficial. The exec department eventually found out about it, and at some point in time they posted a DO out there with his sword.* The word got around that Pop's Place was off bounds, so I think that sort of shut it down. I don't recall what year it was, but I suspect it was about the time I was a first classman. I never got involved in drinking on a routine basis. There was only once or twice that I had a drink around Bancroft Hall, because I was always on the verge academically, and I didn't want to build up a case that would otherwise hurt me if it came up to me having to leave. Consequently, I had very few demerits and stood very high in aptitude.

Paul Stillwell: This month is the 60th anniversary of FDR's second inauguration.† You told me a story when the tape recorder wasn't running about the midshipmen's participation in that inauguration.

Admiral Burke: Well, we left early in the morning, I forget what time, assembled in Bancroft Hall and marched off because it was raining heavily. Marched out West Street to the railroad station, which was where the hotel is now. We took a train and ended up at about Florida and New York Avenue in Washington. It was still raining heavily when we got there. Then we marched on a circuitous route and formed on the south side of the Capitol, I don't know what street it was. It seemed like we waited forever for the inauguration ceremony to end—in the rain!

Paul Stillwell: Again in the rain.

Admiral Burke: It rained all day long, believe me. We must have waited at least an hour and a half over there, and eventually the ceremony was over. There wasn't a luncheon in the Capitol the way it was this year. And off the parade started. The President and his party had gone up the avenue. We got about halfway up the avenue, and then we stopped, because the President and his party went in and had lunch at the White House.

---

* DO—duty officer. On a rotating basis officers in the Bancroft Hall organization had the duty and acted as disciplinarians.
† Franklin D. Roosevelt was President of the United States from 4 March 1933 to 12 April 1945. His second inaugural was on 20 January 1937.

Paul Stillwell: Was this the whole regiment of midshipmen?

Admiral Burke: This was the whole regiment. The West Pointers were there, too, and the Coast Guard; I think the Coast Guard cadets were right behind us. We marched, and we finally got past the reviewing stand. I don't recall what time it was, but it was probably after 3:00 o'clock at least, and we continued marching past the White House all the way up to about 21st or 22nd Street and did a column right and went up 22nd Street. We thought we were going to disband, but pretty soon became disillusioned because we began to quick-time a block and then walk a block and ended up back at the railroad, where we had been dropped off the train. We were carrying rifles with bayonets, and I guess we must have taken the bayonets off after we got off the parade route. But we went all the way back to where the railroad yard was, and I think the object was to make us so tired we'd get on the train and go back to Annapolis.

There was one amusing thing about it. My father had a sister and a brother that lived in Washington. They had rented a suite at the Washington Hotel at the corner of 17th and Pennsylvania Avenue. It was on the second or third floor, and they had all their families and friends in the suite watching the parade. As we marched up the avenue and turned the corner, I could hear my brother shout, "There he is. Julian, look up here." I was in the rear rank of the first platoon of the ninth company. And all these upperclassmen began to yell at me, saying, "Mr. Burke, keep your eyes in the boat." My brother was up there nicely yelling, saying, "Why don't you look up here? Smile, damn it."

But, anyhow, after going all the way back to the railroad yard, I joined my classmate and friend from Orange, Virginia, Stuart Robinson, and we somehow or other had a rendezvous figured out ahead of time with my brother, which was about halfway across town, to which we walked. Then we rendezvoused with a first cousin and his wife and had a pleasant evening. Andy, my brother, drove us back to Annapolis after it was all over. We got in right at the stroke of whenever liberty was up, maybe midnight or 11:00 o'clock or something like that, but that was quite a respite for me.

Paul Stillwell: Did you ever get any lunch?

Admiral Burke: They gave us lunch at about 9:00 o'clock in the morning before we got off the train.

Paul Stillwell: Another story you were mentioning before we started the tape was about Dr. Woods and the case of mumps you had as a plebe.

Admiral Burke: The commanding officer at the hospital in Annapolis was Captain Edgar Woods, who was from Charlottesville, Virginia.[*] He was in med school with my uncle in Washington. Mrs. Woods came from Alexandria, and our parents were friends, and so the Woods family was a refuge for me at the academy. Their daughter Douglas is one of our best friends today.

Well, sometime that spring I came down with mumps. I didn't think it was mumps, because I'd already had them once. But, in any, case they sent me over to the hospital, and they diagnosed it as mumps. I wasn't very sick. In fact, I just had a swollen gland for a couple or three days and temperature for a couple or three days, but they kept me in the quarantine ward for three weeks. I was allowed to go down and walk around the seawall and walk around the yard as long as I stayed away from people. Dougie Woods used to come down there and walk around the seawall with me. She was on one side of the road, and I was on the other. It was a real passionate friendship, I can tell you that.

Paul Stillwell: That must have been after the inauguration, because you couldn't have been in quarantine during that.

Admiral Burke: Oh, I'm sure it was after the inauguration so I guess it was later on. Probably around the first of April, somewhere in that time frame.

Paul Stillwell: What do you remember about the duty officers in general and their role in Bancroft Hall?

---

[*] Captain Edgar L. Woods, MC, USN.

Admiral Burke: Of course, they were the company and battalion officers. I was very fortunate in the company officers that I had. I can still remember their names. Two of them made admiral.

Paul Stillwell: Who were they?

Admiral Burke: Charlie Kirkpatrick, who was a jaygee when he was there during my second-class year.*

Paul Stillwell: He was later superintendent.

Admiral Burke: He was later superintendent and had orders to be Chief of Personnel when he had a heart attack. He was tough, and he was the uncle of one of my classmates, so he automatically became "Uncle Charlie." He taught me a lot about leadership and right as a midshipman, because he knew every single person in his company, and he checked every single person out. Practically every day he came by our room, and we didn't carry on with him.† He was the boss. When I first met him beginning of second-class summer he came in there and put practically everybody on the report in the second-class platoon. I'd never seen such use of a report. A couple of months later I was in what was called the "grease" platoon. I was there during September. I took leave in August and came back in September with a group, and it was to my advantage that particular summer. I wanted to court my future wife, and so I could do it better in August. I got to know him during that month of September, and I put it up to him one day and asked him what the hell he did that for. I said it turned everybody off, because it wasn't necessary. He said, "I just wanted them to know who was in charge." [Laughter]

Paul Stillwell: What was the "grease" platoon?

---

* Jaygee—lieutenant (junior grade). Rear Admiral Charles C. Kirkpatrick, USN, was superintendent of the Naval Academy from August 1962 to January 1964.
† In this context, carrying on means taking things easy, relaxing normal requirements.

Admiral Burke: These were people who volunteered to come back during September leave. They'd let you go in August. You'd get your month's leave in August and come back in September when the rest of the regiment was on leave and take care of the plebes and they called them the "grease" platoon. I had Bill Wylie.*

Paul Stillwell: You mean the other company officer you were referring to?

Admiral Burke: Yes, he was my company officer first class year and both Wylie and Kirkpatrick knew their people. I never fraternized with them, but they made me know that they knew me and knew all about me, and I could go talk to them anytime I needed to.

Paul Stillwell: Any specifics on Wylie?

Admiral Burke: Wylie was a destroyer man.

Paul Stillwell: Very bright man.

Admiral Burke: He left after I graduated. I can remember I did something one day or failed to do something one day on a room inspection, and he came around and chewed me out as a first classman. Up to then he had only praised me, and I was really upset because I'd let him down.

Paul Stillwell: You took it to heart.

Admiral Burke: Yes. I felt strongly enough about Wylie so that first class June week I took Betty, my future wife, and we called on Lieutenant and Mrs. Wylie.† I wanted her to meet him because I felt that strongly about what a great guy he was.

---

* Lieutenant Joseph C. Wylie, USN. The oral history of Wylie, who retired as a rear admiral, is in the Naval Institute collection.
† June Week was the term at the time for the collection of festivities surrounding the graduation and commissioning of the first classmen. Naval Academy classes now graduate in late May during what is known as Commissioning Week.

Youngster year I had another man, who was named Joe Worthington.[*] I don't think he made admiral, but he was an exceptionally good man, and there was a man named Edgar plebe year.[†] When I was a plebe and I was struggling and had so many personal family problems, he was supportive. But I'd say I was lucky. As you go up in the Navy and so forth, you get angry at people who put you on the report or make you do what you don't want to, and I've run into this. As exec of Bancroft Hall, I can tell you I was not necessarily popular. I recall a midshipman who was a friend, dating my daughter. He told me, "Captain Burke, you ought to hear what those guys think about you. I know what you're like, but nobody in Bancroft Hall knows." [Laughter]

Paul Stillwell: Did you encounter Uncle Beany Jarrett?[‡]

Admiral Burke: Oh, yes. He was great. He was a company officer in our battalion. I can remember he put me on report one day for raising my hand in ranks, and I was mad as hell at him, but he did it always with a smile. He never frowned, which, unfortunately, I do. He was a leader, and he had the capacity to talk to people into that they could do it. One year—I think it probably was my first-class year—he talked us into beating Army when we should have gotten shellacked. He got up there and just talked to the regiment at a pep rally before the game.

Paul Stillwell: This was in a football game?

Admiral Burke: Yes. But he always had a smile on his face and it made a difference.

Paul Stillwell: Did you encounter Commander Thebaud, the exec?[§]

---

[*] Lieutenant Joseph M. Worthington, USN. Upon his retirement, Worthington received a tombstone promotion to rear admiral on the basis of combat awards. His oral history is in the Naval Institute collection.
[†] Lieutenant Harold B. Edgar, USN.
[‡] Lieutenant Commander Harry Bean Jarrett, USN, was in the Naval Academy's executive department in the late 1930s and early 1940s. The frigate Jarrett (FFG-33) was named in his honor.
[§] Commander Leo H. Thebaud, USN, was executive officer to the commandant of midshipmen. He had written a widely used textbook, Naval Leadership, With Some Hints to Junior Officers and Others; a Compilation by and for the Navy, First Edition (Annapolis: U.S. Naval Institute, 1924).

Admiral Burke: Yes. Extraordinary man. He came there second class summer, and we were cynical second classmen. He talked to our group two or three times, and I felt that he was a very inspirational kind of person. He knew what example was. My older brother was getting married in the fall and wanted to set the date for the wedding. I was going to be the best man. It came up around Thanksgiving or sometime around there. So I went in to see Commander Thebaud and told him I had this situation and could I get a commitment? "Well," he said, "you'll have to be sat."* Well, that was always a problem with me.

I said, "Thank you very much."

Just as I was leaving, he said, "By the way, Burke, you look like a good midshipman. Where do you stand in your class?" Well, what happened was at the end of youngster year I'd stood about, oh, say, 590. There were probably 600 in the class, and then they flunked out about 30 people. So at that point in time I stood lower than the total number in the class, and I was still sat. [Laughter] And I explained this to him. He shook his head. He said, "I don't know whether you're going to make it." [Laughter]

Paul Stillwell: Did you ever have any doubts whether you'd make it?

Admiral Burke: Oh, yes. I was unsat two Christmases. I spent youngster and second class Christmas there because I was unsat. But first-class year I decided I was going to make it. They used to post unsats at the end of each week in every subject, and first class year I was studying my head off. I used to get up an hour before reveille and study. I would come back and study after class, and the only thing I participated in was choir. I really had a lot of trouble, and we got up to the first-term exams in November sometime, and I got over 3.0 on every exam. I got as high as 3.8 on one, and yet I had hit ten different trees during the fall.† I got the impression that my reputation was so bad on the academic side that they were just automatically marking me down. After that I never hit a tree, and I didn't study any harder. In fact, I didn't study nearly as hard, but I felt like they left me alone. And I've talked to people about this. The rest of the year I went through in a breeze, and I

---

* "Sat" meant being satisfactory in academics.
† The "tree" was a list of students who had failed a particular exam.

gained a modest number of points. I wasn't quite anchor.* I was probably 40 or 50 from anchor.† But I wanted to be a naval officer.

Paul Stillwell: What were your problems in academics?

Admiral Burke: I didn't know how to read—in hindsight. I still don't enjoy reading much, but I can scan read now. Back in the middle '50s I ended up in the front office of CinCLantFlt.‡ I was the administrative assistant to Cat Brown, and I used to have to read this stuff for him.§ He showed me how to do it, so ever since then I can scan read a paper. I don't read it all, but I can pick out the key sentences in a paragraph, and this is how I keep up on world affairs and politics and whatever.

Paul Stillwell: Are there any of the instructors you particularly remember?

Admiral Burke: Yes. "Slipstick" Willie. I forget his name.

Paul Stillwell: Earl Thomson.**

Admiral Burke: Extraordinary guy.

Paul Stillwell: In what way?

Admiral Burke: Well, he knew how to make it fun. I didn't have him. I wish that I had had him, but he taught the class behind me. In those days they used to take the bright guys to go to postgraduate school or to put them in the bureaus, and the rest of the pack would come to the Naval Academy as instructors, where they would have a lead instructor,

---

* "Anchor man" is the slang term for a midshipman who finishes at the bottom of his class at the Naval Academy.
† In the final standings for the 456 graduates in the class of 1940, Burke stood number 388.
‡ CinCLantFlt—Commander in Chief Atlantic Fleet.
§ Vice Admiral Charles R. Brown, USN, Deputy CinCLantFlt.
** "Slipstick Willie" was the nickname given Professor Earl W. Thomson because of his prowess with a slide rule. He taught at the Naval Academy from 1919 to 1959. For details see Shipmate magazine, published by the Naval Academy Alumni Association, June 1982, page 13.

usually a civilian professor, who would teach these guys. They would give them the questions to ask, and you were quizzed every time you went to class. Jack McCain came down there as a jaygee or a lieutenant while I was there and he used pretty salty language. I remember him saying, "Now goddamn it, you take this—" and so forth and he had the place in an uproar.*

Paul Stillwell: Well, Admiral Shear said that his typical greeting was, "Good goddamn morning."†

Admiral Burke: Yes. Well, I didn't meet him until later on and I met him down in Australia. I think he had been transferred off his ship, or maybe he came in off of war patrol. I was exec of a submarine then. He was a colorful figure then, I think. He was a commander or probably a lieutenant commander then. Just about all these guys were acting the way I would have had I ever been assigned to a job like that. They were given questions they were going to quiz, and they were given the answers, and they had to study them. Then they'd show up in class, and you'd go in and see if there were any questions. There was practically no discussion in class. It was all just take the test.

Paul Stillwell: And man the boards.

Admiral Burke: Yes. I can remember one guy I had as an instructor. See, I was a product of the honor system, and there were guys that used to look around to see what was going on and frequently copy. Do you know what getting the dope is?

Paul Stillwell: Yes, that's finding out from somebody who's already taken the test in another section.

---

* Lieutenant (junior grade) John S. McCain, Jr., USN, taught electrical engineering at the Naval Academy from 1938 to 1940. He eventually became a four-star admiral. His son, Captain John S. McCain III, USN (Ret.), is a U.S. Senator from Arizona.
† See the Naval Institute oral history of Admiral Harold E. Shear, USN (Ret.).

Admiral Burke: Yes. That was a violation of the honor system, and I just couldn't bring myself to do that. But it was accepted at the academy. Probably still is accepted. I don't know. Of course, they don't teach the courses the way they did then, and we have educated people with graduate degrees right across the board now, so it's a different ball game now. I was in class one day, and I think it was either history or English, but it was over in that department. There was a lieutenant commander there who came in, and he had half of us sit at the desk, half of us go to the boards, and we drew slips. He walked out of the room while we were writing what we had, and then he was going to come back and have us recite. On the way out he said, "Now, you all keep your eyes in the boat now. You're not looking." And then he walked out.

When he came back in he accused us of looking on each other's papers. He did this a couple or three times, and finally I stood up and let him have it. I said, "If I am cheating, I want you to put me on report and address me, because I have not been cheating, and I resent being talked to this way." He sort of sputtered.

All my classmates looked at me like I was crazy, and when we marched back to Bancroft, my classmates said, "Boy, you really shot your grease today." This was my second-class year, and I was way up in the top 20 in my class in aptitude always. George Lhamon, who was our company commander, came around about a week later, and he said, "What the hell happened to you over there?"[*]

I said, "What's the matter?"

He said, "You just got an unsat fitness report." Kirkpatrick was the company officer and told him to find out, so I told him. So nothing ever happened, but my aptitude mark moved from about a 3.95 down to a 3.75. When I was a first classman, I never ran into the guy again, but later I went to the West Virginia after I graduated. I was in communications, and I was dealing with the flag on board. Fortunately, I was only on there for eight months. In January of 1941 we had a change of flag officers and a new staff. This guy was flag secretary whom I would be dealing with all the time. I had hardly gotten there to see him, and he looked up, and he recognized me right on the spot. He said, "Oh, well, look who's here."

---

[*] Midshipman George M. Lhamon, USN, a member of the class of 1939.

I thought, "God. What's going to happen?" Well, the Lord helped me. About three weeks later I got dispatch orders to go to the North Carolina.

Paul Stillwell: Who was this individual?

Admiral Burke: I can't remember his name. He was on the type commander's staff, ComBatShips.

Paul Stillwell: What do you recall about the marching and drilling at the Naval Academy?

Admiral Burke: Well, I've forgotten how much we did. We used to march to class and did up until sometime in 1960-61 time frame, when I was exec. Before that everybody took the same courses, and it was easy to do. Then when they started shaking up the curriculum and bringing it into the 20th century and letting people have electives and giving people credit for work they'd already done, they couldn't do it anymore. It had the effect that the military bearing, I think, tended to go down. On the other hand, midshipmen are thinking more. I think their education is far better. It's a tradeoff, and I think it's better to have people who think, as opposed to automatons. I think the academy is a great place. I've had two great tours that were different from anything else and both on shore duty. One was executive officer of Bancroft Hall, which is the best job I ever had anywhere. It was the toughest job. The other was ComNavFor Japan, which was shore duty and even though I've had more command at sea than practically anybody you'll find, I would say those two jobs are the two best I had.*

Paul Stillwell: That's interesting. What do you remember about the Army-Navy football games and the pageantry connected with those when you were a midshipman?

Admiral Burke: I just say it was much better in the 1960-63 time frame than it was when I was a midshipman. I was not involved in athletics, and so I had no interface with West Point. The only people who did were the athletes. It was another game, and we were

---

* Commander U.S. Naval Forces Japan.

supposed to beat Army, because we'd been told we were supposed to beat Army. Things were a lot better around Bancroft Hall if you did, particularly if you were a plebe.

We didn't have the hell raising that they had when I was there in '60 to '63, but we did have spontaneous rallies. Milo Draemel was the commandant of midshipmen in my second-class year when we went over, and we had a spontaneous pep rally.* They went up and down Porter Row and stopped at Draemel's house.† I remember Draemel came out and talked to us. He was a friend of my mother's brother-in-law, so Mother came down and took me over to call. Mother was great on calls, and so I called on a lot of people when I was a midshipman, because it was ingrained in my family that you made calls.

I got through plebe year largely because of two families down there. Well, there were three probably. There was a family named Maher. He was a lieutenant commander that lived on Upshur Road, about the fourth or fifth house down from the corner, and he had two sons.‡ Dave in the class of '43 and the older one, I don't think he went to the academy. As soon as I got down there, the Maher family were very nice to me. It was a refuge.

Paul Stillwell: Admiral Shear spoke very highly of Captain Draemel as the commandant. Said he was just the picture of what a naval officer should look like.

Admiral Burke: Well, he was a solid man. Draemel was selected for admiral, and he left shortly thereafter and he took Kirkpatrick with him. I remember calling on Mrs. Draemel. You were supposed to call, and that was one of the families that I called on. Maybe they had me over for a meal, but I remember telling her that I sure wish they wouldn't take Mr. Kirkpatrick. Draemel he laughed, and he said, "Well, he's that good. That's why I want him." [Laughter]

---

* Captain/Rear Admiral Milo Frederick Draemel, USN, served as the Naval Academy's commandant of midshipmen from 1937 to 1940.
† Porter Row is a line of senior officers' residences on the Naval Academy grounds.
‡ Lieutenant Commander James E. Maher, USN.

Paul Stillwell: The Draemels' daughter married a man named Balch out of '39.[*] I still see her around Annapolis from time to time.

Admiral Burke: Is that right? I remember her, but I can't remember what she looks like, but I remember she was a nice young lady. She used to come to the hops when I was a midshipman.

Paul Stillwell: Please tell me about the hops.

Admiral Burke: Well, they were regimented. My roommate, Tate Preston, was on the hop committee. There was a Mrs. Marshall there who was Turner Joy's sister-in-law, and she was the first hostess.[†] Draemel set up this gedunk stand down there under the rotunda.[‡] I don't know whether they still have it or not.

Paul Stillwell: I don't know.

Admiral Burke: When they set this gedunk stand down there to sort of give the midshipmen a place, they decided they wanted to have a hostess, and Draemel offered that job to my mother. It must have been second-class year, but I remember he wanted her to do it, and she was wondering if I would be embarrassed. My mother had been widowed, and her husband was one of five children, and all of the other children were more affluent than we were. We didn't have Social Security or benefits or anything like that, and it was a struggle, so Mother had to go to work. No lady in the family had ever worked before, and she worked the rest of her life until she was about 70 before she retired. She thought about that job, but I think she decided she'd better sit tight where she was, and I'm glad she did.

Paul Stillwell: Why do you say that?

---

[*] Ensign John B. Balch, USN.
[†] Captain C. Turner Joy, USN, later became a flag officer and served as superintendent of the Naval Academy from 1952 to 1954.
[‡] Gedunk is a Navy slang term for candy, ice cream, and sodas—snack-type food.

Admiral Burke: She would have had to move. You've got to realize we're an Alexandria family. The gal across the street was in my teenage group. The gal two doors down—she and I started off in the second grade. I had two brothers, and at that time my older brother had just gotten married. Mother was halfway supporting him while he was getting on his feet. My father also had an insurance business to back up his income, and so my brother dropped out of college at age 21 and started running that. I say we had relatives and friends, and she had lived here ever since she was 18. They wouldn't have had the family support had she moved to Annapolis. I've got all kinds of cousins around here. I've got a brother and he's got three kids. I've got another brother who's dead, but he's got five and four of them live here and so forth. We network.

Now where were we?

Paul Stillwell: Well, we're talking about your time as a midshipman.

Admiral Burke: Oh, we were talking about the dances. Okay. This Mrs. Marshall was there. She used to come down daily and sit in the soda fountain area, so the boys could bring the girls down, and then she would receive at the hops. I don't know what else she did, but those were the things. She was a presence. She would be at all the hops, and usually they would invite some senior officer's wife to be the number-one receiver, but she was always there along with some member of the hop committee.

Paul Stillwell: Where did your dates come from?

Admiral Burke: Most of them came from Washington-Baltimore area. The Holton Arms School. You know that?

Paul Stillwell: I've heard of it.

Admiral Burke: Well, it's still going. They used to be on S Street, not too far from Connecticut Avenue, and those girls used to come down with a chaperone and stay at a drag house or at Carvel.* I started dragging Betty youngster year, but she disappeared in New Orleans. She went to Cathedral School. And there was a Gunston Hall School, which was on the other side of Connecticut Avenue from Holton Arms. Dabney Holloway went there.† Skip Brown, who was the wife of General George Brown, lives here in town.‡ We've gotten to know her and she's a good friend. She and Dabney were there at the same time, as was Dougie Sprunt, the daughter of Captain Woods from the Naval Academy hospital. There were other schools. There were some Goucher girls that came down, and there's a couple of prep school girls that would come down. When Dougie Woods ended up at Sweetbriar, one weekend when I was I think a second classman she came back from Sweetbriar and brought ten girls with her and set up ten blind dates. I think one of the girls eventually married Bill Ingram.§ Another married Crosswell Croft.**

Paul Stillwell: Did the hostesses or anybody provide dancing instruction to some who may not have brought that skill with them?

Admiral Burke: It wasn't the hostesses. We had a dance instructor, and I think we had that probably plebe year during the winter. They would take us up into Smoke Hall, and there would be a male professional dance instructor showing us how to do the one-step and the two-step and so forth. I started dancing when I was quite young, about 12 years old, but notwithstanding that, it didn't hurt to go through the motions to see what everybody else was doing. The various dances we had usually started, I think, about 8:30 in the evening and ended about 11:30, and they were in the armory. The receiving line was about halfway up from the door up in the middle opposite the bandstand, and you had a stag line, and people cut in. The idea was to make sure that your girl, whoever she was, got to dance with a lot of boys to give her a good time. That's the way you did it.

---

* "Drag" was Naval Academy slang for dating girls. A "drag house" was where the young women stayed if they had come in from out of town. Opened at the beginning of the 20th century, Carvel Hall was a favorite meeting place for officers and midshipmen. It has since been torn down.
† She is the wife of Admiral James L. Holloway III, USN (Ret.), who was Chief of Naval Operations, 1974-78.
‡ General George S. Brown, USAF, served as Chairman of the Joint Chiefs of Staff from 1 July 1974 to 20 June 1978.
§ Midshipman William T. Ingram II, USN, graduated in the Naval Academy class of 1938.
** Midshipman William Crosswell Croft, USN, graduated in the Naval Academy class of 1940.

Were there people that went steady in those days? Sure. In my own case, I didn't get involved in the steady business. I just couldn't afford the time to be dating. I didn't have the money. It took more money than I had. My roommate, Bill Howard, who'd been to VPI, was quite a dragger and his father used to send him $50.00 a month, and that was like gold. I couldn't afford that. I finally met Betty in February or March of my youngster year, when she was at the Cathedral School. The choir went up to the Cathedral to sing, and Mother brought her to the service. I met her afterwards, and I've been going steady ever since.

Paul Stillwell: Great.

Admiral Burke: But she went off to Sophie Newcomb College the next fall in New Orleans, so we had a lot of letter writing to do. Generally for the hops, some guys dragged a different girl every week or once a week. It depended on the kind of thing you wanted. They were heavily chaperoned, the girls who went to school. Some of these girls who came down by themselves would stay at a drag house. During my plebe year, a youngster, in the class of '39, was dragging a girl from Holton Arms, and the Holton girls that weekend were staying at Carvel. On Sunday afternoon the chaperone went around to have a room check to tell the girls to get ready to go back on the bus. She walked in one of the rooms without knocking, and there was a guy in the class of '39 in bed with his date. He was gone from the academy before the next morning, and the rules on dragging changed forever.

Paul Stillwell: What were the rules after that?

Admiral Burke: No midshipman could go above the ground floor without being accompanied by his parents. The class of '39 was in the doghouse.

Paul Stillwell: I'll bet. Do you remember the ring dance?

Admiral Burke: The ring dance was special. We had a name orchestra, and I can't tell you what it is now, but we had a big-time orchestra. We may have had Hal Kemp; I don't know. We had a name orchestra. Glenn Miller was there one year.

Paul Stillwell: What do you remember about the summer cruises and the value of those?

Admiral Burke: Well, youngster year we went off in the old battleships, the New York, Arkansas, and, I think, the Wyoming, and these were really old ships.

Paul Stillwell: Which one were you in?

Admiral Burke: I was in the Arkansas.[*] I'd say in a lot of ways you don't learn much, but, after all, I'd never been at sea before, and they teach you the routines. At the time I was there it was demotivating. There wasn't any question about it. I'm sure it's not that way now, and it wasn't when I was on duty there 25 years later. There just wasn't enough challenge for the capability of the youngsters, and so they were pushed around on swabs and so forth in a way for a period of time that probably was unnecessary, and their living conditions weren't anywhere near what they were used to. Perhaps it's a good idea to make everybody go through some of that, but I know that it was demotivating to most of the midshipmen that I knew. It didn't hurt me, because I wanted to be a naval officer, and I was willing to put up with it to be a naval officer.

We started off and went to Kiel, Germany. This was the summer of 1937 when the Germans were getting involved in the Spanish Civil War, and we were supposed to have gone from Kiel over to Livorno, Italy, and then back. But one of the German ships down off of Spain got hit by a bomb, and they sent a pocket battleship down there and shelled.[†]

---

[*] USS Arkansas (BB-33), lead battleship of her class, was commissioned 17 September 1912. Following modernization in 1925-26 she had a standard displacement of 26,100 tons, was 562 feet long and 106 feet in the beam. Her top speed was 21 knots. She was armed with 12 12-inch guns and 16 5-inch guns. She was the oldest U.S. battleship in active service during World War II, eventually being decommissioned in 1946.

[†] Loyalist airplanes bombed the German pocket battleship Deutschland on 29 May 1937 when she was anchored at Iviza in the Balearic Islands. The attack killed 23 German crewmen and wounded many others. On the order of Chancellor Adolf Hitler five German warships retaliated by bombarding the Loyalist port of Almeria on 31 May; 20 civilians died as a result. Germany and Italy then withdrew their naval patrols from the vicinity of Spain.

There was international tension. So they cancelled our Italy visit, and we went to Madeira or a short visit, and then we went back up to Torquay, England, on the southwest coast of England, and then back to Norfolk. As a youngster, from a professional point you just sort of learn the routine of a ship, you scrubbed a lot of decks every day, and you lived in a hammock. We were crammed into a living compartment, and it was just exposing you to what Navy life was aboard a big and an old ship.

Paul Stillwell: What was the relationship between the midshipmen and the enlisted crewmen?

Admiral Burke: We were not as close to them as we should have been, in my opinion. We were segregated. We stood watch. We scrubbed decks every morning with sand and holystones and that sort of business. There was a boatswain's mate out there, and he was tactful, and we always had a first classman up there telling us what to do, but it wasn't something that would cement any relationship. We had an ex-enlisted man in my class named Willy Burgan, who was in my division.* He was at home. He enjoyed fraternizing with the enlisted men, and he could talk their language. He had done things, and I don't know whether he had ever been on that ship, but he had a good time.

Paul Stillwell: What were the living conditions like on a ship that old?

Admiral Burke: Primitive. You had a locker. You had a hammock, and the hammock was strung up right up against the overhead. On two occasions I woke up with a start during the middle of the night and went up like that. I had an I-beam right over my head, and I got whomped in my head. At least one time I think I was knocked out, because I just remember seeing stars, and I woke up the next morning. There wasn't any place that you could sit down and relax. There weren't any seats around or anything like that.

Paul Stillwell: The mess tables got set up just for meals.

---

* Midshipman William W. Burgan, USN.

Admiral Burke: The mess tables were in the overhead, and you brought those down. Everything was right there, and it was all cramped. When you got up in the morning, you had to take your hammock up, fold it up, and put it down in the storage down below. You were living all over the top of yourself, and it wasn't pleasant. What else?

Paul Stillwell: Did you spend any time in engineering?

Admiral Burke: They rotated us around. The cruise started in June, right after June Week, and you got back around the 25th of August or something like that. Then you had four weeks' leave. I think you probably spent a third of that time in engineering. What was engineering like? You had an engineering notebook, and you had to go around and fill it in. The main thing I remember was how hot it was down in the engine rooms and in the firerooms. It was frequently as hot as 115 or 120, and if you really wanted to be somebody to talk about, you go back in the steering engine room on these old battleships. They had a steam-driven steering engine room. There was no ventilation, and it was up to 140, and everybody used to pop salt pills, because that was considered the way to endure it. Now I understand they don't give you salt pills. I don't know whether they do or not. It was the sort of an experience you had to go through just to give you a sense of familiarity. I guess that's what it was. I wasn't inspired by it. I can tell you that.

Paul Stillwell: The good news was that the Arkansas had been converted from coal to oil by the time you got there.

Admiral Burke: The best thing about that cruise was the ports, going to Germany, and we went through the Kiel Canal in daytime and we saw Nazi Germany.

Paul Stillwell: What are your recollections of that?

Admiral Burke: Oh, boy. When we went down there, all kinds of Germans were lining the banks as we went through the canal and the men were up like this, or the men in uniform.

Paul Stillwell: The Heil, Hitler salute.

Admiral Burke: Oh, yes. Then we went to Kiel. We finally got anchored in the middle of the night. I was asleep when that happened but woke up in the morning, and there was that Sea Cloud, the yacht that belonged to Davies.* You know, it's now a charter. People can go around the Mediterranean in it, but it belonged to Marjorie Post Davies. He was the ambassador to Russia at the time. We heard all sorts of wild stories about the size of the crew and all the fancy living over there that we didn't have.

I went up to Berlin on a tour, and we stayed at a hotel there. We had a couple or three nights there, and in the daytime we did sightseeing; at night we went to nightclubs. Bill Howard, my roommate, and I were up there together, but in the daytime we went out to Potsdam and saw all the palaces out there. There was one of them that was called Sans Souci, which was the palace of Frederick the Great. We saw the Potsdam area; that's where the dukes of the realm lived, and it was of that vintage. And we saw the Olympic Stadium, which had been the year before.† Almost anytime you passed anybody they'd be in uniform, and they'd salute you. It was kind of crazy to see how wound up they were on this.

Paul Stillwell: Did you talk to any of the Germans?

Admiral Burke: We talked to a few, but I don't remember anything. We were just looking to see what we could. It amazed us to see how military they were and how they'd click their heels, and I'd say the garbage collector was in uniform. It was that crazy.

Paul Stillwell: Well, Hitler had appealed to their sense of nationalism, especially after the defeat in World War I.

---

* Joseph E. Davies was U.S. ambassador to the Soviet Union in 1937-38. His wife was an heiress of the Post cereal fortune.
† In the 1936 Olympic Games at Berlin America's Jesse Owens earned four gold medals as a sprinter, much to the discomfort of German Chancellor Adolf Hitler, who was preaching a doctrine of Aryan superiority.

Admiral Burke: Well, they have a lot of the same disease the Japanese do. They're sort of turning their backs on what they did. They don't want to own up to it. They were very friendly. When I came back off the cruise, I'd say the Germans were a hell of a lot friendlier than the English were.

Paul Stillwell: How would you account for that?

Admiral Burke: It's the personality. They seemed to be reaching out to us. I mean, just going through the canal they were waving at us and cheering at us and so forth. That didn't happen when we went to England. It just the characteristic of people. Hell, my grandfather was English, my mother's father. Betty has cousins that live over there right now, and we've stayed with them. About 15 years ago we were over there. It's just a different type of reserve and the way they express themselves.

Paul Stillwell: They had just had the coronation of King George VI.[*] Did you see any holdover from that hoopla?

Admiral Burke: I think we ought to get rid of the crown. [Laughter] I think it's seen its day. They don't deserve it, or the royal family doesn't deserve it.

Paul Stillwell: It was still very popular in the late '30s.

Admiral Burke: Oh, yes. It still has a strong sense of support, but it's like a lot of the stuff in the Old South that my family traditions eat up, but it's gone by the board. It's a good tourist attraction, but does it serve any useful purpose?

Paul Stillwell: Well, at least some of the British still think so.

Admiral Burke: Sure.

---

[*] King George VI (1895-1952) was the British monarch from 1936 until his death. His coronation was at Westminster Abbey on 12 May 1937.

Paul Stillwell: Did you get to London?

Admiral Burke: Not on a midshipmen cruise. I didn't have any extra money other than my midshipman allowance. One of my closest friends at the academy, Spencer Wilson, was the son of the dean at Hampden-Sydney.[*] He and I did a tour in southwest England. We sent to Glastonbury amongst other places. We just toured around some of those places. I just couldn't see going up to London on what I had available. I'd shot my wad in Berlin.

Paul Stillwell: Wilson was later killed in the Tullibee.[†]

Admiral Burke: My God, how did you know that?

Paul Stillwell: He married Harry Train's sister. I had an interview with Admiral Train last year.[‡]

Admiral Burke: Spence was a good friend.

Paul Stillwell: What do you remember about him?

Admiral Burke: Well, he was just a hell of a nice guy. This friend of mine that I met at Bullis, Robby Robinson, was from Orange, Virginia. When we got back to the academy, he went around and found all the Virginia boys in our class and made sure that we knew each other, and Spence was one. John Refo was one and Abbot Street.[§] Do you know George Street?[**]

---

[*] Midshipman David Spencer Wilson, USN.
[†] Wilson, then a lieutenant commander, was killed in the loss of the submarine Tullibee (SS-284) in March 1944. She was apparently sunk when one of her torpedoes made a circular run. Only one crew member survived.
[‡] See the Naval Institute oral history of Admiral Harry D. Train II, USN (Ret.).
[§] Midshipman John F. Refo, USN; Midshipman Abbot P. Street, USN.
[**] On the night of 13 April 1945, Commander George L. Street III, USN, commanding officer of the USS Tirante (SS-420), took the submarine into a small harbor on Quelpart Island in the East China Sea, 100 miles south of Korea. The Tirante fired six torpedoes, which sank the 4,000-ton transport Juzan Maru and two 900-ton frigates. She then exited the harbor at high speed. For this exploit and others during the submarine's first war patrol, Street was awarded the Medal of Honor.

Paul Stillwell: I do know him, yes.

Admiral Burke: Well, Abbot was his younger brother. He died, oh, about 1958 of cancer. There were about four of us who were best friends. I'm the only one left. Spence was just a hell of a nice guy. We were all in different battalions, but we hung together. We had a June Week house party both second and first class year, and the parents got involved. His father was a grand guy. His parents were. He was an only child.

Paul Stillwell: Anything else about that first cruise to remember?

Admiral Burke: Well, it was my first look at England, and I went off in the southwest side of it. Strangely enough, the next time I went back to England, which was in about 1984, Betty and I wanted to go to southwest England as a result of having watched a "Masterpiece Theatre" series. I forget the name of it, but it was dealing about southwest. But we love it down there.

I'd say Spence and I traveled around. We went to Sidmouth, and we went to Exeter and Glastonbury. That's all I can remember right now, but we toured around for about four days on our own and spent about $50.00. But dollars were a little more valuable then than they are now.

Paul Stillwell: That is true. What do you recall about the second-class summer?

Admiral Burke: Well, I was living with Bill Howard, and as second class we were over in what was then the second battalion wing, and we had drills and things that we had to do. Youngster year I had started dating Betty, and she'd come down to June Week beforehand. I arranged to get into the grease platoon so I could be with her. Her family had a cottage in North Carolina near Asheville. I was invited to go down there for a couple of weeks in August, so I was able to arrange my schedule so I could get down there. That was my first real confrontation with her family who were family friends of my parents.

Paul Stillwell: Interesting you use the word "confrontation."

Admiral Burke: Well. It wasn't a confrontation. They were very gracious, and we're as close to an arranged marriage as you can get in the modern world. Our families had known each other for a long time.

Paul Stillwell: But evidently willing on both sides.

Admiral Burke: Oh, yes. We got support on both sides.

Let's see. There was another thing that happened. I started smoking when I was about 14, and up to the time I was 20, I was smoking about two packs a day. We had a month's four-stacker destroyer cruise. When we came back, I had a load of cigarettes. They were sea stores, which cost six cents a pack. My roommate, Bill Howard, was taking every weekend, going to Baltimore; he had some girl there. He began to scoop up my cigarettes, because he had used his up, and I wasn't getting paid back. So by the end of second class summer, or before I went off on my August leave, I decided to quit smoking, and it stuck.

Paul Stillwell: Which probably did wonders for your health.

Admiral Burke: When I was about 56 years old, I had an X-ray of my chest, and the doctor who was looking at it said, "You don't smoke."

I said, "No."

He said, "But you did." And he showed the shadow down there in my left lung down at the bottom. He said, "There it is." So I'd say that was the best thing that happened to me next to me meeting and seeing more of Betty.

Paul Stillwell: Right. What do you recall about the four-stacker?

Admiral Burke: Well, it was commanded by a lieutenant. Of course, we thought he was a right old man. By present day standards he was. He was probably in his late 30s, but it was the first time I'd been that close to somebody of that rank exercising authority, and I liked the way things operated there. The captain and the exec particularly—they were both good men. I can't remember who they were.

Paul Stillwell: Do you remember the name of the ship?

Admiral Burke: <u>Fred Talbott</u>.*

Paul Stillwell: Where did the cruise go?

Admiral Burke: Well, it left Annapolis, and at the end of the first day it arrived at the Washington Navy Yard. My mother and brother and his fiancée came down and met me on the dock. So we went off, and we were here for a weekend probably or something like that, a couple of nights. Then I got to come home, which was always nice. In those days you didn't get much time off. And then, where else did we go? We were in Newport. I remember going to Newport, and we probably went to Norfolk but I don't remember doing anything at those other ports. I remember eating lobster for the first time in Newport for a dollar.

Paul Stillwell: What was it about the skipper's manner that impressed you?

Admiral Burke: Well, he was in charge and he knew his ship and he knew his people, and these three things are what make a leader.

Paul Stillwell: Well, it was an exposure for you to an entirely different side of the Navy.

Admiral Burke: Oh, yes. He was good, and I say I liked him. I'd been up on the bridge on the battleship but, gee whiz, that's like going to a funeral almost. Everything is so rigid,

---

* USS <u>J. Fred Talbott</u> (DD-150), a <u>Wickes</u>-class destroyer, was commissioned 30 June 1919. Displacement was 1090 tons, length 314 feet, beam of 31 feet, and maximum draft of 9 feet. Top speed was 35 knots. She was armed with four 4-inch guns, two 3-inch guns, and 12 21-inch torpedo tubes. During World War II she was converted to a target ship for bombing practice and was finally decommissioned in 1946.

and you can't do anything. You've got so many people up there telling you what you can't do, it's very hard to exercise initiative, but this guy was quite good.

Paul Stillwell: Did the idea of serving in a small ship appeal to you?

Admiral Burke: I didn't think about it that much at that time. At the time I was a midshipman, Captain Woods, the CO of the hospital and a family friend, told me that I wanted to be ordnance PG.* Well, I could not possibly become an ordnance PG. You can go back and look at the top section of my class. The chances are those are the guys that became ordnance PGs and/or EDOs, and percentage-wise very few of our class got graduate degrees.† In those days when you got close to graduation you drew for assignment to a battleship, cruiser, or aircraft carrier. The idea was you would stay on there for a couple of years and then rotate off to a destroyer. I had a first cousin who was in the class of '33, and he told me what to anticipate. I know when he moved from a cruiser over to a destroyer he was far happier.

Paul Stillwell: What was his name?

Admiral Burke: Robert A. Dawes. His father was captain of the Houston. Took her out to the Asiatic Station, and when they went out there he used to spend his leaves with us. So for about two years he was spending Christmas leave or the September leave with us until they got back. So that was an influence on me and he used to send us The Log, and we met a lot of his friends.‡

Paul Stillwell: How did the living conditions in the destroyer compare with the Arkansas?

Admiral Burke: Much better. It was much smaller, compact, but we were in a compartment down below the wardroom and forward. As I best remember, we lived in

---

* In the year leading up to World War II ordnance engineering was considered among the most prestigious fields in which naval officers could obtain postgraduate education.
† EDOs—engineering duty officers.
‡ The Log was a magazine put out periodically by the midshipmen.

bunks, as opposed to hammocks, and we generally had hands-on ability to do things. They were probably short on bodies, and so they needed us and so we participated with them.

Paul Stillwell: Still pretty primitive equipment, though, on that vintage destroyer.

Admiral Burke: Well, I see the stuff that's happened since I retired. I haven't been ship's company since '64, and what's happened to the equipment is just dramatic.

Paul Stillwell: Well, that destroyer was World War I technology essentially.

Admiral Burke: Yes. I think when I was a midshipman there was a ship called the Erie that was a gunboat.

Paul Stillwell: Right.

Admiral Burke: Used to be the flagship of the banana fleet. She was air-conditioned and, God, nobody could believe that we would spend money on air-conditioning. I'd say the way things have changed since I retired or in the last 30 years is just amazing.

Paul Stillwell: Any more specifics you remember from that cruise on the destroyer?

Admiral Burke: It didn't inspire me. You were regimented so much. As a midshipman you were regimented even on the cruises. We went to New London. I do remember that. I don't think they put us through the tank, but they took us over and showed us the tank and showed us some of the stuff around, and, of course, there were a couple of modern submarines around.* I don't think they even showed them to us. They showed us the base.

Paul Stillwell: Did that inspire you to go into submarines?

---

* At Submarine School was a water-filled tower in which students had to ascend as training for escaping from a submarine trapped on the bottom.

Admiral Burke: No. I hadn't made up my mind where I wanted to go. Plebe year, when I first entered the Naval Academy, what they used to do was have annual physical exams right after September leave. I had astigmatism and had been wearing glasses to read with for about three years when I became a midshipman. They made the decision sometime during the year that they were going to have annual physical exams right after the mid-year exams. We had about 150 eye unsats as a result of that, and Burke was right in the pack. I had about two or three re-exams which I failed. My left eye was okay, and it was my right eye. Eventually there were so many of us that they let us go on four or five days' leave just to get away from academics. This was in probably early April. So I went on leave, came to Washington.

I had a lot going for me. My father had a brother who was a nationally prominent ophthalmologist. He was the first doctor in the United States to do cataract surgery. He'd gone to Vienna to learn how to do it as a young man, and he had a brother-in-law who lived next door to him who was also a nationally prominent ophthalmologist too. They were both on the National Board, and so they both said that I had normal vision. I had trouble reading 20/20, but I was given a re-exam, and I passed it. And there wasn't any fooling; I passed it. I hadn't done anything except they told me just go out there and look at the sky for four days, and when I got back I passed the exam. But they dropped damn near 100 of my class, and you talk about talent. Some of the best of my class were dropped. It was criminal.

Paul Stillwell: Any that you remember specifically?

Admiral Burke: The one that I remember best was a good friend named Don Andrus.[*] Tom Adams who was from Corpus Christi, was a very good friend, and he would have made a good naval officer. Andrus was terrific. He was a Navy junior. He had been the outstanding student at Western High School in Washington in the cadet corps, and he was just a guy that floated to the top. He was smart as hell. His father was a Navy doctor, and he got discharged and eventually became a doctor, and he's down somewhere around

---
[*] Midshipman Don L. Andrus, USN.

Miami. When he was interning he was here at the Alexandria Hospital, and I saw him a couple of times then, but I haven't seen him since.

Paul Stillwell: The class of '39 lost a bunch because of eye unsat, and a number of them were able to come in during the war as reserve officers.

Admiral Burke: Somebody showed up at a class luncheon. My class secretary, Leigh Winters, died here about two weeks ago.* He came to one of our luncheons with a list of assignments on graduation. There were 30 people in my class that were not commissioned for physical reasons. I think that's crazy to carry people through and then discharge them. A couple of those guys actually made careers in the Navy, because they got back in during the war. I always had to struggle reading 20/20, but I managed to do it at the right time.

Paul Stillwell: Yes.

Admiral Burke: I got commissioned at the end, and when the war started then they began to speed up going to submarine and aviation training. In fact, even before the war one day when I was on the West Virginia—I hadn't been there very long, and a couple of ensigns took me up to Hollywood when the ship was in Long Beach. I'd never been to Hollywood, and we spent the night up there in town. I got back and I found I had to take a physical exam that morning, a flight physical. I miserably failed it because I couldn't see worth a nickel. So I didn't have to worry about going to aviation.

That stuck with me, and then later on, after the war started, I was given a flight physical on the North Carolina, and I didn't pass because of my eyes. I was on the North Carolina down in the Guadalcanal thing when we got hit by a torpedo. When we had come out to Pearl Harbor on the North Carolina, I'd seen my friends around Pearl, particularly in the West Virginia, while it was still there. They were emphasizing that the submariners were the one gang of the Navy that were really doing something against the Japanese, so I just decided to put in for submarines.

---

* Commander Leigh C. Winters, USN (Ret.), died 12 January 1997.

Well, the doctor who had already flunked me once on aviation passed it without even looking at the paper, and then I got ordered. Then he suddenly remembered that I'd flunked and he was really worried that somebody was going to yank his chain, but all I can tell you is that I've got cataract implants now in both eyes. I see like I did when I was a midshipman, except that my right eye is very light sensitive. But some days I can read 20/20 in the right eye. Some days I can't. It hasn't changed that much. But I think the rigidity that they stuck to 20/20 for our graduates was just crazy. Of course, we don't do it anymore, but with all the equipment we have out there and all of the other things you don't need to read 20/20. You need a brain.

Paul Stillwell: Well, speaking of your classmates. Do you have any recollections of John McMullen as a midshipman?*

Admiral Burke: Yes, I sure do. He and I reported to Red Hessel and Ralph Cousins as first classmen. He was in my company. I knew him, but he was light years brighter than me, and he was a lot more mature than I was at that time. He's probably a couple of years older than I am I would guess. I don't know.

Paul Stillwell: What do you recall about his personality?

Admiral Burke: He was a nice guy. He wasn't one of my intimate friends or buddies. I didn't go ashore with him or things like that, but I liked him. He was highly respected.

Paul Stillwell: He was one of those that went into that EDO program.

Admiral Burke: Yes. He's an impressive guy, and he was always somebody that didn't have any trouble with the system. I was always struggling.

Paul Stillwell: Was there any exposure to aviation while you were a midshipman?

---

* Midshipman John J. McMullen, USN, was commissioned with the class of 1940. He served on active duty until he resigned in December 1957 as a commander. That same year he founded John J. McMullen Associates, a naval architecture and marine engineering firm.

Admiral Burke: Yes. Second-class summer we had what they called aviation summer. That was the summer we went on the four-piper cruise on the Fred Talbott. When we got back from that, they had PBYs there or something like them, and they had them stationed at the academy and we went out and flew.* They would put us up in various positions there. They didn't let us fly the planes, but we would sit in the copilot's seat, or we would sit and try to visualize what we were doing. I was never really attracted to flying particularly.

Paul Stillwell: What do you recall about your first-class cruise?

Admiral Burke: We started off at Halifax; it was immediately after the visit of the King George and Queen Elizabeth of England, which had created quite a sensation. This was 1939. I think following that visit they had gone down and been President and Mrs. Roosevelt's guests at Hyde Park, so the town was all abuzz about the King and Queen. They weren't much interested in midshipmen, which was all right. But one day somebody snagged me and sent me on one of these parties that somebody was giving for a group of midshipmen. It turned out to be a Mr. and Mrs. McKeon. He was I think the head of the power company. They were affluent, and it turned out to be a yachting party. They were very nice people, very cordial, and they rounded up about ten midshipmen and had dates for us all, including two of their daughters and the houseguests who were most attractive. And we went off sailing, had a day's sail. They had a couple of Canadians. They had just had their yacht in the Bermuda race so they could share tales with some of our people who had expected to do this next.

Then we went to sea it was foggy and all that, so we went down near Bermuda for a couple of weeks, and then we turned around and went up to Quebec. Going down the St. Lawrence was quite an experience. They always gave us a leave period, and instead of going to Montreal, I went to a place called Manoir-Richelieu on the Saguenay River, which ran into the St. Lawrence. It is a sort of a White Sulphur Springs place: golf course, beautiful hotel, and we were there for about four or five days. I think our bill for that

---

* The PBY Catalina was a twin-engine flying boat that performed extensive service before and during World War II.

adventure was something like $65.00; it was the first time I'd ever stayed at a fancy place like that. I don't think I've been able to afford to do it since. [Laughter]

John Refo and I went up there. Refo was a Navy junior, but he had Virginia roots. That was really the first time really I got to know John Refo well. I'd known him but gradually, and that sort of cemented our friendship. Then after that the cruise went to New York City and spent a couple of nights, and I didn't get ashore in New York. I had something wrong with my foot, so I couldn't go ashore. Then we went on down to Norfolk, and my mother came down, and probably Betty was there too. Betty came down with her and my brother and his fiancée, my younger brother, and we stayed at sort of a B&B. They don't have them anymore unfortunately. And then came on home.

Paul Stillwell: What ship was that?

Admiral Burke: New York.* I learned how to take star sights and things like that, and the next time I took star sights I was the exec of a submarine.† I really had to struggle.

Paul Stillwell: One of the navigation instructors was Roy Benson.‡ Did you get to know him?

Admiral Burke: Everybody knew him. He was great. He was quite a character.

Paul Stillwell: Why do you say that?

Admiral Burke: Well, he didn't take himself seriously. He kidded us along. He made us feel human. In doing it all over again, I wish probably I had been more human than I was.

---

* USS New York (BB-34) was commissioned 15 April 1914. She had a standard displacement of 27,000 tons, was 573 feet long, and 95 feet in the beam. Her top speed was 21 knots. She was armed with ten 14-inch guns, 16 5-inch guns, and eight 3-inch guns. She was eventually decommissioned in 1946 after service in World War II.
† Shipboard personnel use a sextant to take the elevation and azimuth of selected stars as part of the celestial navigation process.
‡ Lieutenant Roy S. Benson, USN. The oral history of Benson, who retired as a rear admiral, is in the Naval Institute collection.

I always thought I was human, but he knew how to relate to the troops, and he did a good job of it. He always had a wry sense of humor that the boys liked.

Paul Stillwell: He was very enthusiastic.

Admiral Burke: Yes. Well, he was closer to the class of '39. I don't know why, but he was. I don't know whether he taught our class or not, but I remember going over to seamanship drills and so forth, and he would be there. Whenever he was around, people liked him and knew who he was. He wasn't just one of these guys with a uniform on.

Paul Stillwell: Admiral Shear has very pleasant recollections of being in the New York, because he met his future wife when the ship stopped in at Maine.

Admiral Burke: Is that right?

Paul Stillwell: Yes. Maybe during that cruise. I don't know.

Admiral Burke: Is Betty Shear from up there?

Paul Stillwell: Yes, she's from Maine.

Admiral Burke: Well, as it turns out, of course, I was on that same cruise, and I'd never been to Maine before.

Paul Stillwell: Well, you undoubtedly had more responsibility in this first class cruise than you had when you were in the Arkansas. What do you remember of your duties?

Admiral Burke: Well, you sort of get to be the platoon leader and handle your men. You get in supervisory positions, like in charge of the compartment to see that the youngsters get the jobs done. On watch on deck, when you go up to the bridge you are standing junior officer of the watch, where you're in an officer-related kind of a duty under supervision, but you're doing things that are more professionally gainful. You also stood watch down on deck when you were in port; you were in charge of inspecting people to see that they were up to speed or checking them in and out and doing some of the details.

I don't recall that these cruises particularly motivated me one way or the other, because there were just too many midshipmen around. Looking at it from then and all these years later and also when I was a midshipman, it seems to me if you want people to get motivated you've got to give them hands-on experience where they're close to it. There are not so many of you in a schoolroom kind of a situation. I suspect they do more of that now than they used to.

Paul Stillwell: Did you find that you enjoyed going to sea?

Admiral Burke: Not as a midshipman. We were packed in there. No, I didn't particularly like it. The thing that motivated me, I wanted to be a naval officer who went places. I'd gotten this idea, as I've said, from correspondence with my mother's aunt. It looked to me like getting in the Navy was a good vehicle to travel, and the longer I stayed in the Navy, I liked the way the thing operated. I got into submarines, and I had the good fortune of wanting to be in submarines. You could participate closely in everything. You had to know your job, and you had to know the jobs of the people around you, and you, by God, saw that they did it, and your bosses saw that you did what you were supposed to. So that sense of things grew into me in a way that I guess it made it pretty hard to work for me later on.

Paul Stillwell: Well, but even as a midshipman you had achieved that objective of getting to a lot of places that most Alexandria boys didn't.

Admiral Burke: Well, I'd gotten there, but I was under pretty heavy supervision. Listen, practically all my friends either went to Charlottesville to college or to North Carolina at Chapel Hill. We used to play Virginia in football every year, and my friends would come up there from the country club, and it was a big lark. We would have to be there and behave ourselves; it's an entirely different operation. These people were very relaxed and just on a weekend outing. We rarely had any sort of a weekend where we were on our own and relaxed and so forth. I don't begrudge it. I've had a rich Navy career, a rich life, but I'd say it's a different kind of a lifestyle. I've enjoyed my life, and I'm very grateful for the experiences I've had.

Paul Stillwell: Well, you talked before about the progress you made as a first classman academically. I wonder if you could describe the life in Bancroft Hall now that you were a first classman and others were reporting to you.

Admiral Burke: Well, I didn't push plebes around.

Paul Stillwell: Just because of your basic belief on that subject.

Admiral Burke: Abbot Street, George Street's younger brother, and I were very intimate friends. First class year he and I sat at the same table, plus a couple of other guys, and we treated plebes like they were one of us. I know every now and then a classmate would join us from somewhere else and get furious because these guys weren't braced up. But I treated them like they were friends. Reuben Woodall, do you know him?

Paul Stillwell: I know of him. He was one of the first Polaris skippers.[*]

Admiral Burke: Yes. He was my plebe, or one of them. You can call him up and ask him. We didn't push them around or anything. We tried to treat them like friends, like I felt it should be done. The only time I ever did anything to a plebe, I hit one plebe once first class year, because he kept on calling me by my first name. He was doing it just to see how far he could push me, so one day I hit him.

Paul Stillwell: Did you whack him with a paddle?

---

[*] When the ballistic missile submarine Robert E. Lee (SSBN-601) was commissioned on 16 September 1960, Commander Reuben F. Woodall, USN, was skipper of the blue crew.

Admiral Burke: I whacked him with my shoe, I think. My roommate Tate Preston said, "Now, aren't you proud of yourself?" And actually I felt like hell about it, because I didn't believe in it.

One of the plebes in '43 whom I spooned was Cabell Moore.[*] His uncle, by the same name, was my father's doctor during his fatal illness. Cabell lives in Richmond, a couple of blocks from my daughter Tina. He didn't make a career of the Navy. He is a close friend, and I didn't see him from the time I graduated until within the past ten years. He introduces me around Richmond as his first classman and best friend at Annapolis. I met him because during my father's fatal illness. His uncle, who had the same name, was my father's doctor up here in this end of the world. But life around Bancroft Hall, I'd just say that the idea of pushing people around the way were doing it I didn't think it was necessary to get to the end result.

Paul Stillwell: Anything else to put on the record about your time as a midshipman?

Admiral Burke: I tried crew and would like to have done it, but I had to drop out because of academics. I tried football, and I know I was as good as a lot of the people that made the varsity. But I really wasn't big enough, and I couldn't hack it academically. I got involved in the choir and that led to my marriage. Not a bad deal.

Paul Stillwell: What do you recall about the graduation ceremony?

Admiral Burke: I can't remember who the speaker was, but it was in Thompson Stadium, and it was a sunny day. I don't recall anything in particular about it. We had been through the numbers and all that sort of thing. See, academic year had stopped over two weeks before. Then there was what they called a drill week, which was to finish up the color competition and sharpen the people up for the parades, I guess. And then we had June Week, so we were sort of glad to get out of there.

---

[*] Midshipman William Cabell Moore, USN. "Spoon" is midshipman slang for the practice of recognizing a junior midshipman and extending a hand of friendship.

Paul Stillwell: Did you feel a sense of relief that these four years were over?

Admiral Burke: Oh, you bet. I was always under pressure as to whether I was going to make it, and it was only the last year after I did well in my exams the first time around that the pressure was not as bad. But I practically never dragged because I couldn't afford the time. I didn't want to get distracted. I was not a guy that went around and dragged every girl that came down the pike. I only had one other girl I was really interested in, and that didn't last very long. It was fortunate because she married a member of '37, but he was not in the Navy. But I was just not one who chased after girls. I liked the girls. I liked to go to dances, and I was always available to go to dances or maybe date somebody as a helper, but I didn't want to get involved until I saw the right girl.

Paul Stillwell: Do you have anything else to add from what we've talked about today?

Admiral Burke: I haven't talked much about my mother. See, my father died when I was 18, and so my relationship with a father was still parental supervision up until the time he got sick. My mother was a giant, and she lived till she was 93. When she finally died here in 1983, she had the largest funeral in Alexandria I've ever seen, and she just enjoyed respect. She didn't go to college, but she was well read. She wrote beautifully, and she knew what was going on. She had an enormous influence, and she backed me up all the way. She had been this way with the entire family. During the time after my father died, she was always there.

Life then was very hard for her. She went to a secretarial school and got a job. She became the secretary for the athletic director at GW.* She did that for about three years, and then she got to be the secretary for the headmaster at Episcopal High. And then when my brother went off during the war, she stopped that and took over the insurance company. She'd never known how to do it, but she did it while he was gone. Then when he came back, she stayed and worked for him. She participated in activities around town, and people just liked and respected her. Whenever we came and went, she kept the family together.

---

* GW—George Washington University.

This is something I'd like to express on both sides. Betty's father died when we were at Submarine School. Our two mothers were very close friends, and they both have kept each side of their families together. Because of those two women we have had very strong bonds in our families, and it's affected both of us. Mother liked the Navy particularly. She dated naval officers when she was a young woman, but she never married one.

Paul Stillwell: Well, Admiral, we got off to a good start today. I look forward to the next one. Thank you.

Interview Number 2 with Rear Admiral Julian T. Burke, Jr., U.S. Navy (Retired)
Place: Admiral Burke's home in Alexandria, Virginia
Date: Wednesday, 5 March 1997
Interviewer: Paul Stillwell

Paul Stillwell: Last time was a sunny day, and today it's kind of gloomy, but we're ready to resume. We talked last time about your graduation. How did you then come to get assigned to the West Virginia?

Admiral Burke: What happened was that you drew numbers, and I don't recall where my preference number was, but I just didn't know enough about the fleet. Captain Woods, the commandant of the hospital, was probably as close a friend as I had. He probably told me I wanted to go to battleships and get into gunnery. So I put my name up there on the West Virginia, and, lo and behold, I was ordered there. The West Virginia, it turns out, was the newest battleship that we had, and it was one of the big 16-inch gun ships in the fleet.* I can tell you about the West Virginia if you're interested.

Paul Stillwell: Please.

Admiral Burke: Well, I went there and I arrived. I wasn't particularly interested at the start in getting zeroed into gunnery.

Paul Stillwell: This is shortly after the fleet moved out to Pearl Harbor.

Admiral Burke: The fleet was in Pearl Harbor and had gone out there.† The families

---

* USS West Virginia (BB-48) was commissioned 1 December 1923. She had a full-load displacement of 33,590 tons, was 624 feet long, and 98 feet in the beam. Her top speed was 21 knots. She was armed with eight 16-inch guns and 12 5-inch broadside guns. She was radically rebuilt after suffering extensive damage during the Japanese attack on Pearl Harbor. She remained in active service until decommissioned on 9 January 1947, following World War II.
† Fleet Problem XXI took place in the Hawaiian area in the spring of 1940. When it was completed, President Franklin D. Roosevelt directed that the fleet remain at Pearl Harbor rather than return to its bases on the West Coast. The idea was that leaving the fleet in Hawaii would serve as a deterrent to Japanese aggression in the Far East.

were all back on the West Coast. There were about 10 or 12 of us from my class that went to the West Virginia, and I arrived with Pete Parlett, a classmate.* We got there on a Saturday afternoon, about two weeks before the rest of our classmates, and the officer of the deck sent me down to the junior officers' mess. I hadn't been there more than a half an hour when the officer of the deck was relieved, and he came down and said, "I told the executive officer, Commander Alexander, that you were aboard and as he was leaving the ship he said, 'Tell those two ensigns not to leave until I have had a chance to speak to them.'"† Well, he didn't have a chance to speak to us until the following Thursday. I had the duty the following weekend, so I didn't get ashore for two weeks, and nobody seemed to care.

Paul Stillwell: Except you.

Admiral Burke: I would have gone ashore over the weekend because there were several people who were going on shore, and the families of most of the married people weren't there. Some of the bachelors had girls, but there were so many fleet people out there the girls in Honolulu were in short supply. But there were things to do around Hawaii. But that kind of framework seemed to exist on the West Virginia at that time.

We had a Marine detachment that was commanded by a captain, plus a first lieutenant and a second lieutenant. Any time the captain had the duty and he wanted to go ashore, he would tell the second lieutenant to take his duty for him. That was routine.

Eventually, when I reported to the executive officer and he asked me what I wanted to do, I made a mistake and told him that I would like to rotate assignments between departments, which was customary at the time, for six months. On the West Virginia that was the wrong answer. I should have said I wanted to be in gunnery. So he chastised me, and I was assigned to communications as a CWO.‡

It turned out to be a stroke of luck for me that revealed itself months later. About eight months later, in the middle of the night, I received dispatch orders to go to the new construction battleship, North Carolina, which was being built in the Brooklyn Navy

---

* Ensign Roger V. Parlett, Jr., USN.
† Commander Boyd R. Alexander, USN.
‡ CWO—communications watch officer.

Yard. And the West Virginia was not a happy ship because the exec, I would say, was the Captain Queeg of all the associates that I encountered in my time in the Navy.*

Paul Stillwell: Any other examples of that?

Admiral Burke: He was just unpredictable. I know that he made people unhappy, and I can tell you this. He was transferred after I was. He was famous all over the fleet, and after he left, the West Virginia wardroom threw a party celebrating his departure, which most of the battleship wardrooms attended.

Paul Stillwell: He was notorious.

Admiral Burke: On the other hand, when I first arrived, the chief of staff on our ship was Captain Kidd, who was selected for admiral right after I got there.† He went out of his way to be nice to me personally. His son Ike was a friend of mine; he lived just about two doors from me first-class year, and I got to know him.‡ He told me that his dad was on the West Virginia before I left, and he had written him. Jesus, I hadn't been there on board more than a week when he personally came down to the JO bunkroom and welcomed me aboard and said he hoped he could see some more of me.§ Every afternoon he would get up on deck and pace back and forth for an hour—I mean, as fast as he could—and he'd catch whomever he could. He caught me one day, and I walked. I was exhausted. But he was extraordinarily nice to me and very considerate. Always a gentleman.

When we were tied up at Ford Island in Pearl Harbor, Admiral Kidd would often take a swimming group before breakfast, and I was included in that. When we were at

---

* Lieutenant Commander Philip F. Queeg, USN, was the fictitious commanding officer of the destroyer-minesweeper USS Caine in Herman Wouk's classic naval novel of World War II, The Caine Mutiny, published by Doubleday & Company in 1951. Queeg was a mentally unstable martinet, so his name has become associated with overbearing, eccentric officers.
† Captain Isaac C. Kidd, USN, became chief of staff to Commander Battleships, Battle Force, in early 1940 after being relieved of command of the battleship Arizona (BB-39). Kidd was promoted to rear admiral while in the billet and in early 1941 became Commander Battleship Division One.
‡ Midshipman Isaac C. Kidd, Jr., USN, was in the Naval Academy class of 1942, which graduated in December 1941, shortly after his father was killed on board the Arizona, which was then his flagship.
§ JO—junior officer.

Lahaina Roads he didn't play golf, but Admiral Pye did, his boss, and I was included in Admiral Pye's golf game.* I don't think I've played with admirals since until I made admiral.

Paul Stillwell: What were involved in your duties as a communications watch officer?

Admiral Burke: Well, as a flagship we had flag circuits, and the flag communicator was on top of us. I stood a watch-in-three or four, I've forgotten. It was down in the bowels of the ship, in radio central. We routed messages, and we had all these radio circuits there. This was before teletype and all of that.

Paul Stillwell: Still CW.†

Admiral Burke: Yes. My responsibility was to route the messages to make sure that the people got them in a timely fashion. There were radiomen on watch, at least a first class radioman, sometimes a chief. We had a chief, and each section was headed up by a first class radioman who oversaw the actual operation. And, by gosh, I'd never typed. I taught myself how to type on the typewriter board.

Paul Stillwell: Did you sit on the circuits at times yourself?

Admiral Burke: No, I did not. We had to learn communications administrative procedures. Because we were a flagship, the flag was on top of us, and we were the decoding board for the flagship.

Paul Stillwell: Typically the ship's communications department is merged with the flag's.

---

* Vice Admiral William S. Pye, USN, served as Commander Battleships, Battle Force, in 1940-41. Lahaina Roads is an area off the Hawaiian island of Maui. The U.S. Fleet often used it as an exercise area and anchorage in the years prior to World War II.
† CW, or continuous wave, referred to a type of radio wave interrupted into the dots and dashes of the Morse code for the purpose of communication.

Admiral Burke: Yes, that's right. Our communications officer was a man named Armentrout, a lieutenant, and he was very helpful and very pleasant to work with.* The communications officer on the flag, his name was Hansen.† I never saw Hansen, who was under a lot of rushes; he was the "pressure" man, I suppose. Armentrout was not, but Hansen was the guy who was putting the pressure on us to be better, faster and so forth.

We had a coding machine that was very primitive by present-day standards. There were rotors and each rotor had little knobs, little pins. I forget the number, but there were at least four or five of these rotors, and you would take them out and with a document based on what day of the month it was, you would have to push the pin either to the right or to the left.

Paul Stillwell: Then they were in sort of a basket?

Admiral Burke: They were in a basket, yes, and shortly before I left they put a more sophisticated machine in there, as I best remember, and I don't recall. A lot of this was made more user friendly and less apt to make a mistake. You had to have somebody check the work and, shortly before I left—I think it was the last time I went to sea—there was an op immediate message that I had to get out. There wasn't anybody to check me, and I screwed up the whole U.S. Fleet. It was a good thing I was going.

Paul Stillwell: Would you have any estimate of what percentage of the traffic was classified in that era?

Admiral Burke: Anything operational was. It could be classified confidential, secret, or top secret. We didn't see much top secret. We were obsessed with the Japanese; this was at the time when the cold war in the Pacific was on. The Japanese fishing vessels were out there; we all perceived that they were tailing us and so forth. I don't know whether they were or not. I didn't have that kind of intelligence.

---

* Lieutenant Erasmus W. Armentrout, Jr., USN.
† Lieutenant Henry O. Hansen, USN, was radio officer on the staff.

Paul Stillwell: Well, security was so tight, for example I think photography of Navy ships was prohibited.

Admiral Burke: This was a long time ago, so I can't remember all of the details, but I know that we were very security conscious, and we didn't talk about when we were getting under way or anything. My cousin, Bob Dawes, had married a girl from Honolulu, and he was off the South American coast on a cruiser.* His wife's family were from Virginia, and they lived in Manoa Valley in Hawaii. They made their home my home any time I was in port. That was another lifesaver as an example of friends that looked out for me. I took other friends up there from time to time, and they had a room where two of us could stay, but they knew I would come and go. They never asked. They and their friends were sort of trained into it.

Paul Stillwell: Did you have much contact with Admiral Pye himself?

Admiral Burke: Not really. Occasionally I took a message to him. Usually the way it worked was that I would take a message to the communicator or to his flag lieutenant, whose name I don't recall, or the chief of staff, and they would take it in to him.

Paul Stillwell: What do you remember about the standards of smartness and cleanliness in the flagship?

Admiral Burke: It was not bad. I think it was okay. You didn't have air-conditioning. There were a lot of things we didn't have that we now just assume that we'll have plenty of, like water, but I don't recall. I feel that the West Virginia was a good example of how a ship should look.

Paul Stillwell: What do you remember about the junior officers' mess? I've heard some compare that to sort of a fraternity house atmosphere.

---

* Lieutenant (junior grade) Robert A. Dawes, Jr., USN, was then serving in the USS Concord (CL-10).

Admiral Burke: Well, I don't recall. When we went in there, the class of '39 was still in there. The fleet was beginning to expand, and so some of the people who I guess we'd have to say were more available were being or had been transferred to make room for us. There were some people in '39 that were in the JO mess when we arrived, plus about a couple or three ROTC officers who had been called on active duty.* I think they were between '39 and '40. We had an aviator who was a Pensacola graduate, and I would guess that altogether we had about 20 people in the mess.

Of the people who went to the West Virginia I had not been close to any of them. I knew most of them. Pete Parlett, who became my closest friend, I hardly knew as a midshipman. Yet he and I reported in to Long Beach to go to Pearl Harbor, ended up on the same ship, and we got to be very close friends. Al Bergner, who was the captain of the football team, and Ace Barton were there.† They were roommates, I think it was their last year at the academy. I'd known Al all the way through but not intimately. But they had girls that followed them. I guess they didn't show up until we got back to the West Coast in October, but they were so preoccupied with the girls from home that we hardly ever saw them socially. My best academy friends were on other ships, and I was still reaching out to them whenever I could. My best friends out there included Tate Preston, my roommate, who was on a cruiser. Spencer Wilson was on the Pennsylvania. Will Morton and Abbot Street were on one of these four-stack cruisers.‡ Morton and Street I used to play golf with whenever we could.

Paul Stillwell: What were the living accommodations like for ensigns?

Admiral Burke: I would say that there was room for at least ten people in our bunkroom. Interestingly enough, about the second day I was in the bunkroom all of a sudden a white-haired captain came in there looking for Ensign Burke, and it was Captain Ike Kidd, making me feel welcome. He was the real smiling face in that arena for me.

---

* ROTC—reserve officers' training corps.
† Ensign Allen A. Bergner, USN; Ensign Wilbur G. Barton, USN.
‡ Ensign William B. Morton, USN; Ensign Abbot P. Street, USN. They reported to the light cruiser Milwaukee (CL-5).

Paul Stillwell: Radar was just then coming into the fleet. Did you have any consciousness of it then?

Admiral Burke: I don't think we had radar at that time.

Paul Stillwell: Your classmate Mike Michaelis said he was involved in the installation of it in the Pennsylvania.*

Admiral Burke: When?

Paul Stillwell: I'm not sure if it was '40 or '41. It was before the war.

Admiral Burke: My guess it would be '41, but I don't remember when we got a radar.

Paul Stillwell: What do you remember about the operating patterns and schedule for the West Virginia out of Hawaii.

Admiral Burke: We would go to sea for a couple or three weeks at a time usually. And on the weekends we would anchor in Lahaina Roads. I guess we probably had the fleet divided up into battleships and cruisers and destroyers. I don't remember having tactical exercises with other ships. It was mainly type training that we were involved in. I'd have to say this, I just don't remember that much, and I think probably that I was so busy just trying to learn the ship and my job I had a very small picture of what was going on.

Paul Stillwell: Well, did you get any awareness of the bigger picture from the messages you were seeing?

Admiral Burke: Not really.

---

* See the Naval Institute oral history of Admiral Frederick H. Michaelis, USN (Ret.).

Paul Stillwell: I guess psychologically you were kind of enclosed in radio, so you didn't get out to see the other ships and the operations and maneuvers.

Admiral Burke: This is hard for me to describe, but we weren't privy, and I don't remember us getting in any intelligence messages that I was dealing with. We didn't have anything about what was going on in the war in Europe or what the Japanese were doing.* Where that information was flowing I don't know. All I know is that we were all on guard. We had this condition of readiness, a defensive readiness. Eventually, it was probably in the late fall of 1940, we started boat patrols and security patrols in Pearl Harbor. We would get the duty, and we would have one of the ship's boats. Ensigns always got this as a boat officer, and you would be patrolling around Pearl Harbor looking out for some sort of a surprise invasion.

Paul Stillwell: Was there a concern about saboteurs?

Admiral Burke: Yes. I don't think there were any Japanese employed inside Pearl Harbor. That was just a segregation kind of a thing. Anybody who was Japanese was sort of suspect, and, of course, we had Japanese all over the place out in town.

Paul Stillwell: You described the type training rather than tactical exercises. It sounds as if there was not a particular sense of urgency about imminent combat.

Admiral Burke: Well, you're talking to the guy who was an ensign who was not in the big picture. I was a mechanical guy—operating, getting messages, and seeing who was routed. I had to route messages and all that sort of business, but the information that was flowing to me wasn't that revealing of any sort of a threat. I don't ever remember seeing anything about movements of Japanese ships or Japanese military forces. Were we concerned about the Japanese? Yes, we were, but it was because the Japanese were moving over in Asia, not where we were.

---

*Japan had been at war in China since 1937; the war in Europe started in September 1939.

Paul Stillwell: Right. They were at war with the Chinese at that point.

Admiral Burke: Yes.

Paul Stillwell: Was there any sort of training program to expose you to the other departments, even though you didn't serve in them?

Admiral Burke: No, to answer your question. I didn't get involved in the other departments until I went to the North Carolina.

Paul Stillwell: Any recollections about being ashore in Hawaii other than the golf and the Dawes home?

Admiral Burke: Yes. When you went up to town, very few of us had automobiles. There was a taxi service, and I forget where you would get in the taxi, but you'd just load up. For probably a buck you could go up, and they'd drop you off at the Navy Y, which was in the middle of town. The big hotel in downtown Honolulu was the Alexander Young Hotel. And I hadn't any more than reported to the West Virginia when some lieutenant from the engineering department called me in. He was an old man; he was a lieutenant. He was in charge of the ship's party, and he said, "You're my number-one helper." This was probably the most important thing I did during the time I was on the West Virginia. He said, "You've got to find a place to get a party, and you've got to find girls and do this and that."

It ended up we had it in the main dining ballroom of the Young Hotel, and I was just going up wandering around Honolulu near the Young Hotel, and I hadn't decided on the Young Hotel or maybe I had. But I talked to them, and the guy said, yes, they would let us have the party there, and then I started walking down looking for the chamber of commerce. I thought that might help me. You've got to remember I had just turned 22 and been locked up in jail for four years, so I was a rather inexperienced person. I was walking across the street, and I saw this gentlemen with a white linen suit, coat and tie, straw hat coming across. I stopped and asked him where the chamber of commerce was, and he said, "You talk like a Southerner. Where are you from?"

His name as Marion Leonard, and after we got playing "Who You Know" and so forth, eventually he invited me up to dinner. He took me over to the chamber of commerce. He and his wife were blue bloods from Charleston, South Carolina, and he was in the Department of Commerce. Very resentful because the Big Five families controlled everything out there in Hawaii, and the Leonards were used to being socially prominent in Charleston. I mean, they were blue bloods in Charleston. My last duty station was in Charleston, and I met their son who had been born when I had been out. But this was another case of meeting a family that sort of helped look after me and provided me another home away from home. But I got to the chamber of commerce, and they told me where I could get some girls. There was some club where single women lived, and they pointed me over there. I was able to go there and persuade the volunteers to come to our dance, and we ended up with a whole pack full of girls.

Paul Stillwell: Great.

Admiral Burke: Then I went down on the waterfront. In those days the steamships used to come in there, and every time they did the Hawaiians were making leis and so forth. I was able to recruit a bunch of natives, and they made leis for us, and they also provided a very large group of gals and music to do hula dancing for us. It was a whomping party, and I learned a lot through that experience about the Hawaiians, how they operated and so forth.

Paul Stillwell: Was this party paid for out of the ship's store profits?

Admiral Burke: Yes, they had a welfare fund, and I don't recall how it was paid for, but it was a whomping party. Everybody seemed to enjoy it, and it helped me get sort of a feel for the Hawaiian culture.

Paul Stillwell: Did you line up a band for it too?

Admiral Burke: Well, the ship's band did the dance music, but the hula gang, they were good. They wanted to do it. I told them I'd like to hire four of them to come in. They brought 20. It was something they just wanted to do to show off. I hadn't thought about that party for years.

Paul Stillwell: What do you recall about that trip back to the West Coast in the fall of '40 for yard work.

Admiral Burke: Well, the fleet went out, as I recall, in the spring of 1940, and there was a fleet exercise. Then the decision was made by the President to keep the fleet out there because the Japanese threat was increasing.

Paul Stillwell: Admiral Richardson, who was CinCUS, objected to that.[*]

Admiral Burke: I know. I was so remote from that, but apparently he objected and eventually was relieved by Admiral Kimmel while I was out there.[†]

Paul Stillwell: What do you remember about that trip to the West Coast in the fall?

Admiral Burke: We had all these married people on the ship, and they were away from their families. Eventually we were told we were going back to the coast for an R&R period, and I forget exactly when it was but probably October.[‡] I imagine that the fleet was divided into sections, and our section went back to Long Beach. And we had happiness amongst the married people for the first time since I'd been there. After we'd

---

[*] For a detailed recounting of Admiral Richardson's difficulties, see his book, written in collaboration with George C. Dyer: <u>On the Treadmill to Pearl Harbor: The Memoirs of Admiral James O. Richardson, USN (Retired)</u> (Washington, D.C.: Naval History Division, 1973).

[†] Admiral James O. Richardson, USN, served as Commander in Chief U.S. Fleet (CinCUS) from 6 January 1940 to 1 February 1941. His relief, Admiral Husband E. Kimmel, USN, was designated Commander in Chief Pacific Fleet rather than CinCUS. Kimmel was relieved of the fleet command on 17 December 1941 in the wake of the Japanese attack on Pearl Harbor.

[‡] R&R—rest and recreation.

been in Long Beach a couple or three weeks, then we went up to Bremerton.* The object was to have some additional antiaircraft equipment installed on the ships. On the way up, the night before we were supposed to get into Puget Sound, we ran into a horrible storm. I don't recall what the winds were, but there was a new bridge that had been installed up there in the Puget Sound area which was the bridge over to Tacoma.

Paul Stillwell: The Tacoma Narrows.

Admiral Burke: That bridge collapsed during that storm.† A number of our officers had rented apartments in Tacoma, and so it affected us very directly. Not being married, I didn't have to worry about it, but I heard about it. Heard lots of complaints, and people had to make last-minute shifts. Being in Bremerton for me was a very enjoyable time, because we had a golf course there right at the yard. We had a nice club and we had a big city nearby that we could catch a ferry at night or late afternoon and go over for dinner and misbehave over in town and go back and get on the ferry and fall asleep in a chair. You'd wake up at 7:00 o'clock in Bremerton and then go to work. We didn't do that every night, but it was there if we wanted to do it. And it was a social time where we got to meet the people on the other ships. The Pennsylvania was there. I can remember Admiral Carney was there with his family.‡ He was the exec of one of the other battleships. He was a commander at the time.

Paul Stillwell: He was in the California.

Admiral Burke: But I remember meeting his daughter, Betty Carney, who later married Joe Taussig.§ The Pennsylvania was there and Spence Wilson, my very good friend, was there, and so I saw a lot of Spence. It rained a lot.

---

* Puget Sound Navy Yard, Bremerton, Washington.
† On 7 November 1940, at approximately 11:00 AM, the Tacoma Narrows suspension bridge collapsed due to wind-induced vibrations. Situated on the Tacoma Narrows in Puget Sound, near the city of Tacoma, Washington, the bridge had been open for traffic only a few months.
‡ Commander Robert B. Carney, USN. As a four-star admiral he served as Chief of Naval Operations from 1953 to 1955.
§ Ensign Joseph K. Taussig, Jr., graduated from the Naval Academy in the class of 1941.

Paul Stillwell: It always does.

Admiral Burke: It was damp and cold, very much like today, much of the time. But socially it was fun. At work we communicators operated whether we were in port or not, and we had the same kind of duty, so it didn't slow down the kind of work we were doing.

Paul Stillwell: Was there any modernization to the ship during that period?

Admiral Burke: As best I remember, we probably had installed 1.1 machine guns. They were four in a mount. My mind boggles me, and I thought I'd never forget some of these things, but I'm sure that that's what we got at that time.

Paul Stillwell: And they were notorious for jamming.

Admiral Burke: Well, that was the best we had at that time. Somewhere along the line we got the 40 millimeters on the North Carolina, but the 1.1s were the original installation.

Paul Stillwell: Did the West Virginia provide a good beginning step for you as an ensign learning to be a naval officer?

Admiral Burke: No.

Paul Stillwell: Was that growing out of the exec's approach to things?

Admiral Burke: Well, I'd say it gave me a step on how the Navy was operating up until that stage. It was too much the discipline that had grown up in the Navy over the years that would be totally unacceptable today. The reserve officers that we had were looked on with contempt. They had a tough time, and we let them know that they were reserves, but I'd say we, the regulars, did not give them the respect that they deserved.

Recognizing this kind of thing has caused me to change my attitude over the years about how you deal with officers who come from other sources and people who come from other backgrounds. We had the first batch of 90-day wonders. I think they came from Columbia University, and I forget the name of the station ship they had up there on the North River.

Paul Stillwell: Prairie State.*

Admiral Burke: Yes, and we had some marvelous people, but the bosses in there let them know that they were second string. They would probably hotly deny it today, but that's the way it was. And we had some real fine people. Later on, when I got to the North Carolina, it existed but not as much as on the West Virginia.

Paul Stillwell: Well, at some point the regulars came to realize they really needed these men.

Admiral Burke: Well, I go back to the plebe system. I've made up my mind I don't like any part of the plebe system, and I think it's this idea of it's just sort of a rate that goes with my rank that I can do things that other people can't do. I don't think that's right. I think you earn the right to do things. Just this idea, for example, where I came aboard on Saturday afternoon and the exec hearing about it said, "Stay aboard until I meet you," and I didn't get ashore for two weeks. This is crazy. It's lousy. It's terrible leadership. It's a terrible administration practice, but particularly leadership.

Paul Stillwell: Lack of consideration.

Admiral Burke: I'd say looking back on different people who were on the West Virginia we had some great guys. We had Claude Ricketts, who came there as the first

---

* The pre-dreadnought battleship Illinois (BB-7) was commissioned in 1901. After her active service she was loaned to the New York Naval Militia in 1921 to serve as a training ship, stationed in the Hudson River west of New York City. In January 1941 she was renamed the Prairie State so the name "Illinois" could be used for a projected new battleship. Construction of the new ship started in January 1945 but was canceled in August of that year because World War II was about to end.

lieutenant.* He was great. But to have a framework that permitted this to operate was no good. After I got to be captain of a ship, if I had ever found somebody pulling that kind of stuff, I'd have fired him. I didn't see that attitude ever at that time.

Paul Stillwell: Do you have any specific memories of Ricketts?

Admiral Burke: Well, he was the first lieutenant, which was not the glamour department, but I do remember talking with him on a business basis about my division at one time, and he was business. He was highly respected by the people around him and who had interface with him. He was only there with me for about three months. There was somebody else in the job, but when he came into that job there was all the difference in the world in that job and how it affected the rest of the ship.

Paul Stillwell: He was credited with counterflooding when the Japanese attacked to keep the West Virginia from capsizing as the Oklahoma did.

Admiral Burke: Yes.

Paul Stillwell: What do you recall about emphasis on damage control in general during your time on board?

Admiral Burke: I can't speak to that.

Paul Stillwell: What do you remember about the quality of the enlisted men in the West Virginia?

Admiral Burke: I thought they were a pretty good bunch. I can remember the names of only a couple. One who was named Shortridge, who was from Louisiana. And my girl was from Louisiana. I can remember the chief. The flag chief was Rhinehart. He had a

---

* Lieutenant Claude V. Ricketts, USN, later became a four-star admiral and served as Vice Chief of Naval Operations in the 1960s.

son who later played for Southern Cal who was a tackle, and I tell you his father would have made a good tackle. He was tough, and he was in charge of that outfit, and we ensigns wouldn't have dared to give him an order. He ran the show. We had old-timers there that had put the ship in commission.

Paul Stillwell: Seventeen years earlier.

Admiral Burke: Those guys owned the ship. It was a good, solid bunch. I wasn't around long enough. I was gone so soon that I really didn't get my feet into the ground.

Paul Stillwell: Well, for some of those long-serving men, the ship was their home. They really didn't have a life away from it.

Admiral Burke: Right. Well, this is interesting. I remember when somebody had broken into these medical kits we had in the lifeboats. They had some sort of drugs in them, and one of the sailors had broken in and gotten caught. We had a court-martial, and he was kicked out of the Navy. They called the crew to quarters, and they read the findings of the court and so forth and they booted him off the ship right there in Pearl Harbor and escorted him out to the gate and let him go.

Paul Stillwell: I've looked at ships' logs from that era, and they're just replete with disciplinary actions: captain's masts and courts-martial.

Admiral Burke: Well, I don't remember a lot of captain's masts and courts-martial. Did I serve on a court-martial? Yes. I guess we had some courts-martial. I don't remember when we were in Pearl Harbor us having a lot of trouble, but when we got back to the base we had some AOLs and I served on a summary court-martial I think they were called.* I was the recorder, and you were the prosecutor and everything. You gave the guy a court-martial not because of the evidence you had but because what he did deserved that much punishment. That's the way it's all worked out.

---

* AOL—absent over liberty.

Paul Stillwell: Anything else to recall about the West Virginia?

Admiral Burke: No. I'd say I was a CWO and the people in our department and the kind of jobs were relatively unimportant in the scheme of things, just being on the team. I didn't realize it at the time, but that's the way it was.

We went back to Long Beach after we left Bremerton, and there was a Christmas leave period. The maximum leave that anybody was allowed was one week, and I wanted two weeks to go to New Orleans to see my girlfriend. I'd been saving up $50.00 a month so I could go to New Orleans if the opportunity ever afforded itself. I had $300.00, which was enough money to go to New Orleans and back by plane. Pete Parlett's girl was up in Bremerton, and so he took my duty. So I put in for two weeks.

The exec, Commander Alexander, didn't think that it had to go to the flag for approval. I don't know whether the exec approved it or disapproved it, but I know he didn't want me to have the leave. It turned out that my request had to go to the chief of staff for approval. I was in the bunkroom there, changing clothes one afternoon, and Admiral Kidd showed up. He said, "Your leave is approved, and I just want you to have the best time possible." The captain's chief yeoman in the ship's office told me later that the exec was mad as hell, but there was nothing he could do about it. So I've always felt very kindly about Admiral Kidd.

Paul Stillwell: That's understandable. And all this stems back to Ike Kidd being nice and writing to his father.

Admiral Burke: Yes. Well, Admiral Kidd was extraordinarily popular with everybody. He was a great leader, and he had the human touch. So I went off to New Orleans and spent Christmas with my gal, and that was one of the things that helped seal it.

Paul Stillwell: So he was very helpful in your future life.

Admiral Burke: Oh, yes. I haven't seen much of Ike, but he lives in Alexandria. I see him on rare occasions, and he knows about this.* Well, I got two weeks in New Orleans, and then I got transferred soon after I returned to the West Virginia. Betty was my girlfriend at that point. I wasn't engaged to her yet, but she was in New Orleans. I got the surprise orders, and that enabled me to arrive in New Orleans on Mardi Gras afternoon on the way to the North Carolina. We spent a week in New Orleans, which I will never forget. Then I came by here and went to see my mother, and she insisted that I go over to the Navy Department.

I said, "Why? I'm an ensign."

She said, "Uncle Bob always went to the Navy Department and conferred. You're supposed to do that." Uncle Bob was her brother-in-law.

Paul Stillwell: What was his name?

Admiral Burke: Robert A. Dawes.† He was the class of '04, and he had a son who was in '33. So I went over to the Navy Department on Constitution Avenue, walked in the front door, and there was a jimmylegs there.‡ I said, "I'm Ensign Burke, and I'm passing through town. I've been told that I'm supposed to report to the Navy Department."

He said, "You are."

I said, "Well, who do I report to?"

He said, "See that book over there? Just go sign it."

So I did. Then I said, "Now what do I do?"

He said, "You go home." So I went home.

Paul Stillwell: And reported that you had conferred.

---

* Subsequent to this interview, Admiral Isaac C. Kidd, Jr., USN (Ret.), died 27 June 1999 at his home in Alexandria, Virginia.
† Captain Robert A. Dawes had by this time retired but was recalled to active duty because of the national emergency then in force.
‡ The Navy Department building was at 17th Street and Constitution Avenue in Washington, D.C. The building remained in use until the early 1970s, when President Richard Nixon directed that it be demolished. Jimmylegs is a slang term used by Navy personnel for civilian security guards.

Admiral Burke: Mother wanted to know who I had conferred with, so she said she knew of a Commander Atherton Macondray, who had married a family friend in Alexandria.* He was on duty in BuNav, so she arranged to have me consult with him, so I went over and consulted with Commander Macondray.† He asked me what I wanted to know, and I said, "How did I get ordered to the North Carolina? This was the lightning stroke of luck for me." So he took me down and bumped into a classmate of mine, Joe Snyder, who was in the detail section.‡ Joe Snyder took me down to the ensign detail, and we asked the officer how come. He went into his file and broke out a letter from the captain of the West Virginia, who submitted a quarterly report. The quarterly report gave the most available ensigns on his ship, and I was number one.

Paul Stillwell: I don't know whether that's good or not.

Admiral Burke: Well, it my case it worked. When I left the West Virginia, I went ashore in the same boat with Lieutenant Commander Lorenzo Sabin.§ He was the ship's gunnery officer, and he was a fine man. I was only there a short time with him, but he let me know that Uncle Bob had written him a letter that I was there. He looked out for me a bit while I was there and as a friend. I just happened to go ashore on a Saturday afternoon when I was detached, and he told me, "You're going to a great ship with great people on it, and I'm going to write Tom Hill that you're coming." And, sure enough, when I got to the North Carolina, I bumped into Commander Hill, who was the gunnery officer.** He told me he had asked for me to be in the gunnery department, but they had a policy that you would go into the department where you had been working so that you wouldn't have to be reeducated.

---

* Lieutenant Commander Atherton Macondray, Jr., USN.
† BuNav—the Bureau of Navigation made officer assignments to various duties in the years prior to World War II.
‡ Ensign Joseph C. Snyder, USN.
§ Lieutenant Commander Lorenzo S. Sabin, Jr., USN, who soon afterward reported to the staff of Commander Battleships Battle Force. The oral history of Sabin, who retired as a vice admiral, is in the Naval Institute collection.
** Lieutenant Commander Tom B. Hill, USN.

Paul Stillwell: You talked about the captain who made you available. Did you have any contact with him during your service?

Admiral Burke: Yes. It was interesting. He was a bachelor. Because I was in communications as a CWO, I was also on the coding board, and I decoded messages and then took them around to these officers. I had personal contact with him whenever we had a classified message that required his initials, so he knew me personally.

Paul Stillwell: Who was he?

Admiral Burke: Henry T. Markland, and I thought he was a fine gentleman.* When I went to tell him good-bye, he said, "You know, Burke, I think we made a mistake in your case." I didn't even know what he was talking about until I got back to BuNav and heard I'd been made available.

Then I went on my way to New York to report to the North Carolina.† The difference between the two ships was the overall quality of the officers and department heads. The new exec and the captain were extraordinarily good people, and the rest of us were below. I sought out and wanted to get into gunnery. They had a lieutenant who was the fire control officer on the North Carolina. His name was A. G. Ward, Corky Ward.‡ He ran the school for the gunnery department, and he was first class.

Paul Stillwell: There's a picture of Ward on a bulkhead down on board the ship now in one of their displays.§

---

* Captain Henry T. Markland, USN, commanded the USS West Virginia (BB-48) from 5 January 1940 to 12 August 1941.
† USS North Carolina (BB-55) was commissioned 9 April 1941. She had a standard displacement of 35,000 tons, was 728 feet, 9 inches long, had a beam of 108 feet, 4 inches, and a draft of 26 feet, 8 inches. Her top speed was 27 knots. The ship had nine 16-inch guns and 20 5-inch/38 dual-purpose guns. Her original armament also included 16 1.1-inch antiaircraft guns and 12 .50-caliber machine guns. She was the first fast battleship commissioned by the U.S. Navy.
‡ Lieutenant Alfred G. Ward, USN, was fire control officer when the North Carolina was commissioned in 1941. The oral history of Ward, who retired as a four-star admiral, is in the Naval Institute collection.
§ The battleship now serves as a memorial in Wilmington, North Carolina.

Admiral Burke: Well, I used to go to his school because I wanted very badly to get into the gunnery department, because obviously that was where the action was, and they had all this new equipment. The equipment on the West Virginia was antiquated compared to what we had on the North Carolina, and I decided I wanted to get into the 5-inch battery, and they had nice computers. They had computers and directors, and they were all hooked up. Things were automatic, and you could see where things could really happen. The antiaircraft equipment in the West Virginia was very primitive.

Corky Ward, for example, obviously had to be the number-one guy, and his opposite number on the Washington was Ed Hooper.[*] They were classmates probably, and both of them were extraordinarily good people.[†] Then we had down through the department and assistant department heads they were really first class.

Paul Stillwell: So you got the impression they'd been essentially handpicked.

Admiral Burke: Oh, sure. You knew they had to be. The exec was Andrew Shepard.[‡] He should have made admiral, and I think what happened was he was such a strong personality when the second captain came there, Oscar Badger, they probably clashed.[§]

Paul Stillwell: Too similar.

Admiral Burke: No, he was not the same kind of officer. Badger was a very dominating guy. Andrew Shepard was an extraordinarily good man, and he knew that ship upside down. He had lots of problems, because we had a lot of crew members that had never been in the Navy, but we had good chiefs, we had good first class. Generally the petty officers who came from other ships were good strong people. The ship had a spirit. Of course, it's down in North Carolina now, and it has an alumni association.[**] I've been

---

[*] Lieutenant Edwin B. Hooper, USN, was the first control officer in the new battleship Washington (BB-56), sister ship of the North Carolina. The oral history of Hooper, who retired as a vice admiral, is in the Naval Institute collection.
[†] Hooper was in the Naval Academy class of 1931 and Ward in 1932; they had been together in doing postgraduate study in fire control at the Massachusetts Institute of Technology.
[‡] Commander Andrew G. Shepard, USN.
[§] Captain Oscar C. Badger, USN, commanded the North Carolina from 23 October 1941 to 1 June 1942.
[**] The ship now serves as a memorial and museum at Wilmington, North Carolina.

down a few times. The last time I went was when we had the 50th birthday, but it had a ship spirit that I think was probably better than any ship that I've served on.

Paul Stillwell: Probably part of that was that she was so much in the public eye for being the first new battleship in almost 20 years.

Admiral Burke: She got plenty of attention, and we were in New York, the center of communications and publicity. The Washington was built down in Philadelphia and got none. They used to call us "The Showboat," and I can remember the first time we passed the Washington at sea or close aboard. In those days you rendered formal honors and all this and broke out the band and lined people up. We passed them close aboard when the ships were down in Hampton Roads. The exec had anticipated this, and he had the band out there. When they were supposed to play the National Anthem, they played "Here Comes the Showboat" and then the National Anthem. He hadn't cut Captain Hustvedt in on it, but, boy, that really went over with the crew, and they've been proud of being called "The Showboat" ever since.*

I remember that the North Carolina began to get radars. We at first got a CXAM, first search radar, and I'm not sure when we got it, but I would suspect that it was in probably the late summer of '41. Gradually about that time they put fire control radar on the 5-inch directors, and then they got them for the main battery.

Paul Stillwell: So it wasn't till the North Carolina that you had much awareness of radar.

Admiral Burke: I don't think so. Of course, we were tied up, but I can remember after getting the CXAM there was a period of time before we got the fire control radar. I remember one day that we had some friends from New Orleans that were in New York, and Mr. and Mrs. Riley were walking around the deck. We didn't even dare mention that radar up there and what it was, because it was so secret. Mrs. Riley looked up there and

---

* Captain Olaf M. Hustvedt, USN, commanded the North Carolina from her commissioning on 9 April 1941 until 23 October 1941.

she said, "Is that a radar?" So I made some stupid remark like, "Well, I'm not sure what it is, but they just put it on."

Paul Stillwell: What are your impressions of Captain Hustvedt?

Admiral Burke: Extraordinarily good man. We had about four captains when I was on there, and they were all fine men. They were all different personalities. Captain Hustvedt, I would say, was as distinguished a person as I have ever come around. He and his wife, who was an exceptionally beautiful woman—I thought they represented the Navy in a way that few couples have. I wish you could have met my mother. She came up to New York, and she said, "Have you called on the captain?"

Paul Stillwell: She was always giving you these coaching tips.

Admiral Burke: She said, "Well, they're friends of Uncle Bob and Aunt Rose's, and we've got to call on them." So we went up and called on them. They had an apartment up in Brooklyn. He put the ship in commission, and he stayed there until he got selected for admiral. He was detached in October and replaced by Oscar Badger. But he knew his people, he knew the ship, and he was always courteous and gentlemanly and never put on an act.

Paul Stillwell: Very dignified.

Admiral Burke: Oh, yes. Terrific guy. And you couldn't help but respect him. Oscar Badger, on the other hand was something else.

Paul Stillwell: What do you recall about the shakedown training in the North Carolina shortly after she was commissioned?

Admiral Burke: We at one stage there were down in the Chesapeake Bay, probably sometime in September or October of 1941, and we went up towards Annapolis and were operating in the bay doing training exercises. Then we anchored out in the bay off of Chesapeake Beach, a resort community, it was then.

Paul Stillwell: Sort of south of Annapolis.

Admiral Burke: Yes, south of Annapolis. We were maybe three or four miles out into the bay, and so I requested special liberty to come home to see my mother. I got an all-day Saturday liberty, which very practically no one else got. I went ashore, and I had to be back at the landing about 10:00 o'clock in the evening.

Well, when I got back there I learned that limited liberty had been granted to some of the crew members and officers. We got back there for the 10:00 o'clock boat and no boat. So, before long, some of these people began to wander off to the nearest bar. The boat finally showed up around 11:30 in the evening, and we got in the boat. It was an open launch, and there must have been 35 or 40 of us in it, chiefs and a few officers and mostly white hats.

The chiefs and the officers were sitting in the stern sheets, and a couple of these chiefs were really under the weather and began to get very argumentative with the officers. One of our officers didn't like it and began to try to discipline these people and make them shut up. Before long we almost had a pitched battle right there in the boat. I was sitting next to one of the more senior officers, I don't recall what job or what he was, it was one of the staff. It was either supply or dental officer. I was sitting between him and one of these chiefs who began to belabor me because I was protecting this officer.

Eventually he turned on me and began to chew me out because I was obstructing his sense of justice. There was a chief sitting right next to him who pled with me to be compassionate, because he was sober, and he said his shipmate was not like that normally. So finally, when we got out to the ship, there was so much noise going on in the boat that the officer of the deck had the boat lie off until people calmed down and were suitable to come aboard a United States battleship. Eventually we came alongside, and I jumped and ran up the ladder and went below. When I came back to the wardroom the next morning to get breakfast, I discovered that there were about ten officers in hack.

Apparently there'd been a free-for-all on the quarterdeck that I escaped from, and I was the only one in the boat that wasn't in hack.

Paul Stillwell: So being quick helped you out. Well, that must not have allowed very much time with your mother, considering the transportation over and back.

Admiral Burke: Well, I'm sure that what happened was I probably communicated with her ahead of time and she came down and met me on the dock.

Paul Stillwell: Oh, I see.

Admiral Burke: It was about an hour-and-15-minute drive each way, and I had a very devoted mother. She was a widow and intensely interested in what I was doing, and so I spent the day with her and it was well worth it.

On that ship I had a marvelous chief named Bill Plusch, who had been in World War I.[*] He had been Ernie King's flag chief, and he had been on a ship that was torpedoed and sunk, I think.[†] I don't know where he came from, but he was living in New London when I went back up there after the war and had a submarine command.

Oscar Badger arrived that fall as the new captain. I was the signal officer, because I had to be in communications. We were in port much of the time, and I remember the first time I took a message up to Captain Badger. There was a chief sitting there in his cabin, and that was Bunny O'Hare. Well, he and Bunny O'Hare had been buddies for years. Anytime you saw Oscar in his cabin, you might see Bunny, who was privy to everything that was going on, and he was running the ship's store. Everybody knew Bunny was his boy. So he had a pipeline in to the chiefs, what was going on, that nobody else had. He also raised hell up there on deck with his officers and pounded on his officers.

He came aboard in October, and then we started operating in December. Went down around Norfolk and then from there we went down in the Gulf of Mexico and

---

[*] Chief Signalman William E. Plusch, USN. He eventually retired as a lieutenant commander.
[†] Admiral Ernest J. King, USN, was Commander in Chief Atlantic Fleet at the time the North Carolina was commissioned.

operated. War started while he was there. He was an explosive personality, and I was up on the bridge getting told how to do my job by this chief who had 25 years' experience. He was very knowledgeable and he kept me out of trouble. I never got in trouble with him, but I'd say when we got into training down there I was on the bridge as much as he was, and I wasn't doing anything, but I was soaking up and watching the various officers that we had try to deal with him. And Corky Ward could deal with him.

We had a navigator named Glisson who was a hell of a nice guy.[*] He got involved in a problem; it was either right before Christmas or right after Christmas. The war had started, and we had mines out and so forth and messages were going. I took a classified message up to the navigator. I knew he hadn't done something that he was supposed to on a chart, and he didn't want me to take it to the captain. I said, "The captain's got to see it." And he pled with me. This officer was a commander, and I was an ensign. I said, "He's got to see it."

So I took it up to him, and I guess we were in port, because he told me, "You call up Captain Denfeld, Bureau of Navigation."[†] So I got him on the phone, handed him the phone, and he said, "I want this officer relieved immediately." Years later, when I began to relieve people, I didn't think about Badger, but sometimes I snapped pretty fast. He was a man that wasn't afraid to make a decision, and when he left I never saw him again. I think he left us and became ComDesLant. I don't know what happened, but I'd say this is the way the life in the Navy goes. You separate from somebody who had a big influence on you for a short time.

Paul Stillwell: After your first navigator left was when you got Joe Stryker.[‡]

Admiral Burke: Joe Stryker came in. Joe Stryker had been a company officer when I was a midshipman the last two years. He put me on a report when he first came there for screwing up the main office. That's the last time I was on report. [Laughter] He was in the fourth battalion my last year when I got transferred over to the fourth battalion. He

---

[*] Commander Charles O. Glisson, USN.
[†] Captain Louis E. Denfeld, USN, who was later Chief of Naval Operations, 1947-49.
[‡] Lieutenant Commander Joe W. Stryker, USN, had been serving as commanding officer of the minesweeper Raven (AM-55).

got passed over for lieutenant commander and had been picked up with the expansion of the Navy. He was then a lieutenant commander. And we got Joe Stryker because he had been captain of a minesweep that was our escort up there in Chesapeake Bay at about the time the war started or just before. And I tell you, he could anticipate what Badger wanted to do, and that took a lot of doing. He came to the ship as the navigator, and here was a guy who had been passed over for lieutenant commander. He could handle Badger better than anybody else up there. It was remarkable.

Paul Stillwell: What was the secret of his success?

Admiral Burke: Well, he'd been a submariner. I didn't know what the circumstances were why he was in the surface ships, but he knew how to handle himself. He was terrific at taking the conn when it was necessary.* He took the conn whenever we were at GQ, and, boy, he was first class.† The trust that the crew had in him was remarkable. And he was a human being. In watching him operate and deal with situations, he always knew the answers. I guess I unconsciously did the same thing years later, but Badger was ruthless in hazing the officers of the deck. I'd say Corky Ward was the only one that could deal with him, and these other officers just didn't study their lesson enough. I guess I got to be the same way years later.

When Joe Stryker came aboard, things calmed down with Badger. We came back after this training period and came into the shipyard at New York for our final checkup. My future wife and her family lived up on East 74th Street. I guess she had moved back from New Orleans to be with her family. The mother and daughter came down for dinner one night in the wardroom, and I guess we went up to my stateroom afterwards. There was a knock on the door, and it was Badger's orderly, who said, "The captain wants to see you." So I went up to his cabin, and he was up there with Mrs. Badger, who had been a patient of one of my two uncles who were eye specialists in Washington. One of them had told them that I was on there, and so she said, "I hear you're engaged."

---

* The individual with the conn—normally an officer—directs the ship's movements in course and speed.
† GQ—general quarters, the time when the crew is at battle stations.

I said, "Yes, she and her mother are aboard." So they had them up, and they were just as charming and relaxed. It was right about this time that there were some transfers in the ship. I was the signal officer, and the captain was very complimentary about the work I'd done with him. I say I wasn't doing anything. I was just up there absorbing. I never had the deck.

The exec got transferred, and we got a new exec who was terrible. He'd been ashore for four years, and he was just out of it. We had the first lieutenant, Thackrey, who later made vice admiral, and he was great.[*] He had been at the Naval Academy as a battalion officer my first class year. I don't know who got transferred in our structure, but the fifth division officer, who had the starboard 5-inch battery, got elevated to air defense. The air defense officer went off to new construction, and so I got the fifth division. Here I was an ensign, and I had seven officers under me and 170 men in my division. All of a sudden, I was on the team. I couldn't believe it.

Paul Stillwell: Do you think that was Badger's doing?

Admiral Burke: I think it was Tom Hill who had asked for me, although the night that I took Betty and her mother up to meet the Badgers, he was very complimentary about how I was doing, and, believe me, I worked hard. I wasn't goofing off. I also had been attending the school sessions. Whenever Corky Ward had a school session on the gunnery department, if I was not otherwise tied up, I would attend it. So I was learning about it, and I was going down to secondary plot to learn how to operate the computer and occasionally went up and would sit in the directors just to learn how to do it. I'm sure he must have known it.

But, in any case, I ended up as the fifth division officer, and I had six or seven officers under me, and all of a sudden I was on the team and I had a big part of the ship. Our classmates were moving up. Some of the lieutenants got transferred to other jobs or other ships. The Navy was expanding. My roommate Bill Laffey got to be the number-two turret officer.[†] He was a classmate. So that's when I felt like I was really getting

---

[*] Lieutenant Commander Lyman A. Thackrey, USN.
[†] Lieutenant (junior grade) William F. Laffey, USN.

somewhere. I didn't have a chief; I had a first class. He was good. He was first class when he came to the ship. I got to know the people on the other side of the ship, too, and a classmate of mine who was really experienced was the division officer on the other side.

Paul Stillwell: Who was he?

Admiral Burke: Speed Simmons.[*] He lives down in Texas. He does not participate in class functions. He was very well liked and very good. He went into aviation. I've written to him a couple of times and never gotten an answer, so I don't know what happened, but we were good friends on board ship.

Paul Stillwell: What are your recollections of Tom Hill?

Admiral Burke: I thought he was great. I had two bosses. One was the air defense officer, who was John Kirkpatrick.[†] Have you ever met him?

Paul Stillwell: No.

Admiral Burke: He is Mr. Oklahoma City. He was in the class of '31. He went to West Point and I think bilged out and then came to the academy. And then I'm not sure when, but he resigned and was in the Naval Reserve. He's a rear admiral in the reserve, but he has done exceptionally well in the oil business. He has given millions and millions to the city of Oklahoma City, and he has been active in the backup of the Navy and so forth and he looks like Gary Cooper. He was a lieutenant when he first came aboard, and I think he worked his way all the way to gunnery officer. Then he got to be the exec of the Oklahoma City when it went in commission. I relieved him as the fifth division officer, and he became my boss. Fine man. Good leader. A real gentleman.

---

[*] Ensign Kenneth G. Simmons, USN.
[†] Lieutenant John E. Kirkpatrick, USNR.

The assistant gunnery officer was Heiny Zemmer, who was about the class of '27.* He was a terrible guy in personnel. He was typical of the era on the <u>West Virginia</u>, where you sort of got hazed. He started off as the main battery assistant, and then he became the senior assistant. He used to run the gunnery department meetings most of the time, because Hill was obviously on a level above that, and Hill didn't get into the intimate details that the main battery officer and the air defense officer did. Eventually Zemmer became the gunnery officer when Hill left. Hill became fleet gunnery officer.

Paul Stillwell: For Admiral Nimitz.†

Admiral Burke: Yes. But I value people on whether they are approachable, and he was very approachable. I could have gone and talked to him any time I wanted to and whenever the need was there I did, but the channel was through Zemmer. Zemmer was the kind of guy where an ensign or a jaygee who was fairly new in those days would go in and have to get permission to go ashore and he would haze them, and he drove himself in the same way. He was married. Had a nice wife named Patsy, and how she put up with the bastard I don't know.

We had been in Guantanamo on our shakedown training, and if you've ever been through a Guantanamo training period it is intensive.‡ You get up early, work hard all day, and come in late. And the gunnery department probably gets as much as anybody. When we got back to New York, of course, all the wives were standing on the dock waiting for us. I was in the wardroom, and Zemmer just stayed on board, because he had work to do. Patsy was aboard. He was down in the office, and he knew she was there. He came up to dinner kind of surly, and so they had dinner together. There were four big tables there, and he was probably at the senior table, and she was being social and nice, and he was being grumpy. After dinner he said, "Got to go back to the office." He went back to the office, and she stayed there in the wardroom with some of the bachelor officers, chatting with them, being sociable, and saw the movie. After the movie she

---

* Lieutenant Commander Harold M. Zemmer, USN.
† Fleet Admiral Chester W. Nimitz, USN, served as Commander in Chief Pacific Fleet and Pacific Ocean Areas, 1941-45.
‡ Guantanamo Bay, on the south coast of Cuba, near the eastern end of the island, for many years provided a fleet anchorage and training area for U.S. Navy ships.

came in, and she asked somebody to do down and get him. He came up, and he said, "Well, I'm too tired to go home," and he went back. That happened.

Paul Stillwell: After being gone all that time?

Admiral Burke: Yes, and I was there when he said it.

I've forgotten exactly when it was, but Andy Shepard was the exec. Shepard was a marvelous guy, and we elected Heiny the wardroom mess treasurer.

Paul Stillwell: That's a job that usually goes to someone who is not too popular with the other officers.

Admiral Burke: When they cast the vote, all the ensigns elected him. They just put the letter "Z" on there. Well, we paid for it because we had the worst meals I've ever seen.

Paul Stillwell: What else do you remember about Tom Hill?

Admiral Burke: Well, Tom Hill was a great guy. He was somebody that was very approachable and somebody I really respected. I guess I'm a people person, and he was somebody I could communicate with. I didn't ever take advantage of it, but I knew that if I had something important enough I could go in and talk to him and lay the cards on the table, and to me this was significant. He was that way the whole time I knew him.

The only other time when I had anything to do with him other than on the North Carolina was in the '50s when I was the captain of the President's yacht, the Williamsburg, for a short time and he was the naval district commandant. He presided over the decommissioning ceremony and was very nice and approachable during that period that I was on the Williamsburg. I went there as executive officer and then succeeded to command. But he was very helpful and provided an approving umbrella on political problems that I had to deal with. He was a friend.

Paul Stillwell: In the engineering department the chief engineer was Fred Edwards, and he had Bill Maxwell with him.* What do you remember about those two?

Admiral Burke: Edwards was first class. Businesslike. I didn't know him personally. Never socialized outside of the ship, but he certainly was well qualified for the job and highly respected by me and the other people that dealt with him. Bill Maxwell—what a character. I'm pretty sure he was an immigrant.

Paul Stillwell: Edwards said Maxwell came over from Russia when the fleet was there after World War I.

Admiral Burke: I think he either came from East Poland or Western Russia, and he enlisted in the Navy. He had the ability to get close to people that he wanted to be nice to him and do favors for them, and they usually would respond. He was a real operator.

Paul Stillwell: Do you have any examples?

Admiral Burke: My memory now is kind of weak on details, but I know he was always good with the JOs. My roommate once said, "He's like a kid." He had the appetites of a JO. He was good at his job, but he was just unconventional the way he did things. He hadn't been brought up in the military system or the academy but, Lord, he ended up in a political job in New York City. You knew that?

Paul Stillwell: No.

Admiral Burke: After he retired, he somehow or other got a job—I forget the name of the mayor who appointed him as the director of smoke control or the environmental kind of thing. Shortly after getting the job he publicly announced that the politics of the system would prevent him from doing his job, and he had the newspapers and the media

---

* Commander Frederick A. Edwards, USN; the oral history of Edwards, who retired as a captain, is in the Naval Institute collection. His assistant was Lieutenant Commander William S. Maxwell, USN.

of New York praising him in a way that you wouldn't believe. He was a popular hero that the politicians hated. He was a nice guy, but every now and then he would do things that seemed almost childish, and I wish I could give you some examples. But I knew that every time I saw him come around, I had to watch out. He was trying to pull a big deal for himself or somebody.

Paul Stillwell: Well, the difference in the North Carolina from your first ship was that there was no JO mess, so you saw the senior officers regularly.

Admiral Burke: We were in the wardroom. We saw them but we sat at different tables. We called them ward one, two, three, and four. When we first got there, the class of '41 was the junior class. There were about six or seven of us from the class of '40, and on up. The exec was from the class of '17, and the department heads were lieutenant commanders from the early '20s. Then the war started, and promotions began to take place, especially in the Marine Corps. We had Mike Fowler, who ranked with the class of '39, was sitting at our table.[*] And all of a sudden he became a first lieutenant, so that moved him up a little bit. And before long he got to be a captain before any of us got promoted to jaygee. Well, that moved him up ahead of some of the people, and then before long he became a major, and he was senior to the class '30 or something like that. I tell you the people's feelings were getting hurt, and they were very irritated about it.

Paul Stillwell: When I served in the New Jersey, it was just that way in the wardroom. We were strictly according to seniority where we sat.

Admiral Burke: I think Mike moved all the way from table four all the way up to table two, and he may have ended up by being senior to Corky Ward.

Paul Stillwell: Ward was out of the class of '32.

---

[*] Second Lieutenant George T. Fowler, USMC.

Admiral Burke: In hindsight I say I never had a good experience that I really appreciated in the JO mess. I remember one day having a conversation about the JO mess with Charlie Kirkpatrick when he was my company officer at the academy. He told me it was just like a fraternity, and I respect him for it, but I didn't see that when I was on the West Virginia. I will say this. I feel the same way about fraternities that I do about the plebe system because they had the same liabilities.

Paul Stillwell: And same hazing.

Admiral Burke: Yes.

Paul Stillwell: Someone who served with Badger told me that he seemed to think he knew everything about everything. Was that your impression?

Admiral Burke: No. He knew how to conn a ship. He stayed up there on the bridge all the time. See, he had been in World War I as a captain of a destroyer, and he talked about it every now and then. Actually I think that he had seen a German submarine go under him, and he had depth charged the guy, but hadn't sunk him. The two captains later met each other. So he knew how to run a ship from the bridge. He didn't wander around below decks.

Now, the last captain of the North Carolina in my time was Wilder Baker.* He was a submariner. He came down, hadn't been aboard long, and, boy, he made a business of getting around that ship, and I was impressed in a way with him I have never been with any other captain of a battleship. When he came into my compartment, he got each enlisted man in charge to tell him how that machinery or that loading machine worked and so forth in a way that Badger would have been lost. Now, I'd have to put myself in Badger's shoes as a captain, because I was not a technical man myself. I came to the top in command so fast I didn't get to be an engineer long enough or a first lieutenant and so forth, and so my short suit has always been depending on somebody to carry me through. I suspect Badger was in the same way. But Wilder Baker made me feel that he would ask

---

* Captain Wilder D. Baker, USN, commanded the North Carolina from 5 December 1942 to 27 May 1943.

enough to get educated, and I've tried to emulate that ever since. I can't remember exactly how long we were together, but when I went up to pay my respects when I was leaving, he let me know that he had met an aunt of mine in New Hampshire, where he had been vacationing, where we go today, and he knew about me.

Paul Stillwell: That's a nice touch.

Admiral Burke: Thirty years later, when we were up there in New Hampshire at a cottage, the man next door to us and his family were Wilder Baker, Jr.

Paul Stillwell: Small world.

Admiral Burke: Do you know Hal Bowen?[*]

Paul Stillwell: Yes.

Admiral Burke: His wife is Wilder Baker's daughter.

Paul Stillwell: Admiral Bowen was a really energetic man.

Admiral Burke: I don't know. I think when he finally checks out, you'd better stuff him and put him in a museum somewhere. He's amazing.

Paul Stillwell: Smart guy.

Admiral Burke: Yes.

Paul Stillwell: The other skipper when you were on board was Captain Fort.[†] What do

---

[*] Vice Admiral Harold G. Bowen, USN (Ret.), who subsequently died of cancer 17 August 2000 at his home in Alexandria, Virginia.
[†] Captain George H. Fort, USN, commanded the North Carolina from 1 June 1942 to 5 December 1942.

you recall of him?

Admiral Burke: I think he may have been a submariner too. I'm not sure. He didn't project his personality to me as much as the others, but he came in after Oscar Badger, and he was a quiet person. I guess he sort of ran the ship the way I would like to do it but try to make sure that the people under him were trained to do the job that they were doing. And he took us through. He had Stryker there, and he had a good man who could do the thing up there on the bridge. He gave us a calming effect after the storm of Oscar Badger.

Paul Stillwell: He'd been, I think, the head of the math department at the academy before that.

Admiral Burke: Had he? Well, he exuded confidence and people respected him. We're Episcopalians by faith, and I often compare the pastor of an Episcopal parish to the captain of a ship. When I tell the pastor this, they look at me like I'm sinning but, it's true, they do. Our previous pastor that we had for 15 years ran it by making all the decisions and so forth in all departments and so on. He and I didn't get along worth a nickel, because I couldn't talk to him. We've got a new guy there now who's been there for about two or three years, and he runs it pretty much the way I would. He makes sure that all of his subordinates are qualified for command. People who are used to being kicked in the tail and told what to do miss the other guy, and I'm very relieved to have somebody you can talk to. [Laughter]

Paul Stillwell: How far along was the ship's construction when you reported? Was she virtually complete?

Admiral Burke: Yes. One month. It wasn't complete when she went into commission, but it was complete enough to have the ceremony that was attended by a lot of people. Somewhere I've got a picture of the ceremony where we went in commission.

Paul Stillwell: Down at the memorial there's a mural photo of the whole crew on the fantail.

Admiral Burke: Yes. I'm sure the CNO was there.* Ernie King was CinCLantFlt; he was there. Fiorello LaGuardia was there.† It was a big spectacle. Adolphus Andrews was the commandant of the district, and they had a big public relations push to make sure that the world knew it was going on.‡

Paul Stillwell: Hanson Baldwin covered for The New York Times, I think, and he later went out on the trials.§

Admiral Burke: Well, we went out on one trial, and it may have been the original shakedown. We had everybody that was anybody in the media along, and Hanson Baldwin was just one of them. I may have somewhere out there in my files a copy of the North Carolina Tarheel, where they had all of these guys writing articles. Winchell was a lieutenant commander at the time, reserve officer, and he was out there and he wrote a column for his paper.** The man who had gotten the picture of the Hindenburg when it exploded was on there, and he did something funny.†† He was professing to be frightened. We were getting ready to test fire all of the main battery plus one side, I guess it was the port side guns, all at the same time, and they had to make a special rig to be able to tie them together.

We had five mounts on each side, so we had ten guns. Tom Hill had Gunner McCrory rig up something so that the captain could pull the trigger up there, or Tom Hill

---

* Admiral Harold R. Stark, USN, was Chief of Naval Operations from 1 August 1939 to 26 March 1942.
† LaGuardia was mayor of New York City.
‡ Rear Admiral Adolphus Andrews, USN, Commandant of the Third Naval District.
§ Hanson W. Baldwin was a 1924 graduate of the Naval Academy. Following several years of naval service, Baldwin began a distinguished career as a newspaperman, culminating as military editor of The New York Times. His Naval Institute oral history includes memories of the North Carolina trials at sea.
** Walter Winchell, who had served with the Naval Reserve in World War I, was a popular newspaper columnist with the New York Mirror and had a radio program with a huge audience.
†† The German Hindenburg was one of the largest airships ever built. Built in 1936, it was 812 feet long and 135 feet in diameter. It created an international sensation on 6 May 1937 when it exploded and burned while approaching its mooring at the naval air station in Lakehurst, New Jersey. That event ended regular airship service between the United States and Germany.

could pull it on the bridge.* This cameraman went around, and he was down talking to Bill Plusch, my chief. Plusch introduced him to me, and he professed to be afraid when this was going on. But what he really wanted to do was to get on another ship and be able to take a photograph of it, and so we eventually arranged for him to move over to another ship, destroyer, and he got a silhouette of this thing and it was dark. It was about 6:00 or 7:00 o'clock in the evening, and it showed up in Life magazine on the center page next week.†

Paul Stillwell: So he knew his business.

Admiral Burke: I forget what the guy's name was, but he was good.

The ship attracted so much attention we had visitors all the time. I was at dinner there one night in the wardroom—or maybe it was lunch—and somebody had asked me to be an escort for some young women. They were employed somewhere. They were down there, and so I took them in the wardroom for lunch. One gal just reached over and took a fork and just stuck it down her dress. I said, "What are you doing that for?"

She said, "I want a souvenir."

So I just said, "You can't take it." So I went over and told the officer of the deck that she had this down her dress and told the Marine orderly, "Don't let her go ashore." The supply officer, Commander Clark, happened along about this time.‡ I told him what happened. He said, "In the first month we have completely replaced the flat silver in the wardroom."

Paul Stillwell: And it was real silver probably.

Admiral Burke: People were just taking this stuff right and left.

Paul Stillwell: So did they get this fork back?

---

* Gunner Thomas S. McCrory, USN.
† See "U.S. Battleship 'North Carolina' Shoots its Guns in Firing Tests at Sea," Life, 15 September 1941, pages 40-41. The two-page spread featured three pictures supplied by International News Photos.
‡ Commander Alfred B. Clark, SC, USN.

Admiral Burke: I don't know whether they did or not.

Paul Stillwell: What do you remember from the commissioning ceremony itself? Was everybody at division parade?

Admiral Burke: No, I think we went to quarters, and then they bunched up on the fantail. I'm in that picture. The ship's officers were lined up, and I don't remember whether they were in two or one line, but I'm in that picture in the front row. My guess is that the captain was out front and maybe the exec and departments heads were in a second row and then the rest of us.

Paul Stillwell: Well, with those catapults back there it was kind of a tight squeeze, wasn't it?

Admiral Burke: Oh, yes. But we probably at the time maybe only had 1,200, and eventually we got about 2,000. Before we went in commission we were living ashore. Three of us, Bill Laffey and Pat Patterson and myself, lived in a room up at the St. George Hotel in Brooklyn for $35.00 a month apiece.* And it was safe to walk from the St. George Hotel down Sand Street. My gal eventually came up from New Orleans, and so I was going ashore a lot. I'd get home three nights out of four after midnight, and I used to walk down Sand Street. There wasn't any problem.

Paul Stillwell: So, it sounds as if you were putting in awfully long days to get the ship ready.

Admiral Burke: Yes. Well, in the communications department we were tied up. So from the signal side of it we were inactive. I was a coding board member. I was learning things like flashing light, teaching myself, or using signal flags. I didn't learn nearly as much as I should have, but we didn't operate enough with other ships. I guess that what I

---

* Ensign William F. Laffey, USN; Ensign DeWitt M. Patterson, USN.

learned the most up there was how my chief operated. We had two first class signalmen, one of whom made chief and went over to the <u>Washington</u>. But I learned a heck of a lot from my chief on how to deal with senior officers, because he was used to dealing with captains of the ships, four-stripers, and he'd been Ernie King's flag chief.

Paul Stillwell: Do you remember any of the lessons he taught you?

Admiral Burke: I guess the main lesson was when he said, "You have a pad with you and a pencil, and you stay close to the cow."* So I got asked to do a lot of things. I was like a flag lieutenant for the captain. I didn't realize it at the time, but I was there and all of these people, the department heads, got used to seeing me around, so I got to be a channel to the captain just because I was up there all the time.

Paul Stillwell: Was Hustvedt friendly or warm? How would you describe him?

Admiral Burke: I never saw him like this in any sort of a conversation. He was up in his separate quarters with his stewards and all that business up there, so he didn't wander around the ship very much. But I remember bumping into him, and he would call me by name, which sort of surprised me.

Paul Stillwell: So it was mostly business?

Admiral Burke: Oh, yes.

Paul Stillwell: It sounds like there was more of a personal touch with Captain Baker, for example.

Admiral Burke: Yes, but I'd say I didn't rub elbows with him. I was only with him not more than two months. It may not have been that long. But he came across to me as a guy who made a point of trying to learn where he was.

---

* In this case, the "cow" refers to the commanding officer.

Paul Stillwell: What do you remember of the sensation when that gun firing took place for the first time and the photographer was off on the other ship?

Admiral Burke: I was on the bridge, standing right behind Tom Hill, and the ship heeled over substantially. I don't remember how many degrees, but I would venture to say it went maybe seven to ten degrees.

Paul Stillwell: That's a lot.

Admiral Burke: During the summer of 1941 we had all these sailors who had never been to sea before and quite a number of reserve officers who hadn't. The number of liberty people coming in late was getting pretty high. So Tom Hill and the exec got together and arranged for the North Carolina to use a National Guard camp up near Peekskill, New York. We sent groups of enlisted men and junior officers from the North Carolina up there for about two weeks, where we lived in sort of barracks and where they had a rifle range up there. We shot the rifle and we were up there for two weeks, but it was a good way to sort of get away from the scene of the ship but to fraternize with the other officers who were there.

It was a two-week camp, and as I remember we could go in town if we wanted to. I don't remember going in town on liberty in particular, but we were not too far from West Point. In a way, for those of us who were up there at that time, it was sort of a bonding experience. Looking back on my experience and the people I've bumped into, I'd say I was extraordinarily fortunate in serving under more experienced people who were good role models for me all my life. North Carolina had an exceptional number of those kinds of people.

In the summer of 1941, at the New York Navy Yard, there was a British battleship that came in there, and I can't remember the name of it, but I think she may have been hit by a torpedo; my memory is so horrible these days. They were in there for a major upkeep and were in there for at least two or three months. Another British light cruiser came in, and you could tell by looking at these ships and what exposure we had to them from time to time how they had been through the wringer. They also served liquor on board their ships.

Paul Stillwell: How were the reserve officers treated in North Carolina compared with what you known in West Virginia?

Admiral Burke: Much better at the start. Not nearly as well as they should have but far better. I was on the North Carolina for almost two years, and so around the time I was leaving they were moving into key jobs. When I came back after I got into submarines I saw the North Carolina on rare occasions, but I could say that the reserve officers had moved in and were carrying the mail. There wasn't any question about it.

Paul Stillwell: So they had earned respect.

Admiral Burke: Oh, sure. Sure.

Paul Stillwell: And the impression I've gotten is that those early reserve officers were really cream-of-the-crop type men.

Admiral Burke: You mean on the West Virginia?

Paul Stillwell: I mean in general that they were from Ivy League schools and they were top guys.

Admiral Burke: I'm just trying to think where they were all from. I know we had Ivy Leaguers. We had a couple from Dartmouth. We had one from Yale. Yes, you're right.

Paul Stillwell: What else do you remember as that year of '41 progressed? The trials and the camp? Then anything more on the shakedown to mention?

Admiral Burke: Well, we didn't get the kind of shakedown cruise that other ships had made earlier. See, up until the time we came along, shakedown cruise meant going off on an extended cruise somewhere with foreign ports, and so we didn't get that. Our shakedown cruise was doing about six weeks or maybe two months down at Guantanamo. And it was an intensive period of gunnery and damage control exercises and engineering exercises.

Paul Stillwell: Did you have outside instructors come in to supervise?

Admiral Burke: I don't remember about that. It wasn't like when I went in years later as captain of a destroyer, where they put instructors on there and they actually supervised the way we were doing things.

Paul Stillwell: Fleet training group.

Admiral Burke: I don't recall that. We did a lot of shooting. Shooting is what I remember the most of, because we were shooting down sleeves in the antiaircraft business, and our main battery was hitting targets in a way that the Navy wasn't used to. From all of the expressions of joy from the captain and the gunnery officer I felt that we were hitting things that way they'd never been hit before.

Paul Stillwell: Would this be attributed to radar fire control?

Admiral Burke: Yes, I'm sure it was. But they were good.

Paul Stillwell: Well, that would make a remarkable difference.

Admiral Burke: Well, it was not only radar fire control. It was also the computer capabilities we had and the gun train order. It was automatic, being fed from the computers up to the guns and actually feeding in the time of burst.

Paul Stillwell: Did you have two separate plotting rooms for main battery and two for secondary or one each?

Admiral Burke: I only remember one each.

Paul Stillwell: Okay. It must have been the Iowa class that went to two each. Were there any droned uses in the antiaircraft so you got some maneuvering capability?

Admiral Burke: Yes. We fired on drones, and the first time a drone came over the ship we didn't hit him, and there was great consternation about it. As I best recall, this happened off of Portland, Maine. I could be wrong, but he came across and it was not too long after the Japanese had sunk one or two battleships over there in Southeast Asia.*

Paul Stillwell: So the war had started.

Admiral Burke: The war had started, and we were terribly concerned that the Japanese had torpedo planes that sank two battleships over there. They brought drones out and made torpedo type passes over the ship, and they got over scot free. We were just horrified, because we'd been shooting down sleeves right and left. And then probably Tom Hill and John Kirkpatrick and Heiny Zemmer got together and tried to figure it out. The drone was controlled by a control plane that was flying overhead. I don't know how far. They figured out that every time that the controller would see a burst he would change course, and he was changing course essentially all the time, and our computer was always playing catch-up, which meant we were always going behind the drone.

Paul Stillwell: Sort of like chasing salvos in surface gunnery.

Admiral Burke: So what we did the next time in anticipation of this, instead of chasing him we fired a spread from one end of the horizon to the other, and he didn't know where

---

* On 10 December 1941 Japanese aircraft attacked and sank the British battleship Prince of Wales and battle cruiser Repulse when the ships were operating off Malaya.

to go, and we shot him down on the next burst. You never heard so much cheering in all your life. Boy, people were jumping up and down and saying, "We got him!"

Paul Stillwell: So that was up at Casco Bay?

Admiral Burke: I think it was.

Paul Stillwell: Was part of the purpose having the ship there as kind of a guard against the German heavy ships in early '42?

Admiral Burke: Yes. We all knew that as long as we were in the Atlantic, that we were to look out for the Tirpitz, so we were sent up there along with the Washington.* I think there was a cruiser up there for a short while and quite a number of destroyers. After we'd been up there and I don't recall how long the carrier Wasp, I think, may have come up there. But anyhow the Washington, and the cruiser and four or five destroyers took off and headed for Scapa Flow. Admiral Wilcox, who was our division commander, either jumped or was pushed over the side.† Interestingly enough, on my last duty station in Charleston, South Carolina, his son was the editor of the paper down there, and we became good friends. He was a rear admiral in the Naval Reserve.

Anyway, we stayed up there for a while longer, and the first of April came along. Well, when I graduated from the Naval Academy in 1940 there was a law on the books that academy graduates couldn't get married for two years. But we had many reserves coming on active duty that were getting married right and left, and we couldn't legally do so. Finally, on the first of April, 1942, the Navy Department, with Congress's assistance, released the information that the ban had been lifted. We were in Portland, Maine, at the time. I was on duty that night, and I got a friend of mine to send a telegram to Betty in

---

* The Tirpitz was a German battleship, a sister of the Bismarck, which was sunk in May 1941. The Tirpitz holed up in Norwegian fiords, tying down Allied forces that would be needed to deal with her if she emerged.
† Rear Admiral John W. Wilcox, USN, Jr., Commander Battleship Division Six, was lost overboard from his flagship, the USS Washington (BB-56), on 26 March 1942, while she was en route to the British Isles. The circumstances of his death were never satisfactorily explained. See Winston Jordan, "Man Overboard," U.S. Naval Institute Proceedings, December 1988.

New Orleans. The telegram said something like, "This is no April fool. We can get married." I think somewhere in our files we still have that telegram.

Lo and behold, her family came up from New Orleans with Betty and my family from Alexandria, Virginia, and a couple of other relatives in New England. We were married in Falmouth Foreside, right adjacent to Portland, at St. Mary's Church, and Chaplain Albert performed the ceremony for us.* We were Episcopalian. He was not, but anyhow we didn't know the people there. We got no counseling or anything like that, but we had the full support of our families and so forth.

Paul Stillwell: What was the date of the wedding?

Admiral Burke: That was 10 April, at St. Mary's Episcopal Church in Falmouth Foreside.

Paul Stillwell: Admiral Shear got married that same month when the prohibition came off.

Admiral Burke: Yes, that was at the same church, a week later. We went to a gathering at Dougie Woods's—she's now Douglas Sprunt—the other night, and there was a couple there named Goodrich. He's a former head of the Bath Shipbuilding Company.

Paul Stillwell: Used to be Under Secretary of the Navy.†

Admiral Burke: Yes. Well, he and his wife were there, and we got talking about this, and it turns out they live right next door to that church.

Our wedding was quite a feat when you consider the restrictions on travel. I think her father was in New Orleans on business, and they drove part of the way. Then Betty hopped on a train and came the rest of the way. The family all got there, and as I best

---

* Commander Francis L. Albert, CHC, USN, was a ship's chaplain for the North Carolina.
† James F. Goodrich served as Under Secretary of the Navy from 29 September 1981 to 6 August 1987.

remember we all got there one night. We were married the next, and I was back on the ship the next. That was our honeymoon.

Paul Stillwell: That situation precluded a lot of the detailed planning that normally goes into weddings.

Admiral Burke: And a lot less expensive for me, but I'm sure it cost the bride's family just as much to rally all that transportation and so forth.

Paul Stillwell: Interesting two Southerners getting married in Maine.

Admiral Burke: Well, we lived there for maybe six weeks. I forget how long it was. Of course, we had a honeymoon, and we spent a night in a hotel. Then the next day or so we moved into a convalescent home on Eastern Promenade in Portland. They'd just gone into business and needed some income, so we were convalescing there for a while. Then Betty went out and found us an apartment, which we had until the ship left. And I've sort of forgotten the dates, but we lived in the apartment about a month, I guess, or six weeks, and then suddenly the ship left. I didn't know it was going to leave, but everybody else in the gunnery department had the word. The ship was staffed with gunnery kind of people. They were the first team, so I suspect they were told and I wasn't.

We went to Norfolk and then went on around to the West Coast. As we were approaching the Panama Canal, the word was passed that there was a battle on out in the vicinity of Midway.* Then when we got either in the canal or just out, they began to give us the results, and that was the first good news that the United States really had. I think the original plan had been for us to go to Hawaii, but they diverted us to San Francisco. We stopped at Long Beach on the way, and so there were rumors around, "What are we going to do? What are we going to do?" So I and a couple of friends called up our wives in Portland, said, "Get to San Francisco." We were in San Francisco, it couldn't have

---

* From 4 to 6 June 1942, U.S. and Japanese naval forces fought a battle northwest of Midway Island in the Pacific. After Japanese bombers had struck the island, carrier-based U.S. dive-bombers attacked and sank the Japanese carriers Hiryu, Soryu, Kaga, and Akagi and the cruiser Mikuma. U.S. ships lost were the carrier Yorktown (CV-5) and the destroyer Hammann (DD-412). The battle was both a tactical and strategic victory for U.S. forces.

been more than two weeks, and at the end of the first week our brides arrived. They had driven across under the speed limit safely, never in dark, and they managed to cross the country in four days and three nights.

Paul Stillwell: You've got a big grin on your face as you're telling me those conditions.

Admiral Burke: You can ask Betty. She swears that it's true. But, anyhow, I think they arrived on a Saturday afternoon, and Betty went to a hotel. It was on a day when I had the duty. Well, the duty was serious business. We had increased readiness. They divided the ship into four sections, and two of the sections had the duty and two sections could get liberty. One section would get an overnight starting at 4:00 o'clock and be back in time for quarters the next morning. The other section would start at 1:00 o'clock and have to be back at midnight. That was called "Cinderella" duty. So we had "Cinderella" duty.

You've got to realize that I was recently married and hopelessly in love, and my thoughts weren't very professional at that time. But Betty was a good sport, and we were living in—why should I remember?—the Canterbury Hotel, which is up in the middle of town. We went through this for a week, and then the following Saturday night I had the duty again. A friend brought her down to the ship for dinner, but I had to go up and man the director. My friend took her to the movies, and then he took her home. I was up there on the director, and I waved at her as she left the ship, and the next morning I found that we were getting under way.

We were supposed to have Sunday dinner the next day up at the Fairmont Hotel with Admiral and Mrs. Woods. He had been a lifelong friend over in Annapolis; now he was in San Francisco.[*] Betty had never met the Woods. She was waiting for me to pick her up to take her to the Woods for dinner. The phone rang in her room, and it was Admiral Woods, who was down there to pick her up. She said I would be there in a while, and when she got down there to see him, he said, "I hate to tell you, but I saw the North Carolina going out through the Golden Gate Bridge about an hour and a half ago."

---

[*] Woods, who by this time was a rear admiral, was inspector for Navy Department medical activities on the West Coast.

So that was how we parted, and Betty moved in with some other Navy wives. There were a lot of Navy wives up at an apartment house at 1060 Bush, and she moved into that apartment building. But she had her own apartment and stayed there for several months before going home.

Paul Stillwell: It's interesting that you had to man a director in port.

Admiral Burke: Well, we got caught with our pants down at Pearl Harbor, and so the routines on board ship were, by present-day standards—see, we didn't have radar, much of it then. We were getting it.

Paul Stillwell: Was this strictly the optical range finder on the Mark 37 director?

Admiral Burke: Well, at that time we had fire control radar on our directors, and we had search radar, but they hadn't been on there very long. I would say we had had them probably nine months. We had exercised with them in January down in the Gulf of Mexico, and they were really effective. It was amazing to see how effective they were over what we had before, but the normal routine when we were at sea was to go to general quarters an hour before daybreak, man the battle stations, exercise. You had gunnery exercises and fire control exercises while you were there, and then finally after daybreak and you were satisfied nobody was coming over the horizon at you, then we set a condition watch. I think that early on it was watch and watch, and it was very exhausting routine.*

Paul Stillwell: That's where youthful stamina comes in handy.

Admiral Burke: Well, I don't know. I don't know whether the young people are any better than the older people on that. Later on, of course, when I got into submarines my stamina really was tested. But my guess is that eventually we went to a watch in three,

---

* Watch and watch, sometimes referred to as port and starboard, means there are only two watch sections, which produces an exhausting routine.

because we went to sea for long periods of time and just had to do it to get other things done.

Paul Stillwell: What sort of practices did you have for surface gunnery when you were in Maine or down in Guantanamo?

Admiral Burke: Well, there were towed targets. They were not very fast, and they weren't maneuverable, but they gave us an idea. It was probably long after we left Guantanamo we and the <u>Washington</u> went down to the Gulf of Mexico between Tampa and Key West and operated there for about a month in advanced training. We shot a lot of AA, and we did a lot of surface shooting.* Usually the surface shootings were offsets and the graduation exercise for the <u>Washington</u> and the <u>North Carolina</u> was getting off at about 40 miles and coming in at maximum speed and firing at each other on an offset, and that was quite a thrill.

Paul Stillwell: I'll bet it was.

Admiral Burke: And I mean we were firing everything we had. The secondary battery didn't get in it, but the main battery did, and I tell you that sort of left you filled with awe when you looked astern of you and saw these salvos landing where you were supposed to be. We both claimed victory.

Paul Stillwell: What do you remember about getting the news of the attack on Pearl Harbor?

Admiral Burke: I was home that weekend. See, my mother was widowed, and she had purchased a townhouse in an area called Yates Garden down in Alexandria. It was a new townhouse. She paid $7,500 for that little townhouse, and today it would cost about $300,000. I was helping her move in from her apartment to the townhouse, and we took a pause for lunch. At the time we didn't have any furniture there, and she had a little desk

---

* AA—antiaircraft.

radio about so big. I turned it on, expecting to get the Washington Redskin game, and we were having a sandwich. All of a sudden the radio announcer announced the news. Mother said, "Son, you've got to go back to your ship." The ship was in dry dock, and I knew she couldn't get under way for a couple of days at the least and maybe a week. I've forgotten why we were in dry dock, but I knew it was something that we could not move in a hurry.

Paul Stillwell: Was this in New York?

Admiral Burke: Yes, it was in Brooklyn Navy Yard. So I said, "In my case it doesn't make any difference." So we went ahead and finished what we were doing.

I know mother had lost her brother in World War I. He had died on the way to France. He got flu and died.[*] But she was very concerned—far more concerned than I was, I think. She had worked as a Red Cross volunteer, and so she had a lot better feel for what was coming that I did. She took me over and put me on the train at the Union Station in Washington. I got there about 7:00 o'clock, I guess, and the ride from Washington to Pennsylvania Station is one I'll never forget. It took, I know, over five hours. But at each station, which was Baltimore, Wilmington, Philadelphia, Trenton, Newark, there were hordes of families seeing off their loved ones. Tears.

The Navy football coach at that time was somebody that I admired. He was a Marine major named Larson.[†] I remember seeing him in uniform in one of the stations, probably Baltimore. There were all of these people crying. I didn't see anything like this ever again, but tears were just all over the place—male and female. I got back to Pennsylvania Station, caught the subway over to the St. George, walked down Sand Street, and it was quiet. I walked down to the ship, and everything was quiet. No extra security around. I mean, we had a fair amount of security, but there was nothing extra that I could observe. The officer of the deck said they were just operating normally because we couldn't move.

---

[*] In the worldwide influenza epidemic of 1918-19 some 20 million people died, including more than 500,000 in the United States.
[†] Major Emery E. "Swede" Larson, USMC, was the Naval Academy head football from the 1939 to 1941 seasons.

Paul Stillwell: How did things change in the ship after that?

Admiral Burke: Andy Shepard was the exec, and I'm sure he gave us a pep talk the next day. You know the Bismarck got loose in the Northern Atlantic.*

Paul Stillwell: She was sunk the end of May 1941.

Admiral Burke: Well, I remember when the Hood was sunk it really shook people up, and there was another one.

Paul Stillwell: Prince of Wales was damaged.

Admiral Burke: That really shook people up, and Shepard gave us a pep talk after that. He was a good leader, and he talked to us and he gave us another pep talk after the war started.

Paul Stillwell: I'm sure he did.

Admiral Burke: I don't recall us having any increased security, but you've got to realize we had a fair amount of security around there and had had it for some time because of the increased tensions that were coming up. We had a lot of people on board. I'd say whenever we were in port it was usually a one-in-four watch schedule, but when we went to sea once the war started, whenever we were in port it was always watch on, watch off. So we had plenty of people. Could have gotten under way with half the crew.

Well, right after the war started, we left New York and ended up in the Chesapeake Bay area just above Norfolk, and we were training. We did some shooting, as I best recall, and, of course, security was really strong then. People were very jumpy.

---

* In May 1941, the German battleship Bismarck, accompanied by the cruiser Prinz Eugen, entered the Atlantic to operate as a surface raider. In a gun duel on 24 May against the British, she sank HMS Hood and damaged HMS Prince of Wales. The Bismarck herself was damaged on the 26th by British torpedo planes and sunk on the 27th by gunfire from the British battleships Rodney and King George V.

I recall I was signal officer and occasionally got involved in decoding messages and taking these highly classified messages to the captain, the exec, and department heads. One of these I had decoded and routed and took it up to the executive officer. It revealed that we were going into Norfolk maybe about the 22nd or the 23rd of December. We got in about 10:30 at night, and the harbor was darkened. We were told to anchor at discretion. We couldn't see the ships. We weren't that confident with radar; we did have a search radar, but we weren't that good with it. We crept into the harbor and got off the Chamberlin Hotel at Old Point Comfort.

Paul Stillwell: Into Hampton Roads itself.

Admiral Burke: Into Hampton Roads. We dropped the hook and began to look around and see where we were and, by gosh, there finally we found a destroyer that was fairly close aboard at anchor. It could have caused a problem when the tide changed and the ships swung around. Captain Badger called me as the signal officer, and he said, "Burke, come over here. You see that destroyer over there? Go over there and pay my compliments to the captain of the destroyer and tell him to get the hell out of my anchorage." So they called away a boat and I went over and went aboard, went into the wardroom. I went into the wardroom, and the captain was Chester Wood, who four years later was my landlord up in Stonington, Connecticut, right after the war.* But, in any case, he was sitting in the wardroom there at the table, and they were having dinner. His exec on his right hand was Bill Wylie, who had been my company officer when I was a first classman a couple of years before.† And I just repeated what the captain said, and Captain Wood said, "Tell Captain Badger we will be out in no time at all."

Bill Wylie followed me out, and he laughingly said, "Damn you. You screwed up the first meal we've had in two weeks." But they were good sports about it.

Paul Stillwell: But they all knew who had the more clout.

---

* Lieutenant Commander Chester C. Wood, USN, was the first commanding officer of the USS Bristol (DD-453), which had just gone into commission on 21 October 1941.
† Lieutenant Joseph C. Wylie, USN.

Admiral Burke: Yes. Anyhow, the next day, I think, was Christmas Eve. I won't go into the details, but I went over to the Woods's quarters. Captain Woods was the commanding officer of the hospital in Portsmouth. So I went over and had dinner with the Woodses and fought my way back through a mass of people in Norfolk trying to get transportation out to the base at midnight. Then when I woke up the next morning, it turned out that there were a bunch of wives aboard. They were all gunnery department or the executive officer. I think the captain's wife and daughters may have been there, too, but the engineer department and the rest of the ship's departments didn't have their families there.

Paul Stillwell: Were these all officers' wives?

Admiral Burke: These were officers, but apparently the message that I had decoded showing that were going into Norfolk had been passed amongst the Gun Club and the captain and the exec and nobody else.*

Paul Stillwell: Just the favored few.

Admiral Burke: Yes. And it created a lot of bitterness, I can tell you.

Paul Stillwell: But you honored security and did not pass the word on to your wife.

Admiral Burke: Well, I wasn't married then.

Paul Stillwell: I see.

Admiral Burke: A day or so later, when we woke up, we found we had the British battleship Duke of York anchored next to us. So Christmas morning, when I went up to

---

* "Gun Club" was a term used to describe the officers—particularly those with graduate degrees in ordnance—who served in battleships, cruisers, and destroyers. They felt that the warships' big guns were, and would remain, the predominant naval weapons. Once aircraft carriers came to prominence early in World War II, the influence of the Gun Club began to wane.

the wardroom, I was told that I was going to be one of three officers that were going to call on the wardroom and gunroom—the gunroom is their JO mess—on Christmas afternoon. So I went over as the junior of the three officers that were calling, and I was escorted to the gunroom. The gunroom had all of these young midshipmen who couldn't have been over 15, maybe as young as 12. After their Christmas dinner they'd been plied with liquor and so forth. They were all passed out, and there wasn't anybody who could talk to me. So finally the officer of the deck who had greeted us came down, and he was a very engaging sub lieutenant, a nice fellow, and he didn't apologize. He said, "We just had Christmas dinner."

But interesting thing, that ship had brought Churchill to confer with our President, and he was over here for at least a couple of weeks conferring with Roosevelt on strategy. I remember going ashore one night while we were in Norfolk over the Christmas period, and I went over to the Navy yard to see Captain Woods. He had been the commandant at the hospital at the academy and was now the commandant of the hospital at Norfolk Navy Yard. On the way back I called up Mother on the phone, not to tell her where I was but just to speak to her. I told her I couldn't tell her where I was, but she must have gotten it when I called her collect. [Laughter] She said, "Son, can you tell me where you are?"

I said, "No, Mother, I can't."

So she lowered her voice, and she said, "Now you can tell me."

Paul Stillwell: That's a good story.

Do you think the reason for the North Carolina's delay in going to the Pacific was a concern about the German ships?

Admiral Burke: Yes. I know that we were worried about the Tirpitz, and I know that there was a decision made in Washington that the war in Europe took priority over the war in the Pacific. When we eventually went around, we were passing through the Panama Canal when the Battle of Midway was announced. The actual engagement probably started about a day or so before we got there, but we were either in the canal or just out when we got word of the results. So we went up to San Francisco and stayed on the West Coast for maybe three weeks. Then we went out to Pearl Harbor along with the Wasp and some destroyers. I'm sure that we were the first significant reinforcement that they got following Midway.

We got there around 5:00 o'clock in the evening, came in, and we went all the way around. We went off to the left and made that circle around Ford Island and came in to Ten-Ten Dock.* We were at quarters, and all the ships of the fleet saw here was this brand-new battleship, and they'd been through hell; it was right after Midway. But we went around Ford Island, and there was the Utah upside down, and the various ships were there.† Everybody manned the rails on the ships, and I get tears in my eyes when I'm talking to you right now, because all of a sudden we manned the rail, and they were cheering back and forth. It was the most emotional experience I had during the war. In 1991 I was invited to talk to the alumni of the North Carolina in Wilmington, and I talked about this. God. These guys got up and said, "Yeah!" And they were cheering then.

Paul Stillwell: Did the other ships blow their whistles and salute?

Admiral Burke: I don't remember blowing whistles, but I do remember the crews were cheering back and forth and waving their hats. And they needed a shot in the arm, I tell you. They needed it badly.

Then I went over to where the West Virginia friends were. There were quite a number of them around, and the officers lived together. It was in the Makalapa area, and it was not the first-class quarters that we know now, but there was an area out there. I don't know whether it was called Makalapa or not, but I went out there frequently for meals and had some of them down for meals. The Oklahoma was capsized and the Utah was capsized, and it was a mess. You had it right there in your face, and you wanted to do something about it.

---

* Ten-Ten Dock, which was part of the Pearl Harbor Navy Yard, was so named because it was 1,010 feet long.
† USS Utah, formerly a battleship, on 1 July 1931 had her hull number changed to AG-16. She capsized and sank at Pearl Harbor during the Japanese attack in December 1941.

Al Bergner, a classmate and later a rear admiral, had gone over on a submarine right away, and a couple of other had moved on over.* The ones that were still there, and without exception, all said, "Well, thank God, the submariners are winning the war." So that began to make me think about it, and then eventually we got hit, so I just decided, "To hell with it. I'll put in for it."

Paul Stillwell: Well, another consideration was that Submarine School was a lot shorter than aviation training.

Admiral Burke: Well, also it was a way to see my wife. I was so worried that she was going to be upset, but she was so happy that I got back that she was willing to put up with it. I don't think that she ever really saw the down side of submarines. I never told her of some of the things I went through, and only within the last couple of years have I told her how close it was. But I lost some very good friends.

Paul Stillwell: Including Spencer Wilson, whom we've mentioned.

Admiral Burke: Oh, yes. Well, there's another good friend in '39, John Shepherd. He lived in Alexandria, and we ran with the same crowd. He dated this girl two doors down from here that I started off with in the second grade. He was a first cousin to a girl that used to live in the house over here, and he was somebody that I really saw a lot of. I didn't see him every day, but I saw a lot of him, and he was a good friend. He was the last exec of the Trigger.†

Paul Stillwell: He was lost right near the end of the war.

Admiral Burke: Yes. But there were a whole raft of them, and the one thing about the submarine thing, though, you got separated from your friends. I saw very little of my classmates once I got into submarines, because we were all in different places, and your

---

* Lieutenant (junior grade) Allen A. Bergner, USN.
† Lieutenant Commander John E. Shepherd III, USN. The submarine Trigger (SS-237) was lost on 27 or 28 March 1945 while moving toward a rendezvous to form a wolf pack in the Western Pacific.

friends became the guys that you might be doing refit with. There was one submarine we refitted with twice, the Grayback, and, gee, what a great bunch of guys they were, and we were all just buddies, and then she didn't come back from war patrol.

Paul Stillwell: What else happened in Pearl? Anything of note there?

Admiral Burke: While we were in port there for probably not more than ten days, a couple of submarines came in off war patrol. They were flying the Japanese flags to show what they'd done. That reinforced what I heard from my friends.

Before long we took off, went to sea. I guess we probably were with the Wasp in a task group and we ended up in the Tonga Islands. I hadn't thought about all these things for years. We were in Tonga for a while, and then we moved over and we joined the carriers. Probably at the start it was the Wasp, the Saratoga, and the Enterprise. They were divided up into three different task groups. They were always in sight of each other but off on the horizon. Then eventually there was an amphibious group that came along, and eventually they had some practice landings somewhere.[*]

You've got to realize that I was junior. I wasn't in on what was really going on. Security was, I thought, unbelievably restricted. To give you an example, we had a British liaison officer on our ship, a commander, at the time. I don't recall when he came aboard but probably came aboard in Pearl Harbor before we headed for Guadalcanal.[†] He was a nice guy, and he was a liaison observer. Here I was in the gunnery department, and we went south. We didn't get briefed on what we were going to do until very close to the time when that landing came off. When all the gunnery department was called in, this guy was with the gunnery department, but they wouldn't let him attend the briefing because it was so secret.

---

[*] There were preparations for the first U.S. offensive action in the Pacific. On 7 August 1942, Marines invaded the islands of Guadalcanal and Tulagi in the Solomons chain. The primary purpose was to gain control of an airstrip on Guadalcanal and thus to prevent the Japanese from achieving control of the surrounding air and sea regions. The campaign was long and difficult before organized Japanese resistance finally ended on 9 February 1943.

[†] On 7 August 1942, U.S. Marines invaded the islands of Guadalcanal and Tulagi in the Solomons chain as part of the first U.S. counteroffensive in the Pacific War. The primary purpose was to gain control of an airstrip on Guadalcanal and thus to prevent the Japanese from achieving control of the surrounding air and sea regions. The campaign was long and difficult before organized Japanese resistance finally ended on 9 February 1943.

Paul Stillwell: And whom was he going to tell?

Admiral Burke: Yes. And we didn't have the picture. We were just right here doing what I was told to do and to be alert for this. Nobody ever came down and gave us a sketch and described what the strategic thing was, as I remember. And our news coverage was limited. It was hard to get your hands on it, and when you finally got mail or occasionally somebody would send you a clipping from home. That's how you found a lot. In a lot of ways you found a lot more.

Paul Stillwell: Do you remember the Battle of the Eastern Solomons?*

Admiral Burke: Yes. That was my real baptism and the baptism of other people. Up to that point, see, the first team on the North Carolina had been the main battery. We were cruising around out of the sight of Guadalcanal, but we were in a support area. It was hard for us to visualize what we doing other than just steaming around and hoping that we weren't going to get torpedoed, because every now and then somebody would sight a periscope or think they did. One day we got an air-search radar contact at about 75 miles. We went to general quarters, and they tracked him right in.

    The carrier in our group was the Enterprise, and their air group launched. So these two strike groups passed each other on the way, going the opposite direction and they talked to us. Joe Stryker had the conn, and I was in my battle station in Sky 3.† I had the after two mounts, and Sky 1 had the forward three. I think that's the way it was, but anyhow the planes came in. Larry Lovig, who was a supply officer, class of '39, was my talker.‡ I was getting orders from sky control, and all of a sudden he said, "Look overhead." Here were planes diving on the Enterprise, and they didn't pull out until they got practically on top of it. They hit the Enterprise. We got into a melee just shooting, and we were zigging and zagging. I remember at one stage Lovig sitting there, and

---

* The Battle of the Eastern Solomons, an engagement pitting U.S. and Japanese carrier-based aircraft against each other, took place on 23-24 August 1942.
† Sky 3 was a fire control director that tracked targets and aimed a number of the 5-inch guns.
‡ Lieutenant (junior grade) Lawrence Lovig, Jr., SC, USN.

yelled at me to look overhead. Here was a plane that was shooting right at me, squirting with his machine guns. He pulled out, and there was a splash not more than 50 feet out from the side of the ship. It seemed like it went on for hours, but actually it was over in about five minutes.

Paul Stillwell: Did you get any protection from the director?

Admiral Burke: Well, see, I could have pulled the metal thing over the top, but we had an outside sight control where I could slew the director around and point the director at the target, and you had to use that to be effective against aircraft.

Paul Stillwell: And you didn't have proximity fuzes yet at that point.*

Admiral Burke: At that point we did not. But we put a lot of shells out, and eventually they went away and everybody was claiming hitting the planes that fell. There wasn't any question about who shot them down. When they added up all the planes we claimed were shot down, it was something like 35 or 40. [Laughter] But I think eventually they gave the North Carolina credit for about five, and they gave my director credit for one, which was probably more than I deserved. But after that experience I can remember going down to the wardroom. There was my roommate and very close friend, Bill Laffey. He was turret two officer, and here they'd been the first team. That evening they weren't the first team, I can tell you. But that made me feel good. In a way, I was a different person from then on.

Paul Stillwell: In what sense?

Admiral Burke: Well, you're going through an experience that you've never been through before. Nobody had ever shot at me before like that in live shooting, and it changes you.

---

* The proximity fuze for 5-inch antiaircraft projectiles was also known as the VT, or variable time, fuze. It contained a small radio transponder that detonated the projectile when it got near a target, thus eliminating the need for a direct hit.

It really has an effect on you. The fact that we had gotten through successfully gave me a sense of confidence that I never had before.

Paul Stillwell: Great.

Admiral Burke: I could observe this both aboard ship and the rest of my life in the Navy. I've seen this operate especially during the war. You have something that is an intangible experience that helps you in dealing with people and being able to make decisions under stress. And there's no substitute for combat, I can tell you.

Paul Stillwell: A lot of stress when those bullets are flying around you.

Admiral Burke: That was my first and only air battle. It was in late August, and after that we steamed around a lot and so forth. There were night actions up there that went against us, and we had a terrible time around there for some time. The submarines began to move in, and eventually we got hit, which was I think afternoon of the 15th of September.

Paul Stillwell: Yes, it was.

Admiral Burke: The <u>Wasp</u> was over in the task group on the horizon, and I was not on watch at the time. One of the unpleasant things we had to do was to censor mail for the crew and they used to pass the word every so often, "Officers gather in the wardroom to censor mail." So that particular afternoon there were three of us, classmates, who were jaygees at that time—Speed Simmons and I and Bill Laffey, my roommate—plus Gunner McCrory. He'd been in the Navy starting about 1920, and he was a buddy to the JOs.

We all hid out in our room. We decided to skip the censoring and go down to our room, which was way up toward the forecastle—just ahead of number one turret—and we were up there telling sea stories. I can remember McCrory used to regale us with some of his stories about how life was when he was an enlisted man. He was telling us about Fleet Week in Seattle, when he'd had too much to drink and had a girl on his arm.

He went to the hotel to go up to the roof garden in the hotel, and he took the elevator and as he got up there the door opened and there was the shore patrol officer waiting for him. And we said, "Gunner, what did you do then?"

He was trying to think of another lie to tell us when we got hit by a torpedo.* I didn't see Gunner McCrory for two days, and when I saw him he said, "You know, if that torpedo hadn't hit us, I'd have had to tell a lie." He and Tom Hill were inseparable, and the last time I saw Gunner McCrory was at the Washington Navy Yard. He was on duty there with Tom Hill. He was a lieutenant commander or a commander at the time. Just as engaging as ever. A good friend.

Paul Stillwell: What was the sensation when the torpedo hit?

Admiral Burke: Oh. It was not a loud bang where we were, but it was a tremendous jolt, I guess, like an earthquake or something like that. We knew we'd been hit by something and so everybody reacted. I mean, we were well trained on what to do, and everybody began to get to the battle stations right away and locked up the ship and so forth. What happened was we were hit about abeam of, I think, either number one or number two turret. We were just on the other side of the ship from where it hit. It went through about five skins and it stopped at the last one. It was that close to really being serious. When we got back in the Navy yard you could have driven one of these big trucks through the hole.

The Wasp had been hit, too, and was burning and had attracted people out on deck to watch the Wasp burning, which was 15 miles away. A bunch of people had gathered on deck, and when the torpedo hit, it put up a wall of water on us. It came down and landed on them and it washed over some people. I don't know how many, but there were two or three people that were lost because they got washed over. Then there were some people who were sealed, watertight, in their compartment, and we had to leave it sealed. They died because we couldn't open it up. I don't recall, but I think we lost

---

* On the afternoon of 15 September the North Carolina was hit and damaged by a torpedo from the Japanese submarine I-19, which also was torpedoed and sank the aircraft carrier Wasp (CV-7). For details, see Ben W. Blee, "Whodunnit?" U.S. Naval Institute Proceedings, July 1982, 42-49.

somewhere between five and eight people. Sure, it had an effect on people. But it brought home the fact that you could get hurt as well as shoot at ships and so forth.

Paul Stillwell: Well, it also showed you could get hurt and survive.

Admiral Burke: Yes. Oh, we went right up to 25 knots. After being damaged, we first stopped at, I think, Tonga, where they put people over the side to take a look. Then we went on back to Pearl Harbor and went in the dry dock to get repaired. This Mr. West, who was my cousin's father-in-law and lived there, had friends that were flag officers, contemporaries, and he had been told about the reports of our air battle. He said there were just people who saw us firing antiaircraft who couldn't believe that that much firepower could be brought and said it looked like the ship was on fire. I'm sure that it made a difference.

We got back, and, as I recall, Tom Hill was transferred up to Admiral Nimitz's, staff, and there were a few other people transferred. I got thinking more about submarines if they were that effective, and so I put in for submarines. Some of my classmates were putting in for aviation. We were in the yard for about a month and a half.*

Paul Stillwell: Did the ship get some additional antiaircraft guns during that yard period?

Admiral Burke: We got 40 millimeters and that was a big plus. They were significantly better than the 1.1s.

Paul Stillwell: Anything else about that yard period you recall?

Admiral Burke: It's hard for me to remember. I was in the yard off and on a number of times, and I can't remember whether it was on a submarine later on or whether it was when I was with sub base, but I had a very good friend named George McDaniel, who

---

* The ship entered the Pearl Harbor Navy Yard for repairs on 30 September 1942 and departed for New Caledonia in the South Pacific on 17 November.

was in the class of '39.* He's from Lynchburg. George was the most nonreg midshipman, and he was a very likable guy. He lived next door to me two out of three years at the Naval Academy. We were in the same company. He was low in aptitude because he was always non-reg; his nickname was "Sloppy." One of his roommates was Wedgehead Zullinger because he did have a wedgehead, and these guys were just fun to be around.† His mother was the secretary to Senator Carter Glass, so we all sort of felt that they were afraid to toss him out on aptitude.

Paul Stillwell: Because he had connections.

Admiral Burke: Because he had good connections. Well, he was on a destroyer that came in that had been in combat. Boy, it had really been chewed up, and they had a fire and lots of damage topside.

Paul Stillwell: That was the Smith. She was with the South Dakota at the Battle of Santa Cruz, and she went into the South Dakota's wake to put the fire out.‡

Admiral Burke: Okay. That's the one. I saw that ship when she came in and, gosh, awful. That would have happened when we were in the shipyard. But he turned out to be a hero. He was, I think, probably the engineer, and he got a Navy Cross, which he well deserved.

Paul Stillwell: I interviewed Paul Backus, who was in the South Dakota during that battle, and he saw the Smith come up behind.§

Admiral Burke: Okay. I forget the name of the captain, but, boy, I tell you they were a mess.** It may have been that a plane landed on deck or something like that. So my

---

* Lieutenant (junior grade) George T. McDaniel, Jr., USN.
† Midshipman John R. Zullinger, USN, class of 1939.
‡ The Battle of Santa Cruz Islands was on 26 October 1942.
§ See the Naval Institute oral history of Commander Paul H. Backus, USN (Ret.).
** The commanding officer of the Smith (DD-378) in that engagement was Lieutenant Commander Hunter Wood, Jr., USN.

friend had it when it counted. I don't know whether George is still living or not, but if he were living around here I'd sure see a lot of him.

Paul Stillwell: What happened then with the North Carolina after you got out of the yard and got back to sea?

Admiral Burke: We went down, and I forget exactly when we got there, but I remember being in Noumea Christmas Day. Somewhere down there I also remember when we were down there in Noumea Joe E. Brown was on a world tour, and he came aboard and it was done as a memorial for his son who I think had been lost in the war or something like that.[*]

Paul Stillwell: There's a picture of him in your cruise book.

Admiral Burke: He came down there and put on a show for us and the remarkable thing about it was that the ship's chaplain introduced him and he, to the surprise of everybody, outdid Joe E. Brown when he introduced him. This was Francis Lee Albert, who had married Betty and me when we were up in Portland, Maine. Chaplain Albert had worked this thing out to get him aboard and then he introduced him.

Paul Stillwell: He went into comedy.

Admiral Burke: Yes, he really knocked a home run. I just remember that.

Paul Stillwell: Was that kind a lull period in the early part of '43 for the ship?

Admiral Burke: Well, the tide was turning. The South Dakota had showed up. I don't know whether the Indiana had showed up yet or not, but ships were coming out from the Mediterranean that hadn't been there before. Cruisers and stuff that had been in the Atlantic. I can't remember what was happening in North Africa, but I guess we had

---

[*] Joe E. Brown was an entertainer, a comedian who appeared in a number of movies.

secured enough of the sea battle in the Atlantic so that they felt they could afford to reinforce the Pacific.* Remembering that, as far as I could tell, we were the first live reinforcements from the Atlantic to get out there.

Paul Stillwell: Well, and the shipyards were starting to kick out a lot of ships by then too.

Admiral Burke: That's true. It was beginning to show, but I can remember right after the war started, I guess when we were up in Casco Bay when I went over one day on a tug. The tug was going to tow a target, and for some reason I was over on the tug to observe the fall of shot or something. The captain had just come from Washington where he had been with somebody and had been told what some of the new construction plans were. They were just mind boggling. Like we were going to build 20 carriers. I couldn't believe it.

Paul Stillwell: Sure enough, they did.

Admiral Burke: I just couldn't conceive—I mean, it took three or four years to build the North Carolina, which cost $75 million. She was the biggest thing that we had ever built up to that time, and I just couldn't comprehend it. That was 1942, and in April of 1944 I was the third officer on the Flying Fish, and we went into Majuro Atoll. The fleet was in there and I counted something like 11 big carriers and something about 10 or 12 battleships and 40 cruisers. It was mind boggling to see that the Navy had grown that far that fast, and, of course, at that stage of the game we were pushing ahead, and that was after some of the real horrible things that had happened in the South Pacific, so you knew you were on the way.

Paul Stillwell: Anything more to wrap up the North Carolina?

---

* Allied forces invaded Casablanca in French Morocco in November 1942. The French forces in the port resisted, so American ships bombarded the port.

Admiral Burke: No, I'd say we didn't get into any more live action after we got torpedoed. We were in support roles, steaming at sea, providing a presence. That isn't the kind of thing where you're interested in combat. You know, it's boring as hell. Standing a watch, being alert for something that's going to happen that either doesn't or catches you.

Paul Stillwell: Was there a fair amount of training in those early months of '43 to keep your skills up?

Admiral Burke: I don't remember us doing any target training. You always did drills on each watch to make sure you were ready. You had planes, you had your own planes and they would run targets for you. But we weren't worried about that; I don't remember that being a concern.

Paul Stillwell: Well, we're right near the end of the tape, so this is probably a convenient stopping place for today.

Admiral Burke: Okay.

Paul Stillwell: Thank you, Admiral.

Interview Number 3 with Rear Admiral Julian T. Burke, Jr., U.S. Navy (Retired)

Place: Admiral Burke's home in Alexandria, Virginia

Date: Friday, 14 March 1997

Interviewer: Paul Stillwell

Paul Stillwell: As we get started on this gloomy, rainy day, Admiral, the thing I'm interested in this morning is what happened after the North Carolina got back from being repaired from the torpedo damage.

Admiral Burke: Well, as I best remember, we got back there, and we were in the support forces off of Guadalcanal. Time had passed. The United States had brought reinforcements from the Atlantic. The battleships Washington and South Dakota were out there. By the time we got back down there, they had had a night engagement right around Guadalcanal, where the South Dakota got shot up because, as we were told, that one of our destroyers was on fire.* The South Dakota turned the wrong way and was silhouetted, and the Washington saved her. The South Dakota had to go back to the East Coast for repairs. She was really badly damaged. The Washington was the hero, and nobody back home really appreciated it.

Paul Stillwell: South Dakota got all the press.

Admiral Burke: And the South Dakota all the glory. We went to sea a fair amount of times. We were based in Noumea in New Caledonia. We were anchored out. It was just sort of a routine kind of thing. Somewhere along the line we got a new captain, who was Wilder Baker, a submariner. He had a style about him in the short time I was with him where he concentrated on his men when he had the opportunity to find out who they were, what they were, and what they could do. I was thoroughly impressed with him.

---

* This was a surface engagement fought the night of 14-15 November 1942. U.S. Task Force 64, under the command of Rear Admiral Willis A. Lee, Jr., USN, comprised two battleships and four destroyers. It managed to prevent a planned bombardment of Guadalcanal by a Japanese surface force.

When we had been torpedoed, I think that finally made me to decide to put in for submarine duty. I wanted to get in on the other side of the war and get going, so I'd applied for Submarine School.

Paul Stillwell: Was that kind of a boring routine that period in early '43?

Admiral Burke: I don't think it was boring, but I'd say I was professionally oriented, and I didn't feel like I was getting into the war. I think in my own makeup I didn't want to be left behind.

Paul Stillwell: You mean in terms of career?

Admiral Burke: Career. I didn't want to be behind. I just knew intuitively that if you wanted to get ahead in the service, you'd better by gosh carry the bricks during the war, and I didn't want to get left behind. The destroyer people and the cruiser people got chewed up down in Guadalcanal, but we, in our particular instance, we were sort of out of much of it. Most of my generation aboard the North Carolina were thinking flight training, which I didn't qualify for and I frankly didn't want to do. I had some weak eyes, and every time I took a flight physical I flunked it. So I put in for submarine duty.

When we were down there under Captain Baker, we did go out on these support cruises. There would be a carrier. We had lost the Hornet. We had lost the Wasp. The Saratoga had taken a torpedo and had to go back to Pearl, and I guess she was back. The Enterprise took bomb damage, and I don't recall whether she went back to Pearl or not. But then during these periods when we would come back into Noumea, the scheduling became such that we could get recreational time on the beach such as softball, picnics, beer, and so forth—both for the officers and enlisted. There were some Army nurses down there, and so somebody arranged some picnics with them.

I can remember one night—it was summertime out there, probably in February—I felt the ship take a list, maybe five degrees. It seemed like five degrees. It may not have been that much, but my curiosity caused me to go out on deck, and here were a boat load of Army nurses coming out to have dinner in the wardroom. Somebody had seen these ladies approaching the ship, passed the word on the 1MC, "Come take a look. There are women out here."* The whole ship's company was gathered on the starboard side by the accommodation ladder. Well, this was interesting, and I was one of them. I resented bringing those women out there, because they were officers' dates. A lot of us felt that way, and we felt it was bad to flaunt that in front of the crew. But it happened, and that's the only time I ever saw anything like that happen, but certainly the picture of women in the military has taken a different twist.

Paul Stillwell: Did you have a flag officer embarked at any time you were on board?

Admiral Burke: Yes, we did but not for long. When we were with the Washington we were BatDiv 6, I think, and Admiral Wilcox was aboard for a short while. He hoisted his flag when the command was first established aboard the North Carolina in Brooklyn. But when the Washington and the North Carolina began to operate, he shifted to the Washington. I don't know why. He was aboard Washington at the time he was lost at sea.

Paul Stillwell: Did you feel a sense of Admiral Halsey's presence when he took over as ComSoPac?†

Admiral Burke: Me personally, no. But he had charisma that projected far beyond where he was. We had a correspondent on our ship—I think his name was Norman Bell—who rode with us for several months. I remember that we had been in Noumea around the Christmas-New Year's period, and he had gone over as one of the members of the press to one of the press briefings that Admiral Halsey presided over, and he came back. I think Halsey had made a promise that we would be in Tokyo by 1 January the next year or something like that, but that was the kind of presence. I guess I also got a feeling from him.

---

* 1MC is the designation of the ship's general announcing system.
† Vice Admiral/Admiral William F. Halsey Jr., USN, served as Commander South Pacific Area from 18 October 1942 to 15 June 1944. He was promoted to four-star rank in November 1942.

I had lots of family connections and friends of friends that I bumped into during the war. I had a first cousin in Washington whose husband was in intelligence and was living on Ford Island in quarters with a bunch of other bachelors, wartime bachelors. He was in the intelligence section of CinCPacFlt, and he told me about Halsey. He also told me about somebody I'd never heard about, Arleigh Burke, who was doing such a great job down there, and that was probably at the time that the North Carolina was being repaired.* That's how I really found out.

Paul Stillwell: Well, anything more to wrap up North Carolina before you went to Submarine School?

Admiral Burke: I would just say in summary I was really fortunate to be on that ship. The four captains that I served under all made admiral. They were good men, and Badger was the most colorful by miles. He did a lot of things that in style endeared himself with the enlisted men at the expense of most of his officers. Notwithstanding that, he was a strong leader. I learned something from every darn one of them, and I was fortunate. Also we had other people who made flag rank, such as Corky Ward, who was a lieutenant then and obviously going somewhere. Those people helped me along the way to learn how to do the job.

Paul Stillwell: What did you learn from Captain Badger?

Admiral Burke: Well, he was a showman. I didn't approve of a lot of the things he did. I mean, he'd chew his officers out in front of the enlisted men in a way that I thought was unconscionable. But on the other hand I was the signal officer, and I was sort of like his messenger. Earlier I mentioned my chief signalman, Bill Plusch; he was steering me on things that I had to do to get along. He was probably as good a coach as I had and taught me how to deal with this. I was an ace at being able to stay out of trouble with Captain Badger, because I saw the mistakes these other people were making.

---

* Captain Arleigh A. Burke, USN, was Commander Destroyer Squadron 23 during fighting in the Solomons in 1943. He later served as Chief of Naval Operations from 1955 to 1961.

Paul Stillwell: Such as?

Admiral Burke: Well, they hadn't studied the lesson. They came up to take the deck, and they hadn't read enough about the operations that they were doing, and Badger probably would quiz them.

Paul Stillwell: He was well named, it sounds like.

Admiral Burke: But when he left the ship, I'll tell, you the ship the crew was worried. But they said, "Well, Stryker is here." Joe Stryker had recently arrived, and he'd made an impact. But you see all of these people, at least I did, and you see how they operate and how they make their successes and failures. I just didn't like the style of chewing out your people. On the other hand, I don't mind chewing out people, but I don't think you ought to do it in front of your enlisted men.

I remember talking to Chaplain Albert one day. I know he didn't tell me he was unhappy, but he said Badger had a style and technique of lionizing himself with the enlisted men at the expense of his officers, and he did.

Paul Stillwell: You haven't said much about Captain Fort. What do you remember of him?

Admiral Burke: Well, he was the least colorful of the ones that I saw. He sort of ran the church the way I would have, I think, or the way I developed my own technique, trying to train the people that were under him to do the job so that if he wasn't there the ship could function. That's sort of the style that I used in time. He came to a ship that was well trained, ready to go to war. He took us, and we got through the first experience quite well, and everything functioned. He didn't get up and take the conn just because he was the captain. He was around seeing what was going on and looking out and letting other people do these things, and I admire somebody for being able to do this.

Paul Stillwell: Takes a lot of self-confidence.

Admiral Burke: Well, I think it's important when you're in charge. I say I always tried to train my officers to take command as soon as they could and let them do all these things. I was criticized twice at Guantanamo when I had my ships in refresher training because I had the junior officers doing things or during an operational readiness inspection that I hadn't taken the conn, somebody else did, and I was criticized for that. And my answer was, "Well, how was the exercise?"

"Outstanding."

"Could you do it as well as that?"

"No."

"Well," I said. "Well what the hell? I have trained that guy so he can do it."

Paul Stillwell: And, of course, that's kind of a hypocritical approach on their part, because their technique is to simulate killing the guy that knows how to do it.

Admiral Burke: Well, I felt very strongly about this, and I got a lot of that from submarine duty later on.

Paul Stillwell: Well, why don't we move you to Submarine School then, please?

Admiral Burke: Okay. I got transferred in Noumea and sent to Cub 13, which was a receiving station that gathered in people being sent back to the States from the sunken ships, from Guadalcanal, from people like me. I ran into people I'd been in high school with who were there. One was Bobby Watts from Lynchburg, good friend in high school, and he'd been on the Hornet. I don't know what happened, but eventually I got transferred and went as a passenger on the SS Wisconsin, which was a merchant ship headed for San Francisco. It took us about three and a half weeks, unescorted, eight knots, zigzagging all the way. We had, I would guess, 35 or 40 officers and probably 150 enlisted men living in the hole.

We were living up in the cabin class, and we were just passengers. My roommates, I had two Marine aviators. One was about my age, a captain; the other one was a major who was an ex-enlisted man. I wish I could remember his name, because he was a marvelous person. He taught me how to play acey-deucy and poker.* He had been in Nicaragua back in the '20s, and he had an intense loyalty to the Marine Corps and to the United States. I think he had also been an immigrant to this country. This was a four-man room. These two guys lived on the other side, and we got to know each other pretty well in three and half weeks. John Crommelin was the major's idol.† He'd been in aviation earlier, but I think he was a ground officer at this time. He was an old man. Hell, he was in his 40s. Red Hessel, class of '37, who had been one of my two first classmen, was on there.‡ He had been on the Wasp.

There were air group people who had come off of Guadalcanal. There were a couple of officers from the Washington who told us about the experience they had when they saved the South Dakota. The senior passenger that we had was a Navy commander, and for the first time in my life I found out how poorly paid we were, because this commander's salary from the U.S. Government was less than the lowest paid able-bodied seaman in the maritime group there on board ship. That's the first time I'd ever heard that, but it came across with a bang.

We ran out of water, so we stopped in Samoa, in Apia Harbor, spent a couple of nights there. We got in about in the early afternoon and tied up to the dock and began to water ship. At 5:30 we had to stop because the governor of the island wanted to take a bath. From where I could see it was a rather primitive place at the time, so I chose not to go ashore. Then we went on our way and got back to San Francisco, which I thought would never happen. And I can remember, as we approached the dock, there was a Red Cross lady down at the end of the dock. It was the first woman these people had seen in months and months, and they began to whistle and hoot and holler, all of our troops aboard. She came up there, and she must have been 65 or 70 years old, and they still whistled.

---

* Acey-deucy is a variation of the board game backgammon.
† Commander John G. Crommelin, USN, was a legendary naval aviator. Among other things, he served during World War II as air officer of the carrier Enterprise (CV-6) and was executive officer of the escort carrier Liscome Bay (CVE-56), when she was lost in the Gilbert Islands in November 1943.
‡ Lieutenant Edward W. Hessel, USN.

I came back home and I flew from San Francisco to Washington. When we got to Washington, there was a snowstorm, so we ended up in New York. I caught the train from New York, and usually it took five hours. That one took about seven or eight for some reason, and I got in about 2:00 o'clock in the morning. Betty and my brother met me at the Union Station, so that was quite a happy reunion.

Paul Stillwell: I'm sure it was.

Admiral Burke: I'd say Betty has been remarkably adaptive all of our lives, and she endured moves, surprises, and so forth, which I don't see how she did. Then Mother gave me her car, and so we drove to New London and checked in. I had to get gas points. Gasoline was rationed, food was rationed, so I had to go by and pick up from the local ration board in Alexandria all those necessary tickets to make the trip and to survive.

Paul Stillwell: Well, please tell me about getting set up at Submarine School

Admiral Burke: Well, I had been in two different battleships, for over two and a half years, and life aboard ship was formal. The uniform regs were adhered to. The enlisted men were very rigid in their formality on those ships. In a sense we weren't hazed, but we were kept in our place by the more senior officers starting at lieutenant. Especially on the West Virginia. It was less so on the North Carolina.

But when I got into Submarine School very quickly I saw the way people operated in a more relaxed manner. While I liked it, it seemed to me that the submarine Navy, at least in New London at that time, was kind of small stuff compared to what was going on in the big fleet operations that I'd been exposed to. And it made me wonder. But it didn't discourage my desire to be in the submarines, because I wanted to hit the Japanese. It did sort of discourage my idea, at that time, of making submarines my future life career.

One of my very closest friends was Spencer Wilson, who was married to Harry Train's older sister. He had been in the Pennsylvania before he came to Sub School. And he came into the Submarine School class after me, and in very short order he recognized the same thing and brought it up to me before I left town. So I sort of packed that and kept that in the back of my head.

Paul Stillwell: Who were some of your classmates in the school?

Admiral Burke: At the Submarine School, as I best remember, the class was about 75 strong, might have been a little larger. About a quarter at the most were Naval Academy graduates. The one whom I knew best was Ben Byrnside out of the class of '41.[*] He and I had been friends at the Naval Academy. I had two Academy classmates, Bill Robb and Mel Abrahams.[†] They were not close friends, but Byrnside was the one that was a real close friend. There was a football player out of the class of '42, Chewning.[‡] He was from Richmond. And there were a couple or three guys from '42 who were friends, Crawford in '42—and now the names have popped out of my head.[§]

Paul Stillwell: Was Crawford the one who later went with Rickover?[**]

Admiral Burke: No, it was not him. This was Bill Crawford.[††] The reason I remember him is that he was sort of the character of the class. He lived out in Noank, as we eventually did, and I used to drive with him. I carpooled with him and one or two others. He got married about halfway through sub school, and his wife came in off the weekend honeymoon and began to vomit, and she was pregnant. Everybody in sub school knew they were pregnant except them.

Paul Stillwell: That didn't take long.

---

[*] Lieutenant (junior grade) Benjamin C. Byrnside, Jr., USN.
[†] Lieutenant (junior grade) William B. Robb, USN; Lieutenant (junior grade) Melvin Abrahams, USN.
[‡] Lieutenant (junior grade) William M. Chewning, USN.
[§] Lieutenant (junior grade) William H. Crawford, Jr., USN.
[**] Lieutenant (junior grade) John W. Crawford, Jr., USN, was also in the Naval Academy class of 1942; he stood fourth in the class of 564 graduates. He later wound up as a long-time insider in the Navy's nuclear power program under Admiral Hyman G. Rickover.
[††] Lieutenant (junior grade) William H. Crawford, Jr., USN.

Admiral Burke: We started off in New London at the Lighthouse Inn, which was very large. It was probably built originally as a residence and then converted. We were in what had to be the master bedroom, in which, I swear, we had the floor space of the downstairs of this house. And we were looking out on the ocean. We stayed there about a week, and then we fortunately saw an ad on the board at the officers' club. It was for a rental in Noank, and so we took that apartment on the Mystic River. That was a very fortunate thing because it introduced us to that side of the New London area.

Going to school, again, you've got to realize people were overly security conscious. We were standing a watch in four, which meant I had to stay aboard one night in four, although I didn't have any duties to perform. But I had to be on base, so I lived in BOQ, and we all did this.* On those nights that you had the duty your wife would come in, and you'd have dinner at the club. That way you sort of socially mixed. There was a forced mixing that otherwise wouldn't haven't have happened, and we made friends there.

Ben Byrnside was a bachelor, and he used to come out with us, and we have been intimate friends ever since. In those days the bachelors were courting girls across the river at Connecticut College, and eventually his wife was one of those ladies. We called them Conn. College Cuties. I think at the time the Conn. College was concerned about having their girls go over to the sub base, but notwithstanding that, a lot of them married submariners.

Paul Stillwell: And Coast Guard Academy men too.

Admiral Burke: Yes. Around New London there were a lot of the wives of submarine officers that were deployed. We saw them at the club particularly. Didn't necessarily meet them, but you saw these people coming and going. I remember the first time I ever saw Roberta McCain, Jack McCain's wife. She was up there, and she was a good-looking lady. She had white hair when she was 30 years old, and she still looks about as young as she did 50 years ago.

Paul Stillwell: That's remarkable.

---

* BOQ—bachelor officers' quarters.

Admiral Burke: Yes.

Paul Stillwell: Who were some of the instructors and the role models that they had in the school?

Admiral Burke: Well, Captain Patterson was the officer-in-charge.* He was a rather austere person, the class of '24. Alan Banister had one of the departments, I can't remember which.† You've got to realize it's over 50 years, so my memory isn't quite as good.

Paul Stillwell: I'm impressed by all that you are pulling out of it.

Admiral Burke: Bill Irvin, who later made admiral, was communications, and they're the only names I can immediately recall.‡ Ted Aylward was one of the commanders up there at sub school.§ He was from the class of '26; I don't recall what department he had.

Paul Stillwell: How much competition was there among the students in the Submarine School?

Admiral Burke: Remember now that I was a horrible student at the Naval Academy. There was competition. I said about a quarter of our class were academy graduates, and the rest were straight out of OCS.** And some of these guys were just bright as they could be but no experience. I think the top two or three people in our class were from OCS. As I recall, I started off about number 8, and I filtered down to about 15 or something like that, maybe 20, but where I began I could see that I could do it.

---

* Captain George W. Patterson, Jr., USN, served as officer in charge of the Navy's Submarine School from December 1942 to January 1944.
† Lieutenant Commander Alan B. Banister, USN.
‡ Lieutenant Commander William D. Irvin. The oral history of Irvin, who retired as a rear admiral, is in the Naval Institute collection.
§ Commander Theodore C. Aylward, USN.
** OCS—Officer Candidate School.

One area that I performed in better than most was in the attack teacher or in the diving machine. I just did it. I can remember looking back on it at the time. The only time I really was good in ordnance and gunnery when I was a midshipman was when I got on the attack teacher when we were having a surface torpedo drill. Somehow or other, I pulled it together. It affected my standing over there, and all of a sudden they stopped trying to flunk me and tried to pass me. At Sub School I don't think people worried too much about class standing. I think they wanted to make sure that the students knew what they were doing.

Paul Stillwell: Well, there was a great degree of motivation.

Admiral Burke: Oh yes. I mean, the war was on and people were coming back from the front to new construction, and I saw friends. For example, John Shepherd, who lived around Alexandria and then eventually in Charlottesville, he was cousin to friends of mine. He was a personal friend. He was in the class of '39. He showed up with his bride, and they lived in Noank. He was in new construction, and so we saw them occasionally and he had been on a couple of war patrols. Phil Glennon who was a very close friend of mine, classmate, he showed up.* He was not married, but he was in new construction. So Betty saw these people and met some of the wives. I don't remember any other names off the top of my head, but they were passing through Submarine School. We had a torpedo department. We all had to learn about the Mark XIV torpedo, and I knew a fair amount about it by the time I finished.†

Paul Stillwell: Were you aware of all the problems it was having in operational use?

Admiral Burke: Not until I reported to the <u>Flying Fish</u> and was told I was the torpedo officer. I'll go into that, but I would say we didn't at the time. The training that we got in

---

* Lieutenant (junior grade) Phillip T. Glennon, USN.
† During the early part of World War II, U.S. torpedoes were notorious for running deeper than the designed settings and for malfunctioning or poorly functioning exploders in cases in which the torpedoes did hit their targets. For details see David E. Cohen, "The Mk-XIV Torpedo: Lessons for Today," <u>Naval History</u>, Winter 1992, pages 34-36.

submarines, we were on O-boats, which were World War I vintage.* They were small, but people were doing things on them, and this really appealed to me. I mean, we had people doing things in the submarines that they never let you get close to doing on a battleship. The battleship is just physically too big; there are too damn many people. Between the captain and the bow there are so many people that you have to have a whole bureaucracy to get the job done, and so you could see this in a submarine. The captain was up there, he let people make landings, and you could see the confidence building up in people. So I liked that. I can't say that I did any better in any of these things, but I went to Submarine School with the idea of getting back out and making war patrols.

Paul Stillwell: I wonder if you could talk some about the attack trainer and how it worked.

Admiral Burke: Well, you've got a periscope. You're looking through the periscope at a little ship model, and they're bringing the ship model closer and closer. And it's all scaled in there, and you take ranges on it.

Paul Stillwell: Did you have a TDC as part of this?†

Admiral Burke: Yes, we must have had the latest TDC. Now, we weren't expert at operating the TDC, but they had somebody there who told us, and we would go over there and fool around. We took the various positions in the fire control party, and in one case they even had it worked up so that, as I recall, there was a diving machine hooked up. You would have to call out the task steps and have a diving officer to give the orders down. Well, we weren't ready to absorb all of that stuff, and we stumbled through it, but it was enough to give you an idea of what was expected.

Paul Stillwell: Did you then get to apply this in making approaches in the school boats?

---

* The early U.S. submarines were designated by letter-number combinations rather than names. O-1 through O-16 were commissioned in 1918. R-1 through R-27 were commissioned in 1918-19.
† TDC—torpedo data computer, a piece of equipment that figures approach courses for torpedoes to take on their way to a target.

Admiral Burke: I don't remember doing that. Sub School wasn't that long. It was only three months, and they had crammed things in there. I don't remember doing that. We may have, but I doubt it.

Paul Stillwell: How much did you get on engineering in that course?

Admiral Burke: It was brief. They told us about diesel engines, Fairbanks-Morse and General Motors. They weren't called General Motors. There was another name, but it was a General Motors. I don't know that we sketched and described, but we had lectures on it, and we had courses and so forth and got examined on it.

Paul Stillwell: What was the balance between classroom work and hands-on type training?

Admiral Burke: Probably I would say about half and half. This is over 50 years ago. The practical stuff appealed to me because I was far better at it, and I performed way above average in the practical stuff. Get me behind a book, I stink.

Paul Stillwell: What choices did you have for your first submarine duty?

Admiral Burke: I was very acutely aware of people who were counting war patrols. By the time I was coming out of sub school, it was the end of June of '43. The war had been going on for a year and a half, and I sort of felt like I was behind. So when the assignment offers came out, I asked to go to Pearl Harbor, so I could get some war patrols under my belt. Because I had classmates who had already been out there a year and had two or three war patrols, and I wanted to catch up.

My year group, the class of '40, was the senior class at sub school. The way they worked it out was they were going to send all people like me in my class out there. Then, about two days before the end of sub school, I got called in with Ben Byrnside and told that one of these training boats down on the river had an exec who had been transferred, and they wanted either one of us to be exec. Which one wanted it? Byrnside had been on the Enterprise and been through a lot of combat, and he was ready to stay home. I said I wanted to go out, so that's what happened. I don't think I told Betty I'd done this.

Paul Stillwell: Well, you got your orders to Pearl Harbor. How did you break that to your bride?

Admiral Burke: Well, she accepted it, and by this time she was pregnant, and so we drove on down here. She had a sister who was married with one child and lived in Chevy Chase. Her husband was too old to get caught up in the draft. He was an old man. He was almost 40. So we came on down here to just touch base with my family, and I guess Betty's family probably were down here by that time. They were living in the Kennedy-Warren in Washington, and so it was convenient.

Then we took a train from here to Chicago and then transferred and went on to California. I will tell you that when Sub School ended, we stayed up at Noank for a week on vacation. One of my four or five best friends, Spencer Wilson, was going to the next sub class. His wife was Harry Train's older sister, Toto, and so we arranged to have them take our apartment. We spent a fair amount of time with them, and then we came on down here.

But I went in to either get paid or something at the pay office in New London. Then I went up to ship's service, and this distinguished-looking, nattily dressed lieutenant commander with three Navy Crosses on his chest came in, had a mustache, very rigid, stern looking, and he was waited on. Then they took care of me, and then a lieutenant or a lieutenant commander came in, and he was a very personable man. He was about the class of '32. I remember him quite well, but his name escapes me. I wish I could dig it up. But he was talking to an enlisted man there and he said, "Did you see Captain Donaho over there?" He said, "Boy, he's been doing a great job."[*]

Well, when Betty and I finally took off from here, we went over to the Union Station in Washington. We had a reservation. That's what I'd gone into the pay office about. We had our reservation to get on the train, and the train had already left. Our tickets were made out incorrectly, and fortunately Betty's brother-in-law, who was used

---

[*] Commander Glynn R. Donaho, USN, was commanding officer of the submarine Flying Fish (SS-229).

to traveling the route to Chicago, arranged to get us on another train that left an hour later that would meet our connection in Chicago. So he persuaded the conductor on another train, the Pennsylvania, that was going out there to take us aboard, and he said he'd get us into something and indeed he put us in an upper bunk in a sleeper, Betty being pregnant. It turned out there were a bunch of Army WACs.[*] I'd never heard of a WAC before and in the middle of the night I heard this girl say, "Hey, Josie. Where is the latrine?" And that's the first time I'd ever heard the word "latrine."

Anyhow, it turned out we were on the same train with Captain Donaho. He had made five war patrols as commanding officer, and they had sent him back for a rest. He was temporarily relieved for the sixth war patrol by his division commander, Frank Watkins.[†] He was back apparently putting on a public speaking tour to promote and sell war bonds. Well, after later getting to know him and so forth, he was the last guy in the world that should have been on a public relations trip. I didn't meet him at the time, but he was on that train, and then later the same train that we went from Chicago to San Francisco. He and his wife had a Chinese amah with them. They would get out at every stop, pace up and down, and then get back on the train. He was very stern, always immaculate. So we made this trip, and it was amazing. Every stop we made, the Red Cross would be out there with doughnuts and coffee. It was an uneventful trip, and we arrived in San Francisco.

Betty and I stayed in the Claremont Hotel across the bay in Berkeley and hoped that we were going to be delayed. But about two days later I got word to report in for transportation, and I was put on a Pan American plane, a flying boat. I took my seat, and there were two seats facing two. The gentleman right across from me was Lieutenant Commander Donaho, and he was just as stern all the way to Pearl Harbor. Hardly opened his mouth.

Paul Stillwell: Did you know at that point he was going to be your skipper?

---

[*] WAC—Women's Army Corps.
[†] Commander Frank T. Watkins, USN. For details on this substitution, see Clay Blair, Jr., Silent Victory: The U.S. Submarine War Against Japan (Philadelphia: J. B. Lippincott Company, 1975), pages 431-432.

Julian T. Burke, Jr., Interview #3 (3/14/97) – Page 140

Admiral Burke: No. I had orders to ComSubPac for assignment.* Donaho was the senior passenger aboard, and the pilot came in and sat down and tried to be personable, but not much happened. So when we got to Pearl Harbor the next morning, we were going ashore in the boat to the landing, and all of a sudden he said, "Where are you going?"

I said, "ComSubPac for duty, sir."†

He said, "Come with me." I went with him to one of the carryalls that carried most of the passengers. Donaho was the senior man, and he told the driver to go to SubPac.

On the way in he said, "Naval Academy?"

"Yes, sir."

"Class? What ship?"

I answered all these questions, and when we got there he took me up and introduced me to the flag secretary, who at the time was the personnel officer. Flying Fish was still on war patrol, and he said, "When's the Flying Fish getting in?"

He said, "Two weeks."

"Who's being transferred?"

Said, "Styer and Gurnee."‡ They had made maybe three or four war patrols.

"Who's replacing them?"

So he named a couple of people who were ensigns out of my sub class in New London.

He said, "I want Burke here."

The guy said, "You can't have him. He's going to the Wahoo."

He said, "I don't like that. You're transferring two academy people, and I need at least one replacement."

He said, "You can't have him. They don't have them."

So he said, "Well, I'll go down and see Sunshine. Where is he?" He was the

---

* ComSubPac—Commander Submarine Force Pacific Fleet.
† ComSubPac—Commander Submarine Force Pacific Fleet.
‡ Lieutenant (junior grade) Charles W. Styer, Jr., USN; Lieutenant (junior grade) Robert L. Gurnee, USN.

chief of staff, Captain Sunshine Murray.* So he went down to Captain Sunshine Murray's, and he came back and said, "Sunshine says I can have him." I had an academy classmate and Submarine School classmate named Willie Burgan. "Oh," he said, "Burgan is going to the Wahoo." So Burgan was put on the Wahoo to replace me, and the Wahoo came in within the next ten days. Burgan showed up some time after that and reported in. I had a very good friend and classmate on there, Richie Henderson, who was from Fredricksburg, and he was a good friend.† He had made about three or four patrols on the Wahoo. The Wahoo went out on the next patrol, then was in for three weeks, and I saw Richie several times. They went out on the next patrol and were lost.‡ So I have had very generous feelings about Captain Donaho.

Paul Stillwell: So just the chance of your being on the same airplane with Donaho probably saved your life.

Admiral Burke: Yes. When I was told that I was going to the Flying Fish and he walked off, satisfied, the assistant flag secretary came over, and he said, "You poor bastard. That's the biggest SOB in the submarine force." That wasn't upsetting to me. Sometime within the next 24 hours he came around and told me that I was going to be torpedo officer. He said, "The ship's coming in in a couple of weeks, and I want you to get all of the training that a torpedo officer can get." They had an attack teacher there, and I went in and worked on the attack teacher a bit, got them to help me on the TDC. Then I discovered the torpedo problems we were having. I guess there were two problems that had surfaced. One was they were running too deep, and the other one was the exploders weren't working right.

Paul Stillwell: Both the magnetic and the contact exploders had problems.

---

* Captain Stuart S. Murray, USN, was chief of staff to ComSubPac, Rear Admiral Charles A. Lockwood, Jr. The oral history of Murray, who retired as a four-star admiral, is in the Naval Institute collection.
† Lieutenant Richie N. Henderson, USN.
‡ USS Wahoo (SS-238) was one of the most successful U.S. submarines of World War II. Her last skipper was Commander Dudley W. "Mush" Morton, USN. She was lost in the Sea of Japan on 11 October 1943, probably the victim of an attack by a Japanese antisubmarine aircraft. Lieutenant Burgan was among those killed when the submarine was lost.

Admiral Burke: Skippers were making statements, "It's a hell of a thing to take a submarine out to test fire the torpedoes on stuff that should have been done at Newport 20 years before." But I think the depth problem had pretty much been settled or the way to deal with it. They just stopped setting them at the normal depth. They'd put them at something less than and it seemed to work. The other side of it was the impact. There was a chief in the torpedo shop there on the submarine base, and I got to be on practically a first-name basis with him. I'd go down there and see what he was doing, and he said he had pressure. He said, "Admiral Nimitz comes down to see me, see how this thing is going." Then they had some tests done. The test was they got a warhead and put an exploder in it. They had some sort of a shipyard crane that would drop them. They did this right in front of ComSubPac's office. Have you heard about this?

Paul Stillwell: Yes, but please continue

Admiral Burke: People would come down there to watch this demonstration of dropping the warhead down this wire and collision. Was it going to work or not? Now, Tom Hill at that time was the fleet gun boss, and his number-two guy was Eller.[*] Eller had taught me at the academy at least once, and I knew who he was. He was a gentleman you wanted to know, just like "Pig Boat Benny."[†] Different personalities, and I got to know him because I was always at these tests.

I went to at least three of these tests to observe them, and they were always down there watching them, so this was a way I worked myself into it. The Flying Fish came in off of war patrol and immediately went in the shipyard at Pearl for overhaul.[‡] About 25% of the crew stayed aboard because they were new people. The rest of them went on leave so the new people could go aboard. One was Andy Anderson, classmate, R. G.

---

[*] Commander Ernest M. Eller, USN. The oral history of Eller, who retired as a rear admiral, is in the Naval Institute collection.
[†] This is a reference to Commander Roy S. Benson, a World War II submariner skipper whom Burke had known earlier when he was a midshipman and Benson was on the academy staff.
[‡] USS Flying Fish (SS-229) was a Gato-class submarine commissioned 10 December 1941. She had a displacement of 1,525 tons on the surface and 2,410 tons submerged. She was 312 feet long, 27 feet in the beam, and had a draft of 15 feet. Her top speed was 20 knots surfaced and 9 knots submerged. She was armed with ten 21-inch torpedo tubes and a 3-inch deck gun.

Anderson.* He had been in the submarine class before me. He had one patrol. And there was another guy whose name escapes me. Bob Gurnee, out of '39, was being transferred, and Charlie Styer, out of '41, was being transferred. That was the nucleus, and everybody else went on leave. The exec was Walt Small, and Shorty Owens was the engineer.† He was a mustang. I think Styer had been the engineer, and so he was relieved by Shorty Owens, and then Styer went on his way. We went in the shipyard, and I was the torpedo officer.

I didn't feel this immediately, but in hindsight I wish I had been the first lieutenant or in engineering, and I'll explain later why. The way they operated, Walt Small apparently was the first exec on our boat that had been able to please Captain Donaho. Walt was from North Carolina down not too far from the Outer Banks, Elizabeth City. It turned out he had gone to Woodberry Forest School, which was the chief rival of Episcopal High School where I went to prep school. And I turned out to be his roommate on the ship. I can see why he was able to deal with Donaho because Walt's as sharp as anybody I've ever seen. A very demanding person and he was good. He had the answers. He was the TDC operator the first patrol that I made. Although the assistant approach officer was somebody else, Walt was the guy that was talking the problem with the captain. I just was standing there as the assistant, learning how to do it and setting the dials to give the train order to the torpedo tubes.

Paul Stillwell: Why do you say you would rather have been the engineer or first Lieutenant?

Admiral Burke: Well, they're the guys that really know the boat. I became exec eight months later, and I just didn't have the detailed knowledge of the boat. I had done the sketches and all of that sort of stuff, but I didn't feel like I really knew the material side of it well enough. I couldn't just pick up a book; I had to go back there. On the other hand, my style of doing things was to go down and talk to people—like Wilder Baker. I'd get them to tell me, to make sure I understood. Every now and then, when we had a casualty,

---

* Lieutenant Roy Gene Anderson, USN.
† Lieutenant Walter L. Small, Jr., USN. Lieutenant (junior grade) Harley G. Owens, USN.

I could dig up and figure out which was a personnel casualty instead of a material casualty that caused this failure.

We were in the yard for two months, and during those two months Eleanor Roosevelt made a tour of the Pacific.* We were in dry dock at the time, and I remember she didn't come aboard our ship. But she came to the side of the dry dock, and Captain Donaho went over and greeted her and talked with her. It was interesting. That was as close as I ever have been to Mrs. Roosevelt. She had a charisma that was impressive, and people felt better by her presence.

Paul Stillwell: She made them feel good about themselves.

Admiral Burke: Well, I wasn't close enough, couldn't hear their voice exchange, but I could see the reaction of the people there who could.

Paul Stillwell: And, of course, her husband had that gift in spades.

Admiral Burke: Oh, yes. Then another thing happened during that time. There were four senators who came out and toured the Pacific to see how the war was going on. They were being given a lot of publicity because they were coming back and telling the world how it was going on, particularly in Washington. One of our officers was Buff Chace.† I used to call him "Chace-Manhattan," which he didn't like, but it turned out his father was on the board. They were a very prominent Rhode Island family and affluent. Buff had been kicked out of Notre Dame and Yale amongst other things, and he'd been in PT boats. He was a very lackadaisical guy but competent on things that he expected to do, but he didn't have the motivation that a regular officer did. He was just doing it, and so he drove Walt Small crazy.

We finally got out of the shipyard, and we were over at the sub base. We were loading out and getting ready to train. Buff Chace had the duty, and one of the enlisted men came down to the wardroom and said, "Mr. Chace, there's some people up there on

---

* Eleanor Roosevelt was the globetrotting wife of President Franklin D. Roosevelt.
† Lieutenant (junior grade) Alden Buffington Chace, USNR.

deck. I don't know what they're doing, but I think you'd better come up." Buff went up and saw a couple of these senators. He didn't know who they were, and they were going around shaking hands like they were on an election tour. Buff said, "Who the hell is that bastard?" and that bastard turned around and said, "I'm Happy Chandler from Kentucky."[*]

The ship's crew was on leave in the States while we were in the shipyard. Captain Donaho had come back, and he had already had his leave, so he was there all the time. A very unfortunate thing happened about the crew. The crew that had leave were men that had had a lot of war patrols, and they came back and blew their stacks. They reported in to the submarine command at Mare Island, and eventually they were sent over as a group to Com 12, the naval district headquarters in San Francisco, for transportation.[†] I don't recall how many of them, but I would say there probably were at least 35 or 40 of these people. And there was a stall and a delay, which can often happen. While they were waiting around, some of these guys for better or for worse went around the corner to the nearest bar, and before long some of these guys got drunk and began to play too cozy with some of the girls in the naval district headquarters. Well, this got up to Com 12 himself, and he sent for the commander submarine administration captain in Mare Island over there and personally chewed him out for the misbehavior of the <u>Flying Fish</u>.[‡]

Paul Stillwell: No doubt things went downhill from there.

Admiral Burke: Donaho didn't know anything about this. And about two or three weeks later Donaho was at a party up on Makalapa that he had been invited to attend.[§] They were probably commanding officers and so forth, and he was up there talking with

---

[*] Albert B. Chandler (Democrat-Kentucky) served in the U.S. Senate from 10 October 10 1939, until his resignation on 1 November 1945 to become Commissioner of Baseball. He is credited with fostering the racial integration of professional baseball.
[†] Mare Island Navy Yard, Vallejo, California.
[‡] Rear Admiral John W. Greenslade, USN, was Commandant of the 12th Naval District (Com 12).
[§] Makalapa is the name of the area near Pearl Harbor on the island of Oahu, Hawaii, where Commander in Chief Pacific Fleet maintains his headquarters.

Admiral Nimitz and Admiral Lockwood, who was ComSubPac.* This gentleman who had been ComSub admin when this incident occurred, that had been chewed out, he had arrived in Pearl Harbor. He came up and saw Donaho there, and, notwithstanding the fact that Nimitz and Lockwood were with him, he personally dressed him down and gave him hell for the behavior of the <u>Flying Fish</u> crew. This had a profound effect on Captain Donaho. He came back and told us about it, and then he called the crew together. He didn't chew them out, but he said he'd let them know what happened. My own perception of this, not having seen him before, it made him a lot more human than he otherwise had been before.

I liked the way he operated. During the exercises that we had, we had intensive training. When I first went up on the bridge to be an officer of the deck, I was standing top watch, and he personally instructed me. He must have talked continuously for about two full watches, and finally he said, "I've told you everything I need to tell you. I'm not going to talk to you unless you do something wrong."

Paul Stillwell: Certainly not if you do something good.

Admiral Burke: Then he took his position whenever we were on the surface on the after end of the bridge—the cigarette deck, we called it. You were there, and the routines that you had were very rigid. For example, the people up on the bridge, including the officer of the deck, had their binoculars at their eyes continuously for four hours. Only to get permission to wipe them off or to do that, but you were expected to keep those binoculars up there. You can argue about whether that was a sensible thing or not, but we came back, and not all submarines did. I never saw another submarine in my experience that had the firmness in detail of operation and supervision.

We always had in the control room an officer backup. The exec backed up the diving officer and checked to make sure, and this saved our lives on a number of occasions. Somebody might forget to shut a valve or somebody forget to do something or flood something. It was the exec's job to do that, and I did that later when I became exec.

---

* Admiral Chester W. Nimitz, USN, served as Commander in Chief Pacific Fleet and Pacific Ocean Areas, 1941-45. Vice Admiral Charles A. Lockwood, Jr., USN, served as Commander Submarines Pacific Fleet from February 1943 to December 1945.

So we went out on patrol via Midway, and then we headed for the Marianas. On the way we got word through a nightly intelligence message that there was a carrier headed for Japan. We had taken on board electric torpedoes, and I had been trained in electric torpedo care and upkeep, as our torpedomen had been. We'd gotten them from the Germans. Before long we had a rendezvous with this Japanese aircraft carrier. It was around midnight, full moon, one destroyer escort ahead. We were pretty far out. We got in to about 2,000 yards, which for an electric torpedo was not close enough, and we fired six torpedoes. The first torpedo came back on a circular run over the ship before the second one got out. It went by like a truck, and you could hear the damn thing circling. Finally, after about seven minutes, there was an end-of-run explosion that lifted us off the deck, and it was a thoroughly frightening experience.

Paul Stillwell: I'm sure it was.

Admiral Burke: From there we heard two explosions, and the carrier went on to Japan.* It was headed from the South Pacific back to Japan. I think we claimed damage, but that's all we could. Then we headed on for Palau and were patrolling off the main port there, I forget the name of it. Before long, after we'd been patrolling there for a few days, a convoy came out and headed towards Japan. We tried to get in, but we were too far out. They had lots of aircraft. This was daytime. We couldn't attack on the surface at that time, but watching Donaho go through his motions as the attack officer for me was an experience.

I was just overwhelmed to see how he operated. He was like a finely tuned machine. He never kept that periscope up more than ten seconds. He could spin, and he could look around and he could drop the scope, and then he would try to remember what he saw, and he would spit it out for the attack party. Finally it was evident we weren't going to get in, so we secured from battle stations, and he turned the conn over to Walt Small, the exec. I was standing next to Walt, who said, "What do you think?"

I had my back to the hatch, and I said, "That bastard is really good." Walt looked over my shoulder, he looked kind of funny, and I turned around and that bastard was right

---

* This attack on the aircraft carrier was on 18 October 1943, north of Saipan.

behind me. He smirked, turned around, and went down the hatch. And I never had a problem with him the rest of his time on there. The rest of the patrol we went after this convoy and caught up with them and made a series of night surface attacks, and I see by your paper here we did sink one.* That was sort of a maze in my learning process. I didn't have the picture of what was going on. Whenever we got on target we did a lot of night radar surface attack. We made two or three attacks, but apparently we only sank one ship.

Paul Stillwell: Would you describe Donaho as an aggressive skipper?

Admiral Burke: He was when I was on there, yes. You have to read a lot of war patrol reports, but he certainly pushed while I was there, and we fired a lot of torpedoes. We fired all of our torpedoes up early, and so then we were sent back to Midway for overhaul or for upkeep. We moved up to the Pan American Hotel—I forget what it was called—and that in itself was an experience.† Donaho was transferred and replaced by Lieutenant Commander Bob Risser.‡ About that time Donaho made commander, I think.

Paul Stillwell: Had you had any contact at all with Frank Watkins during his tenure?

Admiral Burke: Not really, except people liked him. See, he came in as the captain of the ship and was relieved immediately by Donaho, and he was not our division commander. He was the other division commander in our squadron, but people liked him. He seemed easy to work for. Our division commander was Karl Hensel, who had been at the Submarine School before I had been there and a very bright guy.§

Donaho and Hensel didn't like each other, and I remember hearing one of our ship's officers saying they were up on the forecastle one day talking to each other, and you could just tell how they felt by the way they were circling each other they were like a

---

* The Flying Fish sank the 6,550-ton cargo ship Nanman Maru on 27 October 1943.
† Pan American World Airways had a long, close association with the U.S. Navy. Before the war Pan Am developed service facilities on a number of islands that served as way stations for Clippers, the flying boats that flew to the Western Pacific.
‡ Lieutenant Commander Robert D. Risser, USN.
§ Commander Karl G. Hensel, USN.

couple of dogs. The problem I think that existed was that when the war started we had these older people who were in command of the boats, and very quickly they were replaced by the next generation of people. All of a sudden this next generation were sinking ships; they had done it. The men who were their division and squadron commanders hadn't done it, and the younger men resented being told how to do by somebody who hadn't been there.

Paul Stillwell: That's understandable. Human nature.

Admiral Burke: Eventually these division commanders such as Frank Watkins and Hensel, too, were sent out in temporary command so they had the battle experience.

Paul Stillwell: I see.

Admiral Burke: Or they put them in command of wolf packs, and so they had the experience of getting depth charged and went through the sweat and tears that the skippers were going through. But if you've been through hell and you have somebody telling you who's never been there, it's not very inspiring. We had a lot of that, and I'm sure the aviation community had the same experience.

Paul Stillwell: How would you compare Risser with Donaho?

Admiral Burke: I'd better give you more of a personal assessment of Donaho. Donaho was a guy who probably stood almost as low in his class as I did, and he did what I have done over the years.[*] He worked like hell. He realized he was in competition, and when he faced up to something he went down to the nitty gritty of doing the operational aspects of it so it was perfect. And the ship's routines were that way. He never asked anybody to do anything that he wouldn't do himself. For example, submarines don't worry much about honors and ceremonies, but he did. I've been on deck, and I've heard a war hero criticize Donaho jokingly. He said, "That guy's crazy. He was aboard my ship after the

---

[*] Donaho stood number 538 of the 579 graduates in the Naval Academy class of 1927.

war, and he wanted me to render honors just like it was peacetime, like they do on big ships." Well, that was Donaho. He did things exactly right, and if you expected it and anticipated, you got along with him fine. I had been in battleships long enough, almost three years, and I knew how they expected to do things, so this wasn't a sweat for me. But somebody who'd been in the dungaree Navy thought it was crazy.

Paul Stillwell: You also told me last week when the recorder wasn't running that he was immaculate in his military appearance.

Admiral Burke: Oh, yes. That was just the way the guy operated. We had a rule on the Flying Fish. No smoking when the ship was submerged. If anybody got caught, they got busted. And he was ruthless about it. Well, Bob Risser came aboard. He had been in PG School when the war started, and then he went out and made a couple of patrols as a PCO.* Then he came to us. He was a pretty bright guy, but he was more relaxed about things. For example, in the wardroom on the Flying Fish you'd sit down, and there was no conversation until Donaho spoke. I remember when I started talking in the wardroom after I first came aboard and so forth, I got a nudge that we weren't supposed to do that. I never had any problem with Donaho himself.

    I have to go back to the fact that what I said about that bastard being good. Risser when he came aboard relaxed immediately. He was a smoker as Donaho was a smoker, but Risser didn't like this. He'd been on a submarine that the smoking lamp had been lighted the whole time. Well, Donaho had made several war patrols; he had made more than Risser had. Walt Small and some of the others smoked. I don't smoke, so it wasn't a problem for me, but Risser wanted to light the smoking lamp once an hour. Well, frankly, that was a bum deal because people would leave calls to be waked up when the smoking lamp was lighted for five minutes or whatever time. It was crazy.

Paul Stillwell: What was Donaho's rationale for no smoking submerged.

---

* PCO—prospective commanding officer.

Admiral Burke: To save the oxygen. Your endurance. You never knew when you dived in the morning, if you were close in, if you were going to get up. When you got in trouble, the first thing you do is tell everybody not actually on watch to lie down so that it would save oxygen. You had about 24 hours of oxygen. My longest dive was about 20, and I can tell you the air was thin. You couldn't light a match.

Paul Stillwell: So that took a great deal of self-discipline on Donaho's part, being a smoker himself.

Admiral Burke: Well, you do a lot of things when your life depends on it, and I think he looked at it that way. With Bob Risser, life was far more pleasant in the wardroom. He played poker. At sea most days we had a poker game that went for two hours, from 1:00 to 3:00, and he was a pretty good poker player, so he usually won. We kept books and settled at the end of the patrol, but when he lighted the smoking lamp for one hour and so forth, the chief petty officers were upset because they got nervous. Eventually they got over it or were transferred and were replaced, but I can remember a couple of them telling me that they really wanted to smoke. I said, "Well, you don't have to smoke." I was incredibly lucky. Whenever I got nervous, I chewed gum and popped it. That drove them crazy.

Paul Stillwell: What do you remember about the operations under Captain Risser?

Admiral Burke: Well, he was aggressive. A lot of it has to do with luck, on where you are and what's happening. On his first patrol we left Midway and headed towards the passage between the Philippines and Taiwan, I forget the name of it.

Paul Stillwell: Bashi Channel.

Admiral Burke: Probably, and I can remember when we were approaching that channel it began to rain. It rained so hard and so long it knocked the paint off of the superstructure up around the bridge. I was up there for a four-hour watch, and I was drenched to the skin. I had rain coveralls on. That patrol lasted 60 days. We did sink two ships, and the largest was a tanker off of the southern port, of Formosa. I forget the name of the port, something like Takowa. They've changed all the names of those places.

We picked up a small convoy of about four ships and three or four escorts. The biggest ship in it was a tanker, and we picked it up in the middle of the night and managed to hit him, got one hit. That stopped him, and then after dawn I think they had left the ship behind. They may have left an escort there, but we went in and fired again and sank him.* Another ship we picked up in the middle of the night; it was moonlight. We had marked Mark XIV torpedoes on that patrol so they ran straight, and we picked up a convoy of about four or five ships with escorts, and I think this was the first one. Let me see. It was on the 16th of December, and that one was fairly near to Takowa.† We fired at him, and we didn't have radar ranges. We were going on moonlight and just guesstimate. We thought the range was about 1,500 yards and, well, we fired the first torpedo. Before the second one went out, the first one hit.

Paul Stillwell: Closer than you thought.

Admiral Burke: The ship went under so fast it was just amazing. It was hit by the second torpedo, but it just went down like a rock. We got a bit of depth charging. Not much. They weren't close. We didn't get depth charged on the first patrol at all. The frightening thing was a circular run. And then we didn't get anything else to shoot at, but we got two positive sinkings.

We were down off, I think, Hong Kong for a while, and then we got a message that somebody was coming, I mean one of these intelligence top secret messages of a passage of a convoy or something. So we surfaced and started going after it, and apparently there was a typhoon there. We didn't get weather reports or anything. It was just rough weather. And I remember being on the bridge. I had stood the 4:00-8:00 watch at that time. We were going into the seas, and we were taking these seas over the bow. We took a succession of heavy ones, and it was so bad that I was behind the shield

---

* The Flying Fish sank the 10,171-ton tanker Kyuei Maru on 27 December 1943.
† The Flying Fish sank the 8,613-ton cargo ship Ginyo Maru on 16 December 1943.

there, and they were slamming the hatch shut to keep the water from going down and we took one succession there that submerged the bridge. The quartermaster and I both grabbed onto the radar pole. We had two lookouts aft of us, and one of the lookouts was almost washed over the side. He caught his leg in the cable there that went around the after end of the cigarette deck and the poor guy was just screaming, and so I had to relieve him. It so emotionally upset him that we had to get rid of him when we got in off patrol. We couldn't take him up topside again. So we slowed down and didn't get in on that contact that we had the message on.

After that we went into Pearl for upkeep, and when upkeep comes along in Pearl we used to go to the Royal Hawaiian, which was pleasant.* We were up there for two weeks. The routine was that about 25% of your crew would stay aboard. The other three quarters would get the rest camp.

Paul Stillwell: You'd get a relief crew to fix up the boat for the next patrol.

Admiral Burke: The relief crew would come in, and then you would come back and get about three or four days to get yourself back together; I forget the time frame. Then you'd go out for about a four-day training period, and then you'd go back on war patrol.

Well, Small was transferred at the end of that patrol. I was qualified in submarines. This was probably end of January, first of February, and Pete Friedrick out of the class of '37 came aboard and took his place.† I don't know why he came to us, but he had been on, I think, the submarine Peto in the South Pacific. But Small by that time had eight war patrols and needed a rest, so he went back to new construction and gave him a skipper that was very unpopular and not particularly well liked. He went up and complained about it, and somebody said, "Well, he was told you were the only guy that ever satisfied Donaho, and nobody's been able to satisfy Peterson yet."‡

As I say, I qualified at the end of two patrols. The only job I'd had was torpedo officer, and I continued to be torpedo officer for the next patrol. I really wanted to get to

---
* The Royal Hawaiian is a luxury hotel, still in business on Waikiki Beach all these years later. During World War II the Navy used it as a haven for submariners between patrols.
† Lieutenant Ernest S. Friedrick, USN.
‡ Small became the first executive officer of the submarine Icefish (SS-367), which was commissioned 10 June 1944 under the command of Commander Richard W. Peterson, USN.

be engineering or first lieutenant. Andy Anderson, my classmate, was first lieutenant, and he had taken that part of the auxiliary equipment and so forth and hull through the shipyard overhaul, so he had a good handle on it. He was also the diving officer, and Shorty Owens was the engineer, and he'd had a whole raft of patrols. He was a warrant officer.

We went out on the next patrol, which was around Okinawa, and I don't know how many ships we got. We had lots of contacts. We were planning, just for the heck of it, to bombard an island on the way out. There was a Japanese island named Kita Daito Jima maybe 100 miles east of Okinawa. We thought we'd just go by and bombard it, but on the way just before we got there we picked up a radar contact in the night. It was a small ship and we were tailing it to this island. Kita Daito Jima was in sight when we were trailing this contact, and we had to dive because we were too close for air cover. All of a sudden the screws stopped and, by gosh, they had a breakdown. Well, what happened was this ship apparently had an engine breakdown, so we were able to close him and sank him.*

Paul Stillwell: Not much evasion there.

Admiral Burke: He wasn't very big, but it was a kill. Then we went over and patrolled around Okinawa. It's kind of hazy what we did, but we had some night surface radar attacks. I remember in one case we had a large number of radar images, and we began to chase. Then, all of a sudden, we began to get close-in pips on the radar, and before long we couldn't see anything. Then people began to imagine they saw PT boats chasing us, and we dived, and then we didn't hear anything. We came back, and we went through that exercise a couple of times, and the convoy got away.

Another time we actually got in on a convoy and did some shooting, and somebody started shooting back at us and ran right over the top of us. We took quite a depth charging, as I best remember, and we also had an outer torpedo door jam, couldn't get it shut, and we got down to something like 400 feet. Our test depth was 312, and it was quite frightening. We had to break the interlock system to get the outer door shut.

---

* The Flying Fish sank the 5,493-ton passenger-cargo ship Anzan Maru on 16 March 1944.

That was exciting and terrifying. Fazed me a bit and others too. After we got through and tried to figure out what had happened when we had dived, we just guessed our radar probably picked up a covey of birds that were flying low over the water. But we were disappointed because we had a lot of ship targets out there.

Paul Stillwell: How would you describe the sensation of being under a depth charge attack?

Admiral Burke: It depends on how close they are. If you can imagine yourself in one of these big steel drums and somebody hits it with a sledgehammer. That's sort of the way it is—if they're really close.

Paul Stillwell: Did it reverberate through the boat?

Admiral Burke: Well, it depends on how close. When they really get close, they scare you. I don't know anybody that wouldn't be scared. Eventually we got ourselves where we had fired all of our torpedoes forward on that patrol. It's not easy to make an attack with just stern tubes in those type ships. So the captain notified SubPac, who said, "Proceed to Majuro for refit." So we decided to go by Kita Daito Jima, that island, and we were going to shoot. We had a deck gun, and we just decided, well, why don't we shell them? So we were getting ourselves mentally ready and going through a little bit of practice in the wardroom, of how we'd do it. The night before we got there, we picked a pip on radar, in fact we had two pips, a ship and an escort. They were heading for Kita Daito Jima, and we tailed them in. The ship went right up to this dock which stuck out into the ocean from the island. There wasn't any seawall around it.

Paul Stillwell: Kind of like a pier there.

Admiral Burke: It was just a pier, and this escort began to patrol outside, so we went in and went under the escort. He was pinging. You could hear it. It resounded. I mean, every time a ping would go it would just hit me in the belly. I was the TDC operator, had been for two patrols. This was my third patrol. We got in there and turned around, and we fired two torpedoes at this guy tied up at the dock and sank him.* Well, just as we fired the damn torpedoes in the after torpedo room I don't know what happened back there, but you could hear some air escaping. When we fired the torpedo something went wrong in the air system. We put a bubble up there which floated to the surface, and that was a target. That escort came over us, and our keel depth when he went over top of us was about 70 feet. He dropped a whole string of depth charges, and I'm telling you he got our attention.

Paul Stillwell: I'll bet he did.

Admiral Burke: But it was interesting. Here he was. He had us, and after that he dropped a lot more, but after that first burst none of them seemed close. It was really terrifying. It scared the hell out of me and everybody else. We headed on to Majuro, which none of us had ever heard of before, and when we got there the U.S. Fleet was there. I have never seen so many ships in my life. There were at least 10 battleships and I'm sure there were 35 or 40 cruisers, probably 10 or 12 carriers.

Paul Stillwell: This was shortly after the capture of the Marshalls.

Admiral Burke: It was a fleet anchorage. I was the only officer on there who had really been around the fleet, and these other guys just didn't have the experience. It sort of didn't mean anything to them. So we pulled in and went alongside a tender there; I don't recall which one it was.

We always had a squadron commander who oversaw everybody and a couple of divcoms.† By the time we left there, at least four or five submarines had come and gone. As our rest camp instead of going to the Royal Hawaiian, we went over to one of the islands there. They named them after girls, and our rest camp was at Myrna. I looked around, and indeed we had a Betty Island, so I'd have much preferred to be on Betty

---

* The Flying Fish sank the 2,398-ton cargo ship Ninami Maru on 1 April 1944.
† Divcom—division commander.

Island. But we were living in Homoja huts, and they gave us beer. As I recall, whenever we came into port in submarines the officers always had a quota of two fifths of hard whiskey—which none of the surface people had—and the crew drank about as much beer as they wanted. They always had beer available. We always had a ship's party or something like that.

Other submarines came in for refit, and you got to be friends with them. The Grayback was one that we had gotten to know very well in Midway at the end of my first patrol. I think they had come in when we were in Pearl Harbor, so they were really good friends. After one of these patrols the Grayback didn't respond. And you saw different submarines. I remember one of my classmates was Don Scheu, who was in my company as a midshipman.[*] He was engaged to a friend of Betty's that she had gone to Cathedral School over here in Washington with. She was from Jacksonville, and I don't know where he met her. He was on one of the boats that was in upkeep in Midway when we were there, and I saw quite a bit of Don. After about the next patrol he didn't come back.[†]

Paul Stillwell: Did you think about these things while you were on board your boat?

Admiral Burke: Well, in my case you think about them and just hope it doesn't happen. I don't know how to describe it. Spencer Wilson, who was really one of my closest friends, was lost on the first patrol of the Tullibee, which was new construction. They were having a night surface attack, and they had a circular run and they sank themselves. Interestingly enough, about four years later, I was in BuPers in the enlisted division.[‡] The one survivor came in there to get reassigned, and I met him and talked with him. He had been blown over the side and picked up by the Japanese. I'd say I'm sure it can get to some people. I guess I have developed a shell where I can sort of deal with it. My class has the highest casualty rate of any class in the academy, and my roommate for the last two years I was there, Tate Preston, was killed on a destroyer. He was exec of a destroyer at Okinawa that got kamikazed. You think about all of these fine people that didn't make

---

[*] Lieutenant Donald T. Scheu, USN.
[†] Scheu was lost about 16 February 1944 in the submarine Scorpion (SS-278).
[‡] BuPers—Bureau of Naval Personnel.

it just because they got killed. I think there were 17 of my Naval Academy classmates lost in submarines.

Paul Stillwell: But I guess the philosophy you have to have is it's not going to happen to me.

Admiral Burke: Well, it's like driving through Washington.

Paul Stillwell: That's right. Talk about your war zones.

Admiral Burke: When we arrived in Majuro, I was the fourth officer. My classmate Andy Anderson had one patrol more than I did but also he had been the first lieutenant, which from a materiel point of view was really a lot more important than what I did. He was told immediately that he was going to be transferred to be the exec of another submarine, the Kingfish, so I asked the captain if I could take his place. He said, "Sure." I think Buff Chace relieved me in torpedoes, and while we were in upkeep Shorty Owens, the engineer, was also transferred. We didn't have anybody behind me who was qualified, and here I'd only been qualified since mid-February.

Paul Stillwell: I take it you had qualified in command.

Admiral Burke: No, this is qualified in submarines.

Paul Stillwell: How can you have an exec who's not qualified in command?

Admiral Burke: I wasn't exec yet.

Paul Stillwell: Oh, I see.

Admiral Burke: Andy Anderson got transferred. He was third officer. I was fourth. So I took his place, and I became third officer. Then Shorty Owens, the engineer, got transferred. He had a lot of war patrols, more than any of us, and so he was transferred. They gave us Eric Hopley, out of the class of '42, who had just come from Submarine School.* But he had just arrived and had no experience, so I told the captain, "Why don't you let me take engineering, too?" which was what really I wanted, "And then I'll turn it over to Hopley when I can see my way clear." So coming out of Majuro, I was the engineer and the first lieutenant. That meant I was going to have a full plate, but I had a very competent person coming up. Hopley had been commissioned about two years by that time, and he was a sharp guy. I'd known him at the academy.

There was a submarine that came in about a couple or three days before we were leaving. I forget the name of it, but I think it was the Grouper, and the captain fired the exec. We heard about it, but we didn't think anything about it. We were getting ready to go on war patrol. We were going back to the Palau Islands to war patrol and had done our training. We were topping off fuel, and just about a half an hour before we got under way to leave port Pete Friedrick, the exec, came over. I was aft with the oil king checking on the oil coming aboard, and Pete Friedrick came over and patted me on the back and said, "You got it."

I said, "What do you mean?"

He says, "You're the exec." This was about the 15th of April. I had come aboard the preceding, oh, about the end of July.

I said, "What do you mean?"

He said, "Well, I'm being transferred. I'm going over to the Grouper," which had just fired the exec.

About this time quarters was called, and it turned out that they'd given us a PCO, and so he took over as navigator for a short while. He navigated us out of the port. I went down and talked to the captain, and I said, "What happened?"

He said, "Well, the commodore told me I had to provide an exec for that boat, and so I decided to keep you and send Friedrick." I think the rationale was that Friedrick had a lot of war patrols and was due to be rotated back, and I think he figured he could keep me longer then.

---

* Lieutenant (junior grade) Eric E. Hopley, USN.

But who did we have for replacements for losing the chief engineer and the first lieutenant? We got two guys fresh out of Sub School who had never even been to sea. Chace was not qualified yet, but he had the time on board to be considered qualified. He may have qualified by that time, but I'm not sure. But beyond that we had about five officers who were not qualified. Chace was one of the watch officers. The other two were unqualified watch standers.

I don't think Friedrick bothered, but I was brought up that the exec backed up the diving officer, so I started doing all the backup. And it wasn't long before I was tangling with the PCO, who was about four years senior to me. I could see things going wrong in the control room, and he wasn't doing anything about it, so I began to tell him. So after a couple of weeks I relieved him as navigator, so I was navigator, chief engineer, and first lieutenant. I stopped standing watch when I began to navigate.

Paul Stillwell: You did have a full plate.

Admiral Burke: After a month of that, I collapsed, and I went to bed for about two days just to get sleep. I figured out after it was all over that the longest I'd been in bed was something about an hour and 40 minutes, and I was really drained. I'm sure we sank some ships on that patrol. This May and June we sank four ships. I just don't remember what we sank and what we didn't, because it was just all a nightmare. I'm sort of hazy now.

The Philippine Sea battle was coming up in June, and they sent us to be a lookout.* They put a line of submarines off to the east of the Philippines at the various passages, and we were off of Surigao passageway. We were well clear so that we could spot anything. I think about four submarines were assigned to that duty. Eventually, after a period of time, probably a week, aircraft carrier planes began to appear doing searches, and a day or so later here came the whole Japanese Fleet. We went to battle stations and tried to get in. We could not. They were just too far away. The closest ships probably passed at least five miles away, but in any case we got off an alerting message.

---

* The Battle of the Philippine Sea took place in conjunction with the U.S. invasion of the Mariana Islands in mid-June 1944.

Then the Battle of the Philippine Sea came off after that, and we got some of the details but very little of it. But we heard later on that this was the prime alerting message to the U.S. Fleet that the Japanese were coming.

Paul Stillwell: And Herm Kossler in the Cavalla got an aircraft carrier.*

Admiral Burke: Yes. We saw carriers. We saw battleships. We saw cruisers. We saw destroyers and probably some oilers. We also got picked up by a plane in there, and I don't think he bombed us, but he could have had us if he'd have had a bomb.

By that time we'd been on patrol so long because of that extra assignment we were given they sent us to Australia to go via Seadler Harbor. It was the port on the north side of Manus in the Admiralty Islands. There was a fleet anchorage in there, and we went in there and topped off and got enough fuel so we could go on down to Brisbane.

When we got into Brisbane, everybody else went to Sydney on leave, but I just was too pooped out to do anything. We went across the line, and we only had about seven or eight shellbacks, and we had a horrible experience on being depth charged on that patrol. We got pushed down to about 500 feet, and we were lucky to get out. They had us, but I think they must have run out of depth charges. You talk about what do you think about. I thought we'd had it. What was bad about that I didn't have the experience and the knowledge of submarining to be a leader. At least I didn't feel I did. And I don't think I was the help to Bob Risser that I should have been. On the other hand, when we got in off the next patrol he recommended me as command qualified. But that was one patrol that was just a nightmare to me.

Paul Stillwell: That's understandable.

Admiral Burke: We had crossing-the-line ceremony. Now, when I'd crossed the line on a battleship my first time I went to sea on the West Virginia we had a big court. The chiefs and first class were all on the court and beat the hell out of all of us. And there

---

* The message from the Flying Fish enabled the submarine Cavalla (SS-244), under Commander Herman J. Kossler, USN, to sink the Japanese aircraft carrier Shokaku on 19 June 1944.

were a lot of shellbacks there. They seriously outnumbered the pollywogs. Well, this time it was the other way around. There were only about seven or eight of us that had crossed the line, and they had to use me to make up a court. I didn't want to do it, but they insisted, and so they made me the Royal Barber. Well, half the ship had beards, and so I had some electric shears and shaved off half the beards and half the hair and so forth. In fact, one of the guys was so furious when I cut his beautiful beard half off he spit in my face.

Well, after you've been submerged and been through a lot, you accepted it and laughed, but, anyhow, about four years ago one of our crew members did a marvelous job of finding where the crew members were living. He lives out in Phoenix, and he began to get enough people to put a reunion together for the <u>Flying Fish</u>. This was apart from the Submarine Vets. I missed the first two reunions. The first one was out west and the second one, I guess, was going to be in New London. Unfortunately, it conflicted with the graduation of my oldest grandchild in college, so I couldn't do it, but I did help them. I got on the horn and got some doors opened in New London, which they much appreciated.

Well, this guy and I talked on the phone from time to time, and finally one day he called up and he said, "I just want to tell you, I owe you an apology."

I said, "No, you don't."

He said, "Oh, yes, I do."

I said, "Go ahead and apologize."

He said, "I hated your guts for 50 years. But you're not so bad after all."

Paul Stillwell: Was this the guy that you cut the half the beard off?

Admiral Burke: No, but I'd cut his hair in a way that he said that I just ruined the liberty in Brisbane. The girls wouldn't date them, because they thought they were all diseased.

I said, "Were you married then?"

He said, "Yeah."

I said, "Your wife owes me."

Paul Stillwell: Well, that sounds like a great note to end on for today.

Interview Number 4 with Rear Admiral Julian T. Burke, Jr., U.S. Navy (Retired)
Place: Admiral Burke's home in Alexandria, Virginia
Date: Thursday, 20 March 1997
Interviewer: Paul Stillwell

Paul Stillwell: Admiral, when we broke off last time you had just gotten the Flying Fish in off patrol, crossed the equator, and gone to Australia.

Admiral Burke: This was about the end of the Flying Fish. It was the tenth patrol, and we had too many old-timers with too many patrols on.

Paul Stillwell: Too many in what sense?

Admiral Burke: They were burning out.

Paul Stillwell: I see.

Admiral Burke: We had a system in SubPac of rotating people off the ship after each patrol. I think it was something like 12 or 14 men were supposed to be rotated off, and we'd receive replacements. We had a constant school program going on to train the new people. It was good for the officers to have to supervise this, but on the other hand it put a burden on the ship. I was in the personnel business for the first time, and so, working with Bob Risser, the commanding officer, he agreed that we could begin to rotate some of the old-timers off, and we began to systematically rotate them off. Some of them went back to new construction. Some of them went off for a patrol or two and then came back.

Paul Stillwell: Did they go willingly or what was their reaction?

Admiral Burke: It was mixed. I think a few of these guys had been on there almost since the ship had been commissioned. They'd been through one hell of a lot, and I wanted to make sure they didn't burn out. It put the pressure on us to work harder, to train harder, and we got replacement petty officers who were experienced. I remember, for example, we got a chief quartermaster named Wallace. We hadn't had a chief before. He'd been on one of the other boats, I think it was the <u>Spearfish</u>, and he was a very valuable person. He gave us a lot of ideas on how we could do things, just little techniques how we could do better. We got a first class electrician's mate. We tended to not want to let these key people go, because they were people that we knew and trusted and so forth. But I just felt on balance it was better to rotate them off and get replacements in there so that they wouldn't burn out and give them a break. Let them go home.

Paul Stillwell: Was Wallace the chief of the boat?

Admiral Burke: No, he wasn't. He stood chief's watches. He assisted in navigation. One of the things he did is something I've used ever since. We tended to keep people on watch in a job up in the control room and on the bridge. His ship used to rotate these people after an hour, and we instituted that and, by gosh, it made a difference. People were much more alert on the job. Just to give them a change. We rotated the helm, the radar operator, the sonar operator, the lookouts, and people got more interested in what they were doing. They were mentally more alert.

Paul Stillwell: What was your relationship as exec with the chief of the boat?

Admiral Burke: We had two chiefs of the boat. Christiansen was the chief of the boat the last part of my tour, and I can't remember his predecessor. I'll have to go back. I've got a picture somewhere of the boat when went we went to Brisbane. Christiansen was a chief engineman, and he didn't particularly want the job. But he was the best petty officer that we had at the time, and he took it over sometime while I was exec. He did a good job, and we had a good relationship, as far as I can say. There was another chief that we had, though he wasn't chief of the boat. We eventually recommended him for warrant officer, and he made it. We made a mistake and kept him aboard, but it was too tough on him to move from chiefs' quarters to the wardroom. He was Chief Electrician's

Mate Bob Emmons, and Emmons and I are still good friends. He was a terrific officer, but it was too much of a strain to be in the ship that he had made it.

Paul Stillwell: I think usually it's the practice to rotate someone when he becomes a warrant officer for just that reason.

Admiral Burke: Well, it was the practice, and we made an exception because Emmons was the key to our electrical system. We got a first class to replace him, and we didn't know this guy, and we didn't know how good he was. I'd say it was my fault probably because I went up and twisted the captain's arm, and so he said, "Okay."

Paul Stillwell: You talked about the paucity of officer talent when you became the exec. Did that problem get solved?

Admiral Burke: Well, I'm glad you mentioned it. When we got to Brisbane, the captain asked, and we got a qualified officer aboard as one of our replacements, and his name was Dutch Reuther.* He had been on Slade Cutter's ship.† He was a jaygee, ex-chief yeoman. Big, physically big. Confident. Had worked his way up. He knew paper work, and he was an enormous help to me. I can't tell you what a big help he was, but he slung the bull about the heroics of Slade Cutter and the way he ran the Seahorse, and he described Slade.

    I was suffering from a problem called "terror in action," and he told me that Slade in some of the attacks was so terrified he was shaking and they practically had to hold him up to the periscope. Here was a guy who sank probably as many ships, if not more, than anybody else out there.‡ I've always had great admiration for Slade Cutter. Later on I'll tell you an encounter I had with him. But it gave me comfort, realizing that people like Cutter went through this too. Of course, he was a great athlete, well known, but he was an exuberant guy and he was a great leader. So this is just one of the things that I put

---

* Lieutenant (junior grade) Roland A. Reuther, USN.
† Commander Slade D. Cutter, USN, was commanding officer of the USS Seahorse (SS-304). The oral history of Cutter, who retired as a captain, is in the Naval Institute collection.
‡ In the postwar analyses Cutter was credited with sinking 19 Japanese ships.

in my quiver and went home and thought about as I had to go on as exec and later on as captain, some of the things that you get confronted with. Also, Reuther knew the personnel picture and relieved a burden on me at a time when I needed help. I just discovered within the last year that he was still alive and not well, and I wrote him a letter how I thought, and I got the nicest letter back from him. It really warmed my heart.

Paul Stillwell: What was his billet?

Admiral Burke: I think probably he was first lieutenant, but mainly he was cleaning up the paper work, which I badly needed. I had no experience in that department up to that time.

Paul Stillwell: I've talked to Slade Cutter, and he said one thing that stuck in his mind is when he was about to submerge at daybreak he would look up and see the twilight stars and wonder if he'd still be alive to see them that evening.

Admiral Burke: Well, I bumped into him at different places when he was coming in or going out, and he was always exuberant and so forth. But after hearing a description from Dutch Reuther and putting it all together, I tell you, he was a very special guy in my book. I've seen him around in different places, never close except one encounter I'll tell you about later.

Paul Stillwell: He lives in Annapolis now.

Admiral Burke: He does?

Paul Stillwell: He moved here recently.

Admiral Burke: Well, if you ever see him please give him my best. He'll remember me.

Paul Stillwell: I'll surely do that. Well, did you come out of that stay in Australia refreshed for further operations?

Admiral Burke: I was in one heck of a lot better shape. We had the largest turnover of the crew at that time. And, in spite of the fact that I, as the barber, was supposed to have ruined the liberty of the troops when we were in port, I can tell you that when we went down the river at Brisbane to go back to sea I'd never seen so many people standing up on deck, men, crying like babies and watching the girls wave at them and calling to their boyfriends.

Paul Stillwell: Well, the Australian men were fighting the war elsewhere, so the haircuts probably weren't that much of a problem.

Admiral Burke: I had more people having the need for emergency transfers. I think we turned over at least a third of the crew while we were down there. And, as I say, we had too many people on there who had made too many war patrols, and we needed a relief and we got some good people.

So we went on a patrol from there. We went up past New Guinea and on up to Davao Gulf and were patrolling off of Davao Gulf, and there was no shipping going by. Finally one day we were right at the mouth, and a small convoy came by. It was hot as blazes, the water temperature was about 95, and it was taxing the air-conditioning terribly. The water was calm as a millpond, and this small convoy came by. There was a plane overhead, and depth charges were dropped before we got anywhere near the screen. I would say I've had worse; I was used to much closer depth charges. Anyhow, we got through that, but that was the only enemy ship contact we had during that patrol, and we did fire some torpedoes but we got no hits. They were evading. And then, probably a month after we'd been on war patrol, we were directed to go back to an advance base we'd never heard of, the name escapes me, but it was in the East Indies, west of New Guinea, somewhere not to far from Molucca Passage.*

---

* The official history of the <u>Flying Fish</u> says that she refueled at Mios Woendi from 29 August 1944 to 1 September.

We went into a fleet anchorage there mainly of Service Force type ships and went alongside a tender. There was a squadron commander there on board, and we were given a short respite, probably three days in port. There was no place to go ashore, so to give the crew a chance to get some beer, we put them in a boat alongside. I guess we cast them off so they drank beer there. They ran the crew through physical exams, and I found that one of our key second class enlisted electricians had come down with gonorrhea caught in Australia. I didn't want to leave him there, and they wanted to take him off. I had been recently reading New Yorker magazine in an article about a drug I'd never heard of called penicillin. So I went up and asked the doctor, and I said, "What about this penicillin, this miracle drug? Does it work?"

He said, "Sure it does."

I said, "Do you have any?"

"Sure."

"Why don't you give it to my man?" So he shot him, and the next day he declared him okay and he let us take him back to sea.

Paul Stillwell: So your outside reading was helpful.

Admiral Burke: So I've been disposed towards the New Yorker ever since until I recently read a copy.

Paul Stillwell: What can you say in general about tender support during the war?

Admiral Burke: It was good. I can't criticize these people. I know that it was easy for those of us who were going on war patrol to be critical of the people on the beach, because we were getting depth charged and they weren't, but I always found them supportive. I don't ever recall having any disagreement. I have to say this. I had a void in real materiel jobs in submarines during the war. I was really not an engineer. I really wasn't first lieutenant. Those are the two big materiel jobs, so I was always looking over somebody else's shoulder. My own background and experience had a void there that I felt all my life in the Navy.

When we came back to that advanced base, we were given an op order to do coverage for the downed aviators—lifeguard duty. Our station was in Molucca Passage. Sure enough, we got out there and were patrolling out there on the surface, at a safe distance from the beach. Before long planes started coming over and making strikes, and there were a lot of them. They weren't coming over in hordes, but there were enough of them to show that we had control of the air. So we got bolder and moved in, and eventually we could see heavy black smoke at installations.

We knew that there was a Japanese air station over there on the beach not too far. We were in Molucca Passage, and we felt very secure. At one stage of the game there one afternoon, the captain decided to close the beach and see if we could see a little bit more. It was in the mid-afternoon, and we were zigzagging very slowly at about eight knots in case some submarine might take a potshot at us. We were going back and forth, and I was in the wardroom talking with a couple of guys, and we heard what sounded like a splash through the side of the ship. Somebody said, "I wonder what that is."

All of a sudden the diving alarm went, and we ran to the control room. Larry Doheny was the officer of the deck, and he was in shock.* He said, "I could see the whites of their eyes when they passed over." This plane had attacked us, and fortunately we were in a swing when he did. He dropped a bomb where he thought we were going to be, and it was close. That was just one of the episodes that after the war's over you can come back and tell sea stories about. We dived and stayed down for probably an hour or so and then came back up, and it was all clear.

Paul Stillwell: Did you recover any aviators?

Admiral Burke: No. Got no aviators, but we were there, and we got no word of any aviators being in the water. We stayed there for a period of time and ran the course of our op order. Then it was time to go home—60 days was sort of the magic number—but we hadn't sunk any ships. Flying Fish's first and only patrol that we hadn't sunk anything, so we were chopping back from Submarine Force Southwest Pacific back to

---

* Lieutenant Edward L. Doheny III, USNR.

ComSubPac.* SubPac had us go up to the Philippine passageway, between the Philippines and Taiwan, and so we patrolled up there for a period of time. We hadn't run out of provisions, but we were getting down. We still hadn't sunk anything, and I suspect SubPac was trying to help us sink something. So he finally said, "Come on home. You will go on to Hunters Point for overhaul."† We hadn't expected to go to overhaul then. We had five patrols, but the number of days on patrol were quite long that we had had, so we really weren't paperwork ready for it. So the Captain had Buff Chace take over as navigator as soon as we got this word. Then I began to do the paper work to get job orders ready for the yard overhaul.

Paul Stillwell: Presumably Hopley had a big part in that also.

Admiral Burke: Oh, yes. Hopley was in it up to his ears, and he was an enormous help. I had gone through the Navy yard overhaul the year before and had seen how it was done. So I was able to manage it, but I stopped navigating, and Chace got to be the navigator. I was spending all day every day putting the paper work together. Well, before long we got a message—this was early on—got a message that the U.S. Fleet was going up to attack Okinawa from down south, from the Marianas area.

Paul Stillwell: About what month would this have been?

Admiral Burke: Probably end of September.

Paul Stillwell: About a month before the Philippine invasion.

Admiral Burke: It probably was, but we just weren't brought in on what was going on in the rest of the world. But, anyhow, the fleet was heading up towards Okinawa, and we had a track on the fleet. We didn't have anything that showed how big the fleet was or

---

* "Chop" is short for change operational control.
† Hunters Point Navy Yard, San Francisco, California.

how many miles; we just had the PIM.* Bob Risser was a real fine captain, but he hadn't been with the fleet since he had been an ensign. He'd been to PG school and Sub School and qualified, and then he'd come out to us.

Before long we were running into carrier search planes, U.S., so we knew we had to stay on the surface and we probably hoisted the American flag, I don't remember, but we had to because we were seeing too many friendlies. But these U.S. naval aviators began to buzz us, and we got nervous. Gradually we began to sight ships, and I don't recall how close we were, but eventually we were sighting destroyers. They didn't come in close to us, but they were maybe four or five miles away as we were going along. But these planes wouldn't stay away, and it was a very nervous time, wondering whether somebody was going to make a mistake. It was about 4:00 o'clock, and then we changed the watch at 4:00.

We got an unqualified officer who was not too experienced on deck, and the captain had been on the bridge all day.† I was below at the time, and the captain, just as a matter of conversation when our new officer came up there, said, "What do you think? Do you think we ought to dive?"

"Yes, sir." He hit the diving alarm, and there was a destroyer over there about 8,000 or 9,000 yards away. I was in the wardroom with the guy who had just come off watch—I guess it was Hopley—and so we went in and tried to persuade the captain to go back up, but he didn't want to do it. He thought we could ride it out; we were riding at about a 120 feet or something like that. All of a sudden we heard screws overhead, and I can remember Hopley saying, "We're going to get our tails blown off." Sure enough, we took a string of depth charges.

Of course, Hopley and I were in the control room, backing up the diving officer. The first thing that happened, that gun that you fire these flares with jammed. It was probably because the poor guy was so excited. Then we started sending out recognition signals on the sonar. Then this destroyer turned out and came back and dropped another string. By the time he got the second string out, we got the flare up, and so he stood off.

---

* PIM—position and intended movement.
† This means not yet officially qualified in submarines.

I was telling this story to my wife last night; she had never heard it before. She said, "I've heard every other story at least ten times, but this is new."

But, anyhow, we got back on the surface. It turned out that the captain of the destroyer was later Vice Admiral Deutermann, and I think he was as shaken as we because I had contacts with him later on.* When I eventually met him, I told him I had been exec of that boat. He never forgot it, and every time I saw him thereafter, which was probably eight or ten times, he always made a point of recognizing that fact, and he was very helpful to me at a couple of times in my career, once particularly after he had retired.

Paul Stillwell: What so shook him about the incident?

Admiral Burke: Well, hell. He could have sunk us.

Paul Stillwell: Was it essentially the OOD's mistake in taking you under?

Admiral Burke: I don't want to criticize. There are times when you get into a difference of opinion on how something should be handled, and it was easy to second-guess after the fact. I would say we got ourselves into it; we were probably too close to the PIM and didn't realize it. I mean, my experience with the fleet operating units had been in the early days of the Guadalcanal campaign, and we didn't have many ships down there.

Paul Stillwell: Was it a case of stumbling across the fleet?

Admiral Burke: No, we had the word that they were going. I mean, we had some sort of a message, I don't remember seeing the message, but I must have. We had put them on a track, and we thought we were far enough away, but when you give the fleet a PIM, depending on where the wind's blowing, and if they're conducting flight operations they were so big and tough they didn't need to necessarily follow the PIM precisely. My guess

---

* Commander Harold T. Deutermann, USN, commanded the destroyer Cogswell (DD-651) from the ship's commissioning on 17 August 1943 until October 1944.

is they were a little bit west of where the PIM was, and we were a little bit closer than we should have been.

Paul Stillwell: In general did you as executive officer get access to Ultra messages?[*]

Admiral Burke: Not necessarily. What happened was the submarines had these Ultra messages—I think that's what they were called—and the captain didn't show me all of them by any stretch of the imagination, because there had been serious leaks. I know that he was hauled up, not for violating security but to be warned about unnecessary leaks to officers and crew members of classified information. He was very careful about security, but I know that on one occasion, we heard about it, I think ComSubPac came down to greet one of the boats and there were some sailors standing on dock waiting for the boat to come in off war patrol. ComSubPac or somebody like that heard a couple of sailors discussing Ultra messages right there on the dock. And there was the congressman from Kentucky, Andrew Jackson May, who made a tour out to the war area and was informed that the Japanese weren't setting their depth charges deep enough, and, sure enough, that's when our casualties began to increase.[†] Up to that time we'd only lost about four submarines in the first year and a half. Then, all of a sudden, the score went up. So SubPac was really leaning on our people. As I best remember it, on the Flying Fish only the people who did the decoding of an Ultra saw that message and gave it to the captain. So I saw a very limited number of Ultras.

Paul Stillwell: Anything else to mention before going back to Hunters Point for the overhaul?

Admiral Burke: Yes. We went on into Midway on the way home. We got back to Pearl, and I think it was about an 85-day patrol to Pearl Harbor. That included a few days in

---

[*] Ultra—short for ultra secret—was a special security classification given by the British to information gained from breaking the code of the German radio enciphering machine. It has come to be used more broadly to encompass other information obtained from interception and decryption of German and Japanese radio communications.

[†] Representative Andrew Jackson May, a member of the House Military Affairs Committee, revealed this in a press interview in June 1943. See Clay Blair's Silent Victory, page 424.

port at the fleet anchorage. We ran out of everything on that patrol during the last ten days except beef. So about the last ten days we had no bacon, no lamb or anything else. Or Spam. Or ham. And people were getting fed up on beef. Well, we got to Pearl Harbor and, of course, SubPac was down there with a band to greet you. And they had ice cream, and they had steaks and all of this sort of business.

After the party left I had a very pleasant surprise. My older brother, who is two and a half years older, and who had gotten into the Army Air Corps, was a B-24 pilot.[*] He was on his way west from training to go into the combat area, and I didn't know he was out there. He came down to the ship the day we got into port, and I don't know how he found we were there, but he did. I took him down to the wardroom, and so it was nice for me, because he'd beat me up pretty routinely when we were growing up. When he went to the University of Virginia, it was a country club in those days. My last big liberty before going to the Naval Academy was at the University of Virginia Easter week, where I had the pleasure of dancing to Ozzie Nelson and hearing his wife, Harriet Hilliard, do the singing. So I saw the country club life down there.

But, in any case, Andy was aboard. The first thing that was nice was to have these people come in and with respect talk to his younger brother, who was the executive officer. He'd never seen this before. Mind you, he had been living at an airfield on the other side of Oahu in a pup tent, and they were eating out of tin cans. I took him through the ship, and when we got to the galley somebody asked the cook what we were having, and he said, "Oh, we're having steaks."

Somebody else said, "Oh, gee, again?" Andy hadn't had a steak for months. We were together there off and on for a couple of days, and then we went on to California. We were physically beat down. Andy was shocked at my physical appearance. I'd lost a lot of weight. He was surprised that I was as gaunt looking as I was. I didn't even think about it. I'd been looking at myself in the mirror every day, so I saw no change.

Then we got back to Hunters Point, and I went through the joy of getting into the yard, presenting our work orders and so forth. After about a week or ten days I went off on 30 days' leave. Admiral Woods and his family were living in the Fairmont Hotel in

---

[*] The B-24 Liberator, built by Consolidated, was one of the principal heavy bombers used by the U.S. Army Air Forces during World War II. His brother was First Lieutenant George Anderton Burke, USAAF.

San Francisco, and so I checked in with them. My wife had an uncle who lived in San Francisco, and I checked in with him and his family, and then off I went on leave.

I remember the first leg of the flight. As we went from San Francisco to Los Angeles, I happened to be sitting next to a lady whose husband was in the Army. He was in North Africa, and she hadn't seen her husband for two years. Then she got off, and we headed east, and I was sitting next to either an Army or an Air Force guy, officer, and he told me about the landing in the Philippines and what went on in the Philippines out there. He was the one that told me about how the Japanese Fleet broke through and were firing directly on American carriers.[*]

Paul Stillwell: The escort carriers.

Admiral Burke: The escort carriers. He told me that horror story, and that's how I found out. So that shows you how insulated we were, because we just didn't know what was going on. Then I got to New Orleans, and my wife was living with her mother and grandmother in New Orleans. And I saw my baby for the first time after 11 months.

Paul Stillwell: What a thrill that must have been.

Admiral Burke: Well, it was. My wife's side of the family and her mother's side were numerous. In New Orleans she had at least four first cousins and the spouses or the first cousins who were involved in Normandy landings, or one of them was a Marine major who was out in an aviation detachment. The family was heavily involved in the war, so they were very supportive and interested. And we were able, with all of the support that we had from family and friends—one of the families—you probably have heard of Lousianne Coffee.

Paul Stillwell: Yes.

---

[*] On 25 October 1944, during part of the wide-ranging Battle of Leyte Gulf, U.S. forces left San Bernardino Strait in the Philippines unguarded, and Japanese heavy warships came through toward the invasion beaches at Leyte. Japanese gunfire sank two American escort carriers and three destroyer-type ships.

Admiral Burke: Well, the Riley family were intimates, and they had a place across Lake Pontchartrain, so Betty and I took our baby and went over there and stayed for a week, and I have pictures of that experience. All of these things tended to resurrect me. After I'd been on leave about two weeks, I got a letter from the captain telling me that I had been selected for lieutenant commander. I had been a lieutenant since November of the year before. And he said, "You have to go down and get a physical exam and sign a couple of places and send it back to me. You'll be a lieutenant commander, and you can put your leaves on."

So I went down to Com 8 in New Orleans and went to the medical facility there.[*] They had a dispensary, and the doctor said he couldn't do it. I didn't have orders to report to him. But while I was talking to the doctor, somebody else came up and asked me what the submarine insignia was and began to ask me about what we had done and had we sunk any ships. I told him how many ships I thought we had sunk and so forth, and these people had never seen anybody who had been in combat before, so they gave me the physical and passed me with flying colors.

Paul Stillwell: So you must have recovered from your earlier conditional situation.

Admiral Burke: I don't know that they looked at me, but they passed me, and I was a lieutenant commander.

Betty and I went on back to San Francisco, and we were able to find an apartment in government housing. Housing was tight, but one of our bachelor JOs was dating a girl in the housing office at the base, and she steered us to a place where there was a house. I think it was a former house of prostitution that the government had taken over. It was on Bush Street, right near the corner of Mason and Bush, right down the hill from the Mark Hopkins and the Fairmont. This building had about six or eight apartments in it, and the government had redone it. We rented the top apartment on the top floor in back for $50.00 a month. It was all government rental control.

---

[*] Com 8—Commandant of the Eighth Naval District.

We put our name up there, and we were the first people that rented this building, and then I got a second look at Red Cross. The first one had been telling me about my child being born, but Betty's aunt there in San Francisco was a volunteer and she told us about a furniture storeroom Red Cross had, so they gave us basic furniture, no charge. Also, her first cousin was there, and he had a lot of furniture. He was 4-F, but he was a big help, and he gave us some things to dress it up so we did surprisingly well.* We had a bedroom, a bath, and a kitchen and a telephone.

Paul Stillwell: What led you to conclude it had been a house of prostitution?

Admiral Burke: Good question. The doorbell would ring from down below, and we'd have to ring a buzzer to let them in. Then we would look down and they would want to know if Josie was in. It happened too frequently.

When I got back to the ship and got my feet on the ground, I discovered that submarines had lost their priority for repairs in the shipyard. Instead of being number one like we had been in Pearl Harbor a year and a half before, we were at the back of the line, and the carriers and the surface ships had the number-one priority. What this meant was that instead of having a two-month overhaul, it stretched out to four to five months. Well, we were quite happy to have our families, and it gave me all kinds of experience in dealing with the ship's company. In hindsight it was interesting to see some of our crew members emotionally came apart when they got back, and some of the wives came apart. The way it came to me was that these guys came up and said, "I have to have a transfer. I can't make any more war patrols." These were people that up to that point, as long as we had them at sea, were quite reliable.

Paul Stillwell: How would you explain that?

Admiral Burke: Well, I can tell you it happens, and there was one man that the crew was just angry as hell about who they thought was pulling this quitting business. I went out to

---

* 4-F was a classification that kept a man from being drafted into military service because he had one or more medical problems.

a hospital where he was; he was in an Army base hospital that was living and operating in Quonset huts. I made a strong effort to get out to see how these guys were doing and when they were coming back and so forth. I remember one particular guy whose petty officers were really mad at him. They thought he was quitting. I talked to the doctor, and he must have been a psychiatrist because he gave me a lecture on this kind of stuff and why it happened. We had guys that had gone home and their wives had come apart and they had been under a tension that we simply were not aware of. It made me realize over the years that you have problems that are going to come up and—

Paul Stillwell: That aren't visible to the naked eye.

Admiral Burke: No, they're not. But there were enough of these that happened, and I can't tell you the number but it really made an impact on my thinking in personnel.

Paul Stillwell: Possibly this was what's now called post-traumatic stress syndrome.

Admiral Burke: Could be, but we didn't have benny pills to pop to get you through it.

Paul Stillwell: Right.

Admiral Burke: I can remember we had a steward. He was a nice guy, and we didn't give him leave at the start because he wasn't married. When I came off leave, he came in and said he needed some money to go on leave to New York. I said, "Why are you going to New York? You're not married."

He said, "Well, I've got a family there. My wife had bad blood, and she couldn't pass the physical exam to marry." But they had two or three children. He didn't have any money, so I reached in my pocket and gave him $50.00 or $100.00 so he could get to New York. He never came back, and the amount I gave him, of course, by present-day standards would be about $500.00 to $1,000 in change in the value of the dollar. But I felt the guy had to get home, but there was no money there to give him. At that point in time I'd never heard of Navy Relief, and I didn't know whether Red Cross would have helped him out or not. We had no kitty aboard ship.

After Betty and I had been back there for a while and after I saw that our yard overhaul was going to be delayed, we decided to get our child brought out to us. So her mother flew out to Phoenix, I think it was, and Betty flew down there. They traded our daughter, and she came out with us. I think that happened in January, because before she came out we had gone a ski weekend up in Yosemite, which was a nice change of pace. I'd never been skiing before, and that's a part of my life that's never been there before or since. My children ski, but I don't.

Paul Stillwell: Were you getting your war news at that time essentially from the newspapers?

Admiral Burke: Yes. This was 1944 and early '45. Of course, it was obvious that we were going ahead and doing well, and we had landed in France. I guess around Christmas time we had the problem where the Germans reacted.

Paul Stillwell: Battle of the Bulge.[*]

Admiral Burke: The Bulge, and that spoiled Christmas for almost everybody. It was terrible. Betty had a first cousin whose husband was over there involved in that general area. I don't know whether he was directly in the Battle of the Bulge, but the fighting was terrible over there then. It was a strange thing. One of the things we did in San Francisco—have you ever heard of Mom Chung?

Paul Stillwell: Yes.

Admiral Burke: Well, the captain, Bob Risser, was a bachelor, and I don't know whether he took any leave while we were there. Each week, maybe Sunday night or Sunday

---

[*] The Battle of the Bulge was a German counteroffensive in the Ardennes region of Belgium and Luxembourg in December 1944. It got its name from the so-called bulge it created in American lines. The battle, which was fought in bitter winter cold, involved 600,000 American soldiers.

afternoon, Mom Chung would have an at home honoring service people. I don't know where the food came from or the liquor or whatever, but usually she would single out one or two of the heroes and give them some sort of a Mom Chung decoration. And the time that I went there I think Bob Risser was recognized. I don't recall going over there more than once, but he was a regular over there.

When I went there, her sidekick was Sophie Tucker, the singer. The two of them were sort of playing a Huntley-Brinkley, but the gal who was really in charge was Mom Chung.* It was an enjoyable occasion to do once, but I was married and I had other things. I had a child at home, and we had relatives there in town and very close friends like the Woods. We just had our own social group that we were running with, so we didn't feel the need for it.

Paul Stillwell: Anything else to say about the overhaul before you got back into operation?

Admiral Burke: We were struggling. We were out at Hunters Point. We commuted back and forth. The Hopleys had a car, and they lived somewhere in the area near us. We had a driving squad, and I think he was the one that used to drive us, or else his wife drove us to work every day. I can remember there was a meat-packing factory about halfway in, and it's the biggest stink you've ever made. And there was always a traffic jam right there.

Our stay got increased, and then towards the end of our stay we heard that we were going to be sent down to San Diego for about a month. I had an uncle who was the head of Coca-Cola Bottling on the West Coast. His wife was my father's sister, and so the family looked out for us whenever we moved. I'd forgotten to tell you this, but while we were in the shipyard he arranged for us to have a Coca-Cola machine installed in our ship during the overhaul.

Anyhow, he also had a friend who was down in La Jolla at the Casa de Manana, which was a family kind of hotel right on the water's edge, and the manager of the hotel was a personal friend. They had been in the Biltmore Hotel chain 30 years before, and so

---

* Chet Huntley and David Brinkley were two long-time NBC newsmen who did broadcasts together.

he arranged for us to have an affordable room at the hotel. We got to San Diego and had installed what was called an FM sonar. I'm hazy on how long we were there and what month, but it was at least in April. The FM sonar was a mine detection sonar, and we had it installed at the San Diego destroyer base. After it was installed, we went over to the sound lab, and the technicians from Cal Tech, I guess, who were working through the sound lab, came and got the FM sonar connected. Then over a period of time we got into a training program on detecting submerged mines.

Paul Stillwell: This was to get the submarine into the Sea of Japan.

Admiral Burke: Yes. There were other submarines that had already had it installed and gone out on patrol. But we trained and began to have these exercises, and theoretically, the sonar was supposed to pick mines up at 1,500 yards. Well, more practically, depending on the water, the gradients, the temperature changes, and so forth you might pick them up at 300 up to 700 yards, and if you were lucky in some isothermal waters you could pick them up at 1,000 yards. Then the word came out that Admiral Lockwood was going to visit our ship. He arrived with staff members who were involved. Barney Sieglaff was the project officer; it was called Operation Barney.* I think we as a group had nine submarines that had been equipped at this point in time, and that we were getting ready to go up into the Sea of Japan. Admiral Lockwood personally, to the best of my knowledge, rode every single submarine with his key staff members to observe how we were doing.

Paul Stillwell: Did you go through dummy minefields?

Admiral Burke: We went through dummy minefields, and we did this with Admiral Lockwood more than one day. I was amazed to see Admiral Lockwood aboard. Of course, I probably didn't know what the stakes were, and I hadn't had to go through what he had to do and his responsibility. But he rode us while we were doing these penetration exercises. It was not confidence building, because the ranges were not long enough, and

---

* Commander William Bernard Sieglaff, USN.

your ability to maneuver submerged was very limited. You damn well knew that if you got something directly ahead of you, you might not be able to get out of its way. On the last day, on the last run with Admiral Lockwood aboard, when we surfaced we had the mine sitting up on the forecastle. We had entangled it, the cable, in the bow planes.

Paul Stillwell: Good that it wasn't a live one!

Admiral Burke: Also while we were in San Diego, we surfaced one afternoon, and the first word we got was that Roosevelt had died.* We had at least one Republican on there who cheered. We had another Republican on there, Chace, and he said, "I didn't like the guy myself, but he's been a good war leader."

Paul Stillwell: What impressions did you have of Admiral Lockwood from having him on your boat?

Admiral Burke: Oh, he was solid. That was as close as I ever got to him. I saw him coming and going, but I'd say seeing a flag officer of his stature, we knew then that whatever we were getting ready to do was real serious business.

Paul Stillwell: Well, this was an expression of personal concern on his part.

Admiral Burke: Oh, yes. He was concerned. He had to be. And then we went on out to Pearl. Well, before that, I guess it was when we were in the shipyard, Dutch Reuther got transferred. I was concerned about it, but we got an unqualified first class petty officer who was probably the finest yeomen I've ever seen. He was so fine that he offered me a job as an executive in Brazil after the war was over. He had been the secretary and administrative assistant to an executive of a public utilities company in Philadelphia, so he knew how to run things. When I got to a point of writing a letter, he would come up, and I'd say, "Just write him and tell him this." He solved all my letter-writing problems.

---

* President Franklin D. Roosevelt died at Warm Springs, Georgia, on 12 April 1945.

I had been commuting back and forth between San Diego and La Jolla. Finally we left San Diego, and I'd say of all the departures I have ever made—knowing what I was facing—that hit me harder than anything. I didn't know whether I was ever going to see Betty again or Tina.

Paul Stillwell: And I suspect you did not communicate that danger to her.

Admiral Burke: No, no. She didn't know. She had no idea what we were up to, except I just broke down when I told her good-bye. It was tough on the whole crew. They knew what we were up to, but they didn't know the details. Then when we got to Pearl we were given the details.

Paul Stillwell: Of the people who had the mental problems, had they all been taken out of the crew by then?

Admiral Burke: As far as we knew, yes. We didn't have any officers that caved in, but I'd say we probably had at least four enlisted men. There may have been others, but these were the only ones that I was aware of. I didn't go through a screening process to find them, but I didn't know that you could do things like that then.

Paul Stillwell: Those were the overt cases.

Admiral Burke: Yes. We were in Pearl for a few days, and then we went on to Guam. ComSubPac had moved to Guam. He was on the tender Holland, and we tied up to the Holland. Barney Sieglaff was there and provided detailed intelligence; we trained there vigorously.

When we were in Pearl on the way out, my brother Andy showed up again. He had been out in combat, had come back for some R&R, and was living in a pup tent at an Army Air Corps strip on the other side of the island. The ship was able to get a car from sub welfare for the stay, and the captain let me have it, and I went over with my brother

Andy and met his crew. It was an entirely different league. Here was Andy, two and a half years older than me; I was about 26 at the time, and he was 28 or 29.

All of his enlisted crew members were teenagers. I met his officers. He probably had a total of three officers including himself, and the other two guys were about 21. They all called each other by their first names. Very relaxed, casual, and I was shocked to see how you could push people around and go into combat. But Andy had been in enough combat and bombing runs up in the islands there, Okinawa, to be ready to go home. He'd been frightened. I think he'd run up to about 15 missions. Well, at the time he had gone out there, 20 was the magic number for rotation. His squadron had all gone out there at the same time, and they were all approaching 20, and so they grounded half of his squadron, including Andy. They were going to let half of them get 20 and then go home and then replace them. So then the guys that had been grounded would become the experience that would lead them on, so by the time he resumed flying they raised the ante to 25 and then to 30 and then to 35.

Well, when I came back through Pearl there, and we saw each other for a couple or three days. He was based in Angaur, which was the southernmost island of Palau, and he was living in a tent down there. I told him where we were going, and he said he'd see if he could come up and see us. Well, when we got to Guam, indeed he was standing on the <u>Holland</u>, the submarine tender, waiting for me to come in. I got the tender to give him a bunk, and he had his meals on our ship.

Andy had never eaten food like we had since he'd been in the service. Boy, he was really living high on the hog. Bob Risser, our captain, was a bachelor at this point in time and kind of picky about his food sometimes. At dinner one night, he began to give Dick Sly, our commissary officer, a bad time about whatever we were serving. So Andy, being an Army Air Corps officer, told the captain he didn't know what he was talking about. He said, "You haven't lived." And Dick Sly followed Andy around like a puppy dog for that whole week while we were there. Andy was so used to eating out of cans and poor food.

We did some more intensive training. They gave us the best intelligence that I ever saw about where we were going. We had intelligence that had been developed probably by OSS or some group back in Washington.* I'd never seen anything like it. They had the depths of the water and all the charts that had been made of the Sea of Japan and all the depths. We knew what the currents were. We knew what the percentages of chance of getting through. We were going through Tsushima Straits, and there were nine submarines.

It's hard for me to remember the names of the boats now. I can remember some of the people. I think Alec Tyree was one of the captains, class of '36.† Earl Hydeman was the senior commanding officer.‡ I forget the name of the CO of Spadefish.§ The Tunny was one of them; George Pierce, very colorful guy, was the CO.** The Bonefish was lost in the Sea of Japan. The exec was a classmate of mine at sub school and also at the Naval Academy, Fuzzy Knight, great guy.†† But we were getting ready to go, and I guess we were in Guam about a week and then we left and we were divided into three teams of three each.

Paul Stillwell: So these were essentially wolf packs?

Admiral Burke: They were wolf packs to get in. Each team was under the tactical command of a team leader, and they all had a nickname. Ours was Risser's Bob Cats, and I can't remember the others.‡‡ Our particular team was sent up not too far from Vladivostok, but it was still in the Korean side. Water was cold. It was down in the 30s. We were there in June. We were probably the second team that went in. When we went in, I think my maximum degree of terror was operating.

Paul Stillwell: Worse than being depth charged?

---

* OSS—Office of Strategic Services, formed in World War II to collect and analyze foreign intelligence and to carry out special operations under the control of the Joint Chiefs of Staff.
† Lieutenant Commander Alexander K. Tyree, USN, was commanding officer of the Bowfin (SS-287).
‡ Commander Earl T. Hydeman, USN, commanding officer of the Sea Dog (SS-401).
§ Commander William J. Germershausen, Jr., commanding officer of the Spadefish (SS-411).
** Commander George E. Pierce, USN, commanding officer of the Tunny (SS-282).
†† Lieutenant Commander Fraser S. Knight, USN, was lost around 20 June 1945.
‡‡ The other two were Hydeman's Hep Cats and Pierce's Pole Cats.

Admiral Burke: Oh, it was awful. You knew that the currents through there were strong. I forget what they were, but they were at least four knots in some places. We had all of these statistical projections and so forth, but you knew if you hit one of these mines you were a goner. So we dived, as I recall, around 4:00 o'clock in the morning, maybe 5:00 at the latest.

Paul Stillwell: Were these moored mines on cables?

Admiral Burke: Yes, they were moored mines on cables. Our people didn't know where they were. All they knew was that mines had been laid. We knew that we were going to be submerged for a long time, like 12 to 16 hours, and we knew that the conning crew couldn't stay at battle stations all that time. So the captain and I divided it. We had two teams, and so he took the conn at the start. We took two-hour stints because of the pressure. Along with Wallace's suggestion we rotated people around a bit. Our system worked, as far as being able to deal with the pressure. I don't recall who got the first line.

We went through four lines of mines during the day, and I had the conn at least twice. I remember the pure terror of being able to see a mine for the first time at about 700 yards. We picked up one, and all of a sudden this sonar gear was swinging back and forth just like so slowly. When it hit the mine, it would make a ping. Also you had a visual picture on a scope, and it'd make a ping. Then we picked up another one, and the first line of mines I went through we had about ten mines on the screen, and it was going ping, ping, ping, ping, ping, ping. Every damn one of those pings was hitting me in the gut, and in my terror back there in my mind, I can tell you honestly that I spent much of that day on my knees praying that I wasn't going to buckle, because I knew how important to keep my courage and be an example to the officers and crew.

I made a point of getting through the ship a lot during the day to pat the crew on the back and try to let them know how we were doing. I don't know how often I did, but I know that I went through the ship on that day a lot. I was just scared to death, and finally we got through. We were riding along at periscope depth, and I had a disagreement with the captain, because I thought he had exposed the periscope too much. There was a fishing boat in periscope sight. I thought we were too close, and I let him know. I told him, "What we've been through, to stick your scope up that high is wrong." I was wrung out. It's the only time he and I ever had a rift. I felt badly about it, and afterwards he called me in his cabin and he said, "Look, we've been friends. I want to stay that way." So we were.

Paul Stillwell: I take it your intelligence had indicated these were contact mines rather than magnetic.

Admiral Burke: I guess so. Yes. I don't know how close we were, but in the postmortem on this exercise, which was held at the sub base theater, we learned that at least one of the submarines had scraped a mine cable.

Paul Stillwell: Of course, the other thing in your mind, too, is that once you get through that, you know you've got to go through it again to get back out.

Admiral Burke: Well, this was interesting. We got up there, and we had fog and cold weather. It was stinking weather, and we didn't see much in the way of ships. As I best recall, we sank two separate ships. Also we got into a fishing fleet one day and tried to get these guys to give up and transfer, and we were going to blow up their boats. They wouldn't get out, and I don't know how many fishing boats we sank, but we sank a lot of them.

Paul Stillwell: Did you use your deck gun for that?

Admiral Burke: Yes, and it was not good psychologically with the crew and the officers. They didn't like it.

Paul Stillwell: What was your own reaction?

Admiral Burke: I didn't like it. I didn't protest, but it happened.

Paul Stillwell: So I take it it was the captain's decision.

Admiral Burke: Yes. I don't know how many we sank, but I would say 10 or 15 at least; it was terrible. The first ship we sank, we got him at night with radar, and we hit him. He sank, and we were trying to pick up a prisoner. They were all over the place, and they wouldn't come aboard. They'd swim away when you would approach. Finally, by daybreak, we were out of sight of land. We found a survivor who agreed to come aboard. We brought him aboard and kept him up in the forward torpedo room shackled to a torpedo rack. He had been in the deck gun crew of his ship, which was a merchant ship, and he had pictures of himself in the traditional Japanese attire.

Paul Stillwell: Kimono attire?

Admiral Burke: Yes. He sort of looked like the actor Charles Boyer, and so he was called Charlie. Before long the crew began to spoil him, and the captain had been warned about it. He had to get tough, and we had to get tough to try to police the crew.

Paul Stillwell: Well, I've heard of cases where a crew would make sort of a pet out of the prisoner.

Admiral Burke: He became a pet. We, the officers, had to police it, but we couldn't sit on it 24 hours a day. He was aboard for at least two weeks, I think, and the captain was very careful to let the crew know that it was important not to spoil them, because we needed to get intelligence out of them, and the crew just didn't go along with it. I'll finish this part of it.

He couldn't speak English, but constantly they were up there doing sign language with each other. He knew we were coming into port, and he asked for a pen and paper. He wrote something out in Japanese kanji, and it was addressed to the captain, which the captain had translated after we got back to Pearl. He said that because of the fact that he had been captured alive, as far as his family and his community, he was dead and would be of no use in the future. But he wanted the captain to know that he expected to be tortured, and he was treated with humanity and kindness, and he would give his life to the cause of peace forevermore. I wish I had a copy of that letter, but I wasn't thinking that way 55 years ago or whatever time it was.

Paul Stillwell: That's a touching letter.

Admiral Burke: Oh, it was. He had a big impact on us, I think.

Paul Stillwell: It put a human face on the enemy.

Admiral Burke: It was the first time that I had ever been that close to a Japanese. Years later I ended up in Japan on duty and was surprised to find out that they weren't such bad people after all, after I got to know them, but they're like the Germans. They had this thing in their past that you have to always be remembering.

Paul Stillwell: What happened during the rest of your time in the Sea of Japan?

Admiral Burke: Well, we saw a total of two ships, and I don't think they could have displaced more than 2,000 tons apiece. They were coastal inland-sea type ships, and we sank both of those. Then we had the incident with the fishing vessels. Time had run out on us, and so we headed for the rendezvous point, which was west of La Perouse.*

Paul Stillwell: What do you mean the time had run out on you?

Admiral Burke: Well, we had an operation order that we had specified that we would go in there on a certain day and come out on a certain day. So we all rendezvoused to go in, we all went in one at a time, and the idea was that we were going to come out the same way. Captain Hydeman, in the Sea Dog, was the senior officer. He was responsible for

---

* La Perouse Strait runs between the northwest part of the Japanese island of Hokkaido and the southern tip of Russia's Sakhalin Island.

getting us out, and we rendezvoused up in the Sea of Japan, probably as much as 50 or 60 miles west of La Perouse Straits.

We on board Flying Fish were debating how we were coming out and looking at the depth of the water and the channels and so forth. I think all of us just didn't want to go through the agony and terror of running the minefields submerged and were willing to risk it on the surface. When we had the rendezvous, Bonefish didn't show up. I don't recall whether we waited 24 hours or not, but in any case we did wait a while. Then the decision was made to come on out, and the decision was also made to come out on the surface.

Paul Stillwell: Could you still use the sonar when you were on the surface?

Admiral Burke: No. The sonar head was up on deck. But, even so, when we came out on the surface, we came out at maximum speed, and we headed for the straits. Before long we saw some shipping. I'm sure they were Russian because they were lighted. How many I don't recall, but I just remember that there were at least two lighted ships. One of our submarines was lighted up by a searchlight from one of these ships, but we kept on going and we got through. It seemed like an all eternity, but it wasn't nearly as bad psychologically to us as the submerged approach when we went in.

Paul Stillwell: How would you explain that difference?

Admiral Burke: Well, not seeing what you were encountering had some help. If there were mines there, and I'm sure there were, they were laid at a depth that was below the keel of a surface ship. After we got into the Sea of Japan, we did get word through intelligence messages received that Japanese ships had been observed laying mines up in La Perouse, so there were some mines. We didn't know where they were. We came through and went up to the Kurile Chain there and eventually came out into the Northern Pacific and came on home. If I ever felt like a breath of fresh air, that was it. We came on back and stopped at Midway and topped off and then came on into Pearl. Admiral Lockwood, of course, was down on the dock, as he usually was when we came in. He had flown back. A few days later we had a post-operation critique at the sub base theater, where each captain got up and briefed what the ships had done. Admiral Lockwood at the end summarized that we should have come out submerged. He thought that was a mistake, notwithstanding the fact that we made it.

Paul Stillwell: What was his reasoning?

Admiral Burke: Well, you've got to realize he had staff people and analysts up there that were looking at the percentage of chance of and what you could do if. I think their feeling was that it was far safer to come out submerged, because at least if you picked up the mine you could take some evasive action. My observation was you had very little control of what you could do. You couldn't back. You had to keep going ahead. You had a lot of current to deal with in both passageways, and it affected your rudder and so forth. Might be the opposite of what you put on the rudder, based on the current that you had. So there was a fair amount of luck. To my knowledge there were other submarines that went in after we made that operation. They went in singly. I don't know of any that were lost to mines in the Sea of Japan, and I don't know how they came out, but I suspect they came out through La Perouse.

Paul Stillwell: Did you feel, not only in this instance but others, that there was Monday morning quarterbacking from the people up the line?

Admiral Burke: No, I didn't feel that. Of course, Admiral Lockwood's staff was in Guam, and we ended up in Pearl Harbor, so the bulk of his staff that was involved with this included such as Barney Sieglaff and whatever helpers he had. No, my own personal assessment is that Barney Sieglaff's one of the finest people I've ever come across.

Paul Stillwell: So it was strictly a matter of concern for your welfare.

Admiral Burke: Oh, yes. I don't feel there was any quarterbacking on that.

Julian T. Burke, Jr., Interview #4 (3/20/97) – Page 193

Paul Stillwell: Well, it also bespeaks Lockwood's concern that he would come back and see you yet again after you had made that transit.

Admiral Burke: This was a big operation. I would say in hindsight he recommended and all the captains got Navy Crosses, no matter what the tonnage. It was such a special operation that he gave us a card called the Mighty Mine Dodgers. Frankly, almost immediately I would have preferred to have had a Presidential Unit Citation, which I never got. That was a big operation. It was the last really last big operation of submarines during the war. Submarines operated right up to the end of the war, but that was one that caught people's attention.

Paul Stillwell: Were you surprised that there were so few targets in the Sea of Japan?

Admiral Burke: We had gotten to the point where we were running out of targets, and that's what drove us in. Disappointed? Sure. I wasn't surprised, but we were disappointed. I mean, if you spend time on war patrol and do a lot of searching, you're not in action all the time. You're out there looking to get into action, and the percentage of time that you're involved in action is really very small.

Paul Stillwell: Well, you would be disappointed, especially after all the effort and hazard you'd gone through to get there.

Admiral Burke: Oh, yes.

Paul Stillwell: How much longer did you stay in the Flying Fish?

Admiral Burke: Well, we came back and Bob Risser expected to be transferred and detached. I'd forgotten to mention this earlier. He had become engaged to be married to Ruby. She was a widow of a friend of his who'd been lost in submarines, and he had expected to be detached when he got back. I hadn't even given the matter a thought. Then he was greeted on the dock, I think by either Admiral Lockwood or somebody almost that senior, who said, "Bob, what a great job you've done. You've done such a good job we're going to send you back again and detach Burke."

I felt sorry for the poor guy, because I expected to go back and in a way halfway wanted to, because I was professionally motivated. I could see that numbers of patrols, particularly successful patrols, made a lot of difference in career competition. But then I heard, about a day later, that I was going to get command, which I couldn't believe. Bob Risser had recommended me for qualification several months before, I guess after we got back to San Francisco. I hadn't even given the matter any thought at all, because I'd only been in submarines at that point in time two years, so I was astounded.

Paul Stillwell: With good reason.

Admiral Burke: There were too many other people around with more time. They told me I was going to the Guardfish, and so I found that the Guardfish, because the U.S. forces had moved so far into Japan we'd moved out of spaces to deploy submarines. The Guardfish had been taken off of wartime patrolling and put into the training command. In effect, this was a PCO operation, teaching me how to be a commanding officer.* So the way it worked out Bob Risser was given two or three weeks' leave, and he went to San Diego, and he and Ruby got married. When he got back, I was transferred and went over and became commanding officer of the Guardfish.†

Paul Stillwell: That would have been in July 1945.

Admiral Burke: That was probably in mid-July or end of July, and the war was approaching the end rapidly. One of my very close friends, classmates, is Bill Morton.‡ Bill was a real wild hare when he was a midshipman, and like me he stood near the bottom of the class. But when he got to be in combat, he was an aviator, he was in the

---
* PCO—prospective commanding officer.
† USS Guardfish (SS-217) was a Gato-class submarine commissioned 8 May 1942. She had a displacement of 1,525 tons on the surface and 2,410 tons submerged. She was 312 feet long, 27 feet in the beam, and had a draft of 15 feet. Her top speed was 20 knots surfaced and 9 knots submerged. She was armed with ten 21-inch torpedo tubes and a 3-inch deck gun.
‡ Lieutenant Commander William B. Morton, USN.

battle there, he was on one of those jeep carriers. He was the squadron commander on a jeep carrier, and he was called in an emergency to the bridge. He had already done his day's flying, and he was called to the bridge. The captain pointed to a ship over there that he could see firing guns, and he said to Bill, "He's firing at us. Go get him." And so Bill got him.

Paul Stillwell: Very impressive.

Admiral Burke: Bill was on a staff job of, I think, Commander Carriers of either the Third or Fifth Fleet. He was living on Ford Island, and I went over and had dinner with him. Then we went to a movie after dinner, and the movie was about a half an hour along. I think by that time the first bomb had been dropped, and in about half an hour after the movie started, this officer walked in and yelled out, "The Japs are quitting. The war is over."[*] All of a sudden everybody stood up, the lights went on, people looked kind of funny, and we walked out of the movie theater. This was Ford Island, and it was dark, and there were searchlights on in Pearl Harbor. The whole place was lighted up. People were sounding the ships' horns, blowing sirens. You could see rockets going through the air. You could see machine gun tracers going through the air, and this kept up for an unbelievable length of time. Eventually I caught a boat and went on back to the submarine base. When I got back to the ship, there was a message on my desk to the Guardfish, which was the first official message that I had received from Com 14 out there, the naval base commander. It said, "Captains of your ships. Take command of your ships." I would dearly love to have a copy of that.

About that time I went up to SubPac's staff and talked to Harry Hull, who was out of the class of '32 and had been a successful CO.[†] He was not a personal friend, but I had known him through common friends. I threw up to him the idea of my getting out of submarines and going to destroyers, and asked him what he thought. He discouraged me, and so I put the idea out of my mind. It stayed there out of mind for a few years until I

---

[*] In the first combat use of atomic bombs, U.S. B-29 bombers hit Hiroshima, on the island of Honshu, on 6 August 1945 and Nagasaki, on Kyushu, on 9 August. Hostilities ended 15 August in the Western Pacific.
[†] Commander Harry Hull, USN.

got command of my own submarine. Later on I'll tell you how it happened I got a destroyer.

Paul Stillwell: Well, you'd been aiming toward command. With the Guardfish you got it sooner than you expected. What was it like?

Admiral Burke: Well, our ship was providing target services for ASW forces, and so I just went out there and was a submarine target. The World War II submarines were not particularly maneuverable, and you had to conserve the battery and so forth. But we were operating and training the crew, ship's company and so forth. And I had to learn about my officers and my leading petty officers. The ship was pretty much similar to what I'd come from, so learning the ship wasn't that much different. I'd say it was probably a little tough on some of the officers and leading petty officers, because I found that they didn't run as tight as ship as I had been on, and that was the story of my life. But I made some friends, good friends, and I've bumped into a couple of them since.

We were probably around Pearl Harbor for at least three weeks or a month, and then we got word that we were going home. I've forgotten exactly how we got the word, but I remember that there were four submarines. John Middleton was one CO, and Slade Cutter was the other, and I forget who the fourth one was.* We were told to go up and pay a departure call, which we did just before we left on Deputy ComSubPac, Admiral Crawford.† We went up there and Admiral Styer, who was ComSubLant, was in his office at the time.‡ We were there not more than five or ten minutes, and we were being wished the best of luck and thanked for our services. Then Admiral Styer said, "My staff is hard at work figuring out what liberty ports you are going to when you get back."

I was the junior CO by plenty, and without giving it a thought I said, "Well, Admiral, if you have a chance, if you'll put Guardfish down for New Orleans I would be most appreciative." The other guys looked startled, and so I think they conveyed what

---

* Commander Slade D. Cutter, USN, was the first commanding officer when the submarine Requin (SS-481) was commissioned on 28 April 1945. Cutter's oral history is in the Naval Institute collection.
† Rear Admiral George C. Crawford, USN.
‡ Rear Admiral Charles W. Styer, USN, served as Commander Submarine Force Atlantic Fleet from 10 November 1944 to 31 January 1946.

they wanted. When we got to Panama a couple of weeks later, well, the first man that met me said, "I don't know how you worked it out, but you're going to New Orleans."

Paul Stillwell: Where did the incident with Slade Cutter's boat take place?

Admiral Burke: It was about halfway to Panama. Slade Cutter was captain of the Requin, which was new construction. He had passed through all of the training and so forth getting ready to go to war. He'd gotten out to Pearl and done advanced training, and he'd probably already sunk as many ships as anybody in the whole submarine force. I know he's way up on the ladder.

Paul Stillwell: He was second behind O'Kane.*

Admiral Burke: He had his crew ready to take Japan apart, and there was a certain amount of disappointment that they were denied the opportunity. The rest of us were on the way home and had no feelings in the other direction. So eventually he decided he wanted to continue training his people, so one day he asked me to provide target services, so he could train people in his fire control party. When we finished the run, he fired his rocket and then surfaced right by us. He came up with an enormous angle that really was eye catching. I'd never seen a submarine surface with that big an angle so after he came up on deck I sent him a light message and said, "Do that again and we'll take your picture."

He was going to dive and then surface again, so I took my position on his quarter, oh, about 1,000 to 1,500 yards. He went ahead and dived, and we were looking at him through binoculars. He had a high lookout sitting up there in the shears, and the high lookout got left on the surface. All I did was ring up stop and put the rudder over. When I got near the man, I backed down. We threw him a life ring, and he was right alongside there, but the poor guy couldn't grab the life ring. It turned out he couldn't swim.

---

* Commander Richard H. O'Kane, USN, was credited with the largest number of sinkings, 24, of any U.S. submarine commanding officer in World War II.

Paul Stillwell: Was he still hanging onto the periscope shears at that time?

Admiral Burke: Oh, no. The submarine was under and had gone ahead, but he was there in the water. So we put a swimmer in, took the life ring, and got him and pulled him out. Shortly thereafter, Slade surfaced, and he sent us a message that said, "I'm coming alongside. Just tell him to jump in and swim over." When I told him that the guy couldn't swim he almost had a heart attack.

Paul Stillwell: Did you wind up getting his picture?

Admiral Burke: No, I wasn't that fast on the uptake.

Paul Stillwell: But why had he not gotten down in the submarine before she submerged?

Admiral Burke: I don't know. I didn't get into that. I think that probably what happened was the guy daydreaming up there and wasn't aware that they were going to dive again. When you dive, you go down in a hurry, and you've got to be in a position where you can react. If he was just daydreaming up there, it would be very easy under any circumstance to get left up there. He may have been sitting up on top of the shears. I don't know.

Paul Stillwell: Well, you had easier clearance going through the canal in a submarine than you did in the North Carolina.

Admiral Burke: That's true. That's certainly true. I think the Flounder was one of the boats. We were in Panama either one or two nights and had a liberty or so on the Pacific side. Then we got our orders to where we were going. We were in a column going through the canal, and we were obviously a third of the way through. There were no locks around or anything like this. All of a sudden, the submarine in front of us began to back down and they, like we, had people up on deck sightseeing. One of their men was sightseeing, and he leaned against the lifeline and it gave way, and over he went and he was drowned.

Paul Stillwell: Survive a war and then something like that happens.

Admiral Burke: It teaches you that you can never ever let your guard down on procedures.

We were the first submarine to get to New Orleans, where my wife was. We arrived off the delta there and picked up a pilot. By that time the shooting had stopped, but the war was officially not over. You have a bar pilot, and he takes you in over the bar to Pilot Town, which is about a 10-mile stint. Then you change pilots, so when the first pilot went ashore he called up to my wife and let her know that I was coming and where I was going to berth. Then the river pilot took us up the rest of the way.

It was a fascinating experience to go up there. I don't think my whistle had ever been tooted in the time that I had been aboard. Twice as we were approaching large merchant ships coming down, we tried to show that we would pass starboard to starboard. As we put the rudder over to the left, we were only able to get out one beep instead of two, and the pilot said, "That's all right. He knows I'm not going to screw him up."

My mother was raised on a plantation about ten miles below New Orleans, on the other side of the river. For the first time I was able to see where it was, and by then it was a field of oil and gasoline storage tanks. Finally in the mid-afternoon we arrived at the Naval Supply Depot, which was a good mile above Canal Street. My wife and child were on the dock to meet me, and she later told me that when she'd gotten the telephone call she had called up Com 8 and told them that I was coming in, and she wanted to know the ETA.* They said, "Don't you dare break security like that."

Paul Stillwell: Even though the war was over.

Admiral Burke: I have pictures. My child by that time was about a year and three quarters, and she had lived with me sometime from about the middle of November up until April, maybe five or six months. But she was there on the dock, dutifully waving at father and saying, "Hi, Mommy."

---

* ETA—estimated time of arrival.

Paul Stillwell: I'm sure it was a pleasant homecoming.

Admiral Burke: Oh, it was. Interesting thing, of course, being married to a local girl. Although she's not and never has been a resident of New Orleans, she was considered from New Orleans by the locals. So I was a local boy, and I got all the credit for the work that Captain Klakring and Captain Ward had achieved, so you would have thought I'd done it.[*] It was kind of embarrassing, and even though I had been in a fair amount of combat in the preceding two years, the idea of getting into the public arena terrified me. I was interviewed on the radio. I was invited to do a public speaking stint at something like the Kiwanis, and I took a powder and went across the lake to the Riley place over in Slidell. I figured that was much more important. I just couldn't handle public speaking at that time.

Paul Stillwell: One of your enlisted crew members then was Clay Blair.[†] What do you recall about him?

Admiral Burke: He was a quartermaster and he was an attractive, intelligent, thoughtful person. He was, as I recall, third class. He was youthful looking.[‡] Some people are just born with that streak, and I would imagine he looks a lot younger today than he really is.

Paul Stillwell: What do you remember about the quality of his service?

Admiral Burke: Well, he knew his job. He was around the bridge. I don't know that he was the quartermaster. I don't think he was the quartermaster assisting me, assisting the navigator. I'm a great person on asking people who they are, where they're from, and so forth. As I recall, he was from Biloxi. Before the war Betty and I had gone over to Biloxi, and I had a picture of that. My mother's family lived near New Orleans and in

---

[*] Previous commanding officers of the Guardfish were Lieutenant Commander Thomas B. Klakring, USN, and Lieutenant Commander Norvell G. Ward, USN. The oral history of Ward, who retired as a rear admiral, is in the Naval Institute collection.
[†] Clay D. Blair, Jr., later wrote the most thorough book on the subject of U.S. submarines in World War II: Silent Victory: The U.S. Submarine War Against Japan (Philadelphia: J. B. Lippincott Company, 1975).
[‡] Blair was born 1 May 1925.

New Orleans early in her life, and they had gone over to the Gulf Coast and Ocean Springs at Betty's family's, so when any of these things ring a bell, I try to identify and figure out if we have any commonality.

Paul Stillwell: Well, he later made a name for himself with Time magazine and championed Rickover's promotion to rear admiral.*

Admiral Burke: Well, I know that Admiral Rickover deserved it, but I can tell you, I could never have served with him. He wasn't my cup of tea.

Paul Stillwell: You share that with a lot of people.

Admiral Burke: Well, in my lifetime there have been three people in government that knew how to operate the system where they in effect became untouchable. One was Rickover, one was J. Edgar Hoover, and the other was General Hershey.† And maybe John Bulkeley was.‡ But they all were willing to take on the establishment in one way and do it with Congress so that they couldn't be terminated when the time came. I want to say this about John Bulkeley. I really admired his ability to call the shots the way he did when he was the head of InSurv. He served a great purpose for the Navy, because I know that he was probably kept on for political reasons. But he earned his keep in a way that was very valuable, because our budgets were getting hacked to pieces to pay for Vietnam, and he stood up and was counted.

Paul Stillwell: Well, my impression has been that he was kept in that job so long because he did it so well.

---

* Hyman G. Rickover was considered the father of the nuclear Navy. He ran the U.S. Navy's nuclear-power program for many years, from 1948 until he eventually left active duty in 1982 with the rank of four-star admiral on the retired list. Rickover Hall at the Naval Academy is named in his honor, as is the nuclear-powered attack submarine Hyman G. Rickover (SSN-709), which was commissioned 21 July 1984.
† J. Edgar Hoover ran the Federal Bureau of Investigation; Lieutenant General Lewis Hershey, USA, operated the Selective Service System.
‡ Rear Admiral John D. Bulkeley, USN, began serving as president of the Board of Inspection and Survey in 1967, continued after his age-mandated retirement in 1974, and remained until he finally left active duty in 1988.

Admiral Burke: Well, he probably was, but we are in a service where you're supposed to go up and out when you hit the age groups and I don't know how old John Bulkeley was but Admiral Bulkeley I'll bet was in his 80s by the time he finally stepped aside. Or close.

Paul Stillwell: Close. Late 70s.*

Admiral Burke: Well, years later, toward the end of my career, I was Commander Service Force Atlantic, and any time there was a ship being inspected of mine by him and his people, I made a point of riding. I think he appreciated it, and he honored me at the end of one of those trips. He said, "How would you like to relieve me?" I didn't expect anything like that. I didn't want to relieve him, because I didn't want to stay on active duty. That job did not appeal to me that much, but I appreciated the fact that I had gained his respect, and that meant a lot to me.

Paul Stillwell: Yes. Understandably. Well, where then from New Orleans in the Guardfish?

Admiral Burke: We went up to New London. Up to then we'd been in semi-tropical climate, and all of a sudden we got to New London probably around 1 November. Boy, it was cold up there. We had to go into Newport and drop off our torpedoes, and then we came in and reported to the reserve fleet. The submarines were coming in and getting ready for deactivation. We ended up by renting a house out in Stonington. The owner of the house, I think, was Captain Chester Wood.† Although I'd never known the Woods, I knew Mrs. Wood's much younger brother when I lived in Washington. But it was a pleasant year, and for the first time I was going to work in the morning and getting home in the evening and living a more normal life.

Paul Stillwell: Well, Stonington's not exactly next to New London.

---

* Bulkeley was born 19 August 1911.
† In interview number 2 of this history, Burke related an encounter with Wood in late 1941.

Admiral Burke: No, but we made friends. There's one friend who's still there. But housing was short then, and I got a house that had been built about in 1800 and had coal-fired furnace.

Paul Stillwell: One of the newer houses there.

Admiral Burke: Well, when you've been away as long and as much as I had and you're as much in love as I was, you didn't have much trouble keeping warm. We had a large living room, and we had two large living rooms, one of which was heated by the furnace. We had one bedroom that was heated and one other room that was heated by the furnace and that was it. There was a guy named John L. Lewis who was the head of the United Mine Workers, and he had the coal people striking off and on all winter. We were burning hard coal, and we would get down to 50 pounds of coal, and the coal supplier would actually deliver it in bags to the back door.

Stonington at that time was a summer colony. They had a small yacht club. They had a boatyard that had war contracts that usually built yachts, sailing yachts. They had a couple of nice shoreside restaurants. There was a Portuguese fishing family. These were mainly lobster fisherman but not necessarily. There were some affluent people who retired there, one of whom was an artist named Griffith Bailey Coale. In Bancroft over in the messhall is a mural of the Battle of Midway. He painted that. In Stonington we got to know Grif Coale and his wife. He was a Naval Reserve commander who was no longer on active duty. They were very nice to us. We made a circle of friends, and I'd say we lived a more normal life. That was in 1945 we got there, and we lived there for one year.

Before long my wife was pregnant, and her family came up and moved in with us during the summer. Her mother and grandmother and an aunt and a younger sister. We had a big house. They were from New Orleans; most people in New Orleans get out in the summertime. They didn't have air-conditioning then.

Paul Stillwell: Are there any other operations to mention for the time that you were in command?

Admiral Burke: All we did was materiel work getting her ready for decommissioning.*

Paul Stillwell: What was involved in the inactivation process?

Admiral Burke: In the business of decommissioning I can't remember the name of the commander. He was a senior captain, and he had a chief staff officer who was Brooks Harral, who was a very nice guy.† We had engineering supervision and hull and deck supervision and had to follow the rules that they were laying out, and we had inspectors there to help us through it. It was sort of a quasi yard overhaul, but you were putting the machinery to bed instead of to life, and you had to meet certain specifications. To be honest with you, I can't remember the details of what we did. Somewhere along the line we were dry-docked at least once, and we had to paint and prepare the surfaces, both in the tanks and out.

Paul Stillwell: Did you have a floating dry dock at New London?

Admiral Burke: Yes, we did and we were in the floating dry dock. I remember when they put us in they wanted us to open one of ballast the tanks that had fuel in it at one time. We dumped some fuel in the river, and everybody was unhappy. My God, if that happened today I would have been hung at the yardarm, but in those days it wasn't that serious. We just got out the hoses and washed out the floating dry dock, and that was it.

Paul Stillwell: What were the options for you in terms of the next billet from there?

Admiral Burke: Well, the detailer had an excess of people qualified for command, and the people who were in command like me were entirely too young. They had to put the thing back in perspective, so probably sometime around June or July, I was ordered to

---

* The Guardfish was decommissioned 25 May 1946.
† Commander Brooks J. Harral, USN.

Howard W. Gilmore as chief engineer, which I liked.* Only trouble was my family was in Connecticut, living in Stonington, and that ship was in Key West, but I was told that I would be going to shore duty probably within six or eight months. The Gilmore was going into shipyard overhaul in Philadelphia, so I kept my family in Stonington.

So I went down to Key West, and I was down there for not more than a month. Key West at that time had the first touch of polio. I remember Dutch Reuther, my friend. He and his family were living in Navy housing somewhere on the edge of town. I went over and had supper with them one night, and he took me out in the back yard and he said, "See that?" Pointed out three different houses that were a stone's throw from him, and each of them had had a case of polio. That's the first time I'd really come up that close to the problem.

We went on up to Philadelphia, and then I commuted back and forth. We were in the Philadelphia Naval Shipyard for about three months, and that was uneventful. On the weekends I would go home, and Betty was pregnant. I remember one of the weekends I went home at the end of September. She delivered our child so fast that I got involved. I was making coffee, and we couldn't get Betty out of the house. Betty's family had gone home to New Orleans, but my mother was there, so with the help of some other Navy friends we got a nurse named Smitty who was the wife of a retired chief. She was a tough cookie. She really ran the show, and apparently Charlie Styer, Admiral Styer's son, had the same nurse when his child was born, and we somehow or other found out about her.†

Smitty wanted to make sure that we knew who was in charge of that baby of ours. She was trying to over-control us and the baby, and we would only come in to see the baby when it suited her. After a while we discovered that she had given Charlie Styers some of the same kind of thing when their baby was born. So, as related by Smitty, Charlie came in to see her one afternoon when his father was there from out of town, and he said, "Smitty, can the admiral see the baby?"

Smitty said, "Who'd you say?"

---

* USS Howard W. Gilmore (AS-16), a Fulton-class submarine tender, was commissioned 24 May 1944. She had a displacement of 9,250 tons, was 529 feet long, 73 feet in the beam, had a maximum draft of 24 feet, and top speed of 18 knots. She was armed with four 5-inch guns.
† Lieutenant Commander Charles W. Styer, Jr., USN, also a submariner.

"The admiral. He wants to see the baby."

Smitty said, "I told him I don't care if he's King Jesus. He's going to see the baby when I want him to."

Paul Stillwell: His own grandchild.

Admiral Burke: Well, the Navy's made up of a lot of different people.

Paul Stillwell: That's true.

Admiral Burke: I kept up this commute, and then the ship went back to Key West. I was back there for perhaps another month. I had put on my shore duty preference card, which you had to keep up to date, and I think I put first choice NROTC, New Orleans. Second choice, something else in New Orleans, because I figured for Betty it would be the least disruptive. Third choice BuPers, so I was ordered immediately to BuPers. The reason I put BuPers was it was the closest Navy function to my home.

Paul Stillwell: Well, before you get to that could you tell me a little more about the Howard Gilmore and your job on board?

Admiral Burke: Well, I was the chief engineer and we had to do the normal Navy yard engineering work of overhauling equipment. As I recall, we had diesel engines just like the submarines that we tended.

Paul Stillwell: I didn't realize that.

Admiral Burke: We did have a boiler, but it was more of an auxiliary boiler. I think we must have had either four or eight diesel engines. I can't remember the number.

Paul Stillwell: How much connection did you have with the repair department?

Admiral Burke: Well, there was a repair department there, and that rings a bell. The repair officer was an ex-enlisted man who had worked his way up. He was a lieutenant commander. I remember he was a very conscientious guy. He and I didn't see things the same way, but that didn't make any difference. He was effective. We had good capability to take care of the work looking after the submarines when we were able to do it.

Paul Stillwell: Had the workload dropped as a result of the end of the war?

Admiral Burke: Oh, sure. It had dropped. See, we had become a regular squadron support ship. Our homeport was Key West, and we had a squadron down there. The pressures weren't anywhere near the way they were when we operating during the war. I'm sure we must have dropped off in numbers of people.

Paul Stillwell: Well, that went throughout the whole fleet because of the big demobilization.

Admiral Burke: Oh, yes. You had turnover of people and so forth. Stability was not good, and I only stayed there about four or maybe five months. I don't remember whom I relieved, but I had a couple of division officers like the electrical officer, the main propulsion assistant, and so forth. They had been there for some time, and they knew their jobs far better than I did.

Paul Stillwell: Well, you got to learn a little more about engineering that way.

Admiral Burke: Not as much as I would have liked; I wasn't there long enough, really. I was just making sure that the administration was going. I was just checking on the jobs, making sure. I knew how to do that.

Paul Stillwell: It sounds like that was just a place to stick you for a little while.

Admiral Burke: It was. What the bureau did was, I'm sure, with the concurrence of SubLant and SubPac was they sliced out year groups that should have command of squadrons, your divisions, ships, and then what was under them came along there. I finally got ashore about the middle of December of '46. I was ashore for two and a half years, and when I came back I was an exec. The captains of the submarines by that time had worked their way up to the classes of '37, '38 and '39. I guess you could call this the hump. This is the way the hump was reflected. I was an exec for one year. I was qualified for command. I was well qualified for command, and I didn't have to learn how to be a commanding officer. I'd already done enough of it, so I knew how to do most of the things that a CO had to do, but I went back as an exec. I went to the Dogfish, which was one of the lead conversions into guppy snorkels. There were about four of them that were done at the same time on the East Coast. Dogfish was one of them, and Dave Bell was my CO. He was the class of '37. He had relieved somebody in '38, and so I was there a year. I think Dave got relieved right after I did. He had already had combat command anyhow.

Paul Stillwell: Well, before we get that could you talk about your time at BuPers please?

Admiral Burke: Well, it was a learning period, and it turned out I was in the enlisted division distribution, and I hadn't been there very long, less than a month. There was a guy in the class of '38 named Heyden Wells.* He came over and said, "You almost didn't make it."

I said, "What do you mean?"

He says, "Everybody thought you were a Green Bowler." You've heard of Green Bowlers?†

Paul Stillwell: Yes, I have.

---

* Lieutenant Commander Heyden F. Wells, USN.
† The Green Bowl Society was a secret group of Naval Academy graduates that tapped promising young naval officers for membership and then allegedly aided them in getting favorable duty assignments as a means of enhancing their promotion prospects. Many of the Green Bowlers were athletes. The existence of the society became known throughout the Navy shortly after the end of World War II.

Admiral Burke: I said, "What do you mean? I didn't have anything to do with that."

He said, "Well, we've got a list of the Green Bowlers, and if you're a Green Bowler and you come to BuPers you're not allowed to be in the officer division or the enlisted division or anyplace affecting assignments." He said, "There's a guy in your class named Burke who was a Green Bowler, and we thought it was you."[*] So that was my introduction to the politics of BuPers at that time. The Green Bowlers had been discovered, I think, when an officer died in some sort of an accident when he was an ensign before the war, and he had been the captain of the lacrosse team. He was a very popular guy, nice guy. I didn't know him personally, but everybody was high on him. When they packed up his things and so forth, they found the Green Bowl file in his effects. And whoever packed up his things turned it over to his captain, and that's how it got to be known.

Paul Stillwell: What was your specific duty in relation to the enlisted men?

Admiral Burke: I started off as the assistant to the head of the School Assignment Section. We took people that came out of boot camp who were qualified and put them into "A" Schools.[†] We also at that time were running a special program on finding people who were qualified anywhere for electronic training. If they were qualified, we would let them change their rates, and we would put them into schools. One school was at Great Lakes, one was at Treasure Island, and we've got to realize this was at a time when we had two-year enlistments. People were going to the electronic school, which is maybe 45 weeks or 50 weeks, and staying in the Navy and then going out and getting jobs for as much as captains in the Navy working for RCA. It was a terrible time. We had a special desk there dealing with the electronic situation.

I was part of the detail section, which included the overall detailing of enlisted men to the Atlantic and Pacific. We had aviation enlisted detail. Charlie Eisenbach,

---

[*] Lieutenant Commander Louis E. Burke, Jr., USN, who had been a football player at the Naval Academy.
[†] "Boot" is a slang term for a newly enlisted sailor or Marine. Recruit training is known as boot camp. A class A school is one designed to provide specialized occupational training, leading to advancement in a particularly petty officer rating.

who was from the class of '36, ran the aviation detail.* There was a Jimmy Mills, who was about the class of '29, who was an aviator.† He didn't trust me. He was the head of what was called distribution, and then the overall head was a captain. The first captain we had was Karl Thieme, who was a line officer.‡ Then my boss, Brooke Schumm, headed the school section.§ When Thieme left, Brooke Schumm got the head job, and I took over as head of the school assignment section.

Going on in BuPers at that time was a rewrite of the BuPers Manual, and that was a struggle. Everybody participated in it. Brooke Schumm became the head of the Enlisted Distribution Division, and I was the head of one section, the schools. I was the most junior of the section heads, and the real power was Captain Jimmy Mills. He and Charlie Eisenbach had the aviation detail, and Mills, I guess, had all of the rest of mainly blackshoes, and he oversaw Eisenbach. But Mills was an aviator, and I didn't believe in letting people run over me. He and I didn't get along particularly well, but it was a real learning experience.

The BuPers Manual was being rewritten, and we had a tiny part. I had a classmate who was involved in it as one of the project officers. He had had graduate school in personnel management at Stanford, and I think it was part of his baby. I saw enough of it to learn a lot about what they were doing. We had a succession of heads. We had two different heads, as I can remember, of the enlisted division. The first one was Jack Shultz out of about the class of '22 and a very nice gentleman, and the second one, Frederick J. Bell, who's an author.** Maybe you've read some of his books.

Paul Stillwell: He had one called Condition Red, I think, about the destroyer Grayson.††

Admiral Burke: Yes. And he up and retired very unexpectedly.‡‡ He was articulate, good-looking, and seemed to have all the kinds of things that you would like. But he had

---
*Commander Charles R. Eisenbach, USN.
† Captain James Herve Mills, Jr., USN.
‡ Captain Karl August Thieme, USN.
§ Captain Brooke Schumm, USN.
** Captain John Henry Shultz, USN. Captain Frederick Jackson Bell, USN.
†† Commander Frederick J. Bell, USN, Condition Red: Destroyer Action in the South Pacific (New York, Toronto: Longmans, Green and Co., 1943).
‡‡ Bell retired 1 February 1948 and received a tombstone promotion to rear admiral.

some family connections in the McCormick Company over in Baltimore.

Paul Stillwell: The spice company.

Admiral Burke: Yes. I think that may have been why he resigned, but this was the first time I had been thrown into an arena with people, and we used to go up once a week and make our reports. Captain Donaho was head of recruiting then, and we had the enlisted promotion. I had all kinds of problems that I got educated in just by being near them and hearing these people make these weekly reports. On the other hand, even though I'd been in combat a fair amount and had my life threatened, I used to get the shakes having to get up and read my reports or up in the weekly circle. I was about the junior man, and I just lacked that kind of confidence. Before long my brother persuaded me to go to a Dale Carnegie course, and that really bailed me out.[*] It helped.

Paul Stillwell: In what ways?

Admiral Burke: Self-confidence. Learning to hear the sound of your own voice. Learning techniques how better to deal with people. It's the Dale Carnegie course on How to Win Friends and Influence People and how to be positive, how to present things. It was a course that went on about twice a week for about 20 weeks, but it helped me immeasurably and a strange thing happened. After I had gotten through this and was doing fine, all of a sudden I reverted, and it really was upsetting to me. I didn't know what the hell the matter was, and I went down to sick bay in the BuPers Annex. There was a chief down there, and I told him, "When I get in a group or I have to talk I feel uncomfortable. I've been to this Dale Carnegie thing, and now all of a sudden I've reverted."

So he said, "Well, wait a minute." He went out and got me some Phenobarbital, and he said, "Anytime you feel up tight, just take a spoonful of this. In the meantime, I'm a Dale Carnegie man too." He had a group that met once a week over at some church in

---

[*] Dale Carnegie (1888-1955) was a pioneer in training people in public speaking and interpersonal relationships. His best-known work was the popular book How To Win Friends and Influence People, which was first published in 1936.

Southwest Washington near the fish market. These were mainly government employees, and he got me back on my feet. I say it's something that I've had to work on a good bit of my life, but I've got to the point where I can handle it, and right now I can talk so damn long in public I'd kill you.

Paul Stillwell: That was a period when Louis Johnson became Secretary of Defense that there was a real economy kick on.* Did that have an impact on the personnel side?

Admiral Burke: Yes. We were down, as I recall, to about 320,000 enlisted. We were putting ships out right and left. I don't remember the ships or the numbers of carriers, but I'm sure we were down to about eight big carriers. People didn't realize the fact, I think, that we were the number-one power in the world. I'm not sure I did, but the deployment requirements and things like that—I wasn't in the fleet then, but people weren't shipping over. The people who did come into the Navy were mainly draft avoiders, avoiding going into the Army. They were only staying two years, and our reenlistment rates were down around 5-7%.

Donaho was the director of recruiting then and formal as ever, and I paid an office call on him one day. Then I think my mother had him over to the house one time for a party. When he talked to my mother about her son, he said, "Well, Burke did this on the Flying Fish." That was just Donaho.

Paul Stillwell: He wouldn't use your first name.

Admiral Burke: That's the way the Brits do too.

Here's an interesting thing. I was interested in helping the people in New London, and one of the officers who was about at least eight years senior to me was on a staff job up there. Anytime I saw anything on submarines around Pers-6 or BuPers that would be of interest, I would write him and just let him know, and before long he would ask me to check on this. Well, obviously we couldn't do everything to please the

---

* Louis A. Johnson served as Secretary of Defense from April 1949 until September 1950. He cut back substantially on defense expenditures, a program that had to be reversed with the beginning of the Korean War in June 1950. He was removed as SecDef a few months after the war started.

submarine Navy, which was off on the side in those days. One day I had written him something about something that was going to happen, and I don't recall what it was. I knew the submariners weren't going to like it, but I felt I had to alert him. He wrote me back castigating me and all the other stupid people in BuPers, so I wrote him back a note. I shouldn't have done it, but I just wrote him a note and said, "Perhaps you ought to come down here and straighten us out."

Paul Stillwell: Who was this gentleman?

Admiral Burke: I'd rather not tell you. We're friends. He wrote me back a one-line letter, writing off our friendship. And it kind of scared me, because he could hurt me. So I took it over to Barney Sieglaff, who was by that time the submarine detail officer and showed it to him. He said, "I will make sure that you're never assigned around this guy." And I never have been. Then I showed it to Herman Kossler, who was a submarine officer, and he was number two to Donaho.[*] Herman Kossler was a very approachable person, and I think he may have been on the Guardfish somewhere along the way. I didn't know him particularly well, but he looked at it, and he said, "Let me think about it." And he said, "I think you ought to show this to Donaho."

So I made a call on Captain Donaho and showed it to him, and he shook his head. I told him what led into it. He said, "Come back." So I went back about a day or so later and he said, "Don't acknowledge it. Don't let him know you've got it. He'll never know, and someday he'll regret it." Well, that was probably in 1948, and about three years later I was up in New London as commanding officer of a submarine. I went up to the club one Saturday night, and I saw this officer across the dining room.

Paul Stillwell: The man who'd written you the letter?

Admiral Burke: Yes. Later on I went to the bar, and while I was getting my drink he came in. He came into the bar, and he was fairly close to me, and we spoke and went

---

[*] Commander Herman J. Kossler, USN.

back. Then I came to the bar again, and he came back and took his place by me, and he said, "I wrote you a letter some time ago. I really shouldn't have written it."

I said, "I don't know what you're talking about." If you could have seen the relief on his face. And he's got a nice wife. She's a lovely person. The next time I saw him I was down at the Naval Academy and was exec of Bancroft Hall, which was in 1962, which was a dozen years later. They were down there for a reunion, and they came by and called on us.

Paul Stillwell: Well, you got some good advice from Donaho.

Admiral Burke: Oh, yes. He was, I think, an easy man to misunderstand.

Paul Stillwell: In what way?

Admiral Burke: Well, I say he was so regulation. He didn't have a sense of humor. I think he knew what his shortcomings were, but he worked so hard at being able to present himself and his ship or whatever he did. One day when I was in BuPers I had the duty on Sunday, and the duty office in Pers-6 was right next to his office. I could hear him talking as though he were giving a briefing or a speech, and I didn't pay much attention to it, and there wasn't anything going on in the office. I was just a presence. There wasn't any need for me to be there, but I was. It was still too close to the war. It was readiness and watches and so forth. And he finally came in and said, "I want you to do me a favor."

"What's that?"

He said, "I've got to give the Secretary of the Navy and the CNO a briefing on the reenlistment program and what the requirements are, and it's going to be next Wednesday," or something like that. And he said, "I've put this thing together, and I've been rehearsing it."

I said, "Well, I'm not an expert, but I will tell you that I have been taking public speaking with Dale Carnegie, and I do have a little feel for it." So I heard him through about three times, and he had it down pat. There wasn't any question about it. I mean, I don't think I told him anything that he didn't already know. Afterwards, when we had our weekly conference, after he had talked over in CNO with the Secretary, our director, Freddy Bell, had said that the CNO and the Secretary both said it was the finest briefing they'd ever heard.

This is the way I told you when he did that periscope. I said, "That bastard was good." He worked at it.

Paul Stillwell: That period in the late '40s was in turmoil because of the squabbles with the Air Force and the Marine Corps and naval aviation. Did you see any of that?

Admiral Burke: Well, the only turmoil was what I felt there on the job. My immediate boss was an aviator there. He was a hell of a nice guy and very popular, but he didn't trust me and made no bones about it because I was a submariner. I'm the kind of guy if I saw something I would speak up, and I guess you could say I'm not very tactful sometimes. The other aspect of it was that we were so short of electronics technicians at that time my office had a 3-by-5 card on every single electronics technician in the Navy. When they graduated we watched where they went. I would guess we had maybe 15% of the ETs we needed, and they could go out and get jobs just like at the drop of a hat.

We kept in touch with the service schools. I made a field trip out to Great Lakes, where we had one of the electronics schools. The head man there in the Service School Command was Bill Irvin, who had been the head of the communications division when I was at sub school, and he was later a rear admiral.[*] He was a tough guy but very fair. We went out in one these little four-seater, passenger seats, JRB, that the aviators used to get their flight time in. We had a whole raft of them over at Anacostia Air Station, and I went out with Captain Dutch Will, who was the head of training, and Commander Sam Moncure.[†]

Sam is a guy who should have made admiral but didn't. He was a family friend of ours from Alexandria. He was later CO of Com6thFlt flagship and chief of staff to

---

[*] Captain William D. Irvin, USN. The oral history of Irvin, who retired as a rear admiral, is in the Naval Institute collection.
[†] Captain John M. Will, USN. Commander Samuel P. Moncure, USN.

George Anderson, and unfortunately didn't make it.* But I was in the plane with these people coming back, and we had an aviator who was on duty in the training division. This was a training division flight, so I was sent along because I was school assignments. The copilot was a lieutenant commander from training getting his flight time in. There was a commander in there, and we had trouble getting clearance leaving Glenview when we departed.† When we passed over Pittsburgh they were talking to Washington National; I think we were supposed to have landed at Anacostia, but it was fogged in, and we should have landed in Pittsburgh. But he took a chance and came on in, and when we got here we were fogged in and on instruments. Then we headed for Pax River, because we didn't have enough gas to last very long.‡ We got to Pax River, made one circle over the field, and we had to land. We came in, and the ceiling was under 100 feet. We came down and landed and taxied up to the operations building, and the gas tanks were empty.

Paul Stillwell: That'll get your attention.

Admiral Burke: I was in the business of providing ETs for these ground control approach people, so they didn't have any trouble getting ETs from me from then on.

Paul Stillwell: I'm sure they didn't. Well, Admiral, we're right near the end of the tape. Why don't we save the Dogfish for next time please?

Admiral Burke: Okay.

Paul Stillwell: Thanks for another good interview.

---

* Vice Admiral George W. Anderson, Jr., USN, commanded the Sixth Fleet from September 1959 to July 1961. The oral history of Anderson, who retired as a four-star admiral, is in the Naval Institute collection.
† Glenview Naval Air Station, near Chicago.
‡ Patuxent River Naval Air Station, Leonardtown, Maryland.

Interview Number 5 with Rear Admiral Julian T. Burke, Jr., U.S. Navy (Retired)

Place: Admiral Burke's home in Alexandria, Virginia

Date: Wednesday, 16 April 1997

Interviewer: Paul Stillwell

Paul Stillwell: Admiral, we've got a bright, sunny day as we resume this series of interviews. I hope spring is coming.

Last time we were discussing your duty in the late 1940s in the Bureau of Naval Personnel.

Admiral Burke: Well, when I was in BuPers it was a real growing-up experience for me, seeing how the bureaucracy worked. I lived in Alexandria, and I was in a driving squad with two or three other officers.[*] There was a Captain Martin who was in BuPers, and there was a Captain Charlie Brooks, who was, I think, the head detailer in BuPers.[†] In the driving squad you just got a lot of education about what was going on in the rest of the bureau, and it was very informative.

At that time we were non-political or we were supposed to be. In fact, I don't recall voting for President until Eisenhower came along.[‡] We were very sensitive to the fact there would be congressional inquiries about personnel in the Navy. I was told by a friend of mine in detail that if there was a congressional interest trying to get something for an officer, they usually marked his jacket from then on forward with PI to let people know.[§] I always felt like I was serving the President and other people in authority, no matter what their political persuasion is.

Paul Stillwell: Were you expressly forbidden to vote, or was that just something you developed on your own?

---

[*] A driving squad is what is now known as a car pool.
[†] Commander Charles B. Brooks, Jr., USN; Captain Farar B. C. Martin, USN.
[‡] Dwight D. Eisenhower served as President of the United States from 20 January 1953 to 20 January 1961.
[§] PI stands for political influence.

Admiral Burke: I think it was customary in people of that generation and before. We all had strong political feelings, but we kept them to ourselves and didn't advertise it.

Paul Stillwell: So it was an unwritten rule?

Admiral Burke: I still feel this way. It is distressing to me to see how the senior military officers get cranked into the politics of today.

Paul Stillwell: Do you have any other impressions on Brooks? He went on to become a flag officer.

Admiral Burke: He was an exceptionally fine man. Confident. I can't remember whether he was a commander or a captain at the time.

Paul Stillwell: Probably a commander, because he was a captain in the mid-'50s and commanded the New Jersey.

Admiral Burke: Well, I remember that he had been the executive officer of one of the large battleships. The captain was taken ill for some reason, and he became the acting commanding officer for some time and took her through operations.* He was, of course, very proud, but he was somebody who had an extreme degree of confidence and assurance. He lived right across the street from me in Alexandria for several months. I don't think I've seen him since.†

Paul Stillwell: Do you have anything else to finish up on that BuPers tour?

Admiral Burke: Well, I learned a lot just by being there. The organization, and if you had problems, personnel problems, you sort of got the idea of who to go to and you knew people.

---
* Commander Brooks was executive officer of the USS Indiana (BB-58) in 1945-46 and of the USS Iowa (BB-61) in 1946-47.
† Brooks died 28 July 1969.

Paul Stillwell: And it gave you a broader perspective about the Navy as a whole.

Admiral Burke: It did. Perhaps it was a mistake, but I had joined the Navy to leave this area, and I wasn't seeking to come back here. I was seeking to travel and see the rest of the world, but notwithstanding that I learned a lot, picked up a lot. I hadn't been there very long when one day I learned the Admiral Denfeld, the Chief of Personnel, was being transferred.* Ned Beach was his flag lieutenant, and Ned was getting transferred, too, so he was looking for a relief.† He called me up and asked me if I would like to take a look at the job. Well, we had just had our second child, and I don't know whether my third one was on the way or not. I just didn't feel like working that hard, and also I figured that I didn't have Beach's capacity. He was intellectually smart, which I was not, and I knew that it took a lot of ability to do things quickly, and I was not that kind of a person. I guess I was a little big leery of getting into the front office at that stage, because I just had not been around senior people, period, except on the battleship and that was very limited. So I said, "Thank you very much." Ned was surprised when I told him I was passing on it.

In hindsight I don't know that that was for me a bad decision, because somehow or other in my makeup I didn't want what I considered to be a mentor. I wanted to do things on my own. It had some good plusses about it and would have given me some different experience. I never had anybody tell me that I ought to go to the Navy Department early on. I went to BuPers only because I put it on my data card. It was the nearest place to my family home in Alexandria. I'd been away so much I wanted to get some home life, and it worked out fine, but I figured that the fitness report system would recognize me over the period of time. But eventually when I got into the Navy Department I was way over my head, and I was not close enough on a personal basis from that kind of experience where I don't think I made the contribution I could have. I was far more comfortable in command, which I'd had plenty of.

---

* Vice Admiral Louis E. Denfeld, USN, served as Chief of the Bureau of Naval Personnel from 15 September 1945 to 21 February 1947.
† Lieutenant Commander Edward Latimer "Ned" Beach, Jr., USN, later became well known for writing a number of books, most notably the submarine novel Run Silent, Run Deep.

After that I took the Dale Carnegie course, and I won the prize for that class as the most improved student.

Paul Stillwell: I'm glad you can smile when you say that.

Admiral Burke: Well, it was true. I'd forgotten all about it. I remember that they had a meeting, sort of a graduation exercise, and I was one of the key speakers because I was the most improved and got a prize for it. I remember in my remarks at that time I told them that I had been offered a job that was really professionally enhancing, but I was afraid to do it because I was a little bit timid about it, but now that I had taken Dale Carnegie I would have jumped at it. Of course, they all roared and clapped, but nobody ever asked me to be a flag lieutenant again.

Paul Stillwell: Well, you're right. That is an opportunity to get noticed by people in high places.

Admiral Burke: You don't really appreciate that, but you look at the people who get ahead in the senior ranks, and there's a big chunk of them that have been aides or flag secretaries and been around to participate.

That tour was helpful in another way. For the rest of my career, for I would say the next 20 years, I knew people who were career professionals in BuPers or I knew something about the desks. When I was out in the field, I never hesitated to call somebody up to work my way in. I used to be able to find people in desks and would take advantage of it. When you are an exec or a personnel officer or just have somebody you want to check on or do something for, having that knowledge and experience behind you is very helpful.

Paul Stillwell: Well, I've also heard that a BuPers tour is helpful for getting your next sea job as well.

Admiral Burke: Well, when I left there I qualified to go back in submarines. This was postwar when we had the humps, and so my year groups were put back as execs. I had one year exec and then I got a command. I was the exec on the Dogfish, which was one of the first or second Guppy submarines.* The captain was Dave Bell, who was a very experienced submariner.† The personnel on that ship probably were about as capable as any ship I've ever served in. They were really good. They were handpicked.

Paul Stillwell: Please tell me about that experience.

Admiral Burke: Well, I had been off of active submarines for four years, and here I was around a bunch of jaygees, all of whom were very sharp.

Paul Stillwell: And you never really got your engineering training before.

Admiral Burke: And I never got my engineering training. I was apprehensive about this, and I had to work at it.

Paul Stillwell: How much improvement in performance could you see as a result of the Guppy conversion?

Admiral Burke: Well, they had a high-capacity battery for submerged operations, and on the old boats we could do maybe eight knots submerged. I think the Guppies may have been able to get up to 25 knots, but that would expend everything. I don't recall the battery capacity. I think it was about double of what we had before. Of course, the hull was streamlined, and the boat was much more maneuverable submerged.

Paul Stillwell: Did you have a snorkel?

---

* USS Dogfish (SS-350) was a Gato-class submarine commissioned 29 April 1946. She had a displacement of 1,525 tons on the surface and 2,410 tons submerged. She was 312 feet long, 27 feet in the beam, and had a draft of 15 feet. Her top speed was 20 knots surfaced and 9 knots submerged. She was armed with ten 21-inch torpedo tubes. The term "Guppy" grew out of the initials for the postwar modification fitted to World War II fleet boats to give them greater underwater propulsion power (GUPP).
† Commander David B. Bell, USN, had commanded the submarine Pargo (SS-264) during World War II.

Admiral Burke: We had a snorkel, and operating a snorkel you had to watch it. My Flying Fish basic training helped me a lot because I didn't take things for granted. I'd say I worked at everything I did there, but we had such good talent. I was not the navigator. I think the navigator was Bill Nicklas out of the class of '46.* Joe Busher was the engineer, and then he moved over to ops, I think. Bob Hale was aboard. But all these guys had qualified as submariners. I'd never been around so many qualified people, and it took a lot of pressure off of you—the fact that you had that much experience, including marvelous chiefs. I wish I could remember some of the names there, but as time's gone by my memory has dimmed.

Paul Stillwell: What do you remember about Commander Bell?

Admiral Burke: Dave Bell is first rate. He's very smart and a good friend. We would operate around New London a lot of times in the fog and so forth with the kind of talent we had. If I'd have been on the Flying Fish operating like that with the experience level that we had, we couldn't have done some of the things that the Dogfish did. But he inspired a lot of confidence in me and confidence in the people that we had.

Paul Stillwell: Which was something you were short on before.

Admiral Burke: I think we had only one unqualified officer, Al Maynard, and he was terrific. I mean, he qualified in the minimum time that was allowed at that time.

Paul Stillwell: Did this mean that your job was primarily administrative?

Admiral Burke: Well, I was administrative. I participated in all the things, and I took my turn at the periscope. I don't recall taking my turn in landings, because Dave operated pretty much the way I did when I got my own command. I wanted the junior officers to do those things. But he was always there in case anything went wrong.

---

* Lieutenant (junior grade) William C. Nicklas, Jr., USN.

Paul Stillwell: Did you have any encounters with the current in the Thames River?

Admiral Burke: Yes, but I don't remember anything remarkable. I don't remember breaking up the dock or smashing into the dock or whatever, but at various times we had problems with the current.

Paul Stillwell: What do you remember about the mission not only of that boat but the Submarine Force as a whole during that period?

Admiral Burke: Well, the war was over, and there weren't any ships to sink. And most of the thinking in the overall Navy was that submarines were, as far as I could tell at that time, mostly providing services, and so we were around New London a fair amount of the time. We did have the development group with Roy Benson.[*] They were there, and they went off on security patrols and so forth. During that year the Cochino, a Guppy submarine, went off with another submarine and was lost.[†] After we received the report on that investigation, we looked into whether the same thing could happen to us. Dave Bell was a very perceptive person, and we went through "What If?" I've forgotten exactly the circumstances, but I think they developed a short in the after battery.

Paul Stillwell: They had a fire on board.

Admiral Burke: Yes. They had a fire, and when the fire came it turned out to be a short in the after battery. You're going on pure memory from almost 50 years. They did what normally you did, which was to abandon and seal the battery. Well, they had the fire in there, and they had hydrogen gas in there, and they lost control of the boat. Things got out of hand. We on Dogfish went through this by simulation practice.

---

[*] Captain Roy S. Benson, USN, became the first commander of Submarine Development Group Two when it was commissioned in March 1949 and remained in command until August 1950. The oral history of Benson, who retired as a rear admiral, is in the Naval Institute collection.

[†] USS Cochino (SS-345) was lost off Norway on 26 August 1949 as the result of battery explosions and fires. For details see the Naval Institute oral history of Admiral Benson and a book by William J. Lederer, The Last Voyage (New York: Henry Holt and Company, 1950).

Well, in the late fall of 1949 the Dogfish went into the shipyard in Philadelphia for overhaul. We came out of the shipyard probably in February 1950. We had worried about what happened to the Cochino to the extent that we said, "What are we going to do if the same thing happens?" We made the decision if we had a fire in either battery compartment we were not going to abandon it. We were going in.

Right after we left the yard, we ran into some rough weather. We may have had the same set of circumstances that the Cochino had where it was rough. There may have been a little bit of water in the waterways in the compartment. We had a fire in after battery, and we had a crowd of people fighting to get in there. But I remember I was one of those who fought his way in as the people were coming out who were thoroughly frightened, but there were a lot of us that had the sense to go in. We threw the disconnects and it stopped, so they sent us to EB, and they did some modification.* Of course, we were all mad at the Bureau of Ships. They sent some experts up there to look at it. We didn't like what they were saying, and they didn't like us. I was never in that side of it. The guy they sent up there wouldn't give on the design, but I know they fixed it. They did something to fix those disconnects so that they would disconnect and we wouldn't have this kind of thing again, but we were nervous.

Paul Stillwell: Did you have to use any CO_2 or was merely disconnecting the electricity enough?

Admiral Burke: If I remember, all we had to do was disconnect the batteries.

Paul Stillwell: But the point I think that you're making is that because the skipper had thought about this in advance you knew what to do when it happened.

Admiral Burke: Oh, sure. There's nothing like experience to operate on, and Dave was a very perceptive and experienced person. He had been through a lot in the war. He'd had command before. He was a fine CO, and he's been a good friend.

---

* EB—Electric Boat Company, Groton, Connecticut, a shipyard that has specialized in submarines.

Paul Stillwell: Did your boat do any development work similar to what Roy Benson's people were doing?

Admiral Burke: No. As I remember, the Dogfish and Amberjack were the first two Guppies. I believe that's the way it was.

Paul Stillwell: I don't know.

Admiral Burke: The Amberjack under Ned Beach was down at Key West and was called the "Anglejack."*

Paul Stillwell: Why?

Admiral Burke: Because Ned would go down with the biggest angle and come up with it faster and so forth. We didn't operate that way, but Ned did. We knew that this was the stepping-stone to what was coming next in new construction, so we worked very hard on making proposals for modifications to the machinery and hull structure.†

Paul Stillwell: Do you remember any specific recommendations?

Admiral Burke: No, I'm not that kind of a guy, but I do remember that we found that we were sending recommendations up one at a time to SubLant and nothing would happen. We were getting frustrated about these things that we had dreamt up, and there was no action that we could perceive. Dave Bell was a graduate engineer. I forget what his specialty was, but he had been to PG School, and so he went up and paid a visit to SubLant one day. He came back with a letter that Ned Beach and the "Anglejack" had submitted about six months before. Ned had had about 25 recommendations, which

---

* For Beach's perspective on this and other topics, see Edward L. Beach, Salt and Steel: Recollections of a Submariner (Annapolis: Naval Institute Press, 1999).
† This was leading up to a class of diesel-powered fast attack submarines, the first new U.S. submarine design after World War II. The first of the class was the Tang (SS-563), commissioned 25 October 1951.

included everything that we had recommended plus about ten more, and he had beat us to the punch by about six months.

Paul Stillwell: Then Beach got the command of one of those new fast attack boats when it came out, the Trigger.*

Admiral Burke: He did, yes. I knew that well at the time. There were about a half a dozen new attack boats and I, like everybody else, would have given my left arm to have one. I'll tell you about almost getting one later on.

Paul Stillwell: Okay. What can you remember about the operations of the Dogfish in addition to providing services? Did you go make approach training, fire torpedoes?

Admiral Burke: We fired torpedoes. We did approach training. We had an occasional minelaying operation. I'm sort of mixing that in with what I did afterward. I was there for a year, and then I got command of the Sablefish. Admiral Jimmy Fife was ComSubLant.† He used the Dogfish a lot for public relations purposes. I mean, we rode the chamber of commerce and people like that in New London or anytime there was something coming down the river. One day we had a group of people from Westinghouse that came down, and they had an escort officer named Wilkinson that we'd never seen, and, boy, did he pull the wool over our eyes.‡ He was a good actor, and we couldn't believe that this guy was going to get command of a submarine. I think he told us he was going to command a submarine out in San Diego, but he was playing, "I'm a dumb guy." And he took everybody hook, line and sinker.

Paul Stillwell: A little like he's just an old country boy?

---

* USS Trigger (SS-564) was commissioned 31 March 1952.
† Rear Admiral James Fife, USN, served as Commander Submarine Force Atlantic Fleet from 15 April 1947 to 1 June 1950. The oral history of Fife, who retired as a four-star admiral, is in the Columbia University collection.
‡ This was Lieutenant Commander Eugene P. Wilkinson, USN, who a few years later became the first commanding officer of the USS Nautilus (SSN-571), the world's first nuclear-powered submarine.

Admiral Burke: Oh, yes: "I'm a little country boy. Tell me about this. Is that right?" I later got to know him when I was at the war college, and he and I for about two or three months were in the same discussion group. And that's the way he played the thing. He never asked a question he didn't know the answer to. He's sharp as hell, and he's a great credit to the organization. I'm a great admirer of his, but he sure pulled the wool over our eyes. The JOs on that ship were just shaking their heads. They couldn't believe that this guy was going to get command.

Paul Stillwell: Why do you think he did that?

Admiral Burke: Well, that's just the way he operates. Everybody has a style, and it's just a different style. I wasn't perceptive at that point in time. I might have been able to figure it out 30 years later.

Paul Stillwell: Well, one advantage to that approach is that it draws the other person out and gives him a chance to demonstrate his expertise.

Admiral Burke: Yes. That's true. But he's sharp as a tack and smart. I know that I've had a few minor dealings with him over the years later on, but that one time he really fooled us.

Paul Stillwell: I've never heard anyone speak ill of him.

Admiral Burke: Well. I'm sure in the politics I thought he was going farther than he did, and I suspect he was the victim of some sort of politics, and that's the reason he didn't get four stars. He should have.

Paul Stillwell: Well, it's chancy that high.

Admiral Burke: Well, it is. I know that, from personal experience. I've been told I was going to get a certain job, and then it didn't happen.

Paul Stillwell: That comes up in so many of the interviews I do. Just the combination of luck and circumstance and whom you know and where you are at a given time. Who saw you do what.

Admiral Burke: That's right.

Paul Stillwell: Anything more on the Dogfish per se?

Admiral Burke: I've sort of forgotten when the Seawolf keel was laid, but it was laid during that tour of duty that I was up in New London for about two and a half, three years.* Admiral Rickover made several visits up there, and one of them was on the Dogfish. He brought senators up there from probably the Atomic Energy group. He had Senator Bill Knowland of California who I think at the time was the leader in the Senate.† There was also the old senator from Rhode Island, Theodore Francis Green.‡ All of these people were in the papers, prominent people, and Rickover talked to them like they were plebes. It was unbelievable, and they ate it up. I couldn't believe it.

As I recall, Barney Seiglaff was our division commander, and he was riding along sort of as the senior escort officer for the party so that Dave Bell could run the ship. Rickover had most of the enlisted men on the ship furious. He'd talk to them like dirt, and I don't recall having any problems with him myself, but I know that his persona was such that he wasn't a particularly pleasant guy to have aboard. We had at least one, maybe two, rides with him demonstrating. The Halfbeak was our sister ship up there, but we seemed to get more of the stuff. In operations we probably went out on a fleet exercise at least once. I don't remember it, but we were in the shipyard for three or four months, so that was just a one-year stint as a PCO essentially, and then I went on and got command.

---

* The keel for the Seawolf (SSN-575), the Navy's second nuclear submarine, was laid at the Electric Boat Division shipyard on 7 September 1953.
† William F. Knowland, a Republican from California, served in the U.S. Senate from 26 August 1945 to 2 January 1959.
‡ Theodore F. Green, a Democrat from Rhode Island, served in the U.S. Senate from 3 January 1937 to 3 January 1961. He was born 2 October 1867 and thus was in his 80s when he visited Burke's submarine.

Paul Stillwell: Well, please tell me about the Sablefish.

Admiral Burke: She was an old-style fleet boat. We had a shipyard overhaul and got a snorkel while I was aboard.* Sometime after I got aboard, Art Warner, who had been the assistant detail officer, got himself ordered as my exec.† He was a good friend before. I'd known him for about five or six years. We were good friends. And we had a guy named Chuck Griffiths who showed up as a jaygee.‡ He had gotten off the Cochino before she went on her fatal cruise. He went to a six-month electronic course and then came to us. He was our electronics officer.

We had a very experienced engineer named Claypool, and he was well qualified. I'd say we had good talent. I had two unqualified officers and one of them, Al Davidson, qualified shortly after I got there, and the other one, Joe Adelman, was an interesting case.§ He was turned over to me by my predecessor, Sonny Toulon, as being shaky, and he was.** I began to appraise him through my Dale Carnegie eyes, and he couldn't land the boat by himself. He'd been on board pretty close to a year when I came aboard, and he couldn't land it by himself without a lot of help. So after a while, after I'd got myself shaken down, I made him permanent landing officer and permanent approaching officer.

Paul Stillwell: Kill it or cure it.

Admiral Burke: I've never seen such a transformation in a guy in my life. After about two weeks his wife came up, gave me a big kiss, she said, "You've changed my life."

Paul Stillwell: That's amazing.

---

* USS Sablefish (SS-303) was a Balao-class submarine commissioned 18 December 1945. She had a displacement of 1,525 tons on the surface and 2,424 tons submerged. She was 312 feet long, 27 feet in the beam, and had a draft of 15 feet. Her top speed was 20 knots surfaced and 9 knots submerged. She was armed with ten 21-inch torpedo tubes. During the first half of 1951 she was modernized and converted to snorkel operations.
† Lieutenant Commander Arthur H. Warner, Jr., USN.
‡ Lieutenant (junior grade) Charles H. Griffiths, USN. He eventually became a vice admiral.
§ Lieutenant (junior grade) Joseph L. Adelman, USN.
** Commander Alfred J. Toulon, USN.

Admiral Burke: That guy had confidence. He became the best landing officer I had, and it was a heartwarming experience. Paul, I'll tell you another thing. John Tyree was the division commander when I first came aboard, and I relieved the second week of upkeep. John Tyree was getting ready to be relieved by K. G. Schacht, I think.* In any case, he was not to be around very long. The first week I went to sea on the <u>Sablefish</u>, he chose to ride the <u>Sablefish</u> so he could observe me while I was getting shaken down, and I was really ticked off.

Paul Stillwell: Why? Because he didn't give you a chance first?

Admiral Burke: I mean, I'd never seen the fire control party before. We were shooting torpedoes, and I didn't know anything about the capability of the officers other than what I'd been told. Oh, I was ticked off. So I got a lot of advice at the end of that. But I remember after I had been aboard a relatively short time, something came up, and I got a good lesson from John Tyree that's served me well ever since, and I've really appreciated it. I saw him last year when they dedicated the memorial up there in Groton. He was there, and I had the chance to go over and thank him again for what he did. I hadn't been aboard very long when I got some accountable publication that was unimportant, but it was accountable with the Bureau of Ships. It had been lost, and it hadn't been reported in the turnover. So what do you do? I went out and talked to John, and he said, "Well, you can tell them you found it, but you haven't, or you can tell them you've lost it." So I wrote back and said, "We can't find it. We want to write it off."

And they said, "Okay."

Paul Stillwell: That was it.

Admiral Burke: Then a week later the engineer came around with a sheepish look and said, "We had it all the time." But, anyhow, it sort of taught me a lesson of playing your cards, and I've always respected him for that lesson he taught me. It taught me that the

---

* Commander John A. Tyree, Jr., USN; Commander Kenneth G. Schacht, USN.

higher up the pole you go the more your tail gets exposed. If you can't withstand public examination don't do it. Not enough people know those simple truths.

Paul Stillwell: Once you got shaken down in that boat did you feel more a sense of confidence than you had earlier in the Guardfish?

Admiral Burke: Oh, yes. I guess what's driven me is that somewhere along the line I knew I wanted to get ahead, and I wanted to keep going. I guess when I was with BuPers I discovered from my friend Art Warner that they rated the people in each year group one to a hundred or whatever. I knew that if there were fewer command billets, the higher up you got, you were competing with people, and that really got ground into me. So very quickly after I got on board a while, I began to talk to the officers about how good we were. Oh, they'd tell me we were great, but I began to make inquiries. I'd go over and talk to the squadron staff—I mean the working level, not the commanders—to find out who was number one in torpedoes and engineering and whatever. Then I'd make my officers go over to that ship that was number one and get to be at least as good as it was. I followed that routine in every ship I commanded. It paid off.

Paul Stillwell: Do you remember any specific examples?

Admiral Burke: The best example is that by the time I left, having talked to the squadron officers, Sablefish was number one in the squadron. What we needed was to have a good fleet exercise, and we were going on a fleet exercise where the enemy was leaving New York City in a big task force. Sablefish was assigned to the area where it couldn't escape being the hero of the fleet exercise from the submarine point of view. We were just licking our chops, and I was down in the wardroom with the officers going over the exercise. We had been in upkeep. The security watch came down and said, "Captain, you have a telephone call."

I got up, and it was John Tyree, who was the head of submarine detail. He said, "Congratulations."

I said, "What do you mean?"

He said, "You're going to be the executive officer on the President's yacht."

I sort of had mixed feelings about it. I was an anti-Truman person at that time, and he was riding at 25% approval ratings in the polls.[*] I said, "Well, I'm going on a fleet exercise next Monday week. I'll be available just as soon as I get back."

He said, "You're reporting to the Williamsburg next Friday," which was a week away.

So I said, "Well, I don't have a relief."

He said, "He's on the way to you right now. Bob Black." Bob Black had served on the Flying Fish before I had been there, but I knew him.[†] And indeed he walked aboard an hour later. He became the hero of the fleet exercise, and I was really bitter. But we had a good team. I'd say Chuck Griffiths in Sablefish was the first career officer that I served with that had any sense on the electronics. See, we were all makee-learn. The electronics thing came during the war. People were just thrust in there, and the officers didn't know anything about it.

Paul Stillwell: On-the-job training.

Admiral Burke: Yes, and Chuck was the first guy that could go in there and supervise the electronics technicians.

Paul Stillwell: Had he had some postgraduate education in that?

Admiral Burke: No, he had been to an electronics course. He was taken off the Cochino before the fatal patrol, and he went to Treasure Island, where there was a six-month course. Then he came to the Sablefish, and he was a godsend. He was terrific and he took over the electronics job and then in time before I left, I made him the chief engineer and moved the chief engineer into operations. But he was really good. I'd say we had good solid people. Nicklas was qualified and very solid. I'd say all the officers we had were very solid people.

---

[*] Harry S. Truman served as President of the United States from 12 April 1945 to 20 January 1953.
[†] Lieutenant Commander Robert G. Black, USN.

Paul Stillwell: Did you deploy at all during the time in either of those boats?

Admiral Burke: No. There might have been one or two SubLant submarines that deployed to the Med.

Paul Stillwell: A few went out on intelligence missions during that era.

Admiral Burke: Yes. That's right.

Paul Stillwell: We talked last time about Secretary of Defense Johnson and big economy crunch in the late '40s and early 1950. You took command of the Sablefish just about the time the Korean War started.* Did things get better as you observed during that period?

Admiral Burke: Reserves got called onto active duty. I'm just trying to think. I think we must have had a reserve that got called on active duty on Sablefish. Can't remember his name.

Paul Stillwell: Did the mission change at all for you after the war started?

Admiral Burke: I don't think so. We did pretty much what we had done all along, but when we got up to Christmas time, instead of having a Christmas standdown, our squadron went to sea. We were at sea for about two weeks, I think, just before Christmas and were doing continuous ASW operations against submarines. They let us back in port for a very short time, but there was concern I think in SubLant and the squadron commanders that we were not participating in the war and that we might get picked on, I guess.

---

* The Korean War began on 25 June 1950, when six North Korean infantry division and three border constabulary brigades invaded the South Korea. The troops were supported by approximately 100 Russian-made T-34 tanks. In New York that same day the United Nations Security Council adopted a resolution condemning the invasion.

Paul Stillwell: Well, another possibility is that late in 1950 was about the time the Chinese intervened on land, and there might have been a concern that the Chinese naval forces would get involved.

Admiral Burke: Could be. I don't recall going off on any exercises; we did go on a fleet problem every now and then. I went on a big fleet exercise in the fall of '51, and probably we were gone a month but nothing like the deployments I had when I got my destroyer or when I was in the amphibs.

Paul Stillwell: NATO was just starting up its military organization then.* Did you have any NATO-type operations?

Admiral Burke: No. I don't remember any. I don't think I really heard about NATO until I was on the Williamsburg. When I was on the Williamsburg in '53, we went into Norfolk. Admiral Lynde McCormick was the CinC, and he came down.† He and Eisenhower had gone off on a party and played golf, and I think they were talking about the NATO command when they returned from golf.

Paul Stillwell: What were the satisfactions of command for you?

Admiral Burke: Well, I was always acutely aware that I was competing, and I was always trying to have a ship with a high degree of readiness. I took great satisfaction in working the troops, knowing the people. Being in submarines spoiled me for the rest of the Navy as far as personnel. It's interesting how times have changed and things have changed. The submarine people that I served with were capable and intelligent and so forth. I don't think I ran into anything comparable to that until 1990, when I went down to the change of the command of the Theodore Roosevelt. The new CO was Steve

---

* NATO—North Atlantic Treaty Organization, which was established in 1949 as a means of coordinating defense against a potential attack from the Soviet Union.
† Admiral Lynde D. McCormick, USN, served as Supreme Allied Commander Atlantic, Commander in Chief Atlantic Command, and Commander in Chief Atlantic Fleet from 15 August 1951 to 12 April 1954.

Abbot, who is currently Com6thFlt.* Steve we had known since before he entered the academy. He gave us an escort officer, and we went all over that ship. The Theodore Roosevelt had a level of enlisted men that I'd never seen before. I couldn't believe it. I remember going into the avionics shop, and we were briefed by a first class petty officer who talked like he was a commissioned officer, and I asked him if he was a college graduate. He said, "No, sir, but I will be next June." And the non-rated men were equally impressive. I'd say it's a different Navy.

Paul Stillwell: Well, it has to be because it's so much more technical now.

Admiral Burke: But going back to the satisfaction I'd say I just enjoyed being in command. It seems like you're never going to get there, but just before I retired in Charleston the staff had a nice dinner party honoring me. The chief of staff got up and said, "I don't know whether you all know it, but Admiral Burke has had 19 and a half years of commands." So I had a lot of command time in the Navy. It wasn't all sea command, but it was like base commander, it was like NavForJapan. When you are used to being in charge, to me it was very satisfying. I enjoyed it. I don't think I ever took advantage of people or things, but I took great personal satisfaction out of being captain of whatever or the commander of whatever.

Paul Stillwell: Well, changing subjects, were there many blacks in the submarine force at that point?

Admiral Burke: I don't remember any blacks in the crew except the stewards at that time. I don't remember seeing any blacks in ship's company until I got command of the Fremont, and we didn't have many but we had a few. We had one guy named Moaney, who was a second class petty officer, and his uncle had been President Eisenhower's steward. He'd been with him in the Army for years.

---

* Captain Charles Stevenson Abbot, USN, served as commanding officer of the aircraft carrier Theodore Roosevelt (CVN-71) from 9 June 1990 to 27 August 1992.

Paul Stillwell: What do you remember of family life in New London during those years?

Admiral Burke: Not bad. When I was on the Dogfish we had a shipyard overhaul in Philadelphia, and I think I was the only one who kept my family in New London. I had three children at that time, and we lived on the Lower Boulevard in New London, and I just made the choice to keep them there. My oldest child was in school. I'd leave the ship Friday afternoon and get back Sunday night riding the Pennsylvania Railroad. After we'd been a year in that house, the owner wanted to sell it, so I moved to Mystic, into a house that was owned by Russ Kefauver.* It's on Library Street and an enormous house. We much preferred Mystic to New London, although we had no bones to pick with New London. We just liked the smaller town. The people—it's easy to get identification.

Again on the Sablefish I had a shipyard overhaul, and so I went through the same routine. That was disruptive but most of the time when you were operating it was out Monday and maybe back Thursday. Sometimes you operated, you were providing sub school services. You would go out in the morning and back in the evening, but it wasn't extended cruising except when you had a fleet exercise. I remember going to Canada after the overhaul. Sablefish went up to St. Johns. We were probably away from home about a month because of going down to the ship and taking her down to Norfolk for running some sort of a range down there and then going up to Halifax and generally shaking down after the yard.

Paul Stillwell: But nothing like a six- or eight-month deployment.

Admiral Burke: Oh, no. I only remember one submarine doing that while I was up there in that two and a half years. But other than that, occasionally somebody would go down on Exercise Springboard. Maybe stay for probably six weeks to two months, but I don't ever remember people making long, really long trips, except that one patrol.

Paul Stillwell: Did you get involved in the community, in school activities, what have you?

---

* Commander Russell Kefauver, USN, was also a submariner.

Admiral Burke: To some degree. We had friends in the community, particularly in Mystic. And we had our own Navy friends, some of whom had retired there. But we've always had a soft spot in our heart for Mystic—as well as Noank—and we always made a point of driving by our old house on Library Street every time we went through there.

Paul Stillwell: You said you would have given an arm to command one of those new fast attack boats. Were you in the running for one of them?

Admiral Burke: I doubt it. I don't know where I stood in the pecking order.

Paul Stillwell: Well, one thing that you were spared not getting on those fast attack boats was the terrible pancake engines that caused so much problem.

Admiral Burke: Well, I really wanted to get one, but I was not high enough on the pecking order at that point in time.

Paul Stillwell: Well, there weren't very many of them.

Admiral Burke: I felt that I didn't have enough war patrols. I got in and started making war patrols in September or October of '43, and I only made six. So I don't know, but I suspect that most of the guys who got the boats had two or three more war patrols. I was sensitive to that and thinking about what I was going to do. I may have told you earlier, I was also thinking about getting out of submarines and doing other things, because I wasn't sure that submarines were that big in the Navy to get but so far. You bump into older people, and over a drink they might tell you what you ought to be doing to advance yourself. And I talked to Art Warner, the guy who came as my exec on the Sablefish.

Paul Stillwell: From BuPers.

Admiral Burke: From BuPers. He said, "You ought to get yourself a destroyer."

"Why?"

"The guys that are going up and ahead you've got to realize you need that experience." It wasn't until years later, after I got to be a captain, when somebody pointed out to me that the submariners didn't have many votes on the flag board, and you had to make your mark with other people. It wasn't until after I made admiral that I first met one of the members of the board. I called on him in San Diego, and he said, "You're the first guy that I know that has more command in different kinds of ships that I do." I sort of steered away of getting on the inner circle in the submarine family. I felt it might inhibit my getting as far as I wanted to go.

Paul Stillwell: Well, on the other hand, if you had been one of the chosen ones to get that boat then you would have been automatically in the inner circle.

Admiral Burke: True. But I wasn't sure I wanted to be in the inner circle.

Paul Stillwell: Did Warner take his own advice and go into surface ships?

Admiral Burke: He was late getting there, and I think it probably held him back.

Paul Stillwell: Well, anything else on Sablefish before you move to Williamsburg?

Admiral Burke: I say everything was sort of routine. We were providing services. One of the things that I impressed on the ship's officers was that I wanted to get the best people out of Submarine School. So that whenever the students rode us we would treat those particularly well and let them to do as much as they could as students to get a positive feel about the Sablefish. I had no trouble getting volunteers. I mean, for our ship's officers it was a public relations thing. They worked at it, and all the students wanted to come to us, but BuPers wouldn't give us one.

Paul Stillwell: After all that effort.

Admiral Burke: Then the Korean War started, and they gave us another, and we got the anchor guy in the class.

Paul Stillwell: So much for your efforts.

Admiral Burke: He wasn't very effective, and I had to let him go, much to the distress of my divcom. He thought I was being ruthless, but he just wasn't that good.

Paul Stillwell: Well, after having been deprived of that fleet exercise, what was your demeanor when you showed up at the Williamsburg?

Admiral Burke: Well, I reported at the White House, at the naval aide's office, when the Williamsburg was en route to Key West.* The Williamsburg was just a support for the President and his party when they were in Key West.† We provided hotel services for overflow. We also provided the cooks and stewards and supplies at the White House. So I checked in and reported to the naval aide, who was Rear Admiral Robert Dennison at the time.‡ Then they sent me on my way by plane to Key West, and I got there about the time the Williamsburg did.

Paul Stillwell: Did you find why you had been chosen for that billet?

Admiral Burke: Never did. I can think of a lot of different reasons, but I really didn't want the job. Coming from Alexandria I was afraid that with so many friends around that it was a political job. And, going back to what I had said earlier, I didn't want to be tainted with politics. I was naive I guess.

---

* USS Williamsburg (AGC-369) had originally been built in the 1930s as the steel-hulled, diesel-powered yacht Aras for Hugh Chisholm. In 1941 the Navy acquired the ship, renamed her Williamsburg, and converted her to a gunboat. She later was the presidential yacht from 5 November 1945 to 30 June 1953. She displaced 1,806 tons, was 244 feet long, 36 feet in the beam, had a maximum draft of 14 feet, and a top speed of 13.5 knots.
† President Truman had vacation quarters at the naval station in Key West, Florida.
‡ As a captain and rear admiral, Robert L. Dennison, USN, served as naval aide to President Harry S. Truman from February 1948 to January 1953.

Paul Stillwell: What did you encounter when you got down to Key West?

Admiral Burke: Well, let me just tell you one thing. I got short toured about five months, and I was very ambitious to win the E. I knew that about the time that I left Sablefish we should have been standing number one but for a mistake I made in dealing with my boss. My boss at that time was K. G. Schacht out of the class of '35, very nice guy. In the fall Navy was playing Yale in football down in New Haven.* I can't remember whether I went down to the game or not, but anyhow K. G. had come from an assignment in the athletic department at the Naval Academy to be the division commander, and so he was very close to the people at the academy. He had also been a football player, so he went down. We had a for-the-record mining exercise, and, somehow or other, things got screwed up. I don't recall the details, but this was a mining exercise that we could only have that year, that week, that day. When I came in from sea to try to get things rectified so we could go out and do it again, K. G. wasn't there. So I went up to SubLant to get things straightened out.

Paul Stillwell: That would not make him happy.

Admiral Burke: And so Yale and Navy played. He was down in New Haven, and this was on Thursday or a Friday, and he was down there with his friends from the academy. On Monday, when he got back, he got a buzz from SubLant. He and I went round and round, and I read him off. So I thought that I'd been fired when I got ordered to the Williamsburg. That said, when I got down to Washington eventually I went up to BuPers. At that time Mac McCrory was in the detail section.† I went over and asked him if he could find out if I'd been fired, and he assured me I wasn't. But K. G. and I were really circling the wagons there for a short time. But it taught me a life-long lesson, that you don't fight with your boss.

But getting down to Key West, I reported aboard one afternoon. I think the President arrived that afternoon, and the next day there was a press conference. The

---

* In the game at New Haven on 27 September 1952, Navy defeated Yale, 31-7.
† Commander Woodrow Wilson McCrory, USN.

captain and the doctor, who was Red Warden—he was later an admiral—were going.[*] They took me along, and we were standing there in the room. There were probably 20 reporters at the most, and we watched the President being interviewed. Up to that point I had not been a Truman admirer, and I must say I was thoroughly impressed with the way he handled himself and thoroughly unimpressed with how the press behaved. The next day, when the newspapers came out, I learned that what went on in that press conference wasn't accurately reported. That was the beginning of my feeling about how the press functions, because from then on we saw the press corps trailing the President and shooting questions at him and doing things to make themselves obnoxious, and they weren't very high on principle.

Paul Stillwell: Do you have any explanation for that? Do you think it was because he was low in the popularity polls?

Admiral Burke: No, I don't think there's any difference today. I've seen this all along. In the press corps today and what I'm seeing on television operates the same way. The only difference is that up to that time there had been no TV press conferences, and also the press corps was nowhere near as big as it is now. The President knew each one of these people. He could call each one of them by their names, but there were only about 20 or 30-odd of them at the most. But it was an interesting experience to observe this.

You asked what the Williamsburg was like. I was fortunate that I had a great commanding officer, Ed Miller, and he had only been aboard about five or six months when I came aboard.[†] The Williamsburg had been staffed on the enlisted side by a group of personnel that had been on board in the White House structure for years, and I'll give you some examples. In the steward branch it was particularly true. This was 1952. We had a steward who had been there since Herbert Hoover; he had first come aboard in either '27 or '28. We had at least three men that had been there for 15 years. When Ed Miller got to be the commanding officer, he was a destroyer commanding officer, and he had been the executive officer of the Sixth Fleet Flagship.

---

[*] Commander Horace D. Warden, MC, USN.
[†] Captain Edwin S. Miller, USN.

His instructions from Admiral Dennison, who was his boss, were to bring the enlisted men aboard ship down to a normal tour of duty, maximum three years, so that was turned over to me to execute. They had just begun doing this when I came aboard, and so I had some very difficult personnel decisions to make, but I was always supported because I'd been given my instructions. It was particularly difficult with the Filipino stewards, and we had about four our five Guamanians—Chamorros, they were called.

We had about 40 to 45 stewards. Why did we need that many? Well, we also manned the executive mess in the White House, and we also ran the camp, which was called Shangri-La at that time.[*] I think we had at least four stewards at the camp all the time and more when VIPs were there. Truman himself didn't particularly like the camp and practically never went up there, but White House staff members did. But we had people such as a chief electrician's mate who was the President's own movie operator. He'd been there for six or seven years. Hell of a nice guy. Chief pharmacist's mate who was the only guy who was allowed to give him a rubdown or to give him any aid and comfort if he needed it.

Paul Stillwell: Apparently these people had no desire to leave.

Admiral Burke: No, no. And I was not aware of it, but I imagine some of these people also had back-up jobs on the outside. I relieved Bill Hurst in the class of '42.[†] I was told that the reason I had to be there so soon was that he was going to another assignment. It was imperative that I get there in one week, which I did. Well, I got there and relieved Bill, who had been on the ship for about two years. He went to the Pentagon and had 30 days' leave en route.

Interesting personality was Walter Slye, who was the first lieutenant.[‡] Walter had gray hair. He was much older than the rest of us. I would say he was probably in his late 40s or 50 years old. He was the pilot. That was his real job. He was a licensed Potomac River-Chesapeake Bay pilot. Any time the President was aboard or any time the ship was

---

[*] This is a presidential retreat in the Maryland mountains. In the Eisenhower administration it was renamed Camp David in honor of the President's grandson and has that name today.
[†] Commander William J. Hurst, USN.
[‡] Lieutenant Walter C. Slye, USNR.

under way going down the Potomac—ever since the ship and Walter had been there—he always had the conn because he knew the river.* So before long we had a trip down the river. I was up on the bridge continuously, and I watched Walter. Bob Peniston was the navigator, and he was taking bearings, but Walter wasn't watching Bob, and there wasn't any communication between them.† Walter would just go out, he would get to a turn, and he'd put the rudder over. I'd try to find out what he was turning on, and there wasn't anything on the chart to show it.

Paul Stillwell: There was no track laid out?

Admiral Burke: Oh, no. I think he would normally keep the conn down as far as Maryland Point, which is about ten miles beyond Quantico. I was used to a different kind of ballgame on submarines. So I began to ask Walter what he was turning on when we came back up the river down near Mason's Neck, I think it is, which is down where Gunston Hall is, where George Mason lived down in that area. There was a turn down there, and I couldn't figure out what he was turning on. We were coming up the river, and he put his rudder over, and then he walked away and wasn't watching where the ship was heading. He just walked aft, and he said, "See that tall tree back there, and you see that tree down there? When I get them in line, we're in the middle of the channel." When we got up closer to Alexandria, and we took another turn.

I said, "What in the hell are you turning on?"

"Well, you see the Masonic Temple over there?" He had it lined up with a particular tree, and he said, "When they're in line, I put the rudder over." And when we got up to where the Woodrow Wilson Bridge is now or that vicinity and got up to halfway through Alexandria, the buoys were there, but he wasn't paying any attention to them. I discovered he was centering himself on the Capitol dome and the west tip of the Army War College there, now the National Defense University.

Paul Stillwell: How did he do it at night?

---

* The individual with the conn—normally an officer—directs the ship's movements in course and speed.
† Lieutenant Robert C Peniston, USN.

Admiral Burke: Well, I told him I called it cow-pasture navigation, so eventually I put a yeoman up there and made him tell that yeoman everything that he was turning on and doing. I had it written down on a chart so that whoever was overseeing would be able to know what he was doing. It made Walter very nervous, because all of a sudden his mystique was being unraveled. Nobody had ever challenged his mystique before, but I was so used to the procedures in submarines of checking on anybody who did anything I just wasn't comfortable.

It eventually saved my life on the ship after Eisenhower got there, because Walter ordered right full rudder when we were in the channel right off of Alexandria to turn around. I don't know what happened to the quartermaster, who was very capable. He put on left full rudder, and we were right up against the left bank. Fortunately, I was looking at the rudder and saw it going the wrong direction. I went through the pilothouse window, and we got it straightened out.

Having people around who were old hat like that was comforting in one way. I never had any trouble with any of these old-timers. It was just that you were shaking up a routine that was very difficult. For example, we had Filipinos that were married. Their wives were in the Philippines, and they hadn't been able to bring them for whatever reason. They were beginning to arrive just at the time we were transferring their husbands. These were hardship cases.

Paul Stillwell: You did in fact implement the directive?

Admiral Burke: Yes, we were churning them off. We weren't doing it all at once, but we had a program going on. I would say at least half the crew had been on there well in excess of three years, and it was not a comfortable relationship where you had to move these people out.

Paul Stillwell: What other memories do you have of Bob Peniston?

Admiral Burke: Well, Bob was a professional. He stayed on there until about the first two weeks in December, and then he went on his way.* I've hardly seen him since, but he was a very competent, capable person. I've been in touch with him a few times. I discovered that he was down in Lexington and he had a very tragic situation. I think he lost a son.

Paul Stillwell: His son died just when he was due to graduate from Washington and Lee.

Admiral Burke: Yes. I've forgotten the circumstances, but it happened about the time I retired when we were in Charleston. I haven't been in touch with him in recent years, but off and on we've either talked on the phone or exchanged a letter.

Paul Stillwell: Well, he runs the museum down there where General Lee is buried.

Admiral Burke: Well, he was relieved by John Bell, who is a real interesting personality.† John had been in command of a minesweep up in Wonsan Harbor.

Paul Stillwell: What a change!

Admiral Burke: I think he was a jaygee when he came aboard about the 15th or 20th of December. I don't know whether he had a face-to-face contact with Bob Peniston, but John came in and reported. Captain Miller had had a heart attack about a week before, and so I was acting commanding officer. The day that John came aboard and reported, we were due to go up to the White House along with other White House staff to wish the President, First Lady, and Margaret Merry Christmas.‡ They received in the Oval Office, so it was something we had to do. We were White House staff. So about 9:00 o'clock John came in my cabin, which was my office, and reported for duty. He said, "I want to be transferred. I don't want any part of this damn ship." He had come from combat duty,

---

* Peniston went from there to the frigate Willis A. Lee (DL-4). Years later, in 1969, he was commanding officer of the battleship New Jersey (BB-62) when the interviewer was a member of the crew.
† Lieutenant (junior grade) John H. Bell, USN.
‡ Margaret Truman was the President's daughter.

and in a lot of ways he felt like I did when I got ordered there, only more so. I'd never laid eyes on the guy before, and I said, "Well, your first assignment is you're going to come with us and go up to the White House."

So about an hour later we all got in the car, the sedan, and went up there. He was sitting and stewing all the way, and I guess we must have had two cars because Red Warden was there. When the President was aboard, Red was the President's physician, so he knew the White House staff on a personal basis in a way that the rest of us didn't. This exercise was supposed to start at either 10:00 or 11:00, and we were standing out in the rotunda outside the Oval Office. John was standing there off by himself a little bit remote, scowling and thinking nasty things. We were the first to get there by ten minutes.

Pretty soon the door opened to the Oval Office, and out walked Harry Vaughn, who was the military aide.[*] I don't know what you know about him, but he was Truman's administrative assistant when he was a senator. He was a reserve officer and I think a reserve colonel probably. Then when Truman went and became President, he brought him in and made him the Army military aide to the President. And Truman promoted him to general officer. And, oh God, the Army was really upset, and so was the Navy. To think that this guy was being promoted like this, never having earned the rank, and so he was panned in the press royally.

What had happened, Truman's press popularity went to hell in a hand basket, and he was being harassed by the press. And one day Harry Vaughn couldn't take it any longer, and he read off the entire White House press corps and told them what he thought of them. From that day forward he was dead in the press, and he was painted as a drunk and a this and a that and so forth. I had the greatest contempt for the man from what I'd read, and here this guy came out and Red Warden came over. I'd met Vaughn once before, but we re-met him and he was charming. John Bell was just stewing there, and he completely charmed John Bell. After it was over, after we went through and shook hands with the President and his wife and Margaret, we were in the car and John was just bitching all the way back because here this guy had been nice to him and he liked him,

---

[*] Major General Harry H. Vaughn, USAR, military aide to the President.

and he was still mad at the guy. John Bell turned out to be a terrific officer. He was great.

Paul Stillwell: How much of a challenge was there in a job like that?

Admiral Burke: Well, that's interesting that you should ask. I had never before realized what perfection was until I went to the Williamsburg, and this is where Ed Miller was so good to impress on me that when we did things we had zero tolerance on mistakes.

Paul Stillwell: This is the major leagues.

Admiral Burke: And you didn't fool around. Our major league was providing services, and I learned how to do things in a way that was new to me. I had been on a flagship before, the West Virginia. That was child's play compared to the way we played the game.

Paul Stillwell: What would be some examples?

Admiral Burke: Well, Admiral Dennison was the naval aide. He was the commander of the commanding officer. At the time he had the right to bring people down and entertain them on the ship. He used to go up to Shangri-La a lot, and eventually he allowed the ship's officers to go up there if the White House didn't want to use it. I have been up there weekends about three or four times, because off-season White House didn't want it, and it was just a nice place to go. We didn't do a hell of a lot at the time, but it was a nice place to go.

He and his wife were in the social arena of the White House and diplomatic service and so forth and high government officials, and they knew a lot of these people. One night apparently he and Mrs. Dennison were at a dinner party somewhere, and the hostess was complaining about not being able to get beef stroganoff done properly anywhere in Washington. Well, he says, "I can settle that for you. I can do it for you if you can give me the recipe."

So one afternoon I went home, and just as I was leaving about 4:00 o'clock the supply officer told me that Admiral Dennison was bringing a party down. He had his quarters right adjacent to the captain's and he had about four stewards of his own. Whenever he was aboard, they were his. He had his cook and a lead steward plus two servers, and so the messenger arrived with a recipe, and he gave it to his cook. They had a dinner party for about ten people. I didn't think anything about it until I got to the ship the next morning. The captain was already there, and we had a crisis. The recipe got blown. Did you ever read The Caine Mutiny and the strawberry incident?[*]

Paul Stillwell: Oh, sure.

Admiral Burke: Well, we had a beef stroganoff incident. I don't know how to make it, but you have sour cream or something that you pour in beef stroganoff at the right time. Our cook had done it at the wrong time, and so it curdled. Dennison was embarrassed, because he had these very prominent guests. There were at least two ambassadors and their wives there, plus an Assistant Secretary of State, and we had given them the routine business. Dennison just walked all over Ed Miller for this, and Ed Miller walked all over me for this. I didn't even know I was in the food business up to this point. I got pretty horsy with Ed, but he was nice about it. I said, "Look, if Dennison expects me to supervise his mess the way we're talking about now, he is not going to be able to serve anything in that mess without us passing on it first and me in particular."

Paul Stillwell: A reasonable request.

Admiral Burke: I said, "Furthermore, we are not going to have a party. Anything that is served down here in the future when we are having a banquet for whoever [and we had a fair number of these] we're going to keep a source of these things, and we're going to have a dress rehearsal. It's going to be passed on, and we will invite Dennison or

---

[*] Lieutenant Commander Philip F. Queeg, USN, was the fictitious commanding officer of the destroyer-minesweeper USS Caine in Herman Wouk's classic naval novel of World War II, The Caine Mutiny, published by Doubleday & Company in 1951. Queeg was a mentally unstable martinet who demanded an unreasonably thorough search of his ship to find out what happened to a missing quart of strawberries.

anybody else to come down and do it, and that's the way we are going to do it. There's participation in the screwup, but you've got to communicate with us." So eventually we had a beef stroganoff sit-down luncheon and had Dennison down, and he passed on it.

Paul Stillwell: Other than that, what memories do you have of him?

Admiral Burke: He's an interesting man. The memories I have was that he was one of the most able people that Truman had in his entire staff.

Paul Stillwell: He stayed in that billet a long time.

Admiral Burke: He did. What happened was Truman was at the end of his tour and his talent, Clark Clifford and people like that, were leaving.[*] They were being replaced by civil servants from within, and they just didn't have the horses there. I didn't see this directly, but I got it from Ed Miller and from Red Warden—a lot of things that Dennison was doing really were in the political arena that he shouldn't have been in, but he got into by default because there wasn't the competence on the staff at that particular time to handle it.

Paul Stillwell: Do you remember any of those things?

Admiral Burke: I can't tell you.

Paul Stillwell: Well, I have heard Dennison praised for his astuteness in handling the Cuban Missile Crisis, for example.[†] He was very good at operating at the high level.

Admiral Burke: Well, he was the boss, and he didn't project on a personal level to us easily. I mean, he wasn't a hail fellow, well met. A couple of times Ed Miller had parties or supper parties for the ship's officers, and the Dennisons were included. He

---

[*] Clark Clifford, a lawyer and Naval Reserve officer, was a trusted presidential adviser. He later served as Secretary of Defense in 1968-69.
[†] As a four-star admiral in 1962 Dennison was Commander in Chief Atlantic Fleet.

participated, but he wasn't an easy guy to sit down and be able to communicate with. Of course, this is a problem of rank; he was about the class of '23, I think.

Paul Stillwell: Exactly that.

Admiral Burke: Here I was, 17 years later, and I'd never been around him before, but he had a lot on his shoulders. He had a good sense of humor, and I vaguely remember he wrote a farcical thing, a news report for the Washington Star, showing that the Williamsburg had run aground in the Potomac up around Shepardstown or something like that. It was cleverly done. I've forgotten the details and I may have a copy of it somewhere in my files, but I couldn't put my finger on it.

Paul Stillwell: Well, that was probably a parody of the Missouri running aground.

Admiral Burke: Could have been. After Ed Miller had his heart attack, I became the acting commanding officer. Eisenhower had been elected, and things were getting unraveled at the White House.* I don't exactly remember when it happened, but I got word at some point in time that I was going to relieve Ed Miller formally. I went up and paid a short visit in his office and thanked him for endorsing me. He was very nice about it, but I never felt that I was that close to him that he really knew me.

Paul Stillwell: Well, he must have heard about you through Miller.

Admiral Burke: Miller, I think, sensed that I didn't like coming to the ship. As I say, he kept emphasizing the importance of not making mistakes and doing things. It was the same kind of stuff I'd done when I was at sea during the war, to watch what was going on. But you had an entirely different thing to worry about with the White House. When the President and his party came aboard, you had to worry about what rooms they were in. You had to make sure the security was good. We didn't have the kind of security they have now. We had three Secret Service men aboard, on rare occasion four, a supervisor,

---

* Dwight D. Eisenhower became President on 20 January 1953.

and they would stand a watch in three and we provided security. We'd have somebody up and around, but aircraft and helicopters weren't all over the place then, and so it was a rather simple thing.

Paul Stillwell: Doc MacDonald had the command before Miller, and he said out on the Potomac people would come up in pleasure boats and wave.[*] No big deal.

Admiral Burke: Well, one thing was that when McDonald was the CO most of the officers or several of the officers in the wardroom were bachelors. Because they were bachelors and they had been looked at pretty carefully, they were social aides at the White House, so they used to participate up there. When I came in, Dennison was looking to make sure that they were married, and he didn't want social aides up there.

Paul Stillwell: How much contact did you have with President Truman himself?

Admiral Burke: Very little. I might be down on deck when he came aboard. I was invited once or possibly twice to have lunch in the President's mess. That's all. Any time the President came down to the ship, he was always accompanied by his naval aide or somebody who would tell him who these people were, and so he'd call me by name.

Paul Stillwell: Do you have any specific memories of things he said or did?

Admiral Burke: The only thing I remember about it particularly was that he seemed to have a good grasp on historical events. Eisenhower seemed to have the same thing. There weren't a lot of people there when I had lunch with Truman. Maybe eight, something like that. It was a long table. Could handle 20-25 people. One time I was on Eisenhower's right. Another time I was on her right. The Eisenhower people as a group were more impressive than the Truman people. I'd say they had first-team people. As I said, Truman's first-team people had started leaving and so just sizing people up they

---

[*] See the Naval Institute oral history of Rear Admiral Donald J. MacDonald, USN (Ret.).

were more impressive. Of all the people that I saw, the guy that impressed me the most was Milton Eisenhower.[*]

Paul Stillwell: What was it about him that impressed you?

Admiral Burke: Well, he didn't say anything unless it was important, yet he could comment on almost any subject. I later saw him when he was on the board of visitors at the Naval Academy when I went down there for duty. And he was terrific. Made sense. It was at a time when Rickover was pounding on Johnny Davidson; we were getting needled a lot over the quality of the students, the quality of the faculty and so forth.[†] Eisenhower made some very astute comments. He was at that time at Johns Hopkins, and he said, "You don't have to worry about all of this thing that he's talking about. If you look at Johns Hopkins or any other college, the people in the classroom aren't all these Ph.D.s. They're graduate students. The teaching isn't done by the big cheeses with all the degrees." He was a very solid individual.

Paul Stillwell: I've heard that it was Milton Eisenhower who persuaded his brother to give up the presidential yacht because it was perceived as luxurious living by the public.

Admiral Burke: The press secretary, Jim Hagerty, and Ned Beach came down to the ship and had lunch when I was the CO.[‡] I forget what the occasion was. There were four of us. I can't remember who the fourth person was, and Hagerty said, "Boy, we really blew it."

Ned said, "What do you mean?"

He said, "This thing is terrific. We should never have given this up."

Ned said, "Well, can't you reverse yourself?"

---

[*] Dr. Milton S. Eisenhower, the President's brother, was president of Pennsylvania State University, 1950-56, and later president of Johns Hopkins University.

[†] Rear Admiral John F. Davidson, USN, was superintendent of the Naval Academy from June 1960 to August 1962. His oral history is in the Naval Institute collection.

[‡] Commander/Captain Edward L. Beach, USN, served as naval aide to the President from January 1953 to February 1957. Beach's memoir, Salt and Steel, contains interesting material on Shangri-La and the Williamsburg.

"Absolutely not. We'd be torn apart." I know they had already made the decision when they made the mistake of riding the yacht, and Eisenhower used it twice.

When I formally relieved command, the ship was in the shipyard. We went down to Norfolk Naval Shipyard for an overhaul, and when we came back the administration had changed. I forget the sequence of events, but shortly after Eisenhower came in I received word to come up to the White House, so I did. I was going back and forth. Being in the Presidential arena, I didn't have any trouble getting air transportation from Norfolk to Washington, because there were shuttles going back anyhow. I was always given a priority, so I spent a lot of nights at home.

I found that the President would be having a conference on board the <u>Williamsburg</u> about the second day after we returned to Washington from the shipyard. It was with the Prime Minister of France and his Defense Minister and his Foreign Minister plus his ambassador to Washington. Our representatives were going to be SecDef, SecState, and probably the security advisor and head of the CIA. They were going to have the conference on the <u>Williamsburg</u> at 11:00 o'clock in the presidential dining room, one hour. Then they were going to adjourn, go aft to the reception area, have cocktails, receive some more senators and congressmen and Richard Nixon, the Vice President. Then we would have a seated luncheon for about 40 people one hour after they finished the conference. The ship was supposed to go down to Mount Vernon during this time, after all these extra guests came aboard, and then come on back. It went off, and it was going fine. The only trouble was the wind was gusting to 45 or 50 knots across the river. They didn't give us a tug, so I made the decision to only go as far as Alexandria

Most of the town's up on a hill, there's a valley there, and so that gave us a lee. Walter Slye, the pilot, had the conn, and I told him to go over on the left side of the channel, turn around, head into the wind and so forth. Walt worked us over there, and he gave right full rudder and then walked off and looked to see where we were going to turn and so forth and didn't watch the helmsman, which he never did. Fortunately I watched the helmsman, and that was when he turned the wheel in the wrong direction, and anyhow we got back in.

We had to kill time to meet the schedule. It was blustery March weather or late February. It was very uncomfortable, so we were wearing overcoats and things like that; the guests were all inside. We got back to the Navy Yard, and nobody would tell me what it was all about. I suspect it was about Vietnam.

I had another something that happened under Truman's administration that was interesting. One day I came in to work about 8:30, and Ed Miller was already there. I usually beat him in by 10 or 15 minutes, but this time he was already there. It seemed that the Prime Minister of Norway was on an unofficial tour of the United States and had been in Washington for a couple of days, had met the President, but there was no publicity on it, and the senior diplomat in Washington was the ambassador from Norway.

So the President had offered the use of a yacht called the <u>Margie</u>, named after Margaret Truman. It was a cabin cruiser with a crew of three. Had a chief and a first class engineman and a first class deck hand. When I arrived, I found I was the boat officer to take the Prime Minister and his party down to Mount Vernon, and they were going to have a picnic. I didn't get much instruction or anything like that on what was going to happened, except they were telling me what they wanted. There would be somebody there in the party who would inform me. So we had our crew all lined up and rendered honors.

The man who seemed to be accepting the honors wasn't the Prime Minister, as it turned out. It turned out he was the ambassador, so I got the two people mixed up. Nobody introduced me to him, so I thought the ambassador was the Prime Minister. The ambassador was a hell of a nice person. He had been in Washington so long that he was the dean of the diplomatic corps. Anyhow, eventually we started off down the river, and we hadn't gotten much past Hains Point or maybe abreast of the National Airport. I finally was able to identify the first secretary as being sort of the manager for them, and I said, "What are you going to do when you get to Mount Vernon?"

"Oh, we're going to walk around."

I said, "Does anybody know you're coming?"

"No. Don't think so."

I said, "Are you planning to lay a wreath or anything on Washington's tomb?"

"We hadn't thought about that." So he scurried over and whispered in the ear of the ambassador, and pretty soon he came back, and he said, "Is it appropriate for the Prime Minister to lay a wreath?"

I said, "You've been to Mount Vernon?"

"Oh," he said, "many times."

I said, "I used to live on Mount Vernon Boulevard in Alexandria when I was about 12 years old, and I can remember Queen Marie of Rumania went down there and Prime Minister Ramsay MacDonald, and there was a Prime Minister from France. They went down with a whole chain of cars and went down there, and that was back around 1930."

So he went back and whispered to the guy. He came back and he said, "The Prime Minister says that if it can be arranged he would be honored to be allowed to do this." So I got on the radiotelephone from the Margie and called the Williamsburg. I got Ed Miller, the captain, and told him what the situation was. After about half an hour, he called back and said, "The resident manager, Mr. Cecil Wall, will meet you at the dock, and he will escort the party up, and he will have a wreath there for you."

So we were killing time to give them time to get organized, and when we got off of Mount Vernon we could see that there was nobody on the dock. So we went on down a couple of miles and turned around and came back. There was still no one, so I decided to hell with it, and we went in and we made three passes at the dock to kill time. Just as we were securing, Cecil Wall arrived, patting the sweat on his forehead and so forth. He had a homburg on, and he took charge and escorted us to the tomb. They didn't have a photographer with them, so I got one of the sailors to take the pictures. Then on the way up, one of the first secretaries said, "The Prime Minister would like to know if he is just supposed to lay the wreath and then stand in contemplation or should he make a speech?" I think I told him contemplation would be all right, because the gentleman didn't speak English, so it would be easier for him to contemplate.

Paul Stillwell: Right. He could contemplate in whatever language he wanted. Such power you had.

Admiral Burke: Well, you never can tell when something's going to happen where you get to influence events. So we got up there, and here was wreath that he had. Wall said, "I've got a wreath here for you." It was black patent leather leaves with a white flower on it; it was awful looking. It was artificial. It was terrible. And it was sitting on a tripod. So we went through Mount Vernon, returned on the boat and so forth.

Well, my mother was living in Alexandria, and I told Mother this story. Mother was in a bridge group with Mrs. Wall, who was a good friend. Mother told Mrs. Wall about this story from my side, and she said, "Well, I think you'd better hear what Cecil did when he got the call from the State Department that this visitor was coming, and he needed desperately to get some flowers." He called up the DeMayne's Funeral Home that is on Washington Street there, and Mrs. DeMayne was Clover. He said, "Clover, I need a wreath. No questions asked." So he must have taken it right off of somebody's casket. That was all of that business.

Paul Stillwell: You were talking about the concern about the wind when you had that one party on board. I've heard that the Williamsburg was a top-heavy ship, so you would be concerned probably about sail area, wouldn't you?

Admiral Burke: Yes. I only went really to sea in the ship once, and that was when the President and his party flew down to Key West. The ship was like a cork in the sea. I went from Key West back to Washington, and it took us about three or four days. The weather wasn't bad, but I tell you it was rolling and pitching. It was not a ship that you could take out. It wasn't like the Britannia or anything like that.*

Paul Stillwell: Well, I think that it had an extra deck built on it for accommodations, and that made it higher didn't it?

Admiral Burke: I don't recall that.

Paul Stillwell: How did the ship handle?

---

* HMS Britannia was the British royal yacht.

Admiral Burke: It wasn't too bad as long as you didn't have any wind. They must have had tugs whenever we came into the Navy Yard there, but I don't recall using them.* Whenever we came in we always came in headfirst and let the party disembark. Then we'd turn the ship around so that anytime the President came we could run right out, and we did.

One of the times I went out with President Truman. It was about this time of year. I think he had already made his decision that he was not going to run. We got word one Friday afternoon that we were going out. We didn't know where we were going or anything like that. He showed up with a party of four or five, six people. I know Clifford was one of them. I forget who the others were. When he came aboard it was maybe 6:00, 6:30. We told Admiral Dennison we were waiting for rush hour to get over, and then I think it had been raining like cats and dogs. After about a half an hour Dennison came up and told Ed Miller to get under way. So we called the bridge, and they told us that the electric power had been lost, and they had to open it by hand. If you don't think we didn't have a massive traffic jam on the South Capitol Street area. It was awful. I know it made a horrible impression in Washington. That one time Eisenhower went off for four days and came back we got to Alexandria at 8:00. We landed at Alexandria, and they disembarked the White House party there, and then we waited until rush hour was over to bring the ship in.

Paul Stillwell: This is so you didn't interfere with drawbridges?

Admiral Burke: Yes.

Paul Stillwell: Would you have a guess on what percentage of time you spent under way while you were assigned to the ship?

---

* The ship was based at the Naval Gun Factory, now known as the Washington Navy Yard, in southeast Washington, D.C.

Admiral Burke: Very little. I don't remember. Well, it wasn't so bad when Truman was there. I would say he probably went out about four times. I just can't remember. Mrs. Truman's mother was dying in Independence, and so she had moved out to Independence to be with her mother. He didn't want to go out and bached it. I guess he must have flown out there to be with her. He didn't like to go to the camp. Then when I got to be the CO, other than those two times, sometime starting in about April, I think it was, until the ship went out of commission, and we began to have daily cruises I forget how many times a week.* Probably a couple of times a week until we went out of commission on probably the first of July. We were riding the veterans from the Veterans Hospital and servicemen who were in Walter Reed or Bethesda.

Paul Stillwell: Well, that was a nice use for it.

Admiral Burke: It was nice because we would take them down the river below Mount Vernon, turn around, and we'd serve them lunch. Somewhere in my books I've got some snapshots of it. I can't tell you where they are, but I was able one of the times to take our families aboard.

Paul Stillwell: How did you spend the time prior to that when you weren't under way?

Admiral Burke: Well, you've just got normal administration of your ship. In addition to the ship we had two other yachts. One was the called the Lenore, which had belonged to Sewell Avery, and that became Jack Kennedy's yacht. They gave it a Kennedy name, the Honey Fitz. We also had the Margie, but whenever we went off on a trip anywhere we would also take the Lenore with us as an escort vessel, and we had to maintain and keep those. We had to maintain the ship, and I'd say we had the normal personnel things. We also had the White House mess. We had the responsibility of running that, which was under the supply officer. He essentially was the gun boss or the flight officer for the ship.

Paul Stillwell: That was your main battery.

---

* The Williamsburg was decommissioned on 30 June 1953.

Admiral Burke: Yes, it was, and you had to appreciate this. So you got to be very conscious of what was being served and how it was being delivered. We ran the camp, but I don't think the supply officer was in charge of the camp. But we had a chief boatswain's mate up there. His name was Driver, and he was in charge of the camp. He had a crew of about 50 or 55. The Marines from the Marine Barracks had a small detail up there; I forget how many they had. They just had sentries on the gates. Whenever the President came up there, they probably put maybe a company up there.

It was a rather primitive place in those days. There was an area that had been bulldozed where they could land Piper Cubs or helicopters. There was a nice swimming pool. It wasn't flashy or anything like that, but it was a simple swimming pool. The President's cabin was a nice cabin, and also there was one other one. They were the only two that were heated. There were a lot of them that had been built back there in the Roosevelt era; they were unheated. I guess they had water to them, but it was kind of primitive. Now, as soon as Eisenhower got elected, the first thing we did was build a putting green right there in the front. It was probably Ed Miller's idea; he had a lot more imagination than I did. We were using the sailors and technical assistance, so it might have cost $5,000. I defy you to build a putting green for $5,000.

Paul Stillwell: You made a reference earlier to drinking on board the Williamsburg. I presume the normal prohibition on board Navy ships didn't apply there.

Admiral Burke: For the guests they had their own liquor supply. I forget how it was managed, but it was watched very carefully. I mean, ship's company didn't get involved in it, but we were like the Norfolk Steamboat Line from Washington to Norfolk to Baltimore.

Paul Stillwell: But you had an exemption to this rule apparently about serving drinks.

Admiral Burke: I don't think it was the law of the land. I think it was the Secretary of the Navy fiat from about 1914.*

Paul Stillwell: It was indeed, but it must have had an exemption in the case of that ship.

Admiral Burke: I guess so. I probably knew at the time, but the number of years has caused my memory to fade.

Paul Stillwell: What do you remember about the arrangements down in Key West at the Little White House?

Admiral Burke: That was when I first came aboard and I was just looking and learning. I didn't go over there but about three or four times. Our supply officer, at the time was Lieutenant Commander Leo Roberts, and he worried about the stewards and all that and worked out the menus and so forth.† I didn't get involved in it. I was brand new. I went over there, but I went in the building, I would say, at least six times during the period of time we were down there. How long we were down there, I would guess a month, but I don't remember. It was in good taste, and that's about all I can tell you. That's not very helpful.

Paul Stillwell: Well, I'm sort of curious why the ship needed to be down there just because Truman was.

Admiral Burke: Well, we were there to supply logistic support. We were there to provide hotel space for the President if he needed it, and we provided it for some of the guests who were there. There was a Charlie Wilson. There were two Charlie Wilsons then; one was General Electric, and one was General Motors. I think it was the GE guy

---

* On 1 July 1914 a general order from Secretary of the Navy Josephus Daniels went into effect. It abolished the traditional wine messes on board U.S. Navy ships, resulting in a prohibition against drinking alcoholic beverages on board. The ban was relaxed in the 1980s to permit the serving of beer and wine—but not hard liquor—at official receptions on board.
† Lieutenant Commander Leo W. Roberts, SC, USN.

who came down. He may have stayed aboard our ship, but we had several cabins there, staterooms, for guests and they stayed over there or some of the senior White House staff.

Paul Stillwell: I presume protocol was one of those things you had to do at the perfection level every time.

Admiral Burke: Well, it was expected that way. There are little things that happen when you've got the President aboard that become routine. For example, the first morning when I was at breakfast I heard the word passed, heard "Attention" on the announcing system and heard the word "United States" passed. That's the first time I'd ever heard it. The President was passing by. He was great on taking morning walks and, well, he had a troop of secret service there. We got to know some of the secret service and got to know some of the press people. Jim Rowley was the head of the secret service detail, and we all got to know him. We kept our distance. Every morning he went off and took a walk, and it wasn't unusual for him to come by the ship on his morning walk.

Paul Stillwell: So the honors would be rendered just even in his passing by.

Admiral Burke: Yes.

Paul Stillwell: Did you have a band attached?

Admiral Burke: No.
As I say, the camp during the time I was there really wasn't used much by Truman. He didn't care for the camp. I don't think he went to the camp the whole time I was there. But the lead White House staffers could use it. The one who used it the most was Dennison. I think it was her second marriage. I think the Dennisons may have had a couple of children, and they were pretty young for a rear admiral to be having, and I would guess something like 12 to 14 years. I never saw the children, but I heard about them being up there one time because the stewards got too frisky with them and the

Dennisons became upset. Or one of them or she got upset, and so we had to get in business and tell them to watch out.

Paul Stillwell: Well, you had gone to that job with great reluctance. Did you come to enjoy it after a time?

Admiral Burke: I'd say being the captain of a ship was more satisfying than being the exec, but I was never really comfortable with it. I worked my tail off at it. When Ed Miller had his heart attack, he was expecting to be transferred. I think he was told he would be there 18 months, so I think he expected to leave when Eisenhower came in. He had his heart attack and then he was in the hospital at least two months out at Bethesda.

It just happened that we were living out at the end of Wisconsin Avenue near Glen Echo, so once he went in the hospital, I dropped over and saw him frequently and would tell him how the ship was going. I didn't think much about it at the time, but I heard years later from somebody who was a mutual friend that he really appreciated it. But I didn't act like the ship was mine. I acted like the ship was still his. Pretty soon, I guess, he was detached, and then that's when I got fleeted up. Because Ned Beach was there, and Senator Taft was the Bob Dole of his era.* He wanted to downgrade the military around the White House and around the President, and a way to do this was to downgrade the ranks, and so Ned, I think, was probably a commander.

Paul Stillwell: He was indeed.

Admiral Burke: I never really liked the job. I just didn't want it. From a family point of view we ended up by living in Woodacres instead of Alexandria, and I was gone off submarine pay. We had three kids, and there was little that I could afford over here where my friends lived, so we ended up by finding this place at Woodacres, Maryland. That made me more comfortable, because I didn't want my friends to be pressing me to

---

* Robert A. Taft, a Republican from Ohio, served in the U.S. Senate from 3 January 1939 until his death on 31 July 1953; he was the Senate Majority Leader in 1953, after the Republicans took control in the election of 1952.

show them the Williamsburg all the time, and I was able to control our social contacts and ship visits.

From a personal point of view, it worked out very nicely, because we were allowed to use the Lenore on private parties, as long as the White House didn't need it, and it was very nice to be able to have a private party. We didn't do a lot of it, but we did it every now and then during the summer time and take a party down the river. In like manner, after I'd been on board a while we were told we could go up to the camp and spend the night. We stayed in the President's quarters there and had the stewards working. It was pleasant. Interesting experience to be able to do it. We went up there during the Army-Navy game weekend. I took my mother, my three kids and a nephew up there as well as Betty.

Paul Stillwell: What happened to the ship when she was decommissioned? Was she mothballed or just what?

Admiral Burke: Well, I was detached around the first of August, and I left. Then I went off to Norfolk, so I didn't see her until years later, and she was parked across the river here at Blue Plains. I'd say that was at least 20-25 years later when she was over there, and she was kind of rusty and not in the shape she had been.

Paul Stillwell: I imagine the first lieutenant kept her in pretty good shape while the President had her.

Admiral Burke: Oh, yes. She was in A-1. I mean we spared nothing. If we wanted things we got them. There was one feature about the White House. The President at the time we were there frequently passed out trinkets to people who called on him and so forth or were guests as the White House. Much of that came through our quarterly allotment, and we didn't have any trouble getting it reimbursed.

Paul Stillwell: Did you have any feeling whether that was career enhancing duty or not career enhancing or neutral or just what?

Admiral Burke: Good question. As I told you, I thought I'd been fired because of my altercation with my boss in New London. Then I went up and talked to Mac McCrory, who was then a detail officer, and he assured me that I had to be selected. That relieved my concern a bit, but after the ship went out of commission and I was detached, sometime probably in early August, I was invited to come up to BuPers.

Pers-B was the officer section. That was a rear admiral, and the next man under him called me up and said, "We want to talk to you about assignment." So I went up and talked to the captain, and he was very kind and fatherly. I didn't know him. I'd met him down at the ship when he'd come down there when Ed Miller was the captain. Then he turned me over to John Tyree, who handled commanders on down.

So I went in and talked to John Tyree, who was a captain, and we had a nice chat for a minute. He'd been my boss there for a short while in New London, and then he turned me over to the commander detailer, who was Captain B. J. Semmes.[*] So I went in and introduced myself, and he seemed to know who I was. I said, "I've been told to come in and see you about assignment."

He said, "Yes. What do you want?"

I said, "What can I have?"

He said, "Anything you want."

So I ticked off things that I knew that I wasn't qualified for: "MIT?"

"Okay, you can have that."

"Captain of a destroyer?"

"Yeah."

"Captain of a submarine?"

"Probably. You'll have to go over and ask Dave Bell." Dave Bell was then the detailer.

Paul Stillwell: Well, he was a friend of yours.

Admiral Burke: And he was a friend. "You'll have to talk to Dave Bell."

---

[*] The oral history of Vice Admiral Benedict J. Semmes, Jr., USN (Ret.), is in the Naval Institute collection.

I said, "National War College?"

"Yeah."

"Armed Forces Staff College?"

"Yeah."

I said, "There's something fishy here. The Navy doesn't operate this way."

He said, "Well, you haven't embarrassed the Navy since you've been on that job, and the Navy's grateful."

So I said, "Well, let me think about it. How much time?"

He says, "You've got as much time as you want. But I'd like to know pretty soon, because we just don't want to keep you on ice over there where you are."

So I went down and talked to Dave Bell. What I really wanted was one of those new attack submarines, so I said, "I've been told I can get anything I want, and I'd like to get command of one of those new submarines. Can I get it?"

He said, "Yes."

"How long can I have it?"

"One year."

I said, "But I got screwed when I got brought down here."

He said, "That's all you can have, but you can have the Trout." I didn't want to move my family up to New London for one year and then turn around and come back. So I went back and talked to a lot of different people, including John Tyree. He had not gone to a destroyer and seemed to be regretting it, so eventually I came back and said, "I'd like to have a destroyer."

He said, "Okay. Which one do you want?"

I said, "Well, I'd like to be in Norfolk."

"Okay. You go over and talk to Jack Wadleigh."[*] He was the destroyer placement officer. Back when I had been in the shipyard in the Sablefish there was a division up there of destroyers. The squadron commander was the division commander also, named Bony Close.[†] There were four skippers, including Les O'Brien, Bill

---

[*] Commander John R. Wadleigh, USN.
[†] Commander Robert H. Close, USN.

Meadors, and George McDaniel.* McDaniel was a year ahead of me at the academy and same company. I knew him, and he was a good friend. Then a guy named George Street came in and got command of one of these, and they were all nervous as hell to have a glamour boy like George Street there, and I was hearing both sides of it.† What they didn't like—and particularly McDaniel—was all of these submariners were coming in and getting command for one year. Then, just before they had a chance to get dirty, they would go back to submarines. So I wanted to make sure I was going to get a two-year tour.

They were nervous about going to Guantanamo after the shipyard for refresher training. They said the training group down there was merciless and would run you into the ground and make you look bad to your bosses and the type commander. So I decided I wanted a destroyer that I could be on board long enough before the shipyard, so that when I went to Guantanamo I would know my people and have their capabilities in hand. So I was able to pick out the Harold J. Ellison. It was coming off a Med deployment, and so she wasn't going into the shipyard for about a year. That looked okay, and so they gave me the Ellison. I had a verbal commitment from B. J. they'd let me stay there two years, and I'd never met B. J. before. Sometime later I discovered that he had his mortgage at Burke and Herbert Bank, and my uncle, who was the head of the bank, was the guy that got me my appointment from Judge Howard Smith, so I don't know whether that had anything to do with it or not.

Paul Stillwell: Well, we're right at the end of the tape. Maybe we can save the story of that destroyer for the next interview, please. Thank you for a good one today, Admiral.

---

* Commander Leslie J. O'Brien, Jr., USN; Commander Williams W. Meadors, USN; Commander George T. McDaniel, Jr., USN.
† Commander George L. Street III, USN, had earned the Medal of Honor as commanding officer of the submarine Tirante (SS-420) in World War II.

Interview Number 6 with Rear Admiral Julian T. Burke, Jr., U.S. Navy (Retired)
Place: Admiral Burke's home in Alexandria, Virginia
Date: Monday, 21 April 1997
Interviewer: Paul Stillwell

Paul Stillwell: Admiral, last time we talked about your tour in the Williamsburg. Then you went to BuPers, and you got assigned to Harold J. Ellison.* You reported there in the fall of 1953. Was there any difficulty taking command in that you'd not had destroyer duty before?

Admiral Burke: Well, I was apprehensive. They sent me to PCO School in Key West. I was there for a month, and I worked hard, because there were destroyer people there, and these were experienced people. There were a couple of squadron commanders who were going to squadron assignments, and for all of these people it was familiar turf. So I spent an awful lot of time at night studying op orders and general guidance and the rules of the Destroyer Force to try to get myself up to speed.

Paul Stillwell: Were tactics and ship handling two of the main areas?

Admiral Burke: We were involved in tactics and ship handling and ASW and so forth, so I was learning all the way, and everything was a new experience. I made one friend there that I am forever obligated to, Don Dertien, who was going to get command of a destroyer.† My family had moved to Virginia Beach while I was at PCO School. When I finally reported in sometime in September to DesFlot 4 for assignment in Norfolk, I found that my ship was in a Med deployment.‡

It turned out that the ship and one other had been detached and been on the Northern European independent operation, and so I found that she was scheduled to be in

---

* USS Harold J. Ellison (DD-864), a Gearing-class destroyer, was commissioned 23 June 1945. She had a standard displacement of 2,425 tons, was 390 feet long, and 41 feet in the beam. Her design speed was 35 knots. She was armed with six 5-inch guns and five 21-inch torpedo tubes.
† Commander Donald A. Dertien, USN.
‡ DesFlot 4—Destroyer Flotilla Four.

England in about a month after I reported, and there was a major fleet exercise coming up in the North Atlantic. Don Dertien had relieved command, and so I asked him if I could ride his ship to join my ship over there in England.* So we went through a major fleet exercise. Carriers, replenishment groups, hunter-killer groups, and so forth, and the exercise was on the way to and north of Iceland.

Paul Stillwell: Was this a NATO exercise?

Admiral Burke: I remember there was at least one, several British ships there, so it had to be NATO.

Paul Stillwell: There was one around that era called Mainbrace.

Admiral Burke: I don't remember the name. You've got to realize this was 45 years ago. I slept in the captain's in-port cabin down below. Don was up above in the sea cabin. We had the wishbone board on the table in the wardroom to eat all but about four days in that cruise, which lasted at least three or four weeks. It was rough. One of the times we were replenishing alongside a carrier I was up there in the after end of the bridge, and we rolled almost 30 degrees towards the carrier. I don't know how we missed the carrier; it was terrifying. I had a great chance to see Dertien, who had had command of a DE before. This was old hat to him, even though it was a new ship to him. Whether he knew it or not, he gave me an intensive PCO course; it couldn't have been better.

Paul Stillwell: Just by example.

Admiral Burke: Just by example giving me things, "Here's how I do this." Here's one the things that he gave me. Whenever he took his ship alongside, if he was going to let his JOs do it for replenishment, he would give one the conn in the wheelhouse and the other he would give the speed control, so he divided the job in two. Sounds simple, but it worked and it was just something that later on when I went off in a hunter-killer group

---

* Commander Dertien was commanding officer of the USS Cony (DDE-508), 1953-55.

for the first time, in no time at all I was able to go alongside and get outstanding times and be the leader of the pack for the destroyers, simply because I was letting these watch officers do this and letting them participate. They got to be first class at it very quickly.

Paul Stillwell: What was the advantage of separating it?

Admiral Burke: Well, you've only got one thing to look at. I as the captain was overseeing it to make sure things didn't get screwed up. But every time we went in for any kind of a replenishment we would always get a score. At the end of the replenishment exercise, the task group commander would always put out a report on the times that you were involved alongside and hookup. You were in competition with the other destroyers that were doing it. It took me a couple of times to realize that we looked like hell at the start, but in a fairly short time I was the leader of the pack. This was an area where I was competing. After I got to my command, I was competing with people who were experienced destroyer officers.

I had never ever been involved to the degree these destroyers were operating in tactics with voice radio on the bridge. I had seen voice radio before but in a very limited use. I saw the way he was operating, how he was doing it and so having three weeks of terrible weather, seeing how the captain operated, seeing some of the problems they had and how he reacted and solved the problems. It was an enormous help to me.

When I got to my ship, she had been in independent operations and had not been in the task force for five months. We were in Plymouth, England, where I relieved command. I had about a three-day relief, and we were joining up with about three other destroyers plus a couple of auxiliary ships that were returning to the States. Two of the destroyers were going to Norfolk. The rest of the pack were going to Newport. I will never forget I was up on the bridge for the first time under way as a commanding officer of a destroyer. I had a fine exec, Ed Cummings, who's class of '43, but I didn't know any of the officers.* We got under way just about dark and were leaving Plymouth or the external approaches. As we were passing out, we got a long tactical signal by voice to

---

* Lieutenant Commander Edward J. Cummings, Jr., USN.

form up. I discovered that none of the officers, nobody, had copied the message down. These guys had been operating independently. They didn't know how to do it.

Paul Stillwell: So it certainly wasn't habitual behavior.

Admiral Burke: And so I was wild. So the next time I came up, something like this happened, I went to general quarters, and we began to hold school very quickly. One of the destroyers that was going back to Norfolk was commanded by Sandy MacGregor, a classmate and a very close friend.[*] I'd gone to prep school at Episcopal High with him, so Sandy was filling me in on some of the things that he thought were wrong, and he was very kind about it. After we got back, he told me some of his observations, and most of it was around the communications and the unresponsiveness. So I began to drill these people just like I did in submarines and gave that kind of supervision. I drove them crazy, but it worked. We had about 19 officers. Including me and my exec we had about 42 years' commissioned service. On the Sablefish with eight officers I had 43 years' commissioned service, and that had been two years before. So the average officer below the exec had six months' commissioned service.

The engineer was a mustang, but the rest of the officers were from colleges.[†] I had a good slug of ROTC people. I had one from Dartmouth, I think one from Yale, one from Penn State and one from Duke, one from Alabama, and I forget where the others were from. Then I had some OCS.[‡] I had two academy boys. One was top drawer, one was mediocre. But it was interesting to see how they responded once I began to get the ideas across, give them a responsibility, let them do it, make sure that they were studying the lesson. I went back and rewrote the standing orders. Formed them on my Sablefish orders, and I insisted that they reread the standing orders every night or every day before they went on watch. They hated me for it.

Paul Stillwell: Part of your captain's night orders.

---

[*] Commander Stephen H. MacGregor, Jr., USN.
[†] "Mustang" is Navy slang for a former enlisted man who has risen through the ranks to become an officer.
[‡] OCS—Officer Candidate School.

Admiral Burke: Yes. I called them standing orders, and almost everybody calls them night orders. I made them read those standing orders every time they went on watch, and I wasn't fooling. They had to qualify on voice radio and be able to handle it. Apparently they'd had radiomen up there on the bridge doing that sort of thing before I got there. In time it paid off, and they developed a degree of confidence. When we got back to Norfolk following the deployment they had a standdown. Then we just had ISE and that sort of thing until Christmas.* Following Christmas we joined a hunter-killer group with a total of about six destroyers, and we went to Exercise Springboard in the Caribbean for about two months.

Paul Stillwell: Did you have any carrier with you as part of your group?

Admiral Burke: We had one of these jeep carriers, CVEs. The admiral was Briny Temple.† I don't know how I can pull his name out of the hat, but I did. We were doing things in tactics. I'm amazed now thinking about what kind of tactics we did. We used to have tactics in the morning, forenoon, in the afternoon, have dinner, and do it after dark. For me these after-dark tactics were hair raising, because my people were not experienced, and I myself was learning. My exec was up there, and so the only way I could handle it was I'd call the operational group to GQ.

Paul Stillwell: That can be fatiguing.

Admiral Burke: It was, but I had to do it for the safety of the ship, because Briny Temple was having us rotate the axis and reverse course and doing all sorts of crazy things at night.

Paul Stillwell: You weren't confident that your watch sections could handle that.

---

* ISE—individual ship's exercise.
† Rear Admiral Harry B. Temple, USN.

Admiral Burke: At that time my watch couldn't handle it. I was having trouble myself, because I was just learning myself. My XO would come up there and back me up.

Paul Stillwell: Was your North Carolina experience any help at all in this?

Admiral Burke: Not really. We didn't do that kind of stuff. In hindsight I think we were fortunate that some of the ships didn't have collisions, because we were going sometimes at high speeds. Sometimes we rotated the axis, usually 180 degrees, but sometimes we'd do it an odd number like 150 or 90 degrees, and they had us changing station. And we did this night and day. It didn't happen every night, but it happened frequently enough so that I just felt it was important to keep the first team there until I was satisfied that they were able to deal with it.

In the ships that were there, there was Ben Pickett in '38; he later made admiral.* Mark Woods, who was the class of '42, made admiral.† In the other division was John E Dacey, and he made admiral. He was number one in the class of '38—very fine officer and really ran a good ship. All of these people were experienced destroyermen. All of them were in my squadron, and that's whom I was competing with. Later, after I left, Woods told me, "It's made a world of difference in competition since you left." Because I just felt that I had to be at least as good as what they were.

Gradually, we began to come up to it, and our communications became responsive. The officers learned how to do it and could handle it. I expected and demanded first that all the officers of the deck handle it, and then the JOs could do it. So I had all these guys in a relatively short time qualified to handle tactical communications.

Paul Stillwell: And I'm sure the handling of the signal book got a lot better too.

Admiral Burke: Oh, yes. And I think much of this had to do with the style of supervision that I had been raised in on the Flying Fish. We went in and visited Havana. We had an interesting port visit there. I had a very nice guy in the class of '27, Skivvies

---

* Commander Ben B. Pickett, USN.
† Commander Mark W. Woods, USN.

Chamberlain was the squadron commander.* Then from Havana we went down to Kingston, Jamaica, and I think we ended up in San Juan for a short while.

Paul Stillwell: What was Havana like in those pre-Castro days?

Admiral Burke: They allegedly had a democracy. The President was Batista, and things were kind of tight, because you had to be in his pond to get things.† Everybody knew this. I forget how long we were there, but we were there probably four or five days and we met officers, senior officers or contemporaries in the Cuban Navy. It's so long ago that I just can't remember any incidents. There may have been one incident there, but I don't recall anything unusual.

Paul Stillwell: My guess is that there was some forms of entertainment that were not in the United States, such as gambling and what have you.

Admiral Burke: Oh, yes. There were gambling casinos. I remember going to a nightclub there one night. We'd met an American couple who were down there, and he was there on business. They took us to a nightclub that had the finest floorshow I've ever seen anywhere. I mean, it was in good taste.

Paul Stillwell: Singing and dancing?

Admiral Burke: Well, it was a big group of people in it, and they were doing singing and dancing and sort of rockette kind of dancing. I'm just trying to pull it all together. While we were there, there was a young man and his wife, very attractive, who joined us. I think he had graduated from the U.S. Naval Academy. He may have been an officer in the Cuban Navy, but I doubt it, because I think they were really affluent. But I remember after Castro came in this man ended up by living in the United States. He was obviously

---

* Captain Leonard C. Chamberlain, USN.
† Fulgencio Batista, who had been in power since a revolt in the early 1930s. On 1 January 1959 Batista fled into exile, and Castro seized power. Castro became Prime Minister of Cuba on 16 February 1959.

independent in his political views at that time, and his wife was a very attractive person. I think he was in about the class of '46 or '47, sometime in that time frame.

Paul Stillwell: Must have had some way of getting his wealth out of Cuba.

Admiral Burke: Well, I don't know whether he did or not, but during all of this time that we were down there we were going through all kinds of operations. Eventually we did a little bit of type training independent of the carrier, and I recall that we got involved in a torpedo shoot for the record, for competition. We got a hit. I was really shocked.

Paul Stillwell: What was the target?

Admiral Burke: Oh, it was probably another destroyer, but we fired at a long range. I couldn't believe it. I didn't think we had a chance in the world, but we got a hit. We did a lot of type training down there for the record. And by the time we were working toward the end of cruise, our crew was really pulling together and doing well and getting good marks.

Paul Stillwell: Did you have any interaction with the Guantanamo people in training?

Admiral Burke: We did not go into Gitmo, but we were on Springboard, which was sort of a type-training event, anyhow.* One thing that we did not schedule was shore bombardment, because there just wasn't any opportunity. I just didn't know enough about the skills that you needed to have in the competition for the E.†

Well, we were down there for about two months, and when we got back we had a critique exercise up in the CinCLantFlt theater. The chief of staff got up there and started reading off a critique of what we had done. At the end he commended my ship and one other for commanding officer's outstanding performance, which kind of surprised me. I

---

* "Gitmo" is the nickname for Guantanamo Bay, Cuba.
† An "E," for excellence, is generally awarded to a ship or component of a ship as a result of top performance in competition with other ships during a given time period.

was so shaky in confidence, but that really helped me to know that I had pulled that far that fast.

The next quarter we got into another hunter-killer group for a Med deployment, and we were going over for a short one; it was about two and a half or three months. The guy who was the admiral later became ComNavAirLant, a real fine gentlemen. But we had to get ready for a deployment, and I was amazed. You had a checkout and very thorough administrative inspection. First they gave you a preliminary inspection, and then about two weeks later they gave you the final inspection where the admiral came down.

Well, when I had the preliminary inspection, there was a captain who was the chief inspecting officer who was out of about the class of '37. He just tore me apart. I've never seen so many discrepancies, and I was really apprehensive about this. I got my officers together, and we got all these discrepancy lists. We began to work on them and so forth, and I didn't see how we could possibly get through them. When the admiral came down about ten days or two weeks later, he walked through and somehow or other he liked us. He said we were the finest ship he had seen. The guy that inspected us before, the ship's captain, shook his head. He said he couldn't believe it. So the guys really got the message.

Then we went off on this hunter-killer group exercise and a lot of the same type of operation but not quite as intense as had been in Springboard. The first port we went into was Genoa, Italy. When we went into dock, I had an Italian pilot, and he got screwed up on something. I took the conn away from him, and he walked off the bridge. He had tugs there to put us in, and they walked off, and so I had to do it myself.

Paul Stillwell: Was this a Med moor?

Admiral Burke: I guess it was a Med moor.* I just don't remember, but he had screwed the thing. We were going to have a collision, and so I took it away from him, and then all these guys suddenly couldn't speak English. But that turned out for me to be a very fine

---

* In a Med moor, frequently used in the Mediterranean, the ship is moored perpendicular to the face of a dock, rather than being parallel alongside a pier. In the Med moor the stern is near the dock, and one or more anchors keeps the bow in position.

cruise. We worked hard, just like we did down in Springboard, and these officers, particularly the ROTC guys, were really coming aboard. I was amazed how much they improved and how confident they got. After Genoa the next port was Naples. And Barcelona. Then I think we went to Naples. I can't remember the exercises, but we were doing a lot of tactical ASW training and then we went home.

Paul Stillwell: Do you recall the carrier you went with?

Admiral Burke: It was a CVE. <u>Sicily</u> maybe? After we'd been home about a week, our commodore got a letter from the admiral saying that his staff had kept records, had done some scoring on the ships in his group. We had six destroyers over there, and they gave a numerical score to each of the destroyers. The <u>Ellison</u> was number one by so far it was embarrassing. So it was right at the end of the fiscal year. I got recommended for the E, and DesLant wouldn't approve it.[*] Gave it to somebody else because I hadn't done that gunfire support. So I was disappointed, but I say I knew where I stood with my commodore, and I knew I had made the team. I had gotten better scores than the experienced destroyer officers, so I was very comfortable with it.

    My exec had done beautifully over in the Med, and I gave him as much opportunity for the conn and landings as I could, because he needed more of it. I'd qualified him for command, and he got transferred as soon as I got back and was replaced by a lieutenant. He was a former aviation pilot.[†] His total experience on board ship was six months on a destroyer. He was not qualified to stand officer of the deck because they had not been under way. He did not know how to navigate. What had happened was he had been commissioned, I guess, right at the end of the war and sent to Cal Berkeley for a college education. He couldn't hack it, so they put him in General Line School. He was a nice guy. A very good administrator and paper work man.

    My squadron commander said, "Fire him." So I went over and talked to my admiral in DesFlot 4 and said, "Here's what I've got." He just shook his head. I told him

---

[*] DesLant—Destroyer Force Atlantic Fleet.
[†] Aviation pilot was the title for enlisted men who qualified as naval aviators. The practice of putting enlisted personnel through flight training ended during World War II. Many of the aviation pilots were commissioned subsequent to getting their wings.

I wanted to go up to BuPers and see what I could do. The detail officer I got to know as a friend years later. But he was out that day, so I tried to persuade his bosses up there to do something. They refused to do something about it. They said the only way I could unload him would be to write him an unsat fitness report, which I would not do.

Paul Stillwell: How had he gotten assigned to a job like that?

Admiral Burke: Well, I never had it out with the detail officer who did it, but I went in and I talked to his bosses and contemporaries up in BuPers and they all shook their heads. My admiral and squadron commander were familiar with it, and then my squadron commander was rotated off, and we got a new squadron commander. And so we were back from the Med, and we had several months of less intensive operation. We had a stand down and mostly ISE and type training off of Norfolk, and so I used that time for PCO school for my exec. I had to teach him how to navigate, how to pilot, and it was tough because here we had just come back from the Med and all these jaygees I had were really sharp by that time and they knew damn well that they were better ship handlers and had far more confidence operationally. It was a tough thing to deal with.

Paul Stillwell: Tough for them to respect the exec in that situation.

Admiral Burke: Yes. But I would say that he was a good administrator, and he was intensely loyal.

Paul Stillwell: Was he willing to learn in this program?

Admiral Burke: Oh, yes. I couldn't put him up on watch, because I had been through that experience myself during the war on the Flying Fish, but I made damn sure that he knew how to navigate and pilot and tried to get him into the operations as much as I could. But I had a good team of people in operations by that time, and I didn't want him to screw it up. One of the ways I trained him was when we were in type training I would come into Lynnhaven Roads, drop the hook. I was living in Virginia Beach, and I'd leave him out on the ship. I had good experience amongst the department heads operationally. I'd leave him there and go home for the night if the operations permitted it, and then the poor guy would stay up all night long, he was worried about it so.

One night we had a pretty strong breeze up there, and when I got back the next morning a couple of the officers were laughing about how this guy had a very sensitive ear to the wind, because he put everybody on station to get the ship under way. It wasn't that bad, but he was apprehensive and concerned. But gradually he learned, and eventually we ended up in the shipyard at the start of the overhaul in the fall of 1954. We were there through until probably sometime in January and went on to Gitmo.

Paul Stillwell: This was at the Norfolk Naval Shipyard?

Admiral Burke: Yes. I had talked to some destroyer skippers earlier. They were very apprehensive about how nasty Gitmo Training Group could be to somebody coming out of the shipyard, so I had been very apprehensive. When I went to the Ellison I had enough time to get checked out on how to be a destroyer captain before I took my ship into refresher training. So when we were in the shipyard I arranged to get TAD for my department heads and sent them down there for a week at a time during the shipyard overhaul to look over Gitmo, ride the ships, see how they were doing and see what was expected of them.* We worked our butt off on getting our paper work up to date, and so when we finally got to Gitmo, I'd say passing was 75. They gave us a 74, and I remember going up to see the head training officer, whose name was Murphy, who was a friend of our commodore. He told me that we were in such good shape that we really didn't need to go through refresher training.

Paul Stillwell: Then why did he give you a 74?

Admiral Burke: Well, I think that was just an automatic flunk, just to make sure they could improve us.

---

* TAD—temporary additional duty.

Paul Stillwell: That's their game plan typically.

Admiral Burke: Well, it was a good experience for all of us, and I don't know whether he was a captain or a commander, but our commodore called him "Murph." He gave me a good counseling session on things that I could be doing. He said, "One of the things that people screw up on around here is the gunfire support exercise. We have to keep the target area manned. We've got communications, and all you have to do is when you go out in the morning run through the exercise and if you feel like it when you come back in the afternoon reverse course and do the same thing. When you get around to firing for the record when you leave here, you'll find that you'll be up to speed, and it'll be something that you are used to doing." So we did it. So just because we got a 4.0 in the graduation exercise that's how we did it. We did a lot of things like that when we were there, but in the battle for the E competition, you couldn't get credit at Gitmo. You had to be away from Gitmo. So on the way home I managed to get our ship scheduled to go by Culebra and fire it, and so we did quite well.

Paul Stillwell: I'll bet you were right up to speed then.

Admiral Burke: Yes.

Paul Stillwell: That remedied the deficiency from the year earlier.

Admiral Burke: That was the year earlier, but I'd say I knew how to play the game by that time. I missed terribly my previous exec, Ed Cummings, but I was getting the new exec trained in, just as I'd been trained myself. Operationally he never was up to what I would like to have had.

At some point we got ourselves in an advanced ASW exercise, and there was our squadron. I think there were eight ships, versus three submarines of ComSubRon 6 in Norfolk. Each of these submarines had eight Mark 14 expendable torpedoes that they were going to fire at us in a graduation exercise. Our squadron had been in ASW hunter-killer groups, so we thought we were pretty good. Also some of us had just come through Gitmo. The exercise was run by the submarine people because they wanted to prove how good they were in shooting live torpedoes, and these torpedoes were expendables. We would line up usually abreast and come through an area that these submarines were deployed, and they would attack us.

Now, on Monday, Tuesday, Wednesday they were rehearsal runs, and then on Thursday afternoon or Friday morning, I can't remember which it was, we had the real McCoy. The exercise op order instructions said that if we sighted a submarine periscope, we, the destroyers, could run that periscope down. At that point in time, as a former submarine officer, I didn't think I could run down a periscope. So for the first two or three days that we were out there operating, the submarine crews were making attacks, and they were calling us on the underwater telephone and saying, "Bang, you're dead." In many cases we hadn't even made any kind of a contact, and we, the destroyer people, were getting madder and madder.

Finally we got to the graduation exercise, and it didn't work out in the graduation exercise the way they had it in the rehearsals. The first guy that got in on a destroyer fired and missed. That started a general melee, and eventually Ellison picked up a submarine on sonar. Now, each of these submarines had their own division or squadron commander aboard, so they were being intensively looked at by their bosses. Before long Ellison got on top of a submarine, and in order to prevent him coming to the surface I just stopped my inboard screw and tightened up my circles. So I was passing over him about every two minutes, and I was simulating attacks on him so we had essentially written him off as dead. But, of course, he still had his torpedoes, and he hadn't fired. But he had to get up, and all of a sudden somebody spotted a periscope less than 100 yards off my starboard bow, and my instinct was to run him down. I did stop, but it was too late. I hit him.

Paul Stillwell: What submarine was that?

Admiral Burke: It was the Jallao. Somewhere in my records I have a picture of the Jallao's sail. When we went to Guantanamo, we were fortunate to get an outstanding in damage control, which practically no one ever got. We had a fine damage control team, and my damage control got an outstanding down there, and they were commended by the training group for it, those lads were. So, yes, we took some water, but they got it turned off. We had a hole in the bottom. They called off the exercise, and we headed back home. I finally got back to Norfolk. I guess it must have been Thursday night around midnight, and Admiral Frost, the flotilla commander, was on the dock.[*] He met me on the dock, and he supported me to the hilt throughout the entire effort. It was interesting, because the way the different services were organized, Pat Gray, my Naval Academy classmate, was at the time on SubLant's staff.[†]

Paul Stillwell: And he was a lawyer.

Admiral Burke: He was an attorney, and they sent him down right away to represent Jim Mercer, the captain of the Jallao.[‡] Nothing like that happened in the destroyer side of it, but Pat Gray showed up and they had a formal investigation, which was a real learning experience. I don't think you've ever lived until you've been at the green table.[§]

The flag secretary on DesFlot 4 was another classmate, Harvey Seim, and I went over and talked to Harvey about it.[**] Harvey found Wynne Stevens, who was a destroyer captain.[††] I'm not sure whether he still was, but he recently had been, and he was an attorney, so he represented me. We went through a formal investigation, and it was a tough experience to go through this, to ask all the dirty questions they've got to ask. One of the things behind it—I'm sure—is that I was not the most popular captain that ever came down the pike. I wasn't a glad hander, but we had a good ship and a lot of pride.

Stevens and Pat Gray were working this thing so that nobody was going to get hurt. As it turned out, eventually I had to make a statement. I know that when I made my statement I wanted to lay the cards on the table. That's just the way I felt about it, and I did so. Stevens and Pat Gray came over and gave me hell for incriminating myself,

---

[*] Rear Admiral Laurence H. Frost, USN.
[†] Commander Louis Patrick Gray, USN. Years later, in the Nixon administration, Gray was director of the Federal Bureau of Investigation.
[‡] Commander James Mercer, USN.
[§] "Green table" is a slang term for a Navy investigation in the wake of a mishap. By tradition it is conducted at a table covered by a green tablecloth.
[**] Commander Harvey B. Seim, USN.
[††] Commander Wynne A. Stevens, USN.

because I had said that I had not backed down full. I felt that the op order gave me the right to do what I did. I know that I felt that I didn't want it covered up that I hadn't backed down full at the time other people thought I should have.

Anyhow, we all got off, and it was called an operational hazard that had been recognized that might happen in the op order. We eventually got in the shipyard to be repaired. We went over to Newport News.* It's the only time I've ever been there for shipyard repair, and I was very much impressed the way they did it.

Then we went back to sea with another hunter-killer group, and we had a port visit in New York. Entered port and came up past Staten Island at about 7:00 o'clock in the morning, I guess. We were in a line, and the admiral had us running at about 250 to 300 yards between ships. We were blocking the ferries going from Staten Island over to the other side in the river, and one of the ferries tried to penetrate our line. We were causing people to be late going to work, and he chose to go in right on my bow. We almost had a collision, but we got rid of it. Then we anchored up in the North River up around 75th to 80th Street.†

We were there for the weekend and were told that we were going to get under way at a certain time. My wife's sister and her family lived up in Connecticut, so I went up there for the weekend. When I came back and got to my ship, I found that my commodore had decided to get us under way an hour early. When I got there, my ship was still where it was supposed to be, but the commodore was on the flagship and was next door to me. I had to go over and catch hell for getting back a half an hour early or something like that. Apparently he had decided he wanted to impress the task force commander and be down the river before underway time. I was in the commodore's bad graces. Shortly thereafter I got relieved.‡

Paul Stillwell: Who was the commodore?

---

* Newport News Shipbuilding and Dry Dock Company, Newport News, Virginia.
† North River was a name then in use for the lower end of the Hudson on the west side of Manhattan.
‡ Commander Maurice E. Wall, USN, commanded the Harold J. Ellison from July 1955 to July 1957.

Admiral Burke: Don Wilber was then, and he was an entirely different personality from the first guy, Captain Skivvies Chamberlain.* I had learned my lesson up in New London when I tangled with my boss. Stay clear and try to calm things down. That was a great learning experience, and so I got transferred and then a couple of months. Later I heard that the Ellison got the E for the year, which didn't surprise me.

Paul Stillwell: Especially since you'd gotten that gunfire support in.

Admiral Burke: I was gone by that time. After I left the ship I went up to CinCLantFlt staff. I had a month's leave and reported in, and then I was in the plans division.

Paul Stillwell: Well, let me ask you one question about that. You mentioned that when you talked to Captain Semmes, one of the options was to get a fast attack boat for a year compared with the destroyer. In retrospect are you glad that you did what you did?

Admiral Burke: Well, let me tell you. I'd forgotten this. Around Christmastime of '54 we were in port, and one day Len Erb out of the class of '42, who had been in my submarine class, walked aboard.† He called on me, and I said, "What are you doing here?" I hadn't seen Len for years.

He said, "I'm your relief."

I said, "What? I'm not ready to be relieved."

He said, "I'm sorry. You're it." So I went over and talked to my commodore, and he couldn't do anything. Then I went over and talked to Admiral Frost, who was a terrific guy. And I went over and called up B. J. Semmes, who by that time was the readiness officer at ComDesLant and told him that this guy was aboard and so forth. I reminded him he had told me I could have it for two years and gave him a gas pain, but he said, "I'll see what I can do." So he got Len sent to another ship, and then I went out and had the collision. But I must say that having the experience of going through the green table was an experience that helped me in the long run.

---

* Captain Donald T. Wilber, USN. Captain Leonard C. Chamberlain, USN.
† Commander Leonard Erb, USN.

Paul Stillwell: How do you mean that?

Admiral Burke: Well, it's like when I was on the general court-martial board when the <u>Flying Fish</u> had a grounding. You see the questions, and they make you go back and reexamine what you should be doing and how exacting you've got to be.

I'd say pretty generally by the time I got in that collision and went through the green table and so forth, the investigation, and saw how it operated, I think I was pretty well satisfied that I was handling myself and doing the job the way I should have been. The longer I was in the Navy and got more responsible jobs, the more I came to realize, and not enough people think this way, you've got to be ready for public examination, and you've got to conduct yourself this way. It's like an honor system. It was a helpful experience to remind me that you had to do these things, to insist that your officers did these things this way so that you would protect your ship and protect your responsibility. Yes, it was a burden to go through it. Then the thing had to be reviewed, and I probably got a couple of whacks along the way, but it got written off, and professionally I don't think Mercer got hurt. He may have been, but I don't think he did.

Paul Stillwell: Well, let me come back to my question again. Were you glad that you got the destroyer for two years versus one year in a fast attack submarine?

Admiral Burke: Yes. Oh, there's no question about it. I didn't want to move my family. We'd just moved. Been there a year, and I didn't want to turn around and go up to New London and then come back again. I wasn't anti submarine force, but I felt that at that it was in my best interest to have a destroyer for two years and make the team.

Paul Stillwell: Well, it broadened you professionally. No question.

Admiral Burke: Yes. I wasn't thinking at that stage of the game that I might end up being an admiral, although it's the first time anybody ever put the idea into my head. It was B. J. Semmes, and he told me if I kept going and watched the kind of duty I had and was careful about it, I had a good chance. Well, that was too far away, but I was trying to get breadth of experience.

What it takes you away from the submarine community in New London is a club, and we had friends up there. When I was up there as captain of the <u>Sablefish</u>, all I was thinking about was, "Gee, I'd like to go up there and get duty in the Submarine School or SubLant staff and stay here for another couple of years or three years and then get a submarine division right in New London. It would have been marvelous for my family, and we would have been amongst friends, and it wouldn't have expanded my horizons at all. So I'd say from the way the system picked me up and took me out of there from a professional point, it was much better.

Paul Stillwell: Then you went to CinCLantFlt.

Admiral Burke: I started off in the plans division. I was a peon in the strategic plans. I was in a desk which had to do with command relations, 511 Bravo. My immediate boss, was George Pittard, and I don't think I ever came across a more knowledgeable staff officer than George Pittard.[*] He had worked in OP-60 in plans, command relations. For the first time I began to read files and discovered that we were involved with NATO and the British. There were all kinds of records in there telling how difficult the British were to get along with, and for the first time in my life I began to look at things in a different horizon.

Paul Stillwell: What qualities in Pittard did you admire as far as being a staff officer?

Admiral Burke: He was thorough, hard working. I've never seen anybody work any harder, and he had the experience in OP-60, where he had worked for Admiral Arleigh Burke, I think, up in that arena.[†] He just had a depth and sense of commitment.

When I got to CinCLantFlt, this was the first time I'd been on duty around

---

[*] Captain George F. Pittard, USN.
[†] Admiral Arleigh A. Burke, USN, served as Chief of Naval Operations from 17 August 1955 to 1 August 1961. His oral history is in the Naval Institute collection.

aviators, and the chief of staff was Admiral Bob Pirie.* He was then a two star. I don't think he'd been an admiral very long. The head of the plans division was an aviator; the head of ops was an aviator. There were all kinds of aviators around in key jobs and all kinds of destroyer people around.

Walt Small, who had been the exec of the <u>Flying Fish</u> when I first went there, was a commander then, and he was in operational planning. But all the submariners were safely out of sight and in lower jobs. In my particular shop, 51, was Willard Laughon.† He was a section head, and then under him was George Pittard, and then under George we had about four action officers. I was one, Charlie Young out the class of '42 was in there.‡ I was just sort of mumbling along, hadn't been aboard more than two weeks or three weeks, when I got picked for a special assignment which was interesting. I was curious.

There was a captain who was the atomic energy strategic planner in the plans division, Jim Gray, who was an aviator.§ Aviators were the only people in the Navy at that time in the atomic business, and he was apparently a fair-haired boy on the staff. He had two other aviators with him, and the recent selection board for admiral, which were mostly class of '27 vintage, may have been some '28ers in there, they had just been selected. They had their annual charm school in Washington, and then they sent them down to CinCLantFlt, where they were given about a four-day tour down there. Admiral Pirie had Jim Gray as the project officer, and Charlie Young and I were assistants. I was curious to know how the hell I got picked out by Admiral Pirie. I didn't think anything about it at that time, but he told me later that he had been in Washington maybe on a selection board or something, and he had seen my record.

So that time was the first time I'd ever been thrown around admirals. Jim Gray had probably just made captain, but he knew how to operate around these guys, and he was good on his feet. I didn't get to be buddies with these admirals in four days, but just being around them and hearing them talk was an experience.

---

* Rear Admiral Robert B. Pirie, USN, whose oral history is in the Naval Institute collection.
† Commander Willard R. Laughon, USN.
‡ Commander Charles M. Young, USN.
§ Captain James S. Gray, USN.

Shortly thereafter I got picked for something else. Jim Gray again was put at the head of the detail. I don't know whether he called me up, but he said that Pirie had put me on this project, and I think Charlie Young was also on it, and he was a submariner too. He was Cassin Young's son.*

Paul Stillwell: Yes, and he had had the Redfin before that.

Admiral Burke: Yes, he was somebody I'd known as a midshipman. I don't think I've seen him since CinCLantFlt duty, but I knew him fairly well as a midshipman, and we got along fine. But it turned out that there was a proposal being made by Martin-Marietta. At that time Martin was all in the Baltimore area.

Paul Stillwell: That was still just Martin at that point.

Admiral Burke: Yes. There was a proposal where they were trying to develop a jet seaplane.

Paul Stillwell: P6M Seamaster.†

Admiral Burke: Yes. You know all about that.

Paul Stillwell: Didn't work too well.

Admiral Burke: Well, we were put together as a team to try to present it to CinCLantFlt. Maybe to OpNav. This was one of the few times I've ever gotten up against Beltway

---

* Commander Cassin M. Young, USN, received the Medal of Honor for his heroism as the commanding officer of the repair ship Vestal (AR-4) at Pearl Harbor in December 1941. As a captain he was killed in November 1942 while serving as commanding officer of the cruiser San Francisco (CA-38) during the Battle of Guadalcanal. His son, Charles M. Young, was in the Naval Academy class of 1942, two years behind Burke.

† The Martin P6M Seamaster was a swept-wing seaplane powered by four J-71 engines. It was designed for mine laying and reconnaissance flights. It made its first flight in July 1955. Plagued by technical problems and competing priorities, the plane was limited to prototypes. It never went into production or fleet service.

banditry, but gradually I could see the way the thing was perking.* I don't know whether it was dreamt up in OpNav on the aviation side or whether it was dreamt up in Martin, but when you looked and saw who the players were on both sides, they were buddies and it made me suspicious. We were on this special team of presentation, and Jim Gray was the guy who did it.

Paul Stillwell: Was he for it?

Admiral Burke: Oh, sure. He was also selling Jim Gray, but he was good on his feet and he was close to Admiral Pirie, and I'd say I was just doing some of the legwork. I've forgotten now what the concept was.

Paul Stillwell: These planes were supposed to haul troops, weren't they.

Admiral Burke: No, the idea, they were looking for special weapons delivery, and there would be a submarine tender at an advanced base. You'd have a submarine that would go and refuel this guy, who would fly maybe from the United States out to halfway to his target or two-thirds of the way there. He would land and get fueled by the submarine and then go on, and that was the reason that Charlie Young and I probably were involved in it. They were probably going to have a submarine tender.

Well, the thing eventually died of its own weight, but it was a learning experience for me to see these different players who formerly had been naval aviators who were now working for Martin. They were all on a first-name basis, and I don't whether they had been paid and had a contract, but they had a big study on how this was going to be executed. Well, that came off probably early fall of '55, and then I was just in a driving squad from Virginia Beach. There were about four of us that went to the CinCLantFlt compound. We would get to work about 8:00 and leave about 5:00 o'clock.

---

* "Beltway bandits" is a nickname for consultants that work for the Department of Defense. The name comes from their office locations near the Capital Beltway that surrounds Washington, D.C.

Paul Stillwell: Why would that be a CinCLant thing, as opposed to, say, BuAer?*

Admiral Burke: Well, I don't know. I don't know the politics of it, but I was just involved in normal staff projects that involved command relations. Once or twice I went up and talked to people in OP-60 to learn more about what I was supposed to be doing. It was all a learning experience. Then sometime right after Christmas, I called in one day and Willard Laughon said, "Something marvelous has happened to you. This is great. You're going to go up to the front office. You've been asked for by Pirie by name. You better go up there and call on him."

It was at that time, I guess, that Pirie was getting transferred to a carrier, and his job was being upgraded to three stars and given a double title as Deputy CinCLantFlt and chief of staff.† So he was being replaced by Cat Brown, who came in with three stars and was chief of staff and deputy.‡ Then there was a deputy chief of staff, who was Charles Melson.§ So I went up and they had an office for me there. I was the administrative assistant to the chief of staff. That was my title. Actually most of the work I did was for the deputy chief of staff.

Cat Brown was there for five months, and I'd say in no time at all I was invited into the flag mess. CinCLant was Jerauld Wright, and he rarely showed up for lunch.** The department heads were there, plus Bill Keating, a classmate who was flag secretary.†† I don't recall whether the flag lieutenants were in there or not. I don't think they were. So that gave me quite good exposure, just listening to what was going on. How things were operating. How the politics of it or how things were done. I was in that job for about probably from about February or end of January for the next almost 18 months.

Paul Stillwell: What examples do you remember of the politics or how things were run?

---

* BuAer—Bureau of Aeronautics.
† Rear Admiral Pirie commanded Carrier Division Six from March 1956 to July 1957.
‡ Vice Admiral Charles R. Brown, USN.
§ Rear Admiral Charles L. Melson, USN. The oral history of Melson, who retired as a vice admiral, is in the Naval Institute collection.
** Admiral Jerauld Wright, USN, served as Supreme Allied Commander Atlantic, Commander in Chief Atlantic Command, and Commander in Chief Atlantic Fleet from 12 April 1954 to 28 February 1960.
†† Commander William J. Keating, USN.

Admiral Burke: Well, I was working for Melson, who was a cruiser-destroyer sailor. First thing I had to do was get me another car, because I was on different hours from everybody else. I'd have to get to work about no later than a quarter of eight, probably 7:30, and brief all the messages in the line of key stuff for him and for the chief of staff.

Melson did not have a flag lieutenant, and so I in effect became an administrative assistant to Melson, and he would task me for certain things to do. We also had all these JCS papers that had to be briefed, and I'd never seen a JCS paper.* I didn't know what they were, and Cat Brown, bless him, sat down with me one day and showed me how to underline the important issues. And so when I say brief, normally what I would do is just underline the stuff that they had to read, and that's the way I read papers today. When I read a paper I can the read the front page of the Wall Street Journal or the Washington Post or the Washington Times in just no time at all, but I just read the key sentences and go on. I did that for a year and a half intensely. What else?

Paul Stillwell: Well, please tell me about the personalities of Brown and Melson. You said before that you really admired Melson.

Admiral Burke: Well, I do. He taught me a lot. Was he easy to work for? Not particularly, because Jerauld Wright was up there, and he was a tough individual. My only association with Jerauld Wright before I got there was when I was a first classman and he was the battalion officer. He was the duty officer one night, and when he left the main office to inspect my battalion I met him there, saluted him, and I thought smartly. I accompanied him while he was around, and later on I found out he'd turned in an unsat fitness report on me. [Laughter]

Paul Stillwell: What was he like when you were at CinCLant?

Admiral Burke: At CinCLant I have never ever seen anybody sharper. We had all kinds of problems that I was able to sit in the arena when he would come in, sometimes when

---

* JCS—Joint Chiefs of Staff.

there would debates amongst flag officers. I remember doing this at least a half a dozen times, and there would be different opinions on how to approach the problem and to solve it. He would sit over there and not say anything during all the debate. And then he would get up and in a very few short words say, "This is what's going to be done," and he was always right. He would have these pithy sentences, and he would say, "This is the apple." He could define what the object was better than anybody I've seen on what had to be done, and I had great admiration for the man.

Paul Stillwell: So a great analytical mind.

Admiral Burke: Oh, yes. And, of course, he was in the job, as I recall, for six years. He was a towering figure for my money, and I think there was a certain amount of awe and fear. I don't know whether there was or not, but he was a hard man to stand up to. When I was down in the plans division at 511-B I had to write some things. I drafted a couple of letters that eventually got up to him and they came back to me with X's in red ink and gave me a couple of short lines on what to say. Then every time I gave it back to him he'd sign it in a minute. [Laughter]

Paul Stillwell: Do you have any examples of his ability to figure out the problem and the solution?

Admiral Burke: I can't, but I just remember in things like ASW or whatever, there were always opinions on how we ought to address a problem and where we ought to put our resources. And, of course, the aviators think they know best, the submariners best and the destroyer people, and you've got these conflicts. He seemed better able to pull it all together than any person I've been close to, and I wasn't that close to him. On the other hand, my office was directly under his flag lieutenant, Peter Belin, and I used to write personal mail for him.* When I got to work for Admiral Melson, I used to write some of his personal mail, but I rarely got a chance to see him or speak to him.

---

* Captain Peter Belin, USN, was an intelligence specialist.

Paul Stillwell: What was Melson's working style like?

Admiral Burke: Well, when I first went up there, the aviation community were really running that staff. Admiral Wright was spending at least half his time with SACLant, and so the guy who was running the thing was the chief of staff, and they were sort of settling into it with this new three-star job.* Well, Cat Brown came in, and he was only there for five months and then went off to be Sixth Fleet. But Melson was the continuity, and I think he was tense. But I watched him in a lot of things that we did, and he taught me something that I've never forgotten, and I still use it today. When you're getting ready to put out a new policy or a new directive, call the people that are going to be affected and see how they go along with this. Now, he had a classmate, Caldwell, who was the chief of staff of AirLant.† And Admiral Melson would call Admiral Caldwell or the cruiser people or whatever, but he wasn't that close to the submariners. I had a submarine pin on, and I don't know that he didn't trust me, but the submariners just weren't up in the front office, I mean in rank.

Paul Stillwell: And the man who had picked you was gone—Pirie.

Admiral Burke: Pirie was gone, but that didn't bother me. But Cat Brown was a hell of a nice guy, and then we got up to around first of May or middle of April, and I was wandering along. All of a sudden it turned out there was a NATO conference in Paris, and Jerauld Wright said he wanted to send all of his flag officers over to this NATO conference. I don't know how many, but there were at least 15. But he didn't want a bunch of satchel aides going along with them. Cat Brown was going, and I think he was the only three-star in the group, so Admiral Melson worked it out that I would be sort of the tour guide or the administrator. So I had to manage the plane, which was easily made available, and get in contact with all these contacts that were going. There were some 15 of them. I can remember some of them. Wellborn, who was Com2ndFlt.‡ I forget what

---

* SACLant—Wright's NATO command title was Strategic Allied Commander Atlantic.
† Rear Admiral Henry H. Caldwell, USN.
‡ Vice Admiral Charles Wellborn, Jr., USN, commanded the Second Fleet from June 1955 to July 1957. His oral history is in the Naval Institute collection.

Chief Masterson was; of all the group he was better personally organized than all of them put together.* I've always been impressed the way he handled himself in getting ready and what he was going to do when he got over there.

They were a fine bunch of men, each one of them. We left in a Navy transport plane and flew from Norfolk. I think we landed first in Argentia, and then we flew from Argentia over to Ireland in Shannon. Arrived in Ireland about 6:00 o'clock in the morning, and somebody came up and offered us some Irish coffees, first time I've had it. We had all these flag officers wandering around the terminal there, and this American civilian came up and asked me, said, "What are all these admirals doing here? Is something wrong?"

I was a bit evasive, because he sort of caught me by surprise. Finally the guy said, "Damn it. My name's Bill Hearst. I demand to know what's going on here."† And then he stormed off before I could answer.

We went on into Paris and stayed in a very nice hotel that wasn't too far from the Arch. We were in Paris for about five, probably five, six days, and the conference was out at the NATO headquarters. I got to sit in on some of them. Some of them I was excluded, but Field Marshal Montgomery was the host.‡ He was the deputy to Norstad at the time.§ Norstad was the commander and, my gosh, I don't think he was quite yet 50.** He was a young man when he made general officer. But the guy who was running the show was Montgomery, and I've never seen quite such an ego in my life.

These various sessions went on, and I say as I best remember I got to attend about half of them and they were talking about grand strategy, et cetera. Then at night we did a little bit of Paris night clubbing. Also had a chance to visit the Louvre and other places around town. I was impressed with the fact that people weren't tooting horns at each other in all their traffic, and apparently there was a very heavy fine. They behaved themselves, and it had an effect on the traffic and how they drove. I remember that

---

* Captain Kleber S. Masterson, USN. The oral history of Masterson, who retired as a vice admiral, is in the Naval Institute collection.
† William R. Hearst, Jr., was publisher of the New York Journal-American.
‡ Field Marshal Sir Bernard Law Montgomery (1887-1976) was a controversial British Army officer who had played a substantial role in World War II.
§ General Lauris Norstad, USAF, served as NATO's Supreme Allied Commander Europe from 1956 to 1962.
** Norstad was born 24 March 1907, so he was 49 at the time.

Admiral Pirie arrived. He was relatively junior, and he came separately and brought his flag lieutenant with him and went back separately commercially and ended up in New York, presumably because that's where his carrier division was.

Paul Stillwell: Why do you have such a smile when you talk about Admiral Pirie there?

Admiral Burke: Well, he was trying to beat the system. He came up to me just before we were leaving and asked me if I would take back some whiskey for him. I said I'd be glad to, but I'd like to see that he had a bill of sale in case I got challenged, and he was affronted. But if we got tagged, I did not want to have to pay the price.

Paul Stillwell: Which is understandable.

Admiral Burke: One of the things we did, one night Admiral Pirie and Admiral Brown and I and two or three others went to a French nightclub. Admiral Pirie had had duty over there and knew a lot of the people around town. There was a stripper there, and he had finagled the stripper after she was completely stripped to come over and grab Admiral Cat Brown and take him out on the floor and dance with him.

Paul Stillwell: How did Brown react to that?

Admiral Burke: Oh, he was horrified. This was so far and away from his behavior. Admiral Brown was the kind of guy that read the Bible every night, and Admiral Pirie pulled this on him unexpectedly. [Laughter]

Paul Stillwell: I take it he was embarrassed by it.

Admiral Burke: Oh, yes. He got red as a beet, but he was a good sport about it.

Paul Stillwell: What can you say about Admiral Brown in general and working with him?

Admiral Burke: I found him to be a very compassionate, gentle person. I didn't know him that well, but I found him easy to talk to. He was not the least vindictive on a personal basis. I would like to have seen more of him, but I'd say the way we were operating there and so forth he came from other duty to CinCLantFlt, and I think the purpose was just to get him into the "what's going in the fleet," and then he went off to Com6thFlt.*

Paul Stillwell: And did an excellent job during the Suez crisis that fall.

Admiral Burke: I was working more with Admiral Melson than I was with him, but I'd say everything I saw about Admiral Brown I admired and liked.

Paul Stillwell: You were mentioning a story when the tape wasn't running about the reenlistment situation in the Atlantic Fleet. If you could discuss that please.

Admiral Burke: As I best remember, the reenlistment rates in the fleet at that time were about 7%, and people were constantly worried about what are we doing about it and trying to tell us to put on more pressure. The basic problem was when you sat up there where I was and saw the exercises that were being cranked on and laid on on top of exercises those ships weren't in port. Bill Keating, who was a classmate, was the flag secretary, and we saw a lot of each other because we had mutual responsibilities. We sat down one day and took out the CinCLantFlt current op order and added up the operations for each type, such as a carrier, such as a destroyer, such as a cruiser or amphibs or service force ships. If you were a married man on a carrier in the Atlantic Fleet and standing a watch in three you could expect to be in your home port on liberty with your family not more than 18 days a year. And I think the destroyer force, it ran up to about 25 to 28. The cruisers were perhaps about the same or a little better, and the service force and amphibs similar kinds of problems. I think that the submariners were the ones that got the most time in port. They were around 45 days.

---

* Vice Admiral Brown commanded the Sixth Fleet from August 1956 to 30 September 1958.

So we put this in a memo and said, "If you want to do something about reenlistment, you'd better take a look at this and do something about it so that the people can have a reasonable life." I signed the memo and put it on Admiral Melson's desk one day when he was at lunch. When he came back, he was in shock, but it got the message across. Unfortunately, nothing happened, and I think it was just the culture in the Navy at that time. The way you got readiness was by sending people to sea and keeping them there. It took many, many years before they got unwound, but I see right now evidence that we're going back to that, because we don't have enough ships.

Paul Stillwell: Right. We have maybe a third of the ships we had back then or just a little more. What were some of the issues that passed through the front office during those years that you were there?

Admiral Burke: Oh, brother. The submarines were beginning to generate more political clout. As I best remember, we were getting into the business of nuclear missiles in submarines. Up to that time the aviators had a lock on the nuclear weapon delivery. The submarine Regulus program was evolving.* That was one issue that I saw a bit of. Reenlistments were always there. We were struggling with ASW. I remember Admiral Wright was constantly frustrated because the Russians were patrolling in the Atlantic, and our ASW was so ineffective that we could not force any of them to the surface. Admiral Wright offered a case of whiskey to the first captain who could bring one up. I don't know whether he ever had to pay off or not, but he would have been glad to. I believe from a readiness point of view from where I sat that was a significant issue.

Politically I saw evidence of the struggle between England, which had diminished power following World War II and not wanting to give up the command responsibilities and the Americans pressing forward to do it. In parts of our Navy certain people felt very strongly that we needed to push harder.

---

* Two Regulus missiles were designed to be fired from surface ships or surfaced submarines. Regulus I, which entered the fleet in 1952, was 34 feet long, weighed 12,000 pounds, and had a speed of Mach 0.9 and range of 500 miles; Regulus II, which had its first flight test in 1958, was 57 feet long, weighed 22,000 pounds, and had a speed of Mach 2.0 and range of 1,000 miles.

Paul Stillwell: Do you remember any reaction in Norfolk to the Suez Canal Crisis in late '56?[*]

Admiral Burke: Well, I was there. Cat Brown was over there at that time.

Paul Stillwell: He was Com6thFlt, yes.

Admiral Burke: Yes. My memory of that right now is rather dim, but we weren't directly involved in it so I just don't remember.

Paul Stillwell: Another thing you were mentioning at lunch is that after he left Admiral Goldthwaite came in and had a flag lieutenant whom he found attractive.

Admiral Burke: I think McFall was his flag lieutenant.[†] Admiral Goldthwaite came in and relieved Cat Brown.[‡] McFall and I just clicked. His wife was out of town, so he came out to the house a few times, and he clicked with my family equally as well.

Paul Stillwell: What qualities did you find appealing in him?

Admiral Burke: Well, he was just a first class gentleman, and professionally he was superb. At that point in time we had one son, and we were beginning to think in terms of prep school because the constant moving was causing him to have academic problems. Dodge was encouraging me to send our son to the same prep school that he had gone to, St. Andrew's in Delaware, and ultimately we did that. But I'd say we just seemed to have the same principles of everyday life, and he was a superb flag lieutenant. He was an aviator and had had good aviation duty. We just hit it off.

---

[*] On 26 July 1956 President Gamal Nasser of Egypt announced that his country was nationalizing the Suez Canal Company. Israeli forces invaded Egypt's Sinai Peninsula on 29 October 1956. Britain and France then intervened militarily on behalf of Israel in an unsuccessful attempt to secure the Suez Canal, which was damaged and closed to traffic. Rather than support the British and French, the United States asked for a United Nations resolution to end the fighting. A cease-fire took effect on 6 November.
[†] Lieutenant Albert Dodge McFall, USN.
[‡] Vice Admiral Robert Goldthwaite, USN.

Paul Stillwell: Do you remember any issues about the retirement of the battleships along around that era?

Admiral Burke: No, I don't have any recall of that.

Paul Stillwell: The Forrestal got commissioned, and so the big-deck carriers were coming into the fleet.

Admiral Burke: We lived in Virginia Beach in the Bay Colony area amongst aviators. Fred Turner, for example, lived right across a little lane next door to us, and his son and our son were about the same age.[*] Peter Aurand lived next door.[†] Pierre Charbonnet was Fred Turner's squadron commander.[‡] I think Alan Shepard may have lived over in what we called the Pea Patch, which was about a half a mile away as the crow flies.[§] I didn't know him at the time. There were all kinds of aviators in the area that we lived, but they were on a different circuit. Most of them were based at Oceana, and I was, of course, based in Norfolk and so on a professional basis we didn't bump into them.[**] Fred Turner did come to CinCLantFlt, and I did ride with him for a while, and I certainly highly respected him.

Paul Stillwell: What recollections do you have of Aurand?

Admiral Burke: I would say he's an intellectual. He played his cards close. I didn't see a lot of him, because he was on a different track than I was. I forget how long they lived next door to us. There were about three different families that lived there during the four years that we were in that house next door. As I recall, he was Eisenhower's aide wasn't he?[††] He relieved Beach.

---

[*] Lieutenant Commander Frederick Turner, USN.
[†] Commander Evan P. Aurand, USN.
[‡] Commander Pierre N. Charbonnet, Jr., USN.
[§] Lieutenant Commander Alan B. Shepard, USN, who in 1961 became the first U.S. astronaut in space.
[**] Oceana Naval Air Station in Virginia Beach.
[††] As a captain, Aurand served as presidential naval aide from February 1957 to January 1961.

Paul Stillwell: Right.

Admiral Burke: But he was a smart guy, and he had good ideas about things he thought the Navy ought to do. He was not afraid to push them, and I respected him for it.

Paul Stillwell: Well, he was an innovator too. I think he had one of the first jet squadrons, if not the first, in the fleet. I had hoped to get his oral history, but he never responded and then he died not too long after I had asked him.

Admiral Burke: There was an aviator who lived across the street there for a while named Bossom. He had a son same age as my son, and he was the exec of a squadron, and he was killed on a Med deployment. These things happened every now and then in my neighborhood.

Paul Stillwell: Yes. Anything else from that tour of duty that you want to put on the record?

Admiral Burke: I think that it was a growing period for me in that it exposed me to a lot of different parts of the Navy and Navy thinking that I'd never been exposed to. When I was living in Virginia Beach I was always in a driving squad. Until I worked in the front office at CinCLant, when I was in the driving squad in destroyers. That saved my life because my buddies in the driving squad were other destroyer skippers. In one case it was a division commander, Kenny West.[*] Others were Ben Blee, who had been a destroyer skipper, and Mark Woods, and we used to share our experiences. I can remember many times hearing somebody having a problem, and as soon as I got aboard ship I would call my exec and say, "Check into this," and he'd wonder where I got this perception from.

Paul Stillwell: Well, how did they save your life?

---

[*] Commander Kenneth M. West, USN.

Admiral Burke: Well, they would cause me to find things before they got too far along. I don't remember any one in particular, but it happened that way.

Paul Stillwell: Well, Blee was another alumnus from the battleship North Carolina. What recollections do you have of him?

Admiral Burke: I didn't know him on the North Carolina. I met him when I was in PCO School in Key West, and he had married a girl who was from Virginia Beach, Martha. Martha's parents lived about, oh, less than a half a mile from where we lived, and so we got to be social friends by living in the same community. It was a very friendly social community, and people our age and younger gathered every weekend at somebody's house, and that's how I got to know him. Before long we were driving together. He was an intelligence specialist or graduate, and he ended up by relieving Peter Belin as Jerauld Wright's flag lieutenant. He's been a good friend, and I'm still in touch with him.

Paul Stillwell: Well, you went from there to the Naval War College. Please tell me about that experience.

Admiral Burke: Well, as I was finishing CinCLantFlt duty. I figured that it was time for me to get a submarine division if I was high enough on the list. I checked, and I was, but they told me that the policies had changed, that if I had had a destroyer command I wouldn't get a submarine division command because they were equated to each other. Did I qualify for it? Yes. Well, I wasn't very happy about this, and I didn't want to go to Newport, but it turned out for me to be a very good year off.

We went up there and lived in the city, and it was interesting to participate with the student body—I mean, meeting these people. I had a roommate who was an Army officer and another one who was an aviator and so forth. Early in the fall we got into seminar groups where we studied world history, and we went around various parts of the world. I was assigned a project to give a one-hour dissertation on the Mid-East. The subject was "Is Islam a Bar Against Communism?" I'd never been there, and I still haven't been there, but I'm an expert.

Paul Stillwell: Vicariously.

Admiral Burke: It was for me a very interesting experience because it was then an explosive time. I can't remember whether we had an Arab-Israeli War when we were there, but most likely we did.

Paul Stillwell: Well, there was one in '56 which was shortly before.

Admiral Burke: Yes. But in any case when I did this study for this dissertation the librarians provided me with all the books I had to read and so forth. I went into this thing on the side of the Israelis and came out on the side of the Arabs, and it's always affected a lot of my thinking about the way things were. Essentially there were no Jews in the Holy Land from around 70 A.D. until 1915 when the Balfour Declaration, and then gradually the British opened it to get the Zionist Movement on their side. Then they opened the spigot gradually, and when World War II started there were maybe 75,000 Jews in that area. Today we probably have several million, largely because the United States has been the sponsor. Well, if you think in terms of the Caucasians have been in America since about 1600 and if the Russians had won the Cold War and turned this United States back over to the Indians we'd be pretty unhappy too. That sort of has colored a lot of my thinking about that area ever since.

We had one particular student whom I rated the outstanding officer; his name was Hazeltine.[*] I was in a driving squad with him. He was an Army officer out of the class of '40 at West Point, and he obviously had been a golden boy. If he wasn't the First Captain he was pretty close to it. He'd commanded a battalion in Burma and been on Mountbatten's staff for a while, and he'd been a special assistant to Omar Bradley when he was the Chairman.[†] He knew all the right people and he'd done all kinds of things. When he was working for General Bradley he had had to do studies on nuclear submarines. He knew more about nuclear submarining from a strategic point of view

---

[*] Lieutenant Colonel Charles B. Hazeltine, Jr., USA, who stood ninth in the West Point class of 1940.
[†] General of the Army Omar N. Bradley, USA, served as Chairman of the Joint Chiefs of Staff from 16 August 1949 to 14 August 1953.

than almost anybody I'd met up to that time, and he was a really impressive person. Yet he did not make general officer.

Paul Stillwell: Do you have any explanation?

Admiral Burke: I think he was too aggressive. I've met people around his vintage. Nobody has acknowledged that's been the reason, but that's my impression. He lives in the area. I've seen him a few times, maybe four or five times in the last 20 years, but it really surprised me when he didn't make it. There were others there that made flag rank in the Navy. I don't think I got any surprises, but that was the one surprise that I got.

Paul Stillwell: In what ways was that year helpful to you professionally?

Admiral Burke: Well, I think everybody needs to step back. We did some manufacturing of plans. That didn't help me. I'd already learned how to do that at CinCLantFlt staff. I knew how to put plans together, but I did a lot of professional reading. We had to write a term paper, and mine was about the civilian-military relationship in the United States. My paper wasn't any good, but it caused me to read about people. This was just before the liberals really got into high gear in the Vietnam era, and it gave me an appreciation of what was happening on the college campuses or what happened later on. I did a fair amount of reading. There were books in the library on the subject which I was surprised to find out about. At the end we had the global strategy session, and there were some big cheeses from business there. We were in seminar groups, and it was interesting and a learning experience to rub elbows and talk with these people on some of the problems they dealt with.

Stuart Ingersoll was the president of the war college, and Charlie Lyman was the chief of staff.[*] I can remember one day we were having a lecture or a presentation from a group from OpNav, probably OP-60, on strategic planning. All the students were gathered, and all of a sudden the back door of this room opened and Ingersoll stormed in

---

[*] Vice Admiral Stuart H. Ingersoll, USN, served as president of the Naval War College from 13 August 1957 to 30 June 1960. Rear Admiral Charles H. Lyman, USN.

in a rage, got up on the platform and took over from the speaker and pointed a finger at the student body and said, "The next goddamn guy that opens his mouth to the press without my permission is going to be hanged." Then he stormed off and said a few other golden words that were equally as impressive.

Well, we didn't know what the hell he was talking about, and we were kind of embarrassed because we had Air Force and Army people and Marines in the class. There had been a revolution in Venezuela the day before, and the guy who ended up on top had been a student at the Naval War College foreign officers' course the year or so before and had lived out in town somewhere. His next-door neighbor, who was a naval officer, was interviewed by or called on the telephone by one of the New York papers to find out what about him, and so he told him.

Admiral Lyman was a genuinely warm person. I don't know whether you've ever interviewed him or not.

Paul Stillwell: No.

Admiral Burke: But a real gentleman and somehow or other we knew something about the Lymans. They had a reception for the students and they were neighbors of a sister-in-law's family here in Alexandria at one time. I will never forget when Betty and I were out on the Ocean Drive one Sunday afternoon, with our youngest child who got to the point she couldn't wait to go the bathroom. So we just told her to go behind a bush there and go, and while she was going Admiral and Mrs. Lyman walked up on us. That was our personal introduction.

Paul Stillwell: I gather he had a good sense of humor.

Admiral Burke: Yes. But somewhere along the line he had a heart attack, and I think that yanked his bell and held him back, but he was a really fine gentleman.

Paul Stillwell: Did you have distinguished visitors who would come in and speak to the student body?

Admiral Burke: We did, and I don't have any in mind. Oh, let me go back to this discussion group, seminar group. Dennis Wilkinson was in mine, and although I'd met him before, this was the first time I got to sit down across the table and talk with him. He was an impressive person and smart as a whip. While we were at the war college, Sputnik went up, and, of course, the whole world changed.* Everybody was nervous and jumpy and so forth. Dennis was transferred back to OpNav, and that's when the decision was made to accelerate the Polaris submarine program.† He went on back, and so we didn't see him anymore. We had a couple of other officers. I remember Jim Osborn.

Paul Stillwell: He was the first skipper of the George Washington.‡

Admiral Burke: Yes. Well, he was in our class too. I don't think he went back early, but Dennis did, and there may have been some others.

Paul Stillwell: Any examples of what impressed you about Wilkinson?

Admiral Burke: He's got a mind like a trap. He was good at asking questions, but I never saw him ask a question that he didn't know the answer to. I think it was his way of evaluating the people that he was with. I was not personally that close to him, but I was in his seminar group and I saw him operate. I don't recall when he left, but I know I was keenly disappointed when he left, because I felt like I had been on the way to form a relationship with him.

Paul Stillwell: Did he have that same dumb country-boy approach that you had seen earlier?

---

* On 4 October 1957, the Soviet Union launched Sputnik I, the first artificial earth satellite. It caused great uproar in the United States, which had expected to be first in space.
† Polaris was the name for the U.S. Navy's first submarine-launched ballistic missile, which became operational in the early 1960s. Its more-capable follow-on was the Poseidon missile, which entered the fleet in 1970.
‡ When the ballistic missile submarine George Washington (SSBN-598) was commissioned on 30 December 1959, Commander James B. Osborn, USN, was commanding officer of the blue crew, and Commander John L. From, Jr., USN, was commanding officer of the gold crew.

Admiral Burke: Well, it was more sophisticated.

Paul Stillwell: Did you have war games at the war college?

Admiral Burke: Yes, we had a war game eventually, and this is one of the things that particularly impressed me about my Army friend, Hazy Hazeltine. He played Mr. Bad Guy, and he was really good. I guess he had been involved in things like this, so it was old hat to him, but he was first class in that.

Paul Stillwell: What kind of scenario did you use?

Admiral Burke: I just don't recall; look, this is 40 years ago.

Paul Stillwell: I'm amazed by the stuff you come up with. I'll keep asking.

Admiral Burke: That's intellectual.

Paul Stillwell: Well, you were talking about the idea of teaching planning, which you'd already had. Were there other areas of the course work that were useful to you?

Admiral Burke: Well, it helped me a lot to brush up against these people. For example there were foreign officers there. We'd meet them in the bowling league. That seemed totally inconsequential to me at the time. I couldn't figure out why these guys were there because they were all googy [phonetic]. I mean, they had never bowled this kind of bowling before and we had Japanese there, we had South Americans, we had some European.

Well, when I got to Japan in 1970, which was 12 years later, I called on the Chairman of the Joint Chiefs, and we had been classmates at the Naval War College. The CNO had been to the Naval War College, also, and though I didn't know him at the time but the Chairman, Admiral Itaya, claimed to have remembered me. I didn't remember him, but he claimed to remember me and that we were in Japan classmates, people who go to school the same year are considered classmates. They tend to be loyal to their classmates or whatever, they are family. It helped.

Paul Stillwell: So did that give you a bond with him when you got over there?

Admiral Burke: Yes. I never took advantage of it but, I mean, I knew I had a friend. I don't recall how long he stayed there but my principal contact in Japan was always their CNO.

Paul Stillwell: What do you remember about Henry Eccles, the great guru of logistics?[*]

Admiral Burke: Gee, I'd forgotten all about him. I was impressed with him, and I remember I had some idea, and I can't remember what the idea was, but I remember going and talking to him about whatever that idea was, and he encouraged me to develop it as something that deserved development.

Paul Stillwell: Well, you probably had not had too much exposure to logistics at that point, had you?

Admiral Burke: No. I'm not a logistician, and I've heard people say, and I think they're right, that logistics wins the war. But I was never motivated to get in that side of it. It was only when I got ordered to ComServLant that I really got into it to my eyeballs.

Paul Stillwell: Any other courses that you studied? Anything in the political arena? Geopolitical?

Admiral Burke: No. I think I'm a more of a people contact person. I played golf one day, and somebody brought his buddy along. His name was Alan Shepard. He was a

---

[*] Upon retirement from active duty in 1952, Rear Admiral Henry E. Eccles, USN, began a 25-year second career as head of the logistics department of the Naval War College; he was a prolific author.

lieutenant commander in the junior course. He was a nice guy, and we had a nice foursome over at the Newport Country Club. I was a golfer when I was a youngster and I didn't get to play again really until I got to the War College and I played several times and probably with Larry Heyworth, Jim Holloway's brother-in-law, but I remember playing with him and enjoyed it.* I may have played a second time, and the next time I asked about Shepard he had been transferred in the middle of the year to go off with something called space. I'd say there were different people that entered my life that have made a difference up there.

Here's something else. Let's go back to my destroyer tour where I did well, but I wore my submarine pin. I don't recall that we were in uniform at the war college. I think we wore civilian clothes. After I'd been up there a while I heard that ComDesLant, whose flagship was down at the waterfront in Newport, had held a gathering of all the destroyer skippers in the war college class. Well, I wasn't invited. I think B. J. Semmes was gone, or I would have gone over and needled him a bit about it, because I figured he was a friend. I forget the name of the guy who had relieved him, but he had been on the <u>West Virginia</u> and was a fair-haired fire control officer and eventually made admiral, but he was the guy. He was one of these destroyer people that hated submariners, and that cult pervaded the Navy and the destroyer Navy for a long time. I'd be curious to know how it is now, but I'll tell you later of a confrontation that I had.

Paul Stillwell: I suspect there are very few people in the Navy today who have commanded both a destroyer and a submarine.

Admiral Burke: Well, I don't think you'll find anybody in the Navy that has the breadth of different kinds of commands that I've had. The way it's structured and the technology to learn all that you have in your ships now, it's very hard to do it. It's a different ball game.

Paul Stillwell: How much did you learn about naval aviation and its role during that year?

---

* Commander Lawrence Heyworth, Jr.; Admiral James L. Holloway III, USN was CNO, 1974-78.

Admiral Burke: I don't think I learned too much. I mean, we had people that came up and addressed this; I remember we had LeMay came up and talked to people.* I remember Jerauld Wright came up. Generally speaking naval officers at that point in time were lousy speakers. Jerauld Wright, however, had a script in front of him, and he knocked a home run because he had been a CinC for about five or six years at that point in time. He knew his job and he knew how to articulate it, but naval officers in those days as a group were very poor speakers.

I'm glad this came up because over the years after I took my Dale Carnegie Course when I went up to New London and eventually got <u>Sablefish</u> one of the chaplains on the base had a speech class in the evening once a week maybe, and I got involved in it just to keep going. Back when Eisenhower first came in, the <u>Williamsburg</u> was down in the Norfolk shipyard, and I knew I was getting command. I was concerned that I was going to be thrust in the public arena and that I wouldn't be able to handle it well enough. So I went up and talked to the chaplain in the shipyard, and he gave me two tips. One, he said, "You want to read the Sermon on the Mount. That has all of the vowels and syllables that you need to be able to public speak. The second thing is you want to get yourself a recorder [they were wire recorders then] and read into it, practice read into it. When you're going to make a speech, write it out and give it, then play it back so you'll get used to it." So I did that, and it was an enormous help.

I got up to the war college, and they had a speech class up there at night that was voluntary, and I participated in it. There were a couple of Air Force people. The aviators generally were far better speakers on their feet than the non-aviators. The reason I came to conclude was that you have to be able to brief your gang before they go fly, and they learn this at a very young age. The Marines seemed to be able to do it, too, but I don't know when the Navy has started or if they have started teaching their people how to speak. But I was working on it all through those years and felt that it wasn't until I got to

---

* General Curtis E. LeMay, USAF, served as Commander in Chief of the Strategic Air Command from 19 October 1948 to 30 June 1957. He was a lieutenant general until 29 October 1951. The original title was Commanding General, changed to Commander in June 1953 and changed to Commander in Chief in April 1955.

be a flag officer that I was comfortable. I didn't get completely comfortable, I guess, until I got in the reserve business, where I was like a politician.

Paul Stillwell: Ceremonial a lot of times.

Admiral Burke: Yes. But it caused me to work at it, and eventually when I had situations that came up I got good enough so that sometimes people would come around and give me a pat on the back. I know from other things I've done that if you work hard enough, you can usually manage to cope and then eventually do damn well.

Paul Stillwell: Well, when you get to the point beyond comfort and actually enjoying it, then you've really achieved something.

Admiral Burke: Then you don't know when to shut up.

Paul Stillwell: Well, I don't know how much you've got to say on your submarine division time. Do you think we can fit that in in the next 30-40 minutes?

Admiral Burke: Yes.

Paul Stillwell: All right. Well, you said that you had been disappointed not getting a division before. How did that come about?

Admiral Burke: Okay. Here's what happened. When I was in Norfolk before, at CinCLantFlt, I went up and talked to Ebby Bell, who was the submarine detailer.* He said I couldn't have it. Explained why. Then I got up to war college, and he called me up one day and he said, "Hey, we've changed the rules. You can have a submarine division if you want it."

---

* Commander C. Edwin Bell, Jr., USN.

I said, "Are you kidding?" I didn't believe him. But I'd cussed him out, called him four-letter words and everything I was so furious. I couldn't believe that he would be so compassionate as to call me up after the way I'd talked to him.

Paul Stillwell: That's a generous man.

Admiral Burke: Apparently what had happened was they had upgraded the squadron commander of a submarine to being a major command. It had not been up to that, and they upgraded the division command to be same thing as equivalent to a destroyer division, and so I said, "Let me think about it," and I said, "What division are you talking about?"

He said, "ComSubDiv 63."

I said, "What do they do?"

"It's a Regulus division." I didn't know anything about missiles. I'm the least technical guy in the Navy in the submarine force. So after a while I called back. I probably thought it over and said, "Okay."

"You're going to relieve Charlie Styer," whose father was Admiral Styer, who had formerly been ComSubLant.* Before long Charlie called me up on the phone. He was in Norfolk, and he said, "This division is going to deploy to Puerto Rico."

"Why?"

"Well, the Regulus missiles. There's a missile range down there, and that's where they can shoot the missiles and recover them and so forth, and the set-up down there is much better. We're going down there to look it over, and we want you to go down with us." So this was probably in May, and I was finishing up about the first of July, so I was given at least a week. I went down and joined Charlie and a bunch of people, and we went down to San Juan. The concept was there were six submarines in the division. Most submarine divisions had four. Two of the six carried missiles, and the other four had the ability to guide. Each of these four guiding submarines had a radar that would lock onto a missile and steer it.

---

* Commander Charles W. Styer, Jr., USN.

Paul Stillwell: So this is essentially terminal guidance.

Admiral Burke: Yes. The idea was that the guidance submarine would get in off the beach. The missile would launch it from maybe a couple of hundred miles out, steer it in, and then the guidance guy would pick it up and steer it in and drop it in over the target. There was a GMU, a guided missile group, and this was a logistics outfit that prepared the missiles, got them ready to shoot, and so forth. These were missile technicians; the groups were various sizes that probably had 75 to 100 people. Then there was a guided missile squadron or something like that.

There were chase planes that when they would fire one in practice would go out and pick it up and bring it back and land it. We didn't own the chase planes, but they had to work very closely with us. The only reason they probably wouldn't give them to us was we were submariners. They were aviators, and AirLant probably wouldn't let them go, but we worked very closely together. So we went down to Roosey Roads.* It was kind of primitive but fascinating, because Roosey Roads had been an alternate headquarters underground for the British Navy when they were getting ready to be chased out of England in World War II.

Paul Stillwell: I did not know that.

Admiral Burke: There were caves in the mountain down there and so forth at Roosey Roads, and it wasn't very well developed. It was really out in the boonies, but we got set up there. As I say, we were doing all the planning, and then when I left the war college we went to Norfolk. Virginia Beach was home for our kids down there, and so we rented a cottage for about two months in Virginia Beach. I relieved command in Norfolk, and all of this had been arranged before I got there. A troop transport came in, made a stop in Norfolk, and we loaded all our families aboard, Betty and the kids. We went down there, and all the troops went down there on their submarines and the families went down on the

---

* U.S. Naval Station Roosevelt Roads is located at the eastern edge of Puerto Rico. Its land mass consists of 31,000 acres: 8,600 acres on the island of Puerto Rico and 22,400 acres on Vieques Island, seven and one half miles southeast of the main station. The facility was completed in 1943, and Roosevelt Roads was commissioned as a U.S. Naval Operations Base. It has served as both a training facility and base for Navy ships and aircraft since Word War II.

transport. We just sailed right alongside, and when we went into port the families in the transport went in ahead of us. The trouble we had there was that the local people, I think it was particularly the chief of staff, resisted giving us support as we deserved.

Paul Stillwell: Was this Com Ten?

Admiral Burke: Com Ten. The chief of staff was a submariner named Ramsbotham.* The admiral was an aviator, Dan Gallery.† We were there for a year, and it was a real adventure. The base had organized to meet us. The captain of the station, who was named Chamberlain, was from South Carolina and a very nice guy. But they put our officers—the commanding officers of the ships, maybe the execs, and me—in a sort of a barracks kind of apartment complex. It was over near the Carib Hilton in a section of the naval station, but it was away from the naval station. These were really junior officers' quarters. There were spaces there on the main base where there were lots of adequate quarters, but they didn't give them to me at the start. But I kept my mouth shut because they didn't have quarters for our enlisted men. I had some staff officers there who really got to work and found military housing that was not being used, forced them to give it to our people. I didn't go after anything myself until I made sure all these other people were taken care of. Eventually they offered to let me move on the base around Christmas or right after.

Paul Stillwell: Did you have any contact with Admiral Gallery yourself?

Admiral Burke: Oh, not much. He was sort of remote. The one that I had the most contact with was Rammy Ramsbotham. He was from the class of '29. I'd known Ramsbotham and his wife before. They had lived in Stonington right down the street from us when we were there right after World War II. We had known them socially there. I never served with him before.

---

* Captain Robert S. Ramsbotham, USN.
† Rear Admiral Daniel V. Gallery, Jr., USN, served from 1956 to 1960 as Commandant of the Tenth Naval District and Commander Caribbean Sea Frontier. In 1957 he gained an additional title as Commander Antilles Defense Command.

There was a fairly strong Navy League there. The driving force in the Navy League was a Puerto Rican named Frank Crocco, and he worked for the Barker Dry Dock Company that was right next door to us. One of our concerns was that when we had to get shipyard support, that we'd have to go back to the States because we didn't have a submarine tender down there. So eventually we got them certified to dry-dock a submarine, and there were at least one that was dry-docked there while I was there.

It was a fascinating experience for me because it's hard to believe that San Juan is 100 years older than Jamestown, Virginia. There are two or three of the edifices there in town still being lived in that were built to take care of Ponce de Leon and/or his daughter. It took us a period of time to shake down, but we got our people into Roosey Roads, the guided missile unit, and then we had to begin training. We had two submarines, the <u>Runner</u> and the <u>Argonaut</u>, that were homeported in San Juan. The other four submarines were still homeported back in Norfolk, but they would come down and operate with us in rotation.

Paul Stillwell: So you had only the crews of two submarines and the staff to accommodate in Puerto Rico for housing.

Admiral Burke: Yes. Well, let's see. Roosey Roads was about 50 miles down the road, so they were remote and that gang of people lived down there on the base. But in San Juan we had my own a reinforced submarine division staff too. I had an ops officer and a couple of people in ops, one in admin and one in logistics plus some yeomen.

Paul Stillwell: And a chief staff officer?

Admiral Burke: No, not really. My ops officer essentially. He was a lieutenant commander.

Paul Stillwell: Did you have a missile officer?

Admiral Burke: Not on the staff, but one of my officers was checked out for it. Now, the actual missile submarines, the Barbero and the Growler, were homeported in Norfolk. The Barbero was a World War II submarine that had been adapted, and then I think the Growler, which came along later, was a fairly new one. It was cut in two and expanded a bit to be able to take this.

The missiles were carried in tanks on deck and had to be pushed out on deck and launched like an aircraft. They were nothing more than a pilotless aircraft. My guess it took at least a couple of minutes to get one of those missiles in the air, and it was a very cumbersome operation. About three or four months after we were down there, around Christmas time or maybe January, our program in the Atlantic was cancelled. We did some firing, but much of it wasn't particularly satisfying. It did give me a chance to do a lot of the things that a commander has to do. I was still a division commander.

We used the Air Force missile target. They had a target on the edge of San Juan, and so we used to have planes that belonged to the missile squadron. It was a guided missile squadron that was moved from over here on the Eastern Shore down to Roosey Roads. We would steer those planes like we would steer a missile. In order for us to do that, I had to go out to Ramey Air Force Base, which was one of the bomber bases. I called on the general officer who was a West Point classmate of mine—he was a brigadier—and to get his permission for us to use it.* They were a bit apprehensive and suspicious that the Navy had missiles that were going to use their training target. So eventually he said he would like to have his ops officer come out. The following week we were out off of Ramey, and his ops officer came out on a helicopter and watched us steer over the target and use it, and so thereafter we regularly used it. During the winter ComSubLant, who was Freddie Warder, came down for a Springboard visit.†

Paul Stillwell: Now, this would be the winter of '58 & '59 probably.

Admiral Burke: Yes. And Admiral Warder brought several of his staff members. He also had a submarine tender down there for the duration of Springboard. There were

---

* He graduated from the Military Academy the same year Burke graduated from the Naval Academy.
† Rear Admiral Frederick B. Warder, USN, served as Commander Submarine Force Atlantic Fleet from 24 September 1957 to 13 January 1960

several submarines brought down from up north, so one of the things that happened was when I took him out to Ramey to meet the Air Force commander out there, we got off the plane and were met by the general. As we walked past an open hanger, we noticed that there was a very sleek looking plane with long wings and very small body. Admiral Warder asked the general, "What's that plane?"

The general said, "Admiral, that plane is so secret that they don't even tell me anything about it." Sometime shortly thereafter Gary Powers was shot down over Russia, and that was the plane that we were looking at.[*]

Paul Stillwell: So that was the U-2.

Admiral Burke: Yes.

Paul Stillwell: How effective were the missiles when you used them in the tests?

Admiral Burke: It was cumbersome. We participated in several exercises with fleet units, but we didn't fire them then. We would only fire them when we were out in a very structured situation. When you launched it, you had to have a plane coming in overhead about the time of the launch and chase it and pick it up and bring it back to the airfield. Before Freddie Warder came down there to the demonstration shot we had several successful shots. He came to view it, and the missile went in the drink right in front of him, so we weren't very happy.

Paul Stillwell: This was still the Regulus I, wasn't it?

Admiral Burke: This was the Regulus I. While we were down there, the Regulus II was just about ready. I think it was the Growler that came down and was supposed to be

---

[*] On 5 May 1960 Soviet Premier Nikita Khrushchev announced that Soviet forces had shot down a high-flying American U-2 reconnaissance plane on 1 May near the city of Sverdlovsk in the Ural Mountains. The American pilot, Francis Gary Powers, was tried for espionage and sentenced to ten years' confinement. He was later returned to the United States in exchange for a Soviet spy. On 16 May, 1960, because the United States refused to apologize for the overflight of Soviet territory, the Soviets cancelled their planned participation in a multinational summit conference and withdrew a previous invitation for President Eisenhower to visit the Soviet Union.

getting ready to take the Regulus II. But then our program was cancelled, and immediately we began to lose some of our key people that were being transferred to the West Coast because that's where they were putting what was left of the Regulus program.

Going back to the politics, in the business of getting people transferred down there or different units down to support our operation, I got a fair amount of resistance at the fleet or AirLant level moving onto that air station at Roosey Roads. I can't remember the details of it. The minute our program was cancelled, they started sending their own people down there right and left after they had told us there wasn't room. In my opinion, they were fearful of the missile program as being conflicting with their objectives, and I sensed that.

Paul Stillwell: Well, the thing that was really the undoing of Regulus was the need to fund Polaris.

Admiral Burke: I didn't disagree with that decision to cancel Regulus, but I'd say I was struggling with just getting our group organized. At the time I didn't know that Polaris was in the cards when we went down there. It was a wonderful year. It was a great adventure for my family to go down there, and we loved it.

Paul Stillwell: Well, please tell me about the family life.

Admiral Burke: We hadn't been around long before we met a woman whose family was in Norfolk. Her husband had gone down there years before because of the tax breaks in business, and they had set themselves up a glove factory or something like that. We had mutual friends back in the Norfolk area, and before long we got to be good friends and their children were the same age as our children, and they introduced us to some of their friends. The Pattersons were the names of the people that I'm talking about, and they lived in a suburb of San Juan. They expanded some of our social contacts with their friends.

San Juan had a mayor, Dona Felisa Rincón de Gautier, and she was sort of a female edition of Franklin Roosevelt.* At the time, I guess, she was pushing 50. I think she may still be alive. She was somebody that enjoyed enormous popularity with the Puerto Ricans. When we first got down there, I took my skipper, and we made an office call on her just to let her know we were in town, and shortly thereafter we received an invitation. There was a convention of beauticians, and she wanted me and my staff and my commanding officers to show up to help entertain all these beauticians. So I let them know that we had wives in town, and it would be inappropriate, so we got to take our wives. They weren't much wanted, but it gave them a chance to attend this event, which I believe was held in the city hall. The mayor lived in an apartment in the top of the city hall, and so Betty got to know her. We would see her at some of the official parties that either the naval station or Com Ten had. Dan Gallery had converted his band to a steel band. Have you ever heard about this?

Paul Stillwell: Yes.

Admiral Burke: Well, they used to play all the time, and we all got to be steel band fans. I forget the dance they did, but all these young people did it. The steel band played over at the club all the time, and it was a general joyful occasion to have them around. Dan Gallery had a big reception on New Year's Day, and Christmas is a real religious occasion in the Catholic countries. They don't do the celebrating of presents and all that sort of thing and partying until Three Kings' Day, which is the 12th day after Christmas. And they're all talking about what are we going to do on 12th Night, and so Betty spoke to the mayor at the New Year's reception asked her where we could see Three Kings' Day celebrated. She said, "Well, come with me."

Well, Betty came back and said, "She's invited us."

I said, "She doesn't realize we've got three children and your mother and my mother here." So I called up her apartment. This was over the Christmas period, and she was on holiday. Her sister, who was down from New York, answered the phone and I said, "Dona Felisa invited us to accompany her on Three Kings' Day or invited my wife

---

* Felisa Rincón de Gautier was the dynamic mayor of San Juan from 1946 to 1968.

and me. I want to let you know that if she wants to withdraw the invitation fine because we have this big party."

She said, "Oh, no indeed. Bring them."

Paul Stillwell: The more the merrier.

Admiral Burke: And she said, "Just be there at the city hall at 5:00 o'clock in the morning. It was either 5:00 or 5:30 and she got the age and sex of each child. Well, we got to the city hall, and there were a couple of limousines out front plus a pickup truck. We fell in behind the pickup truck, and we walked into the foyer there in the city hall, and it was just an office building. She lived on the top floor, and there were a couple or three Puerto Ricans there with big hats, had guitars, and they were just sort of strumming like so. We waited there, and after about ten minutes she arrived. She had a tray of coffee with her and cups and served us all coffee. Her husband was with her, and she had an appropriate present for each child. I remember she had a baseball uniform for my son, who was about 12 at the time. She had a tin horn for my mother and one for my mother-in-law. They were pushing 70, I guess, at the time.

Then she said, "Just follow me." So we got behind the truck where the guitar players rode, and the truck had an announcing system on it. We started through San Juan and first went to the cathedral. And what was happening was she was going around her constituency, and there was a service going on in the cathedral. By this time it was 5:30 or quarter of 6:00. She went into the cathedral for a while. We didn't go in, but she did. And then she came out, and then we got back in and we went up to the Candado Beach section, which is just beyond the Carib Hilton. It was the Chevy Chase of San Juan.[*] She pulled up in front of a couple of very large houses.

Then she told my mother and Dottylo, Betty's mother, "Now I want you to go up." We went up, and she had a horn herself, and they were holding reveille on these friends. One of these friends finally woke up, came out, and she had them get their own car and get in the line. We had a couple of more stops and did the same thing, and then eventually we worked our way out to the edge of town.

---

[*] Chevy Chase, Maryland, is a ritzy suburb of Washington, D.C.

We left the highway and went up a horrible road and got to where we couldn't go any further and we stopped. We were on the top of a small hill, and there was a big party going on in a small pavilion and it was a Three-Kings' Day party. Dance, food, orchestra and it was a large shed, almost like a barn, but there were nice-looking people there and they were well dressed, having a good time. By this time it was getting daylight. We were looking over the ocean, which was miles away, and there was a great big picture window there without any glass in it and people were eating, oh, fried chicken and things like that and throwing the remnants out the window. There was a great enormous hog that was staked there, and that was the garbage disposal.

Paul Stillwell: Well, the climate's okay not to have a window.

Admiral Burke: Well, we kept on going, and, as I say, we stopped at a number of places. Her family's been there so long, and she was stopping at relatives and friends. Around 11:00 o'clock we arrived at a town that was beyond and south of Roosey Roads. It was a good-sized city or a town, and we pulled up in front of a house and it belonged to her niece and her husband, who had a child. They were having a christening party, and it's a big party there. I remember when we walked in you sort of go into an atrium, it was that kind of a house, and somebody came out with a plate of what looked like hors d'oeuvres we'd never seen before and offered them to us. We took them and started to take a bite and somebody said, "What is this?"

They said, "Blood sausage." Have you ever heard of blood sausage?

Paul Stillwell: I've heard of it. I don't know what it is.

Admiral Burke: Well, the kids immediately disappeared. They found a dog there and Mother and Dottylo just sat there. They were afraid to touch it. I don't remember whether I ate it or not, but the Catholic priest was there, and eventually the parents disappeared with the child. There was a Catholic priest present, and he refused to have these non-Catholics participate in the baptism, and so they went off and baptized the child and Dona Felisa, who had come down there just for the baptism, wasn't included and, oh, she was upset.

Paul Stillwell: Was she not Catholic?

Admiral Burke: Yes, sure, she was but, in effect, I guess we were intruders. The priest was the problem.

Paul Stillwell: She had shown the poor judgment of bringing you heathens.

Admiral Burke: Yes. We hung around for about two or three hours, and then we were so exhausted we went home. She was still going strong and was very disappointed that we had to go home to another engagement. We just had burnt out.

You know, at the beginning of each school year, the teachers ask you to write about the most interesting thing during the summer. Well, that was the subject that our children used the rest of their lives in school.

Paul Stillwell: Did you get out and ride your submarines much?

Admiral Burke: Yes, I rode them frequently. I did something that I'd never seen done before. I can't remember the size of my staff, but I had four people, while most sub divisions did not have more than one. I began to give each boat what I called a free operational readiness inspection. I had qualified submarine officers in command that were in my guided missile group, so I used them, too, so I gave all these boats what I called a free ORI as a training vehicle.

Paul Stillwell: Well, training is a traditional function of the divcom.

Admiral Burke: Yes, and it was very helpful. In one case, however, one boat did so poorly that ultimately I got the CO relieved. I just didn't think he had a firm enough hand.

I was able to pull it off by getting him relieved after one year, but the boat did not have firm command control.

I had another incident where the XO of one of the boats went into St. Thomas, and the XO had too much to drink, and he got into a squabble. It wasn't a fistfight, but he was not popular amongst his chiefs and so they had quite a row, open row, after they got back to the ship. It was so bad that the captain was really upset about it, and I insisted that we unload him. It's too bad, because that guy had been on the West Virginia when I was a boot ensign, and he was one of the students that I had taught in preparation to go the Naval Academy Prep School.

Paul Stillwell: He was an enlisted man then, I take it.

Admiral Burke: He was an enlisted man, and at this point he had just made lieutenant commander. He was trained in missiles. He was a sharp guy, but he had drunk too much and got into a nasty, almost a fistfight with his chiefs.

Paul Stillwell: Who were some of the skippers you remember from that division?

Admiral Burke: Paul Purkrabek had the Runner.[*] I'd rather not name the one that I had replaced. Cal Dew had the Barbero, and he got a new exec on there, who in no time at all turned out to be the best exec we had, and his name was Jim Watkins.[†]

Paul Stillwell: I've heard of him.

Admiral Burke: Interesting thing, he was the youngest exec we had. He had been ashore for I think three years at Postgraduate School. And about the first or second week they came down from Norfolk.

Paul Stillwell: That's all the tape we have, so let's get the rest of the story next time.

---

[*] Lieutenant Commander Paul V. Purkrabek, USN.
[†] Lieutenant Commander Carlos Dew, Jr., USN. Lieutenant James D. Watkins, USN, later became a four-star admiral and served from 1982 to 1986 as Chief of Naval Operations.

Interview Number 7 with Rear Admiral Julian T. Burke, Jr., U.S. Navy (Retired)
Place: Admiral Burke's home in Alexandria, Virginia
Date: Wednesday, 30 April 1997
Interviewer: Paul Stillwell

Paul Stillwell: Admiral, it's a real pleasure to be with you again on this sunny spring morning. The last time we were talking about your experience as a submarine division commander, and I think you also wanted to mention something about your extracurricular activities as it were in Puerto Rico.

Admiral Burke: It's a foreign culture or a Hispanic culture. Puerto Rico is not a state. It's a territory or a commonwealth. If you buy things down there, they're tariff free or frequently tax-free. For example, you could buy liquor, both U.S. and foreign liquors, down there at much, much less than you could in the States. At the officers' club, for example, you could get a fifth of Bacardi rum for 80 cents. I don't know what the going rate is now, but it presented a problem because we were constantly being pressed to help people get liquors aboard their ships to get back into the States without going through customs. We were cautioned by the local command there that there had been some very sad cases where career officers had tried to make a big haul and had been apprehended, and it was a big no-no.

Paul Stillwell: By the local command you mean Com 10?

Admiral Burke: Com 10 and also the naval station commanding officer, who was very helpful and supportive. So all of our people knew this was a no-no to get involved in this. When Exercise Springboard came along, I found that a couple of my staff officers had been designated by my superior to load up liquor. I told them that they did not have to obey the order. Then I went over and told my superior, and he was most unhappy with me. I don't know whether they did or did not, but I told them they did not have to do it. I went up and looked him in the eye and explained why, and he was very unhappy with me.

Paul Stillwell: Was that the base commander or the squadron commander?

Admiral Burke: The squadron commander. But I think this was one of the few times in my life when I had to look a senior in the eye and tell him. It wasn't the last, but it was good training. [Laughter]

Paul Stillwell: That's tough.

Admiral Burke: Well, as a matter of fact, I had a similar experience. It wasn't over liquor. I think I told you when I was in Gitmo when I was captain of a destroyer, when a squadron commander, not my own, wanted me to take his brother, a Catholic priest, from Gitmo back to Kingston. Did I tell you?

Paul Stillwell: I don't remember that one, no.

Admiral Burke: He sent me a message and asked me if I would do it because my ship was going to Kingston. So I sent him a message back and said, "If he qualifies in accordance with the OpNav instruction, I will be very pleased." Well, and then he sent an emissary, and apparently he didn't qualify in accordance with the instruction, because they hadn't got permission, and I wouldn't take him. This gentleman came over and just raised hell with me, but I held my ground and checked out. My boss was in Gitmo, and he supported me, as did the base commander. I didn't take him, and that gentleman later on became the chief of staff of ComDesLant. I don't think it hurt me, but that was an uncomfortable situation.

Paul Stillwell: Understandably.

Admiral Burke: I dealt with the Air Force, because we used their target for training. Also, I think there were a couple of Dutch islands down there where we had some navigational sites on their beach that we were using. Precise navigation was very important to us in launching of these Regulus missiles.

Paul Stillwell: Was there any connection at the time between that and Polaris testing?

Admiral Burke: Not at that time. We were not involved in Polaris.

Paul Stillwell: I wondered if they used the same ranges, for example.

Admiral Burke: If they did, I was not aware of it. My understanding was it was all up at the cape.* But we had a few firings of Regulus down there. About half of them were successful. We had our guided missile group down there, a squadron of planes. I can't remember the squadron commander, but I know he's from Biloxi, Mississippi, and I knew him when he was a plebe. He was the class of '43. They used to chase the missiles, take control of them after they got over the target and then bring them back to Roosey Roads and land them. And we did some demonstrations. We did this a few times to let the Navy League and VIPs in the local areas see it done. They didn't actually see the shooting, but they saw the landing.

Paul Stillwell: So the missiles were sufficiently expensive they wanted to recover them for reuse?

Admiral Burke: Oh, you bet. They were pilotless aircraft and very cumbersome in comparison with what we do now. They were really bow and arrow in comparison with what we have now.

Paul Stillwell: Well, you said that the tests were only 50% successful. What constituted a non-success?

---

* Cape Canaveral, Florida, has been the site of many U.S. missile launchings, including the earliest in the space program in the early 1960s. In November 1963, following the assassination of President John F. Kennedy, it was renamed Cape Kennedy. The name was changed back to Cape Canaveral in 1973 in deference to the wishes of Floridians. It is the site of the John F. Kennedy Space Center.

Admiral Burke: They would go in the drink and a total loss. I can remember that happening twice. The first time it happened ComSubLant was down there, Admiral Warder, and we were giving him a demonstration when it happened. I mentioned his visit last time. He's a fine gentleman.

Paul Stillwell: Any specifics you remember about him?

Admiral Burke: Not really, but he was very supportive. One of the things that I did that I'd learned from Admiral Melson there is to be sure that your bosses know what's going on. I knew this was a big project when I went down there, and I used to send weekly sitreps on how we were doing. I'd been out of submarines for about six years when I got that job, and so there was a whole new team of people in New London, most of whom really didn't know me. So once we left Norfolk I began to send a sitrep, copy to the squadron commander, copy to SubLant.

I had a yeoman—I forget his name—but after we'd done this a while he said, "We need to get a different kind of typewriter that has print that's eye-catching." So I thought he was crazy, but he did it. It was rather small print, but it was sophisticated, and we started banging that out. Then when Admiral Warder came down during Springboard the first thing he said to me, he said, "I really like to see those different sitreps." [Laughter] So I guess it made a point.

Paul Stillwell: Was this an electric typewriter?

Admiral Burke: I don't recall.

Paul Stillwell: They were in their infancy, I think, around then.

Admiral Burke: But it was an interesting lesson. It taught me the importance then of telling your people what you're doing, people who are interested in and you're remote from. Years later when I was in Japan in very difficult negotiations I sent almost weekly reports back to OpNav, and I know it helped.

Paul Stillwell: Going back to these missiles that were unsuccessful, was there a concern about the technical capability, the maintenance, or how did that work out?

Admiral Burke: We had good people. I can't tell you why they went in. Of course, we didn't recover them, so we couldn't find out. But the Polaris was coming down the track, and we hadn't been down there more than about four or five months and our program was cancelled in the Atlantic. Immediately they began to pull our key people and send them to the Pacific, because they kept the Regulus program going a little bit longer in the Pacific. I think it was just plain too cumbersome.

Paul Stillwell: Well, when we finished up the tape during our last interview you were in the midst of a story about an operational readiness inspection and Jim Watkins. Could you pursue that one?

Admiral Burke: We had submariners in the guided missile unit, and I had a staff of about three or four officers in addition to myself. So when the ships were down there I used to give them operational readiness inspections to get them ready for it. When the <u>Barbero</u> came down, she was not homeported down there. She came down from Norfolk. We gave her an operational readiness inspection, and I think this is where I met Jim Watkins, who had been aboard a very short time. He was cool as a cucumber and far and away the best exec that I saw. And he was far and away the youngest.* He was a lieutenant, and most of the other execs were lieutenant commanders.

Paul Stillwell: Any specifics on the ORI itself?

Admiral Burke: Well, no. We fired torpedoes, we did all the exercises and so forth, and we had emergency drills. We had ASW exercises. We could get services locally for that.

---

* Watkins was born in 1927, so he was in his early 30s.

Paul Stillwell: In the general business of rating those who reported to you, the skippers, you had a reputation in BuPers as a tough grader. What was your philosophy on fitness reports?

Admiral Burke: I didn't know that.

Paul Stillwell: Well, I heard it from a detailer.* [Laughter]

Admiral Burke: Well, in a way I'm surprised, but I don't believe in carrying people. I've had a long-time idea. I've seen a lot of fitness reports in my lifetime. I have not been on many selection boards, but I have been on enough boards to see that the real stuff doesn't get in there. I'll give you an example. There was somebody that had done something that was really not right. I can't remember what it was. But years later, after I made admiral, I was on a major command selection board for surface ships, and I saw this guy's record. I don't recall that I knew him, but I heard about whatever he had done. There was hardly a blip in his record for it. Now, he should have been hammered, but nobody wanted to for some reason. I began to think then that you ought to grade the reporting senior on how he evaluates his people. Because if you're counting on somebody who's passed a certain screening and he's been carried, you're in trouble.

Paul Stillwell: And you're doing a disservice to the profession.

Admiral Burke: Well, you're doing a disservice to the country if you carry somebody. If you look at my record, I've spent most of my time at sea or seagoing jobs, and I have a thing about the politicians who come up through the bureaucracies and see people who are somebody's fair-haired boy; they get put on a ship that is loaded with talent. Then they get carried, and they put their minimum time. As soon as that time is up, back to the front corridor they go, and they're doing a great job as an administrative assistant for somebody. Then they get selected for a big job, and they've never been through the mill

---

* This is in the oral history of Admiral Harry D. Train II, USN (Ret.).

on how to deal with people, make judgments. They've been carried. They might be very good administrative assistants or aides and so forth, but they are not tough SOBs.

Paul Stillwell: And the profession is about command at sea.

Admiral Burke: I will admit that I have fired people where others wouldn't, but I think I've saved lives.

Paul Stillwell: As a ship's skipper, you were in contact with the officers on a daily basis. When you were a unit commander, how did you evaluate people on other boats who were not in your physical presence?

Admiral Burke: Well, I'd say the way I dealt with this, I rode every single boat, and I also gave every single boat what I called a pre-ORI before they had an ORI. I can't remember the name of the guy who was my ops officer and a terrific submariner. Snuffy Jackson was the head of the guided missile gang. He and all of his officers were qualified, so I used all these people as my team. Then we sat down and talked about these people, how they were functioning and so forth, how they did it. For example, I can remember the one boat where Snuffy was in the control room and I was in the conning tower. He described to me what happened in the control room, and we were lucky we didn't sink. He saved us, because the exec was just sitting there with his teeth in his mouth and didn't do anything.

Paul Stillwell: And I would think the other thing would be the flow of reports that you get.

Admiral Burke: Oh, yes. You see how people operate. You get your reports from the material people and the personnel people. You go down and you've done all these things. You don't have to look at all of it, but you've done so much of it that you get a feel for how they're functioning. If you look at the kind of business I've been in, I've been judging people all my life.

Paul Stillwell: And the system sort of forced you to do that.

Admiral Burke: And you're forced to evaluate. And you're evaluating your bosses as well as your contemporaries and your subordinates. I haven't been to any school on how to do it, but I just had to do it.

But going back to Puerto Rico, though, I say was dealing with another culture. You had to be careful that you didn't step on the local culture.

Paul Stillwell: And you didn't want to unwittingly offend people.

Admiral Burke: We learned how to deal this it. It was the first time that I had ever lived outside the American culture. It was an interesting experience and told me that you had to find out who you're operating around and living with and deal with it and respect the people in those kinds of situations. At the time Puerto Rico was shipping people up to the United States for jobs, and they were doing their best to get people to come down and develop with new industries, and they were giving them tax breaks. But eventually our program got cut, so we were getting ready, and at the end of one year we were sent back to Norfolk.

Now, when I first went down to Puerto Rico I was on a one-year tour as a division commander. But when I saw the nature of getting settled into Puerto Rico and all of the dealing with the different people, both in the civil side and the military side and also the other services, I felt it was important to get some stability. So I recommended that I be extended an additional year, and it was approved.

Paul Stillwell: So this would just be working with submarines in an attack mode, not the missile mode.

Admiral Burke: Well, you've got to realize that ASW was the prime reason for submarines at that point in time.

Paul Stillwell: And they were part of the hunter-killer groups.

Admiral Burke: Yes. And they were making ASW patrols. The missile submarines were sent back after a year, so I called up the detail officer and told him that we were coming back. I asked him what I'd do at the end of a year, and he said, "Well, it's been approved and I don't want to shake the bush," so I had a second year.

We came back to Norfolk. It's an interesting way we came back. My family came back on a Navy transport. I traveled with them. Took our car aboard. For some reason we got off-loaded up in Narragansett Bay at the Seabee base. It may have been for personal reasons, because sometimes our family used to go up and still do go to Squam Lake in New Hampshire, and maybe it may have been an excuse to visit relatives up in that neighborhood. But we came back to Norfolk, and we moved back to Virginia Beach, settled there, and we had one more year during which time we were exercising. We had lost our missile submarines and some of our guidance submarines.

Paul Stillwell: Did you get different submarines as replacements?

Admiral Burke: We lost the missile submarines, and I think we took on one or two others. We were just doing normal ASW and submarine attack training based in Norfolk. During the spring of 1960 I took three boats, and we went down to Fort Lauderdale on a cruise. I think it was a training exercise, and it took us about two weeks. It took us a week to get down there, and then we were in for a port visit. And then we were supposed to come back.

I rode one of the submarines down, and on the way down we were providing snorkeling targets. We were alternating targets. One target would snorkel through the other two, and the other two would detect, track and attack and then we were just playing leapfrog on the way down. On one of these exercises, where we were getting ready to be the target, we dived. Since we were going to be target, I went up into the wardroom and sat down with my division engineer, and we prepared to snorkel. We were just about ready, and I don't recall whether the word was to commence snorkeling, but all of a sudden we had an emergency surface. Somebody had made a mistake, and the snorkel head valve was locked open. We ducked under and took about 30,000 pounds of water, and we almost lost the boat. We had two engines, two generators that were flooded out.

This was probably around 2:00 P.M., as I best remember, and it took time to get the water out of the engine room. I was waiting for the captain to get himself ready to do something about reporting his casualty, and nothing was happening. I didn't want to take command of the ship. So finally I got my division engineer to prepare a casrep and had it all ready to go. I got hold of the captain and I said, "I've got this message here unless you want to send your own." He didn't want to send it. I said, "All right if you don't send it, I will."

So finally he said, "I'll send one." But he stalled, and it took him about two hours before he would agree. So we got the casrep out. I think it probably took at least six hours before we got it out, and I was very upset about it. Finally we got into port, and while we were there a commodore came down.

Paul Stillwell: By that do you mean a squadron commander?

Admiral Burke: Yes, mine. He came down, and I don't know whether he rode one of the other boats back or not, but I told him. He may have come down to see what happened. I told him that this thing was going to require an investigation. He agreed, and he said, "It looks like you're it."

I said, "Well, I was a passenger."

He said, "It's your turn." We had three division commanders, and the other two were either on investigations or getting ready to come off or whatever.

Paul Stillwell: Given your mindset, you would hardly be impartial in that case.

Admiral Burke: Well, as soon as I heard the emergency surface I got to the control room, so in a sense I was a witness or I felt like I was. And so we had an investigation. I've forgotten the details of the findings, but I could sense in my investigation that I was talking with people, in particular the chiefs, who really didn't trust the captain. They were worried about him. This was just a gut feeling. But, anyhow, I put my recommendations in, and the investigation went to SubLant. Got past the commodore all right.

After a while, the man who was the chief of the watch in the control room when this thing happened retired from the Navy. I was living at Virginia Beach, and one day I was driving home and I was low on gas. I just stopped at a gas station, and it turned out this guy was working there. So we chatted, and so I made a point of just dropping by and getting my gas there because I wanted to help him out. I sensed from the way things had happened that there had been another flooding or something was wrong that hadn't been reported.

Paul Stillwell: You mean prior to the one that you experienced?

Admiral Burke: Yes. I just sort of got this from intuition, talking with the enlisted men. So when I had the captain on the stand I asked him very carefully, had anything ever happened before? "Absolutely not." And so, as we were going along, my investigation got to SubLant. One of the officers on the staff wanted something for some technical reason to be looked into further. It was unimportant, but they sent the investigation back to be reopened. The second time around, well, the captain had a guy in the class of '39 who I knew and liked and respected to be his counsel, but he also got a Navy lawyer. I couldn't understand why he got this help. The exec was the son of either a three- or four-star retired officer or somebody who was just about retiring and was a contemporary of CinCLant's. So there was a certain amount of pressure there. The exec had been in the control room. He hadn't been on top of it either.

I was riding home one day during the reopening of this thing and stopped and got some gas. The ex-chief came over and he said, "Commander, I've been thinking about this." I'd asked him if earlier there'd ever been a prior flooding, and he would give me an evasive answer. This time he told me about when it happened. Sure enough, they'd been in some rough weather about two months before out in the cape area and taken a big slug of water down the conning tower hatch. Some machinery in the pump room was flooded and out of commission. It was in the ship's log, but they hadn't reported it to higher command.

Paul Stillwell: Was it a similar circumstance of not having the snorkel capped?

Admiral Burke: No, no. They just took a slug of water down the hatch, and they grounded much of what they had in the pump room down below, but it hadn't been reported. So I went around and talked to my friend who was his counsel. I guess he was a captain. I said, "I've got this information, and I'm going to ask him again, on the record, under oath." And the CO denied it that he had ever had any problem before. I said, "All you've got to do it lay it on the table." But he refused. So then I broke out the ship's log and laid it on the table and made it part of the record. And I had him fired. I think I had the exec fired too.

Paul Stillwell: Did you call the chief as a witness?

Admiral Burke: Didn't have to. It was in the log.

Paul Stillwell: Which the captain had signed, of course.

Admiral Burke: Yes. That was as tough a thing as I've ever dealt with, because the captain had a son who was married to a daughter of very close friends. He was a Navy junior. I think the exec had had apparently a good record up to that point. He'd had a job in the Pentagon, and people seemed to think he was doing a good job up there as far as I could find out. But I felt badly about it, and I lived with this problem for months and months and months.

Paul Stillwell: But you were given no choice in the matter.

Admiral Burke: Well, I say I just felt the guy had been lying, and he was trying to cover up. If I hadn't have been there, he wouldn't have reported it, I don't think. I had evidence, and he refused to acknowledge that he'd had another flooding just shortly before that and he hadn't reported it. It was in his log.

Several months later I'd been transferred to the Naval Academy, and I was standing on the chapel steps. Now, this was about in late fall of 1960, about five or six months later. I was standing on the chapel steps, and this nice-looking gentleman came up in civilian clothes, and he said, "Captain Burke?"

I said, "Yes, sir."

He said, "I'm So-and-so's father. I just wanted to see you," and turned around and walked off. [Laughter]

Paul Stillwell: The father of the fired skipper?

Admiral Burke: Yes. He was a retired captain. I discovered later he lived in the area here, where we live now, and knew people that I knew. As I say, it was an exceptionally tough thing, but I know that nobody came around and said, "You had to do it." But finally I remember bumping into a couple of people, contemporaries of mine, who knew him from other times. They told me separately that it was time that somebody had lowered the boom on him. But I said, "It was no fun." I know members of his family, and he's got a nephew that's a member of the plebe class who's a real fine young man going places. [Laughter]

Paul Stillwell: Well, being the tightly knit organization that the Navy is, those connections are bound to be coming up.

Admiral Burke: Oh, there was another thing that was unfortunate. In the spring of 1960 there was a group of officers coming from CinCNELM staff, one of whom was Captain Bob Carroll, who was a contemporary.* He had been a division commander, and I think he was in some sort of plans. He and two other officers were coming from CinCNELM to Norfolk, and they were riding a Capitol Airlines plane from Washington to Norfolk. It crashed over very near Newport News and everybody was wiped out. Bob was a good friend. I had a classmate on there, too, whose name I can't remember right now, but I did

---

* CinCNELM—Commander in Chief U.S. Naval Forces Eastern Atlantic and Mediterranean. The headquarters for CinCNELM were in London. Captain Robert M. Carroll, USN.

not know him well. But that wiped out a good chunk of the planning section of CinCNELM's staff.

Then, during the summer, I got word that I was finally going to the Naval Academy, and I found out from the wife of a friend across the street down at Virginia Beach that I was going to be the exec of Bancroft Hall.

Paul Stillwell: Well, you've told me before—and I'm not sure whether the tape recorder was running—all the uncertainty you had for a while on what job you had. Maybe we could cover that to be sure.

Admiral Burke: Admiral Melson was the kind of person that didn't like to tell you something ahead of time.[*] He wrote me when we were in Puerto Rico about a year ahead of time and asked me if I would like to come to the Naval Academy for duty. Dodge McFall was his flag lieutenant, and I suspect I may have given him a nudge, but, in any case, I wanted the job as XO of Bancroft Hall.[†] It was the only one I wanted.

Paul Stillwell: Why did you have that strong desire?

Admiral Burke: Well, I thought that the XO job was a first-string job. I would obviously get quarters on the base there, and it was not until I had been in the Navy 18 years that I had gotten quarters or that we used the facilities. When I went to Puerto Rico that was the first time. And my family and my kids were getting up in age and expense. And I wasn't particularly interested in coming home. Then after we got back to Norfolk, so I wrote him and said I'd love to.

That was in the summer of 1959, and then sometime during the winter Admiral Warder was down in Norfolk for a visit. We had dinner aboard the tender in the commodore's cabin. Admiral Warder asked me to step aside, and he told me he would like me to be officer in charge of the Submarine School. I told him of my commitment, and he said, "Well, think it over."

---

[*] Rear Admiral Charles L. Melson, USN, was superintendent of the Naval Academy from June 1958 to June 1960. The oral history of Melson, who retired as a vice admiral, is in the Naval Institute collection.
[†] Lieutenant Commander Albert Dodge McFall, USN.

I said, "Well, I've written to the academy and said I want to come, but I'll look into it." Well, then I started going around touching base with different people whose judgment I respected, and one of whom was Red Ramage, who was then a cruiser division commander on the waterfront, and he said, "Absolutely not. Don't go to the Naval Academy. Go to OpNav. That's where you get your ticket punched. You're not going to gain anything at Annapolis."[*] But in the end I decided to keep my word, and I wrote Admiral Melson that I had been pressed a bit, but I was still committed. I just wanted to let him know. So that's the way it worked out.

Well, by the time I got there Admiral Melson had been relieved by Admiral John Davidson, a submariner, whom I had known, not well, but I'd met him in years before up in New London.[†] But Dodge McFall was still there for one more year as his aide. So we got there, and sometime during the late spring my wife became pregnant. We moved in and occupied 29 Upshur Road, right by the gate. That began the three years there, probably professionally and from a family point of view the best we had in the Navy.

Paul Stillwell: What made them so enjoyable?

Admiral Burke: Well, the exec job was the toughest job I had by miles. It wasn't anything else. But it was the kind of thing I liked to do. We had fine officers in Bancroft Hall. And when you're dealing with about 4,000 midshipmen, which we had at time, you've always got problems. I didn't have to plan my day. The problems walked in every day. I relieved Doc Abbot, class of '39.[‡] During the turnover period, which was probably about three or four days, he said, "There's something funny going on. I don't know how it's happening, but there are things that are appearing in the Log, conversations or information, where the only place they have been transmitted in Bancroft Hall is in this office."

---

[*] Rear Admiral Lawson P. Ramage, USN, was Commander Cruiser Division Two in 1958-59. The oral history of Ramage, who retired as a vice admiral, is in the Naval Institute collection.
[†] Rear Admiral John F. Davidson, USN, was superintendent of the Naval Academy from June 1960 to August 1962. His oral history is in the Naval Institute collection.
[‡] Captain James L. Abbot, Jr., USN.

Paul Stillwell: The Log is a midshipman magazine.

Admiral Burke: Yes, that's the weekly magazine. He said he'd tried to have things traced, and he couldn't figure out how it was happening. Sure enough, it began to happen to me after a while, so I quickly learned if I were going to have a clandestine conversation I'd get out of my office and go talk in a busy office. But you were always interviewing midshipmen for one reason or the other. You saw all of the people that were very bad boys, and you also saw and dealt with the very good ones, and it was a strange mix.

Jack Creamer was one of our battalion officers.[*] He later was on my staff in NavForJapan and performed better than any staff officer that I've served with. But that's where we got to know each other. We had a fine bunch of battalion officers, and I'd say I had nothing but respect for the hard work those people did and their ability to help me. We had one Army exchange officer for a one-year tour and one Air Force. The Air Force officer I think may have been there for a three-year tour. But the Army really had top-drawer people. Denny Roush was one.[†] Bob Koch was one, and there was a third whose name was Shultz.[‡] Shultz was a Navy junior. His father had been a division head when I was first in BuPers back in '47. And I've bumped into him once or twice since. But each one of them was good. I used to have a battalion officers' conference about three times a week so we could talk over what we were going to do and so forth. That was the first time I'd really gotten together with the Marines.

We had Bob Twisdale there for the first two years as a battalion officer.[§] He was called "The Green Machine" and was a character the midshipmen loved to needle, but he was good and they liked him. Then he was relieved by another Marine who I can't remember. He was not as colorful as Bob. But I learned over a period of time that the Marines really paid more attention to the academy in their way than the Navy did. When Bob was the senior Marine at the academy and they picked officers for the academy, each year at a certain time he would go up to the headquarters and he would review the jackets

---
[*] Commander John J. Creamer, USN.
[†] Major Maurice D. Roush, USA.
[‡] Lieutenant Colonel Robert J. Koch, USA; Major John M. Shultz, USA.
[§] Lieutenant Colonel Robert H. Twisdale, USMC.

and say, "I'll take this one and that one and that one." Then they would go up and have a conference with the Commandant.

We didn't get that kind of service from the Navy. And looking at the quality of the people we had and where they went, I would have to say that the Marines did a better job. Maybe the Navy thinks about this now, but what happens is when you see better leadership the midshipmen are going to follow that and want to be Marines instead of in the Navy.

One of the Marine company officers was Dick Dean.* He was the class of '54. At the time I was there he'd only been out of the trade school six years, but he was obviously an outstanding man. He may have been the six-striper when he was there. But while I was there, maybe during the second year, he was picked out of the blue as far as I know for an Olmstead Scholarship, which was three years. Off to Brazil he went, and I didn't see him again until he was a BG, when I ran into him out in the Sanno Hotel in Tokyo about 1978. [Laughter] I think eventually he made lieutenant general; he was an exceptionally fine company officer.†

What happened at the time I graduated was interesting. My class was mad at the executive department about graduation, and a disproportionate number of people wanted to go and fill the Marine quota. Well, you can't find anybody now in my class or five years later who would admit that he had just wanted to go into the Marine Corps in preference to the Navy and ended up in the Navy. But I think it's important to have the best possible people that you can have in those billets as an influence.

Well, after leaving the submarine division, we went up to Annapolis about the first of August in 1960. It was right toward the end of plebe summer, and we walked right into family weekend for the plebes, and I'd never seen anything like that before. It was a great event. Then academic year started, and all their enthusiasm and motivation and everything went down the drain, as I suspect it still does every year. That began to reinforce the opinion that I had. I hadn't even thought about this plebe thing until I got back there, but gradually over a period of time I said, "Why do you want to kill that enthusiasm?" I think it's stupid. Every year the families come there. They are so

---

* Captain Clyde Dixon Dean, USMC.
† Dean retired as a lieutenant general 30 September 1987. His final billet was as Chief of Staff, Headquarters Marine Corps.

pleased with their sons, and their sons are so proud of what they've done in such a short time, and then, bango, you turn them loose on these animals who come back there to have to straighten them out.

Paul Stillwell: Did you do anything during your tenure to try to change that?

Admiral Burke: Yes, I did. I don't know whether it was my second or third year, but I tried to persuade Charlie Minter, who talked to the superintendent, Charlie Kirkpatrick, but they just shook their heads.* Said it was too radical an idea at that time, and I know the present superintendent feels that way, because I've written him a letter.

Paul Stillwell: What was your observation on Admiral Davidson as superintendent?

Admiral Burke: Well—

Paul Stillwell: One of the events I heard about during that period from Admiral Davidson was about a ticket-scalping scandal involving the football team. What are your recollections of that?

Admiral Burke: Well, we had a great football team that year, probably as good as we've ever had.

Paul Stillwell: Including a Heisman Trophy winner, Joe Bellino.†

Admiral Burke: Yes, Bellino was there, but there were a lot of other good players. I've forgotten exactly when it happened, but one afternoon a couple of weeks before the Army-Navy game it came up. It floated to the surface, and I don't know how, but it

---

* Captain Charles S. Minter, Jr., USN, served from 1961 to 1964 as the Naval Academy's commandant of midshipmen. Rear Admiral Charles C. Kirkpatrick, USN, was superintendent of the Naval Academy from August 1962 to January 1964.
† Midshipman Joseph M. Bellino, USN, was awarded the Heisman Trophy as the outstanding collegiate football player of the 1960 season.

seemed that the football players were given tickets for quote their friends. Apparently some of those guys were selling the tickets for money, which they were not supposed to do.

Now, I'm not sure whether this was a breach or what kind of a breach it was. I didn't know the athletic department rules or the NCAA rules or whatever.* But I know it was a serious problem, and I remember meeting with the superintendent, the commandant who was Jim Mini, Sneed Schmidt, who was the secretary of the Academic Board, and probably Rollo Miller, who was the chief of staff, and maybe Red Coward.† I don't recall whether Red was in the group, but he must have been.‡ I was along, too.

The discussion was about what problem this presented, and what are we going to do about it? It was a short time because apparently if we floated this thing probably half the football team, the first team, would have been knocked out of the Army-Navy game. We talked about it at some length, and then the meeting broke up. Admiral Davidson asked me to stay after the meeting, and the others left. He chatted about it a little bit, obviously in great distress, and asked me what I thought we ought to do.

I said, "I frankly don't know. I just don't have enough feel for it." Walked out and then a day or so later—or it may have been that night—we had a meeting of the first class when he told them what was going to happen. Essentially Admiral Davidson was wiping the slate clean. I know that after the meeting, perhaps the next day, some of the first class came around to their battalion officers and were outraged. I don't know that I had any that came to my office, but I know that they were very upset about it. Thought we should have blown the whistle.

Paul Stillwell: Even at the expense of public embarrassment.

Admiral Burke: At that same time, I had a pregnant wife and we were expecting. Before long, during the middle of the meeting, Dodge McFall, the flag lieutenant, came in and

---

* NCAA—National Collegiate Athletic Association.
† Captain James H. Mini, USN, served as commandant of midshipmen, 1960-61. Captain John Sneed Schmidt, USN, academic aide to the superintendent and secretary of the Academic Board. Captain Charles K. Miller, USN, administrative aide to the superintendent.
‡ Captain Asbury Coward III, USN, was Naval Academy athletic director from 1959 to 1962.

announced that Betty had gone to the hospital apparently in labor. I could have been excused, but I made the decision to stay there. I didn't get to the hospital until about 7:00 o'clock that night. When I got to the hospital, Betty was in delivery, and they wouldn't let me see her. After about a half an hour or three-quarters of an hour Dodge McFall came over and sat with me for about a couple hours and then went home.

Finally our youngest child, Charly, was born. Then the doctor came in shortly thereafter and told me there might be a problem. Apparently he had been short on help and he had delayed her delivery. Charly was short on oxygen and he had blue spots on his face. The doctor was concerned, but it worked itself out in a couple of days, and after a couple of days he was fine.

Paul Stillwell: In your role in the executive office what types of issues came to you as opposed to the commandant of midshipmen?

Admiral Burke: Well, I didn't have as big a job as the commandant. The commandant was also on the athletic council, I think, whatever it's called. So he was involved with athletics in a way that I was not. But I was more directly involved with the individual battalion officers and the internal administration. We ran the fitness report system, the evaluation system. We oversaw the honor system, and we oversaw the discipline. We also fed them and tried to develop them as they were coming up. So I say I had extraordinary respect for the body of midshipmen. We have people from all walks of life. We had them in my class, but the academy is a lot, lot bigger than it was when I was there. It's interesting to see where these people come from and what they develop into.

Paul Stillwell: You mentioned that you had contact with the very good ones. Any of those that stand out in your memory?

Admiral Burke: Well, Jerry Smith was one of the six-stripers.[*] He was there, I think, the first year. John Knubel was one.[†] I think they're all the names. I can remember the

---

[*] Midshipman Jerome F. Smith, USN, Jr., class of 1961.
[†] Midshipman John A. Knubel, Jr., USN.

faces because each year while I was there we used to invite them over for dinner. We had groups of them that we would have over, and this is one of the things that they get done that did not occur when I was there that we gave the battalion and company officers an allowance. I don't recall whether I got an allowance or not, but we were able to have them in our homes and meet them, know them socially outside of the regimen of the hall. I think it had a lot to do with easing the tension between the exec department and the various midshipmen in the first class.

Paul Stillwell: Well, they got to know you as an individual rather than just as somebody in a billet.

Admiral Burke: Yes. Well, I've always felt like I know Jerry Smith. In recent years I've seen Jerry Smith over at the National Defense University, and he's a respected individual.[*] He's smart as hell. We had one man who—I think he was in the class of '62, I can't remember his name—who was particularly outstanding. He was the number-two guy in the brigade. He was the class vice president. He had had a couple of years at Yale before he enlisted in the Marines. The last time I saw him was a long time ago. He was either a light colonel or a colonel and he was an aide to either the VCNO or the CNO. And he was a really impressive guy. He was so much more mature than I was at that age I couldn't believe it.

Paul Stillwell: What are some of the most memorable disciplinary cases you dealt with?

Admiral Burke: The toughest ones were always honor. You see, I go back in my mind to the fact that I was involved in an honor system at my prep school. When I was a midshipman we did not have an honor system. It was beat the system. And yet you ask my classmates today—and I've had discussions recently at the class lunches; they thought we had it. Today they think we had an honor system. But notwithstanding that, the kinds of problems that you get into usually have to do with breaking of privileges.

---

[*] Smith later earned a Ph.D., became a rear admiral, and served as commandant of the Industrial College of the Armed Forces.

Signing out. Somebody wants to go somewhere and he's got a girl out there, and he wants somebody to cover for him. These things happen. They're cheating. When I was a midshipman, cheating rarely was reported and only by the officer corps, not the midshipmen themselves. The worst case that I can remember happened probably my third year at the academy as exec. It was a cheating case. The boy called home and his father was incensed. Wouldn't speak to his son again. He would disgrace the family.

They hadn't made the decision in this case, but there had been decisions short of expulsion in the past if people would acknowledge, "I did something." It was above the commandant and me. It was up with the superintendent and the commandant and a couple of other people, probably the secretary of the academic board. This guy had done it, and he came in to me, and he was wondering what he could do, and I said, "Well, I'll talk to your father, but it seems to me that you did it and you know you did it. The best thing for you to do is clear your conscience and put yourself at the mercy of the board." There had been similar cases like this where the board had given them a bunch of demerits and so forth, and I felt they'd let him off because he did seem repentant. They kicked him out. And I tell you, I felt terrible. I thought, based on other cases at that time, that he would get a break. But each case is different.

What was bad about it was the fact that the boy's father disowned his own son and had called me up. He was outraged with his son, and I talked to him at length and I pled with the father to be compassionate and support the kid, but he would not. So I went over to Jim Kelly and he helped me at a time when I really needed help.[*]

Paul Stillwell: Because essentially you'd asked the midshipman to trust you.

Admiral Burke: Yes. I'd asked him to trust me, and I thought that based on other cases of the same kind of degree of violations where people had owned up, that they would let him stay, but they didn't. But I'd say overall I feel that the honor system has been very good for the academy. It's improved the leadership of the midshipmen. I do have a strong bone to pick with the fact that the conflict with the plebe system. Have I talked to you about this?

---
[*] Captain James W. Kelly, CHC, USN.

Paul Stillwell: Yes.

Admiral Burke: And I think it's wrong. Upperclassmen are quite ready and willing to put plebes on the report for violation of honor when they come up with a white lie when they're under pressure. At the same time they won't come clean with their own roommates or their own classmates when they know what they did and that won't do it. I'd say in general I think you've got to get rid of the plebe system as it now is constituted.

Paul Stillwell: Was Chaplain Kelly helpful to you in that situation?

Admiral Burke: He was sympathetic, and he said, "I know exactly what you're talking about. I've had to deal with the same thing."

Paul Stillwell: Do you know if the young man ever made peace with his father?

Admiral Burke: I don't know. Never heard. But at the academy, you meet a lot of different people. You see people from past years who come. My mother dated at the academy when she was a young woman, and we were at Annapolis when the class of '12 had its 50th anniversary. Well, that sounded like a long time, class of '12 to 1960. Well, we have the same spread now. [Laughter]

Paul Stillwell: Well, while we were changing tapes you recalled the name that you were searching for, and that was Pappy Weems who lived near the State Circle in Annapolis.*

Admiral Burke: Right. He was a colorful person, I mean, lots of enthusiasm. Betty and I were fortunate enough to be invited to dinner. I guess it was my last year over there, my third year. I remember Admiral and Mrs. Kirkpatrick were there and probably the

---

* Captain Philip Van Horn Weems, USN (Ret.), had graduated from the Naval Academy in the class of 1912 and retired in 1933. He was later recalled to active duty in 19142-46 and 1960-61. He was an expert in navigation and ran his own navigation business in Annapolis while not serving in the Navy. He died in 1979.

Minters and the Burkes and maybe six or eight couples. It was a nice evening, and he was a very enthusiastic kind of person, and he also had a reputation as a wrestler. He used to go over to the wrestling loft and occasionally wrestle with some of midshipmen on the team. Now he was in the class of '12 and he was wrestling people in the class of '62 and '63.

Paul Stillwell: Fifty years later.

Admiral Burke: He was in good shape. Jack Kennedy was the President at that time, and we started off on the physical business. People began to get in shape more, and there were requirements to get fit. I was excused from this. I was over 40, but there all of a sudden we began to get word that you had to be able to run a quarter mile and so forth and do different things. For the first time in my life in the Navy, people began to get in shape and think about it. So apparently he went out and did the run, whatever the specified run for a 40-year-old man.

Paul Stillwell: But he was in his 70s probably by then.[*]

Admiral Burke: He was probably in his 70s and he was getting a lot of publicity about it. Well, about this time Charlie Minter ended up in the hospital probably with a back problem. I don't recall what it was, but he was over there. It was not a fatal thing by any means. I used to go over and see him to tell him how Bancroft Hall was. He was in the hospital for a week or ten days at least, and I'd go over there to bring him up to date.

I remember one day when I was leaving I left Charlie's room, went down to the basement to go toward wherever my car was parked, and as I passed a room where the door was open, the lights were off, and I heard this voice say, "Hey, Burke. Hey, Burke." I looked in there, and there was Pappy Weems.

He said, "Shhh. Don't tell anybody I'm in here."

I said, "What are you doing in here?"

---

[*] Weems was born 29 March 1889.

"Oh," he said, "You remember that quarter-mile run I did the other day? I pulled a muscle in my leg, and I don't want anybody to know it." [Laughter]

Paul Stillwell: I have heard lots of wonderful things about Admiral Minter. What are your recollections of him?

Admiral Burke: Well, he's big, but I look on him as being big no matter how you look at him. He has a heart and sensitivity for human relations, and to me he was a most inspiring person to work with. He didn't ask anything of me that he wouldn't or couldn't do it himself. I found him a very marvelous boss and a good friend, and I still feel that way.

Paul Stillwell: The Naval Academy had fired a football coach shortly before you got there in Eddie Erdelatz, in part because he was setting up his own empire.* He felt that the football team was somehow separate and didn't have to do all the things that the other midshipmen did. What was the atmosphere when Coach Hardin was there?†

Admiral Burke: Well, he was working hard to do it. I would say I heard a lot about Erdelatz, but I usually I found Hardin not too hard to work with. The best coach I found to work with was the lacrosse coach, Bilderback.‡ Most of the coaches felt that we were too tough in Bancroft Hall. Bilderback told us, "The tougher you make it on them, the better I like it." [Laughter]

Paul Stillwell: Why did he say that?

---

* Edward J. Erdelatz was the Naval Academy's head football coach for the 1950 through 1958 seasons. The team's overall record in those years was 50-26-8, a percentage of .643.
† Wayne Hardin was the Naval Academy's head football coach for the 1959 through 1964 seasons. The team's overall record in those years was 38-22-2, a percentage of .629.
‡ Willis P. Bilderback was varsity lacrosse coach at the Naval Academy, 1959-72. His teams in those years won 123 games while losing 22 and tying one. His teams won or shared in eight intercollegiate championships and became the first to win four straight national championships.

Admiral Burke: Well, he thought it was good discipline, and he thought the discipline helped them in performance on the field.

I'm sure they've made a lot of changes now, but each year that I was there, there was a conflict between athletic department, exec, and academics. The midshipmen used to call the Maryland Avenue the Yalu.* I don't know whether they still do or not. The athletic department felt the athletes, if they didn't have to study and didn't have to go to school, we'd put them in the Sugar Bowl every year. The academic people said if they didn't have a Bancroft Hall we could make Rhodes scholars every year. And we said if they didn't have to go to class and go to play football or whatever, we'd make good officers.

We had an explosion each year I was there. It usually started in the academic side but not always. The pressures on the midshipmen are considerable, and you require special tutoring to keep up, in the football especially, but I'm sure it's just as bad in basketball and other sports now, for those guys to compete in the level that they are expected to compete they require special tutoring. They weren't getting it then in the way that I think they may be getting it now. I don't know what they're doing, but they should be getting summer school ahead of time. I don't know how Joe Bellino passed the course because he was just being yanked around all over the place to satisfy politicians.

Paul Stillwell: Well, Admiral Davidson said he had to deliberately put a stop to the public appearances in order to save Joe's academic career.

Admiral Burke: Yes. Oh, it was terrible.

Paul Stillwell: I suspect that that term "Yalu" no longer holds over there because it's so far in the past historically by this time, but it would have had a fresh meaning then that soon after the Korean War.

---

* The Yalu River separates North Korea from Communist China. The rules of engagement during the Korean War prevented offensive action across the Yalu, because President Harry S. Truman did not want to risk setting off a still wider war. The people at the academy were thus using Maryland Avenue as a figurative dividing line.

Admiral Burke: Yes.

Paul Stillwell: Any recollections of Roger Staubach from your time?*

Admiral Burke: He was in the class of '65. The plebe team that he was on was really great. I remember they had a fullback, I forget his name. In his own way I thought he was just as good as Staubach. I remember watching them play a game where the varsity had come over to watch the plebes who were undefeated. Staubach was running around the field escaping tacklers and so forth, and I was sitting very near Hardin and his coaches. They were laughing. They said, "Boy, when he gets up on the varsity they're going to kill him."

Well, the next year we started off and he was a youngster and we had another quarterback. I don't think he'd been first string the year before, but he had played enough so he had the deck on it and was playing. I forget how we started out, but we had a game with Cornell at the academy. At the half the score was nothing to nothing, and nothing had happened. And so at the beginning of the second half—I don't think Staubach was put in until after the first exchange—and he put Staubach in and when the game was over it was 40 to 0. [Laughter] But that guy was really good.

Paul Stillwell: You mentioned the academics briefly. Any other impact that that had on your office?

Admiral Burke: Well, looking back on it, I don't think I did enough, but we tried to communicate with the other departments. I don't know when it started, but I used to meet with my opposite numbers in the various academic departments and athletics just to try to be on frequency, know each other, try to be mutually supportive. Were we successful? Not completely.

---

* Roger Staubach, who won the Heisman Trophy in 1963 and graduated from the Naval Academy in 1965, played professional football for the Dallas Cowboys from 1969 to 1979.

Paul Stillwell: Admiral Davidson said one of the interesting things was hearing from the old grads who, of course, figured that any change from their time is a terrible thing, and one of the changes during that period was doing away with marching to class. What do you recall about that change?

Admiral Burke: Well, it was essential to do it because the curriculum had changed, and no longer could we box people in. The midshipmen were just a lot better educated than we were. And you could tell. They asked questions. In my day we did everything by rote. It had an enormous effect on the military posture of the brigade, so all of a sudden you would see people strolling to class instead of marching to class. There's a difference, so you're going to have a different kind of a person. I don't think that's all bad, but you're not going be nearly as military as you used to be.

Paul Stillwell: Right.

Admiral Burke: And, of course, we knew we could see that girls eventually were going to come in the brigade, because I think at that time they were in the ROTC units, and it was just a matter of time before we would.* I may have told you this before and it contributed to my everlasting desire to do something about the plebe system. I noticed that, in time, that I didn't think our people were socially mature enough. We had the Naval Academy Dairy, and I got a nephew a summer job out there, and he used to come into the quarters and visit us at night. He was about 16, not more than 17. He was socially more mature than second classmen that were dating may daughter. Now, it is true that he was sort of a sophisticated guy, but this caused me to look at what causes this.

Their basic problem is there are so many restrictions on midshipmen that they don't get a chance to socially mature. About the same time or maybe shortly before that I'd been on a train somewhere coming from New London down here. In the car was a bunch of young Catholic students. They were studying for the priesthood, and they were let out going somewhere and they were in the car. Well, those guys were whooping it up like a bunch of sailors, and it made me realize that this was very much what happens

---

* In the summer of 1976 women were first admitted to the Naval Academy as midshipmen.

when you lock people up. They have to express themselves. It amazes me the privileges that we have down there now, the automobiles we drive and all of that sort of stuff. But when I was growing up none of the kids in the local high school had automobiles, and now they have parking reserved for the seniors up here at the local high school.

Paul Stillwell: The same where my son goes to school.

Admiral Burke: I did get a lot of calls from friends who had sons who were midshipmen because somebody was making it too tough for them, but somehow or other they all seemed to survive.

Paul Stillwell: Well, I've about run out of questions on that tour of duty. Do you have any other topics?

Admiral Burke: Well, I'd say we made a lot of friends there over the years. I mean Red Coward and Jean. He was the athletic director. He was relieved by Bill Busik.[*] And I'd known Bill. Bill was a plebe in my battalion, so I knew him, not well, when he came back there. I'd met him off and on over the years, and I have high regard for him. Harry Hahn was the secretary of the academic board, and then he was relieved by Bob McNitt.[†] Bob I'd known before, and he was there with us for two years. My own assessment is that he's done more for the Naval Academy than any officer that we have.

Paul Stillwell: And he's a prince of a man.

Admiral Burke: Yes. I think he has been just magnificent, and we ought to put something up there and name it after him because he has done so much. He was the guy

---

[*] Captain William S. Busik, USN, was the athletic director from 1962 to 1965. Following his retirement from active duty in 1971, Busik served as head of the Naval Academy Alumni Association until 1994.
[†] Captain Harry B. Hahn, USN. Captain Robert W. McNitt, USN. The Naval Institute's oral history of McNitt, who retired as a rear admiral, goes into valuable detail on the changes made to Naval Academy academics during his tour of duty in the 1960s.

that brought the first dean.* And he had the respect of the academic community in the colleges and universities, and that took a lot of doing.

Paul Stillwell: What do you recall about President Kennedy and the commencement speech in 1961?†

Admiral Burke: Well, I remember it, that it was the day after the final ball, and Sneed Schmidt was the secretary of the Academic Board. The President started to speak, and we were all in white service uniforms. Sneed crossed his legs and he had on black socks. [Laughter] He just had gotten up late that morning. [Laughter] And all the wives who were sitting down there on the front row who had been with us at the final ball just broke out and started laughing. [Laughter]

Paul Stillwell: Anything about Kennedy himself you recall?

Admiral Burke: No, he was relaxed, charming. I remember he made some remark that he'd got a lot of laughs when he said that he'd started off in the Navy and then PT boats and look where he got. [Laughter]

Paul Stillwell: And a shipwreck on top of it.‡

Admiral Burke: Yes. But I don't recall anything other than that.

Paul Stillwell: Well, it's an interesting note to end on. Another fine interview today, Admiral. I look forward to our next meeting.

---

* Dr. A. Bernard Drought was officially appointed as the first civilian academic dean of the Naval Academy on 1 July 1964 after serving a year in the position on a pro tem basis.
† President John F. Kennedy made the principal address at the Naval Academy graduation ceremony on 7 June 1961.
‡ Shortly after midnight on 2 August 1943, while Lieutenant John F. Kennedy, USNR, was in command of PT-109, the motor torpedo boat was rammed and cut in two by a Japanese destroyer while operating in the Solomon Islands. Kennedy towed one of his crew members to safety after the collision and was awarded the Navy and Marine Corps Medal as a result.

Interview Number 8 with Rear Admiral Julian T. Burke, Jr., U.S. Navy (Retired)
Date: Tuesday, 10 February 1998
Place: Admiral Burke's home in Alexandria, Virginia
Interviewer: Paul Stillwell

Paul Stillwell: Admiral, we've got a beautiful sunny day on which to visit today. We're going resume discussion of your tour as executive officer of Bancroft Hall at the Naval Academy.

Admiral Burke: The people were what made the job, and it was a tough job because when you're handling a student body of 4,000 Americans who are tied up behind the four walls of the academy, you're going to have problems. I found that the clergy were around Bancroft Hall as much as I was almost, much to my surprise, but they were needed.

Paul Stillwell: What sorts of things did they do?

Admiral Burke: Well, they were counseling midshipmen. I know it was not unusual to see Chuck Greenwood or Si Rotridge or Jim Kelly around Bancroft Hall when you least expected it, and they weren't over there just because.* They were talking to midshipmen who they knew had some problem that they needed to unload about. Oftentimes the midshipmen would go over and talk to the clergy when they had serious problems, which could be a variety of things.

Now, let me see. I'll give you an example of a serious problem. I think it was the class of '62. We have an honor system now, which we did not have when I was a midshipman, and I'm very grateful that we have it. In the spring of probably 1962 Jim Kelly came in one day and told me we might have a problem with the graduating class, and this is a long, detailed explanation. We were approaching graduation, probably six weeks or two months ahead. When the class graduates, they want to get sworn in, get on

---
* Lieutenant Charles L. Greenwood, CHC, USN; Captain Henry J. Rotridge, CHC, USN; Captain James W. Kelly, CHC, USN.

the road and get married or whatever, and go on leave. Commander Dick Brega was my administrative officer and an exceptionally fine person.* He was at the end of his third year there and knew the routine, and so he decided to put in a package so that they could get all of these signatures done before graduation. It turned out that one of the forms these young men were signing listed next of kin. And it turned out that a number of them either had signed or were getting ready to sign forms on which they were not going to include their wives, whom they were legally married to while they were midshipmen.

Paul Stillwell: Legally married in the eyes of the nation or state but not in the eyes of the Naval Academy.

Admiral Burke: Right. So if they signed this piece of paper and they were married, they had committed an honor offense. So Jim told me about this, so I took him over to Charlie Minter across the hall, and Charlie took him over to see the superintendent. The superintendent asked, "How many people are we talking about?" Well, it turned out there was something like 70 or 80 of these guys were married. [Laughter] I can't remember whether it was Admiral Davidson or Kirkpatrick, but I'd say whoever was superintendent almost had a heart attack.†

Paul Stillwell: Well, how did you find out—just because they wouldn't sign?

Admiral Burke: Well, these people that had signed had a guilty conscience. "What do I do?"

Paul Stillwell: What was the resolution when this committee went to the superintendent?

Admiral Burke: Well, I think they just looked the other way. I don't think there was a decision that they weren't going to get tough about it.

---

* Commander Richard E. Brega, USN.
† Rear Admiral Charles C. Kirkpatrick, USN, was superintendent of the Naval Academy from August 1962 to January 1964.

Paul Stillwell: And presumably something that a midshipman told the chaplain would be in confidence because of the religious aspect of it.

Admiral Burke: Yes, but he just wanted to let us know it wasn't a handful. But I remember when the superintendent asked Jim, "How many of these? Ten? Fifteen?" No, more than that." Well, we got up to something like 80. [Laughter]

Paul Stillwell: Well, I think another role of the chaplains is that they're facing people in a culture shock kind of a situation and a sympathetic ear can often be very helpful.

Admiral Burke: Yes. There were other problems. When I relieved Doc Abbot as exec he told me that he was surprised to learn that there were a number of midshipmen who didn't get along with their parents, particularly their fathers. Usually they were Navy juniors, and he said, "You might know some of them." Well, I couldn't believe this, but over a period of time I began to meet some of these people.

The first year I was there we had a young lad who had attended Episcopal High School, which was a prep school I had gone to. He had also attended Bullis School, which I had attended. And he had absolutely no respect for his father. He eventually left the Naval Academy. He either flunked out or he was a misfit, but his father came in, and it was not a pleasant experience to deal with that. During the three years I was there, I had about eight or ten situations that occurred, and at least three of them I knew the father. They were not intimates of mine, but I knew them.

Paul Stillwell: Did you try to act as an intermediary?

Admiral Burke: No. It's too personal, and none of the parents ever indicated there was a problem. Now, we had a group there that the mids called the "shrinks." Maybe you know about them.

Paul Stillwell: No.

Admiral Burke: It was a team of a psychiatrist and two psychologists. I think they were attached to the sick bay down in Bancroft Hall, and any time we got somebody who was behaving out of the ordinary, getting too many demerits or any unusual behavior, we would run them down before the shrinks. I forget what the official name of them was, but they were enormous help, and I got some experience and education in their insight. If I had it to do all over again, I think I'd take some courses in psychology. My training in psychology has been trial and error all my life and just like playing the stock market. [Laughter]

Paul Stillwell: Some wins, some losses.

Admiral Burke: I've had some bear markets. [Laughter]

Paul Stillwell: What do you remember about handling disciplinary cases, both infractions against midshipmen regulations or more serious things?

Admiral Burke: Well, the things that came up to my level were serious just to begin with.

Paul Stillwell: By nature.

Admiral Burke: You were talking usually of class-A offenses. Or if you had somebody like Joe McCain, Admiral Jack McCain's youngest, who was a plebe my first year there.[*] He just was one of these guys that accumulated demerits, and he eventually went out at the end of the year on demerits. I think he took pleasure in getting demerits. He's a family friend, and all the family were crazy about him, but it ended up he's an example of a type of Navy junior. I don't think he wanted to go to the Naval Academy, but he

---

[*] Midshipman Joseph Pinckney McCain, USN, entered the Naval Academy with the class of 1964 but left in the spring of 1961, at the end of his first year. His brother, John S. McCain III, who graduated from the Naval Academy with the class of 1958, is now a U.S. Senator. Their father was Admiral John S. McCain, Jr., USN.

thought his family wanted him to go. His parents were not intimates of ours, but we knew them.

Paul Stillwell: And he had an older brother who had graduated from the academy.

Admiral Burke: Right. But he just had the devil in him, and he was unsat. I guess his father came up at the academy to see how he was doing. His father was a terrific guy who could put himself on the level with anybody. Sneed Schmidt had me come over, and I talked to him in front of Sneed, and Sneed thanked me later on for being as candid as I was. I said we weren't persuaded in Bancroft Hall that he really wanted to be there. Then he was unsat at Christmas, so we invited him to come over to the house whenever he could and he did. And he just endeared himself to my family. Helped decorate the Christmas tree. The ceilings in those quarters are maybe 12 or 14 feet; they're very high. He got up on a ladder and his fingerprints, I'll bet, are still on the ceiling. Our son Charlie was born there that year, he was special and attracted all kinds of attention. His next oldest sibling was his sister. His sister was about 12 or 13, and his brother was maybe 14 or 15, and the next older sister was 17 or 18. We had lots of hands to help us, and he was smart as a whip and he got used to adult companionship very quickly.

Paul Stillwell: Well, I think your observation that he wasn't really cut out for the academy is accurate. Admiral Davidson said that he was given one chance after another, and the final straw was when he took his shoes off in class one day.

Admiral Burke: Well, he was a rebel, and there are a lot of people that are rebels. I've got some in my relatives. They enjoy shocking people.

Speaking of our son Charlie, one day when he was about two years old he disappeared from the house. We had a beagle hound named Happy. It was about 10:30 in the morning, and Betty took her eye was off of Charlie for a short while, and all of a sudden he disappeared. Well, this was in the spring, I think, and she ran around the house. He wasn't there, and she went on to the parade ground, and she immediately ran down to the water's edge, where Alumni Hall is now. When she got down there, the delivery postman was down there, and he said, "Are you looking for a little child and a dog?" Well, I just saw them over in that direction." Well, she caught up with him as he was passing the bandstand headed for Bancroft Hall. He had been to my office, and he and Happy were going to my office. [Laughter]

Paul Stillwell: You alluded briefly to the honor concept. How did that differ from the honor code at the Military Academy?

Admiral Burke: Well, our concept said you don't lie, cheat or steal, and if somebody did something that was a lie or a cheat or a steal, that was it. At West Point they had a code that said, "This is it," in terms of what was an honor offense. Where we ran into this was at the exchange weekends for the midshipmen and cadets. A West Point cadet was with us in Bancroft Hall, and he signed out and got a privilege and went to Washington and then didn't do what he said he was going to. For us that's an honor offense and a kickout. It wasn't in their code at West Point. It wasn't defined. If the guy had done this at West Point, it would have been an honor violation, because it was in the code, but they didn't codify the fact that the offense could not be done at Annapolis. Well, that's too hard for me to deal with, but that's the way the Army operates.

While we're talking about this, it was a great learning experience for me to be exec and oversee the battalion officers' conferences that we had about two or three times a week. They made all sorts of recommendations. This was a great learning experience for me to see how the different people operated. We had some Army officers. One was Bob Koch, who had been deep selected. He was a real fine officer, but he wanted a battle plan for everything, and the Marines weren't far behind. [Laughter] It was awfully hard to get us naval officers to put it on paper. But it taught me a lot about how the different services operate.

One of the times it came up was when the Kennedy inauguration came up.[*] We didn't have a battle plan to match the weather conditions or something like that, and it really was upsetting to the Army guy. I think the Marines were quite ready to slog through, but the Army guy didn't like it. [Laughter]

---

[*] Kennedy was inaugurated as President on 20 January 1961.

Paul Stillwell: It was very cold that day, as I remember.

Admiral Burke: Oh, it was terrible. It was also tied in with Rickover. Sometime during the fall of 1960 the decision was made in the Navy Department that Admiral Rickover could interview prospective nuclear submariners and select them for assignment to his program on graduation. This was a really dramatic shift. As I recall, he had about a quota of 80 that he was going to be allowed to take, so a board of officers was set up. I think Walt Small, who was the head of math, science and engineering, was probably the chairman.[*] They interviewed the individuals, and I think they sent up about 120 people for Admiral Rickover.

The day that they were to be interviewed was the day of the inauguration of President Kennedy. And, of course, the weather went to worms, and they called up Rickover's office, and they asked if they wouldn't cancel it because of the transportation difficulties, and he held firm that they had to be there. When the midshipmen returned, they had all kinds of stories about his infamous interviews. Since I wasn't interviewed, I can only give you second- and third-hand reports, but I would say they were typical of what I'd heard in the fleet.

He had selected his 80, and then about a week or so later Jimmy Dunford, who was his number two, called me up and said, "Admiral Rickover has a list of ten people that he interviewed in excess of his quota. He would like you to tell them that he plans to have them ordered into the program as soon as he's allowed to by the Navy Department."[†]

I said, "Fine, Jimmy, that's okay with me, but I'd like you to give me something in writing." I'd written the names down. Well, Jimmy couldn't believe that I would ask for it in writing, but something told me I ought to do it. Then I reported it up the line, and I thought when the superintendent heard, he said, "You did!?" [Laughter] He wasn't very happy about it.

---

[*] Captain Walter L. Small, Jr., Director of Science and Engineering.
[†] Captain James M. Dunford, USN.

Paul Stillwell: He wasn't happy that you'd make the request?

Admiral Burke: That I wanted it in writing. However, when it did come in writing, half the names had been changed [laughter], so I don't think that made any difference. It didn't then. But this was essentially the beginning of service selection. And we had the Air Force—I told you earlier—oh, at lunch I guess it was.

Paul Stillwell: Right. It wasn't on the tape.

Admiral Burke: Okay. Well, 25% percent of the graduates of both service academies, of Naval Academy and West Point, for several years had been going to the Air Force, and frankly this was disruptive. It was particularly disruptive because I found that the Air Force offered something the Navy either couldn't or wouldn't, which was if an individual applied to a graduate school of his choice and was accepted, the Air Force would send him to that graduate school and not require any additional obligated service. This was a very attractive feature to some of the young men there.

I told you last time about Bob Twisdale, a Marine who was a battalion officer, who apparently had the pick of the Marine Corps in choosing company officers for the academy. I can remember two Marines who were company officers. I think one of them was in the class of '56 who had probably been the brigade captain, and he ended up as a lieutenant general. He was selected for some graduate program that sent him to Brazil for three years. I don't even think he applied for it. We had another one, I can't remember the gentleman's name but he was an extraordinarily capable person. Paul Slack was another one. He ended up as a brigadier. I don't recall any of our Navy company officers making flag rank.

I've been thinking about the people who were the role models when I was in Bancroft Hall as a midshipman, and I had four company officers in four years. They were exceptionally fine men, including future flag officers. Also in Bancroft Hall at that time we had later Rear Admiral Lyman Thackrey, he was battalion officer, and Commander Jerauld Wright. And Beany Jarrett.

Paul Stillwell: So what you're saying is that when you came back as executive officer there was not that level of talent in Bancroft Hall.

Admiral Burke: Well, let me say this. I wasn't looking for it, but shortly after I got there I found that I was on the Navy Uniform Board, and I went up to a meeting with Herman Kossler.* He was on the board too. One day he told me that he had been on a selection board and found that the fitness reports at the Naval Academy were reflective of people who were not necessarily going to get ahead. I don't have any reason to downplay people that we had. They looked like they were good solid officers to me. But they spent 70 to 90 hours a week on the job. They really worked hard, so I could not complain about their performance.

Paul Stillwell: Did you have a hand in writing these fitness reports that Admiral Kossler found disappointing?

Admiral Burke: Oh, no. This was right at the beginning of my tour.

Paul Stillwell: I see. Well, did you make an effort after that to separate out the best and give them a better chance?

Admiral Burke: All I can tell you is that in my own writing of fitness reports I never gave people a free ride. I did not believe in marking everybody at the top of the heap. I believed in recognizing performance. So I'm not answering your question, but I didn't boost them just to take care of inflation.

Paul Stillwell: Did you have a dialogue with BuPers to try to get better people assigned?

Admiral Burke: We tried, but I think what we were competing with was graduate school and special programs such as Rickover's. Rickover's was not the only one. There were other programs.

---

* Captain Herman J. Kossler, USN.

Paul Stillwell: You mentioned before the tape started that Admiral Davidson had performed a useful function in shielding those below him from Admiral Rickover. What specifically was involved in that?

Admiral Burke: Well, Admiral Rickover really had a thing on the Naval Academy. I don't know how frequently, but he called up Admiral Davidson at a regular routine basis just to harass him. I know it happened, because I walked in his office one day right after he hung up, and he was just shaking his head. Rickover was telling him how sorry he felt for Davidson because who was not competent to be the head man down there.

Paul Stillwell: How did Davidson react? Did he just take this in stride?

Admiral Burke: He took it in stride. There are so many Rickover stories. I heard these stories when I was back in submarines when other people were getting ready to go. I would never have ever have thought of applying for his program. I think it's interesting that Bill Crowe, I've been told, was wanted by Rickover, and Crowe turned him down.[*]

Paul Stillwell: Harry Train was in that same category.[†] What else do you remember about that first football season that you were there when Joe Bellino got the Heisman Trophy?

Admiral Burke: It was a winning season. I think we lost one game, but we had a good team.[‡] Bellino was, of course, the star. The big thing that year was we played Air Force for the first time.

Oh, I forgot. [Laughter] The day I arrived on the scene at Annapolis to report for duty was the day our goat had been kidnapped out at the dairy farm, and I couldn't get

---

[*] Admiral William J. Crowe, Jr., USN, served as Chairman of the Joint Chiefs of Staff from 1 October 1985 to 30 September 1989.
[†] See the Naval Institute oral history of Admiral Harry D. Train II, USN (Ret.).
[‡] The Midshipmen had a 9-1 record in the regular season, losing only to Duke, 19-10. Navy lost to the University of Missouri, 21-14 in the postseason Orange Bowl game.

excited about it.* Well, I can tell you everybody in Bancroft Hall and the superintendent and so forth—everybody was really upset about it. I was amazed to see how upset they were. I wasn't getting into it because I was so new on the job, but Jim Mini was upset, and there were telephone calls from probably Red Coward.† I don't know whether Red was upset. I really hadn't gotten to know him at that point in time.

In any case, the dairy farm belonged to the commandant and came under us, and I wasn't any help.‡ But eventually it turned out, and I've forgotten exactly, the Naval Investigative Service got involved in it. Somebody had seen a car out there, and they'd recorded the license number, and it turned out that it was the car of a family that lives about a mile from here in Alexandria.

When the Investigative Service agent came down and talked to us, he told us how he found this goat. It turned out that the family either had a son or a nephew who was a cadet at the Air Force Academy. They had loaned him the car, and the cadets had gone over there and picked it up and taken the goat to Andrews Air Force Base and put it on a special plane to fly out to the Air Force Academy in Colorado Springs.§ So when the thing finally broke in the paper and Drew Pearson got it and everybody started raising hell about using a big government plane, they wouldn't dare put it in an Air Force plane to fly it back.** [Laughter] The plane that took it out was already back here. So they had to take up a collection. [Laughter] So eventually they got the thing flown back.

As I recall, this was about the fourth game in the season, and the emotion that was going back and forth between the two schools was just unbelievable. In hindsight I was just amazed, but it was there. It was very tough on Roger McLain, who was our Air Force exchange officer.†† And, of course, the Air Force wanted to beat us so badly they could taste it. Even after we found out they had the goat, it took them some period of time to get it. I was in Jim Mini's office at least once when he called up his opposite number and asked him about it. They didn't acknowledge they had it for a long time,

---

* The Naval Academy's mascot is a goat. It is a sporting tradition for the service academies to kidnap each other's mascots.
† Captain James H. Mini, USN, served as commandant of midshipmen, 1960-61.
‡ The goat lived at the Naval Academy dairy farm outside Annapolis.
§ Andrews Air Force Base is located approximately ten miles southeast of Washington, D.C., in Prince George's County, Maryland.
** Andrew Pearson was a muckraking syndicated newspaper columnist, the predecessor of Jack Anderson.
†† Captain Roger McLain, USAF.

although we knew they did. Finally they admitted it, and then they didn't want to send it back, because they didn't have the money to send him back. [Laughter] It was all just a lot of child stuff.

Then we got to the day of the game, and as I recall they didn't have their whole student body there. It was over in the old stadium in Baltimore. And they tried to do something like light some smoke or smoke makers, and they ran some cadets down on the field, but it didn't work. They trying to obscure either our march-on or the team's arrival on the field, and fortunately that didn't work. Then finally the game got going, and they made a touchdown first. Then finally we got our act together with Joe Bellino and we beat them; we got about four touchdowns, I think.[*] But everybody was just thoroughly drained after it was over.

Paul Stillwell: What do you remember about Bellino specifically from that year?

Admiral Burke: Well, he was a winner. He was a great running back. I remember in that game he played exceptionally well. But the problem was he was All-American and he was at the Naval Academy. He was forced to attend special events away from the academy. Even a good student would have had trouble, and he was having troubles keeping up academically as many of the football players did.

Paul Stillwell: Too many distractions.

Admiral Burke: Oh, yes, it was terrible.

Paul Stillwell: Last time you mentioned Sneed Schmidt's black socks when President Kennedy made the graduation speech in 1961. Anything else about that occasion?

Admiral Burke: The other thing I particularly remember was after it was over Kennedy noticed there were practically no black faces in the graduating class, and so we were questioned and pressured to start doing something about it. We did have a few blacks

---

[*] Navy won the game, 35-3.

who were midshipmen but not many. I don't recall the number, but when I relieved Doc Abbot he gave me a handwritten list of the numbers that we had. We tried to watch how they were doing and to make sure that they were getting the benefit of being given fair treatment and so forth. I think by the time we left there the plebe class began to reflect a little bit more in the way of black midshipmen but not much.

Paul Stillwell: Were there some specific recruiting efforts made in the black community?

Admiral Burke: I was remote from that, so I don't know, but I know that these things were happening. One year we had a young black who was from the state of Maryland who was in the first class. When he came up to graduation he failed his final exams. There had been quite a large amount of publicity by the NAACP that wanted to make a big thing out of it and show up and recognize this.[*] Up to that time, in order to sit with your class at graduation you had to be a legitimate graduate. I'm sure this was the class of '62, because I think Admiral Davidson made the decision that he could sit with his class. The board sent him to summer school, and he graduated at the end of the summer. I kind of think there had been other people who sort of fell in this category of being sent to summer school. But I don't believe anybody who hadn't yet made it was allowed to sit with the class at graduation. I think Admiral Davidson, to his credit, handled that about as diplomatically and politically as you could.

Paul Stillwell: Because there probably would have been a furor if he hadn't.

Admiral Burke: Oh, it would have been terrible. Yes.

Paul Stillwell: That was during some of the very ugly incidents down South in terms of racial relations.

Admiral Burke: Right.

---

[*] NAACP—National Association for the Advancement of Colored People.

Paul Stillwell: What do you remember about deaths of midshipmen? You told me previously that there had been a couple of suicides.

Admiral Burke: Well, I say again, going back to what I said before, when you've got 4,000 people I don't care what their qualifications are, you're going to have some things happen that you don't want. We probably had at least three midshipmen that were killed in automobile accidents going home on leave. One of them I remember happened somewhere on the way to Philadelphia at Christmas leave. There was a snowstorm and the driver got blinded; the car ended up in the ditch, and this young lad was killed. Then the family were notified and they didn't believe it.

There was another one out in Kentucky, and we had a terrible time getting the word to them; we didn't want to just send them a telegram. We wanted somebody to go in there, and we finally got somebody who was head of the ROTC in that area and he went over. This guy later worked for me. When I was in the phib group, he was my operations officer, and he told me that the father thought he was kidding.

We had an honor case, I think it was the last year I was there in the spring, and this midshipman had previously done something that wasn't right in the honor department but had gotten a reprieve. Then he had signed out for a privilege, saying he was going to do one thing and had done something else instead. His plans came apart, and so he was found out. He committed suicide.

There was another one. I remember his father was in the class of '38. I knew his father as a midshipman. When I say I knew him, he was not an intimate. He just showed up at choir practice and was on the other side of the choir from me, but I remembered him quite well. His son had gotten involved in signing out for a privilege and came in late and didn't do what he said he was going to do and somehow or other beat the rap. He got let off the hook by the Navy Department, I think, not us. I guess the guy was a second classman when he committed the earlier offense. By the time he was a first classman, I had left the job and was out in the fleet. I got a copy of the Navy Times, and I saw where this guy had committed suicide. And he, too, apparently had done it again.

It's very tough dealing with these cases. I can't remember having dealt with suicide after I left the academy, but I've certainly dealt with a number of deaths of people under unfortunate circumstances. And all of them, I guess, supposedly harden one on being able to take things that are very unpleasant.

Paul Stillwell: But it would be especially hard when it's somebody that young just snuffing out all future promise.

Admiral Burke: Well, that's true. People can recover, I think, but when you're in an honor system environment you think that the world has come down on you forever. I think people can overcome adversity. I believe that.

Paul Stillwell: Well, the other side of the coin is that there are probably some people who felt a lot of adversity, but they were helped out by the chaplains to sufficient degree that they got by it.

Admiral Burke: Not everybody's smart enough to go talk to a chaplain.

Paul Stillwell: That's right.

Admiral Burke: Looking at my notes here, I wanted to mention more about one of the chaplains. Chuck Greenwood was a lieutenant, an academy graduate. He had been an aviator and crash-landed, I think, on a golf course down at Jacksonville somewhere. Somebody had been killed, and so he converted to being a chaplain. He was extraordinarily effective and usually at least twice or three times a year while I was there with him a midshipman would come in and want to resign because he wanted to be like Chaplain Greenwood. [Laughter]

Paul Stillwell: That's being too much of a role model.

Admiral Burke: There was another thing. We had visiting clergy for sermons, and Jim Kelly did an extraordinary job of getting people. Had Billy Graham there one time, and quite frankly he was a disappointment. As Jim said later, "He needs a half an hour to warm up, and I gave him 20 minutes."

Paul Stillwell: For the whole thing. [Laughter]

Admiral Burke: But we had another guy, I think it was the first year I was there, named Sloane Coffin. Did you ever hear of him?

Paul Stillwell: He was the chaplain at Yale.

Admiral Burke: When he got up there he didn't give a sermon. He gave a civil rights speech.

Paul Stillwell: Very liberal.

Admiral Burke: And, sure enough, he was picked up and jailed in Selma, Alabama, shortly thereafter. We had another one, Peter Marshall. He came down a couple of times. There were others but these are the names that I remember particularly.

Paul Stillwell: And that was a time when chapel was still mandatory for the midshipmen.

Admiral Burke: There were people that made a difference that we met or had to deal with. Did you ever meet Pierre Bernard?[*]

Paul Stillwell: No.

Admiral Burke: Well, he was an academy graduate who lived on Hanover Street, the first street right outside the main gate. He lived down towards the end in a very nice Georgian type house. He was head of a local bank. When I relieved Doc Abbot, he

---

[*] Jean Pierre Bernard, a 1923 graduate of the Naval Academy who resigned his commission and went into the Naval Reserve.

made sure that I met Pierre Bernard, who was a good friend. I'm sure that Pierre was a member of the Naval Academy Foundation or the Academy Foundation there. But he was somebody that was a good civilian friend that helped in the public relations sector. He was discreet, and his advice was always sound. Turned out he was from New Orleans, where my wife's family was, and I don't recall whether it was then or it was probably a while later my mother-in-law and Pierre's brother turned up in the same retirement home, so I met his brother.

There were a lot of exceptional people there that were at the academy while we were there that I enjoyed serving with and dealing with in different ways. Bob McNitt came while were there and relieved as secretary of the academic board. I had known him. I guess I first met him when I had a destroyer. He ran an ASW school down at the waterfront at Norfolk. I think he lived at Virginia Beach, and we went to the same church.

Paul Stillwell: Coincidentally I've just been interviewing him alternatively with you.

Admiral Burke: Well, I think in my book Bob has done more for the Naval Academy than anybody in my lifetime. His manner of dealing with people and his background—he was, I'm sure, highly respected in the civilian academic community, and we were extraordinarily fortunate to have him there. Later Bob came back to the academy and I think was a role model for getting things done that kept us on track.*

Paul Stillwell: A true gentleman.

Admiral Burke: Yes. I don't know whether he's told you about the tragedy in his family or not. His wife was killed in an accident.† She was a lovely person.

Paul Stillwell: Did you have any part of the changes that led to bringing in a civilian academic dean?

---

* After he retired from active duty, Admiral McNitt worked for many years as the Naval Academy's dean of admissions.
† This is covered in Admiral McNitt's oral history.

Admiral Burke: Oh, no. I was fenced into Bancroft Hall. I had nothing to do with it.

Paul Stillwell: Was there any connection in your organization with the people who were kicked out for not being up to par academically?

Admiral Burke: No. We were like scoutmasters, I guess; that was just something the academic department took care of. We couldn't go over there and plead there. I suspect we put something down there on their fitness reports or their aptitude, but I don't know. I just don't recall. We're talking about something 35 years ago, and my memory recall isn't quite as good as it used to be.

One person I met when I first got there was Emmy Marshall, and I don't know how long she had been there. When Admiral Draemel was the commandant when I was a midshipman he established the first female presence inside Bancroft Hall when he brought in Mrs. Marshall, who was the sister-in-law of whoever was the head of the weapons department. They put up this soda fountain that was directly under the rotunda to sort of humanize and give us some place to be sociable within Bancroft Hall, which we had not had before that. So whenever it was open and during liberty hours she was supposed to be there, and she was a nice lady. This job had been established to sort of emulate what West Point had. Emmy was an extraordinary person, and she had at least two or three ladies that helped on occasion, one of whom was the mother of a very good friend of ours. Mrs. Lehardy was her name, and she too was a Navy widow. They used to be the hostesses at tea dances and hops and so forth and have a presence. And in the ceremonial side of it they were always very good advisors.

Because we lived on the parade ground, we always got heavily involved in the color presentation and so forth, and Emmy or one of the other ladies was always involved in that, and so we saw the color girl.* The color girl used to come over to our quarters and dress and then appear on the field from our house. It was very convenient to live over there when you had these dress parades, because frequently there would be friends

---

* As part of each year's graduation events the top company of midshipmen is designated as the color company. The girlfriend of the commander of that company is designated as the color girl and takes part in the ceremonies.

from the service from out of town that might be there that would drop in. It was nice to be able to go up and sit under the canopy there. We were on the second row. And we had a beagle hound, Happy, which I've referred to. Have I told you about Happy?

Paul Stillwell: Well, you told me that Charlie was chasing him over there to meet you in Bancroft Hall.

Admiral Burke: Well, one day, I think it was Governor Tawes who was the Governor of Maryland; he was the reviewing official for the Wednesday afternoon parade.* The troops were already all lined up for the present arms and so forth. Betty and I were sitting under the canopy, and all of a sudden everybody started to laugh and turn around and look at us. [Laughter] Somehow or other Happy had gotten out of our house, and he was down there challenging the Second Regimental Commander. [Laughter] Our daughter Sally, who was about 14, ran out from the house. I don't know if she saw it. She was laughing so hard she could hardly stand up. [Laughter] She ran out and recaptured Happy. [Laughter] But we took a bit of hazing over that incident.

  Well, it turned out that a year before we went up there for duty they had a dog incident that really could have gotten serious. Our beagle wasn't all that big, but somebody had a fairly big dog like a boxer or something like that that got out in front of the reviewing canopy, and a Marine was sent out to retrieve him and he turned on the Marine. [Laughter]

Paul Stillwell: One thing you mentioned before the tape started was the changes that came about when people started taking different classes instead of virtually identical schedules.

Admiral Burke: Well, we used to march to class because everybody took the same course except foreign language, and it was easy to slice us up into different battalions. But then we got in the situation where we had electives and some people were taking more courses than the other and so forth, and it was difficult, and it became impossible to

---

* J. Millard Tawes, a Democrat, served as governor of Maryland from 1959 to 1967.

schedule that and maintain the military posture. So the decision was made to stop marching to class. We did and there was a gradual decrease in the military posture of the midshipmen. There wasn't any question about it.

I'm sure the superintendent and the commandant took some heat about the lowering of the military bearing of the mids. But it stuck, and we were committed to going the route we did. Also involved was the business of pressuring us to do something about our faculty. The officers who came there did not necessarily have graduate degrees. They were just there on a tour of duty like being a division officer or being a desk officer in OpNav. They needed more education than they had, and so gradually the Navy began to send more people to graduate school. As I remember, the first year I was there the Navy had programmed for that year only 15% of a particular year group to go to graduate school during the whole time they were on active duty. I think it's up around 60 or 70% now or it was by the time we left. They were having trouble finding people who were qualified who really wanted to go to graduate school. It's interesting in reviewing today versus when I was a mid. Coming up to graduation, the opportunities for graduate education were either in ordnance or engineering and perhaps a little bit in electronics, but I don't think electronics was a word that anybody knew anything about then.

Paul Stillwell: Right.

Admiral Burke: And the people who were ordnance engineers were considered the glamour people in the fleet.

Paul Stillwell: The Gun Club.

Admiral Burke: The Gun Club.* They really were. When I went to my first ship, they weren't interested in me because I was not high enough in academics to be considered.

---

* "Gun Club" was a term used to describe the officers—particularly those with graduate degrees in ordnance—who served in battleships, cruisers, and destroyers. They felt that the warships' big guns were, and would remain, the predominant naval weapons. Once aircraft carriers came to prominence early in World War II, the influence of the Gun Club began to wane.

Paul Stillwell: What were the advantages in the education of the midshipmen by getting a more varied curriculum?

Admiral Burke: Well, I want people who can think and be able to react to the world in which we live. This is a long, involved answer. I could talk on for hours on this subject, but essentially at the time I went to the academy, and before that particularly, the military lived behind a fence and were isolated from the civilians. The Navy was a very small organization. We probably had fewer than 100,000 people in the Navy when I first graduated. I've forgotten what my signal number was, but I think it was around 7,000 when I was first commissioned, so I was right at the bottom of the heap.[*] There weren't more than 7,500 or maybe 8,000 line officers then.

We were dealing with people who had all come up in the same mold. This doesn't happen anymore. We had segregation in our country. We had also a class system within the white community. Living right here in Alexandria I was brought up in a strongly class system. The people who ran Virginia were Episcopalians, and I didn't have any Catholic friends essentially until I went to the Naval Academy. I think you need people who can think, reason, and reach out. We were taught to memorize and recite. I didn't start thinking until I was over 30.

Paul Stillwell: And now there are earlier opportunities for graduate education as well.

Admiral Burke: Oh, yes. I think it was the first year I was down there the Arleigh Burke scholarships were started. I've forgotten how they were selected, but we had selection boards, so we had input on it, but they were also academic. And then we had people who were recommended for Rhodes Scholarship, and I'd say we, the service, had to make exceptions. Once we got into the Rhodes Scholarship business we discovered that West Point was number two in the country behind Harvard. We found that West Point had more academic honors than we did, but we started doing something about it. I think all

---

[*] The Navy Register of 1 July 1940 indicates a signal number of 7112 for Burke; that represented his relative standing among the unrestricted line officers of the Navy at the time. The number for the junior-most ensign was 7172.

of these things started when Admiral Davidson was there, and to his credit he gave it a big push.

Paul Stillwell: Well, as I remember talking to him, he said he had objected initially but has since come to see the value of the changes.

Admiral Burke: Well, any time you promote change you're going to get a reaction. There's just no getting away from it. I was comfortable with the idea. I liked the idea. I'd say when I was in class with people who had already had this stuff that didn't make sense to me. They weren't developing.

Paul Stillwell: It was a waste of their time.

Admiral Burke: And it didn't seem right to me to just keep retreading somebody just so that other people could catch up. It's just like I told you before, I believed when I was a midshipman and even more strongly after being exec I'm going to get rid of the plebe system as it's constituted because I think it restricts the maturing of these people.

Paul Stillwell: What do you recall of the reaction on the part of the alumni when midshipmen no longer had to march as companies to class?

Admiral Burke: Well, they didn't ping on me, but I heard about it. They felt the place was going to hell. You know, Admiral Smedberg had been the superintendent.* He was Chief of Personnel, and so he and Admiral Davidson and later Admiral Kirkpatrick used to talk to each other frequently on the phone. He was their boss—"Smeddy," as he was called. I really didn't know him, but he said that there should be a rule that anybody who has been superintendent of the Naval Academy should not be allowed within 100 miles of the Naval Academy. [Laughter] And the same thing could be applied to almost any flag officer at certain times. [Laughter] Well, I won't tell you who it was, but an

---

* Rear Admiral William R. Smedberg III, USN, was superintendent of the Naval Academy from March 1956 to June 1958. From 1960 to 1964, as a vice admiral, he was Chief of Naval Personnel. His oral history is in the Naval Institute collection.

ex-superintendent was living around there, and he used to drop in and give unwanted advice or unsolicited advice. I think you know who I'm talking about.

Paul Stillwell: Harry Hill.*

Admiral Burke: But we had other old grads that did too. We had one of our six-stripers. This six-striper was a hell of a nice guy. He was a Navy junior. I think it was the first year I was there. His father used to drop in on the commandant and tell him how to run it every so often. [Laughter] How he could put up with that stuff I don't know. I was just glad I was the exec and was across the hall. [Laughter]

Paul Stillwell: Well, what kind of demands on your stamina did that job pose?

Admiral Burke: It was just about the most exhausting job I've had. I'd say during the war on war patrol where I came apart, that was one thing. I didn't come apart here, but my day was full. I used to be in the office about a quarter of eight. The corridor boy would bring up my lunch from the galley, and I'd eat my lunch there at my desk, and I might get home around 5:30 or 6:00 o'clock. I'd stick around and have dinner and get back to the office about 7:30, I'd say at least three nights a week, sometimes four.

Paul Stillwell: How late would you work then after dinner?

Admiral Burke: I'd say till 11:00 maybe. The problem is that I was usually dealing with very serious cases, either honor and/or discipline or both, and I'm just a believer in doing it directly. I used to interview these people. I didn't have to, but I just believe in knowing whom I'm dealing with. You get into a lot of situations. One year, and I forget which year it is, you know when you get up into around the first of March the first class sort of gets an idea that—and it happens every year, I'll bet it still does—"They're not going to flunk me out." This is also in demerits. One of the years we had a surprising

---

* Vice Admiral Harry W. Hill, USN, was superintendent of the Naval Academy from April 1950 to August 1952.

number of people who were first class who were up around 75 to 100—I forget what the number of demerits is but it was too high and too many. I interviewed every one of those mids who were high in demerits. I had them up in my office and talked to them just to let them know that they weren't going to get a free ride.

Paul Stillwell: Did those visits have a beneficial effect?

Admiral Burke: Well, they probably hated my guts for it. [Laughter] As far as I know, it probably helped, but what I wanted to do is convey to them the fact that we had a personal interest in them. You know, when I was a midshipman in Bancroft Hall it was so regimented that you were not close enough to your bosses to get a personal feel for them. They come up and see you when you're lined up at formation and so forth and they're looking at you but you don't get to know them.

Paul Stillwell: Very impersonal.

Admiral Burke: Yes. You're walking down there, and some officer puts you on report because you scratched your head or something like that. Uncle Beany, God bless him, put me on report for turning my head in ranks or something and I had hardly turned it, but he was laughing when he put me down. But these kinds of things, it's an impersonal kind of atmosphere and I'd say the longer I was in the service after I got on ships I made a point of trying to interview everybody that served under me.

Paul Stillwell: What sort of toll did this pace take on your physical well-being after a time?

Admiral Burke: Well, I was going full blast all year, and I say I did fine. Then I got up to summer, and Jim Mini was transferred and replaced by Charlie Minter as commandant right at the beginning of plebe summer. I've forgotten exactly when it happened, but it probably happened before the plebe summer started. The summertime is when you have your leave program for your personnel, and here we had the plebe summer, and I just decided that it would be a good idea if I stuck around to make sure Charlie got the support he needed. It was good for me because I got to know Charlie, and I was very impressed with him. Then I got up to, oh, about October, and I ran out of gas. I was just hanging on for dear life the rest of the academic year.

Paul Stillwell: Just in terms of fatigue?

Admiral Burke: I just didn't have the energy. I'd run out of energy. My gas tank was empty. I'd say when we got around Christmas that helped, but there's always something going on there to keep you busy. It put a strain on me, but it really taught me a lesson that I have never forgotten, because I have been very careful ever since to make sure that not only I take my leave but the people under me.

Paul Stillwell: Were you able to scale back on your hours after a while?

Admiral Burke: I don't know that I did. I guess I'm a slow person. [Laughter] My wife has said that I'm a workaholic. While Charlie was there I did for a while try to go over and take a swim at the pool during lunch hour, but I didn't do it on a regular basis the way I should have. I just felt it was taking too much time away.

Paul Stillwell: Well, what do you remember about Captain Minter as the commandant?

Admiral Burke: I think he was great. No matter how you look at him he's a big man. He's got extraordinary judgment, and he's got a good sense of humor and very fair person. One of the things I was amazed was his ability to get up and talk to the visitors when they came through, the VIPs and so forth. I really envied his ability to do this.

Paul Stillwell: I've never encountered a person who didn't like Admiral Minter.

Admiral Burke: Well, personal, I'd say this is part of leadership to me, having the charisma that he has or his ability to communicate in a friendly manner. And Mary supported him to the hilt and in her way she's just as great as he is. Ever since we've met them, they've been good friends. Unfortunately, they live in another town, so we don't see them very often, but they're good friends.

Paul Stillwell: What do you remember of Admiral Kirkpatrick who succeeded Davidson?

Admiral Burke: Well, he was my company officer and he is an exceptional man in the people department for my book. He remembers you. He was my company officer for one year as a second classman, and then off he went as a flag lieutenant with Captain Draemel who was selected for admiral. The next time I saw him was about 1944 in the submarine officers' club at Pearl Harbor. He was Admiral Ernie King's personal aide and a war hero, and I walked into the bar there and he was sitting there having a drink with somebody, and he looked up and saw me.* He hadn't seen me since 1939, and he called me by name. He remembers you. Then I saw him in New London when I had command of the Sablefish. He was a squadron commander for a while up there, though he was not mine. But he's a tough guy to work for, and what I like about him he means what he says and he makes damn sure that you do what he means.

Paul Stillwell: Did you see examples of that when he was superintendent?

Admiral Burke: Well, I just knew him from the little contact that I had with him as a midshipman and feel by the way he operated that he wanted things done in a hurry. If I were a four-star admiral, I would want Kirkpatrick as my number-one assistant because I could be a good guy all the time. He's interested in people, but he had this thing born into him. He knows how to relate with people, but he lets you know if you're not cutting the mustard. Well, I appreciate this. When he came in as the superintendent, I told the battalion officers, "This guy is going to be looking into Bancroft Hall, and if ever you hear of anything that he's interested in I want to know about it and I think whoever is the

---

* Admiral Ernest J. King, USN, served as Chief of Naval Operations from 26 March 1942 to 15 December 1945 and as Commander in Chief U.S. Fleet from 20 December 1941 to 2 September 1945; he was promoted to the rank of fleet admiral in December 1944.

action person must know that he wants it done yesterday." And he hadn't been there very long before he was walking the halls. I told Charlie Minter that this was going happen, and he said, "Well, I'm not going to walk the halls."

I said, "Well, I just want to let you know it's going to happen, and I'm not sure how we're going to deal with it." But he would go in and walk the halls and open a door and go in and sit down and talk with the mids. They'd tell him how the place was running. Well, that's a good way to find out.

Sometime during the year, we had a screw-up in the menu, or there was something that the mids didn't like in the menu planning, and they began to start bitching about it. So as soon as I heard about it, I figured he was going to hear about it. I knew this was going to happen so I got with the commissary officer in each battalion or regimental staff, and I set them up so that they could review the menus that were being submitted, and I had a whole plan there that was in operation. Well, I was sitting at my desk a few days after it was all set up and going, and I got a phone call and Kirkpatrick was on the phone. He told me about the complaints from the mids and said, "What are you going to do about it?" And so I told him what we'd done. He said, "You've already done this?"

"Yes, sir."

So he said, "Thank you very much."

Paul Stillwell: Disarmed him.

Admiral Burke: But I'd say that's the way you had to operate. It was just sizing up the guy you were working for. But I say I really liked working for him because you knew where you stand all the time. He was Uncle Charlie. As far as I know, he became Uncle Charlie when he was a company officer because his nephew was in my class. When he came back he was still Uncle Charlie. I remember when he relieved as superintendent it was at a ceremony on the parade ground; I think it was just a plebe parade. I don't know whether we had the second class out there or not. He talked to them and he talked to them one on one, and it sort of shocked some of our company and battalion officers because he told them he was going to know them personally, and he did. And so when we went down to the Oyster Bowl and he walked across the field at the half, the midshipmen got up and cheered him, and he'd only been aboard about two months into academic year when that happened.

Paul Stillwell: I think you mentioned once before when we were talking you were disappointed that he did not become the Chief of Naval Personnel.

Admiral Burke: Oh, I think he would have been great for the Navy. But he had this heart attack the night before he was to be relieved as superintendent. Happens to all of us sooner or later. But that's the luck of the draw, I guess.

Paul Stillwell: Do you have anything else in your notes to recall about the Naval Academy period?

Admiral Burke: Here are a couple of things. The first class lectures, you know. I don't know what night they were on but Tuesday nights probably. And I'm not sure what department. Probably English, History and Government probably sponsored them. They'd have wheels from the Navy Department down, and it turned out that immediately after the Bay of Pigs Arleigh Burke had been scheduled to speak, and I mean it was within a week.* Washington was still in an uproar, but he kept his date and came down with Mrs. Burke. Betty and I attended that lecture.

I've always felt that Arleigh Burke in a prepared address was not very good, and on the other hand I have never seen his equal on being able to stand up and respond to questioning. He was terrific. That night, when he finished his prepared address, which was, I would say, at best mediocre, we had a recess. Then we came back in, and he began to take questions. And I tell you, several of the midshipmen first class jumped up and really wanted to know how did we get into this mess. The mids wanted to know who the hell was responsible for this screw-up. He gave an answer that was I thought unusual

---

* In mid-April 1961 a force of 1,400 Cuban exiles, secretly trained by U.S. personnel in Guatemala, landed in the Bay of Pigs, on the southwestern coast of Cuba, in an attempt to overthrow Fidel Castro, that nation's Communist dictator. The invasion attempt was a disaster. President John Kennedy decided that U.S. naval intervention would worsen the situation, so ships and aircraft offshore were prohibited from taking part.

and effective. He said, "I'll tell you what happened, but it's not to go outside this room. I attended the meeting where the decision was made, and we were asked certain questions and went around the table, one at a time, and each of us responded. When my turn came, I gave my input, and it went on to the next person. At the end everybody was silent." He said, "My silence was assent, so if you're looking at who's responsible here, I am." Have you heard this before?

Paul Stillwell: No, I hadn't, but it takes a big man to say that.

Admiral Burke: He didn't say what he recommended, but I thought that was one of the finest things I've ever heard.

Paul Stillwell: He's universally admired.

Admiral Burke: Let's see. We ran the dairy farm. We ran the mess hall. We ran the midshipmen's store. Sick bay. The shrinks. What I have learned, I'd say every job I have had in the academy was a learning experience. Like I told you about the shrinks. I had never known anything about that before or even considered it. I never had to worry about a store before in a sense until we had the midshipmen's store. We had an enormous extracurricular activity there that was largely funded by the profits from the midshipmen's stores.

The mess hall was an interesting operation, and in order to speed things up, we installed serving carts. It wasn't my idea. I think the stewards were in the mess hall then. But running all that operation was a big-time do, and in order to make it more efficient they got these serving wagons, they probably still have them, where they bring the food to the tables.

Oh, one other thing I'd like to talk about is the exchange weekends with West Point. When I was a midshipman I didn't know anybody up there. The only people that had any contact were the athletic teams, and I don't think they really knew the people they were playing against other than as competitors on the field of honor. But now we have exchange weekends, and when I was there the superintendent came down with his wife and stayed with our superintendent. Their deputy commandant came down, and he and his wife were our houseguests. And we went up there; we became good friends. It's a nice thing, and I believe it fosters the ability to later on to work together when they get in joint duty.

Paul Stillwell: And especially now with the Goldwater-Nichols Act it's made it that much more important to have joint service.*

Admiral Burke: Well, at the time I came up the line joint service was something that you didn't necessarily want to get into. It helped practically no one to get along. The first team stayed at home.

Paul Stillwell: Well, OpNav duty was much better than joint duty in that era.

Admiral Burke: Oh, yes.

Paul Stillwell: You mentioned the Bay of Pigs. Do you have any perspectives to offer from the Cuban Missile Crisis, which took place in late '62?

Admiral Burke: I'm trying to think where I was. I guess I was at Annapolis then. It was the fall of our third year. I really don't. I remember it happened just about the time of the Oyster Bowl game, and for some reason Betty and I didn't go down. I have lots of questions about the whole deal and why didn't we do what we were supposed to do but the politics of it, I could speculate but it would only be speculation.

Paul Stillwell: Well, do you have anything else on the Naval Academy from that tour of duty?

---

* The Goldwater-Nichols Defense Reorganization Act of 1986 went into effect on 1 October of that year. It mandated a good deal more in the way of joint-service relationships than had been the case up to then. For details, see "DoD Reorganization," U.S. Naval Institute Proceedings, May 1987, pages 136-145.

Admiral Burke: Well, all I can say is that it was personally rewarding, professionally rewarding. We made enormous numbers of friends. As a result of that tour of duty, we have since whenever we could gone back to homecoming on Friday night so that we could mix with the other classes and see as many old friends from around the service. Strangely enough, the rest of my classmates don't like Friday night.

Paul Stillwell: Why not?

Admiral Burke: I don't know. They hardly show up on Friday night. They go off and party somewhere else, so the people that show up at that Friday night that we know are less and less. Just an interesting observation, the only people left on active duty today who were midshipmen when I was the executive officer are a very few flag officers. Steve Abbot, who is in the class of '66, was probably a plebe or a youngster when we left. He's the only person that we know personally on active duty. He's Com6thFlt.

Paul Stillwell: Well, that's all the questions I have. Why don't we save the <u>Fremont</u> for next time please?

Admiral Burke: Okay.

Paul Stillwell: All right. Thank you for a good interview again, Admiral.

[Tape recorder turned off]

Paul Stillwell: All right. Here we go with a little postscript.

Admiral Burke: We had a number of VIPs that came through, and invariably most of them eventually visited Bancroft Hall. One of the VIPs was Prince Juan Carlos and his bride, who was the daughter of the former Queen of Greece.[*]

---

[*] In 1962 Prince Juan Carlos of Spain married Princess Sophia of Greece. In 1975, after the death of Spanish dictator Francisco Franco, he became King Juan Carlos I, Spain's first King since the country became a republic in 1931.

Paul Stillwell: When did they come through?

Admiral Burke: They came through during the summer of '62, right after Admiral Kirkpatrick had become superintendent. Charlie Minter and Mary were not available, I don't know why, so Betty and I were subbing for them. He came over to Bancroft Hall, and then there was a luncheon at the superintendent's. Probably the ambassador was there from Spain plus a couple of others, and I had the good fortune to sit next to the princess. They were on their honeymoon. They'd gone around the world and had been to Hawaii shortly before they came to Washington, and I asked her what the most fun thing that they had done during their honeymoon trip.

She said, well, when they had been in Hawaii that they had a night off from their official schedule where they could get out and do what they wanted. So they went out by themselves and she said, "You know, when I was growing up and up until the time I was married, I had never before spent any money. That night was the first time I had ever been able to spend money." [Laughter] But she was a lovely young lady. I remember when they came into Bancroft Hall I was up on the steps to greet them and escorted them into the rotunda and up to Mem Hall. One of our secretaries in our office there on the right was Anna Samaris, an Annapolitan who was Greek by heritage, so I introduced her to Anna, which pleased her very much.

Paul Stillwell: You certainly had a variety of chores in that job.

Admiral Burke: Well, I did, but I was fortunate to watch Charlie Minter and learn under his tutelage. He knew how to handle it, and I wish I were half as good as he is in dealing with the public.

Paul Stillwell: Okay, thank you.

Interview Number 9 with Rear Admiral Julian T. Burke, Jr., U.S. Navy (Retired)
Place: Admiral Burke's home in Alexandria, Virginia
Date: Thursday, 26 February 1998
Interviewer: Paul Stillwell

Paul Stillwell: Well, Admiral, you've arranged some delightful sunny weather for today's interview. Last time we talked about what I know was an enjoyable tour for you at the Naval Academy, and from there you went back to sea again, so let's resume at that point please.

Admiral Burke: Well, first I had to decide where I wanted to go, and I don't remember the details, but I decided that I wanted to go try to get a command of a cruiser ultimately. But I had to get a deep draft ahead of time, and I shopped around with my friends up in BuPers. I was assigned to the Fremont, which was an APA in the amphibious force.* She was based in Norfolk. She was in the Norfolk Naval Shipyard in Portsmouth, Virginia, and they'd just commenced an overhaul.

I relieved a classmate, John Greenbacker, as CO, and in the short time we had our turnover.† This was a completely foreign environment to me, amphibs. I was interested in the amphibs because looking back on my experience I had been doing different things almost whenever I went somewhere. It didn't bother me trying something new and different. Also, when I was on CinCLantFlt's staff a number of years before, I was impressed with the articulate value of the amphibious force that the then ComPhibLant had in letters that came up to the CinCLantFlt. I was up in the front office and frequently read them, and I observed the value of the strategic importance of them.

Paul Stillwell: Was that Spike Fahrion?‡

---

* USS Fremont (APA-44), a Bayfield-class attack transport, was commissioned 23 November 1943. She displaced 8,100 tons, was 492 feet long, 70 feet in the beam, had a maximum draft of 26 feet, and a top speed of 18 knots. She was armed with one 5-inch gun and carried a variety of landing craft for amphibious warfare operations.
† Captain John E. Greenbacker, USN, commanded the Fremont from 13 July 1962 to 2 August 1963.
‡ Vice Admiral Frank G. Fahrion, USN, served as Commander Amphibious Force Atlantic Fleet from January 1952 to April 1956.

Admiral Burke: Yes, it was. He was exceptionally articulate. There was another person that I had bumped into, I don't know whether he was still on active duty, but it was Joe Stryker, class of '25, who had been a company officer when I was a mid and later was on the North Carolina.* Joe Stryker eventually worked his way to exec on the North Carolina. The enlisted men didn't mind the captains coming and going, but as long as Commander Stryker was there that was great. I'd bumped into Joe Stryker a couple of times, and he had told me the importance of the amphibs, and I just remembered that. I was ambitious, and I wanted to get ahead. I didn't think I was on the first team in the submarine Navy, so I thought I'd like to go for a cruiser if I could, and so there I went.

Well, when I got down to the shipyard the ship, of course, was in dry dock and looked like hell, dirty. I had never really operated around the Marines except the few company officers and the battalion officer there at Annapolis. Greenbacker was not very complimentary about the Marines and told me how difficult they were to deal with. Eventually I relieved him, and he went on his way and I took charge. The Fremont was a flagship for the squadron, I think it was Squadron Four.

Eventually we got out of the shipyard, went up to the base at Norfolk around the first of November, and we were getting ready to go to Gitmo for refresher training. By that time Admiral Jack McCain had relieved as ComPhibLant.† We were at the base on the 22nd of November 1963, which happened to be my son's third birthday, my youngest child, and he and Betty came down for lunch. We were supposed to get under way at about 1:00 or 2:00 o'clock in the afternoon. They had lunch with us, and we had a birthday cake, and then Betty and Charly left and went up to Ward's Corner. Then they were going to come back and wave at us as we left the dock. As we were being pulled away from the dock by the tugs, Betty drove up and called up to me and told me just as I got it from my sound-powered telephone that Jack Kennedy, the President, had been killed. So I rang up "All stop." Made the announcement on the 1MC. We were backing away into the channel with two or three tugs alongside and the pilot aboard, and the pilot was nervous and we had a minute of silence, of respect, and then we went on our way.

---

* Captain Joe W. Stryker, USN, commanded the Fremont from 18 June 1948 to 27 May 1949.
† Vice Admiral John S. McCain, Jr., USN, served as Commander Amphibious Force Atlantic Fleet from 1963 to 1965.

Paul Stillwell: And this was the first time you'd gotten under way with the ship?

Admiral Burke: Well, I had come up from the shipyard to the Norfolk Naval Base.

Paul Stillwell: I see.

Admiral Burke: And then we went down to Gitmo. While we were there, Admiral McCain was making a tour of all of his arena and he ended up in Gitmo. He came aboard, and I greeted him with side boys, and he said, "Don't you know we're in a state of mourning?"* [Laughter]

Paul Stillwell: What else do you remember about him?

Admiral Burke: He's a good friend. He's somebody I've always from the first day I met him been able to talk to. He had a magnetic personality that was extraordinary. I think he was the kind of guy that got the best out of people because they wanted to please him very hard. I never had any trouble with him. But I think I told you earlier about my first time I ever heard of him when he was an instructor over in the skinny department.

Paul Stillwell: I don't recall that.

Admiral Burke: I was a second classman, and one of the third classmen in my company came back one morning from the lecture at Sampson Hall. He said, "Boy, we really heard it today." McCain, who was then either a jaygee or a lieutenant, had given a lecture that day to the third class. I don't know what the course was, but it was in physics or electricity. And he used a number of words, profanity, that weren't allowed by gentlemen. The midshipmen started laughing and raising so much hell and enjoying it so much that the department head, who was a crusty old four-striper, came out and stood in

---

* Side boys are crew members stationed in two ranks at a ship's gangway on the arrival or departure of officers or officials for whom side honors are rendered. The number of side boys varies from two to eight, depending on the rank of the individual.

the door and quieted it down. We heard later that he was never allowed to make another lecture. [Laughter] But everybody knew the next day who Jack McCain was. [Laughter]

Being in the amphibs was a learning experience for me, because everything I was doing was new and the type of ship and the type of people. The quality level of the personnel in the amphibious force was light years below what I'd been used to serving with in submarines.

Paul Stillwell: And destroyers, too, probably.

Admiral Burke: Yes. My senior watch officer was a lieutenant commander. I learned that the previous summer, before I got transferred from the academy, one of our officers had been aboard the <u>Fremont</u>, and they were asking about this guy from Annapolis. He cheerfully told the senior watch officer that the new captain ate lieutenant commanders for breakfast. [Laughter] And I'm sure he believed it. [Laughter] But when I got there that senior watch officer wasn't qualified to stand a top watch. I was used to the officers I had on my destroyer or on my submarines; they could do circles around what we had there.

I had an exec who administratively was quite good, and he kept me out of trouble in that department, and I watched the operations carefully. But the general level of competence of these people was very limited, and I had to be around and on top of it. When we got back from Guantanamo just before Christmas I found we were deploying to the Med on a normal six months' deployment. In early January we went down to Morehead City and loaded out. We had the flagship, so the squadron commander moved aboard.

Paul Stillwell: Who was he?

Admiral Burke: Bob Merritt out of the class of '39.* I had never served around him before. He had a small staff, and the arrangement was that we had the battalion commander on board and his staff plus one company plus some other units of one

---

* Captain Robert G. Merritt, USN.

company of Marines. Early on, after having heard from my predecessor about the difficulty with Marines, I worked very hard at getting to see what they were doing and how they were doing it and so forth. When we went down to Morehead City, going alongside and watching them load out was quite an experience.

Paul Stillwell: Could you just describe that little bit please since it was so new to you?

Admiral Burke: Well, I went through some short courses or briefings over at PhibLant to begin with, but when we went down to Morehead City we went alongside the dock, and they started loading stores and bring people aboard, and it took overnight. It was a 24-hour exercise, and they were loading things like Jeeps and heavy equipment and so forth in the space that we had. We had an LSD and, of course, they flooded down and would get things in their landing craft and bring them in the tailgate. We had at least one LST in the group. We had six ships—an AKA, an APA, an LSD and an LST plus the Fremont.* Is that six?

Paul Stillwell: Well, maybe you had two APAs, the Fremont and one other.

Admiral Burke: But we were the flagship, and we had at least 450 Marines aboard. We had a total of about 800 to 900 people on board ship when we were fully loaded. There was a helicopter detachment that went along with the squadron. We had a SEAL detachment. We had a Marine recon detachment.

Paul Stillwell: Did you have an APD with you?

Admiral Burke: No, I don't remember an APD. But I'd say everything I saw was new to me, and so I was learning all the way, and we headed for the Med.

Paul Stillwell: What had you picked up about handling the deep-draft ship, which was part of the reason for sending you there?

---

* AKA—attack cargo ship; APA—attack transport; LSD—dock landing ship; LST—tank landing ship.

Admiral Burke: Well, it wasn't like being on a destroyer where you were maneuvering around all the time or on a submarine where you were diving. You were sort of kind of trying to keep the ship in a rather stodgy formation. You didn't get involved in tactics of that kind. It was sort of like a convoy I guess.

Paul Stillwell: Well, for going in and out of port you had two problems, a single screw and a lot of sail area.

Admiral Burke: Well, around the piers we normally had a pilot to get us in and out. I don't remember making an unassisted landing for the first time. I wasn't used to that, but I also wasn't used to doing with a single screw. I don't recall having any narrow scrapes just from doing things like that.

Paul Stillwell: What else do you recall about the crew?

Admiral Burke: The Fremont was the biggest ship I ever commanded, and I made a conscientious attempt to get through the ship a couple or three times a week and to give a presence there. There's segregation on those ships between sailors and Marines, so I wanted to make sure they knew me. I wanted to do things to make sure that they knew that I was looking after their interest. Not everybody does that.

Paul Stillwell: That's true.

Admiral Burke: Consequently, I tried to run my ship like I had my submarine. I tried to interview every single man on my ship when he reported aboard and when he left. When I was on the transport we had about 450 people in the crew. I know I missed some because I didn't have that kind of time, but almost everybody had a face-to-face meeting with me. The kind of thing I was concerned about was unwarranted assumption of authority on people. I was a CO of a ship back during the racial problems. This was back in the '63 time frame. I wanted to make sure the blacks knew that if they felt they were frustrated they could come up and talk to me.

Paul Stillwell: That's an important thing for them to know.

Admiral Burke: I never had anybody come up, but I told every single person I interviewed if something was wrong and it wasn't being fixed, he had the right to come directly to me. Nobody ever told me that, but I felt that under the circumstances in our country it was important that they know it. I didn't get to interview all the Marines by any account, but I knew all the officers. But my Dale Carnegie training made me concentrate on knowing the men, knowing who they were and what their capabilities were, and I think they appreciated it.

I went around the ship by myself oftentimes to look it over, and I ended up in the chiefs' mess, once or twice in the first class mess. I also found out that the Marine battalion commander, anytime I dropped in on him the sergeant major was always sitting there by him, and the sergeant major was a member of the chief's mess. So I had a pipeline from the chiefs' mess through the sergeant major through the colonel. I began to work that way and this was before we had command master chiefs. I made a command chief.

In the first class mess, we had a very unusual man in Pop Meehan, who was a first class. He was in his 60s, I'm sure. He had been in the Navy in World War I, and this was 1963-64. He was an old man. But he happened to be there the day I walked in, and we sat down and had a cup of coffee. We told some sea stories, and then he started dropping by my cabin almost every few days to tell me what was going on and what was needed, and it was a pipeline that probably the officers hated my guts for it.

While we were in the Med we had a visit from Paul Nitze, who had recently become Secretary of the Navy.[*] We were conducting a landing over on an island that's just west of Italy. It was Italian territory, and we were at a landing beach when Nitze came aboard. His aide was a Captain Zumwalt.[†] That was the first time I ever heard of

---

[*] Paul H. Nitze served as Secretary of the Navy from 29 November 1963 to 30 June 1967.
[†] Captain Elmo R. Zumwalt, Jr., USN, executive assistant to the Secretary of the Navy.

Bud or saw him. When Nitze came aboard, I had Pop Meehan up there to greet him, and Pop presented him with a coffee mug with the SecNav's name inscribed on it, and he said, "I want to tell you. I don't want to do what the captain did. He dropped his and broke it and we had to give him another one." [Laughter] When we got back from that cruise, Pop ended up in the hospital. I guess he—I wrote Bud and asked him to get an autographed picture of the Secretary, which he did, and Pop had that picture of the Secretary there in his hospital bed, and he made a lot of impression. [Laughter]

Paul Stillwell: How could he stay in the Navy so long? He must have been in 45 years.

Admiral Burke: He got out and he was out for a number of years, and then he came back in.

Paul Stillwell: I see.

Admiral Burke: We were living in Bay Colony in Virginia Beach at the time I had him aboard. I had my car bring him out for dinner one night, and he was just a genuinely nice guy that was a friend. After he retired he went home and I kept in touch with him until he died. He was one of these morale builders that we were fortunate to have in the ship and people would rally around. He could find information or get things done that otherwise wouldn't be—just little things that made a difference.

As I say, once we got all the Marines aboard I made a concentrated effort to get around the ship daily, as near as I could, and go through the Marine spaces and let them know I was around. Also I used to have Marine officers in the detachment up to my cabin at practically every meal so that I could get to know them and find out what made them tick. John Adams was the commanding officer of the company, and he's an academy graduate and somebody I have the highest personal regard for.[*] I had him up on the way to Gibraltar. I had him up for a meal at least three times, so we got to know each other very soon, and it turned out that after we got through Gibraltar he wasn't around,

---

[*] Captain John A. Adams, USMC.

and I asked where he was. They said he was on leave. So when he got back after a couple of weeks I said, "Where have you been?"

He said, "Oh, I went to see my grandparents."

"Where?"

"Greece."

I said, "Greece? John Adams?"

He says, "The name's Adamopolous." [Laughter] And he told me this story. His father lived somewhere north of Athens; he was one of quite a large number of children. He was the oldest and at age 17 the family scraped together enough money to send him to America, and so he went there and landed in New York and began to send money back home to keep the family going. After 17 years he wrote to the family and said, "Send me a wife." And they did.

I said, "How many other are you?"

He said, "There are five of us, four boys and a girl."

"Where do you stand in this?"

He said, "I'm the middle one."

I said, "Did they pick out your wife?"

He said, "No, but they did pick out the wife of my younger brother and my sister's husband."

I said, "Well, how did the marriages work out?"

He said, "Actually, I think the ones that got picked out worked out better." [Laughter]

But I was learning through this. I have been into so many new places all my life that whenever I get into a bunch of people I start right off and find out who they are, where they came from, where they went to college, what their backgrounds are, and I just do this intuitively. It doesn't make any difference whether it's a church or whatever, but it enables me to get to figure out people a lot faster than perhaps the average person can.

Another guy, Mike Wodarski was the battalion commander. Really interesting guy and smart and shrewd. Turned out his parents immigrated; I think his father was a Czech, his mother was Hungarian. They happened to end up together in Pennsylvania, and they met up there and got married. He was a graduate of Penn State College. His father ran a little beer parlor alongside a small recreational lake somewhere up in Pennsylvania. They had slot machines, and Mike didn't know they were illegal until after he'd graduated from college. But that's what paid his way through Penn State. There were about six or seven brothers and sisters; all of them were college graduates, and the parents were immigrants. Mike graduated from Penn State, and I think he had a graduate degree in personnel from Stanford. He was somebody that was teaching me about what the United States was all about, and we became good friends. I haven't seen him in years now, but we were good friends and he taught me a lot about the Marine Corps. But we went on our way into the Med.

Paul Stillwell: It sounds as if you developed a better relationship with the Marines than your predecessor had.

Admiral Burke: And they loved me. I'll tell you why later. [Laughter]

Paul Stillwell: All right.

Admiral Burke: Well, I worked at it. I didn't like the idea of having each other in such confinement when you're supposed to be mutually supporting. I had never heard this before but, oh, it didn't surprise me in a way because we're different cultures in a way.

Paul Stillwell: But they're also your main battery.

Admiral Burke: Well, that's right. Somewhere along the way it turned out that the problems on Cyprus blew up, so instead of making our first port in the western Med we ended up by going straight off of Cyprus and started patrolling.*

Paul Stillwell: Now this would be in early '64?

---

* The constitution of Cyprus, adopted in 1960, created a republic and provided for government officials of both Turkish and Greek nationality. In December 1963 the island experienced a constitutional breakdown, resulting in the separation of Greek and Turkish Cypriots.

Admiral Burke: This was early '64, yes. We never came in sight of the island, but we were always over the horizon. There were maybe 1,000 or 2,000 Americans on the island. There was, I think, an American electronics security station there. There were a number of Greek-Americans that had gone home for retirement. As I went around the rest of the Med during that cruise, I discovered in talking to American consuls that much of the work that they did was supporting those kinds of people, making sure they got their Social Security checks.

But, in any case, we were there, and eventually we never got into actual combat. We almost got ready. The Marines were just champing at the bit to go ashore, and this was the first time I had ever in my life seen troops trying to get ready. We had a small flight deck on there, and the Marines would go back there and do sitting-up exercises to stay in shape. For the first time in my life I saw captains and majors and lieutenant colonels out running around with the troops, which I'd say I never even thought about this before. But it made sense. And they were usually leading them. Then eventually Com6thFlt, Vice Admiral Gentner, came down and paid us a visit.* And he sent our first nuclear carrier, Enterprise, down there so that our troops and personnel could go on liberty on board the Enterprise. [Laughter] And they did. They went over there and had milkshakes and all that sort of thing. The only thing they were lacking were girls and beds. [Laughter]

Paul Stillwell: A major difference though. Well, and alcohol too.

Admiral Burke: Well, while I was on board we were lying to, it was a nice sunny day very much like today, rolling easily and the liberty boats were going back and forth, and our crew and the Marines were eating it up and the other ships were getting the same benefit. And who showed up but Dodge McFall; he was in an A-1 squadron on the Enterprise.† So I took Dodge around and took him all through the ship and down into the compartments where the Marines were, and they were stacked in there knee deep, believe me. We had a nice visit, and then it went on her way.

---

* Vice Admiral William E. Gentner, Jr., USN, commanded the Sixth Fleet from March 1963 to June 1964.
† The Douglas A-1 Skyraider was a propeller-driven attack plane.

Then when Admiral Gentner came down he told the commodore and also the Marines, Mike Wodarski, the battalion commander, he said, "When you get out of this mess I'm going to let you go to any port in the Med of your choosing."

Wodarski spoke right up. He said, "Admiral, we've got to be careful. My Marines are ready to tear anything up. They can't be trusted to go into any port." So, oh, we were furious. They finally sent us to Malta. We all wanted to go to a good liberty port!

Paul Stillwell: Malta might not have been your first choice.

Admiral Burke: It wasn't ours. No, I would have said probably one of the French ports, but the decision was taken away from us. And so the squadron went up to Malta, and for me it was a fine learning experience. Have you ever been to Malta?

Paul Stillwell: No.

Admiral Burke: Of course, from a liberty point of view for the troops I think it's the last place in the world that they would like to have gone. But from getting historical education of what's been going on before and what's been happening since, it was ideal. We went in there, and, by gosh, they had a British commodore who was there, and he invited the commanding officers over and the commodore over for lunch in the castle there. Then we began to read all about the great siege of Malta back in about 1415. I read a couple of books about Malta and the history of it and how they got that way. Of course, it was run by the British. We met a few British people.

One of the British officers that I met down there was a lieutenant commander; he and his wife had a few of us out for dinner. They had a son who was in school in England and coming back for Easter vacation, so I said, "Well, bring him out to the ship with his friends." Well, these kids were about nine years old, had been packed off to England to go to school, and that's common in their culture. My God, I thought it was cruel and inhumane punishment, but it's their expectancy. I don't recall much after that.

Paul Stillwell: Did the crew enjoy Malta at all?

Admiral Burke: I don't think they enjoyed it the way we did. I think they were glad to get their feet on the ground, but they were limited in what they could do.

Then from there we went on up to Naples, and we were assigned an Italian Navy liaison officer who was a commander. I forget his name, but he had an English name or Anglican name like Taylor or something like that. But he looked Italian, spoke Italian, and spoke English with an Italian accent. It turned out that his Taylor ancestor had settled there during the Napoleonic Wars when the British were taking over the Mediterranean, and he just stayed and he was a hand-me-down and he was in the Navy. Well, he was a very nice guy.

One day while we were there, some of us went into Pompeii. We drove off the road about a mile away from the gate and back into an orchard and on private property, but there was no fence there and we were just sitting under the trees eating lunch. Out of nowhere came this Italian talking to us in broken English, very broken English, and I started chatting with him. It turned out that he was a deserter from the U.S. Army in World War I. He'd married an Italian girl. [Laughter] He was from somewhere in West Virginia.

At that time, my oldest child, my daughter Tina, was on a year aboard at the Sorbonne in Paris. And I'd written to her, urging her to come down if she could when I was in Naples. I had a classmate, Bill Morton, who was on the staff of the NATO commander there, a distinguished gentleman.[*]

Paul Stillwell: Admiral Russell?[†]

Admiral Burke: Yes. He was there, and anyhow Bill Morton and his wife, Sis, lived out at Basillibo, which is off on the Naples Bay to the left of and when facing Naples from the sea. It's a beautiful area. And my daughter the last I'd heard was she couldn't make it because of studies and so forth. Well, it turned out that on a Friday afternoon she and a

---

[*] Captain William B. Morton, USN.
[†] Admiral James S. Russell, USN, served as Commander in Chief Allied Forces Southern Europe from January 1962 to March 1965. His oral history is in the Naval Institute collection.

classmate, who was also Navy junior, decided they would come after all. It was too late to cash any checks or get any money, so they just went down and hopped a train in Paris and headed for Italy. They got on a first-class train. Just walked on and didn't get thrown off until they got to Milan. Then they hitchhiked down the autostrad and ended up in Naples about 3:00 o'clock in the morning.

The family of my daughter's classmate had had duty there, so she was familiar with the lay of the land. She got to the Mortons' area, which was a beautiful villa that had been turned into three or four apartments. You had to walk through a gate, down a sloping, winding lane through trees and so forth and they arrived there at 3:00 o'clock in the morning. When the word got around the local Navy people about what my daughter and her classmate had done, they thought those two girls should have been whipped, but they got away with it.

I had a classmate, Jake Heimark, who was on the staff there; he was an intelligence specialist.* Jake was at sea but his wife, Betty, had Tina and me out for dinner one night, and Tina was telling about her experience and what she'd done and Betty Heimark began to scold her. Then she stopped and she said, "Well, maybe that wasn't so bad after all." She was a Navy junior, and her father had been stationed in Shanghai, and she had done something ten times as bad, going over the fence into the International Settlement. [Laughter]

But from there we went into Barcelona, sort of the passing of time. We had a landing with, operated with the French, probably in Corsica. This was at the time right after the French were pulling out of NATO. They were very picky about whom they would operate with or what the command relations were, but I wasn't dealing with them because I was the ship's captain, not the commodore. And from there we went into Barcelona. Saw a bullfight.

Went to a mountain out in some place called Montserrat, which is where Christianity first started in Spain. I don't know whether it was St. Paul that brought it there or not. Probably. And it's up on a high mountain peak. It's a very impressive area and a big church. I was up there on a tour bus, and one of the things that you did was to, after you went through the cathedral there or the basilica, was to go up on the high peak

---

* Captain Jacob V. Heimark, USN.

and they'd take you up in a lift, up straight up. And I remember there were a bunch of sailors who were whooping it up on there like sailors shouldn't have done in this particular situation, and all of a sudden one of them looked through the window that was in the floor. We were up about 1,000 feet and all of a sudden they became deathly quiet until they got off that elevator. [Laughter] I don't remember anything more about that.

During those landings around Corsica, I learned that the British wanted to participate, and the Italians didn't want them. Later on, somewhere along the line, the French were there, and they didn't want the British either. The next year when I was back there I ran into the same thing again. The problem was that this was the twilight of British power, and they had exercised their power around there, but they no longer had the clout. These European NATO navies were much more interested in working with us. I suspect people were just tired of English clout. I imagine there are a lot of countries around the world that are tired of Americans, too, for the same reasons.

Paul Stillwell: Was this because they perceived the British to be arrogant, do you think?

Admiral Burke: Well, usually the British had staked out a toehold somewhere and taken something away from them. Best example of that was the Spanish that we ran into. The Spanish still want Gibraltar back, and while we were there we saw some examples of that. We had a Spanish liaison officer aboard, and his contempt for the British was strong. This was the next January. We were over in Spain over Christmas of '64 and then in January of '65 my family was over there at that time. They were planning to leave, and they got held up going into Gibraltar. It was a stall. I've forgotten the exact circumstances, but it took them a long time to get through. This was just deliberate harassment by the Spanish on something that the British have a toehold on and don't want to let go. I suspect if you took a vote amongst the people who live in Gibraltar, they'd still like to stay with England, but that is Spanish territory, and the Spanish won't quit wanting it back.

Paul Stillwell: You can understand that.

Admiral Burke: Well, it's similar, and people wonder about the Israelis and the Arabs. Same problem. After my reading about the Mideast, I've often thought that if the Russians had won the Cold War and turned this East Coast back to the Indians we'd be in a hell of a problem.

Paul Stillwell: What do you remember about that intricate choreography of an amphibious landing with the assembly circles and the line of departure and so forth?

Admiral Burke: Well, not much in detail except it took a lot of learning to watch it. It was different from anything I'd worked, because there was so much of everything you couldn't control it. You could only say, "Here's what we want to do," and you'd go out and train to do it, but if your people out there weren't instructed and trained to do it, it wasn't going to get done. You had to get all of these assembly circles you're talking about and so forth and getting up and it took a lot of preparation, briefings and training to get these people to know what they were going to do, where and when they were going, and how. And the weather didn't always cooperate

Paul Stillwell: Your deck crew was a very important factor in getting the boats in the water.

Admiral Burke: Yes. And this was very disturbing to me when I got there and saw the quality level of the officers versus what I was used to. We got what was left over, and it was very disturbing to me to see that we had so much committed to this kind of warfare. Now, I kind of think we're doing a lot better in this department now than we were then. From all the literature I'm getting from the Navy Department these days, it looks like we are playing more into the amphibious side of projecting U.S. power than we were then. But if you don't put your best people there you're going to get hurt.

Paul Stillwell: Well, another factor since then was the creation of the Surface Force as a type command, so it sort of homogenized the personnel situation.*

Admiral Burke: Well, I left the fleet just as that came off. When I had the Fremont, the cruiser-destroyer people were the people that ran the surface Navy. The service force and the amphibs were running well behind them. At least that was the impression I had.

One thing I'd learned when I was in submarines, our squadron commander was Chuck Triebel, C. O. Triebel.† When I first had the Sablefish as commanding officer he used to bitch all the time about how terrible it was to communicate with ships and find out what the captains were thinking. That started me working on the problem, and so when I went to different ships I made sure that our officers could pick up that telephone and talk coherently with knowledge. It made a difference because you're advertising yourself every time you do it. I know that when I first started working on it, particularly in my destroyer, the guys hated me because I put a lot of pressure on them, because they didn't know how to talk on the radio. But by the time I got back from a two and a half months Med cruise they were marvelous. My commodore received an evaluation of each of the ships in our squadron that went along, got it from the task force commander who was an aviator admiral, and they gave each of the ships a numerical score. We were number one so far it was embarrassing. I just worked on trying to make these guys be able to do that.

Paul Stillwell: And that's especially important in the ship-to-shore movement.

Admiral Burke: Well, the ship-to-shore thing was something I never directly got involved in and never had to do it. When I look at these movies and hear what happened on D-Day at Normandy or any of these places like Tarawa I don't know that I could have cut that.

Paul Stillwell: Well, you never know.

---

* Naval Surface Force Atlantic Fleet was created 1 January 1975 by combining the Cruiser-Destroyer Force, Mine Force, Service Force, and Amphibious Force of the U.S. Atlantic Fleet.
† Captain Charles O. Triebel, USN, served as Commander Submarine Squadron Eight, 1948-50.

Admiral Burke: I did different things, but I'd say I wonder whether I would have stood up and been able to deal with it.

Paul Stillwell: How did your next assignment come about?

Admiral Burke: When the Fremont was in the shipyard, I had gone up to BuPers and told the detail officer, who was in the class of '39, that I wanted to get a cruiser. His question was, "Who's your sponsor?" I didn't have one. He said, "Well, I can't give it to you. Unless you've got somebody from over in OpNav pushing for you, you're not going to get it." Well, I didn't have that. I had not had that kind of a career pattern. I'd just gone out and sort of done it on my own, and I figured that I would make it based on my previous command performance.

Paul Stillwell: Which is as it should be.

Admiral Burke: But, in any case, he said, "You can have a submarine squadron, or you can have an amphibious squadron or a service squadron."

Right off the bat I said, "I'd rather have an amphibious squadron."

He said, "Why?"

I said, "Well, that's where I'm serving now, and I'm beginning to learn something about it, and I think I can do a better job there. I don't think I can help myself professionally by going back to submarines." The unofficial word around was that there was a quota for submarine officers because of the makeup of the selection board. That was the impression that was coming through. You could look back, and never more than two were selected.

As I went through my time in the Navy, I just felt I wanted to be more knowledgeable about more things in the Navy than just submarines, because in the submarine Navy that I'd been in, the diesel side of it, politically it was a very small part of it. I had friends that had gone all the way to flag rank, but it didn't appeal to me just to get to be in submarines. I wanted to try something else. So I was signed up to go to

ComPhibRon 6 at the end of the Fremont tour. Then I received a letter from the detail officer telling me I was going to get it. About a month later he called me up and told me about one of my classmates, Andy Anderson, Roy Gene Anderson, who was a submariner and had been in the Polaris program, he was a postgraduate in ordnance.[*]

Paul Stillwell: He was the chief staff officer for the first Polaris squadron.[†]

Admiral Burke: Yes. He was checked out as a nuclear submariner, but not ever had a command. We were classmates, and I'd known him quite well at the Naval Academy. We'd been shipmates on the Flying Fish. He should have been the exec, but he got transferred and was exec of another boat. So we were good friends, and he said, "Andy Anderson needs some surface experience; he hasn't had enough to compete for flag rank. We want you to take the submarine squadron he was going to get, and he can have yours so he can be better qualified.

I said, "Well, I'll think it over." So I went around and talked to people. At the time there was a submariner who was my amphibious group commander. I went over and talked to him, and I talked to a couple of other submarine people, and I just decided to hell with it. I said, "Andy had a chance to pick his career and he did, and I had a chance to pick mine and I did, and this is how it's going to come out."

I never had a chance to talk to him about it, but it all got taken care of by the selection board that spring, because he got selected a year ahead of time before getting a major command, and they gave him the stars immediately. But I was advised by at least two flag officers to go ahead and don't try to fight the bureau. So I never discussed it with Andy, and he made flag rank and I don't know whether he was surprised or not but he did.

Paul Stillwell: Well, you said that you made the Marines happy on board the Fremont. How did that happen?

---

[*] Captain Roy G. Anderson, USN.
[†] See the oral history of Rear Admiral Norvell G. Ward, USN (Ret.), who served as Commander Submarine Squadron 14, the first squadron of ballistic missile submarines.

Admiral Burke: Well, I say I took the effort to know them personally, and I knew all of the platoon commanders, I knew the heads of the units. I had these guys up, and I knew enough about what they were doing so I could talk to them about it and be sympathetic and supportive.

I used to be around the ship a lot at night. I started insisting that we have soup and sandwiches for the midwatch and this made the supply officer very unhappy. Occasionally I'd be up in the middle of the night, and I'd go by and check, and I found frequently that the sandwiches weren't very good and the soup wasn't very good, and it was cold. So before long I had the supply officer meeting me there every night at 11:30. Eventually the soup and sandwiches at midnight got so popular that the Marines used to line up for it. [Laughter]

Paul Stillwell: Well, also you said that your senior watch officer was not all that great. Did you get that situation squared away?

Admiral Burke: Well, I didn't have a replacement for him. He just was not a strong person. He was a hell of a nice guy, but I had to be there pushing him. I had one Naval Academy officer. I've forgotten who he was, but he did not compare with any of the officers I had on the destroyer, for example. You had to be on top of things more then, but I didn't know enough about things, and I felt like I was riding a lot in a vacuum. My exec was quite good in administration. He had been in destroyers I think, in DEs, and he knew how to run things. But he was so involved in the administration he didn't get much involved in the operations.

Paul Stillwell: What about cleanliness? That's usually a problem on an amphibious warfare ship.

Admiral Burke: Well, it wasn't what I was used to, but when you've got Marines lying around on the ships all the time it is not easy to deal with. We went off in January, and we got extended up to over seven months because of this Cyprus crisis. So when we got back around, gee, I guess it was up in July, we were pretty thoroughly wrung out. Then I was relieved within three weeks after we got back.*

Shortly thereafter I became the squadron commander of Amphibious Squadron Six. Then within a month we went back over again. I never felt like I was really on top of the job the way I got on top of my destroyer. I didn't know anything about destroyers when I went into it, but, by God, I learned in a hurry. I had to. Well, this was a different kind of a learning. I was learning all the way on how to get along and deal with and support Marines. By the time I got over to my squadron I'd been on a flagship, which was an old ship, and moved over to a squadron flag, which was the La Salle, which was a brand-new ship and, boy, what a difference.†

Paul Stillwell: Amazing. Now she's the Sixth Fleet flagship, and she's got some age on her by now.

Admiral Burke: Well, that was over 30 years ago, so she was brand new then. Right after I took over, off we went on a major fleet exercise where ComPhibLant was in charge.

Paul Stillwell: Steel Pike.‡

Admiral Burke: Yes. And Admiral McCain was the commander. My group of ships, Squadron Six, and the Marines embarked. Operationally we were not in Squadron Six. I was just going along as a passenger on that exercise. It was probably as big an exercise as we've had since World War II. We got over there, and Admiral McCain was in

---

* On 14 August 1964, Captain Charles K. Schmidt, USN, relieved Burke as commanding officer.
† USS La Salle (LPD-3) was originally commissioned 22 February 1964 as an amphibious transport dock. She served as an amphibious warfare ship until 1 July 1972, when her designation was changed to AGF-3, a miscellaneous flagship. She was flagship of the Middle East Force from 1972-80 and 1983-94. She subsequently became flagship for Commander Sixth Fleet.
‡ On 26 October 1964 a full-scale amphibious assault exercise, Steel Pike, began in southern Spain. It involved 80 ships and 60,000 men from the Navy, Marine Corps and Spanish armed forces. It was the largest peacetime amphibious exercise ever held. In addition to the Navy ships, ten U.S. merchant ships transported Marines from the United States to Spain. Landings took place at Huelva, 50 miles northwest of the U.S. naval base at Rota, Spain.

command. Things were going along fine at the landing, and then apparently the SEAL team or the UDT team got in trouble.*

It was right next to a Spanish resort beach, and these SEALs at night, whenever they were supposed to be sleeping and so forth, would go over the boundaries and go over into the Spanish resort area and start fooling around. Eventually they got caught up by the Spanish police. I never heard the exact details of it but it was embarrassing to the commanders and the U.S. Government. After the exercise was over, I went over to pay my respects to Jack McCain. We were being detached from his group of ships and going into the Med for our regular deployment. He said, "Now goddammit, I want you to make sure that those guys, those damned SEALs that screwed up over on the beach get punished properly and never get ashore."

I said, "Admiral, they're under your command. It's up to you do to do it." [Laughter] And he didn't do it. [Laughter] But I say he was a marvelous guy and a good friend.

Paul Stillwell: What do you remember about the exercise itself?

Admiral Burke: I can't give you any details of it. No.†

Paul Stillwell: They even had a bunch of merchant ships involved in it just to test that part of the amphibious mix.

Admiral Burke: I say I was just a passenger in that thing. My staff and I were involved in planning the Med tour. This was a diversion to us that we didn't get into. Let me just finish up this McCain story.

Paul Stillwell: Sure.

---

* SEALs are Navy personnel trained for sea, air, and land operations. In previous years similar individuals were designated as part of underwater demolition teams (UDTs). In addition to that specialty, the SEALs have a broader mission that includes commando-type operations ashore.
† For details, see James B. Soper, "Observations: Steel Pike and Silver Lance," U.S. Naval Institute Proceedings, November 1965, page 46.

Admiral Burke: We went into the Med and ended up in Barcelona for Christmas. The SEAL team detachment that we had in our squadron came from some of the SEALs that were on Steel Pike. They were on one of the LSDs. I guess it was the day before Christmas. I can't remember whether we were anchored out or not, but anyhow the LSD was anchored out, and the captain sent an urgent message he had to confer with me personally. So he came over and told me that the preceding night he had been just taking a tour around the ship. He got back to the flight deck, and there was a drunken brawl going on the flight deck of his LSD being led by three SEAL officers. These were the boys that had participated there in Spain in getting in trouble.

So I said, "Okay, we'll fire them." So I disqualified them and sent them back to PhibLant, and I requested replacement. Eventually they got there, but we sent them back, period. I didn't hear anything more about it until the following year. Let's see, this was January of '65. Well, in about November of '66 I was a rear admiral, had become ComPhibGroup 3 in San Diego. Champ Blouin, who was the new PhibPac, said he wanted me to go out and take a look at Vietnam because I was responsible for training certain boat crews and things like that.* So I was in Vietnam for about three weeks and flying around visiting everywhere and one of the times, it was toward the end of the tour, we ended up in a place was about 30 or 40 miles down the river from Saigon.

When I landed, there was a commander that came up to greet me who was the senior naval officer. He said, "Admiral, I'm real happy to have you here. We have just had the most successful operation of our team since we've been out here in this particular area, and I want you to pin on some medals." So the first three guys I pinned medals on were those three guys that I kicked off our ship. [Laughter] We were all laughing about it as we went down the line.

Paul Stillwell: So they had the same qualities. They just worked better in another context. They were rough and ready guys.

---

* Vice Admiral Francis J. Blouin, USN, served as Commander Amphibious Force Pacific Fleet from July 1966 to May 1968.

Admiral Burke: Yes. When I went over to the Med with the squadron, I had been separated from my family right much. Mike Hanley was a classmate of mine who had command of one of the big carriers.*

Paul Stillwell: <u>Forrestal</u>, I think.

Admiral Burke: Yes. He told me about these commercial cargo ships that carried up to 12 passengers, unscheduled, and so I was able to work out something for my wife and our two youngest children. Our little boy, Charly, was approaching his fourth birthday, and we took our daughter, Sally, who was about 16, out of school. My mother and Betty's mother, too, came along and they just waited there in Virginia Beach until they got a telephone call, and they drove down to Norfolk, boarded a ship, and later arrived in Savona, Italy, I think. It was a port near Genoa, and they had a Hertz U-Drive meet them, and they put 3,000 miles on that car. My mother was a voracious reader, and she always had a book that she was reading. She could read a book a day. One of the books she made sure I read was <u>The Agony and the Ecstasy</u>, which taught me a lot about the Italians I didn't know. Another one was called <u>Adrianne</u>, which was the biography of Lafayette's wife. Taught me a lot about the French and the politics of the French and their culture.

Paul Stillwell: <u>The Agony and the Ecstasy</u> was a historical novel about Michelangelo, wasn't it?

Admiral Burke: Yes. It was a memorable experience. My mother, when she was engaged to my dad, had been in Europe just before they were married when World War I broke out. I think they were in Italy when it happened. But she had been in Italy in 1914.

In Europe at that time it was safe for women and men to go around by themselves at night in cities. My wife and our family group went to Venice, and they were staying in

---

* Captain Michael J. Hanley, USN, commanded the aircraft carrier <u>Forrestal</u> (CVA-59) from March 1964 to March 1965.

a family hotel. The first night, there was a man at an adjacent table who was an American. He had been there and realized that they had just gotten to Italy. He took my mother and mother-in-law and daughter on a tour, walking tour, around Venice, and they got home around 10:30 or 11:00 o'clock. My wife was at home with Charly, who was approaching his fourth birthday, and she was beside herself wondering where they were. Sally was so excited at what she had seen, and so she took her mother and led her around Venice after 11:00 o'clock for about an hour and a half, and it was perfectly okay.

They visited places that I couldn't go to, and they would tell me about them. It wasn't until about five or six years ago that Betty and I went to those places together, and it was quite a memorable experience. Also, our little boy, who was born almost the same day that John-John Kennedy was, looked very much like him.* More than once an Italian would come up and just pick Charly up and carry him across the street, and he'd pick up an apple off a fruit stand and give it to him. We'd always given him a lot of attention but not like the Italians did. It gave us a warmth of feeling about the Italians that has never left us.

We had exercises with the Italians. We had a couple of NATO exercises. Professionally also I got to be involved in a couple of fleet exercises where, believe it or not, I was the task force commander. So I got thrust into task force antiaircraft defense and so forth, and it was quite a learning experience for me that I would never have gotten sitting on a desk as a submarine squadron commander.

Paul Stillwell: Any of your individual ship skippers that you particularly remember?

Admiral Burke: One of the LSD commanding officers, Howard Moore, was an aviator; he ended up as a flag officer, ComFAirWestPac, and came to Japan shortly before I departed.† He was the class of '43. Tex Winslow was the captain of my flagship.‡ He was the class of '42, and occasionally I've seen him here in town. He had been captain of the Secretary's yacht when he was a young officer, maybe a lieutenant commander. We

---

* John F. Kennedy, Jr., was the son of the President-elect when he was born 25 November 1960, three days after the Burkes' son.
† ComFAirWestPac—Commander Fleet Air Western Pacific. Rear Admiral Howard S. Moore, USN.
‡ Captain Edward H. Winslow, USN.

had Ernie King's son. I guess he was captain of the LST, I think, when I had the Fremont.* He seemed like a very solid citizen, but he was younger than the rest of us. My contemporaries were all captains. He was a commander. That's about the best I can do for you right now.

Paul Stillwell: What can you say about the new capabilities that the LaSalle offered, a new type of ship, the LPD?

Admiral Burke: Oh, they were great: their capacity, the living conditions, air-conditioned throughout. I don't recall that we had air-conditioning in the Fremont. Possibly in the captain's and the commodore's cabins but not much beyond that. But all of the living spaces were air-conditioned and, boy, what a difference. I'll tell you, when we went down for the load-out I was not directly involved as the ship's captain, but when we tied up to the dock at Morehead City and things didn't move the way they were supposed to move.

I learned a lot then about Marines, because the battalion commander who later made general officer, when he came on board La Salle to check out with me and so forth, he was telling me what a great job his men did. They were not doing a good job. They only got the job done because the ship's company got in there and helped them. It taught me something. What had happened was they were going on this deployment, and they'd had a big party the night before. They weren't up to getting moving, and they didn't show up until the early afternoon. They were supposed to have been there at 8:00 o'clock in the morning, and we had to bail them out. It taught me a lot to see how the sailors would use their initiative when there were unwritten directives to get the job done or the Navy people do. They're much better at that, I think. I saw enough of this in those two years. It just happened that way.

Paul Stillwell: On the other hand it's surprising that Marines would not be where they were supposed to be at a given time.

---

* Commander Ernest J. King, Jr., USN.

Admiral Burke: Well, I'd have to say it probably meant that their leaders weren't there either, and all I can say is that we left on time, but it was only because our sailors got in there and bailed them out.

I think the whole exercise, the whole battalion was like that. On the other hand, I made a point of having a balance of Marine officers with naval officers participating in my commodore's flag mess so that they felt included. And this kept us going throughout that cruise. I had a second one when I was in the Caribbean, too, and had a similar experience there. I wanted to make sure that our staff and their people knew each other on more than just a remote contact, and it seemed to work.

Paul Stillwell: Did you have a chief staff officer with some good amphibious experience?

Admiral Burke: I can't remember his name. He was a very solid guy. He probably didn't get selected for command. I had a superb operations officer whose name I can't remember. He was a lieutenant commander. He had been passed over twice, and he got selected for commander and then he later on worked for Admiral A. G. Ward.[*] He eventually made captain, and he was a crackerjack. I wish I could remember his name. I haven't seen him since, but he did a fine job.

We went into Nice before Christmas, and we had two unpleasant things. One was we had a couple of sailors that raped a young single mother. These two sailors had gone to the movie, and she was the ticket collector. When she finished, they tailed her home and were trying to date her and whatnot. When she finally got to her house and started heading in they grabbed her and threw her over the hedge and raped her. And it got reported. I think her son came back and reported it to the police.

The police went down to the waterfront immediately—it was towards the end of liberty—and they began to check everybody that came back, and they were able to pull out the two guys who had done it. They were black, as I recall, and they had enough on their uniforms to suggest they'd been in a wrestling match, and she identified them. And

---

[*] Admiral Alfred G. Ward, USN, served from April 1965 to September 1967 as U.S. representative to the NATO Military Committee.

here we had an international incident. It turns out what we did was we turned the people over to the French authorities. And in talking with the consul there, he told us that when somebody like this did something there wouldn't be any reprieve later on, the parole the way we have. In the European countries, particularly France, on something like this it's the duty of the family to feed the person when they are in jail. And so one of his jobs was to see that American citizens who were in the local jails, that they got fed. Just interesting.

The other thing that happened while we were there, we were anchored outside the seawall. I think it was at Nice where we were, and if it wasn't Nice it was the next port to it. I was expecting to go ashore that afternoon about 1:00 o'clock, but about 10:00 in the morning, all of a sudden, I heard the second anchor drop. We had a sudden gale that came up, and it was about 60 knots. It was a mistral that came down over the Alps and hit every so often. Boy, it blew like hell. Nobody got in trouble, but I tell you, if we hadn't dropped the hook we could have been in deep trouble.

Paul Stillwell: Were there some positive aspects?

Admiral Burke: When my family was there at Christmas, we had first gone to Nice and been at Nice for about a week, and my wife and daughter went up to Paris to see my older daughter. Then Betty came back and Sally, my daughter, and Tina joined us in Barcelona at Christmas. I don't remember any operations with the Spanish Navy, but I'm sure we must have had some. Then we went from Barcelona to Valencia and spent the New Year's week there at Valencia.

We're Episcopalians, and we went to an Episcopal service in Barcelona, and we were told that this was the only Episcopal Church or Protestant church in all of Spain. When we went to Valencia we had the American consul and his family out on Sunday dinner and to attend church, and this was the first time they had been able to go to a Protestant type service and were quite grateful for it.

I can tell you one of the events. We went up to the city square at midnight New Year's Eve, and people for some reason were eating grapes. That was a sort of a Spanish custom. And then my family left, and we went out on a major fleet exercise in the

Western Med. And then we proceeded over to Greece and went into the port of Athens, Piraeus. The first night ashore we went to the yacht club where our boat was landing. We went to the bar and had a drink before we went into Athens. A civilian club member came over and began to chat with me. He asked me about my family and so forth, and I told him, and he said, "You're the luckiest person I ever heard of."

I said, "What do you mean."

This man was about a contemporary. He said, "I haven't yet received permission from my father to get married." [Laughter] He said, "In our society the father rules the family, and my father has not given me permission."

I said, "Do you have any brothers and sisters?" Well, he had a sister who was married, and he had a younger brother who was a doctor and married. They were happy. "Why not you?"

"Because I'm responsible for the family and my father has not turned over the responsibility to me yet." And he said, "I am a big shot. I have recently been to the United States and the houseguest of the chief executive officer of IBM for two weeks. I made some very good deals for our company, but when I got back it wasn't approved and final until my father got the complete facts and approved it, and then that was it. Since then I've been up to Germany and done the same with them and I had to come back?" You know, I'd say that kind of thing and then going back to John Adams, the Marine, that conversation I told you about, made me realize the importance of cultures to what people in countries will do.

Paul Stillwell: It's a great illustration.

Admiral Burke: I've run into situations since then where behavior patterns of certain people sort of reflected that mentality or that culture, and I was able to react to it.

Years later, when I was in Japan, I discovered it took about six months before the Japanese would begin to really accept you for what you are or before they understood and figured they could trust you. Once they got to that point, they're usually your friends for life, but just because they smile at you and are very pleasant and polite on the surface at an introduction encounter—believe me, that's not friendship. And that's the way with most Orientals that I've met.

Paul Stillwell: What other experiences did you have in command of the amphibious squadron?

Admiral Burke: We had operations down in Crete. I can't remember whether they were before or after we had been to Athens, but I know that there was good rapport between the Marines and their counterparts in Greece. We had an amphibious landing on the south side of Crete. We had a horrible storm. Several of the Greek ships that were participating had dragging anchors, and the radio circuit was full of foreign language and frustrations, but nobody got hurt. The Marines were on the beach there for at least a week. I went over and toured their facilities and had a very interesting experience encountering what the Greeks had. I went over at least twice and was shown what they were up to.

At the end of the exercise we were in the area where Cat Brown had operated when he was Com6thFlt. His personal messages sent back to Admiral Wright always contained biblical quotes that created a humorous reaction. So I sent for the chaplain when the exercise was completed and told him because of the storm we had I would like to find something appropriate for my sitrep that I'd send Com6thFlt. So he hadn't been gone very long and he came back. He had the perfect quote. It seemed that St. Paul had been shipwrecked by stormy weather in the bay where we had our landing and had wintered over in that community. And his comments were that the locals were varlets, harlots and all sorts of things, terrible things. [Laughter] So when I sent my sitrep to Com6thFlt I just put the reference, "St. Paul's umpty-ump, paragraph umpty-ump. No change." [Laughter]

Well, we did that exercise after we left Athens, and from Crete we departed and went all the way home. As we passed Italy, Com6thFlt sent a Marine colonel out, a liaison officer, as we sailed by, on a helicopter to visit us and touch base and give us a pat on the back and say, "Thank you." And he said, "By the way, what the hell was that message all about?"

Paul Stillwell: So you told him.

Admiral Burke: He said, "Oh."

We went back from the Med after we had our full six months' deployment, not extended thank goodness, and we probably got back the middle or end of March.

Paul Stillwell: This would be 1965.

Admiral Burke: Yes. And then around the first of June I was deployed to the Caribbean. There had been trouble in the Dominican Republic.* There'd been an uprising there, and we had landed troops, and things were pretty well contained so we were the follow-up and relieved the amphib squadron that had been the busy people. We still had the same La Salle flagship, but we had something new, the CH-46 helicopter, which was just coming.† This was the first time they had deployed. It was a test deployment, so we had lots of VIP visitors looking at us.

Paul Stillwell: That was a helicopter that was really a mainstay in Vietnam.

Admiral Burke: Yes, but at this time it was being tested and evaluated. Our battalion commander was Bob Bohn, who later made general officer.‡ The helo squadron commander was a crackerjack. He was a major, and he later made general officer, I think. His wife turned out to be a Navy Relief volunteer who was a crackerjack. I remember running into her out at the El Toro Marine Air Station in California, just south of Los Angeles. But we had a horde of evaluators come down while we were deployed. I think our first stop was San Juan, and it was a come-back-home visit for me because I

---

* On 28 April 1965 President Lyndon Johnson dispatched a 400-man expeditionary brigade to the Dominican Republic to protect the lives and property of American citizens caught in a military revolt in that nation. By 29 April, 1,600 Marines had landed, and by 7 May 6,000 Marines were ashore and another 2,000 offshore. They were followed by Army troops, bringing the U.S. combat presence by 11 May to more than 11,000 troops. Navy ships evacuated more than 4,300 civilians during the operation.
† Official trials of the CH-46 Sea Knight helicopter, manufactured by Boeing Vertol, were completed by November 1964, and five Marine Corps squadrons were equipped with them by mid-1965.
‡ Lieutenant Colonel Robert D. Bohn, USMC.

saw a few old friends. Most of them had left, but I did see a few. From there we went around to Roosey Roads and to then to the two small islands there, Vieques and Culebra.

Culebra was where we did the gun shooting, and Vieques was where the Marines landed. The Marines landed and were ashore an extended period of time there, and the helicopters were operating. My classmate Andy Anderson, who had made admiral around the first of June, came down, and I think the Marine division commander also came to take a look at what was going on. We were there at Vieques, as I recall, for around two weeks. Whenever we had those landings I usually went ashore sometime during and got briefed on what they were doing and how the hell they were coming, and they were very pleased with the operation. The helicopter was meeting the expectation. From there we went down to Curaçao, and that was an interesting place. Have you ever been there?

Paul Stillwell: No.

Admiral Burke: They had a pontoon bridge across the harbor entrance so you could get from one side of the island to the other because inside there was an enormous opening. So to let us in they had to break the pontoon with a tug and haul it aside and let the ships in. And it was Dutch.

We went to a couple of receptions there, and it was interesting to see the Dutch. I'd never been around them before, and they reminded me very much of Germans I'd met before World War II. The American consul general was a gentleman that had been a neighbor of mine in Yates Garden in Alexandria back in 1948-49. He now resides over in Beverly Hills here, and I see him occasionally. But it was a very pleasant experience going in and sampling another culture, which was colonial. The people that we encountered were very loyal to the Dutch Government.

Then after that we probably went back to Vieques and returned to San Juan, and then I was relieved. My family had been in Virginia Beach, and I was relieved probably around early August by a classmate, Art Berndtson.[*] My family annually goes up to Squam Lake in New Hampshire, the Golden Pond, and my mother-in-law at the time was

---

[*] Captain Arthur H. Berndtsen, USN.

having her children and grandchildren and in-laws as her guests. So my family were moved out of the house in Virginia Beach and gone up to Squam Lake, and I joined up there after they had been there a while. Then we came back here and moved into this house about that time, in the middle of September '65.

Paul Stillwell: What was your next duty station?

Admiral Burke: I reported to OP-60. Previously I'd gone up to BuPers, and what I'd wanted to get was a senior officers' management course at Harvard Business School. It was a short course, something like three to six months. I thought it would be nice to have that since I was not a PG of any sort. So I went up and talked to the detail officer, and I don't remember who it was, but he said two things. One, "Who do you know?" [Laughter]

Paul Stillwell: That same problem.

Admiral Burke: And the second thing is he said, "On your record you need to be at the seat of the government. You have no experience at the seat of the government."

I said, "What do you mean?"

"Washington duty."

I said, "Well, when I was a lieutenant commander I was in Washington at BuPers, and then I was on the President's yacht."

He says, "That doesn't count. You've got to get to the Pentagon."

Paul Stillwell: That was probably good advice.

Admiral Burke: Well, it was late in the game, because when I got there I was a naïve captain and around people who knew how to operate. I went to OP-605, which was in plans. I've forgotten what 605 was, it was strategic plans I guess, and Art Esch, classmate, was in 601 I think.* I was a branch head, and I had about 15 or 20 officers

---
* Captain Arthur G. Esch, USN.

under me, and in addition to that under them were about 10 or 15 really first-line action officers. I think 603 was across the hall; they were doing the planning for Vietnam. Ace Lyons was the junior action officer in my shop.* He was a lieutenant commander.

Paul Stillwell: Please tell me about him.

Admiral Burke: [Laughter] Ace was an interesting person. I've never seen anybody work harder than he did.

Paul Stillwell: Very aggressive.

Admiral Burke: And he turned a lot of people off because he was so aggressive. But he never went in when he didn't know at least as much as the guy he was sitting across the table from. He usually knew the other guy's job better then he did. He used to come in and work Saturday and Sunday. He wasn't the only one. There were several action officers in OP-60 who had the same characteristics. They were highly competitive, they were good at what they were doing, and they knew how to do it. They wouldn't hesitate to steal each other's action on an item if they knew it was going to get them front-office exposure. Most of these officers, and Ace was one of them, were known by their first names by the CNO, VCNO, OP-06, OP-090, and all of the top people. All the three and four stars knew these people by their first names.

These officers were exceptionally good. They worked hard, and I'd say Ace Lyons is probably the one that went the farthest and worked the hardest. To give you an example on Ace, he routinely came in and worked all Saturday afternoon and late in the evening and frequently on Sunday. Now as I recall, we were strategic plans, but Ace had a way of working his way into the active plans of what was going on across the hall, with I think it was 603 or 602. They were the people working the Vietnam problem.

I remember one Sunday Ace came in and was working at his desk and had all these top secret documents out on his desk. During the course of the afternoon he went

---

* Lieutenant Commander James A. Lyons, Jr., USN. Later, as a flag officer, Lyons served as Commander Second Fleet, OP-06, and Commander in Chief Pacific Fleet.

out in the hall and across the hall and locked the door behind him like he was supposed to do, but left all his junk out there on the table. He was in with one of his buddies working the Vietnam problem, and while he was gone the security watch came in and found all of his documents exposed in violation of security regulations, and it took the VCNO to get him out of trouble. But being on a first-name basis, he didn't have any. [Laughter]

Paul Stillwell: And this was Rivero at that time?

Admiral Burke: I think it was Rivero.[*]

Paul Stillwell: What were some of the cases and issues that came to you in strategic plans in that period?

Admiral Burke: Oh, me. Well, we had a group there. Walt Small, who was in the class of '38 and was in my job before I got there was over in Paris.[†] He was in a special shop, but his shop reported to my shop even though he was a flag officer. He was involved in some NATO negotiations. I forget the name of it, but we had a NATO group of ships.

Paul Stillwell: The Standing Naval Force Atlantic.

Admiral Burke: I think he was working on those negotiations. His family lived here, but he was over in Paris for a long time and was going back and forth.

Paul Stillwell: Were you involved in the relocation of the fleet homeport from south France over to Italy?

---

[*] Admiral Horacio Rivero, USN, served as Vice Chief of Naval Operations from 31 July 1964 to 17 January 1968. His oral history is in the Naval Institute collection.
[†] Rear Admiral Walter L. Small, Jr., USN.

Admiral Burke: I don't remember that. I'm trying to think. I believe it occurred while we were there, during that period.* It may not have. I know it happened in the time frame about the time I was over there in the Sixth Fleet or right after I got back. But I don't think that was the issue. I think it was this standing group that had something to do with it. As I recall, it was a group of ships with NATO crews and so forth.

Paul Stillwell: Multi-national.

Admiral Burke: Multi-lateral force—MLF. That was the code word. We got involved in command relations problems. Also, as I recall, was there was a desire in OP-06 to separate CinCLantFlt from CinCLant. There was a proposal, I've forgotten what it was, that I was opposed to the party line and had been stomped on within OP-06. Then when they got up and briefed the CNO on it, the CNO on the weekly briefing for the VCNO and CNO, the CNO wanted to know what jackass had proposed this, and not a single one of my bosses stood up, so I took the rap for it. I was really ticked off at my bosses about it for not having the guts, and one of them I've hardly spoken to civilly since.

Paul Stillwell: Do you have any recollections specifically of Admiral McDonald, the CNO?†

Admiral Burke: No, I didn't know him then. He was relieved by Admiral Moorer after I left. But I was not an aviator, and the aviators ran the show. I'd say I became acutely aware of what at least seemed to me to be the politics of the Navy; that the Navy was being run by the aviation community at that time. OP-06 was an aviator, I think OP-03 was, and the CNO was. I didn't get the feel that the submarine and destroyer people had

---

* In 1966 and 1967 French Prime Minister Charles de Gaulle gradually withdrew his nation's naval and military forces from NATO because he believed the United States had too much control over those forces. He also demanded that all NATO headquarters, bases and troops be removed from France by April 1967, which was done. France remained a member of NATO politically but not militarily.
† Admiral David L. McDonald, USN, served as Chief of Naval Operations from 1 August 1963 to 1 August 1967. His oral history is in the Naval Institute collection. Admiral Thomas H. Moorer, USN, was CNO from 1 August 1967 to 1 July 1970. His oral history is in the Naval Institute collection.

the push in the policy and the money. But I was only around for about eight months, and so I was not close enough to it. I was still learning when I was selected and transferred.

Paul Stillwell: Well, please tell me about getting the news that you'd been selected for rear admiral.

Admiral Burke: Well, I guess I knew that I had to be competitive just on the job I had, because the officer before me had made rear admiral. I was in one of a number of jobs that seemed to be screened as a prerequisite for flag rank. There were a lot of people around, and I figured that I was going to have to serve some time up there before I was able to carry my weight, because I didn't really feel like I was carrying my weight. I knew that I had carried my weight in the fleet and done well in the fleet. But I was a babe in arms and learning.

I was doing very limited participation in some of these JCS debates. I was normally not expected to go down there. We had special people to go down in the JCS papers. I did go in one, and I went down with Ace Lyons, and the reason I got it was that the guy who was expert in it knew it was going to be bad for the Navy, and he didn't want to be in a position to come in. He found an excuse to be sick that day, and he told me ahead of time he was not going to go there. So I took it because nobody else would take it, and it was my first time. And it was interesting to see how it worked.

I can't remember what the question was, but Ace Lyons, I think, went down as my assistant. He knew 20 times more about the subject than I did. And it came out about the way we expected. We were on the short end of the stick. But it was a learning experience for me, and you see in my career I had been going from one learning experience to another. I had not repeated. Consequently, I've gotten used to asking dumb questions in an arena.

One of the things I observed very quickly when I went into the Pentagon, you'd get into an arena with some of these conferences where there might be 20 or 30 people. Most of the participators were interested in letting people know how much they knew, but they were afraid to ask or show how much they didn't know. Well, I've been in the "I don't know" position ever since I started off, and I don't mind asking people. I'd say I had a tough year there, and by the time I left I felt like I was getting somewhere, and I hoped that I could come back into OP-60. It never worked out that way.

Paul Stillwell: Let me ask you again. What do you remember about getting the news that you'd been selected?

Admiral Burke: Well, I had some indications. What happened when our board came up, it sat in the White House for a long time, like two weeks. I forget why it happened, but there was some reason. In any case, Lyndon Johnson was the President, as I recall, and a couple of people had told me that my name was on the list. I said, "How do you know?"[*]

"Well, I just know." One guy that I remember was Jim Hingson out of the class of '39, who was a submarine friend that was up in one of the front-office echelons.[†] I was up on a staff problem, and he brought the subject up, "You know you're on the list."

I said, "Oh?" I figured that I wasn't going to make it that year. I figured I had to wait to do a full year before I'd be a serious contender. I had a classmate, I won't tell you who it was, who was really worried about it and was competitive and thought he was going to make it. I thought he was optimistic at the time, because he had been into submarines too long and hadn't done enough other things, but he'd been in the Pentagon a lot longer than I had.

Anyhow, I went down to lunch one day, and just before I went to lunch, my brother at Burke & Herbert Bank called me up and said, "Congratulations."

I said, "What do you mean?"

He says, "You're an admiral."

I said, "Aw, horse crap."

He said, "No, that's right."

I said, "How do you know?" Well, there was a social friend of his who was a civil servant in the White House. He took the list in for the President's signature, and the President signed it. The guy called and told my brother, who called me. Well, I thought, "Aw, baloney." But anyhow then I went to lunch and somebody came along and told me

---

[*] Lyndon B. Johnson served as President of the United States from 22 November 1963 to 20 January 1969.
[†] Captain James M. Hingson, USN.

that the list was out. I was down in the Pentagon cafeteria, and when I got back Betty was off somewhere and I called her. Well, she had heard before I had from my brother, and she wasn't even excited. [Laughter] This was maybe a Thursday, and the next day Betty and I took off for Hollins College, which is near Roanoke. Our daughter was graduating, and so we went through that weekend down there and got back.

The first thing I did was to go up and talk to my boss, who was Al Fleming, who was OP-60B.[*] Big John Victor Smith was OP-60.[†] What I was concerned about was whether I was going to be transferred, and Al Fleming said, "No, you're going to be here for another year, and we want you here." I breathed a sigh of relief, and that was in the morning. About 2:00 o'clock that afternoon a guy named B. J. Semmes called me on the phone and said, "Congratulations."[‡]

"Thanks very much, sir."

He says, "Your bag packed?"

I said, "What do you mean?"

He said, "I want you in San Diego on Friday morning."

I said, "Are you fooling? I just got the word I was going to stay for a year."

He said, "No. You're going to San Diego. You're going to be ComPhibGroup 3." So I came home and told Betty that, and she broke into tears, as did Sally. So it was a blow, because we had expected to be here for three years. I only had only one other tour in the Navy Department. But I think they did extend me and let me get there the following Monday instead of Friday.

We had the usual personal question of what do we do? Rent the house? What are you going to do for the summer? As long as we're talking about this, I think I may as well go through with it. Our summer plans were to go to New Hampshire as my mother-in-law's guest in August or end of July. I guess it was sometime in July. I went out and became PhibGroup 3, and I've forgotten exactly when it was. There was a Fleet Week up in Seattle and we had a group of ships that went to Seattle for Fleet Week. I

---

[*] Rear Admiral Allan F. Fleming, USN.
[†] Rear Admiral John Victor Smith, USN.
[‡] Vice Admiral Benedict J. Semmes, Jr., USN, served as Chief of Naval Personnel from 1 April 1964 to 31 March 1968. His oral history is in the Naval Institute collection.

was the task force commander, my first group command at sea, and there were quite a number of ships.

On the way up there I got a personal message from ComPhibPac, telling me that my son, Charly, our little boy who was then five, had had some sort of problem with losing balance and so forth. He was hospitalized and was on the way to Bethesda.[*] I gave the message to the doctor there on the ship, who was a lieutenant, and he told me this looked like some sort of a brain tumor. So I believe what happened was I came back on emergency leave. I was in Seattle for a couple of days, and then I took a plane and came on back to Washington. It happened that it was coinciding with the charm school that you have for rear admirals, the selectees, so I was able to participate in that.[†]

We got the news that Charly had something that was inoperable and that his life expectancy was limited. He was in Bethesda for about a month. We were very lucky that Red Warden, who had been our doctor on the Williamsburg, was the commanding officer of the hospital at San Diego.[‡] He was a family friend and able to counsel us on what to do and how to do, and Bethesda did all they could in the time. Eventually we got Charly back. He had all kinds of tests done that were essentially surgery and X-rays. They drilled a hole in his head and put things in his system so that it would show better, but there wasn't anything that could be done for him at that time.

At the time I was in a combination of duty and emergency leave. After the conference was over, I went on leave and drove out to California with my other son, Jud, who had just finished freshman year in college. I'd never driven across the continent before, which in itself was an experience. We stopped at Omaha at the SAC base, and we also stopped at Nellis, the base right outside of Las Vegas.[§]

But it was a tough experience. Then eventually we rented a house in Coronado from the then commandant of the Eleventh Naval District there in San Diego. A very nice person and we lived on Seventh and A Avenue. Our friends directly catty-corner from us were the Hansens that remain lifelong friends. They really looked out for us.

---

[*] National Naval Medical Center, Bethesda, Maryland.
[†] "Charm school" is a nickname for an indoctrination class for newly selected flag officers.
[‡] Captain Horace D. Warden, USN.
[§] SAC—Strategic Air Command, then based at Offutt Air Force Base near Omaha, Nebraska.

But the whole time we were in San Diego, Charly was terminal, and he finally died in early June of 1967.

Paul Stillwell: Did he go out to California?

Admiral Burke: Yes. Betty came out sometime in September, as I recall, and we moved in there. Amongst our neighbors were Admiral McCain's sister, and Joe McCain was living with her, Admiral McCain's youngest child, whom we'd gotten to know as a bad-boy plebe. Joe was an extraordinarily good friend during that time. He used to come over and pep up the family. He was just good fun and kooky as hell, but he was good for us. There were countless others. Jim Watkins was a commander then.[*] He was exec of a cruiser, and they lived across the side street. He had two boys. One was, I think, a little older than Charly and one a little younger. After Charly died we got a letter from Jim's 12-year-old son that's unbelievable and unforgettable.

Paul Stillwell: You have shown me that. Yes.

Admiral Burke: It's very hard for me to talk about him over a period of time with you without getting sentimental. He's buried over here in the family plot in Ivy Hill, which is about half a mile from here.

There was another friend, Jauncey Sweet, who was about the class of '54.[†] He and his wife lived around the corner from us. He was a company officer when we were there, and we had served together in Puerto Rico. And we've stayed close to them. But, as I said, it was a very, very tough year.

Our daughter Tina had graduated from college, and she came. She had been living here in Alexandria with some of her classmates, but came home to be with us. She was engaged to be married, and she eventually was married there in Coronado, about two months after Charly died. Our son Jud was in college out there, and then he went off to Tulane after Charly died. And Sally came back to Virginia to college, so Betty was by

---

[*] Commander James D. Watkins, USN, was executive officer of the cruiser Long Beach (CGN-9).
[†] Lieutenant Commander Harry Jauncey Sweet III, USN.

herself for about three months when I was deployed, and then I was relieved and came home and came on back to OP-01R.

Paul Stillwell: Well, why don't we end the session with that, and we can talk about the phib group per se the next time?

Admiral Burke: Okay.

Paul Stillwell: Thank you.

Interview Number 10 with Rear Admiral Julian T. Burke, Jr., U.S. Navy (Retired)

Place: Admiral Burke's home in Alexandria, Virginia

Date: Tuesday, 17 March 1998

Interviewer: Paul Stillwell

Paul Stillwell: Well, Admiral, it's great to see you again. We're ready to go now to your job as amphibious group commander in the Pacific Fleet. If you could resume there please.

Admiral Burke: Well, I went out to Coronado, and I was ComPhibGroup 3. I later became Group One, and I get them mixed up. This essentially was ComPhibGroupEastPac.* Of course, the war was on out in Vietnam, and so PhibGroup 1 was permanently deployed and homeported in the Philippines.

Paul Stillwell: At Subic Bay.

Admiral Burke: My responsibilities as ComPhibGru 3 had been expanding. What we were doing was overseeing the training of the boat people for the rivers and offshore or close inshore patrol. That was done up at Mare Island.† Then Vice Admiral Champ Blouin became ComPhibPac just shortly after I arrived. He had me go out to Vietnam, and I was out there for a good three weeks in country, plus stops in Hawaii, Japan, Okinawa, Guam, and the Philippines.

Paul Stillwell: When was that trip?

---

* ComPhibGroupEastPac—Commander Amphibious Group Eastern Pacific.
† Mare Island Naval Shipyard, Vallejo, California.

Admiral Burke: As I best remember, it was maybe October or November of '66. Just about the time I left, Dodge McFall, who was a very close friend, was killed in an air accident. Dodge was very close to the family.* He was our son Charly's godfather.

Paul Stillwell: What else can you say about Dodge McFall?

Admiral Burke: Dodge was one of the finest people I've ever known. It just happened that we met when we were together down at CinCLantFlt. He was an aviator, and he was about ten years younger than me.† When he first came there, his wife and family, children, were somewhere else, so he came out to the house a couple of times and hit it off with the family right away. We just liked him and we fit. We're still good friends of his widow and his children and keep in touch with them. We don't see them very often, but we always send them Christmas cards. She lives in Jacksonville, and we always make a point of seeing her if ever we're down there. But he had an extraordinary ability to write and articulate things. I'm sure that he would have been a four-star admiral if he had stuck around.

He had had one deployment out in WestPac in an AD squadron as an exec. He was getting ready for another deployment when he was killed. By that time my son Charly had developed a brain tumor and was not expected to live. Dodge came down to San Diego to see Charly. I just happened to be away that day. I didn't know he was in the area, so I didn't get to see him, but all the family did. He gave us a big boost. He went back to his airfield and was having a final training flight off of San Diego before they deployed, and he went off the end of the flight deck and flew in the water, and they never found his body. It was devastating to everybody that knew him.

Anyway, about this time I went out on this trip. I went all over Vietnam. The only place I didn't go was the DMZ at the very most northern part.‡

---

* Commander Albert Dodge McFall, USN, commanding officer of Attack Squadron 74 was lost on 6 December 1966 while leading his squadron off the carrier Bon Homme Richard (CVA-31) during a training mission on a foggy night. Gardner McFall has written a book of poems about her father; it is titled The Pilot's Daughter (St. Louis: Time Being Books, 1996).
† McFall was in the Naval Academy class of 1950; Burke was in the class of 1940.
‡ DMZ—the demilitarized zone that divided North Vietnam from South Vietnam.

Paul Stillwell: Did you talk to Admiral Ward out there at ComNavForV?*

Admiral Burke: I was his houseguest for a while. I visited General Westmoreland's headquarters.† I'd known him when he was the superintendent at West Point. He was not there, but I talked to his chief of staff. I saw all the wheels. I went down in the Mekong Delta and visited—I forget the names of these sites, but where we had boat people. I remember one of them in particular. Our people were quartered in a hotel. They had the first three floors, and on top of that was a whorehouse and a nightclub. [Laughter] But it all seemed to work. [Laughter]

Paul Stillwell: What was your impression of the state of the war in the rivers at that point?

Admiral Burke: Well, these people were working and working hard. They were patrolling. They'd been in combat. Some of them had been fired at. At the time I couldn't get a handle on how they were doing, because the Viet Cong were all around in the woods and so forth.‡ It was a very eerie feeling. But they seemed confident in what they were doing. The morale seemed good.

Paul Stillwell: But you didn't have a way to measure just how worthwhile it was?

Admiral Burke: No. One of the more impressive people I met was Hank Mustin, the operations officer down at one of these bases.§ He was a commander at the time. I think his family lived in Coronado, and Betty had met her while I was away. But he was a very impressive young man, and it didn't surprise me at all to see where he ended up.

---

* On 10 May 1965 Rear Admiral Norvell G. Ward, USN, became chief of the Naval Advisory Group Vietnam; on 1 April 1966 he got the additional title of Commander U.S. Naval Forces Vietnam when that command was created. He fulfilled the two roles until relieved on 27 April 1967. His oral history is in the Naval Institute collection.
† General William C. Westmoreland, USA, served as Commander U.S. Military Assistance Command Vietnam from 20 June 1964 to 2 July 1968.
‡ Viet Cong was a derogatory term for Vietnamese Communists in South Vietnam.
§ Commander Henry C. Mustin, USN, who later became a vice admiral.

Paul Stillwell: That's quite a Navy family.*

Admiral Burke: I was being helicoptered around so I could see what was going on. Oh, I wish I could remember the names of the places. I visited about five sites in the delta. There was one on an island, An Thoi, where the seagoing people were Coast Guard, and they were really with it. And from there we flew on back, and as I recall we ended up at Vung Tau. That's where a boat patrol had come in very successful, and I pinned the medals on the three SEALs that I'd fired over in the Med about a year and a half before. They were grinning, and so was I.† [Laughter]

Paul Stillwell: Did you get any impressions from this trip that you were able to crank into what you were doing when you got back to the West Coast?

Admiral Burke: Well, it was a very hard task to do. We were developing the various "how you do it" manuals for these people.

Paul Stillwell: Doctrine.

Admiral Burke: Doctrine. And the people who were doing it were out there, and the people who were writing the manuals were thousands of miles away, and they hadn't done it, and it was a very difficult thing to do. We had a group that was getting ready to deploy that was up in Mare Island, commanded by a very aggressive guy. He didn't want to be bothered by ComPhibGroup 3 and didn't make any bones about it. So I don't think the way we were structured we were able to be very helpful. I went up to Mare Island two or three times, as did other staff members, but I think they felt we were more of a hindrance than a help.

Paul Stillwell: Why was the training there instead of at Coronado?

---

* His father was Vice Admiral Lloyd M. Mustin, USN (Ret.), whose oral history is in the Naval Institute collection.
† For the background to this event, please see pages 405-406.

Admiral Burke: It was already settled when I got there, and I didn't question it. It was done because they had rivers up there. We didn't have them in Coronado.

Paul Stillwell: Makes sense.

Admiral Burke: They eventually got out there, and, as far as I could tell, they performed well. The problem was that our Navy was deepwater, and things like SEALs and the riverboats and so forth was just foreign to our kind of thinking. It was hard for them to get the sympathetic support that they needed.

Paul Stillwell: Were you able to get any people back from over in Vietnam to help you write the doctrine?

Admiral Burke: I don't recall any that came back, but I think practically all these people were reserve officers and when they served their time they wanted to get out and go home. I remember when I was in OP-60 as a captain, all of the special warfare planning in the Navy was being done by very junior people, and if you bumped in against the Army you were dealing with fairly senior people. I think it was not until sometime in the '80s before we coughed up a flag officer, Chuck Lemoyne.[*] He's a good friend. He died about a year ago.

Paul Stillwell: Well, then when the Special Warfare Command was created that really put an emphasis on it.

Admiral Burke: Yes.

Paul Stillwell: It was a joint product.

Admiral Burke: Well, we knew the people. I had met the guy in Coronado who was the commanding officer of the group. I guess it was a warfare group. He was a captain, and

---

[*] Rear Admiral Irve Charles Lemoyne, USN.

I had met him years before when we'd been in Puerto Rico, so I knew him, and so I had that going for me.

Paul Stillwell: Frank Kaine.*

Admiral Burke: Yes. He was a good friend, and so it was easy to be talking with him.

Paul Stillwell: Well, and he was running the school there in Coronado, which was helpful also to get some of that expertise in.

Admiral Burke: But it was a real educational course for me. One thing I've enjoyed about the Navy I've kept getting into new arenas and being exposed to new things and being the new guy on the street who asked all the dumb questions. But it was a great opportunity for me to get exposed to the special warfare people and more with the Marines than I had in the past.

I did get to command a Marine-Navy amphibious exercise in August of '67, and it was very helpful. It had lasting help to me, because most of the Marines were reserves. We had a Naval Reserve public affairs group, and I went out of my way to meet these officers and talk with them. One of them was a commander or a captain, and his place of business was KNX-TV in Hollywood. I told him my concern about public affairs. When I'd been out to Vietnam I saw some very good things being done. You would never know it by what you were reading in the papers, and this was very disturbing to me. So shortly after that exercise he arranged a dinner for me at the Jonathan Club in Los Angeles and had about ten reserve officers there. The object of the exercise was to school Burke in public affairs. These were prominent people. Herb Klein, does that name mean anything to you?

Paul Stillwell: He was in the Nixon Administration.

---

* Captain Francis R. Kaine, USN, served as Commander Naval Special War Group Pacific, based at Coronado, California, from November 1966 to April 1970. Captain Kaine's oral history is in the Naval Institute collection.

Admiral Burke: Yes. He was the first Director of Communications. He was the editor of the San Diego paper. There was another man named Herb Mendenhall who was owner-publisher of the Van Nuys Daily, which at the time was reputed to be the largest suburban daily in the country. Also a Republican. There was a CBS type man who had a program on the CBS West Coast, sort of a Mike Wallace type. He was a very feisty guy, but I remember him particularly because during the evening these people made the point to me that the Navy didn't know how to make friends with the press. The Navy, because it was so defensive with the media, tended to push them away and be unfriendly with them. So it was reflected in the press we were getting. Then they cited people who were good at it, Jack McCain, Chesty Puller, and others.[*] I never met General Puller, but they told me some stories that they kept from getting out to the public because they liked him.

They also told me that when you visit a naval base the media guy is usually low ranking and doesn't have access to the commander. They beat upon me that I should get a senior public affairs officer on my staff and have him in as a member of my mess. I had a public affairs officer I wasn't particularly happy about, so I put him under the number-two guy in planning and operations and brought him into my mess. I had that officer go out and deal with the press. In a very short order I began to get compliments from the media people. I say it was so darn easy I couldn't believe it.

Paul Stillwell: Who was the number-two man that you had do that?

Admiral Burke: I can't remember. It's only 30 years ago. But he did a good job.

Paul Stillwell: So you took aboard the lessons that these men had given you at the dinner?

Admiral Burke: Yes, indeed, and I'd say it really helped. It changed my life in dealing with the media. I told you earlier on I'd been to Dale Carnegie. Well, this was a PG in Dale Carnegie. [Laughter] It really was, because it made a big difference.

---

[*] Lewis B. "Chesty" Puller was a highly decorated Marine Corps officer who fought in anti-guerrilla actions in the Caribbean in the 1930s, in World War II, and later in Korea. He eventually retired as a lieutenant general. The frigate Lewis B. Puller (FFG-23) was named in his honor.

Paul Stillwell: Would it be fair to say that by you meeting them halfway they came the other half?

Admiral Burke: Yes. I've got a letter from a retired chief petty officer, reserve, who worked for the <u>Charleston Ledger-Dispatch</u>. When I retired he wrote me one of the nicest letters I ever received, and I know it helped me in dealing in the public arena.

Paul Stillwell: Did you do any training specifically for the ships that were going to be in the Market Time patrols off the coast of Vietnam?[*]

Admiral Burke: I personally didn't get involved in it. All of that was done up at Mare Island and up in the rivers up there. I'd say it was not a satisfactory situation, but it was something. I guess they figured they had to put it under a flag officer, and so I was it. I did not do a good job at it.

Paul Stillwell: What do you remember about training for the bigger ships that would be deploying, like the LPDs and the LPHs, APAs?

Admiral Burke: I can't give you an answer on that. I was not directly involved with that kind of training. The training and operations when they were back in the West Coast really came directly under the squadron and type commander. If there were big exercises coming up, I got involved in them. There weren't many at that time, because there were so many people deployed. Quite frankly it was not a professionally satisfying experience.

Paul Stillwell: Was the main thrust of it the training of these units up near Mare Island?

---

[*] In the summer of 1965 U.S. ships and craft began working with the South Vietnamese Navy to establish the Market Time patrol off the coast of South Vietnam. Its purpose was to monitor coastal traffic and thus to prevent North Vietnamese craft from infiltrating South Vietnam to deliver weapons and other supplies to Viet Cong forces.

Admiral Burke: Where we were, that was an add-on that had started with the war. We had the interest, but it was remote. I suppose what they should have done in hindsight was send us up there so we could have overseen it more directly. On the other hand, if we'd have gone up there we'd have driven their captain wild when he was trying to get his squadron ready, so I'm not so sure. I don't believe myself personally in creating a bureaucracy or an echelon just because you've got somebody available. I saw too much of that in the Pentagon.

Paul Stillwell: What would you say was the main role that you had in that job?

Admiral Burke: Planning exercises and performing exercises. We didn't get the chance to do much, but we were ready. We had the capability to operate on a regimental, possibly all the way up to a division level. We had a big staff. And we had a reserve battalion. I don't think it was a regiment. We had a regimental exercise up at Camp Pendleton. It was a good-sized operation, and it took planning. We also did a test for one of the command ships.* I think they were getting ready to build one, and we were given the task to show how we would manage and operate this command ship in operations. We set up our staff and went through this dummy exercise with people looking over our shoulders. We got severely critiqued, and I disagreed with one of the critiquers. But it was a very helpful thing, and some of the things that we tested out and tried they put into command ships that came along and the later big assault ships.

Paul Stillwell: Well, the LHA and the LHD.†

Admiral Burke: Yes. See, those ships were, they were just dream ships then, those big ships, but that they were talking about them or getting ready to build them.

---

* During World War II the Navy converted commercial cargo ships into specialized amphibious command ships. In the 1960s the Navy designed a class of ships specifically for the purpose. They were the Blue Ridge (LCC-19), commissioned 14 November 1970, and the Mount Whitney (LCC-20), commissioned 16 January 1971.

† LHA is the designation of a type of amphibious assault ship. The first of the type, USS Tarawa (LHA-1), was commissioned 29 May 1976. LHD is the designation of a similar amphibious assault ship. The first of the type, USS Wasp (LHD-1), was commissioned 29 July 1988.

Paul Stillwell: The command ships came out so well, the Blue Ridge and the Mount Whitney, that they were seized by fleet commanders and taken away from the amphibious force.

Admiral Burke: Yes.

Paul Stillwell: But I understand that the LHAs and the LHDs now essentially perform that role because they have sufficient capability. Do you remember anything specific about those tests and critiques?

Admiral Burke: The only thing I can remember was that we went through a sort of a dummy battle situation. You're talking 30 years. It's just too long for me to get into the details of it.

Paul Stillwell: How much computerized and automated equipment did you have on board the flagship in that era?

Admiral Burke: Oh, boy. We had very little. I guess it wasn't until I was ComServLant, sometime after that, when I went down on some of the ships there at DesFlot 4 and saw the dramatic change I just couldn't believe it.

Paul Stillwell: The amphibious force flagships then in PhibPac were the Estes, Eldorado, and Mount McKinley, which were World War II merchant conversions.

Admiral Burke: Right. Well, Eldorado was one of my flagships. Probably the Mount McKinley the other one.

Paul Stillwell: What do you then remember about going out to WestPac in that job subsequently?

Admiral Burke: Well, in the WestPac job I really didn't get engaged in combat. I remember a fair amount because I was always available there. We did a lot of cruising around, but we went out there to operate. We were essentially ComPhibForce Seventh Fleet, and we were there in case there was a regimental- or division-size landing. They didn't have them. Battalion was about the largest thing they had, so we were overseeing. I would go when there was a landing. The first time I went out was in 1967, January probably up until April. We observed a couple or three landings, and I say the Marines went in and it was tough sledding.

Paul Stillwell: And those were probably under the tactical command of the ready group, weren't they, which would be a captain?

Admiral Burke: Yes, the squadron commander. And I visited particularly amongst the I Corps, because there were Marines up there, and I visited most all of the Marine command sites except up around the DMZ.[*] I knew or got to know all those people. I made it a point that I was going to, so they would know who I was and vice versa. I visited some Army posts and commands. I sensed a certain amount of rivalry between the two. What else? The landings when they were held were held by squadron commanders and, of course, they were under my administrative command for these exercises, not tactical.

I had one operation there, where one of my contemporaries who didn't make admiral was my subordinate. We were looking over the shoulder, and it was a landing that went off fine. When they were in fairly close to the beach, they were within range of the rockets that were known to be held by the opposition. After all the boats returned and so forth, they sat there. So my ops officer came up and wanted to know what to do, and I said, "Well, just call up his ops officer." He did, and nothing happened, so after a reasonable time I sent the squadron command a request to please move and so forth. I didn't think anything about it, but as captains he was a lot of numbers higher than I was.

---

[*] South Vietnam was divided into four corps tactical zones. The northernmost was I Corps (pronounced eye). It ran from the demilitarized zone on the north, past Danang, and down to Quang Ngai Province at its southern limit. Included in it were Hue, Khe Sanh, Quang Tri, and Chulai. Because of their initial landing at Danang in 1965, the U.S. Marines operated largely in I Corps throughout the war.

I ran into him at a reunion about, oh, maybe 20 years later, and a mutual friend said, "You realize that guy hates your guts?" I think this is the classmate system. I couldn't believe it, but then I began to add up, and I could understand a lot of avoidances. But it's a hand-me-down, I think, from the "You don't report a classmate" or at least that's the way it was when I was there.

Paul Stillwell: But did that mean he thought that you shouldn't be in command?

Admiral Burke: I never talked to him about it. He's dead now. I was real sad when it happened. I'm devoted to his wife, and she's a good friend, but it happened, and it's one of the very sad personal experiences that I've had.

Paul Stillwell: But you saw an operational responsibility that wasn't being fulfilled.

Admiral Burke: Well, it may have been. This guy was a good friend when we were midshipmen. After that we didn't see a lot of each other because we went different career paths. If somebody had been expecting either one of us to make flag rank he would have been the one that they would have guessed years before. But this is the way it came out.

Paul Stillwell: Well, that may have been a part of the resentment as well.

Admiral Burke: Well, I'm sorry, but the reason I'm mentioning it is this. When I was a midshipmen having come from an honor system school this business of covering up for your classmates. This was rampant when I was a midshipman, and it was something I found very difficult. In fact, I never did it, but I know that there were plenty of people who did and as a practice.

Out there when I was phib group commander it gave me the opportunity to visit Okinawa, meet the general officers up there and become friends. I mean, I took advantage of visiting all the sites and the Marine aviation places, too, and the training sites so I had a good feel. It was a real educational experience for me and just so that I could absorb the knowledge. I remember that while I was out there I was approaching the end of my tour. I saw Admiral Blouin, and Baumberger was with him.* He was CruDesPac, I think, at the time and both of them very fine gentlemen. I told Admiral Blouin that I felt like on the completion of that tour from all I'd learned about the Asiatic station, the people who were out there, the strategic elements involved, I felt like I was finally qualified to make admiral. [Laughter]

Paul Stillwell: Did you find that job in WestPac as unsatisfying as the one back on the West Coast?

Admiral Burke: Well, I was just out there and not in charge of the operations. I wasn't unhappy. I had a lot of things that were difficult to deal with. On the home front not only Charly had died, but Betty was by herself at home. The other three children, one had gotten married and the other two had gone east to college, so Betty was by herself, and she is extraordinarily good at being able to take care of herself. Notwithstanding that, that was in my mind. As it turned out, I went out there twice. First I went out in January and came back in April. Then I went back out maybe at the first of October, the end of September, somewhere in that time frame and was relieved on the first of December, so I had another couple or three months out there.

Paul Stillwell: Are there any events you remember from that second stint out there?

Admiral Burke: We had an exercise. We had something with the Philippine Navy. I've forgotten what it was.

Paul Stillwell: Well, part of your role must have been to go around and visit the individual ships, because I know you came to our LST that fall.†

---

* Rear Admiral Walter H. Baumberger, USN, served as Commander Cruiser-Destroyer Force Pacific Fleet from 1965 to 1967.
† Paul Stillwell was then a junior officer serving in the tank landing ship Washoe County (LST-1165).

Admiral Burke: Well, I did. I visited all of the commands out there I could, because I felt the people and Admiral Ward out there wanted presence, command presence. I was his houseguest there probably off and on for almost a week. I didn't see much of him. He was doing other things, but I would come in and spend the night and then go off somewhere, and he was very helpful.

Paul Stillwell: Any specifics you remember about him and his help?

Admiral Burke: Well, he was steering me around as to what I ought to look at, since I'd never been in Asia before except in a submarine when I went out there, and so my information on the subject was very limited. We went through Japan when I went out there in the fall of '66 just on that three-week tour. As I recall, we went down to Yokosuka and visited there and then went on down to the Okinawa. I say "we." It was my ops officer and aide. We also went down to the Philippines and then over. Somewhere along the line I went to Danang. I visited there, and then as I recall we went back. There were a couple of other places there in I Corps and then between there and Saigon and then went on down to the delta. It gave me a feel for what it was all about, because all of my orientation since World War II had been back east. So it was more informational, and I was not really, at no time out there was I participating in any direct command exercises.

Paul Stillwell: I can see where that would be frustrating.

Admiral Burke: Well, I'd say it was a learning experience of meeting the people, learning the problems. I worked hard at trying to learn what it was all about. And, heck, I had to do that in every job I had. About the time you get transferred you feel like you've gotten to the point where you're ready to take on the world, and then they transfer you and give you another one.

Paul Stillwell: Anything more to say about your phib group duty?

Admiral Burke: I'd say I was essentially a type commander for the amphibs in the WestPac, and so I didn't get directly involved in any operations. But I did get involved in overseeing. I visited a lot of ships, and I observed from the sea these exercises, at least two landings while I was out there. But another thing I got involved in was a SEATO conference in '67. That was in Manila. I remember the Brits were there from Singapore, and there were some Australians there too.

The political scene in the Philippines was not good. I remember we were staying in a hotel in downtown Manila, and this conference went on for a couple of days. The conference actually met somewhere out in the suburbs at some sort of place, but you could hear gunfire. We stayed off the streets. It was like going into Southeast Washington, so we were much relieved to get out of town. It wasn't anything particularly significant that came out of it that I could see, but we did meet people from other countries and in the Navy. I did meet some of the Philippine Navy officers, but there was nobody there that I ever saw again or had seen before.

Later sometime during that same tour I went to Baguio the first time because a subcommittee of the House Armed Services Committee was touring Vietnam.[*] I don't think Mendel Rivers, who was probably the chairman, was there. I don't recall who the chairman of this subcommittee was. The House minority leader of the Republicans was there.

Paul Stillwell: Charles Halleck.[†]

Admiral Burke: Yes, that's who it was. Heck of a nice guy. I'd never met him before. But this was a learning experience for me. They had all of the commanders in the fleet. Bush Bringle was Com7thFlt, I think, and Ralph Cousins was commanding the carriers off of Vietnam.[‡] I forget who the others were, but it was interesting to watch this hearing go on. They were soliciting all they could out of us about what was happening from our

---

[*] Baguio is the site a summer resort about 130 miles north of Manila on the island of Luzon in the Philippines.
[†] Charles A. Halleck, a Republican from Indiana, served in the U.S. House of Representatives from 29 January 1935 to 3 January 1969. At various times he was majority leader and minority leader in the House.
[‡] Vice Admiral William F. Bringle, USN, served as Commander Seventh Fleet from 6 November 1967 to 10 March 1970. Rear Admiral Ralph W. Cousins, USN, was Commander Task Force 77.

point of view. I think the biggest impression I came away with was the guy who was really running the show was their staff counsel. He was an arrogant son of a bitch. He was a reserve officer, and I believe he later made brigadier general in the Marine Reserve.

Paul Stillwell: Russ Blandford.[*]

Admiral Burke: Yes. But he was in charge, and I mean he was pushing these congressmen around. I was surprised. I had a nice chat with Mr. Halleck. Told him I'd been appointed to the Naval Academy by Judge Smith, who was probably a contemporary of his, from our district here. And he began to spin tales. Judge Smith was a Democrat but as conservative as they come. He eventually ended up as chairman of the rules committee, so he was a power. And Mr. Halleck told me how he and Smith would deal behind closed doors or when people were away so that they'd get legislation through. That's all I can recall. It was an interesting experience, and it introduced me to my idea of heaven in the Philippines, Baguio. [Laughter] Have you been there?

Paul Stillwell: No. I've certainly heard about it.

Admiral Burke: There's an American Embassy summer place there or there was then. And, oh, it's beautiful. Well, I just wanted to mention that because that sort of introduced me to the congressional thing and then sometime later, it wasn't too long later, I was OP-01R in the reserve business.

Paul Stillwell: What were the considerations that led to your next job?

Admiral Burke: Well, what happened was I went from phib group back to OpNav. Because of the family situation, I just felt we had to come home, and so I asked to come back to Washington. I was told that I was coming to OP-01R, the reserve job, and we came back to this house, which we had purchased in 1965. I reported in one day, and

---

[*] John Russell Blandford served as chief counsel to the House Armed Services Committee, 1963-72.

during that night they had the Pueblo incident, and when I got to work the next morning I found out about it.* Nobody had called me, but reserves had been called to active duty. I also found out very quickly that I was something like the sixth or seventh officer that had been offered to be OP-O1R.

Paul Stillwell: Why was it such an unattractive job to most people?

Admiral Burke: Well, the reserves at that point in time were sort of looked on with scorn. I don't think as badly as it was at the time pre-World War II. When I was on the West Virginia the reserves were treated almost with contempt, and it was better than that on the North Carolina, particularly after the war started, but it was not a career-enhancing place to be in.

Paul Stillwell: Well, you told me that Admiral Blouin had some adverse comments in that regard.

Admiral Burke: Well, he thought I was going ruin whatever chance I had of going farther. To go back to Washington and take that job he thought it was the end of the line. Well, what happened was we had a reserve call-up that was just a symbolic call-up. The Navy called up, I think there was a Seabee battalion and maybe a couple of air squadrons and a couple of other things. The Seabees I think eventually were deployed to Vietnam and did a very creditable job. The air squadrons that were called up were essentially non compos mentis, and they were just not militarily capable. Most of the reserves of the other services were in the same boat.

So eventually a study was performed directed by OSD, and I was made the director of the Naval Reserve study, and practically no money was given us to do it.† I mean, this was a period when there was lots of money for studies because McNamara wanted studies going all the time at the drop of a hot, but this didn't affect military

---

* USS Pueblo (AGER-2), an electronic intelligence ship, was seized on 23 January 1968 in the Sea of Japan by North Korean naval forces. The ship's crew members were held as prisoners until 23 December of that year. Of the 83 officers and men on board, 28 were intelligence specialists.
† OSD—Office of the Secretary of Defense.

readiness as far as the Navy. The Navy was being shortchanged to supply the various divisions of ground troops that were taking on the war in Vietnam, and the Navy was really hurting.

My number two was a captain named Earl Greer.[*] My office staff were all reserve officers on active duty, TARs, and they were all specialists.[†] Earl Greer was in the Naval Academy class of '42. He was a TAR, a very capable officer, and he led me around. He was the guy that told me the things that we had to do, and he was the guy that I put over there on the study and put it together and made the thing go. I got probably most of the credit for what was done, and I'd have to say I'm proud of it, because I think a lot of the things in the reserves today were started in that reserve study.

Paul Stillwell: What was the methodology for the study?

Admiral Burke: Well, we didn't have any money and so forth, so Earl went around and got people. With the help of the reserve section in BuPers, he found reserve officers who had special talents, one of whom was a guy named Charles who was a reserve lieutenant. He was an associate professor in business at Georgetown University. Earl got him over there for his two weeks' training, and I think we were able to get him to do some active duty there more than his annual training. He knew how to do all these attitude surveys. I remember when he came in there we did an attitude survey on all of the personnel of the Naval Reserves, and you know normally they take about a slice of 5%.

Well, the reserves had a problem, which I became very quickly aware of. They had a political problem. The guys who controlled the reserves, the political side of the reserves, were inactives. They were very nervous because all of their goodies that they had been working around for years were being threatened. We had a lot of reserve units that there was no excuse to have simply because some congressman or senator wanted them. A senator from Illinois had a totally useless place that we wanted to put out of commission. There was no excuse for it being there, but we tried to get it out of commission, and it wouldn't go and wouldn't fly.

---

[*] Captain Earl M. Greer, USNR.
[†] TAR—training and administration of reservists. Those individuals designated as TARs are reservists on active duty. Most of their duty involves the reserve program rather than the active-duty Navy.

Apart from that, I'd say a lot of these reserve units around at that point in time were sort of like little local clubs. The club members organized it and took care of themselves, and they operated their organization as the Reserve Officers Association and the Naval Reserve Association. Well, the Naval Reserve Association are pikers. The guys that are really political as far as politics, at that time they seemed to be pretty interested in the reserves, but the ROA was just political as it could be, and I learned a lot about politics very quickly.

Again, I was going into an arena that I was a babe in arms. Within the first two or three weeks I was on the job I had to go over to Capitol Hill with a prepared text and testify before one of the committees. We had to testify before the Senate and the House Armed Services Committees, the Appropriations Committee and one other, so I got a lot of practice. My Dale Carnegie training was a big help. But I tell you I was over there talking from a script that Earl Greer wrote. I would go over with Earl Greer, and he had all the answers, but I had to get up there and sit across from Eddie Hebert.[*] We had a congressman, Porter Hardy, who used to live down here three doors.[†] I didn't know him particularly well. I hardly knew him, but he slugged me over there, and laughed at me when I got home. [Laughter]

Paul Stillwell: Slugged you in what way?

Admiral Burke: Well, I've forgotten what it was, but he was doing it trying to embarrass somebody else.

Paul Stillwell: Well, what would be the purpose of these visits to Congress, to justify budget requests?

---

[*] F. Edward Hebert (1901-1979), a Democrat from Louisiana, was elected to the U.S. House of Representatives in 1932 and came to Washington as part of the Democratic sweep that led to the "New Deal" legislation of 1933-1935. He retired from office in 1976 after being stripped of his chairmanship of the House Armed Services Committee.

[†] Porter Hardy, Jr., a Democrat from Virginia, served in the U.S. House of Representatives from 3 January 1947 to 3 January 1969.

Admiral Burke: Yes, these were annual events; everybody has to do it. Not everybody but in certain jobs, and I was over there. The reserve budget was pitifully small. I mean really small. So I was learning all of this, how do you do it. Then one of the things I was assigned to was the Reserve Policy Board of DoD. I got to know all of the opposite numbers in the Army, Air Force, and Marines. There were civilians as well as military on there. I got to know the people in the other services. The head of the National Guard Bureau was Wimpy Wilson, who was a real political animal.* He was a major general and very likable. He went over to testify about the Kent State incident.†

Paul Stillwell: They reacted to the Cambodia invasion in 1970.

Admiral Burke: Yes. Do you remember that?

Paul Stillwell: Oh, yes.

Admiral Burke: Well, a week or so after it happened, we, the group of reserves, went over to the Senate Armed Services Committee to testify in support of the annual budget. Wimpy Wilson was the senior one of our group, and he was the first one up to be interviewed, and Senator Stennis said, "This meeting is now off the record. Wimpy, tell us what happened out there in Kent State."*

And so Wimpy did. He told things that were completely off the record, I mean were sensitive that never came out in the press. Such as there were known Communists that were out there stimulating that exercise. It wasn't something that just happened. He said before the shots were fired some of the National Guardsmen had been physically injured. A couple of days later I went down to his office to talk to him and to get more of an expanded account. He had some rocks on the table, and these rocks had hit some of

---

* Major General Winston P. "Wimpy" Wilson, USAFR, was with the National Guard Bureau from 1950 to 1970; he is considered the architect of modern air guard.
† Beginning on 29 April 1970, U.S. and South Vietnamese troops launched attacks into Communist staging areas in Cambodia. The invasion sparked widespread antiwar demonstrations throughout the United States. On 4 May 1970, at Kent State University, Kent, Ohio, a detachment of Ohio National Guardsmen opened fire on a group of protesters and killed four students.

the National Guardsmen and injured them to the extent that they were hospitalized. This never got in the press.

But let's leave that now. About the time I went in there, the Reserve Officers Association dedicated the building that they have over there on Capitol Hill. I got invited over there all the time. They have a Navy section and an Army section and an Air Force section. The Navy section was headed up at that time by a rear admiral (retired); he was a tomb-stoner, Andrew Jackson.[†] He's still living. I just checked in the book. He lives down near Orange, Virginia. But he had been in that job for a good 20 years and was the real political mind in the Reserve Officers Association. He knew all these congressmen. There would be events over there or a luncheon and we would be invited, so I'd go over there, and he would have John McCormack from Massachusetts because he was Speaker of the House.[‡] John McCormack would come over there and praise all these reserves like they were the finest people that ever came down the pike. While all of this kind of thing was going on, the people back in the Pentagon who were active duty Navy I don't think really saw it or could feel it. I could tell them about it, but they wouldn't believe it.

Well, we were working this study. Earl Greer was getting these people in. We needed some guys to help us in the legal aspects of us. Well, I couldn't get any help out of JAG.[§] They were too busy. So we got some lawyers out of a law group down at Atlanta. I can't remember the guy's name, but he was a captain, lawyer, and he was commanding officer of a law company down in Atlanta. I'll dream up his name sooner or later. He took on the job of a lot of the legal aspects.

Now, one of the troubles I had with Andy Jackson was that he had so much prestige and so forth. Anytime you'd start to make any changes in the reserves, he would all of a sudden say, "Well, the legislative history of this prevents you from doing what you're after."

I'd say, "What is the legislative history?"

---

[*] John C. Stennis (1901-1995) was a Democrat from Mississippi. He was in the U.S. Senate from 1947 to 1989, including service as chairman of the Armed Services Committee. The aircraft carrier John C. Stennis (CVN-74) is named in his honor.
[†] Rear Admiral Alexander Jackson, Jr., USN (Ret.).
[‡] John W. McCormack, a Democrat from Massachusetts, served in the U.S. House of Representatives from 6 November 1928 to 3 January 1971; he was Speaker of the House from 1962 to 1971.
[§] JAG—the office of the Navy's Judge Advocate General.

He said, "Well, that's in the notes, informal notes that are done in the committees when they're putting this together." Andy Jackson professed to be the super knowledge of all the legislative history involving reserves, particularly naval reserves.

Paul Stillwell: There were a lot of people that didn't want the applecart upset.

Admiral Burke: Right. That's right. So I got this guy down from Georgia. He came up here and did his two weeks, and I got to be friends with him. He was an ROA guy, but I told him, "Here's the problem. One of the annexes to this study is going to be legislative history." His reserve law company in Atlanta took that job for us. So that took care of a hell of a lot of problems and enabled us to begin to structure the organization.

Paul Stillwell: Did you have the sense that Jackson was bluffing?

Admiral Burke: I didn't know, but I was again a new boy on the street in an organization that was highly political. To give you an example of what I'm talking about, the Reserve Officers Association have an annual meeting in the wintertime. They have two big dos a year, and they had it here. They usually recognize a high politico with their Minuteman award or something like that and make a big hero out of him and make a big fuss over him. This guy could be the Secretary of the Navy, or it could be the Secretary of Defense, or it could be somebody like that or some key congressman or senator. Then he makes a nice speech, and they all get up and cheer and all feel good and pat him on the back and just hope that the next time around he'll support them.

Paul Stillwell: Well, there was also a practice that some of those congressmen who were also reservists got selected for flag rank like Craig Hosmer.

Admiral Burke: Well, there was something that had been started before I got there, but it was to me very helpful because I met some very interesting people. For example, Edgar Shannon, who was the president of the University of Virginia, was a captain in the Naval

Reserve, and he did his two weeks in my office.* Now, what we did whenever these special people came in, we would make up a good briefing schedule, and we would run them all around the Pentagon. We would send them around and get them up in the E-ring, all departments, and they would come back just really impressed.† We had one guy who was a senior vice president in North American Insurance. He was a naval reserve and later he became president of the Naval Reserve Association. The same thing with him. There was a congressman from New York, Republican. God, he was a nice guy, and we did him.

Paul Stillwell: Stratton?‡

Admiral Burke: That's probably who it was. Really a nice guy. Well, you got to know them. And this Reserve Policy Board. I got to know some really impressive people. We were having trouble in the ROTC units around the country, all services. An interesting thing, the Ivy League dumped the ROTCs except the University of Pennsylvania. I'd be interested to see if they still have it. I think Pennsylvania had the ROTC in engineering instead of arts and sciences. I've sort of lost track of when it happened, but we had a committee studying the ROTC problem. They had about five university presidents as members. One was the president of Tulane. I think Edgar Shannon was one; probably that's where I met him. And there was the president of Claremont College in California and Wisconsin, and St. Louis University.

The people on this committee did an evaluation of ROTC and came up with a very sensible explanation of why we were in such a fix. They pointed back to the time when Kennedy was President. There was pressure to get rid of the draft, and so the solution was—I don't know who made the decision, but I guess he did—that they would give academic deferments, which meant as long as you were in academia, in college or if

---

* Captain Edgar F. Shannon, USNR.
† The Pentagon has lettered corridors, going from A at the innermost to E at the outermost. E-ring offices, which go around the perimeter of the building, are considered the most prestigious.
‡ Samuel S. Stratton, a Democrat from the state of New York, served in the U.S. House of Representatives from 3 January 1959 to 3 January 1989. He served on active duty as a Naval Reservist during World War II and eventually became a captain in the reserve.

you were teaching. It was about the time of the Sputnik or just after that.* If you were in a faculty, that would give you a draft deferment. So they told us that they found from their experience that the colleges and universities and seminaries were loaded with people who would not normally be there in order to avoid the draft, particularly when the war came along. They said that the leaders in this disruption on the campus were the faculty members who were trying to justify what they had done to their students. It's interesting.

Paul Stillwell: Rationalizing.

Admiral Burke: Yes. I'm involved in the Episcopal Church, and we have a seminary out here in Alexandria. It's on the edge of town. I could tell from what I was hearing that there was a certain amount of that. They had students up there that shouldn't have been there. I don't know how many they were or what's happened to them but I know it happened.

Paul Stillwell: What were you trying to achieve in relation to these NROTC units?

Admiral Burke: Well, the NROTC units were under fire. They were getting a lot of bad times. There were lots of disruptions on the campuses. There was a big disruption down at the University of Virginia. Edgar Shannon got out in front of it and sort of led it. I thought he was going to be run out, but he had been a very successful president up to that time and the authorities down there let him off the hook, and the power brokers in Richmond decided you give him one mistake. And so that's what happened.

Paul Stillwell: What was his mistake?

Admiral Burke: Because he got out in front of the rioters and led them.

Paul Stillwell: Oh, I see. Even though he was a captain in the reserve?

---

* On 4 October 1957, the Soviet Union launched Sputnik I, the first artificial earth satellite. It caused great uproar in the United States, which had expected to be first in space.

Admiral Burke: Yes.

Paul Stillwell: That is curious.

Admiral Burke: He wasn't on active duty, but I'd say up to that time I felt confident he would have probably made admiral, but he didn't make admiral.

Paul Stillwell: No, not after that.

Admiral Burke: I haven't seen him since the times he was up here on active duty or reporting in that committee. He was a very fine guy. But it was tough time, and during those years my own son was in college, and he went the ROTC route. On the other hand, I have two nephews who managed to keep themselves in college and graduate school until they got to the right age, and then they were home free. I know a number of people that did that. So it was a way of trying to avoid something that we were dealing with. We were all relieved when early in the Nixon Administration the draft was abolished, and it made a difference.*

Paul Stillwell: Well, our President was one of those who kept in grad school and didn't have to go.†

Admiral Burke: Well, don't get me on that.

Paul Stillwell: Okay. [Laughter] What were the findings in this study that you commissioned or led?

Admiral Burke: We came up with, as I best remember, a number of recommendations on what to do about the Naval Reserve. They came up with the idea—and I think it's

---

* In 1972 the Defense Department announced it would end draft calls in mid-1973. Secretary of Defense Melvin Laird announced on 27 January 1973 that the use of the military draft had ended as of then, several months prior to plan.
† Bill Clinton was President of the United States at the time of the interview.

standard practice now—of having the reserves do their active duty right alongside active units. You go down to CinCLantFlt or possibly even here in the Pentagon there are reserves in the local area who come in and get their reserve time just by working in the shop there and so the people know them and they know the job. When I was on active duty I first went to the <u>West Virginia</u> we began to call in reserves. They were just like foreigners almost. You have to start off from scratch.

Paul Stillwell: Well, in 1974 a new system was put in so that units were formed to support specific gaining commands, as opposed to a unit going all different places.

Admiral Burke: Well, this was one of the features of our study. I'd forgotten the gaining command, but that was one of the things we were trying to sell. Our part of the study was just about finished when I left there in the end of July of 1970. But you just couldn't implement all of this kind of stuff.

Now, I can tell you there was a reaction amongst the reserve community of not liking it, and I did a lot of traveling around the country. When I got involved in this study there was a reserve admiral, TAR, over in BuPers. He was an aviator, Ace Parker. He lives over in Maryland now. But the aviation community seemed to be the center of the political opposition that we were encountering. But he one day told me that I ought to go down and talk to Admiral Felix Johnson.[*] He was a vice admiral, retired. Had formerly been chief of the naval reserves or he had done a reserve study years before and that was the last, I think back in the '50s.

He lived down in Maryland just off, not too far from the bridge down there. And every time you mentioned Felix Johnson in a reserve gathering they all clapped. So I called him up one day, and Betty and I went down to have lunch with him, and I had a nice talk with him. I also got hold of Admiral Deutermann.[†] He was the class of '27. Johnson was in '20. Both of them were exceptionally nice to me and gave me a lot of advice on how to deal with the reserve community.

---

[*] The oral history of Vice Admiral Felix L. Johnson, USN (Ret.), is in the Naval Institute collection.
[†] Vice Admiral Harold T. Deutermann, USN (Ret.).

Paul Stillwell: What was their advice?

Admiral Burke: Well, just get around the country and try to tell people what you're doing, not hard sell, and I did.

Paul Stillwell: Did the opposition come from those people who were comfortable with the status quo and didn't want it upset?

Admiral Burke: I would say so, but anyhow as I went around the country I met these people, and we liked each other, and I got along fine with them. And I was persuading people this was all right.

Then there was a TAR officer named Armie Armistead who was a captain, the senior TAR in OP-05.* I was there for two and a half years on the job, and the study was on for practically the whole time I was there. One day during the study Armistead came around and was storming, telling me that he thought this study stank and so forth. I named a guy that I'd just been with out in Chicago who was very enthusiastic about it. His name, I think, was George Shultz. I'm not sure about the name, but he was a surface guy and not an aviator. He was an ROA type, and I said, "He said he thought we were doing a great job."

Armie he said, "He said that?"

I said, "Yeah." And he turned around and stormed out of the office. Within an hour Charlie Duncan, who was Chief of Personnel called me up and said, "Do you know a reserve officer named Shultz from Chicago? He just called up and said you were wrecking the Naval Reserve."† [Laughter] And that was one example.

Paul Stillwell: So had Shultz changed his tune after Armistead talked to him?

---

* Captain Reginald G. Armistead, USNR. OP-05 was the office of the Deputy Chief of Naval Operations (Air Warfare).
† Vice Admiral Charles K. Duncan, USN, served as Chief of Naval Personnel from 5 April 1968 to 21 August 1970. The oral history of Duncan, who retired as a four-star admiral, is in the Naval Institute collection.

Admiral Burke: Well, I never asked Armie about it, but I'd say that kind of thing happened. So you had to keep your guard up.

Over at Andrews they had a reserve unit that was really loaded with political kind of people.* There was a Capitol Hill unit too. I don't know whether they still have that or not but to enable people on Capitol Hill, the congressmen and their the staff members, to get active duty.

One day, just by accident, I discovered that somebody from over at Andrews wanted to meet with the Secretary of the Navy. He was a reserve over in that unit. I guess the way I found out about it was an assistant to the Assistant Secretary for Reserve Affairs just happened to be talking to somebody, and I heard the name, so I got him to repeat it. I said, "This guy wants to see the Secretary? Do you know what about?" Well, I knew about this ROA aviation upset, and I said, "After he gets through I want to get a read on this thing if you can."

So the guy came back and said, "I can't tell you what was said, but you wouldn't like it." So I went in and I went over and talked to Charlie Duncan and told him that this stuff was going on, that he was trying to get to the Secretary, who was Chafee then.†

He said, "Well, I'm not going to go talk to him."

I said, "Okay, do you mind if I do?" So I got an appointment, and I went over what was done and I said, "My guess is you were told by somebody that I was wrecking the reserves with the way the reserve study's going."

He said, "That's right. That's what he said." Sometime after that we had some sort of reserve gathering at the Del Coronado, and Chafee was one of the featured speakers, along with Ike Kidd, I think.‡ When he got up there, the first thing he did was give me a strong pat on the back the way the reserve study was going.

Paul Stillwell: So did you have a chance to present the rebuttal position when you went to see Chafee that time?

---

* Andrews Air Force Base is located approximately ten miles southeast of Washington, D.C., in Prince George's County, Maryland.
† John H. Chafee served as Secretary of the Navy from 31 January 1969 to 4 May 1972.
‡ The Hotel Del Coronado is a landmark in Coronado, California. Vice Admiral Isaac C. Kidd, Jr., USN, served as Commander First Fleet from 30 September 1969 to 1 August 1970.

Admiral Burke: I just told him. He knew what we were doing. I guess he was briefed but he gave me a big backup. That was a big help in getting things down the pike. We were trying to structure the reserves. This gaining command concept came out of our study. I know that we were talking about it, and Earl Greer was the man that was really working on it. There are politics in the reserves. I sat on a couple or three selection boards of the reserves while I was there. Earl Greer had the finest record in the reserves, and he didn't make admiral.

Paul Stillwell: Are you suggesting that was a political payback?

Admiral Burke: Yes, I think so.

Paul Stillwell: Well, one advantage of your approach would be that you matched specific billet requirements on one hand with billets in reserve units on the other.

Admiral Burke: Yes. And to me the payoff was what happened over in Desert Storm.[*] It looked like everything we dreamed of as a possibility came to fruition with the reserves the way they got called in. I know they got called in. I was a Red Cross volunteer at the time coordinating between Red Cross and the Army and Air Force, Navy and Marine reserve requirements and I tell you, there were people all over the country that needed help.

Paul Stillwell: Well, when you were making these selling tours around the United States did you point out how abysmal the response had been in '68?

Admiral Burke: Well, no. You can't go back and tell reserves they stink. You've got to tell them, "Here's where we're going and we need your help." And at the working level they responded.

---

[*] In January 1991 U.S. and Allied Coalition forces attacked Iraq to get it to retreat following its August 1990 invasion of neighboring Kuwait. The holding action in the meantime was Operation Desert Shield. The conflict itself became known variously as Operation Desert Storm and the Gulf War. Coalition forces won the war in February 1991.

My reserve lawyer friend from Atlanta used to come in fairly frequently and was an enormous help. One day he came over and he said, "Admiral, suh, you ought to know that I'm hearing things about you that aren't very good. There are a lot of people out there that want to get you." [Laughter] And they had clout because it was during that time the reserve community, and mainly aviators I think, behind the scenes went after McNamara and succeeded. I got the inference from comments from some of my reserve contacts that this is what happened.

Paul Stillwell: Well, Johnson had a lot of reasons to be unhappy with McNamara.

Admiral Burke: Well.

Paul Stillwell: That may have been a contributing factor.

Admiral Burke: It could have been they were taking a lot of credit. [Laughter] But I'd say this experience of dealing with them on how to get things done politically taught me lessons on how to get things done in Japan, and if I hadn't have had that reserve experience, I'd have struck out in Japan.

Paul Stillwell: Well, it probably toughened your skin a little bit too.

Admiral Burke: Well, interesting thing—I wanted to get back into OP-06, and after I'd been there for a couple of years and could see the end of the line. When a billet in OP-60 became available, I wanted to get it. I had friends over there that saw that my experience level might give me a chance, but I didn't have a chance because I was not in that structure; I didn't know the people really. In hindsight it's just a well I didn't, because, you see, in my career I kept going into new places. You're always making new friends, but your depth of contacts, there were people in OP-06 on their second and third tours of duty. There's a big difference in having somebody there. I couldn't have been nearly as effective as some of those kinds of people.

Julian T. Burke, Jr., Interview #10 (3/17/98) – Page 456

Paul Stillwell: How much relationship did you have with Admiral Duncan when you were in the reserve job?

Admiral Burke: Not much. I used to see him at the weekly staff conference and when somebody like I told you called him up, but I rarely got into anything with him.

Paul Stillwell: So you had a fair degree of autonomy.

Admiral Burke: I kept him cut in. I don't remember specifically that I did, but other jobs I've had I've always written memos, sort of situation reports. I've always done that.

Paul Stillwell: Well, presumably he supported what you were doing, or you wouldn't have kept on doing it.

Admiral Burke: Oh, yes. Well, I got a Legion of Merit after it was over. [Laughter]

Paul Stillwell: Well, there's another indicator. What was your relationship with the reserve commanders out at Glenview and Omaha?

Admiral Burke: Omaha, excellent.

Paul Stillwell: George Muse.

Admiral Burke: George Muse.* I had known him. We were in the same war college class. He was not a close friend, but I knew him and respected him.

    Bill Guest was the aviator admiral at Glenview, and I'll tell you a story.† We were going out to Las Vegas to a reserve convention, ROA convention, and we had to go through Chicago. We left here about 7:00 o'clock in the evening, and a line squall went through Chicago just about the time we took off. So we ended up in St. Louis and had to

---

* Rear Admiral George R. Muse, USN, Commander Naval Reserve Command, Omaha, Nebraska.
† Rear Admiral William S. Guest, USN, served as Chief of Naval Air Reserve Training from March 1967 to December 1969.

wait there until the weather cleared, and then we got into Chicago about 11:00 o'clock in the evening. There must have been 10,000 people that had got screwed up because of this line squall. So I was going with somebody else, and we ended up at Glenview for the night.

The steward there was a sleepy Filipino, and he gave me a key to the VIP room down there. I walked down there and opened the door, and there was a guy in my bed wrapped around this girl. [Laughter] So I went back to the desk. I apologized. I said, "I'm real sorry," and went back to the desk. [Laughter] Said, "Give me another key. There's somebody in that room." So he gave me another key. I went down there, and it turned out to be the room next door. Opened up and the same guy was in the bed in the next room. [Laughter]

So I went back to the desk. I said, "I want to find out where the ensigns sleep."

[Laughter] My guy that was with me said, "Oh, Admiral, you can't do that."

I said, "I want to go to sleep." [Laughter] So I went and got an ensign's room, and I got to sleep. But when I went down to breakfast the next morning I could hear somebody mumbling at the next table, at a table over there about, "Some damn guy came in my room last night." [Laughter]

Paul Stillwell: Twice.

Admiral Burke: So when I got out to Las Vegas the admiral out there was there, and I told him what happened. He said, well, he had a commander on his staff who had been transferred, and they had moved out of their quarters. So he had his own set of keys to that suite, and so he gave the new guy his set of keys, and the front office didn't know it. [Laughter]

Paul Stillwell: What was the command relationship between you and those two commands?

Admiral Burke: They were divided. It was surface and air. To be honest, I can't remember.

Paul Stillwell: Well, I wonder if it was a case where you would make the policy and they were to execute it?

Admiral Burke: Well, it was sort of that way. In hindsight I didn't command anything. I was OP-01R. I was a staff man. We developed policy, and it always got approved up really above my level when it was serious business. George Muse commanded the surface reserve, and they commanded the air reserve and we formulated policy. We got together from time to time. I went out to Omaha a couple or three times, and I went out to the air reserve place a couple or three times. But the air desk, Armie Armistead, was OP-05R.

Paul Stillwell: Did you bring Muse and Guest in on your selling program for the study and the changes?

Admiral Burke: I don't remember. I went out there. I know that they were told what we were doing, but as I best remember the answer to that is probably not. I know that we didn't have any disagreements. We had very good relations with them. Muse and I got along fine, and I didn't have any trouble with Guest at Glenview. But the guidelines for the aviation really went out of OP-05. But we cut them in on what we were doing and tried to get them aboard with what we were doing.

Paul Stillwell: Is there anything else to remember about that tour of duty in OpNav?

Admiral Burke: Well, there are names that I can't remember of people that I got to meet, know, respect. Mr. Packard, I didn't get to know him, but he was the Deputy Secretary of Defense.[*] He came down to our reserve policy meetings. Of all the various executive political appointees like that, I would say I'd rate him number one.

---

[*] David Packard served as Deputy Secretary of Defense from 1969 to 1971. He was a co-founder of Hewlett-Packard Company and over the course of years held a number of positions, including chief executive officer and chairman of the board.

Paul Stillwell: Well, I think that's a widely held opinion. He's highly admired.

Admiral Burke: There were other people that I met, but I just can't remember the names.

Paul Stillwell: Well, maybe we ought to save the Japan tour for the next time, because I think that's going to be fairly long and involved, and we can get it all in one piece.

Admiral Burke: Yes. When I got appointed to this study people were shaking their heads. "It's a hopeless job," and so forth. And I wasn't getting any serious support within the Navy Department either on money or personnel. So I went over and called on Arleigh Burke and told him my dilemma. He was over there in that Georgetown think tank, and he was very kind. I didn't know him, but I'd met him. I'd shaken hands with him was I was a CO of a destroyer. But he was very kind. I asked him questions like, "Is it worth the trouble? How do you get--?" And he gave me some tips, which I generally followed by going out and doing a selling job around the country. He was one of them. The same thing happened with Vice Admiral Felix Johnson and Vice Admiral Deutermann, too; they actively helped. I've forgotten exactly when it was, but I got them to come in and they attended some meetings with some of these reserves when we were briefing. They stood up and supported what we were doing. That kind of support caused a lot of these reserves out there who were ambivalent to get on board.

Paul Stillwell: Who appointed you to do the study?

Admiral Burke: I don't know whether I ever got a piece of paper or not, but I was told I was it. That came down from probably Charlie Duncan. But the Secretary of the Navy knew that I was running this study. It was a political kind of a study.

Paul Stillwell: I think Admiral Semmes might have been Chief of Personnel when you went there.*

---

* Vice Admiral Benedict J. Semmes, Jr., USN, served as Chief of Naval Personnel from 1 April 1964 to 31 March 1968. His oral history is in the Naval Institute collection.

Admiral Burke: Yes, I think he was. Boy, I thought you were older than me, and you've got a sharper memory than I have. [Laughter] Yes, I remember he was there and Charlie Duncan came in sometime during the tour.

Paul Stillwell: Anything else?

Admiral Burke: No, I'll think about it tonight.

Paul Stillwell: All right. Well, I look forward to the Japan story. I know that'll be exciting. Thank you.

Interview Number 11 with Rear Admiral Julian T. Burke, Jr., U.S. Navy (Retired)

Place: Admiral Burke's home in Alexandria, Virginia

Date: Wednesday, 25 March 1998

Interviewer: Paul Stillwell

Paul Stillwell: Admiral, we have a bright sunny morning today for this discussion. Please give me the background on how you got the job in Japan.

Admiral Burke: When my tour of duty was coming to an end, I was told probably by the flag detail officer was that I had two choices of duty. One was to be ComNavPhil or to be ComNavForJapan.* I knew nothing about Japan. I had seen NavPhil. Herman Kossler had been out there, I think, when I had been out there and then also Phil Gilkeson out of '37.† And I'd visited both of them out there. I was inclined to go for ComNavPhil simply because I knew something, but I began to ask around. Dennis Wilkinson had been the chief of staff, U.S. Forces Japan, and I talked to him.‡ He gave me a very good briefing on why I should go to Japan.

Paul Stillwell: What was the rationale he offered?

Admiral Burke: Well, he said strategically he thought it was better. We were tied into the defense of Japan, and we were over committed down in Vietnam at the time. We were trying to pull out, and the future in the Philippines was just not stable. But I came away from that, and then I just decided. I'd talked to Admiral Burke when I'd gone over and called on him when I first got involved in the reserve study, and he had been helpful, so I just decided to go over and talk to him. He told me that he thought Japan would be unquestionably the best place to go.

---

* ComNavPhil—Commander U.S. Naval Forces Philippines; ComNavForJapan—Commander U.S. Naval Forces Japan.
† Rear Admiral Herman J. Kossler, USN; Rear Admiral Filmore B. Gilkeson, USN.
‡ Rear Admiral Eugene P. Wilkinson, USN, had served as chief of staff for Commander U.S. Forces Japan, a joint-service command. See Wilkinson's Naval Institute oral history.

He said, "You know, when the Korean War broke out, I was on the staff of CNO and he sent me out to be his personal representative with MacArthur.[*] I had a separate set of code wheels so that I could talk directly to CNO without having to go through the Army code system." I forget how long he was there, but while he was there the peace settlement occurred and Japan was allowed to reorganize their military services. It was against the law to have an Army, Navy, and Air Force, but it was not against the law to defend themselves, so they called them the Maritime Self-Defense Force and so forth. He said the Navy people came to him and asked him to help them how to set it up, so he did. So after listening to him for the better part of an hour, I thanked him very much, and I came back.

Betty didn't want to go to either place. You've got to keep in mind this was three years after Charly had died, and we were still recovering emotionally from that. We'd come home to get over it. It was interesting. Betty made no bones about it. She didn't want to go to Japan. Well, it turned out about three years later she didn't want to come home. [Laughter]

I made the decision, and then eventually I got detached. Zumwalt came in the first of July, and I got detached about three weeks later.[†] I don't think I had any leave. I just got proceed time, and I was working right up until the day I got detached. One of the days I was home here, the packers were here, and we were moving out. I received a call from John Tyree, who was the Inspector General.[‡] He had also been my division commander when I was commanding officer of the Sablefish. He called me up, and he said, "Come in. I've got something to tell you."

I said, "I've been detached. I'm not coming in. We're in the midst of moving our stuff out of the house, and I've got to be here."

So he said, "Well, if you don't come in, I'm going to get the Chief of Personnel to send you dispatch orders." [Laughter] So I wasn't very polite to a guy who was a vice admiral. I was really upset, and Betty wasn't happy either. I drove in reluctantly, and

---

[*] General of the Army Douglas MacArthur, USA, Commander in Chief U.S. Forces Far East.
[†] Admiral Elmo R. Zumwalt, Jr., USN, served as Chief of Naval Operations from 1 July 1970 to 29 June 1974.
[‡] Vice Admiral John A. Tyree, Jr., USN, Naval Inspector General.

when I got there, there was an officer in the class of '37. I can't remember his name. He was a flag officer in OP-03. A hell of a nice guy. He was doing the briefing.

It turned out that 17 days after Zumwalt got to be the CNO the decision was made to withdraw U.S. Navy forces from Japan. And nobody told me. I had been briefed by everybody in preparation to go. I'd been all over OpNav. I'd been in OSD, NSA, CIA, and the State Department.[*] Nobody had mentioned anything like this. And I knew everybody in OP-06. His answer was that there had been this secret study done some time before Zumwalt became CNO. Tom Moorer was the CNO, and he ducked it.[†] He didn't want to have it happen right at the end of his watch and stuck Zumwalt with it. And I think that was fair enough.

So it was placed on Zumwalt's desk, and he waited until the 17th and executed. Oh, it didn't just get executed period. It had to be negotiated with the government of Japan. This problem had to be negotiated on a government-to-government basis.

Paul Stillwell: It's just not like giving an order to a ship at sea. There's more to it.

Admiral Burke: That's right, so what this meant was that the State Department was going to have to tell the embassy to negotiate it. I didn't know any of this sort of procedure. John Tyree just told me, "You're going to find that everybody in Japan is going to be mad, and you're just going to have to bite your tongue and tell them to shut up and carry out orders when you execute." So in thinking about myself, I could see I was at the end of the line. I was being sent to a job that was a nothing job.

Paul Stillwell: Just turn off the lights and shut the door.

Admiral Burke: Yes. I didn't know how long this was going to take. I had no idea, but I figured it would probably take at most a year. And I had no feel for what we had in Japan.

---

[*] NSA—National Security Agency.
[†] Admiral Thomas H. Moorer, USN, served as Chief of Naval Operations from 1 August 1967 to 1 July 1970. His oral history is in the Naval Institute collection.

Paul Stillwell: Even after all those briefings?

Admiral Burke: Well, the briefings weren't covering what we had there. It was more about what the strategic situation was in the Western Pacific or what the intelligence thing was and what our capabilities were. I did hear a lot about our capabilities out there, and I'd never been involved in special intelligence before. So then we went to Pearl Harbor, and they were in on it. That is, the front office did, but it was still hush-hush.

Paul Stillwell: Admiral McCain?

Admiral Burke: He was CinCPac.[*] Admiral Hyland was CinCPacFlt.[†] He had been OP-60 when I first went into OP-60. We spent about four days in Hawaii getting briefed and meeting all of the necessary people that I had to contact. I'd say I knew Admiral McCain, not intimately but somebody I always got along with. And then we departed. We landed in Tokyo and spent two nights in Tokyo. We stayed at the Sanno.[‡] Our daughter Sally was still in college, but she was 21, and so the government wouldn't pay for her or give me the money to go out commercially. Through my Air Force Reserve contact I got her on an Air Force flight. She came in about 24 hours after we did. She had flown out on a troop plane, only girl on it, and they were going to Vietnam. She said they were all well behaved. [Laughter] Then we went to Yokosuka, and I met for the first time Dog Smith, who was my predecessor.[§] He was quite a character.

Paul Stillwell: Very colorful. I met him out in Yokosuka one time.

Admiral Burke: I'd like to talk to him again, but the poor guy died within a year. But he was an engaging person, and his idea of a turnover and mine were entirely different. I

---

[*] Admiral John S. McCain, Jr., USN, served as Commander in Chief Pacific from 31 July 1968 to 1 September 1972. His oral history is in the Naval Institute collection.
[†] Admiral John J. Hyland, USN, served as Commander in Chief Pacific Fleet from 30 November 1967 to 5 December 1970. His oral history is in the Naval Institute collection.
[‡] The Sanno Hotel in Tokyo was run by the U.S. military for members of the services and their families.
[§] Rear Admiral Daniel F. Smith, Jr., USN, served as Commander Naval Forces Japan from June 1968 to August 1970.

think he was doing his best to keep from going down a shopping list of "what do you do and so forth." On the second or third day he said, "Well, now it's time to go to a hotsy bath," so we went to a hotsy bath out in Yokosuka about 4:00 o'clock in the afternoon. [Laughter] Betty and I were, at that stage of the game, living in the Togo room at the officers' club.* And that was quite an experience in itself to live in the Togo room.

I relieved command, and I told you I always seemed to be moving into a different field. So I had to work like hell to learn more about still another field in the Navy. I had to learn to depend on and evaluate people. It wasn't until I got to Japan towards the end of my career that I suddenly realized that I had acquired the ability of making instant evaluations of people that were about 80% correct. I didn't flaunt it, but I was in a job where practically anybody from the Navy Department and most people from DoD had to pay a courtesy call on me. Well, I saw a wide spectrum of people, civilians as well as military. And it was very interesting talking with these people, getting them to reveal themselves.

Among all these people I met were lots and lots of Japanese officials, civilian and military, and they all bowed and so forth. It's just a culture that I wasn't used to. In preparation Betty and I had taken some Japanese language training over in Crystal City from a Japanese lady who was a student at Georgetown University.† I couldn't take very much of it, and so when I wasn't there she would get more into the culture. Then I went up to the office as soon as Dog Smith left town, and a column of people began to call on me, all Japanese. After a couple of days I couldn't remember a single one.

Paul Stillwell: Couldn't sort them out in your mind.

Admiral Burke: No, I couldn't. But the first guy who walked in was a little guy named Ichiro Masuoka. It turned out I heard about him later. He was a short black-haired man, and he gave me his card. They all give you a card. There's English on side, Japanese on

---

* In the 27-27 May 1905 Battle of Tsushima Strait (which connects the Sea of Japan with the East China Sea), Japanese forces under Admiral Heihachiro Togo overwhelmed the Russian Baltic Fleet led by Admiral Zinovy Rozhdestvensky.
† Crystal City is the name for a large modern office complex in Arlington, Virginia, not far south of the Pentagon.

the other. And Kasano, Kasano San. He was the president of the chamber of commerce. That was his official title. I would say he was the unofficial ambassador to the United States Navy in Yokosuka. It turned out that Masuoka was the ambassador to the U.S. Navy, period. And there was Mayor Nagano. These people we got to know over a period of time and became friends. There were lots and lots of others. The Japanese CNO who was named Uchida and his VCNO was Ishida. There was a Vice Admiral Kitamura. I had to pay office calls around the Department of Defense, and up in town Nakasone, who was later Prime Minister, was the Defense Minister.*

Paul Stillwell: Did most of these individuals speak English?

Admiral Burke: Yes. They start teaching English in about the fifth grade. Right after I relieved command, I met the deputy to Nakasone. His name was something like Tsuchia. He had daughters about the same age as my daughter Sally, and they invited Sally to spend a weekend with them up at their home in the country. So she went off with them right there at the start and had a very interesting experience with them. Whenever Sally came back from college she got together with the girls. We had the girls down at our house as guests once or twice. We discovered that they had never sunbathed, which is why they don't have wrinkles. [Laughter] But I'd say we got thrust into the culture out there.

Of my staff, none were going to make admiral, but they were very solid people. One of them, my N-4, Jack Creamer, had been a battalion officer at Annapolis and he had been out there for about a year, year and a half.† He was a very solid performer at Annapolis, and he was brilliant in that job in Japan. There was Captain Fred Berry, class of '45, who was the N-1 at the start, and then I moved him to N-3. He was a submariner. He'd already had a squadron. He had been out there about a year when I got there. The intelligence officer, I can't remember the top guy. I had Jim Eaves as my public affairs officer.‡ Can't remember my intelligence officer. I'll dig it up sooner or later, but the

---

* Yasuhiro Nakasone served as Japan's Prime Minister from 1982 to 1987.
† Captain John J. Creamer, USN.
‡ Commander James S. Eaves, USN.

number two, Commander Lou Martinez, was the really effective one.* Emmett Riera was ComFAirWestPac.†

Paul Stillwell: He was at Atsugi.‡

Admiral Burke: He was at Atsugi. Al Bergner, a classmate, was homeported at Sasebo.§ He was the Service Force Seventh Fleet. That's about all I can remember. Strat Wentworth, who I think had been chief of staff of Seventh Fleet, made admiral, and then he got the MSC job out there in Yokohama.** Mickey Weisner was Com7thFlt.†† And there were some homeported destroyers at Yokosuka, and we also had a tender there. Negotiations were going on under the table up in Tokyo, and finally, just before Christmas, the negotiations were completed for the drawdown. I think the only thing that was going to be left out there was ComNavFor Japan staff plus a communications station.

Paul Stillwell: Would the Fleet Activities Yokosuka have been closed down?‡‡

Admiral Burke: I don't recall. They would have had to maintain something there, but they were going to give up the shipyard, the supply center, the public works, and the ammunition depot. We had an enormous ammunition storage out there.

Paul Stillwell: Did you hear what the reason was for this plan to close it up?

Admiral Burke: Admiral Clarey was the VCNO at the time the decision was made. He had orders when I left OpNav to relieve Admiral Hyland who was retiring as CinCPacFlt.§§ He came out to Japan in '71, probably in March or April. I was going to

---

* Commander Lucian C. Martinez, USN.
† Rear Admiral Robert Emmett Riera, USN, Commander Fleet Air Western Pacific.
‡ Atsugi is the site of a U.S. naval air station near the port of Yokosuka on the island of Honshu, Japan.
§ Rear Admiral Allen E. Bergner, USN.
** Rear Admiral Ralph S. Wentworth, Jr., USN, Commander Military Sealift Command Far East.
†† Vice Admiral Maurice F. Weisner, USN, served as Commander Seventh Fleet from 10 March 1970 to 18 June 1971.
‡‡ Essentially the U.S. Navy has a large base at Yokosuka, but it is titled "fleet activities" as a euphemism.
§§ Admiral Bernard A. Clarey, USN, served as Commander in Chief Pacific Fleet, 5 December 1970 to 30 September 1973.

brief him on where we stood with what we were doing. And we didn't make any bones about it. We couldn't figure out why those dumb guys had reversed themselves. This was after the reversal.

Paul Stillwell: When did the reversal take place?

Admiral Burke: Oh, wait a minute. I'd better answer that question later on.

Paul Stillwell: All right.

Admiral Burke: Two days before Christmas the Prime Minister announced in Parliament—and it was given lots of publicity throughout Japan—that the U.S. Navy was going to withdraw, and the Japanese Government thought it was good for Japan. And right away we started executing. We started sending people home and closing up shops and so forth. There were some homeported ships there, and I don't recall how soon they left, but they left quite soon. I think the goal was to get out of there within six months.

Towards the last week in January a quarterly scheduling conference for Seventh Fleet was going to be held at Baguio. Apparently they alternately held them one in Baguio and one in Yokosuka or something like that. So everybody went to Baguio, and many of them took their wives. I took leave and took Betty down there on space available and introduced her to that life. It was like going down to Hot Springs, Virginia, almost. It's a very pleasant vacation.

Well, when I arrived down there, I had just hadn't been there more than a half an hour when I bumped into Bobby Inman, who was a commander at that time and the special intelligence officer for Com7thFlt.* He said, "Admiral Weisner wants you to look at this message." It was a message from CNO himself saying that they had a new plan, which was to homeport a carrier group in the Western Pacific. There'd be a carrier, probably six destroyers, and probably a support ship.

Paul Stillwell: When would you say it was that you learned of that?

---

* Commander Bobby R. Inman, USN, later director of the Central Intelligence Agency.

Admiral Burke: It was probably around the 23rd of January of 1971 and said that Vice Admiral Champ Blouin and a party would be visiting Tokyo to talk to the embassy staff.[*]

Paul Stillwell: He was then OP-06.

Admiral Burke: He was OP-06. Well, also at the conference, sort of wandering around as an agent from CNO, was Dave Bagley, who was a rear admiral then.[†] I think he was in charge of these special programs. I've forgotten the umbrella that he was under. But I'd like to go back and say we had Z-grams that were coming out all the time, which were shaking up the Navy.[‡] I'd met Dave. Either he had been in Yokosuka before the meeting or not, but he was there and I saw him down there.

Paul Stillwell: But he was sort of CNO's emissary?

Admiral Burke: Yes. And Mickey Weisner told me that he wanted me to get back to Yokosuka and attend the meeting with Champ Blouin as his representative. I wasn't an addressee on this. This is how I found out about it. So Betty and I got back on a plane. I was on leave, so to take care of Betty presented a temporary problem, but as it ended up I was able to get a flight out and made it.

Paul Stillwell: Well, you were not in Weisner's chain of command. What was the relationship between your command and his?

Admiral Burke: I had two bosses. One was CinCPacFlt, and the other one was U.S. Forces Japan. I forget his name but he was three-star Air Force, and I was Commander Naval Forces Japan under him. Actually, I commanded practically nothing out there.

---

[*] Vice Admiral Francis J. Blouin, USN, served as Deputy Chief of Naval Operations (Plans and Policy) from July 1968 to July 1971.
[†] Rear Admiral David H. Bagley, USN, Assistant DCNO (Personal Affairs).
[‡] Z-grams were consecutively numbered policy directives from Chief of Naval Operations Zumwalt that attempted to deal with such issues as enlisted rights and privileges, equal opportunity, and Navy families. Junior personnel viewed them much more favorably than did their seniors. See U.S. Naval Institute Proceedings, May 1971, pages 293-298.

Paul Stillwell: What was the nature of the association you had with Com7thFlt?

Admiral Burke: I would say I supported him wherever it was necessary, but the FltActs belonged to ComServPac.* ComFltActs, if he chose to, could ignore me and sometimes did. It was sort of an odd thing, but on the other hand it was helpful, very helpful. While we were regaining control I wouldn't have had time to fool with FltActs. It was a pain in the neck to have ComServPac come out there and take charge of his FltActs and want to exercise his muscle when I was the boss guy in the area, and I had one uncomfortable experience. Notwithstanding that, it turned out to be a good arrangement, but I wasn't in a situation where I could force people to do things. So my experience in the reserve business was very helpful, and I used that experience to get things done.

Paul Stillwell: Well, that's the background. Let's return to Weisner deputizing you to go to this meeting with Blouin.

Admiral Burke: Well, he was a three-star, and he was the boss guy in the Western Pacific, and I did what he wanted.

Paul Stillwell: What came of the meeting?

Admiral Burke: We went to the meeting, and the ambassador was Armin Meyer.† His deputy was Dick Snyder. Howard Meyers was his political-military man. When the package was presented that we wanted to homeport and so forth, this was a problem, because we were giving up a whole raft of quarters and capability in Yokohama too. The biggest chunk of our quarters were in Yokohoma. They exploded, particularly Armin Meyer and Dick Snyder. Snyder had done the negotiating. Armin Meyer was a career diplomat and Dick Snyder was, too, and Snyder was the real dean of the college and did most of the work in that department. They were outraged, and they flatly refused to talk

---

* FltActs—Fleet Activities Yokosuka; ComServPac—Commander Service Force Pacific Fleet.
† Armin H. Meyer, a Foreign Service Officer, was U.S. ambassador to Japan from 3 July 1969 to 27 March 1972.

to the Japanese Government unless and until they got a directive from the State Department.

Now, Dave Bagley attended that meeting, and he and I and Champ Blouin were living in Tokyo. I moved up to the Sanno for the duration of the discussions. I don't think it was just one meeting, but we were there overnight, and so I got to know Bagley a little bit. I think Bagley came back down to Yokosuka and stayed for a day or so to look over Yokosuka and see how we were doing. I got to know him fairly well through these visits. He came out two or three times while I was there, and I developed a very good relationship with him. I felt like I could communicate with him anytime.

Anyhow, I came back from this meeting. It was on a Friday, and I called together my key people in the staff, Creamer, Stroud who was my chief of staff.[*] His replacement was on board, Pappy Fruin, and Fred Berry.[†] He was N-1 and my ops officer, I forget his name. We talked about this problem late on Friday night for about two or three hours. Because I had formerly been in OP-60, I sort of had a feel for how things were done. I said, "All I can tell you is I know that this is what OpNav, according to CNO wants, and we've got this stone wall. We've got to find out if this is amenable to the Japanese Government."

Paul Stillwell: And you weren't going to get any help from the ambassador.

Admiral Burke: No, no. We concluded, and I said, "Well, somehow or other we've got to get into the Japanese Government."

Jack Creamer said, "If you do, you're going to get sent home if you get caught." So we kicked this thing around about what to do and what not to do. We didn't take a vote. But during the night I decided to get hold of an interpreter who worked in the intelligence department. He was Doug Wada, a Japanese-American, born and raised in Hawaii. I'd heard that he had been out there for about 15 years at least and knew where all the bones were buried, and I just laid the problem bare to him. I said, "Do you have any idea how to get inside the Japanese government to find this out?"

---

[*] Captain George W. Stroud, USN.
[†] Captain Jack L. Fruin, USN.

He came right back. He said, "Oh, it's easy. You remember that little guy that was the first person that called on you? His name is Masuoka. He's the secretary to the speaker of House of Representatives. I can get to the speaker of the House of Representatives anytime I want to. All I have to do is call up Masuoka, and he can arrange it."

Paul Stillwell: He was a useful man to have around.

Admiral Burke: Well, it was extraordinary. I had my car take him up to the train, and about three hours later he called down to the opcon center, "Tell Admiral Burke everything's okay. I'll see you Monday morning." When he came in Monday morning, he told me he had gone up and had lunch with Funada and Masuoka. He said Funada nodded his head and said it was okay.

I said, "Well, what was his reaction?"

He says, "He wished to hell that the Americans would make up their mind and do what they ought to do in the first place." [Laughter] I got to know Masuoka quite well while I was there, and every CNO and every Com7thFlt and every CinCPacFlt and every ComNavFor Japan before and after me have known him. He called himself "Mister Navy." He died here about eight months ago. He knew more American flag officers than I ever did, whether I was on active duty or retired. So after I heard from Wada, I passed the word to OpNav back channel what I'd done.

Paul Stillwell: Why back channel?

Admiral Burke: Well, because I didn't want people to have access to communications on what I was doing.

Paul Stillwell: Especially the State Department people?

Admiral Burke: Yes. I didn't want the wrong people to become privy to it. So I'd say for the next two years practically everything I was doing on the subject was back channel for that reason. And the fact that I had been in OP-60 I had a feel for how they operated. Lou Martinez was my number two in intelligence, and I set up what I would call a command team.

The main thing that we had to do first was to save this SRF Yokosuka, the ship repair facility, because we needed that shipyard desperately to keep our capability in the Northwest Pacific and Western Pacific. So that's what we worked on initially. I got through to Funada, and then I had a meeting with Admiral Uchida shortly afterwards, I'd say within a week.* He had been on a tour I think to Europe and to the U.S. He was Zumwalt's guest. He asked for an emergency meeting with me one Sunday.

He and his VCNO, Ishida, and Nakamura, his operations officer came down in my quarters there, and he told me that he had been rendered honors over at the Navy Yard.† He and Admiral Zumwalt were riding to the Pentagon thereafter, and on the way Zumwalt told him about this plan that he had of homeporting a carrier task group in the Western Pacific. Uchida couldn't believe his ears. He came down to talk to me about it. I told him what I knew at that point in time; we had what the Japanese call frank discussions. So it was timely that he came down, because I didn't have to worry about wondering whether I could talk to him about it. But he wanted us. They were on our side. There wasn't any question about it.

Paul Stillwell: So then was it a matter of convincing the political side?

Admiral Burke: And I told him that I had this informal indirect communication with Funada, and that reassured him. I never did ask him who his political ties were. But from then on I could cut those three people in on what we were doing. I'd say what was unusual about it over a period of time as we worked the problem, I got into a situation where I'd send back a situation report about once a week back how things were going. Before long, I was telling OP-06 what to do. That's pretty heady wine.

---
* Admiral K. Uchida, JMSDF, Chief of Maritime Staff. Vice Admiral Teiji Nakamura, JMSDF.
† The Washington Navy Yard is on M Street in southeast Washington, D.C. For many years it was an industrial facility known as the Naval Gun Factory. Since the late 1970s the residence of the Chief of Naval Operations has been in the Washington Navy Yard.

Paul Stillwell: Yes, it is.

Admiral Burke: We sort of carried this kind of thing out over a period of two years. Eventually, and I forget when it was, we got the decision on saving SRF.

Paul Stillwell: Where did that decision come from?

Admiral Burke: Well, it came when we thought things were ready on the Japanese side. I guess probably Uchida was the one that would tell me this, that they were ready to receive it, and he had to go political to find this out. Then I would tell OpNav, "Now it's time to make a recommendation." Then they would run it up through OSD and over to the State Department. I guess it had to be passed by the National Security Council. Then a message would come from State telling the embassy to negotiate this. Well, they didn't like it, and they suspected what was going on, but they couldn't prove it.

There was a Japanese Foreign Service officer who was a personal friend of Dick Snyder's. They had served together somewhere before, and about this time he was brought in as the head of the North American section of their Foreign Office. Before long he invited me to have a one-on-one luncheon at a restaurant in Tokyo, and we played golf together a couple of times so we had what the Japanese call frank discussions. I told him Snyder was not in on what we were doing. Eventually I heard from one of my guys. I guess I heard from Jack Creamer, who had a lot of work to do with the embassy. They said Burke was just like Dick Snyder. [Laughter]

Paul Stillwell: What did he mean by that?

Admiral Burke: Well, that was a negative pat on the back. [Laughter]

Paul Stillwell: Was it your perception that the State Department involvement would make it more difficult for the Navy to negotiate?

Admiral Burke: I don't think the State Department was the problem. The embassy was the problem.

Paul Stillwell: Okay.

Admiral Burke: They were frustrated. Now, there was an Under Secretary of State who was a Navy friend. I forget his name, but he was on very good terms with Clarey or had been and others in the Navy Department. He was sort of, from that point of view, steering the Navy Department. After we got the SRF saved, boy, there was a sigh of relief all over the place, including the Japanese, too, because we had all these Japanese employees. They didn't know where they were going to end up. I think Dick Snyder realized that eventually we were going to get what we wanted. I don't know whether he was trying to help me or not, but one day in a conversation he said, "The way that you always get what you want, you've got to package it so that you don't do it all at once." And that was good advice. I mean, we had to retrieve a lot. The key things were the SRF, and then we had to get destroyers there. We had to recover Atsugi.

Paul Stillwell: There was a communications station.

Admiral Burke: I don't think the communications station had been given away.

Paul Stillwell: I see.

Admiral Burke: And we had a security station.

Paul Stillwell: Kamiseya?

Admiral Burke: Kamiseya, but I don't think we'd given that up. But we'd given up Atsugi, and we'd given up Yokohama, as well as just about everything on the base there at FltActs. So we started packaging things, and before long we got the destroyers out there. Then I guess the next thing we had to do was save Atsugi. The Japanese were prepared to give us actually what we wanted. I knew what Dick Snyder's instructions were, and he didn't negotiate what he was told. So he let the Japanese into Atsugi. Just wanted to share the bases in a minority role, but they were there. When I went up to talk to Admiral Uchida after it was all over, he said, "Mr. Snyder didn't ask for what we were prepared to give." But I couldn't do anything about it.

Paul Stillwell: What about Sasebo and the Marine Corps Air Station at Iwakuni? Were they part of the package?

Admiral Burke: Sasebo was, and I just don't remember how we did on Iwakuni. I was mentally so preoccupied with what I was doing, but I know Sasebo was part of the package.

Paul Stillwell: That was given away and had to be retrieved?

Admiral Burke: Yes. And then the final step was to get the carrier out there. There were all kinds of emotional things. As I best remember, the destroyers got out there probably in the fall of '71. I think that's when. I'm sort of vague on that. It may have been in '72. Some of the people involved didn't want to come, and it screwed up their planning, so you we had all kinds of individual problems like that. But when they finally came we had a squadron out there and a good bunch of people.

Then we had to work at least a year on the carrier, which we finally got approved in the summer of '72 with the word that the carrier would take a year before it could get out there.* There was a lot of politics on that because of whether or not they had nuclear weapons on board. Our policy was we didn't confirm or deny. Any time we had any sort of ship that had nuclear capability of any sort in port, there would always be a demonstration out at the front gate. I forget the name of the parties, but the mayor was a

---

* The aircraft carrier Midway (CVA-41) and her escorts arrived in Yokosuka, Japan, on 5 October 1973 to begin the first overseas homeporting of a complete carrier task group. The forward deployment was the result of an accord arrived at on 31 August 1972 between the United States and Japan. In August 1991, after nearly 18 years of service out of the Japanese port, the Midway left Yokosuka for the last time and was replaced by the Independence (CV-62) as the forward-deployed carrier.

practical Socialist. One of the things I discovered very early on—which I previously discovered in the reserve business—you had to go down to the grassroots and sell the program to get the heads going up and down so that their bosses wouldn't be afraid to commit themselves, even though they agreed with what you wanted. You would go talk to the top people about what you wanted to do, and they would all smile and agree with you on what you wanted to do. But then nothing would happen. So gradually Jack Creamer and I came to the conclusion that we would have to start at the lowest common denominator and work up. And the technique worked. I had a lot of help from a lot of people.

Paul Stillwell: Now, where were you doing this lowest common denominator selling job?

Admiral Burke: I wasn't doing it. I'd tell Creamer, "Find out where the thing starts in their department." Then either he or one of his people would go in there and start selling it.

Paul Stillwell: Are you talking about selling to the Japanese people?

Admiral Burke: Yes. It's a bureaucratic concept, and they would have to find out who the next level of responsibility was and work the thing up. There's so much time since then that it's hard for me to pull all this back together, but I had this team of people, and I would meet with them from time to time. We would talk the issues, and it was a no holds barred. I told them they could disagree anytime they wanted to. But it helped me come up with a sounding board.

Early on I felt and needed a political-military staff officer, which I didn't have, so I designated Martinez as that. He was in intelligence, and he was very valuable. I also needed more than he had and I was talking to Tiny Atkinson, who was the naval attaché.[*] He said, "There's an officer up here. He's a graduate student." And he sent a man

---

[*] Captain Wilton L. Atkinson, USN.

named Jim Auer.* Jim was probably a lieutenant commander at the time. He was a Navy graduate student at Tufts, and he was out there working on his thesis, "Postwar Japanese Navy." He had a letter of introduction from Arleigh Burke when he came out and probably Zumwalt, and he knew more big shots in town then I ever did. But he was extraordinarily helpful in putting me together with different people.

Paul Stillwell: Such as whom?

Admiral Burke: This guy right here, Taoka. This picture was taken at a dinner one night. We got together at the Sanno and had dinner. This is Jim Auer right here. This is my flag lieutenant, Curley. This is Nakamura, who was the operations officer for Uchida, but by this time Uchida had retired, and Nakamura was now the Commandant of the Kure Naval District. Jim Auer is brilliant and very capable guy. He had ideas abounding, and he knew people around town. He put this meeting together. This is Masuoka right here and this is Taoka.

Taoka was a newsman who had operated between Kyoto and Tokyo and he was highly respected. He was sort of a college professor type. He was somebody that you could consult with for advice as a father figure, and they respected him. I don't know how Jim got to know him, but he knew different people around Tokyo and occasionally these things were extraordinarily helpful. This is Pappy Fruin here. Nakamura eventually ended up as chief of staff of the Navy and became the Chairman of the Joint Chiefs. He was somebody I had a very good relationship because he was the class of '40 there and they call you classmates.

When I arrived out there, it was hard for me to realize how big a shot in their culture I was. They knew all about me. When I called on the Chairman of the Joint Chiefs, Admiral Itaya, he knew all about me from A to Z, and it turned out that we were classmates at the Naval War College.† He was in the foreign officers' section. I didn't recall, but he reminded me that we were classmates. But this gives you an entrée in their culture that's far different than or far stronger I think than it is in ours. But this meeting

---

* Lieutenant Commander James E. Auer, USN.
† Admiral Takaichi Itaya, JMSDF.

helped. I don't recall exactly what we talked about, but I'm sure we talked about the objective of what we were after. This led on to other things.

I discovered there were U.S. Naval Reserve officers in Tokyo. One was a man named George Purdy, who had been in the class of '31 at the Academy.* His wife was Japanese. Before long he invited me to speak to the ROA, the Reserve Officers Association, meeting at one of their dinners, and so I met a lot of these gentlemen who were Americans representing foreign companies out there. They were GE, Getty Oil, DuPont, so I got to meet a number of them. Purdy was with Dresser Industries, a big U.S. corporation based in Texas. One time I said, "What's your job with this outfit?"

He said, "Well, I'm like the base commander." He had been out there for many years. He said, "My job is when one of our company heads for Japan or the Far East, I find him a place to live, give him logistic support until he can go on his own." A good example of that was a classmate of mine named Jim Smith.† Jim had resigned from the Navy. He was an EDO.‡ He'd gotten involved in the space program, I think, and he had been the head of a project down in Louisiana; I think it was with Chrysler. Then he got transferred out to Japan, and he worked for Dresser also. He was involved in some oil development, in chemicals and oil, and he went to Europe frequently, but he was based in Tokyo.

Turned out his wife had been the widow of somebody that Betty knew in New Orleans, so we got to be pretty good friends and saw a fair amount of each other over a period of time. Eventually I told George Purdy what I was interested in. I didn't tell him exactly, but I told him that we had this problem of trying to get ourselves back in, and I was running into a lot of problems, and I needed to know inside the government.

He said, "Well, I think I can help you on this. You know, the government and industry are very closely married in Japan. I belong to a business group of Japanese and Americans that meets about once a quarter, and so I can bring you in as my guest." So very soon I was invited to this dinner up in Tokyo, and there were Japanese businessmen with the chairman of the board of Mitsubishi and Mitsui, and there were about 15 of these

---

* George I. Purdy had resigned from the Naval Academy prior to graduation and subsequently was commissioned in the Naval Reserve. He reached the rank of lieutenant commander in the reserve.
† Captain James C. Smith, USNR.
‡ EDO—engineering duty officer.

Japanese there. They were all presidents of companies. One of them was Morita, who was one of the two people that put Sony together.* Morita at the time was on the IBM board and spent as much time in New York as he did in Tokyo.

Of all this group Morita was the only one who was my age. All the others were much older. Whenever the Japanese sat down to have a what they called friendly discussion with the Americans the Japanese were on side and they had a pecking of the table and we were on the other, and they always sat based on their age. Morita was the one I wanted to do business with, but he was always down at the other end of the table. And he was a man with extraordinary ideas. One of the Americans was Bill Geyser. He was DuPont. He had married a Japanese lady who was the president of Ichibana International. He was the only one of the bunch that could conduct negotiations in Japanese. He'd been out there that long. Then there was a man from Getty Oil. I can't remember the other names. Westinghouse. Bill Young was not there. Bill Young was a reserve officer, a retired or reserve officer. He had married Japanese, and he was the Virginia Port Authority representative in Japan.

Paul Stillwell: In what way were these individuals helpful to you in your effort?

Admiral Burke: Well, it gave me a feel for the culture. Purdy had a yacht, and occasionally he would bring these people down on a weekend, come down to the base, and they were all reserve officers: Army, Navy, Air Force. Before long, I got a letter from the president of the Navy League, asking me to do what I could to get a Navy League established in Tokyo, so I passed it on to Purdy, and he got one going. A few months later I got a letter from Ralph Cousins, who was the VCNO at this time, saying that he'd heard that they were passing around free memberships to the Atsugi Golf Course if they joined the Navy League.† [Laughter] I showed the letter to Purdy, and he hotly denied it, but it stopped. [Laughter]

---

* Akio Morita (1921-1999) served during World War II on the Japanese Navy's wartime research committee. In May 1946 Morita and Masaru Ibuka founded The Tokyo Telecommunications Engineering Corporation. In 1958, as the corporation reached for global markets, it changed the corporate name to Sony. Besides managing Sony, Morita was a member of the Japan-U.S. Economic Relations Group.

† Admiral Ralph W. Cousins, USN, served as Vice Chief of Naval Operations from 30 October 1970 to 1 September 1972.

Paul Stillwell: Were these businessmen able to give you any influence with the Japanese Government?

Admiral Burke: No, but it gave me a feel for the culture, the various things that were there. I never felt that any of these people had their hand in the government, but they were all close enough to what was going on. One time they had a session down at a hotel on Izu Peninsula, which, oh, it's about 100 miles away, and it was at one of these golf outings, sort of a Hot Springs or White Sulphur kind of a place. It was interesting to watch this thing. The Americans would gather in late afternoon about 5:00 o'clock and have cocktails, and then we'd have dinner. After dinner they would have quote friendly discussions. When the Japanese were hosting, they'd have it at one these fancy places. One time they had a nightclub star there, a woman who did some singing.

The senior man there was the board chairman of Mitsubishi, and he looked to me like he was at least 80 years old. He had his flag lieutenant by him standing over around behind a potted palm tree as the presidents of the subsidiaries would come in. They would come in the entrance, look around, find out where he was, and then they would go over and bow to Mr. Mitsubishi. I think his name was Sutsumi. The angle of the bow related to the order of the peck. No kidding.

When you call on a Japanese in his office, he's all smiles and acts like he wants to please you. And you come away thinking that everything you wanted is jake, but it isn't that way. They have to decide they know and like you and trust you before they will do business. It took me about six months, but I felt over a period of time that I won the confidence of the people that I was dealing with. I had so much to learn about Japan, and after a while Betty made a point of getting a book on Japanalia, I called it. I must have read 30 books about Japan. How we got into the war, how the war was fought, how the war ended. All of these things contributed to my ability to deal with them and to gain their confidence so they would communicate with me and tell me what I wanted to know.

If you read the books, there are different books about how the war was fought. One is The Rising Sun, and one's called The Chrysanthemum and the Sword.* One of them describes in detail how the war came to a conclusion. They were losing the war, and there were people in the cabinet wanting to turn it off, but the military people wanted to keep it going. When the nuclear weapons came, it finally shocked them to the point that they had to do something, and so there was a description in probably The Chrysanthemum and the Sword about how the war ended.

They had a cabinet meeting, and it was a tie vote, and so the Emperor cast a vote to turn the war off. General Anami, who was the War Minister, voted to keep the war going. But his loyalty to the Emperor caused him to go back to his headquarters building at the Army headquarters. He got his bureaucratic staff, who were in open revolt, to behave themselves and to follow orders and put the necessary instructions out to the Japanese Army to comply. At the end of the day he got in his sedan and drove out to his house, where he had his own private home. He was living in the suburbs and it describes how he came in.

In those days the husband when he returns from work the first thing he does is get a hot bath, go through a ritual and maybe have a cup of tea. It described how he put on his ukada and walked out in the garden and sat down in his garden. He had seven sons, and the youngest was a baby. His wife brought the baby out, and he played with the baby for a while. Then he called for his wife. Passed the baby back to her, and she took the baby on back into the house and he went out on the edge of the garden and committed hara-kiri in the most painful way, which is considered the most noble in Japan.†

Meeting these people and reading about them and so forth was helpful. Another couple we met early on was the Satos. Mrs. Sato's family owned the Buddha that's in Kamakura and they live on the place. Her husband was the bishop.

Paul Stillwell: The great daibutsu.

---

* John Toland, The Rising Sun: The Decline and Fall of the Japanese Empire, 1936-1945 (New York: Random House, 1970). Ruth Benedict, The Chrysanthemum and the Sword: Patterns of Japanese Culture (Boston: Houghton Mifflin Company, 1946).
† General Korechika Anami committed hara-kiri on 15 August 1945, shortly before Emperor Hirohito announced Japanese acceptance of the Allied peace terms.

Admiral Burke: Yes. Betty and I just went over there early on to see the daibutsu. I'd heard about Mrs. Sato, but we hadn't met her, and so we just went over and knocked on her door. It took her about a half an hour, and we sort of invited ourselves in, but she was very gracious. She spoke excellent English. Her husband didn't. But she was, I would say, an ambassador between us and them. She was always very cordial and very friendly and seemed supportive, and it wasn't until I got my orders for detachment she suddenly became more interested in who was going to replace me. [Laughter]

Paul Stillwell: Well, you started to talk a while back about Admiral Clarey and you had a discussion with him on this whole process. What did that involve?

Admiral Burke: He and Mrs. Clarey came out for a tour around the Pacific. They were our houseguests, and I talked to them privately there, and then I had him down for a briefing in my office. I would say there was a certain amount of frustration in my staff and me too. We couldn't figure out why the hell this decision to pull out in the first place had ever been made. It didn't seem to us to make sense, and at the briefing this sort of came out in spades. Admiral Clarey, rather than let it take over, said, "All I can tell you is, based on the assumptions that we were given in this study that was done, there was no alternative than to shut down in Japan."

Paul Stillwell: Do you know what those assumptions were?

Admiral Burke: He didn't say, but I can say my guess is that if you look at the Navy at the time we were decimated. The naval appropriations, I'm sure, were being emasculated to support additional divisions of troops in Vietnam. I know one year there we didn't get a carrier because there was a division of Army. That was while I was in OpNav.

Paul Stillwell: Well, I wonder if this was part of the drawdown as the Vietnam War was winding up because the withdrawal started about 1969.

Admiral Burke: It could have. But that's all he said. He just wouldn't talk about it, and I'm sure he was privy to information that he couldn't share.

Paul Stillwell: That's intriguing that you would be sent out to execute a plan and not even given an explanation for the reasoning.

Admiral Burke: Well, that's true, but we had two plans that passed in the night, one going one way and one reversing, and it just seemed to us it was a crazy situation. I couldn't understand how it was being executed and the planners and executors weren't closer together.

Paul Stillwell: It's curious.

Admiral Burke: I've said a lot of things like I would have kicked a lot of butt. [Laughter]

Paul Stillwell: Well, while you were having this process of turning around the withdrawal, how much contact did you have with the Japanese Speaker of the House?

Admiral Burke: The kind of contact I had was a formal arrangement. I wasn't buddies with him, but every so often, I would say probably twice during my stay, I had him down as a guest for luncheon. Took him out in my boat and rode him around the harbor. But a number of times, though, he would have a luncheon up in his official quarters, which were not too far from the Sanno. He was very cordial to us, and it was interesting to go up there because there were times when I needed to see him to determine how the U.S. Navy plans for Japan were progressing in his government. And he would tell me.

I was doing this through my interpreter, Doug Wada, and Masuoka was always present. I don't think I ever took advantage of him. I do remember one time. Gromyko was making the first state visit of a Russian official to Japan.* He was there for two or

---

* Andrei A. Gromyko was a long-time Soviet diplomat. Among his posts were ambassador to the United States, Ambassador to the United Nations, Deputy Foreign Minister, and Foreign Minister.

three days. During that period we were in a critical time when we were going to send a recommendation through State to the embassy to do something. I really had to get the word on it where they stood so that I had confidence it would be received. So I asked for an interview and asked to see Funada. I was told to be back at 4:00 o'clock or something like that on a weekday afternoon. I couldn't believe it because that was the time they were having a state reception for Gromyko. When I arrived, I started off and apologized; I didn't mean to interfere with his social life. He said, "I didn't want to go." [Laughter]

Paul Stillwell: To the reception, that is.

Admiral Burke: Yes. He was pro-American. And I'd say that I met people because my name was Burke. These people, particularly amongst the higher echelon in the Navy or civilians who had been associated with government, assumed that I was Arleigh's son or his much younger brother.* After about six or eight months I gave up trying to explain. They just would not accept it. So doors got opened to me, and I met people and they would go along with things I felt because my name was Burke. I was embarrassed about it at first, but it was so damned helpful I stopped being embarrassed. [Laughter]

Give you an example. There was a retired vice admiral named Hoshina. He was vice admiral Imperial Japanese Navy. He was 80 years old. He'd gone to Yale as a graduate student. He was one of those that opposed the Japanese striking us. He knew what our capability was. He'd served in the upper house of the Diet, and he was considered their preeminent Navy elder statesman. He was a hell of a nice man, and one day he asked for an appointment with me. Somebody told me who he was, and I invited him to stay for lunch fortunately. Well, he came down and very polite but he was very firm. I couldn't believe how firm he was on his message, "We want you to do what you want." That was sort of the message.

Paul Stillwell: So since he was in the Diet was he sending a signal on behalf of the government?

---

* Admiral Arleigh A. Burke, USN (Ret.), was a former Chief of Naval Operations. He was treated with great respect and deference by the Japanese because of his chivalry during World War II and because he had an instrumental role after the war in establishing the Japanese Maritime Self-Defense Force.

Admiral Burke: Well, the upper house doesn't have any clout. It's like the House of Lords in Britain.

Paul Stillwell: I see.

Admiral Burke: But he was a father figure to their Navy at that time. He's dead now. At least twice while we were there he invited Betty and me up for dinner, and we went to a fairly good-sized spread with prominent Japanese. I had no idea who they were, but it was recognizing me as ComNavFor Japan. It gave me entrée into things that I didn't even know about.

After I'd met him, the next time I saw Admiral Uchida, with whom I played golf about once every two or three months, he was the CNO at the time, and I told him I'd met Hoshina. He said, "He was polite to you, but he means business."

There was another couple we met out there were very interesting. He was Air Vice Marshal Sir Cecil Boucher, RAF.* His wife was the daughter of a British businessman, and I don't know what happened to her parents during the war. They had shipped her to Bermuda when she was a college student. Her mother was American. It turned out Betty has some first cousins in Bermuda. She knew them. [Laughter] This is connections. The Bouchers turned out to be probably our best friends out there on the civilian side. They lived in Kamakura in her family home, which is on the shore right next to the Kamakura royal palace, which was a summer palace that the royalty had. It wasn't ostentatious but it was a very nice home. It was a second marriage for Boucher, and she was about our age. Boucher had been in World War I, so he was a good bit older.

It turned out that, towards the end of the war when Mountbatten was the British commander in Southeast Asia, Boucher was his air deputy.† And then during the occupation he was involved in the British occupation of Japan. That's where this couple met. His marriage had come apart, and so they were married and so we got to know

---
* RAF—Royal Air Force.
† Admiral Louis Mountbatten, RN, Supreme Allied Commander Southeast Asia, 1943-46.

them. He somewhere along the line knew Arleigh Burke and other Navy people. And she was an artist and a television personality. That gave us a gate to events and people whom we hadn't met.

Paul Stillwell: Well, one other factor in all of this is that I would think it was in a Japanese self-interest to have a strong U.S. military presence as protection for their islands since they did not have a strong military.

Admiral Burke: They did. That's true, but also—and I don't know whether it was Communists or Socialists—they didn't want any part about nuclear weapons. I'd say the samurai instinct seemed to have disappeared with World War II, but they still had it during World War II. You'd meet a Japanese and you'd ask him his name, and he'd let you know like, "My family were samurais," and they said it with pride like a Virginian would say, "I'm from Virginia."

But while we were there, and it was within the first four or five months I was there, some Japanese political nut who had a small group of followers took over the War Ministry. I forget the guy's name. He was like some of these nuts we have out West that have taken over places. They had a standoff up there, and eventually he committed hara-kiri right in front of the public.*

Paul Stillwell: I think he was a poet or something wasn't he or an artist or author?

Admiral Burke: He was an author. But I can remember when the event happened I was on the way up to Tokyo to call on Admiral Uchida, and it had just happened when I arrived. Admiral Uchida was devastated to think that somebody would be doing hara-kiri in that age when actually it had only been a short time before. I mean, the hara-kiri thing wasn't all that out of date in World War II. They believed in it up to and through World War II, that if you couldn't get what you wanted you gave your life.

---

* Yukio Mishima, considered a writer of world stature, committed suicide 25 November 1970 at a Self-Defense Center in Tokyo after failing to enlist the support of troops there for a planned coup d-etat.

Paul Stillwell: Well, as I remember this man had his aides cut his head off after he was dead or something like that.

Admiral Burke: I don't remember. We visited different places. I can't tell you in the order that we did, but we went down to Sasebo. That happened very soon. And we've been to Iwakuni. We've been to Kure, the Japanese Naval School. They had a Defense School in Yokosuka, and apparently they would graduate from there and then send them to the Naval School at Kure. We went down to Kyoto.

The World's Fair was on at Osaka when we arrived in Japan. We went down to that, and the biggest impression I had about the World's Fair was that I saw one obese Japanese. I couldn't believe it, but when I saw that it was towards the end of the day and I don't remember all the things that we did, but we just went down because we'd heard about it. We were guests of the Japanese and were taken over to a naval base over on the Sea of Japan, and I can't remember the name of the place, but we were there for a weekend. We were the guests of the CNO when Uchida was the CNO. We went up to Northern Honshu and visited a Japanese airbase up there. We went up in a Japanese Navy plane. Betty went with me and then they took us over into a resort hotel in the mountains, Japanese style, which was quite interesting. And then there was some sort of a Japanese celebration, Mardi Gras celebration going on in this port city.

Then we parted company, and they flew us in a helicopter across over to Hokkaido and we visited Sapporo. We had a naval security station over there, I think. We had one at Misawa, which was in Northern Honshu. We went there. Then we took a couple or three days' leave. We sent to Sapporo, and we visited the American consul and then we went to another Japanese resort area. We were the only Caucasians there.

Of course, at every Japanese hotel you've got these hotsy baths where they have mixed bathing and so forth. Well, Betty had had her reservations about doing something like this, and as it turned out they had a boy side and a girl side. This particular hotsy bath was supposed to be the largest of its kind in Japan. They had at least ten pools that were quite large. A couple of them were maybe 50 feet long, 30 feet wide, where you could swim. They had different temperatures and different kinds of things in the water. This is the male side. At one end they had a lot of palm trees in pots and on the other side were the ladies. They had a very small pool over there, but there was room enough for them to do it.

Well, I was on the men's side. Betty was in the ladies' side. I persuaded her to go down, and before long I saw Japanese women on the men's side. So I went down towards the end, and there were, oh, at least eight or ten women. They were in this crowd, and they were talking as though nothing was wrong. They don't mind baring their breasts, but they managed to keep their crotches covered with a towel. Everybody gets a hand-sized towel when they go in there. So I called Betty with a family whistle, and so she came over and I persuaded her to come in. I said, "It's all right. Nobody's going to pay any attention to you." Well, apparently when I had my towel I had my towel above my crotch. [Laughter] And I walked out. [Laughter] Betty was laughing about it, and she mentioned it to one person when she got back to Yokosuka, and soon they were talking about it all over the base. [Laughter]

When we left there, we flew in a helicopter back to our plane. We ran into one hell of a storm, and I was terrified. You know, even in Japan the international language for pilots is English. But they were talking Japanese. They really got excited. [Laughter] When they started talking Japanese, I was scared, but we finally got out of it and came on home.

Well, when I got back, I talked to the American consul general in Yokohama. I can't remember his name, but he was a heck of a nice guy. I was telling him about being in Hokkaido and our experiences. He said, "You know, my first assignment in Japan I was a consul in Sapporo. After I'd been there for about a month or so, my wife and I decided to take a weekend off and go up to one of these small places at an inn where they had a hotsy bath. What happens is you get your bath before dinner." So he said they waited, and they decided to go down early so that they wouldn't have to encounter the mixed bathing. So he went down and found that everything was all clear and nobody was there. So he came back and told his wife and so they got all set, got ready and went on down to the bath. When they got down there they opened the door and walked in, and there was the mayor and the city council and their wives all bare-assed. [Laughter]

Paul Stillwell: Welcome to Japan. Well, they just treat it as no big deal.

Admiral Burke: No, it's what they're used to; they don't have the puritanical kind of life. For example, it's not unusual in Japan to be driving along somewhere on a country road, and you'll see a man relieving himself right there on the road. When we were detached and left Yokosuka to catch our plane back to Honolulu, unfortunately it turned out to be rush hour and instead of taking an hour and 15 minutes to get to the airport it took us about three hours. We got stalled in Yokohama, and we were sitting in this one place for about 20 minutes. We were alongside a canal and the driver in the car in front of us just hopped out of his car, climbed up on the wall and relieved himself into the canal as though there was nothing to it. And that's Japan.

Paul Stillwell: Well, I recall that it was not uncommon to have women in cleaning the men's restroom while the men were using it.

Admiral Burke: On one of the trips Betty and I left Kyoto and drove across Honshu to the Sea of Japan. We stopped at a gas station or someplace to freshen up. She asked our driver, Kabaya-san, where she could go and he pointed to her, and so she walked in there and of course there were a row of urinals there. But right by the door beyond that were the stalls. As she passed by the first urinal, the Japanese there looked and saw her and tipped his hat to her. [Laughter]

I never experienced any animosity towards Americans, but I came to the conclusion that in the Orient—and particularly it's true in Japan—that they don't care whether you're a Republican or a Democrat or a Communist or a Catholic or a Jew or whatever. They want to know who the boss is, and they want to please the boss. And if they can please the boss, things are better. You've got to be careful to realize this, and I'll give you a for instance. When I first got there, we hadn't been there very long when somebody called on us, and this man had a presento. That's customary in Japan.

Paul Stillwell: It's obligatory, isn't it?

Admiral Burke: Yes. And sometimes these presentos get out of hand. I guess because I was ComNavForJapan the title I had gave me a presence in the minds of the Japanese that I didn't have. I began to receive presentos from shopkeepers and things like this. I sent them back. But there were some people I couldn't do this for. For example, Kusano, who was head of the Chamber of Commerce, was extraordinarily helpful to us. I could talk to him about things when we needed. He was helpful politically, and he really helped us on the change of homeport. Because the mayor, although he was for us, he was Socialist and the Socialists were against us coming there. But it was good for business. So what I worked out was when he would give me something I would give them a bottle of Scotch whiskey, which was something that was very dear to them. I could get Scotch whiskey through the package store there on the base much, much less expensively than it was on the economy.

I worked this very hard so that I didn't want to violate what I considered were the rules of the game in the U.S., but I had to do something. I remember I got a sizeable present from somebody I'd never heard of the first Christmas that I was there, and I sent it back, and I was told I was crazy but I just couldn't see it. When I found out I was going to leave around the first of August of '72, I was told that I would be leaving in time, in about four or five months. There was a tailor out in town, Tom Andoh. He was not too far from the main gate. So I went down there and got measured for a lot of suits and so forth. I got a blue service uniform, a civilian suit, a blazer with my family crest put on it, and a couple of pairs of slacks. When he finally delivered these things to me, there wasn't any bill. I had my aide contact him and he said, "There isn't anything." And so I sent for him and told him I wanted his bill. He said, "Admiral, I can't send you one."

I said, "Why not?"

He said, "You don't realize how much business I get because I'm your tailor." [Laughter] He said, "This is the best advertising I can get in Japan." So we argued some more, and he was very firm, and I said, "Suppose you had made all these clothes for a captain. How much would you have charged him?" Well, he thought a while and he said, "Oh, maybe $50.00." So then we played this game down to an ensign by rank and he said he'd charge an ensign $250.00, which was a steal. But I finally paid him $250.00.

That was all he'd accept. At present, of course, prices in Japan are out of sight now, but my total take was about $20,000 a year at that time. When we went out there, it was 360 yen to a dollar. A year or so ago it was down to 80 some yen.

Paul Stillwell: Well, it's recovered. It's back up above a dollar now.

Admiral Burke: It's about $1.40, I think, now.

In the summer of '71 my son was getting married, and so we came back then for the wedding. He was out on the West Coast. Then I came on back here to touch base at the Pentagon. During the time I was back here President Nixon made the decision to float the dollar, which had the impact ultimately of the dollar losing value. It went all the way while we were there down to 320 yen. We were really upset, and in fact they even gave some of the people out there a small allowance to help compensate for it. But when we got back, I had one of these Japanese friendly American meetings that I told you about, business meetings. They specifically asked me to join them as a member so I was a member from then on. And they made me the honored guest. They wanted to know what I'd talked to President Nixon about on this trip, [Laughter] what he had said. [Laughter] During that period of time China was opening up a little bit.

Paul Stillwell: Kissinger made the trips over there and met with Chou En-lai.*

Admiral Burke: Yes. While we were there, one of the bankers, either Mitsubishi or Mitsui, had gone to China and been the guest of their government's top people and had talked with the top people in their government. He was the principal guest at one of these dinners and gave us his impressions before it was put in the papers in Tokyo. So I'd say this was sort of the kind of stuff I was getting involved in. While it didn't directly affect us, it gave me a feel for what they were doing in a way that I otherwise wouldn't have.

---

* Henry A. Kissinger was the President's national security adviser, 1969-73 and later served as Secretary of State, 1973-77. Chou En-lai became Premier and Foreign Minister of China when the Communists won control of the nation in 1949. He was replaced as Foreign Minister in 1959 but still remained the country's most influential spokesman in foreign affairs.

Paul Stillwell: Did you file regular reports on this sort of thing back to OP-06?

Admiral Burke: I don't know that I told them about that specific incident, but I sent situation reports back. It turned out that Jack Creamer was an extraordinary message writer. I'm not very good. I would come back from conferences and discussions, and we would have a meeting of this group, what I would call the command group. We'd talk over what was going on. It wasn't only me. It was other people participating.

Paul Stillwell: Sort of your kitchen cabinet.

Admiral Burke: Yes. But we had a marvelous relationship, and then I'd ask Jack to write up the message. And he could knock a home run. When I came back to OpNav, I got more than one compliment about the message writing we had. I was appropriately modest until I ended up with Jerry King, who was 03 at the time.[*] He wasn't even discreet about the way he asked. He wanted to know the name of who the guy was that was writing. I think Jerry knew I didn't have this capability. I told him right off, but I said, "Forget it. He's happy where he is, and he's going to retire in a year."

Paul Stillwell: You got the idea he was trying to filch him from you.

Admiral Burke: These meetings were loaded with emotion and frustration, and Jack had the ability just to lay it on the line. I did my best to cut in CinCPacFlt, and I don't think I got them upset.

Paul Stillwell: Did you ever get anything directly from CNO's office other than that visit from Admiral Bagley?

Admiral Burke: Well, Admiral Zumwalt and Mrs. Zumwalt came out there in the summer of '71. It was not too long after we had saved SRF, Yokosuka. They were

---

[*] Vice Admiral Jerome H. King, Jr., USN, served as Deputy Chief of Naval Operations (Surface Warfare) from 6 July 1971 to 19 July 1972.

living in Tokyo, but they came down and spent one day in Yokosuka. He talked to the troops, all the gathered enlisted there. He told me sometime during that visit that he had been told by somebody in State—that's the guy who was the under secretary who was close to the Navy—that we had a 20% chance of reversing this thing.

Sometime within the next year Bagley was back out there and told me that the homeporting project was Zumwalt's number-one priority project, and he said the next goal was to get the same thing into working in Greece. He also told me that I was on the list to make vice admiral. I told Betty. She said, "Don't spend the money yet." [Laughter] When he was out there on that visit he asked me what I wanted to do on my next assignment. I said, "I'm in a job that I know, I'm handling it well, and I think it would be a mistake to replace me unless you can advance me. I know the people, and they trust me, and trust is very important out here to get what you want." I've forgotten the timing of that, but my guess is that would have been probably sometime early in '72.

Paul Stillwell: I don't know if he was the Chief of Naval Personnel yet by that point or not.

Admiral Burke: No, I don't think he was. I worked very hard when I was out there on doing things that related to the Z-grams. They were stirring up the race issue, the black-white thing. And we had a Z-gram on drinking. He had that shop in BuPers that handled all kinds of things like alcohol abuse and black-white things. I can't remember. There was a lot of stir-up in the Navy at that time.

In the race issue, as I best remember, I reached out and had a committee. I don't know whether they were all black or whether it was some white, some black, but I had some of those men up in my office. I told those people, just like I had told the individuals on my ships, that if they didn't like things come up and talk to me, and they were comfortable with this. Dealing with this kind of thing was hard. Socially I had never mixed with blacks, and I'd say that I was raised in a strong Southern background. But I worked like hell at it out there of making sure that these blacks could come in and talk to me if needed.

Some of these things were disturbing to all hands. See, I did not command anybody except my staff, which was fairly large, probably 50 or 60 people, officers and civilians and enlisted. But I did create and followed all of these directives and had the race relations committee. I had them up in my office and talked to them.

I didn't talk to all of them, but I also had them up and conveyed to them that if they didn't like things they could come to me either as a group or individually and talk to me. The command master chief, who was Hispanic and a very fine man, was someone I saw regularly on how things were going. One always wonders how well you're doing. I did get around a bit but the big activities on the base were like me, they were tenants on Fleet Activities and they didn't belong to me. Their boss was ComServPac, so they were careful not to rope me into their command chain problems.

Most of the COs there in FltActs had additional duty with me, and I wrote them a concurrent fitness report, but I saw the insides of what they were doing very little. We had a chain of visitors out there for all sorts of reasons. Most often they were headed to Vietnam, and they would stop by Japan on the way or they were returning from Vietnam, one of whom was Assistant Secretary of the Navy Johnson, who was black.[*] He'd been a Korea Marine, and he came to Yokosuka. He must have been accompanied by somebody. But I had never before entertained anybody at my table who was black.

He came up for breakfast as oftentimes these visitors did, whoever they were. I had them come up for breakfast, and then we'd take them down to the office and brief them on our operations or what we were doing. He had the same routine and when we went down there I had him in my office, just me, one on one for a short while. Then I took him into my conference room, where I had the race relations committee, and introduced him and told the committee they were free to talk to him about anything that bothered them, and I walked out. When he came out, he seemed very pleased with what he had heard.

Betty and I were going to a festival that afternoon somewhere, oh, 50 or 60 miles away, and we took him along as our guest in the car with us and enjoyed his company. We attended the festival, and then we came on back. Festivals are usually accompanied by fireworks, and we've seen all the fireworks we ever want to see. But after he returned

---

[*] James E. Johnson, Assistant Secretary of the Navy (Manpower and Reserve Affairs).

to Washington and the Navy Department, I got a note from Bill Behrens, who told me in the note that at a meeting of SecNav and the senior people in the Navy Department when Secretary Johnson reported on his trip he gave glowing reports of the way things were going in race relations in Yokosuka.* I think looking back on it, it was probably much easier in that oriental culture to be able to do this than it would have been back home.

Paul Stillwell: Do you have any overall observations on Admiral Zumwalt's tenure as CNO?

Admiral Burke: [Chuckle] Yes, I would say on the plus side he initiated some things that were badly needed to pay more attention to the human needs of the troops. I can think early on that—all my career probably—the families did not seem to be considered, and for the first time they were given structured support. I suspect that the Army and Air Force were light years ahead of us in this.

Alcohol abuse. I was initially frustrated when we began to hear about alcohol abuse, but I'd have to say after a period of time and over a period of several years that I remained on active duty I saw enough evidence of alcohol abuse both by the man on active duty and/or his wife where something had to be done. The best example of that I can think was the second man to be the commanding officer of the Marine detachment at Yokosuka, at FltActs. He was a fine young man. He was a light colonel. He had been a college athlete. I think he was a star halfback at Virginia. I personally liked him and thought a lot of him and watched him around the base and so forth, and I thought he was doing a great job.

His name appeared on the binnacle list.† He was in the hospital one day, and I found out just by reading the morning dispatches that he was hospitalized, so I called the CO of the hospital and asked him what the problem was, and he said that he'd have to come up and talk to me. He said, "He's got an alcohol problem."

I said, "What do you mean?"

---

* Rear Admiral William W. Behrens, Jr., USN.
† "Binnacle list" is an old Navy term for those with medical problems.

He said, "He has had an alcohol problem for some time, and his next-door neighbor is one of my doctors. He's been treating him to get him through problems. The time before this incident that has just occurred my man told him if he did it anymore, he was going to turn him in to the hospital because he was threatening his own life."

And that's what happened. So I called up the top Marine in Okinawa, I forget who he was, and told him there was a problem up here, and I thought he ought to send somebody up and take a look. Well, he sent a colonel up who reported in to me, and I chatted with him and told him what I'd been told. He went down and took a look, and he came back and said, "Oh, I think the medical people have the wrong slant on this young man."

I said, "I don't think they do."

He said, "Oh, yes, they do." So he went on back to Okinawa. In the meantime, I had gone up and talked to the officer's wife, who was distressed and insisted that he did not have an alcohol problem. This happened about six weeks or two months before I was detached at Yokosuka. A month after I departed, I heard that the same thing had happened all over again. I heard after I'd been back in the States that he had been relieved for cause. That was tragic.

Also, when I left Yokosuka and became ComServLant, I began to look at the people who might be involved in alcohol and/or overweight. I began to detect it just by looking at the troops when I went aboard ship. I also found that in Yokosuka there were probably two or three alcoholic wives of captains there, at least two that I can remember. It was not a happy situation. So I think I'm all for keeping an eye open for it.

Paul Stillwell: Anything else on Admiral Zumwalt that you want to mention?

Admiral Burke: Well, he undoubtedly had guidance from his civilian masters to do certain things. The reenlistment rates were awful at that time. They were, as I recall, probably around 8%, but we were getting ready to lift the draft. They had to improve the quality of life, and he was working vigorously to that.

In his efforts to convey what he wanted to the Navy, he was going over the heads of his chain of command. I saw it in Yokosuka, because he talked to the body of enlisted men there, and it was a very popular CNO talking to the troops. But there were things said that really were going over the head of the boss of the people. It undoubtedly was not the intention but letting the people know that the bosses were in the way of getting them to do what they wanted. That was essentially the way I listened to it, and it sort of frustrated you.

There were people who apparently were working up in his office. He had a special office up there on the front corridor that were handling these Z-grams or these reforms, or at least that was the impression I gained, and there would be operatives who would show up who were trying to find out what was going on. I didn't get any adverse reaction from these, but later on I had a problem in Charleston that I'll tell you about.

Paul Stillwell: Well, as ComNavFor Japan you said you didn't have an operational role and you didn't have jurisdiction over the base. Was it considered primarily or almost exclusively a political-type job.

Admiral Burke: Political-military. There were time when I was in operational control, but I really didn't control anything like before I went out there, the Pueblo. He was under opcon of ComNavFor Japan. Or occasionally there would be a special operation making a sweep through the Sea of Japan. There was an ASW group that went through. They were under our opcon, but we really didn't run them. I mean, we had the setup there in our opcon center and watched it carefully, and they came through and got a briefing but the Pueblo, I think that was more under direct control.

Paul Stillwell: All right. You described the political-military aspects of it.

Admiral Burke: For me it was essentially learning and meeting and knowing the Japanese, and I worked very hard at that. We had a broad spectrum of friends. I mean, here it is 25 years later and those that are still alive that we knew we are still exchanging Christmas cards. I invited Funada to my retirement ceremony, for example, and I got a nice short brief note of regret. Masuoka, who just died about six or eight months ago, came to this country about every two years until he retired. The last time he came through that I really got a chance to see him—he came back since then—but I was one of four people that he specifically had told the Navy Department that he wanted to see, and so we had a dinner party for Masuoka and his wife. We had the Holloways here. We had Bob and Sarah Long and two or three others.* At the time I left Japan Funada-san gave me a couple of silver liquer cups with his name inscribed and so as is customary with the Japanese you always have toasts.

Well, when I had toasts I gave Masuoka one of these Funada cups and I had the other, and I made a nice toast and for the first time in my life I saw a Japanese break into tears. He cried like a baby. That was probably about eight or ten years ago. We've seen him about three times since. He has a party when he comes or did at the Japanese Inn in Washington, and we'd always be invited. He continued to know all of the flag officers possible in the Navy, especially the higher ranking ones. When he died last fall I was concerned about his being properly recognized until I got my Christmas letter from Admiral Uchida, and it turned out that I think CinCPac and CinCPacFlt went to his funeral. He was awarded some Secretary of the Navy recognition, and since then they have dedicated a new carrier pier at Yokosuka, as the Masuoka Park and Pier, so I think he's been recognized.

Paul Stillwell: Sounds like it.

Admiral Burke: And he deserves it. [Laughter] What's the place where Commodore Perry landed?

Paul Stillwell: I don't know. Well, there's something they call the Black Ship Festival. Is that it?

---

* Admiral Robert L. J. Long, USN, served as Commander in Chief Pacific from 31 October 1979 to 1 July 1983. His oral history is in the Naval Institute collection.

Admiral Burke: Yes. Well, this Black Ship Festival celebrates Commodore Perry.* The Black Ship Festival we went to probably in the spring of '71. It's hard to believe, but after I'd been there a while I sort of felt like I was the successor to Commodore Perry.

Paul Stillwell: In a sense you were.

Admiral Burke: But I remember Skid Masterson, who was the captain of the ship that rode a lot of us down there.† I think most everybody were American that rode down on the ship. Then Admiral Uchida, who was still the CNO, met us down there. There was a big parade and there were all sorts of ceremonial situations, wreath layings and a lot of things that we just didn't know and fireworks always. Then we drove back. But it was an interesting occasion just seeing how Japan works. If you ever want to get the details of it, which I did while I was there, read the biography of Commodore Perry.‡

Paul Stillwell: By Samuel Eliot Morison.

Admiral Burke: By Morison. It was really revealing and it was one of the many books I read, and we were right there. I guess if I'd have stayed out there I wouldn't have had any trouble going native. I can't remember anything specifically except we visited all the holy places out there that had anything to do with it. It was particularly interesting to read the book, which I probably did afterwards because I had had so many things on my agenda. I can't recall anything of specific other than the fact there was a parade, which we rode in in an open sedan. This was just typical because the Japanese have a festival at the drop of a hat almost anything, anytime.

When we first went out there in 1970, Buck Shaw, who was in command of FltActs at Sasebo, insisted that I come down and pay him a visit.§ And thank gosh he did

---

* In 1854 Commodore Matthew C. Perry, USN, landed in Shimoda, Japan, with hopes of establishing an effective trade relationship between the United States and the Far East. His visit is commemorated in the annual Black Ship Festival at Shimoda.
† Commander Kleber S. Masterson, Jr., USN.
‡ Samuel Eliot Morison, "Old Bruin:" Commodore Matthew C. Perry, 1794-1858; the American Naval Officer who Helped found Liberia (Boston: Little, Brown, 1967).
§ Captain Claude B. Shaw, USN, served as Commander Fleet Activities Sasebo from 1968 to 1972.

because Betty and I went down. As I best recall, we flew down to a city some maybe 75 or 100 miles away, and Buck met us at the plane and then he arranged for us all to stay at a Japanese inn, which we had never even heard of, the concept. The manager of the inn was named Den O'Coach [phonetic], and his parents lived there.

It turned out that Buck had been there a number of times and thought it was a good stopping-off place. And it was, believe me. We went there, and it turned out that Den O'Coach's father had retired. He was a big businessman, and he had turned his business over to number-one son, who was operating in Tokyo. Number-one son designated his younger brother to be in charge of this Japanese inn that the family owned and he was to take care of his parents. This is the way the Japanese do it. We had dinner that night in a fairly large room sitting on these zabutons in Japanese style, and it was quite an interesting introduction into that kind of culture. Then the next day we went on our way to Sasebo and met Buck Shaw.

Al Bergner was in port at that time. He was Commander Service Force Seventh Fleet. He was in port and lived on the base there. Buck Shaw was the FltActs and the base commander. We met all of the local businessmen at a dinner that they had for us. We were welcomed in a way I just couldn't believe. I'd never seen this sort of thing before. It was overwhelming. There was much to be briefed about, what the capability of Sasebo was, and, of course, there was concern because we were giving up a lot down there. It was the gateway to the Sea of Japan. Then we came on back afterwards, but that again was part of my education on what Japan was all about. The last time I'd seen the Sea of Japan was at the end of World War II.

The longer we were there, the more friends we made and particularly amongst the Japanese. Betty used to play bridge with some of the Japanese wives. They were all flag officers's wives. There was one, Admiral Ishikuri. Turned out he was a classmate in their Navy.[*] He was also a submariner. During World War II, in the month of July 1945, his submarine had been assigned to the Sea of Japan to go after those American submarines, one of which I was in in the Sea of Japan. And we became friends 25 years later. While we were there, he became the commander of the naval activity at Kure, and we were his houseguests. We were both glad we didn't meet each other in 1945.

---

[*] That is, he had become an officer in 1940, the same year Burke did.

Paul Stillwell: Right. [Laughter]

Admiral Burke: We still get a Christmas card from Admiral and Mrs. Ishikuri. It was a good lesson and showing that if you have a common goal that you will try to work together and get along and frequently end up with great respect.

Paul Stillwell: Well, I think we've covered it quite thoroughly today, and I'm grateful for all your recollections.

Admiral Burke: Well, I'll probably dream up a few more after you leave. [Laughter]

Paul Stillwell: Okay. We'll get those the next time. Thank you, Admiral.

Interview Number 12 with Rear Admiral Julian T. Burke, Jr., U.S. Navy (Retired)
Place: Admiral Burke's home in Alexandria, Virginia
Date: Wednesday, 3 June 1998
Interviewer: Paul Stillwell

Paul Stillwell: Well, here we are for the final interview concerning your career. Last time we talked extensively about your tour in Japan, and then you came ashore back to the United States. You mentioned that there might have been a chance for three stars. If you could recount that please.

Admiral Burke: Well, I don't think Dave Bagley was Chief of Personnel at the time, but he seemed to be a wandering ambassador for the CNO.* He was out in Japan, oh, I would say, nine or ten months before I eventually got transferred and asked me what I was interested in for my next tour of duty. I told him at the time that I knew the Japanese, they knew me, and we trusted each other. We had gotten some remarkable things done, and we were working on getting the carrier homeported in Yokosuka. I said, "You don't want to upset this." The carrier had not been approved yet. We had the destroyers out there, and I said, "I would not like to leave unless I can improve on my job and position."

He told me right up front that I was on the list of those who were being considered for three stars. I told my wife this. She said, "Well, don't put them on your uniform yet until you get it." I was eventually transferred in early January of '73. But around the first of August I got a call and was told I was going to be detached and gave me the name of my replacement. I said, "Where am I going?"

"Well, we haven't decided yet." This kept up for a couple of months. Betty and I celebrated our pending transfer by going up to the top of Mount Fuji. But, anyhow, we were kept on. Ace Lyons was the administrative aide to OP-06, and I talked to him several times.† All he would tell me was that my name was in the pot. He wouldn't tell

---

* Vice Admiral David H. Bagley, USN, served as Chief of Naval Personnel from 1 February 1972 to 10 April 1975.
† Commander James A. Lyons, Jr., USN.

me what it was for. Eventually I got word, oh, probably around the first of December, that I was going to be ComServLant and relieve my classmate, Roy Gene Anderson.*

Paul Stillwell: Well, one of the things I think you mentioned at some point was that PhibLant was one of the things you were in consideration for.

Admiral Burke: Well, I figured that because of my experience I would be well qualified for either PhibLant or PhibPac. I would have been well suited for that, based on my experience in the amphibious force.

Paul Stillwell: Sure.

Admiral Burke: On the other hand, I didn't have the Pentagon experience to get the nod to get that kind of job. At the time I was quite—I can't say I was upset. I was sort of surprised. But we were going through a significant change of picking younger people, and so the fact that I didn't get it didn't surprise me. In hindsight I think I was able to do more for the Navy and the people in the fleet after I got back because I was willing to speak out on issues that needed to that other people were afraid to.

Paul Stillwell: Well, please tell me about that.

Admiral Burke: Well, I had never been in the Service Force, but that kind of never having been there before was not new to me. I'd go out and begin looking at what was under me and trying to meet the people. At the time I was in the Service Force we had at least 45 ships. We had naval stations in Newport, Norfolk, Charleston, Mayport, and Key West. They all came under me, and so I was the logistics officer for the fleet. All of the supply and ammo depots came under me, and so did the Seabees. I'd never really known anything about Seabees. So I spent the next 22 months on the road a lot, meeting people and types of things I'd never encountered, and people talked very frankly to me.

---

* Rear Admiral Roy G. Anderson, USN.

Shortly after I came aboard, John Bulkeley, who was InSurv, was inspecting one of our ships, the Seattle, which was an AOE.* She was fairly new and was the pride of the fleet, and I just went on board to see John Bulkeley operate. People were sort of apprehensive, so I said, "I'll go down there and ride with him and get to know him." I told the captain I'd be aboard, and I would just look around. I'd never been on an AOE before, and while they were going through all of their inspections and so forth I did my own informal inspection. I observed a lot of things that I felt were not under firm command control.

Paul Stillwell: Well, what might be an example?

Admiral Burke: Well, I went down to the bottoms, all the way down into the magazines, and I could tell that the captain had never been down there. And I didn't just go down into one; I went into several. I went all over the engine spaces. I went up into the anchor area and the steering engine room. I didn't go all the way to the tops. I talked to a lot of the troops, and I was up on the bridge at night while they were there, and I could see that I wouldn't have let my people run a ship the way they were running it.

Paul Stillwell: Was it too loose?

Admiral Burke: I would say it was lack of command control. I had firsthand knowledge that it wasn't, and I told the squadron commander. I don't think his squadron commander was aboard, but I was just aboard there for familiarization.

Paul Stillwell: What was the problem in the magazines, for example?

Admiral Burke: Well, I don't recall the details, but I didn't see any indication on any directives that he had been there, which I would have thought he would have. When I was on the bridge, just watching things go on, it was I felt very loosely done. I called the

---

* Rear Admiral John D. Bulkeley, USN, began serving as president of the Board of Inspection and Survey in 1967, continued after his age-mandated retirement in 1974, and remained until he finally left active duty in 1988.

squadron commander in and told him to give this guy a shake. It wasn't long thereafter they went up to Yorktown to load out for a deployment, and they decided to go under the Yorktown bridge without getting it to draw.* So they took off the top of the radar mast. So I had the captain relieved. That was the first time somebody had been relieved in a long time in the Service Force.

Paul Stillwell: But that got the attention of everyone else.

Admiral Burke: That got attention, and the answer was, well, his navigator told him he could get under the bridge. [Laughter]

Anyhow, the decision was made, either just before or just after I got to Norfolk, that they were going to decommission some of the naval stations. I've forgotten exactly how many, but Newport was one. Key West, I think, was one. But there was some major situation, which forced me to go around to each of these places and look them over carefully.

Paul Stillwell: That was a round of cost cutting in '73. Elliott Richardson was the Secretary of Defense, and he said this was not going to make him popular back home in New England, because of the closing of Newport.†

Admiral Burke: The one in Newport was caused by the phasing out of the fleet units there. I went up there at least three times during my tour. I went to Charleston, Mayport, Key West, and the naval station at Norfolk. I got to meet the people. I was meeting aviators as well as submariners and surface people who were managing.

All the mine and ammo depots came under us. I'd never really seriously been around Yorktown before and discovered that the oldest house in the state of Virginia is right in the middle of the most sensitive part. And the state of Virginia, if it knows, it can't do anything about it. It's a little red-brick house that was built around 1620. It was right in the midst of their most sensitive area. [Laughter] I guess I had been to Yorktown

---

* Ships load ammunition at the Yorktown Naval Weapons Station, Yorktown, Virginia.
† Elliot L. Richardson served as Secretary of Defense from 30 January 1973 to 24 May 1973.

before when I was ComSubDiv 63, and we had the guided missiles. Our guided missile unit was stationed there because we had the nuclear weapons.

Paul Stillwell: What was your role in connection with shutting these places down?

Admiral Burke: Well, it was just they were phasing out or transferring authority to somebody else. They probably gave them to the district commander, because later on I went to Charleston as the base commander, and the station came under me. It worked out all right, and it gave me the opportunity to go down and see the command relations and see how people were working and how they were running the show. Each one was different.

Then I rode ships. As I say, I had about 45 ships. I didn't ride them all, but I rode as many as I could. I met a lot of different kinds of people: the aviators, the submariners and the surface people who were getting their deep-draft commands. It was the first time I had run across aviators in large numbers at that level, and I was impressed with the ones that they selected for command. I very early felt that they were probably better quality than the black shoes overall.

Paul Stillwell: How would you explain that?

Admiral Burke: Well, that's the way they came across. For example, Hunt Hardisty was one of our COs.[*] There was another one who made flag rank, I can't remember his name, who was quite good. I'd go back to it on their ability to be able to speak and present. I discovered this when I was in amphibs. The aviators were better at presenting things, and they learn as young officers to be able to give a briefing to the pilots, what they're going to do in a day's operations.

Paul Stillwell: Well, another factor would probably be that the aviators would send their best and brightest intending them to get the aircraft carriers.

---

[*] Captain Huntington Hardisty, USN, took command of the replenish oiler Savannah (AOR-4) in 1973 and command of the aircraft carrier Oriskany (CVA-34) in 1974. He eventually became a four-star admiral and served as Vice Chief of Naval Operations and Commander in Chief Pacific.

Admiral Burke: Yes. But I would say by and large the impression I got on these ship visits was they could articulate what they had, even though their experience level made you wonder how they could do it. I think they were using the system that they had been brought up in on accountability and also in the machinery of aviation. They applied the same principles and it worked.

It sort of irritated me that we didn't get more good people in ServLant. But I'd say that's the way it appeared to me. And I know that in the staff level more of the stars in the surface area were over in CruDesLant.* They weren't interested in coming over in the Service Force.

Paul Stillwell: Well, it was a kind of a self-perpetuating system in that the reputation was that the Service Force didn't get the best people, so the good people didn't want to go there because it might hurt their careers.

Admiral Burke: That's right. And when I went into the amphibs I didn't know anything about the amphibs. I was concerned about it. But I had to get a deep draft, so the choices were limited to service force or amphibs. Then I got in there, and I wanted to get a cruiser, but I didn't have a mentor. [Laughter] So I didn't realize it, but looking back on my career I think the only time I had a mentor—and I didn't know it at the time—was when I left the Williamsburg and went over to BuPers to find out what my next assignment was going to be. I didn't even know I had a mentor, and I got what I wanted.

Paul Stillwell: Who was your mentor in that case?

Admiral Burke: The White House. [Laughter]

Paul Stillwell: Well, you said earlier that when you got into this ServLant job it gave you a chance to speak out on things. What did you mean by that?

---

* CruDesLant—Cruiser-Destroyer Force Atlantic Fleet.

Admiral Burke: Well, we were in the era of Z-grams and the social revolution within the Navy that had been started. People began overtly, I think for the first time, really caring for the troops in a way they never had before. The Navy was investing in this effort, and this has had a dramatic effect, I think, on long-term retention. Looking back on it, I think compared to the other two services up to that point we'd done a pretty poor job of caring for our people. Anybody in my generation can recite chapter and verse of lack of thinking of people, and this was a dramatic turn-around. But in order to do this he created a system, and I don't whether he could have done it any better. He had these human relations teams in each port or centers, I forget what they were, who had license to steal practically.

Paul Stillwell: Very confrontational.

Admiral Burke: They went around in effect spying and reporting directly back, not through the chain of command or not necessarily to the commanding officers. There was fear amongst many of the commanding officers. I discovered in visiting them that they didn't know where they stood. These guys would come down from Washington. Dave Bagley was their boss in BuPers, and he was relieved by Chick Rauch.[*] Rauch was the boss when I got to Norfolk. When I would visit the ships, some of the captains would say that enlisted men would come aboard as sort of spies really and wander around and talk directly to the sailors. Without even reporting to the captain or the officer of the deck, they'd find crew members and say, "Tell me what's going on here that you don't like." This kind of stuff.

Well, as soon as I found this out within the Service Force I took a very firm stand. The PCOs for our ships came in to our staff for indoctrination, and then before they left they came in and called on me. I extended that call for about at least two or three hours. I had a tape recorder, and I told the PCO I was going to tape our conversation. At the end I gave him the tape, and I said, "It's private, between you, me and your executive officer." But I told them how I wanted them to command their ships. I described these incidents that had been reported to me by the captains and by my chief of staff, who was

---

[*] Rear Admiral Charles F. Rauch, Jr., USN, Assistant Chief of Personnel for Personal Affairs.

also very concerned about it. I told them, "The first thing is if you have anybody like this, get their name, serial number, and you call me," and I gave them each my telephone number. "And if you can't get me," I gave them a backup, "You are not to let these people leave. I want to hear about it immediately. And I want you to send me an official dispatch that you've done it."

Paul Stillwell: Did you tell them to prevent these people from coming on board the ships?

Admiral Burke: I said, "They have got to come through the captain of the ship and whatever they do, you're in command of your ship. If they don't have orders there, they are off that ship."

There was an incident that occurred shortly after I came aboard. We had a type commanders' conference at surface. Rojo Adamson was the DCNO for Surface Warfare, OP-03.[*] I had previously met him. The type commander representative of ServLant was Burke. ServPac was Jack Barrett, a submariner; Ebby Bell was PhibLant.[†] We were all submariners. Rojo spent the whole damn two days there cussing out the goddamn submariners. Nobody said anything. Finally, about halfway through the second day, I stood up and chewed him out in four-letter words. I wasn't fooling. After it was over, the session ended, we went into his office. I apologized, but I told him he asked for it, and I told him he was being unethical. I dressed him up. He's been saying "Sir" to me ever since.

Also, I called up Dave Bagley, who was Chief of Personnel, and Dave assured me it wasn't their policy. I said, "Dave, you guys that are running the Navy, you, Zumwalt and this guy, you're doing it and you're allowing it go on."

"Oh, we don't."

Paul Stillwell: You mean an antisubmarine prejudice?

---

[*] Vice Admiral Robert E. Adamson, Jr., USN.
[†] Rear Admiral John M. Barrett, USN; Commander Service Force Pacific Fleet; Vice Admiral C. Edwin Bell, USN, Commander Amphibious Force Atlantic Fleet.

Admiral Burke: It was an antisubmarine prejudice within the guys running our Navy. So I decided not to bring it to Zumwalt's attention, but he came back at the end of the conference to talk to us. I told him of at least one incident that occurred of his people down there, Rauch's people, and he assured me that it wasn't supposed to go on. That wasn't right. But believe me it did.

It was infected in their culture to do this. The problem was that it affected good order and discipline, and it was breaking down morale, and you could see it in the troops. They looked awful. I mean, we shifted to being a dungaree Navy when Bud came in. And we shifted to beards. And we shifted to not having the haircuts. People looked like hell, and the general attitude and respect that people had previously went to hell in a hand basket. I was shocked when I got back to the fleet.

I noticed it before when Bud Zumwalt came out to Japan, when he talked to the assembled enlisted men down in an auditorium. He was a very popular speaker for the enlisted men because he in effect was asking, "How many of you want to get rid of—" I've forgotten what he was doing, but it was a good political speech. There wasn't any question about it. But he wasn't supporting the chain of command that was out there running it. He was being a popular leader. He might disagree with this, but I can tell you it happened. I saw it. I could see out there that in general, the fleet units and so forth, for the people their general appearance and military bearing were going down.

So I started having personnel inspection there in Japan. I went out and did it. I don't recall exactly when it was. Nobody grumbled to me face to face, but I know they didn't like it. When I got to ServLant I started right away having personnel inspection, and I can tell you it made a difference. Our people were so much sharper looking than CinCLantFlt staff it was embarrassing. I jacked them up and got them looking the way they should have. I told Ralph Cousins about it.[*] I think he thought I was being probably a little bit stuffy about it, but I began to tell these guys to get in shape and get the potbellies off.

When I was riding the ships, I was looking for alcoholics and so forth, and I found them. I was surprised. All you had to do was go down and look at people more carefully

---

[*] Admiral Ralph W. Cousins, USN, served as Supreme Allied Commander Atlantic, Commander in Chief Atlantic Command, and Commander in Chief Atlantic Fleet from 31 October 1972 to 30 May 1975.

in a different way and you'd find them. I had a feeling that we were turning things around. And I began to speak out when we'd get together. There was a weekly meeting at CinCLantFlt, attended by the local flag officers. I used to speak out every now and then. Strat Wentworth was there.* I remember when I finally got transferred he said, "I'm going to miss you. I like hearing you bitch and bring out these things. Nobody's going to do that anymore." But I say if I had gotten three stars I'd have had to go along with the Zumwalt program, and I didn't want to. I wanted to shake it up and get them back where they ought to be going, and I think I had some effect.

Paul Stillwell: Why do you believe that you couldn't have done that with three stars?

Admiral Burke: Well, I knew I was a short-timer. I didn't know how long I was going to last, but I could tell that the people who were getting three stars were men like Stan Turner—all the guys were at least three years younger than I and some more than that.† I was only about 55 or 56 then myself, and I could see they were pushing the older people out. So in the case of my flag officer year group something like 60% of the people had been pushed out at the first look for retention. By the time I came up for the first look, they told us, I think, it was 30% retention. I didn't expect to be retained, but I was in a job out there in Japan. They couldn't let me go.

Paul Stillwell: So your feeling was that you were no longer bucking for promotion, so there was no need to hold back.

Admiral Burke: Yes. When Zumwalt came in at the end of that tycom conference and I told him what had happened and he said, "Well, it's not supposed to be this way." And he jumped on Rauch, and Rauch came around and said, "We didn't do that."

---

* Rear Admiral Ralph S. Wentworth, Jr., USN, Commander Cruiser-Destroyer Flotilla Two.
† Vice Admiral Stansfield Turner, USN, served as president of the Naval War College from 30 June 1972 to 9 August 1974. He had graduated from the Naval Academy in the class of 1947, seven years junior to Burke.

I said, "The hell you didn't. It's going on, and you don't know what's going on in your own shop." I was really ticked off because it was affecting the old-line chief petty officers and first class. They were throwing in the towel and getting out.

Paul Stillwell: They felt that their authority had been undermined?

Admiral Burke: Yes. Yes.

Paul Stillwell: What about drugs during that era?

Admiral Burke: I don't remember drugs as the problem.

We were embarked on race relations. Oh, here was another thing that happened. We had one of these black-white seminars that went on for at least two, three days. I forget how long it went. I was the junior flag, and flag officers were ordered to go through it. They came and gave us this session; the head of the group was a chaplain, a commander. He may have had one officer with him, and then all the rest of them were enlisted. There were blacks and whites.

They had a group of us there, and Walt Small was a flag officer there.[*] I don't know what job he could have had, but he was there. There were about seven of us. I'd say actually I learned a lot from it, but I had been working on race relations myself, just by trial and error. For example in Japan I told you about the visit from the Assistant Secretary of the Navy Johnson, who was black, a former Marine. I know that when he went back he told the gathered group there in one of the CNO conferences or SecNav conferences that NavFor Japan really had first-class race relations. So I'd been working at it and trying to establish rapport with the blacks. But I was really offended by the group that gave this presentation. The group of admirals decided after it was over that we were going to have a critique with this commander chaplain and that I was going to be the spokesman to tell him off. [Laughter] And I said, "How come you want me to do it? Because I'm the most junior?"

---

[*] Rear Admiral Walter N. Small, Jr., USN, Assistant DCNO (Plans and Policy).

"No," they said, "Because you're the biggest SOB in the group." [Laughter] So I told him off. But I will say this. That program shook people up and made them look in a different way than they had in the past. And I think it helped, so I don't have any bad feelings. It was just the fact that at that point in time I wasn't ready to be treated the way I was there. I mean, there were things that are accepted today. For example, I think there were two officers, a commander and then a lieutenant. They were talking back and forth on a first-name basis, and that was just foreign to me.

Paul Stillwell: Did they do anything that was demeaning to you personally?

Admiral Burke: I don't remember that they did, but I don't think they did anything personal, but it was just the way it was done. They had a job to do that was tough, but I don't know how else they could have done it. I forget what they called these groups.

Paul Stillwell: Well, I've heard that they were confrontational in nature.

Admiral Burke: Well, I remember when Arleigh Burke was CNO and I was at Annapolis he got Admiral Davidson to accept a group to come down there and around, a committee of people to test out your feelings on leadership and so forth and get the juniors to tell the seniors that they don't like you and why and so forth. And we rejected it. We thought it was too revolutionary. I'd say I always have made an effort to go around, talk one on one with my people so that they would communicate with me. I'm a real traditionalist in chain of command and things like that, but I think it's up to the boss man to know his people. Not all of them do.

Paul Stillwell: Well, one explanation for what you encountered is that subordinates sometimes get overzealous in carrying out what they believe are the wishes of their seniors.

Admiral Burke: Well, while I was in Japan there was a black officer, who showed up out there. He did not come up to see me. He was a lieutenant or a lieutenant commander, and he wandered around the place as a spy and out in town and so forth talking with the troops, and I don't think he ever reported in to anybody. I didn't get close enough to him because out there I did not command the CO of FltActs. FltActs was the naval station commander, and his boss was ComServPac in Pearl Harbor. I was a tenant so I didn't get directly involved in it, but I heard about it.

Later, when I went through Charleston, there happened to be one of these spies. I'll tell you about it when we get to Charleston.

Paul Stillwell: What do you remember about the business of providing fleet support, the underway replenishments, beyond that initial visit to the AOE?

Admiral Burke: Well, I was an administrative kind of a guy, and I went out and watched them when they did it. I didn't make deployments. I made trips. I know more about underway replenishment from having been replenished at sea when I was in amphibs. I did ride a couple of ships during replenishing. The AOE was a new kind of a ship. I told you that my first nasty act was to fire the captain of the Seattle. A year later we had another captain, and they got the Arleigh Burke award for the most improved ship in the U.S. Navy. So I think I did the right thing.

Paul Stillwell: Sounds like it.

Admiral Burke: Well, I can't say anything about the equipment and the techniques and so forth. We did it, and we did it successfully. I had service squadron commanders reported to me; we had a squadron commander out of Newport, Norfolk and Mayport. They might have had two squadrons in Norfolk. I think we did. The squadron commanders were the people that I operated through. They were an enormous help and I got with them.

I had one problem in Jacksonville. When I got there, I found that we had the first ship that was a test ship for women.

Paul Stillwell: Sanctuary.

Admiral Burke: Sanctuary.* It was being fitted out at Hunters Point in San Francisco, and it came around to Mayport and was in our squadron there. As I soon as I found out we had a test ship, I went out there to take a look at it, and it was interesting. I visited that ship at least four times. And I was always in communication with them, not personally but through the chain of command, and we watched it like a hawk.

About a third of the crew were women. They were all handpicked. The men I don't think were. I could not see that they were handpicked. Officers only. The living accommodations for the individual women, lowest enlisted rank, seaman apprentice, were better than for the males on the ship, and they had privacy and space that just for my money wasn't right. But that's the way they were set up. This had all been put together before I got there, and so I don't recall exactly when it happened. The ship eventually left San Francisco and came around to Mayport, which was their homeport. The goal was that the CNO, Zumwalt, had planned to have a deployed carrier group in the Mediterranean, just like we had set up at Yokosuka, with the families and so forth.

Paul Stillwell: They were planning to base it out of Greece, I believe.

Admiral Burke: It was going to be about 25 miles west of Athens or along the coastline.† We were going to construct a pier there so that we could have a support ship such as a tender or repair ship. But the ships were going to anchor out. I don't think the carrier was going to be allowed to berth there.

Paul Stillwell: I think the Sanctuary was intended as a dependent support ship, wasn't she?

---

* USS Sanctuary (AH-17) was originally commissioned as a Navy hospital ship in 1945, then decommissioned the following year. She was recommissioned for service off Vietnam in the late 1960s, then decommissioned in 1971 for conversion to a dependents' hospital and commissary/Navy exchange. When she was recommissioned on 18 November 1972, the Sanctuary became the first U.S. Navy ship with a mixed crew of men and women.
† In 1973-74, the U.S. Navy home-ported six destroyers in the port of Elefis, Greece, near Athens. They were part of a plan that envisioned putting a carrier task force of up to 30 ships in the port. Before the remainder of the program could be implemented, it was cancelled because of strained relations between the United States and the Greek Government. See The Washington Post, 30 April 1975, page A2.

Admiral Burke: Yes. The Sanctuary was going to be the floating naval station, and as I best remember it had a hospital, it had a Navy exchange, and I don't know that it had a commissary, and it had a certain amount of limited machine capability. They were all enthused about it. This project went down the drain politically because the Greek Government couldn't accept it. But in any case it was the test ship for women. I was never brought in to what was going on up in the Navy Department, but obviously there was a lot of interest up there.

Sometime after they got to Mayport one day the service squadron commander called up and said that there was a problem. I said, "What's that?" There was a carrier admiral whose office was on the dock right next to the Sanctuary. He had suddenly gone over to the ship unannounced, and that's all he knew. Well, to make a long story short, we had probably the first official female harassment case, and it didn't become official.

Paul Stillwell: Was this Beetle Forbes?

Admiral Burke: This was Beetle Forbes, and he had been in BuPers before he went to the carrier.[*] The complaint had hit Dave Bagley, and he called up Beetle to look into it. A while later the commanding officer of the naval Jacksonville hospital, it was a flag officer, medical officer, came aboard unannounced. I don't recall the succession of events, but we got bits and pieces of what had happened. On Friday night the Sanctuary's wardroom had happy hour over at the officers' club. When the officers went over there, the head doctor allegedly took a pass at the head nurse, and so the head doctor was replaced.

By the time I got in the act, it was all over. So we started looking into it, and as soon as I found out, I felt this was just the way the Navy had been running here lately, so I convened an investigation, and I called up the flag officer in Medicine and Surgery. I think he was their Inspector General, a doctor, and he was somebody I knew. I asked him what the hell, and he said, "Well, you know. We've got to put this thing to bed, and we got told to do something about it, so we did."

---

[*] Rear Admiral Bernard B. Forbes, Jr., USN, Commander Carrier Division Six. The Naval Institute collection includes the oral history of Captain Louis Colbus, USN (Ret.), who was on Forbes's staff in the early 1970s. Colbus has interesting recollections about the Sanctuary from that period.

I said, "Well, when are you going to start talking to the chain of command?" I must have called Bagley because I was—I don't know whether I did or not. Anyhow, I got the report of what happened and sent it on to Ralph Cousins who was the CinC, and he stopped it right there. But they didn't want to hear it.

Paul Stillwell: What was the finding in the report?

Admiral Burke: I guess the doctor may have taken a pass, but what happened was the head nurse was angry, and so she asked for TAD orders to go to Washington.[*] And it hit us at a time that we were hard pressed for that kind of money. So we asked what the reason was, and she wouldn't tell us. So she was mad enough to go up there at her own expense. She contacted a senior woman officer, Fran McKee.[†] Fran went right in and told Zumwalt, and Zumwalt got the machinery going. I guess he told Bagley to take care of it, and that's what happened.

Paul Stillwell: That's what led to your investigation?

Admiral Burke: Well, when I heard that this guy was being replaced, and so they replaced him immediately. He was relieved for cause, but there was nothing official about it. It was all unofficial. I felt that if they were going to do something like this, they should have gone down there through the chain of command and investigated and made the recommendation.

Paul Stillwell: So what I'm getting essentially is that you felt in your investigation the doctor had not gotten due process.

Admiral Burke: He hadn't gotten due process.

Paul Stillwell: You reported that to Admiral Cousins, and he did not forward your report.

---

[*] TAD—temporary additional duty.
[†] Captain Fran McKee, USN.

Admiral Burke: Right. I didn't expect him to, but I didn't like the way they handled it. It was just like Chick Rauch's guys coming down on the ship, and it undermines your good order and discipline and leadership. So eventually I had the nurse up in my office. I gave her a lecture, and she was an attractive gal, about 40 years old. I don't know what happened or not or why or how it happened, but possibly the guy had too much to drink.

I'm just trying to think of other things that came up. I'd never had any real relationship with Seabees except when I'd been in the amphibs.* But I was the boss of the Seabees, so I visited their two main camps, one of them was at Davisville, Rhode Island, and the other in Gulfport, Mississippi, and got to see a bit of them. Also they were reconstructing the Bermuda airstrip, so I went out to Bermuda and saw what they were doing out there. Then they were also building the base out there in Diego Garcia, and I remember when I went out to Diego early on I never heard of the place.† I requested to go out there, and Ralph Cousins couldn't figure out why I wanted to go. Well, it turned out after I went out there I was the first flag officer to spend more than one day. I stayed out there three or four nights and it was a real experience.

Paul Stillwell: Please tell me about that experience.

Admiral Burke: Well, we flew out to Thailand. What's the capital of Thailand?

Paul Stillwell: Bangkok.

Admiral Burke: Bangkok. Went out to Bangkok and then caught a plane from there. That's where the air supply came in from. The British had leased to us a tip of this island, which was a large copra plantation, and I guess they had some barracks. They must have had a small pier there. But it was really camping out. The idea was there'd be a base for Indian Ocean operation, and all the work was being done by Seabees. You've

---

* Seabees is the nickname applied to members of the Navy's mobile construction battalions (CBs).
† Diego Garcia is an atoll about 1,000 miles south of India; it was formerly British territory. In the 1970s the U.S. Navy made a significant investment in facilities there to support ships operating in the Indian Ocean. See Kirby Harrison, "Diego Garcia: the Seabees at Work," U.S. Naval Institute Proceedings, August 1979, pages 53-61.

got to realize this is 25 years ago, and my memory isn't as keen as it was. They were building barracks. I don't recall whether they had actual barracks then or not, but some of the people were living in tents. They had bulldozers and things, and they were moving things around. It was really primitive and interesting to see these men rolling up their socks. They were really a can-do outfit.

Paul Stillwell: Why did the Seabees work for you rather than Facilities Engineering Command?

Admiral Burke: They provide support for the fleet. Then the battalion commander said, "How would you like to go over on the British side of this?" So we drove several miles in a Jeep towards the fence. There was a barbed-wire fence there. Then we went down to the beach and there wasn't a fence on the beach and so we drove around it. Before long we saw a PBY from World War II on the beach.* It had run out of gas and there he was. [Laughter] There he was.

We went a bit farther, I don't know how far, probably five or six miles. We came to a vacated plantation, which had been the home of the owner. There was a good-sized house, but it was all on one floor with the out buildings around it and not unlike what you would see in delta country down the Mississippi River. We walked in. There was no furniture in this house, but it was unoccupied. Obviously had not been for many, many years. On the table in the middle of the room was a log dating back to around 1815. The log was in French. This had been a French possession, and then as a result of the Napoleonic Wars the British gained possession.

Paul Stillwell: And a PBY's still there.

Admiral Burke: So just watching the Seabees do the work and the gung-ho attitude and so forth they were impressive, and they were getting the job done with minimum numbers of people. They went out there on a deployment and came back to Davisville or

---

* The PBY Catalina was a twin-engine flying boat that performed extensive service before and during World War II.

to Gulfport. And I'll say this. When I was in the reserve business, I bumped up against the Seabees, and those were the best-organized people I've seen in the Navy as a group from top to bottom.

Then when we flew back we flew back to Bangkok, and I stayed there a couple of nights just to look at the town and sightsee and then we came on back. We came back through Europe. We landed maybe in New Delhi first, and then we were headed on for Beirut. But we didn't land in Beirut. We ended up in Athens. There was some sort of an incident in Beirut between the bad guys and the good guys, so we missed it. And then we were on our way home.

Paul Stillwell: Well, Athens it not a bad consolation prize.

Admiral Burke: Well, we didn't stop in Athens and visit. We didn't have a port visit. We just kept on our way.

Paul Stillwell: Oh, I see.

Admiral Burke: I don't remember. I didn't take a look around Athens. Then later on I went down to Bermuda and saw the operation they were doing in Bermuda, and I've been to Gulfport and seen those people. We had some Seabees out in the Philippines at that time, and the commanding officer of the detachment out there or the battalion was assassinated by some guerillas and they were front-line people.

Later on I made a Med tour. Went all over the Med visiting the various locations we were stationed at or had activities. Rota, Spain. We went in to Naples. Maybe I did go to Athens on that trip. And there's an airfield down in Sicily.

Paul Stillwell: Sigonella.

Admiral Burke: Yes, I went down to Sigonella.

Paul Stillwell: Did you have any role in support for the ballistic missile program?

Admiral Burke: No. Only admiration. [Laughter] But I'd say then before long the word came out that we were going to reorganize the fleet. We were going to merge, form SurfLant, and ServLant went out of commission eventually.

Paul Stillwell: I think SurfLant officially stood up on the first of January in '75.*

Admiral Burke: Well, I hauled down my flag before Christmas. I know I went down and relieved in Charleston before Christmas. I could have been relieved by my chief of staff or somebody like that just to get me out of town.

Paul Stillwell: What was your reaction to this consolidation?

Admiral Burke: As we started getting ready to consolidate ServLant, PhibLant, and CruDesLant into the Surface Force, it seemed to me like it was going to be a big, big organization that would probably be dominated by the CruDesLant people. I was concerned primarily about the amphibs because I didn't think the culture of the Navy would change that much about the Service Force. I did have first-class people in supply, and I had a fine chief of staff, but he was not going to make admiral, and I think he knew it. But overall I felt that the amphibs were the ones that were going to get hurt in this thing and I'd be interested to know whether they have.

Paul Stillwell: Well, as I understood the philosophy it was to bring the Service Force and the amphibs up to the level of the CruDesLant.

Admiral Burke: Well, nobody ever brought me in on how it was arranged, but if that's happened so be it. That's great. But I've watched the Navy in my lifetime, and the first team in the Navy when I first joined was the gun club, and if you weren't a gun clubber you didn't belong. In those days there weren't very many postgraduates. Then it became

---

* Naval Surface Force Atlantic Fleet was created 1 January 1975 by combining the Cruiser-Destroyer Force, Mine Force, Service Force, and Amphibious Force of the U.S. Atlantic Fleet.

the aviation club, and it was dominated by aviation for a long, long time. Then it became the submarine club. I'm not sure what club is in charge right now, but one of the reasons I chose the course that I did at the time I did was to get enough experience so I would be known well enough in other things than my specialty. But today that doesn't seem to make any difference, and I just wonder how these people who get up there who are members of clubs, how they can spread the thing out. I don't understand it.

Paul Stillwell: Well, also, one of the things that came on about that same time was the establishment of the surface warfare officer designator and the qualification program.

Admiral Burke: Well, that was true and that came up. I guess we, the type commanders, got involved in this. That was a necessary thing to do because the submariners in my opinion in the junior officer business were light years ahead of junior officers in the surface Navy. And they got the intensive training. I can remember when either Dave Bagley or the CNO came down and announced to us that they were creating this pin and they were all wearing them. My attitude was you haven't earned it, because when I went through the submarine I didn't get to wear that pin until I'd been through the school and gone through and knew my ship valve by valve and circuit by circuit. I don't know what's happened in the surface Navy, but I hope they have been just as demanding and I so stated at the time.

Paul Stillwell: Well, two things I'm aware of. One is that they established an initial school comparable to the Submarine School, and the other was that there was a specified set of standards to get that pin. The senior people who had it were sort of grandfathered into it.

Admiral Burke: I was grandfathered. They sent me a letter and congratulated me. [Laughter] And I didn't think that was fair. Well, actually when I was out in Japan I got a letter from Dave Bagley. He told me that there were not enough top-quality people at that time in the Surface Navy, and they were afraid that the submariners were taking over. Would I be glad to shift my designation from submarines to surface? So at that point in time I'd had probably as much command time in the surface Navy or maybe more. So I called up Fred Turner, who was Pers-B and a personal friend, and I asked them to look into it.* He wrote me a note back and said it didn't make any difference, so I said okay. So I was changed at that time.

I don't know where they're carrying me now, but I have always felt that I knew so much more about submarines that I served in than I ever did about the surface ships and the people operating in them. I just couldn't convey this idea into the surface tycoms even though we had submariners on there, on the board at the time.

Paul Stillwell: How would you characterize your overall relationship with Admiral Cousins?

Admiral Burke: Oh, we're friends.

Paul Stillwell: Any incidents you remember from the time that he was the fleet CinC?

Admiral Burke: Yes. I'd forgotten about it. [Laughter] I probably upset him once. One of our ships was getting ready for deployment and was not in good shape. It was commanded by an aviator who had been a wing commander out in Vietnam, and I'm sure probably had a good combat record out there. But they were so screwed up that we had to put half of our engineering staff down there to get them ready to meet their deployment date. They were going to deploy on a Monday, and he gave all of his people the weekend off after they'd been working so hard. Our people got that ship ready to deploy.

Paul Stillwell: This would not sit well with you. What was your reaction?

Admiral Burke: I said he wasn't ready for a major command.

Paul Stillwell: Did he get one?

---

* Rear Admiral Frederick C. Turner, USN, Assistant Chief of Naval Personnel for Personnel Control.

Admiral Burke: No.

Paul Stillwell: Well, how did Admiral Cousins figure in this?

Admiral Burke: Well, I don't know that he talked to me personally, but I got word that he thought I ought to take another look at it. But I didn't talk to him face to face. No, I have the very highest regard for Ralph Cousins.

Paul Stillwell: Well, the thing I've heard a number of people say is that when he was the VCNO he was extremely loyal to Admiral Zumwalt.

Admiral Burke: Well, you have to be, and it's a very difficult role. I mean, you've got to realize he was class of '37, and Zumwalt didn't have the kind of experience that Cousins had.[*] He hadn't been in the fleet that much, and it makes a lot of difference in the way you think and operate. I can point to all kinds of people like that. I'd say this experience of doing this oral history exercise I'm going through right this minute has caused me to think a lot about things. I think it's probably just as well that I didn't go any farther than I did because I didn't have enough experience in how to operate in the bureaucracy of the Pentagon. And if you don't have that you're not as effective.

Paul Stillwell: On the other hand you're saying Admiral Zumwalt had a lot of that but was short on the fleet side.

Admiral Burke: Well, that's true. I'm not familiar with all of his duty tours, but he would be an example of these people—I mean, I read in the New Yorker magazine the writeup on Admiral Boorda sometime after he died.[†] I don't know whether you ever read that article.[‡]

---

[*] Admiral Zumwalt had graduated in the Naval Academy class of 1943.
[†] Admiral Jeremy M. Boorda, USN, served as Chief of Naval Operations from 23 April 1994 to 16 May 1996. He committed suicide.
[‡] See Peter J. Boyer, "Admiral Boorda's War," New Yorker, 16 September 1996, pages 68-75, 77-86.

Paul Stillwell: I did.

Admiral Burke: I don't see how he ever got to be CNO. I saw him twice over at these retired briefings, and I thought he was very effective in handling himself in front of the flag officers. He seemed to know all of the questions that were being asked and so forth, and he frequently was speaking for his DCNOs there, and he did I thought an exceptionally good job. He spent more time over at those flag officer briefings, and I was impressed with him. On the other hand, after reading that article and seeing what his background had been, I don't see how he got the job. Or if he did the job he was missing so much, I guess in the growing up of having to make tough decisions.

Paul Stillwell: Well, I think it was a case where wherever he had been before he had just met with so much approval. Then he got to be CNO and was presented at that level with all the insoluble problems and the criticisms that go with them.

Admiral Burke: I had another experience on relieving somebody. One of the times I went to Newport, and I think it was probably the last time I went up there, I went aboard one of our ships. It was I think a repair ship, and they knew I was coming some time ahead. I went aboard with the squadron commander and from the time I got to the quarterdeck just the receiving the party aboard was done in a very sloppy fashion. On the way to the captain's cabin I asked the commanding officer a couple of questions, and I've forgotten what they were, but he didn't seem to know the answers. I got into the cabin and asked him several leading questions and he always gave me sort of dud answers. And as we looked around the ship and so forth, I wasn't impressed.

I spoke to the squadron commander about it later, and he was shocked. What he was hearing, he couldn't believe that this guy was acting the way he was and he had been there for some time. So I took another look. I had the squadron commander take another look and did the write-up on him. We sent what we found up to BuPers and recommended he be replaced. Dave Bagley was I think, one, irritated that I'd do something like that again. But he later told me he had never seen a combination of inept things on somebody like that, and he thanked me for letting the guy go. I didn't go around looking to fire people. I just felt that this was the result of not being careful enough to look at the command training of our people, and I'd say I really worked on it during the time I was ServLant to try to reinforce the commanding officers to know that they were in charge of their ships.

I had another experience up in Newport that was funny. It was on my first trip up there. My flag lieutenant was a very fine young man named Doug Holladay.* If you're in a certain circuit in Virginia, you know a lot of people. I'd never met any of his family, but it turned out he was a graduate of ROTC at Virginia and he'd gone to Woodberry Forest School, which is in Orange, Virginia, which is the chief rival of Episcopal High School where I attended. Now, those schools had been playing football since about 1900, and so the rivalry is pretty intense, and everybody in Virginia knows about it.

When I called up from Japan to talk to Doug, who was a flag lieutenant, we introduced ourselves to each other. I needed something up in my home in Alexandria, and I asked him if he knew anything about it, and he let me know that he knew about Alexandria because he had gone to Woodberry, and they used to play football up at Episcopal. So I just told him I said, "You better watch out. You're going to be in trouble. I'm going to be giving you hell from here to breakfast." Well, we've been friends ever since, good friends. He was a very attractive guy. Married to a lovely wife.

Back to the incident. We were about to depart. There was a dinner the last night we were in Newport. The hostess had too much to drink and was getting too close to me, and so I suggested that I was too old and sleepy. She'd better get to Doug. And she went over and started taking a pass at Doug. [Laughter] So when I finally saw Doug's concern, I told the host that I had a busy day tomorrow, and I thought we ought to go home. On the way home Doug said, "Admiral, I really appreciate that." [Laughter]

Let's see. What else? I list these things about these replacements because over the years I have felt we haven't done enough of it in the Navy. The few times I have observed fitness reports in large numbers I have not seen enough recognition of poor performance or less than satisfactory that I've been aware of.

Paul Stillwell: Well, are we ready to move on to your tour as commandant then?

---

* Lieutenant Douglas S. Holladay, Jr., USNR.

Admiral Burke: Almost. Just about a week before I was getting ready to be transferred, the retired admiral who was the director of the Virginia Port Authority announced that he was going to retire. When I was going to Charleston, I knew that I was going to have to retire in a year and a half or two at the most and that port authority job was something that I'd been aware of since 25 years. A neighbor of mine in Virginia Beach had held the job when I was captain of the Ellison, and I always thought, "Gee, what a nice way to finish out your life."

So here I was going to Charleston, and I wondered if it was going to hurt me if I threw my hat in the ring for port director. So I talked to BuPers, and they said go ahead. I talked to probably Pers-B, whoever was in the job, and I sort of got the idea that they would have been relieved to let me go because they were looking to get younger people in, and here I was 56. [Laughter] So I threw my hat in the ring and got into the politics of "What do you do?" I'd never looked for a job. This was a real experience. And apparently I had to go around and ask questions on how you do this, and this was getting mixed up in my getting ready to transfer.

Well, we went ahead and got transferred and went on down there. But I had to do a lot of things in a hurry, and I went down to the port authority and talked to them. I talked to the people down there and I talked to the man who was about to leave the job. And I talked to Admiral Clark, who was my neighbor. He gave me a lot of good advice on how you go about it. There was going to be a search committee, but they hired a consultant to do the search. And I had to get people to give me endorsements. So I got a number of people, both in and out of the Navy. The ones that really counted were the ones that knew me from home, Alexandria. Then I was transferred and went on down to Charleston and Charleston had a port authority too. [Laughter]

I don't know how long it was before I'd been in Charleston, but everybody in Charleston knew about it. I didn't tell anybody, but all of a sudden they knew it, the port authority community up and down the coast knew it. So before long we were there in Charleston. I relieved about the 15th of December. We didn't take any leave when we were en route. I relieved very quickly. Then we took a couple of weeks' leave immediately and went to New Orleans to visit my mother-in-law and her family down there.

I had lunch with the husband of Betty's first cousin down there, and I told him what I was up to. He gave me the name of a couple of people at the port authority in New Orleans. I don't recall whether I met the head man or not, but there was a retired Army officer who has worked for them, and I talked to him on it, how it worked out and how he did it. Of course, the politics was different. Betty's grandfather had been in the shipping business in New Orleans. He's been dead since the '30s, but he was very prominent in shipping. They had family contacts. So I had at least three different interviews with people giving me advice on how do you do it.

The thing that concerned me was what do I have to offer somebody like that? Particularly there were a couple of them that had military experience gave me on how to do it. Then when I got back to Charleston I went over and met the port authority people there, and they were helpful. So eventually, along about May, I got a call from the headhunter, and he wanted to interview me. It was the first time I'd ever been interviewed for a job. [Laughter] I wish I could have had the experience before I talked to him. I felt like a plebe. I really did. But when I got through I said, "What do you think? Do I have a chance for this?"

He said, "No, you're too damned old. They're looking for somebody 48, and you're almost ten years too old."

Well, as it turned out before that because I was the commandant we were invited to many local events. The Citadel is there. General Mark Clark was the emeritus president and George Seignious, a lieutenant general in the Army, retired, was the president, and Doug Plate was on the staff over there.* So I got invited to a variety of social events and otherwise at the Citadel. When they had the board meeting, Arleigh Burke was on the board at the time. They had a big reception out at Mark Clark's residence. I think he probably had quarters out there. They really revered him. And Clare Booth Luce was there, as was the president of the Seaboard Railroad, which was

---

* General Mark W. Clark, USA (Ret.), was president of The Citadel from 1954 to 1965; Lieutenant General George M. Seignious, USA (Ret.), was president from 1974 to 1979; Vice Admiral Douglas C. Plate, USN (Ret.).

headquartered in Richmond.* There were at least three board members there, including the president of Seaboard Line that I met for the first time and they said, "We hear you've got your hat in the ring for the port authority job," and they all volunteered to send in letters of recommendation. Well, I said to this guy who was with Seaboard, "You don't know anything about me."

He said, "The hell I don't. I'm a reserve major general in the Army. You were in the reserve business and we look out for reserves. [Laughter] And besides you've been doing fine here and we like you." So I had people like that, and I had people here in Alexandria. One of my very close friends who's dead now was the head of the First United Virginia Bank in northern Virginia, and another one was head of a shipping company right here. I mean, he did a lot of importing and owns a terminal. Clarence Robinson was a close family friend of my father's. When this guy who interviewed me said, "I don't know whether I need to interview you because you've got so many people who know you already I've gotten all the information I need. All these people in the port business checked you out. You've done the right things."

But eventually they selected somebody from in house and then fired him within a year. I got a call when they fired him and said, "Throw your hat in again."

I said, "No." [Laughter] But also on the horizon was the fact that the retirement benefits on retirees were accelerating fast because the COLAs were going up and the active duty people were not.† I don't know whether you've heard about this.

Paul Stillwell: No.

Admiral Burke: But about the time I went up to one of these type commander conferences at OpNav it was mentioned there. Apparently sometime around 1968 or '69 Congress passed some sort of law giving military retirees the same COLAs as the civil servants once a year. We had not been getting that in the active services. Finally I think Senator Stennis was able to get it through Congress. In the meantime people who were retired were getting these very nice COLAs, because it was a relatively high inflation at

---

* Clare Booth Luce was the widow of Time, Inc., chairman Henry Luce. She was a playwright and had been ambassador to Italy.
† COLA—cost of living allowance.

the time, and the active duty were not. We had situations where flag officers who were getting retired were making more than the active duty people. By the middle of the first year I was there I was thinking about turning my suit in, because if I retired then I would have a $250 a month benefit over waiting for another year. Means Johnston, who was CinCSouth, up and retired about that time and it made over a $450 a month difference in his monthly pension.* Finally they got this legislation through.

Ed Brazwell, who was the staff director for Stennis, lived here in Alexandria. Jack Ticeler worked just under Brazwell, and I called him up, and he said they were going to get the thing corrected, and so I decided to wait. The correction was that we in our particular category would not make anything less than people who had already retired when we retired. So that was stirring up things in the background.

I got off the track. Neither Betty nor I had ever been to Charleston before, but when we went there we had Episcopal High School connections. There were a number of Charleston boys who go there or did when I was at Episcopal, and there were still a half a dozen that I could find in my alumni book, and I made sure they got invitations to the change of command. These were old Charleston people.

Paul Stillwell: What was the role of the commandant? That was a time when the naval districts were sort of being phased out.

Admiral Burke: Well, I was double-hatted. I was a base commander and a naval district. I was the reserve overseer for Com Six and Com Seven and Com Eight. So that was new. So I did a modest amount of traveling visiting these places. I think I was overseer for Com Five, too, because I made a field trip up into Richmond and western Virginia, down through North Carolina.

As far as the base activities, I had two different base commanders, and they were both very fine people and did first-class jobs. When I was ServLant two of the three that I bumped up against made flag rank. But I did not get immersed in it. I did oversee. We

---

* Admiral Means Johnston, Jr., USN, served as Commander in Chief Allied Forces Southern Europe from November 1973 to September 1975.

had a law office there, so we got involved in some legal matters. I was worried more about the public image.

I was on the board at the United Way. I just decided so I could meet a cross section of leaders and I did. I knew the mayors and the movers and the shakers and the Navy Leaguers. I joined the Rotary Club. I knew a pretty wide assortment of people, which probably my immediate predecessor hadn't done. Herman Kossler was a former commandant; he lived in the area and he was a big help and a very nice person. I had known him in my tour in BuPers. He had been in the recruiting area, and so I didn't know him well but I knew him.

We met people all over town. The mayor was Palmer Gaillard, and he was a Republican, conservative, and he accepted a Pentagon job after I got there.[*] He was one of the Deputy Assistant Secretaries. He had been mayor for a long, long time and he was replaced by an elected guy named Joe Riley, who was a Democrat.[†] Joe Riley was a young fellow. He's now about 50, so this was 25 years ago. He was a young attorney. His father was in real estate and was also very political. Joe is still mayor.

But I had access to all those people. Joe Riley was not really socially acceptable to all these people who lived in what was called South of Broad, in the big mansions down there, but he's made a very fine mayor. And so I say we knew the people in the politics. I had never known anything about South Carolina history. I had it ground into me, the history up here in Virginia and north, but it's real interesting to find that the church we attended, I think, had three signers of either the Declaration or the Constitution. And the conclusion of the war in Yorktown, the campaign started in Charleston.

Paul Stillwell: Would it be fair to say that you had primarily a public relations job?

Admiral Burke: Yes, I think so. And we worked at it hard, and when I got there I had to be a Burke [Laughter] and straighten a few things out.

---

[*] John Palmer Gaillard, Jr., was mayor of Charleston from 1969 to 1975. He was Deputy Assistant Secretary of the Navy for Reserve Affairs, 1975-77.
[†] Joseph P. Riley, Jr.

Paul Stillwell: Such as?

Admiral Burke: Well, when I got down there, things were kind of slipshod and less military than I would like to see and very casual. People used to come up essentially undressed into the admiral's office, and I'd let them know that they didn't do that, and I had to really tighten up. Maybe they all thought I was an SOB. I began to inspect the troops, and they were a bunch of fat slobs.

Paul Stillwell: Sounds like a repeat of your ServLant experience.

Admiral Burke: It was much more so. I didn't raise hell with them, but I tried to set an example. Gradually the bellies began to diminish, and they looked better, and I had routine inspections. We had a Marine detachment, and I'd have a small parade there at colors and invite people like the mayors and the Navy League people to participate. It was very popular with the local people to see some of the ceremonial functions restored.

I used to make a point of when the enlisted men, the chiefs, retired I'd receive them in the office. If they wanted to bring their families with them, they could. Shortly before I retired there was a couple that came in, a chief and his wife. We had a nice cup of coffee and chatted. Finally she broke in. She said, "Admiral, I want to thank you. My husband was a fat slob, and he's really come around." [Laughter] She said, "I really appreciate it." [Laughter] She said, "I couldn't do anything with him." He just looked sheepish and laughed. [Laughter] But I'd say those kinds of things, there weren't many of them that happened. But I felt like I did lot more for the Navy when I got to ServLant and down in Charleston in doing things like that in presenting what I felt was the relatively old-fashioned stuff.

Paul Stillwell: Well, by then also Admiral Holloway had taken over as CNO, so some of the Zumwalt influence was fading.

Admiral Burke: Well, not as much as you'd think. When I reported to Charleston to relieve I was there for about maybe two or three days, and then we had the command relief, which was on a Friday. My predecessor had retired before I got there, so somebody else was double-hatted temporarily.

I went up to the office after the ceremony, and it was about 2:00 or 3:00 o'clock in the afternoon. The chief of staff said, "I think I ought to tell you there's a lieutenant from OpNav and CNO that's been in the area here. He's black and I think you ought to know that he's here. He's been wandering around talking to the troops informally."

I said, "Does he have a set of orders?"

"Not as far as I know."

"What's he doing?"

He said, "Well, he's leaving this afternoon for Washington."

I said, "Do you know what he's doing?"

"All I know is he's been here."

I said, "Tell him I'll be in the office at 8:00 o'clock tomorrow morning, and I want to see him, and if he doesn't like it tell him, put a security guard on him." [Laughter]

So he said, "Aye, aye, sir."

So the next morning I made a point of getting in at 8:15 instead of 8:00. He was waiting for me. So I invited him in, and I said, "I understand you've been here in the area. What are you doing down here?"

He said, "Admiral Bagley told me to go down to Charleston and look it over."[*]

I said, "Let me see your orders."

"I don't have any."

I said, "Do you realize who's the commanding officer down here?" I had him in there for about 45 minutes or an hour, and I gave him a lecture on command relations and so forth. I said, "Please, when you return tell Admiral Bagley I expressed my respects, and I hope that next time you come down here that he'll issue orders so that we can ensure that you get requisite support."

Sometime after that, we had a commandants' conference up there. It was run by whoever runs the shore establishment in OpNav. It was probably a two-day conference.

---

[*] Admiral Worth H. Bagley, USN, served as Vice Chief of Naval Operations from 5 June 1974 to 30 June 1975.

At the end there was a lot of bitching about some of these things that were happening like that and some other things that were happening. It turned out that Worth Bagley was going to come down and talk to us before we left. So that whatever these gripes were came up. They didn't say anything, so I brought whatever the gripe was up, and I've forgotten. He defended whatever the gripe was. I've forgotten what it added up to. But I made the point, I said, "If you want the thing, this is how you've got to do it."

But, anyhow, when I got back about three days later I got a letter from Worth Bagley informing me that these were the wishes of the CNO. Well, I know Jim Holloway, and he would have never do this, whether he was trying to push it or not. He was my next-door neighbor in Japan, and we've stayed in touch since, and I know damn well that Jim Holloway wouldn't have put up with that kind of stuff.[*]

Paul Stillwell: Well, Bagley of course was a disciple of Zumwalt.

Admiral Burke: Yes.

Paul Stillwell: The one event I remember from that period that you and I attended was the commissioning of the USS Spruance in Pascagoula.[†]

Admiral Burke: I went to two commissionings. That was one. One was the first LHA.

Paul Stillwell: Tarawa.[‡]

Admiral Burke: Senator Stennis was there and I participated in the event. I don't think I participated in the Spruance ceremony. Maybe I did.

Paul Stillwell: I think you spoke at it.

---

[*] Admiral James L. Holloway III, USN, was Chief of Naval Operations from 1974 to 1978. He had served as Commander Seventh Fleet from May 1972 to July 1973. During that time he had quarters in Yokosuka, Japan.
[†] USS Spruance (DD-963), lead ship of her class, was commissioned 20 September 1975 at Pascagoula, Mississippi.
[‡] USS Tarawa (LHA-1) was commissioned 29 May 1976.

Admiral Burke: I don't remember that. These kinds of exercises were old hat or something, because this was something that came under the commandant of the district, and I think it's written that way in the Navy Regs. Each of the two times that I got involved in these things I got nudges that somebody else like the type commander wanted to come in and do it for me.

Paul Stillwell: I remember Admiral Kidd was at the <u>Spruance</u> event also, because I saw him escorting Mrs. Spruance.[*]

Admiral Burke: She was a gracious lady. It was the only time I'd I ever met her.

Paul Stillwell: And her grandson was there.

Admiral Burke: I remember her. And one of the times Betty accompanied me. I don't know whether it was that time or not. But there was a fair amount of public relations in that job.

For example, I went over to Atlanta on one occasion, and because of my previous reserve contacts I got involved over there with Naval Reserves. I remember going out to Chattanooga to some big celebration out there, to which normally I would not have gone. There was a parade, and all the services were there. I went down to New Orleans at least once, because I had quite a reserve responsibility. I've forgotten all that I had. I had it up in the Fifth Naval District too. I remember going up to Richmond and Raleigh and out to Lynchburg, I think over to Roanoke and then back. So I'd meet these people and meet reserves, and I was used to doing it. I met a wide span of people as a result of it.

Paul Stillwell: What were your responsibilities as the base commander?

---

[*] Admiral Isaac C. Kidd, Jr., USN, served as Supreme Allied Commander Atlantic, Commander in Chief Atlantic Command, and Commander in Chief Atlantic Fleet from 30 May 1975 to 30 September 1978. Margaret Spruance was the widow of Admiral Raymond A. Spruance, USN (Ret.), for whom the ship was named.

Admiral Burke: Well, really the guy who ran the base was the naval station commander. Various people like the CO of the hospital had additional duty to report to me. It was not unlike what I was doing in Yokosuka, where I didn't command the base commander. The supply depot, his boss really was NavSup, and the shipyard commander the Sea Systems Command and so forth. I didn't get inside. I knew these people. I talked with them. I visited their commands, but I couldn't tell them how to run to the shipyard, and I couldn't tell them how to operate the fleet. The fleet people came under the fleet, and they were all very courteous and so forth. Occasionally I got involved in the housing of senior officers, but the CO of the station really ran the housing, and I didn't want to get involved in the details of it.

Paul Stillwell: Well, from a nostalgia point of view it's sad that Charleston has now gone away as a Navy center.

Admiral Burke: Well, it was interesting. For a southern boy, which I considered myself to be, it was a nice place to end up. Those quarters were terrific. It was a beautiful setup where we made friends with a lot of people that we didn't know, both in the civilian side and the Navy side. And we looked with a considerable amount of affection on that. I felt strongly enough about it if somebody had offered me a job I would have stayed there if it was appropriate. I did get one job offered me, but it was not up to what it should have been. I didn't think it was up to me to look for a job, and I didn't want to do that. I just decided I had strong pull to come here, so we came home.

Paul Stillwell: How much entertaining did you do in that job?

Admiral Burke: A modest amount. You see, they had cut us back on stewards. I only had one steward there, and so I had to keep that in mind. Whenever we entertained I don't think we pulled in stewards to help us out, but we had receptions there. We had guests that would come to town. For example, the governor of Virginia came down with a few people, and I was asked by some of my local friends to have him out. They knew I was a Virginian, so I had him out for a stag luncheon. We did things like that I would say three of four times.

When I was in Japan I was taking at least $1,500 a year out of my pocket, and I had three stewards there. By the time we got to Norfolk, I think we started off with two, and they cut us back to one. Stewards allowed people to socialize in a way that they probably don't now. I don't know who has stewards and who doesn't now, but I think it sort of causes people to socialize less. My daughter was down in Charleston with her daughter looking at the College of Charleston here this year, and she went out to show her child where her daddy used to live and she used to visit. She arrived at the gate, and they wouldn't let her get in that area because it was shut.

Paul Stillwell: What was the sequence of events that led up to when you actually retired?

Admiral Burke: Well, I received a letter probably signed by the Chief of Personnel, letting me know that my time had run out and to make plans for it. See, when I first got selected I expected to stay on until I would be 62.* Then we came in for charm school, and I think they told us that they had decided to shorten it to ten years. I had just turned 48 when I was selected. By the time I got to charm school, which was two or three months later, they announced that it would be ten years max, and that at the end of seven you'd be looked at for retention. The rule than was that 70% would be retained, and 30% would have to retire.

We were riding along with that until Zumwalt became CNO. On the first selection he came up with, we were told that they were changing the rules. They said that a flag selectee year group would be reviewed for retention after three years and that 30% would be retained, and 70% would be retired. This new policy was activated about four years after I became a flag officer. As I recall, I wasn't screened for about another year. It became apparent that some very good flag officers were retiring. I had the good fortune to be working closely with the Japanese on a high-priority project. So I survived and served a full ten years as an active-duty flag officer.

---

* The mandatory retirement age for U.S. military personnel is 62.

Paul Stillwell: Were you ready to go psychologically, or did you have regrets?

Admiral Burke: Well, the problem is when you're 58, psychologically I wasn't ready. You see, I had never thought about doing something else. I was an operator. I wasn't a technician of any sort. I didn't have a specialty. When I was in that reserve study I had met a faculty member from Georgetown University. He was an associate professor in the business school at Georgetown, and he was a reserve officer. He did a lot of the work on our reserve study. I had the idea that when I got out of the Navy I'd like to go to business school. I figured that would be a good thing for me to do. He said, "Sure, we'll be glad to take you on." And we've kept in touch.

When I was in Charleston, I was in touch with him and told him I was interested, so he talked to the dean. And the dean said, sure, he'd like to have me. So I called the dean. I said, "What the hell? You haven't even looked at my credentials. I wasn't that good a student."

He said, "Listen. You've had better all-around experience than any of these graduates are ever going to have. Having you sit in the classroom will be invaluable to backing up what the professors are going to be telling them." So they wanted to take me in. I was going to retire on the first of July 1976, and they wanted to take me in August. All I had to do was show up.

I said, "Look. I've got a family vacation coming up with my family in New Hampshire, and I can't do it. Can you take me in January or February?"

"Sure. Be glad to." Well, when I got back I found out that the dean had been fired, and my friend had been fired with him. [Laughter]

Paul Stillwell: Well, timing is important, isn't it?

Admiral Burke: And so that went down the drain.

Paul Stillwell: Well, can we dwell just a minute on the retirement itself? Did you go out with the flags and the bugles?

Admiral Burke: Oh, yes. Ike Kidd, who was CinCLantFlt, came down. He was a personal friend, and I hadn't seen much of him over the years, but as I told you earlier he and I had been friends since we were midshipmen. He came down very kindly and much to my surprise I got a DSM.* I'm sure Ike was the guy that did it. I was embarrassed, because I didn't feel like I earned it. But he said some nice things about me, and my mother was there and my children, my mother-in-law, and a couple of grandchildren were there, so it was a nice event for us.

It was a brief ceremony. Because I was retiring, I'd had my going-away reception about a week before in my quarters. So Ike just came in and flew in and flew out and went on home. There was a reserve admiral, Jed Smith, who came down from Baltimore, somebody that I'd met when I was in the reserve business years before. And there were a couple or three people that showed up like that. But other than that, I thought there wasn't anything heroic about it.

Paul Stillwell: What have been the highlights of the years since then?

Admiral Burke: Well, I came home, and we occupied this house, which needed fixing up, and I did a lot of work on the house. About the end of March of '77 I was beginning to think in terms of going back to work and talked around town a little bit. I wanted to work in Alexandria. My desire was not to get involved in beltway business but to work in Alexandria so I'd be better able to get back into the Alexandria community. I had a couple of suggestions, but I could tell that what was available I didn't think I wanted to try.

Then I got a phone call one day, it was probably around the first of April. Jim Holloway called me up and said that he wanted me to do something for him. I said, "What's that?"

He said, "I want you to be the vice president of the Navy Relief Society."

I said, "Is there a salary?"

He said, "I don't know, but I'll let you know."

---

* DSM—Distinguished Service Medal.

I said, "Well, I've got to make some money." [Laughter]

So he called back in a while, and he said, "Yeah, there's a salary. I'm not sure exactly what it is." I think it was about $18,000 a year at the time. Well, I tacked that on my retirement, and that would give me about what I would have made if I were on active duty so I said, "That's okay. That's all I'm looking for."

Donn Robertson was the president when I got there.[*] He was a second lieutenant on the West Virginia when I was an ensign.

Paul Stillwell: Small world.

Admiral Burke: I relieved Ray Hunter.[†] He was a company officer at the academy I think my last year. I didn't know him. I'd met him I guess when I was on CinCLantFlt's staff. He used to come over from time to time. And there was a Marine whose name escapes me now who was the financial manager. But I relieved Hunter, and Hunter had been there for a long time. He'd been there almost since he had retired up until '77.[‡] He was probably in his high 60s or approaching 70. Rod Badger was there, and he was maybe 67 or something like that.[§] I could tell in talking to the people up there that the Navy had changed so much in the past five or six years over the Navy they had been in, and I just decided very quickly I was going to retire when I got to be 65, which I did.

Donn Robertson was there for a year. Bob Salzer came after him.[**] As it worked out, I traveled about two months a year, not all at once, but I would go out on field trips. It was really a rewarding job, and I feel forever grateful that I was able to visit as many places that I'd never been to, particularly aviation and marine installations like Whidbey Island, like the air station up in Brunswick, Georgia and Brunswick, Maine. Like Corpus and a couple of other outlying fields down at Corpus, I forget the names of them. And around Pensacola the same thing, Meridian, Mississippi. I think I may have been to

---

[*] Lieutenant General Donn J. Robertson, USMC (Ret.), served as president of the Navy Relief Society from October 1973 to March 1978.
[†] Rear Admiral Raymond P. Hunter, USN (Ret.).
[‡] Hunter retired from active duty in November 1959.
[§] Captain Rodney J. Badger, USN (Ret.), who was born in July 1912.
[**] Vice Admiral Robert S. Salzer, USN (Ret.), served as president of the Navy Relief Society from April 1978 to September 1982.

Dallas. And all the Seabee activities. I saw a lot of places I'd been to when I'd been in ServLant. I made a trip to the Med and England. I did not go up to the submarine place at Holy Loch.

Then I made a WestPac trip in probably '78, something like that. I took Betty with me. I paid for her way. We went to Pearl, Japan, and then I took about four or five days' leave in Japan so we could see our friends. Lando Zech by that time was ComNavForJapan.* Then we did Navy Relief at Okinawa, and we had probably an overnight stay there. Then we went down to the Philippines. I guess we probably stayed in a hotel in Manila and then we drove on down to Subic. Flew to Guam. Then went on to Pearl. I visited Pearl and came home.

Paul Stillwell: What was the substance of these visits?

Admiral Burke: To get a feel for the size of the local operations, know the employees, size up the volunteer picture, let the command know who we were and why. The relief assistance money came from headquarters, as did the compensation for employees. It was always good to get the idea on improvement in administration and relief policies.

When I was ComNavFor Japan and ComNavBase Charleston, I was not as close to and supportive of Navy Relief as I should have been. A visit from the president or vice president of the society would have helped. Personal contacts with local commanders are always beneficial.

Paul Stillwell: What were the procedures in the home office?

Admiral Burke: The wives of the CNO, VCNO, Commandant of the Marine Corps, and other senior officers volunteer and serve once a week as case workers. They form the relief committee and are also board members. They are very helpful in the contribution to oversight and development of policies that are transmitted by the president. The head caseworker administers the policy that's formulated to ensure that the various chapters do

---

* Rear Admiral Lando W. Zech, Jr., USN, served as Commander Naval Forces Japan from August 1978 to June 1980.

what they're supposed to be doing. We have field representatives. There were four of them when I was there. They would come in from the field during the summer to rewrite the volunteer guidance and get the new guidance. Then in the fall, starting in September or late August, they would leave town and go on the road until spring, going from place to place, staying usually about two to two and a half weeks. They held school on volunteers and checked the performance of the individual offices.

Paul Stillwell: This was to make sure that the policies were consistent and executed fairly?

Admiral Burke: Yes, and they would teach the new volunteers.

Paul Stillwell: I see. So you depended primarily on volunteers in the field offices?

Admiral Burke: Yes. Now, at big places like Norfolk, San Diego, Pearl Harbor, Camp Pendleton, and Camp Lejeune, you might have one or two professional caseworkers. San Diego. The big stations. Pearl and so forth. We were talking on the phone to them a lot. Now, what caused me to up and really retire was we were getting ready to compute, and I didn't want to get involved in computing.

Today they work it a bit differently, all by e-mail. When they'd have a case before, they'd have policies on how to deal with them. Then if they exceeded those policies they'd call up headquarters to get permission to exceed or "What did I do with?" and the phone was going in that department all the time. We had the head caseworker. She was the voice of Navy Relief to all the volunteers around the country and overseas.

One of the nice things about this constant traveling I was doing was that I got to know just about all the people. I met the base commanders and frequently people on their staffs. This was the first time I'd really on an executive level gotten to know women who were executives. I got along with most of them quite well, but occasionally I would bump into somebody who was used to running the things the way they wanted and you had to do something.

For example, we had a lady in Norfolk who was in charge. Her name was Betty Burton, and she had been there for years and was a fixture. When I was down to talk to her and asked her about her association with the fleet, she didn't think it was necessary to go down and make Navy Relief known to the fleet. It was the other way around. I tried to encourage her in a lot of different ways to do things, as did my bosses, both Donn Robertson and later Bob Salzer, and she would resist these. She wanted to do it her way.

Eventually we had enough of this, and I put together a letter of her deficiencies and recommended that we unload her. And Bob Salzer bought in, bless his heart. She got herself a lawyer. It was not the first time we had had to deal with a lawyer, but we had these kinds of problems to deal with. Each time we forced somebody out, we usually had lawyers involved in it, because it was very important to be able to back up the reasons for it. This was quite an educational process for Burke, I can tell you. It wasn't like handling your men in the Navy. [Laughter]

That was one example. Another one in Charleston. We had a lovely lady down there who could charm anybody anywhere. She happened to be our longest employee in years of service, and everybody loved her. She was probably totally inefficient, but she was a great lady and when she finally retired we ended up with a problem. Having been in Charleston, I knew somebody down there that would have well fit the job. But the commandant, who was the local president, went for this lady that had been selected. So we accepted that. Shortly thereafter I went down to meet her. I was the personnel officer for the entire organization.

I had hardly sat down when she had told me she needed to have a private secretary and needed a raise. When I came back, I told my boss that we got the wrong person in there, and somehow or other we ought to unload her. It took another year and a half before they unloaded her after I had left, but they unloaded her because she continued to perform in a way that was outside the rules of the Navy Relief Society.

At the time I was there, there was a long-standing history of the San Diego office doing pretty much what it wanted to. We got a new head out there who continued in that tradition, so I went out there. I had looked it over pretty carefully, and they also not only have the main auxiliary, but they have sub-stations at North Island and outlying stations. It's a big outfit. They and Norfolk are the two biggest field offices that we had. They have quite a number of employees to keep it going. But I interviewed all the employees and had one on one with them to make sure that they were satisfied and so forth. After we got back, the head man sent a letter in, saying that I had promised one of his employees who was an outstanding employee a pay raise, which I had not. And had recommended that it be given to her immediately. That didn't cause him to be fired at that time, but he continued to commit all these acts on his own horse, and eventually he was replaced after I left, not by me but by the commandant, who got fed up with him. So these things happen.

Paul Stillwell: Can you provide some specifics on Admiral Salzer's contribution and how he got the organization better known?

Admiral Burke: Donn Robertson stepped down after four years. As I recall, it's a three-year tour, and he was reelected by the board. He stepped down after four, and then Bob Salzer came in. I had never worked with or been close to him before I went to the Navy Relief, but I'm as much impressed with him as any naval officer I've ever known. He knew his stuff, he could articulate it, and he knew how to manage.

His wife was a vigorous Naval Relief volunteer, and I think she probably educated him in the details. She had previously been on a relief committee, but when he came there she stayed at home and did not do it. I'm sure she was probably giving Bob some guidance, much like Betty helped me. Jane Salzer is a very sharp lady herself. He traveled a lot, and he was an exceptionally able writer. Any of the directives that he had anything to do with were easily understood and made sense.

He was very anxious to get better participation and strongly pushed the business of getting Navy Relief into the fleet. It was his idea that we establish units aboard ship. We started off with carriers and then gradually moved it down to the ships that were smaller. We trained enlisted men, chiefs, as volunteers, and they administered it so that if a man was on emergency leave overseas he could get Navy Relief support on his ship. So they became more aware when it was in their hands. We saw it immediately was at the annual Navy Relief fund drive. The carrier that had the number CV-64 set as a goal of $64,000 for the annual fund.* We received that amount from that ship.

Paul Stillwell: You mentioned setting up the offices on board the bigger ships such as carriers. I would think that a benefit of that is that men can see that their shipmates have been helped by Navy Relief, and they're more likely to contribute.

Admiral Burke: Well, that's true and they did. All of a sudden other ships heard about it, and we established them on other ships. Then we set up a Fleet Navy Relief office and had a retired captain in charge right down on the waterfront so that we were getting interface with the waterfront in a way that they never had before. It was particularly effective when the ships were deployed. Probably now they're down on ships as small as a submarine maybe or a minesweep or something like that. Of course, submarines are so much larger now than they were in my day.

Paul Stillwell: Well, they still have probably no more than 150 men in a crew.

Admiral Burke: Well, that's a lot of people in my book. [Laughter]

Paul Stillwell: And a lot fewer than an aircraft carrier.

Admiral Burke: I know that when I was a division officer, in that level, pretty generally the sailors didn't have much sympathy for Navy Relief because they didn't seem to understand their problems. I think the minute you got it on board where the sailors and Marines can talk to them, there's an entirely different attitude.

  The job that I had at Navy Relief taught me somewhat about business management in the civilian community, things I'd never even thought about. For example, when I went there I discovered that we had a crazy pay system. You went to work, and you got automatic pay increases every year just like the Japanese. These people who had been working there the longest time, not necessarily in the most

---

* USS Constellation (CV-64).

important jobs, were amongst the highest paid. I'll give you an example, Gladys Beetack, our key social worker. She was the one who was the voice of Navy Relief. She made less money than her secretary did because the secretary had been working for us for 20 or 25 years and had all these fogies. That was not the only case like that, but we had several.

Shirley Giles was our executive secretary for the president and vice president and a superb person. I think she came to work for Navy Relief when she was about 18 or 19, and she has only just retired. Had she stayed there under the old system she would have been making more than the president. So what we did was we made a compensation study, and I was the chairman of the compensation committee.

Paul Stillwell: And not very popular, I would guess. [Laughter]

Admiral Burke: We hired a consultant who led us through it. But I learned about how to do a compensation study and how it was put together and related to position descriptions and so forth. It took months and months, but it has been an extraordinary help to me in other activities. When I was on the vestry of my church we had compensation problems. When I joined the board of the American Red Cross chapter, after I retired from the Navy Relief, the first assignment I was given was to do a compensation study, and I copied the Navy Relief system, and it was implemented.

Each year we had to come up to a review on our so-called manual. One chapter has to do with the policies on granting aid, and that's looked at very carefully. Also in the time I was there twice redid the entire manual, and I was the driver behind that. The shape of the Navy Relief and participation has gradually changed. I'm sure it's a lot different now than it was when I was there because they have become automated. They have centralized and eliminated a lot of field billets and do the work at the headquarters. We used to keep files on every single case in a regular file drawer, so you can imagine how big the files were and now they have that computerized and you can get that information very quickly. We had access to, what was it, autovon?[*]

---

[*] Autovon is the name of the military's telephone system.

Paul Stillwell: Yes.

Admiral Burke: And so we could call around the world and did. We talked to overseas. Japan, Philippines, Naples, Rota, Spain. That was not unusual so we knew those people by voice, and when we went out there we reinforced it with getting to know them face to face.

Paul Stillwell: What might be an example of a case that somebody would come in with a plea with a need? How was that processed?

Admiral Burke: Well, if they're at an auxiliary, say, Long Beach, they go in for an interview. They may have emergency leave, or they need some food on the table, or they need a rent deposit. They state what the need is and why, and then they sit them down and do a budget on them and find out their ability to repay, find out if they have been repeat need people, as much as they can about the history. The individual auxiliary has a level of what they can grant within policy, and if the amount exceeds that policy they have to call and get permission from headquarters. Or it may be outside, the reasons for it may be outside of policy. It may just be an unusual situation.

Paul Stillwell: How long did the process take? Did you try to do it in 24 hours, let's say?

Admiral Burke: They tried to do it as fast as they could. Sometimes these things got to be real sticky and because they were sticky they might take a period of several days, and they'd refer it to the relief committee, who were active duty people. Or they would refer it back to either the president or me to make a decision. I didn't get into much of that myself. Usually the head caseworker would come to me, and she would give me her recommendation and I would say, "What do you think?" and she would tell me, and I don't ever recall having a problem with the head caseworker over it.

Paul Stillwell: Well, I would see a disadvantage in the automated system that's done remotely that you can't talk to the people and get an assessment face to face.

Admiral Burke: Well, it's like going to the airport and getting a seat on a plane at another airport. [Laughter] I mean, when you automate you get a lot of things. You get speed. You don't get the human hands or you don't see the human hands. But they seemed to work. I'd go over there a couple of times a year to have a social visit.

Shirley Giles, bless her heart, has been doing all of my desperately needed clerical work for me or typing. Now that she's retired although she says she's equipped to do all my stuff at home, I haven't been able to find her at home since she left and I'm like a lost sheep. She is a superior person and she was the corporate memory and she really knew where the bones lay. I really respected her.

She only got mad at me once. She used to take a week's leave with her husband and go down to Pinehurst so he could play golf in the wintertime. One year she forgot to tell us. We had something critical coming up like a board meeting that she was key to and some reason that we needed her presence there, and she had committed herself to this, so we went ahead and let her take the leave although we needed her. Then we hired a temporary, and she didn't like that at all. [Laughter] We gave her a two-day contact, and she wouldn't speak to the captain. [Laughter]

Paul Stillwell: What safeguards did you have against embezzlement or other kinds of fraud?

Admiral Burke: Well, we had auditing. To the best of my knowledge nothing like this happened at the headquarters, and I can't remember any of it happening in the field, but I'm sure we had a few cases. We had problems that occurred in the field from time to time, but the ones I remember were the ones of difficulty dealing with individuals or dealing with the implementation of policy.

It was surprising how good some of the executive directors were. We had one executive director in New London. Again I can't remember her name, but she was so capable she went to business graduate school at a nearby college, and we paid her tuition. I wanted to move her down and run the Norfolk office, but we couldn't get the gal to resign. It just went on and on, and I think she eventually left and went off and did something else, but she was really good.

Paul Stillwell: Did you deal strictly in loans or did you also have grants?

Admiral Burke: We had grants, and these were done with a review situation. I didn't get into the casework as much as the president did. They had the relief committee. Always the relief committee had a volunteer each day plus Gladys, and if anything got too sticky they knew they could come to the officers. Bob Salzer took a more personal interest in it than I did, but it was a busy job and an interesting job.

Paul Stillwell: Well, I would think it would be very satisfying, too, to know that you're helping all these people when they really need it.

Admiral Burke: Well, that's true, and I'd say it was a people business. Their corporate structure is like a club, and they all keep in touch.

Paul Stillwell: Any recollections of your contacts with Admiral O'Connor?[*]

Admiral Burke: Yes. I first met him when I was ComServLant just on an office visit when he was making a tour down there, and we seemed to hit it off. Then I secondly met him when I got interviewed for the job, and he was the only one that asked me any penetrating questions, and I really respected him.

We had a very sticky issue. This was during the time when it was government policy to fund abortions, and he opposed this vigorously, and we had all kinds of paper work going back and forth for exceptions to policy and so forth. We went along with federal policy until it was changed. He had to buy in on it, because he was a member of the board. He didn't like it. Then he retired and became a bishop somewhere in

---

[*] Rear Admiral John J. O'Connor, CHC, USN, served as the Navy's Chief of Chaplains from July 1975 to June 1979. As a Catholic Cardinal, he was Archbishop of New York from 1984 until his death in 2000.

Pennsylvania, and before long he was a Cardinal, and then he was giving us a bad time. [Laughter] Then we all laughed.

Paul Stillwell: Well, that's a matter of religious principle.

Admiral Burke: Oh, yes. But I thought he was a very effective person, and I'm amazed; I don't know what age he is, but he's got to be close to my age.

Paul Stillwell: He was born in 1920, I'm pretty sure. He faced a mandatory retirement date in 1995, but that just came and went, and he's still in New York.

Admiral Burke: Well, it's interesting. He's probably a year older than the Pope, and it's evident that he's in far better physical shape.

Paul Stillwell: Well, of course, he has the advantage that he didn't get shot.

Admiral Burke: True.

Paul Stillwell: But he's a very vigorous, very intense man.

Admiral Burke: Yes.

Paul Stillwell: Anything else to say about Admiral Salzer and his role there? You said he was a very effective manager.

Admiral Burke: Well, he was an effective manager. He knew the people. He knew how to attract good people. We expanded the headquarters staff a little bit while he was there to make sure that we responded better to the volunteers. We hired a couple of people that we hadn't had before in volunteer support. He was acutely aware of the need to support the volunteers and in a way that I don't think headquarters always had been.

I think it had a lot to do with Jane Salzer being very sensitive; she was a very vigorous volunteer in her day. She did not get her hands inside the office, but she was good and a very sharp person. I never saw him when he couldn't sit down and deal with people knowledgeably on any subject. Finances, relief policy or anything like that he knew what he was doing. He never sat down with people that he couldn't deal with them. He knew the personnel at least as well as I did, and when he went out in the field I'm sure he did exactly what I'd done as far as getting to know the personnel in the field.

There were a lot of things we wanted to do, but we were hesitant because of the dollars and cents in travel and cost of getting people together. Now they have moved on. I don't know whether it's because they are wealthy or whatever, but they bring their executive directors together, maybe east and west, about once a year and I think that's real good. It makes them feel closer to what's going on.

When you're dealing with volunteer organizations the compensation is different from in business. This is something I learned when I did the compensation review. When we finally got the package, the consultant came around and gave it to me, and he said, "I want to tell you. Your pay scales, because you're a volunteer service and also because you're Navy Relief, are less than what they could get on the outside. But you've got to realize that the work you're doing is in itself compensation and job satisfaction." He said, "In interviewing I've interviewed people all over the society, and I have never ever seen an organization for which I've done a compensation review that enjoys such high approval by its employees. That in itself is compensation."

Paul Stillwell: An interesting concept.

Admiral Burke: When I got over into the Red Cross board, I sprang that on the leadership. I had the same problem there where they were paying everybody on longevity and not on job. We had a greeter who was doing nothing but greet people, and she was a lovely person. She was the highest paid employee, and she was greeting and taking money down to the bank once a day, and that's all she did. So I had to level her off. This is what we did. We didn't cut anybody's pay, but we just put them in a position where they wouldn't get any more pay raises and most of those people went ahead and resigned.

Paul Stillwell: Which is understandable if they don't face a future of increases.

Admiral Burke: Well, they don't necessarily get more money outside because they're not equipped for it.

We had a student loan program, and that was run under the secretary's office. These were children of officers and enlisted, active and retired. I think they have expanded that to actually make it available to the officers and/or their wives. Before it was just their children or dependents. I don't know what the circumstances, but I think it was a very good worthwhile program, and I endorsed the idea.

We had a retirement system that we ran and we got—you remember something called ERISA? Does that mean anything to you?

Paul Stillwell: I've heard of it.

Admiral Burke: But we ran into ERISA and had to review our retirement system early on when I was there. We had an attorney who had worked for us for years, and I was helping them. I needed legal advice from them, and I called up this attorney or his number-one assistant, who was doing most of our work, and finally he said, "Do you realize every time you call up I'm charging you $50.00?" [Laughter] I'd never heard of that before.

Paul Stillwell: That's the way they do it.

Admiral Burke: I had to deal in health insurance, and eventually I found that one of the companies we were dealing with who had most of our insurance, it was longstanding, I've forgotten what the problem was, but I was not getting satisfaction out of the company. The head of that company or the local agents there in Washington was a friend of some relatives of mine in Washington. They dropped the bricks, and so I called up

John Hancock in Boston and demanded they change the agency, which they did because they were embarrassed. But these kinds of business practices were so foreign to me. It was a learning process and I enjoyed it.

Paul Stillwell: How long did you stay, all told?

Admiral Burke: I originally planned to stay for six years and then when we had the change Bob Salzer left in April, and that would have been my six years, so I agreed to stay on six more months, so I was there six and a half years. I left in October 1983.

Since then I've been involved in retirement and trying to work on the stock market and learned a few things through bitter experience in the crash of '87. [Laughter]

Paul Stillwell: Well, other than that, the trend has been mostly up, so I hope you've done well.

Admiral Burke: Well, I learned something that was interesting. With three college-age children and three marriages there in a narrow time—and a mortgage—I was fairly heavily in debt when I finally retired. My last child got married. Then, since I had no outside income over a period of about seven years I eventually came out of debt, and I began to invest, and I learned one thing about the market. I was churning my stocks right and left with the advice of my good friend Merrill Lynch.

Then the crash of 1987 came, and it wasn't as bad as it could have been. It wasn't anything like happened in '29, but the value of my portfolio went down. This happened in the end of October or early November, and at the end of the year my account executive made a big mistake. He let me know that he'd had a good year and received a bonus. I got to think about it, and then I got out all my sales slips.

Paul Stillwell: That's how he makes his money, on the transactions.

Admiral Burke: I couldn't believe how much I'd made money for him or him and/or Merrill Lynch. On top of that were the capital gains, which at that time were much higher than they are now, I think. So I made up my mind that I was going to buy and buy things that were solid and not sell. That's been my policy since, and within two years my portfolio was back; it only took two years to come back after the crash.

Paul Stillwell: There's a lesson in there.

Admiral Burke: I notice that the rest of the market has been following my advice ever since. [Laughter] But I'd say in hindsight it's been very rewarding to come home and live in this community where there are friends around and family that I grew up with. Unfortunately, a lot of these friends and family have departed, but their children and grandchildren are around.

Paul Stillwell: Well, and the fact that it's near where you grew up has to have a special meaning as well.

Admiral Burke: Oh, yes. There were four other families that I grew up with right here on the street when I first bought in. By the end of this year there will only be two of us left. We will be here and the other one is a widow. Her husband practically grew up in my house. But we love it. And I'd say that I think I've said everything and I appreciate your hearing me out.

Paul Stillwell: Well, I thank you for all the contributions. I just wonder if there's any summing up you want to do of the 40 years in uniform and some of the changes you saw in the Navy during that period.

Admiral Burke: Well, I tell you. In the 40 years I'd say I got through the academy in large measure because of my mother, the kind of support she gave me and the friends she had who were Navy connected. They looked out for me. I was on the verge of flunking out practically the whole of my first three years at the academy. After I got out in the fleet, I was hopelessly in love with Betty, and I kept wanting to eventually get married, which we did after two years.

Her support and her willingness to adapt to all of the changes have been significant, because we have moved a lot. I think I may have told you we counted up the changes of residence that she endured, which was 32. Most of my Navy friends or contemporaries usually staked out a house somewhere and came back and forth to it. We did not. I wanted to go after the jobs and did, and we had interesting tours. Once we were married I don't ever remember having a bad tour except the duration when our young son was dying. But we could never have done it if Betty hadn't supported me the way she did.

Looking back on it, I wouldn't trade what I had for anything else. I would not have qualified for the Rickover program. I met the gentleman. I wouldn't have worked for him, but he wouldn't have had me. How many people could say they were captains of the ships, commanded the ships that I did in different parts of the Navy and done the different kinds of things that I have been able to do and enjoy? I don't know of anybody else who's had as many different kinds of commands as I have and that's given me a tremendous amount of satisfaction.

I chose deliberately to go into new things. It makes you work harder. When you get there, you can't coast because you've got to work to catch up with the people who know. I felt this mostly when I went to my destroyer, the Ellison, because I was operating in a very competitive squadron. Mark Woods ended up as CruDesPac, and a good friend, and he was in the same squadron, and he told me after I was transferred he says, "The competition is a lot easier now that you're gone."

Paul Stillwell: That has to be very satisfying.

Admiral Burke: I didn't want to get left behind. But I wasn't smart enough or shrewd enough to realize you had to get those command jobs inside the Navy Department in the Pentagon. Nobody ever sat down and talked to me and said you've got to do this and do that.

Paul Stillwell: Would you single out the experience in Japan as the thing that had the most lasting impact?

Admiral Burke: On the Navy? You bet your sweet life. Here we got thrust into something. Betty didn't want to go. I had to practically grab her by the hair and take her, and once she got there she really got with it. I really had no feel for Japan and through a succession of good fortune I met people who would help me. But as far as personal achievement, that was it. For our government, I'd say, in actuality what it did for naval presence and so forth it was significant.

Paul Stillwell: Well, I thank you very much, Admiral, for the summary of your life and your naval career. The career itself was a legacy to the Navy and the nation, and this oral history is a further legacy that will probably outlast both of us. I thank you very much.

Index to the Oral History of
Rear Admiral Julian T. Burke, Jr.
U.S. Navy (Retired)

Abbot, Captain Charles Stevenson, USN (USNA, 1966)
In the early 1960s was just starting his time as a Naval Academy midshipman, 382; in 1990, as commanding officer of the carrier Theodore Roosevelt (CVN-71), had an outstanding enlisted crew, 234-235

Abbot, Captain James L., Jr., USN (USNA, 1939)
In the late 1950s and early 1960s served as executive officer in Bancroft Hall at the Naval Academy, 336-337, 354, 363-364, 367-368

Adams, Captain John A., USMC (USNA, 1955)
In early 1964 made a deployment to the Mediterranean as commander of a company of Marines on board the attack transport Fremont (APA-44) and visited his grandparents in Greece, 391-392

Adamson, Vice Admiral Robert E., Jr., USN (USNA, 1944)
In the early 1970s, as DCNO (Surface Warfare), demonstrated what Burke felt was a prejudice against submariners, 510

Adelman, Lieutenant (junior grade) Joseph L., USN (USNA, 1947)
In the early 1950s got off to a shaky start on board the submarine Sablefish (SS-303) but then improved dramatically, 229-230

Air Force, U.S.
In the late 1950s Submarine Division 63 used an Air Force target and Air Force base near San Juan, Puerto Rico, while conducting Regulus missile tests, 314-315; in the early 1960s the Air Force offered inducements for Naval Academy graduates to receive Air Force commissions, 359; in 1970 Burke's daughter Sally was the only woman on a plane full of troops headed for the Far East, 464

Air Force Academy, Colorado Springs, Colorado
In 1960 cadets from the Air Force Academy stole the goat mascot of the Naval Academy team prior to that year's football game between the schools, 361-363

Albert, Commander Francis L., CHC, USN
Served during World War II as the senior chaplain on board the battleship North Carolina (BB-55), 102, 121, 128

Alcohol
In the late 1930s some Naval Academy midshipmen drank in speakeasies in Annapolis, 17-18; in the autumn of 1941 a number of crew members of the battleship North Carolina (BB-55) became unruly in a ship's boat after hitting bars near

Annapolis, Maryland, 80-81; while on leave in San Francisco in 1943, several crew members of the submarine Flying Fish (SS-229) were drunk and disorderly, 145-146; beer and liquor available in the spring of 1944 at a rest camp on Majuro in the Marshall Islands, 157; serving of alcohol on board the presidential yacht Williamsburg (AGC-369) in the early 1950s, 259-260; in 1956 Rear Admiral Robert Pirie tried to get Burke to smuggle some whiskey into the United States for him, 294; in the mid-1950s Admiral Jerauld Wright offered a case of whiskey to the first skipper who forced a Soviet submarine to surface, 296; in the late 1950s liquor was available at cheap prices in Puerto Rico, leading to temptations to smuggle it into the United States, 322; in the early 1970s, Burke focused on cases of alcohol abuse among his subordinates, 496-497, 511-512

Alexander, Commander Boyd R., USN (USNA, 1916)
In the early 1940s, as executive officer of the battleship West Virginia (BB-48), was a difficult man to deal with, 57-58, 70, 73

Alexandria, Virginia
During the Civil War in the 1860s, 2-3; in the 1920s still retained the flavor of the Old South, 1-2, 7-9; operation over the years of the Burke & Herbert Bank, 1, 4, 9; in the late 1930s there was an issue on whether to honor a black servant in the Burke plot of an Alexandria cemetery, 3; schools in the 1920s and 1930s, 2, 5-7

Amberjack, USS (SS-522),
Submarine that skipper Ned Beach operated aggressively when he had command around 1950, 225-226

Amphibious Group One
In 1967 this group served essentially as Amphibious Force Seventh Fleet and commanded landing operations in Vietnam, 436-440

Amphibious Group Three
In 1966-67 this command oversaw the training of Navy boat personnel near Mare Island, California, to prepare them for operations in and around Vietnam, 426, 429-430, 433-434; in the summer of 1967 planned and conducted an amphibious warfare exercise that was held at Camp Pendleton, California, to test concepts for new ships, 431, 434-435

Amphibious Warfare
In the early 1960s, the attack transport Fremont (APA-44), operated her landing craft during amphibious exercises, 399-400; in the summer of 1967 Amphibious Group Three planned and conducted an amphibious warfare exercise that was held at Camp Pendleton, California, to test concepts for new ships, 431, 434-435

Anami, General Korechika
Japanese Army officer who committed hara-kiri in August 1945 when the war was lost, 482

Anderson, Rear Admiral Roy G., USN (USNA, 1940)
    Served during World War II in the submarine Flying Fish (SS-229), 142-143, 154, 158, 402; in the mid-1960s was selected for flag rank without having had a major command, 402; in the spring of 1965 visited the Caribbean, 415; in the early 1970s served as Commander Service Force Atlantic Fleet, 504

Andrews Air Force Base, Maryland
    In the late 1960s had a Naval Reserve unit that was filled with people who had political connections, 453

Andrus, Midshipman Don L., USN (USNA, 1940)
    In the 1930s failed to pass the Naval Academy eye test and had to drop out, 45-46

Antiair Warfare
    Gunnery practice in 1941 by the AA batteries of the battleship North Carolina (BB-55), 100-101; gunnery by the North Carolina in August 1942, during the Battle of the Eastern Solomons, 115-117, 119

Antisubmarine Warfare
    Use of depth charges in 1944 against the submarine Flying Fish (SS-229), 154-155, 168; Japanese air attack against the Flying Fish, 170; in 1944 the destroyer Cogswell (DD-651) inadvertently depth-charged the Flying Fish, 171-173; in 1943 Representative Andrew May revealed in an interview with the media that Japanese antisubmarine forces were not setting their depth charges deep enough, and casualties increased afterward, 174; in late 1950 submarine Sablefish (SS-303) was involved in ASW exercises against other submarines, 233; in the early 1950s hunter-killer task groups exercised in the Atlantic, 271-272, 274-275; in 1955 a number of destroyers and submarines in the Atlantic took part in an ASW exercise that resulted in a collision, 279-280; in the mid-1950s Admiral Jerauld Wright offered a case of whiskey to the first skipper who forced a Soviet submarine to surface, 296; in the late 1950s the boats of Submarine Division 63 were involved in antisubmarine training missions, 329-331

Argonaut, USS (SS-475)
    Submarine that was based at San Juan, Puerto Rico, in the late 1950s during missile tests, 313

Arkansas, USS (BB-33)
    In the summer of 1937 made a summer training cruise to Europe for Naval Academy midshipmen, 34-40

Armistead, Captain Reginald G., USNR
    Reserve officer who worked in OP-05 in the late 1960s and objected to a planned reorganization of the Naval Reserve, 452-453

Army, U.S.
In early 1943 a number of Army nurses visited the battleship North Carolina (BB-55) at Noumea, New Caledonia, 125-126; during the Korean War, Rear Admiral Arleigh Burke had a special set of code wheels to avoid going through the Army communications system, 462; in 1957-58 Army Lieutenant Colonel Charles B. Hazeltine was a top-notch student at the Naval War College, 301-302; in the early 1960s had exchange officers at the Naval Academy, 337, 357

Army Air Forces, U.S.
During World War II, Burke's older brother Andy was a B-24 pilot, , 175, 184-185

Atkinson, Captain Wilton L., USN (USNA, 1945)
In the early 1970s served as U.S. naval attaché in Tokyo and advised Burke on an officer who could be helpful in negotiations with the Japanese, 477-478

Atlantic Fleet, U.S.
Planning functions carried on in the mid-1950s by various sections of the fleet staff, 285-290; efforts in the mid-1950s to improve reenlistment rates in the fleet were hampered by heavy operating schedules, 295-296; in January 1975 the Naval Surface Force Atlantic Fleet was created by merging several commands that had previously been separate, 522-523

Atsugi, Japan, Naval Air Station
In the early 1970s the U.S. Navy ceded partial control of this facility to the Japanese, 475-476

Auer, Lieutenant Commander James E., USN
In the early 1970s, as a graduate student in Japan, was very helpful to Burke in facilitating contacts with Japanese officials, 477-478

Aurand, Captain Evan P., USN (USNA, 1938)
Intelligent naval aviator who lived in the Virginia Beach area in the mid-1950s, then went to become naval aide to President Dwight Eisenhower, 298-299

Australia
In the spring of 1944 the submarine Flying Fish (SS-229) visited Australia while between war patrols, 161-162, 168

Badger, Captain Oscar C., USN (USNA, 1911)
Experience in World War I, 90; was a dominating individual when he served in 1941-42 as commanding officer of the battleship North Carolina (BB-55), 77, 79, 81-84, 90, 92, 109-110, 122, 127-128

Bagley, Vice Admiral David H., USN (USNA, 1944)
In early 1971 represented CNO Elmo Zumwalt at a Seventh Fleet scheduling conference in the Philippines, 469; soon afterward met with U.S. embassy people in

Tokyo about a program to homeport an aircraft carrier and her escorts in Yokosuka, Japan, 471; in 1972 talked to Burke about a possible promotion to vice admiral, 494, 503; from 1972 to 1975 served as Chief of Naval Personnel, 509-510, 517-518, 523, 526

Bagley, Admiral Worth H., USN (USNA, 1947)
In the mid-1970s, as Vice Chief of Naval Operations, sent a representative to observe the personnel situation in Charleston, 534-535

Baguio, Philippines
In 1967 a U.S. congressional subcommittee held a hearing in Baguio on the subject of the Vietnam War, 440-441; in early 1971 the U.S. Seventh Fleet held a quarterly scheduling conference at Baguio, 468

Baker, Captain Wilder D., USN (USNA, 1914)
Competent officer who in 1942-43 commanded the battleship North Carolina (BB-55), 90-91, 96, 124-125

Barbero, USS (SSG-317)
Submarine used in the late 1950s for Regulus guided missile tests in the Caribbean, 314; in the late 1950s Lieutenant James Watkins was an outstanding young executive officer, 321, 326

Bay of Pigs, Cuba
In the spring of 1961 Admiral Arleigh Burke, the Chief of Naval Operations, spoke at the Naval Academy about the failed Bay of Pigs invasion, 379-380

Beach, Commander Edward L., USN (USNA, 1939)
Intelligent officer who served in the late 1940s as flag lieutenant to Vice Admiral Louis Denfeld, who was Chief of Naval Personnel, 219; demonstrated his aggressive qualities around 1950 when he commanded the submarine Amberjack (SS-522), 225; submitted ideas to be incorporated in a new class of fast-attack submarines, 225-226; as naval aide to President Dwight Eisenhower in the early 1950s, wanted to reverse the decision to decommission the presidential yacht Williamsburg (AGC-369), 252-253, 262

Bell, Commander C. Edwin, USN (USNA, 1939)
In the mid- and late 1950s served as a submarine detail officer in the Bureau of Naval Personnel, 309-310

Bell, Commander David B., USN (USNA, 1937)
In the late 1940s and early 1950s drew on his World War II command experience while serving as skipper of the submarine Dogfish (SS-350), 208, 221-222, 224, 228; in 1953 served as submariner detailer in the Bureau of Naval Personnel, 264-265

Bell, Captain Frederick J., USN (USNA, 1924)
Retired to private business in 1948 after service in the Bureau of Naval Personnel, 209-210, 215

Bell, Lieutenant (junior grade) John H., USN (USNA, 1948)
In late 1952 reported aboard very reluctantly to become navigator of the presidential yacht Williamsburg (AGC-369), 245-247

Bellino, Midshipman Joseph M., USN (USNA, 1961)
Top-notch Naval Academy football player who earned the Heisman Trophy for the 1960 season and made a lot of public appearances, 339, 347, 361, 363

Benson, Captain Roy S., USN (USNA, 1929)
In the late 1930s taught navigation at the Naval Academy and made summer cruises with midshipmen, 49-50; in the late 1940s commanded Submarine Development Group Two out of New London, Connecticut, 223

Bergner, Rear Admiral Allen E., USN (USNA, 1940)
As a junior officer, served in the battleship West Virginia (BB-48), 62; went into submarines soon after World War II started, 113; in the early 1970s commanded Service Force Seventh Fleet, 467, 501

Bernard, Mr. Jean Pierre (USNA, 1923)
Naval Academy graduate who became an Annapolis banker and was very supportive of his alma mater over many years, 367-368

Berry, Captain Fred T., USN (USNA, 1945)
In the early 1970s served well on the staff of Commander U.S. Naval Forces Japan, 466, 471

Beverley, Major General William Welby, USA (Ret.) (USMA, 1938)
After failing to get an appointment to the Naval Academy, in 1938 became a West Point cadet at the age of 16, 11

Bilderback, Willis P.
Tough individual who was highly successful while serving from 1959 to 1972 as lacrosse coach at the Naval Academy, 346-347

Black, Lieutenant Commander Robert G., USN
In 1952 became commanding officer of the submarine Sablefish (SS-303) and did well in a fleet exercise, 232

Blair, Clay D., Jr.
Journalist who covered Navy topics and had previous experience in World War II as an enlisted man on board the submarine Guardfish (SS-217), 200-201

Blandford, John Russell
　In 1967, as staff counsel to a congressional subcommittee, ran hearings held in the Philippines on the subject of the Vietnam War, 440-441

Blee, Commander Ben W., USN
　Destroyer skipper who was in a car pool with Burke in the mid-1950s and later served with him on the Atlantic Fleet staff, 299-300

Blouin, Vice Admiral Francis J., USN (USNA, 1933)
　In late 1966, as Commander Amphibious Force Pacific Fleet, sent Burke on a training tour to Vietnam, 406, 426; in 1967 met up with Burke in the Western Pacific, 438; recommended against Burke taking the OpNav job of overseeing the Naval Reserve, 442; as OP-06 in early 1971 talked to the staff of the U.S. embassy in Tokyo about a program to homeport an aircraft carrier and her escorts in Yokosuka, Japan, 469-471

Boorda, Admiral Jeremy M., USN
　Was effective in speaking to retired flag officers while serving as Chief of Naval Operations in the mid-1990s, 525-526

Boucher, Air Vice Marshal, RAF
　British officer who lived with his wife in Kamakura, Japan, in the early 1970s, 486-487

Bowen, Vice Admiral Harold G., USN (Ret.) (USNA, 1933)
　Energetic officer who was married to the daughter of Admiral Wilder Baker, 91

Brega, Commander Richard E., USN (USNA, 1943)
　In the early 1960s did a fine job as administrative officer in the Naval Academy's Bancroft Hall, 353

Bristol, USS (DD-453)
　In December 1941 had to move out of her anchorage at Hampton Roads to make way for the battleship North Carolina (BB-55), 109

Brooks, Captain Charles B., Jr., USN (USNA, 1931)
　In the late 1940s served in the Bureau of Naval Personnel and in the 1950s as commanding officer of the battleship New Jersey (BB-62), 217-218

Brown, Vice Admiral Charles R., USN (USNA, 1921)
　Assessment of his role in 1956, when he served as Deputy Commander in Chief Atlantic Fleet, 25, 289-290, 292; in 1956 went nightclubbing in Paris while there for a NATO conference, 294; working style, 295; in 1956 commanded the Sixth Fleet during the Suez crisis, 297; sent witty messages to Admiral Jerauld Wright, 413

Bulkeley, Rear Admiral John D., USN (USNA, 1933)
For many years served as president of the Navy's Board of Inspection and Survey, 201-202, 505

Bullis, Lieutenant William F., USNR (USNA, 1924)
In the 1930s operated a school in Washington, D.C., to prepare young men for service academy entrance exams, 6-8

Bureau of Naval Personnel
After World War II controlled the seniority of officers commanding submarines, 208; role in the late 1940s in the assignment of enlisted personnel, 209-216; substantial drop-off in the number of active-duty personnel following World War II, 212; senior officers who served in the Bureau in the late 1940s, 217-220; in 1953, while serving in the Bureau of Naval Personnel, Captain B. J. Semmes told Burke he could have essentially whatever he wanted for his next assignment because he hadn't embarrassed the Navy while serving in the presidential yacht Williamsburg (AGC-369), 264-265; in 1963 Burke learned from his detailer that he couldn't get command of a cruiser because he didn't have a high-ranking sponsor, 401; in 1964 BuPers tried to get Burke to swap squadron commands with his classmate Roy Anderson, 402

Burgan, Lieutenant William W., USN (USNA, 1940)
Ex-enlisted man who fit in well in 1937 during a summer training cruise on board the battleship Arkansas (BB-33), 35; died in October 1943 when the submarine Wahoo (SS-238) was lost, 141

Burke, Admiral Arleigh A., USN (USNA, 1923)
In 1943 commanded a destroyer squadron in the Solomons, 127; during the Korean War had a special set of code wheels to avoid going through the Army communications system, 462; in the early 1950s gave strong support to the formation of the Japanese Maritime Self-Defense Force, 462, 485; in the spring of 1961 spoke at the Naval Academy about the failed Bay of Pigs invasion in Cuba, 379-380; as CNO sent a group to the Naval Academy to get juniors to express their feelings about seniors, 514; in the late 1960s and early 1970s provided useful advice on reorganizing the Naval Reserve, 459; suggested the value of a tour in Japan, 461

Burke, First Lieutenant George Anderton, USAAF
Rendezvoused with his brother Julian in January 1937 on the occasion of President Franklin Roosevelt's inauguration in Washington, D.C., 19; as a B-24 pilot in World War II, visited Julian in Hawaii and Guam, 175, 184-185

Burke, Rear Admiral Julian T., Jr., USN (Ret.) (USNA, 1940)
Family background, 1-5, 8; parents of, 3-10, 13-14, 16, 19, 29-31, 42, 45, 49, 53-54, 74-75, 79-81, 106-107, 131, 199-200, 212, 344, 407-408, 540, 555; siblings, 6, 9, 19, 24, 31, 42, 49, 54, 131, 175, 421; wife of, 11, 21-22, 32-33, 38, 40-41, 55, 73, 74, 83-84, 95, 101-105, 113, 131, 135, 138-139, 176-178, 180, 184, 199-200, 203, 205,

206, 303, 311, 317-318, 336, 340-341, 356-357, 379, 381, 385, 407-408, 411, 422, 424-425, 438, 451, 462, 465, 468-469, 479, 481, 483, 486, 488-490, 494-495, 501, 503, 529, 536, 542, 545, 555-557; children of, 23, 53, 180, 184, 199, 205, 219, 236, 282, 297-299, 311, 317-320, 335, 341, 356-357, 370, 385, 396-397, 407-408, 411, 422-424, 427, 438, 450, 453, 464, 466, 492, 538, 540, 554; boyhood in the 1920s in Alexandria, Virginia, 1-6, 11; education of, 2, 5-7, 10-12, 24-26; in the 1930s attended the Bullis School as preparation for the Naval Academy, 6-8, 11-12; from 1936 to 1940 was a midshipman at the Naval Academy, 8-10, 12-54; in 1940-41 served in the crew of the battleship West Virginia (BB-48), 27-28, 46, 56-75, 321; served 1941-43 in the battleship North Carolina (BB-55), 46, 75-129; marriage of in April 1942, 101-103; return to the United States in early 1943, 129-131; was a student at the Submarine School from April to July of 1943, 131-137; in the summer of 1943 was transferred to the submarine Flying Fish (SS-229), even though he was destined for the ill-fated Wahoo (SS-238), 140-141; service from 1943 to 1945 as torpedo officer and executive officers of the Flying Fish, 142-194; for nearly a year in 1945-46 commanded the submarine Guardfish (SS-217), 194-204; during the latter part of 1946 was chief engineer of the submarine tender Howard W. Gilmore (AS-16), 204-207; from 1946 to 1949 had duty in the Bureau of Naval Personnel, 209-220; in 1949-50 was executive officer of the submarine Dogfish (SS-350), 221-228; from 1950 to 1952 commanded the submarine Sablefish (SS-303), 229-239, 285, 400; in 1952-53 was executive officer and then acting commanding officer of the presidential yacht Williamsburg (AGC-369), 239-266; from 1953 to 1955 commanded the destroyer Harold J. Ellison (DD-864), 267-284, 323; in 1955-57 was on the staff of Commander in Chief Atlantic Fleet, 285-300; was a student at the Naval War College in the school year of 1957-58, 300-309; from 1958 to 1960 was Commander Submarine Division 63, 309-335; served 1960-63 as executive officer of the Naval Academy's Bancroft Hall, 15, 23, 28, 335-383; in 1963-64 commanded the attack transport Fremont (APA-44), 384-404; served in 1964-65 as Commander Amphibious Squadron Six, 404-415; was head of the Navy Plans Branch in OpNav in 1965-66, 416-422; in 1966-67 was Commander Amphibious Group Three, 422-426; during much of 1967 commanded Amphibious Group One in the Western Pacific, 436-441; served 1968-70 as Assistant Deputy Chief of Naval Operations (Naval Reserve), 441-460; from 1970 to 1973 was Commander U.S. Naval Forces Japan, 12, 461-504; in 1973-74 was Commander Service Force Atlantic Fleet, 504-528; served 1974-76 as commandant of the Sixth Naval District, 6, 529-540; retirement from active duty in 1976, 539-540; from 1977 to 1983 served as vice president of the Navy Relief Society, 540-554; post-retirement activities, 554-557

Busik, Captain William S., USN (USNA, 1943)
In the early 1960s served as athletic director of the Naval Academy, 350

Byrnside, Lieutenant (junior grade) Benjamin C., Jr., USN (USNA, 1941)
In early 1943 was a student at Submarine School in New London, 133-134; after graduation opted to stay with a school training submarine in New London, 137-138

CH-46 Sea Knight
    Helicopter that underwent operational testing in early 1965 in the Caribbean, 414

Canada
    In the summer of 1939 the battleship <u>New York</u> (BB-34) visited Halifax and Quebec during a midshipman training cruise, 48-49; in the early 1950s the submarine <u>Sablefish</u> (SS-303) visited St. Johns, 236

Carnegie, Dale
    In the late 1940s the Carnegie course proved very helpful to Burke in enabling him to master public speaking, 211-212, 220

Carroll, Captain Robert M., USN
    In the spring of 1960 was killed in the crash of an airplane near Newport News, Virginia, 334

Chace, Lieutenant (junior grade) Alden Buffington, USNR
    Served during World War II in the submarine <u>Flying Fish</u> (SS-229), 144-145, 158, 160, 171, 183

Chafee, John H.
    As Secretary of the Navy in the late 1960s-early 1970s, supported Burke's plans to reorganize the Naval Reserve, 453-454

Chaplains
    Value of chaplains in counseling midshipmen and staff members in the early 1960s at the Naval Academy, 343-344, 352-354, 366-367

Charleston, South Carolina
    As commandant of the Sixth Naval District in the mid-1970s, Burke had many contacts with the people and institutions of the city, 529-533

Charleston Naval Base
    As commandant of the Sixth Naval District in the mid-1970s, Burke was double-hatted as the base commander, 531-535, 536-538; mid-1970s visit by a black naval officer whom Burke perceived as a spy from Washington, 534-535; the admiral's quarters were sumptuous, 537-538

Citadel, Charleston, South Carolina
    Military school that in the mid-1970s had a number of associations with Burke as the local naval base commander, 529-530

Civil War, U.S.
    Burke's ancestors and their associates fought in the 1860s war on the side of the Confederacy, 1-3; in the 1920s there were still elderly war veterans living in Alexandria, Virginia, 2

Clarey, Admiral Bernard A., USN (USNA, 1934)
In 1971, as Commander in Chief Pacific Fleet, directed Burke to reverse the process of turning U.S. naval forces in Japan over to the Japanese Government, 467-468, 483-484

Clark, Commander Alfred B., SC, USN
In 1941, as supply officer of the new battleship North Carolina (BB-55), had to replace silverware that was stolen by guests, 94

Clark, General Mark W., USA (USMA, 1917)
In the mid-1970s was president emeritus of The Citadel in Charleston, South Carolina, 529

Classified Information
While working in the plans section of OpNav in the mid-1960s, Lieutenant Commander Ace Lyons inadvertently left classified material exposed when he left his office for a time, 417-418

Coale, Commander Griffith Bailey, USNR
Served as a Navy combat artist during World War II and lived in Stonington, Connecticut, after the war, 203

Cochino, USS (SS-345)
In March 1949 the submarine was lost as the result of a fire caused by a battery problem, 223

Codes
Use of in the early 1940s for radio communications by the battleship West Virginia (BB-48), 60; limited distribution of Ultra messages on board the submarine Flying Fish (SS-229) during World War II, 174; during the Korean War, Rear Admiral Arleigh Burke had a special set of code wheels to avoid going through the Army communications system, 462

Cogswell, USS (DD-651)
In 1944, while operating with the fleet, inadvertently depth-charged the submarine Flying Fish (SS-229), 171-173

Collisions
In 1955 the destroyer Harold J. Ellison (DD-864) and the submarine Jallao (SS-368) collided during an ASW exercise in the Atlantic, 280-281

Commercial Ships
In early 1943 the SS Wisconsin transported Burke and other servicemen from Noumea, New Caledonia, to the United States, 129-131; a Navy commander

traveling on board the Wisconsin found that his pay was less than that of the lowest paid able-bodied seaman in the crew, 130

Communications
Use of radio by the battleship West Virginia (BB-48) in the early 1940s when she was flagship for Commander Battleships, Battle Force, 59-61, 64; in 1941 by the new battleship North Carolina (BB-55), 95-96; during the Korean War, Rear Admiral Arleigh Burke had a special set of code wheels to avoid going through the Army communications system, 462; use of voice radio in 1953 by destroyers for tactical communications, 269-270

Congress, U.S.
In 1943 Senator Albert Chandler visited the submarine Flying Fish (SS-229) at Pearl Harbor, 144-145; in 1943 Representative Andrew May revealed in an interview with the media that Japanese antisubmarine forces were not setting their depth charges deep enough, and casualties increased afterward, 174; In September 1953 members of Congress were present at Electric Boat for the keel laying of the Navy's second nuclear submarine, the Seawolf (SSN-575), 228; in 1967 a subcommittee held a hearing in the Philippines concerning the Vietnam War, 440-441; political influence on the structure of the Naval Reserve required annual naval testimony to Congress, 443-447; testimony following the May 1970 incident in which National Guardsmen shot and killed antiwar protesters at Kent State University, 445-446; in the late 1960s Congress instituted cost of living allowance raises for retired military personnel, 530-531

Cony, USS (DDE-508)
Destroyer in which Burke received valuable training in 1953 before taking command of his own ship, 268-269

Cousins, Admiral Ralph W., USN (USNA, 1937)
In his last year at the Naval Academy, 1936-37, was compassionate toward Burke and a bit non-reg, 15-16; served as Vice Chief of Naval Operations in the early 1970s, 480, 525; from 1972 to 1975 commanded the Atlantic Fleet, 511, 518-519, 524-525

Coward, Captain Asbury III, USN (USNA, 1938)
Served as Naval Academy athletic director from 1959 to 1962, when various problems arose, 340, 350, 362

Crawford, Lieutenant (junior grade) William H., Jr., USN (USNA, 1942)
Married while a student at Submarine School in early 1943, and his bride was soon pregnant, 132

Creamer, Commander John J., USN (USNA, 1944)
   In the early 1960s did a fine job as battalion officer at the Naval Academy, 337; in the early 1970s was superb while serving on the staff of Commander U.S. Naval Forces Japan, 466, 471, 474, 477, 493

Crete
   In early 1965 U.S. forces held an amphibious landing in the vicinity of the island, 413

Cuba
   In the early 1950s the destroyer Harold J. Ellison (DD-864) made a port visit to Havana, 272-274; refresher training in 1955 at Guantanamo Bay, for the crew of the Harold J. Ellison, 278-279; in the spring of 1961 Admiral Arleigh Burke spoke at the Naval Academy about the failed Bay of Pigs invasion in Cuba, 379-380

Cummings, Lieutenant Commander Edward J., Jr., USN (USNA, 1943)
   In the early 1950s served as executive officer of the destroyer Harold J. Ellison (DD-864), 269, 271-272, 276, 279

Curaçao
   In 1965 received a visit from the amphibious transport dock La Salle (LPD-3), 415

Cutter, Commander Slade D., USN (USNA, 1935)
   During World War II compiled a top-notch record while commanding the submarine Seahorse (SS-304), 166-167; was in Pearl Harbor in the summer of 1945 as skipper of the submarine Requin (SS-481) and then took her to the East Coast once war was over, 196-198

Cyprus
   In early 1964 the attack transport Fremont (APA-44) patrolled off the island during a crisis there, 393-394

Davidson, Rear Admiral John F., USN (USNA, 1929)
   In the early 1960s served as superintendent of the Naval Academy, 336, 339-341, 356, 514; in the fall of 1960 the academy football team was involved in a ticket-scalping scandal that Admiral Davidson decided to keep quiet, 339-341; shielded those below him in the chain of command from Admiral Hyman Rickover, 360-361; in 1962 decreed that a black midshipman who had not yet completed all the requirements could sit with his class during the graduation ceremony, 364; opened up the curriculum for a wider range of choices, 372-373

Dawes, Lieutenant (junior grade) Robert A., USN (USNA, 1933)
   First cousin of Burke who preferred destroyer duty in the 1930s to that in a larger ship, 43; while Dawes was serving in the cruiser Concord (CL-10) in the early 1940s, his family provided hospitality to Burke in Hawaii, 61

Dean, Captain Clyde Dixon, USMC (USNA, 1954)
In the early 1960s did a fine job as a company officer at the Naval Academy, later promoted to lieutenant general, 338

De Gautier, Felisa Rincon
Energetic mayor of San Juan, Puerto Rico in the late 1950s, 317-320

Dennison, Rear Admiral Robert L., USN (USNA, 1923)
In the early 1950s, while serving as naval aide to President Harry S. Truman, he also supervised the presidential yacht Williamsburg (AGC-369), 239, 242, 247-251, 257; he had political acumen as well, 249; children of, 261-262

Depth Charges
Used in early 1944 against the submarine Flying Fish (SS-229), 154-155, 168; in 1944 the destroyer Cogswell (DD-651) inadvertently depth-charged the Flying Fish, 171-173; in 1943 Representative Andrew May revealed in an interview with the media that Japanese antisubmarine forces were not setting their depth charges deep enough, and casualties increased afterward, 174

Dertien, Commander Donald A., USN
In 1953 went through PCO training before taking command of the destroyer Cony (DDE-508) and then provided valuable shipboard experience to Burke, 267-269

Destroyer Force, Atlantic Fleet
In the 1950s long-term destroyermen expressed resentment against submariners who came in briefly and took destroyer commands, 265-266, 307

Deutermann, Vice Admiral Harold T., USN (Ret.) (USNA, 1927)
In 1944 commanded the destroyer Cogswell (DD-651) when she inadvertently depth-charged the submarine Flying Fish (SS-229), 171-173; in the late 1960s and early 1970s gave Burke useful advice on reorganizing the Naval Reserve, 451-452, 459

Diego Garcia
In the early 1970s Seabees were involved in construction projects to set up the Indian Ocean island as a fleet support facility, 519-521

Disciplinary Problems
Various infractions in the early 1940s on board the battleship West Virginia (BB-48), 72; while on leave in San Francisco in 1943, several crew members of the submarine Flying Fish (SS-229) were drunk and disorderly, 145-146; in early 1960 Burke, while serving as Commander Submarine Division 63, Burke had to investigate a casualty on board one of his boats that took aboard large amounts of water on two different occasions, 330-334; disciplinary system and honor violations in the early 1960s as the Naval Academy, 342-344, 354-356, 374-375; in the fall of 1964 a group of SEALS got in trouble in Spain and had to be disciplined, 405-406; while on

liberty in Nice, France, in December 1964, two U.S. sailors raped a French woman, 410-411

Dogfish, USS (SS-350)
In the late 1940s had an overhaul during which she received the Guppy modification that made her faster and more streamlined in appearance, 221-222, 236; operations out of New London, Connecticut, 222-226; in 1950 avoided disastrous results from a battery room fire because of training and precautions beforehand, 224; received a visit from Captain Hyman Rickover, who was unpleasant to the enlisted crew, 228

Doheny, Lieutenant Edward L. III, USNR
In 1944 served as officer of the deck on board the submarine Flying Fish (SS-229), 170

Donaho, Captain Glynn R., USN (USNA, 1927)
In his dealings with other people, he projected a stern demeanor, 138-141, 143, 214; in the summer of 1943 arranged for Burke to be transferred to the submarine Flying Fish (SS-229), even though he was destined for the ill-fated Wahoo (SS-238), 140-141; was a highly capable submariner as commanding officer of the Flying Fish, 143-151; in 1943, Eleanor Roosevelt, the President's wife, visited Pearl Harbor and talked with Donaho, 144-146; disagreement with his division commander, Commander Karl Hensel, 148-149; in the late 1940s served as head of recruiting in the Bureau of Naval Personnel, 211-215

Draemel, Rear Admiral Milo F., USN (USNA, 1906)
In the late 1930s served as the Naval Academy's commandant of midshipmen, 29-30, 369, 377; offered a job in Bancroft Hall to Burke's widowed mother, 30

Draft
When John Kennedy was President in the early 1960s, students were given academic deferments from the draft, which led to discord during the Vietnam War, 448-449

Duke of York, HMS (British Battleship)
In December 1941 the ship was at Norfolk after having brought Prime Minister Winston Churchill to the United States, 110-111

Duncan, Vice Admiral Charles K., USN (USNA, 1933)
As Chief of Naval Personnel in the late 1960s, heard from people who objected to a planned reorganization of the Naval Reserve, 452-453; Burke routinely informed Duncan on the progress of the reserve plans and received his support, 456

Dunford, Captain James M., USN (USNA, 1939)
In the early 1960s assisted Admiral Hyman Rickover in selecting Naval Academy midshipman for the nuclear power program, 358-359

Eastern Solomons, Battle of
Operations of the battleship North Carolina (BB-55) during the battle in late August 1942, 115-117

Eaves, Commander James S., USN
In the early 1970s served as public affairs officer on the staff of Commander U.S. Naval Forces Japan, 466

Eisenbach, Commander Charles R., USN (USNA, 1936)
In the late 1940s handled the detailing of enlisted aviation personnel while serving in the Bureau of Naval Personnel, 209-210

Eisenhower, President Dwight D.
Burke assessed Eisenhower's inner circle people as being more impressive than those of his predecessor, Harry Truman, 251-252; in 1953 was in Norfolk for golf and a NATO meeting with Admiral Lynde McCormick, who was Strategic Allied Commander Atlantic, 234; decided in 1953 to decommission the presidential yacht Williamsburg (AGC-369), 252-253; in 1953 had a conference on board the Williamsburg with representatives from France, 253

Eisenhower, Dr. Milton
Impressive individual who was president of Pennsylvania State University in the early 1950s, 252

Electric Boat Division, General Dynamics Corporation, Groton, Connecticut
In September 1953 was the site of the keel laying for the Navy's second nuclear submarine, the Seawolf (SSN-575), 228

England
See: Great Britain

Enlisted Personnel
In the early 1940s an enlisted man from the crew of the battleship West Virginia (BB-48) subsequently attended the Naval Academy and became a submariner, 321; role of the Bureau of Naval Personnel in the late 1940s in the assignment of enlisted men and women, 209-216; during that period people were taking Navy electronics training and then leaving for the civilian job market, 209, 215; in the early 1950s, many of the enlisted crew members on board the presidential yacht Williamsburg (AGC-369) had been on board for many years until Burke began making changes, 241-242, 244; in 1990 Burke visited the aircraft carrier Theodore Roosevelt (CVN-71) and was very much impressed by the professionalism of her enlisted crew, 234-235

Enterprise, USS (CV-6)
In the summer and fall of 1942 operated in support of the Guadalcanal campaign, 114-115

Enterprise, USS (CVAN-65)
 In 1964, while in the Mediterranean, hosted visits from crew members of the attack transport Fremont (APA-44), 394

Equator Crossing
 Ceremony held in 1940 on board the battleship West Virginia (BB-48), 161-162; in the spring of 1944 by the crew of the submarine Flying Fish (SS-229), 161-163

Erb, Commander Leonard, USN (USNA, 1942)
 In late 1954 was ordered as commanding officer of the destroyer Harold J. Ellison (DD-864) but was subsequently detailed to another ship, 283

Fahrion, Vice Admiral Frank G., USN (USNA, 1917)
 Wrote articulate letters while commanding Amphibious Force Atlantic Fleet in the mid-1950s, 384-385

Fife, Rear Admiral James, Jr., USN (USNA, 1918)
 In the late 1940s, when he was serving as Commander Submarine Force Atlantic Fleet, he used the submarine Dogfish (SS-350) for public relations purposes, 226

Fire
 In March 1949 the submarine Cochino (SS-345) was lost as the result of a fire caused by a battery problem, 223; in 1950 the submarine Dogfish (SS-350) avoided disastrous results from a battery room fire because of training and precautions beforehand, 224

Fire Control
 Role of fire control radar in the shooting by the North Carolina in 1941, 99-100

Fitness Reports
 In assessing people over the years, Burke was rated as a tough grader because he didn't believe in carrying people who weren't doing their jobs well, 327-328, 360, 527; in the early 1960s Captain Herman Kossler told Burke that the fitness reports given to officers serving at the Naval Academy were not likely to get them promoted, 360

Fleming, Rear Admiral Allan F., USN (USNA, 1936)
 In 1966, while serving as OP-60B, assured Burke he would be in the Pentagon for another year after being selected for rear admiral, but Burke wound up being transferred right away, 422

Flying Fish, USS (SS-229)
 Transfer of personnel between patrols in World War II, 142-143, 153, 158-160, 164-168, 178-179, 184; Eleanor Roosevelt, the President's wife, visited Pearl Harbor and talked with Commander Glynn Donaho, skipper of the Flying Fish, 144;

shipyard period at Pearl, 144-145; while on leave in San Francisco in 1943, several crew members were drunk and disorderly, 145-146; rigorous adherence to correct procedures under Donaho, 146, 149-150; Pacific war patrol in late 1943, 147-148; rules concerning smoking, 150-151; patrol near Formosa and China in late 1943 and early 1944, 151-152; patrol in the early spring of 1944 near Okinawa, 154-156; patrol in May and June 1944 near the Marianas, 160-161; between-patrols visit to Australia in the spring of 1944, 161-162, 168; role of the petty officers who served as chiefs of the boat, 165-166; war patrol in the summer of 1944, 168-172; in 1944 received an inadvertent depth-charge attack by the U.S. destroyer Cogswell (DD-651), 171-173; limited access to Ultra messages within the boat, 174; visit in the autumn of 1944 to Pearl Harbor en route the West Coast, 174-175; in late 1944 and early 1945 underwent had an overhaul at Hunters Point Navy Yard in San Francisco, 175, 178-182; some crew members requested transfers because they couldn't take combat any longer, 178-179, 184; installation of FM sonar and appropriate training in early 1945 to prepare the submarine for Japanese minefields, 182-183; in the summer of 1945 joined wolf pack operations into the Sea of Japan, 186-192; in the summer of 1945 captured a Japanese prisoner, 189-190

Food

During World War II the submarine Flying Fish (SS-229) was on short rations at the end of a long war patrol, then did much better once in port, 175, 185; in the early 1950s the stewards on board the presidential yacht Williamsburg (AGC-369) had difficulty making beef stroganoff properly, 247-249; varieties available in the late 1950s during a Christmas celebration in Puerto Rico, 319; in the early 1960s, while in command of the attack transport Fremont (APA-44), Burke got the ship's supply officer to improve the quality of midnight rations, 403

Football

In the fall of 1960 the Naval Academy football team was involved in a ticket-scalping scandal that the superintendent, Rear Admiral John Davidson, decided to keep quiet, 339-341; in 1960 cadets from the Air Force Academy stole the goat mascot of the Naval Academy team prior to that year's football game between the schools, 361-363; success in the early 1960s of Joe Bellino and Roger Staubach, who earned the Heisman Trophy while playing for the Naval Academy, 347-348, 361

Forbes, Rear Admiral Bernard B., Jr., USN (USNA, 1945)

In the early 1970s, as Commander Carrier Division Six, was called upon to investigate a complaint of sexual harassment that involved officers from the dependent support ship Sanctuary (AH-17), 517-518

Fort, Captain George H., USN (USNA, 1912)

Calm, quiet individual who served for six months in 1942 as commanding officer of the battleship North Carolina (BB-55), 91-92, 128

Fowler, Major George T. USMC
   Officer who was promoted rapidly while serving with the Marine detachment on board the battleship North Carolina (BB-55) during World War II, 89

France
   In early 1953 senior French officials met with President Dwight Eisenhower on board the presidential yacht Williamsburg (AGC-369), 253-254; in the mid-1950s a large group of NATO's senior officers gathered near Paris for a strategy meeting, 293; sights and sounds of the city of Paris, 293-294; in the city of Nice in December 1964 two U.S. sailors raped a French woman, 410-411

Fremont, USS (APA-44)
   In the summer and fall of 1963 was overhauled at the Norfolk Naval Shipyard, 384-385; was in Norfolk when President John Kennedy was killed in November 1963, 385; in late 1963 went to Guantanamo Bay, Cuba, for refresher training, 386-387; the quality of personnel was lower than that Burke had encountered in submarines and destroyers, 387, 399-400, 403; load-out at Morehead City, North Carolina, 387-388; handling characteristics of the ship, 389; during the first part of 1964 deployed to the Sixth Fleet in the Mediterranean, 390-398, 403-404; Burke's meetings with crew members and embarked Marines, 389-392, 402-403; port visit for the crew in Malta, 395-396; port visit in Naples, Italy, 396-397; port visit to Barcelona, Spain, 397-398; operation of the ship's landing craft during amphibious exercises, 399-400; got a top score for performance during the Med deployment, 400

Friedrick, Lieutenant Ernest S., USN (USNA, 1937)
   In 1944 served as executive officer of the submarine Flying Fish (SS-229) before being transferred abruptly, 153, 159-160

Frost, Rear Admiral Laurence H., USN (USNA, 1926)
   In 1954, as Commander Destroyer Flotilla Four, enabled Burke to retain command of the destroyer Harold J. Ellison (DD-864) after another officer was ordered in, 283; was supportive of Burke in 1955 after the Harold J. Ellison collided with the submarine Jallao (SS-368), 281

Gallery, Rear Admiral Daniel V., Jr., USN (USNA, 1921)
   As Commandant of the Tenth Naval District in Puerto Rico in the late 1950s was famous for his steel drum band, 312, 317

Genoa, Italy
   Visited in the early 1950s by the destroyer Harold J. Ellison (DD-864), 275-276

Gentner, Vice Admiral William E., Jr., USN (USNA, 1930)
   As Commander Sixth Fleet in early 1964, visited the attack transport Fremont (APA-44) in the Mediterranean, 394-395

German Navy
    In May 1937 the German pocket battleship <u>Deutschland</u> shelled a port in Spain during the Spanish Civil War, 34

Germany
    In the summer of 1937 the battleship <u>Arkansas</u> (BB-33) transited the Kiel Canal and visited the port of Kiel, 34, 36-38

Glenview, Illinois, Naval Air Station
    Embarrassing mix-up in BOQ room assignments in the late 1960s when Burke stopped over at the air station during a trip, 456-457

Glisson, Commander Charles O., USN (USNA, 1921)
    In late 1941 was replaced as navigator of the battleship <u>North Carolina</u> (BB-55) after the captain lost confidence in him, 82

Golf
    Burke played golf as a youngster in the 1930s, then, after a long hiatus, resumed as a senior officer, 12; played against future astronaut Alan Shepard in the late 1950s in Newport, Rhode Island, 306-307

Gray, Captain James S., USN (USNA, 1936)
    In the mid-1950s was involved in atomic energy planning on the staff of Commander in Chief Atlantic Fleet, 286-288

Gray, Commander Louis Patrick, USN (USNA, 1940)
    As a lawyer on the staff of Commander Submarine Force Atlantic Fleet in the mid-1950s, Gray represented the commanding officer of the submarine <u>Jallao</u> (SS-368) after she collided with the destroyer <u>Harold J. Ellison</u> (DD-864), 281-282

Great Britain
    In the summer of 1937 the battleship <u>Arkansas</u> (BB-33) visited England during a midshipman training cruise, 38-40

Great Lakes, Illinois, Naval Training Center
    In the late 1940s the Service Schools Command provided training to electronics technicians and other ratings, 209-210, 215

Greece
    In early 1965, the amphibious transport dock <u>La Salle</u> (LPD-3) visited Piraeus, the port of Athens, 412; a plan in the mid-1970s to homeport large numbers of U.S. Navy ships in Greece did not come to fruition, 516-517

Greenbacker, Captain John E., USN (USNA, 1940)
In 1962-63 commanded the attack transport Fremont (APA-44) before turning her over to Burke, 384-385, 388; was not complimentary about the Marines on board, 385, 388

Green Bowl Society
Secret society of Naval Academy graduates that looked out for each other in terms of assignments prior to and shortly after World War II, 208-209

Greenwood, Lieutenant Charles L., CHC, USN (USNA, 1950)
Former naval aviator who was very helpful to midshipmen while serving in the early 1960s as a Naval Academy chaplain, 352, 366

Greer, Captain Earl M., USNR (USNA, 1942)
In the late 1960s, while stationed in OpNav, had a major role in a study that led to the reorganization of the Naval Reserve along functional lines, 443-444, 446, 454

Griffiths, Lieutenant (junior grade) Charles H., USN (USNA, 1946)
After surviving the sinking of the submarine Cochino (SS-345) in 1949, joined the Sablefish (SS-303) and demonstrated proficiency in electronics, 229, 232

Gromyko, Andrei
Soviet diplomat who visited Tokyo in the early 1970s, 484-485

Growler, USS (SSG-577)
Submarine used in the late 1950s for Regulus guided missile tests in the Caribbean, 314-316

Guadalcanal
Operations of the battleship North Carolina (BB-55) during the summer of 1942 while in support of the campaign, 115-117; on 15 September 1942, the Japanese submarine I-19 torpedoed the battleship North Carolina (BB-55) and the aircraft carrier Wasp (CV-7), 117-119; night battle in November 1942 involved the battleships Washington (BB-56) and South Dakota (BB-57), 124

Guantanamo Bay, Cuba
In the early 1950s the fleet training group at Guantanamo Bay was perceived as merciless by skippers of ships that went there for training, 266; site of refresher training in 1955 for the crew of the destroyer Harold J. Ellison (DD-864), 278-279

Guardfish, USS (SS-217)
By the summer of 1945 this submarine had been taken off war patrols and was serving at Pearl Harbor as a training boat for prospective commanding officers and as a target for training ASW forces, 194-195; journey to the East Coast after the conclusion of the war, 196-198; port visit in New Orleans, 199-200; in late 1945 and

early 1946 was at New London, Connecticut, to prepare for decommissioning, 202-204

Guest, Rear Admiral William S., USN (USNA, 1935)
In the late 1960s, as Chief of Naval Air Reserve Training, maintained frequent contact with the reserve office in OpNav, 456-458

Gunnery—Naval
In 1941-42 the new battleship North Carolina (BB-55) conducted firing trials and training, 93-94, 97, 99-101, 105-106; antiaircraft fire by the North Carolina in August 1942, during the Battle of the Eastern Solomons, 115-117, 119; in early 1944 the submarine Flying Fish (SS-229) shelled the island of Kita Daito Jima, near Okinawa, 155; in 1944 the Flying Fish fired at fishing boats in the Sea of Japan, 188-189; in 1955 the destroyer Harold J. Ellison (DD-864) practiced naval gunfire support in the Caribbean, 279

Guns
In the early 1940s old battleships had inadequate guns installed for antiaircraft defense, 69, 77

Guppy Program
In the late 1940s the submarine Dogfish (SS-350) received the Guppy modification that made her faster and more streamlined in appearance, 221-222

Gurnee, Lieutenant (junior grade) Robert L., USN (USNA, 1939)
During World War II served in the submarine Flying Fish (SS-229), 140, 143

Halleck, Representative Charles A.
In 1967 was a member of a congressional subcommittee that held a hearing in the Philippines concerning the Vietnam War, 440-441

Halsey, Admiral William F., Jr., USN (USNA, 1904)
In 1942-43 provided an inspirational presence while serving as Commander South Pacific Area, 126

Hardin, Wayne
Successful in the early 1960s as head football coach at the Naval Academy, 346, 348

Harold J. Ellison, USS (DD-864)
In mid-1953 was completing a European deployment when Burke took command, 266-269; need for training of the ship's inexperienced officers in operational practices, 269-271, 276-278; in the early 1950s took part in hunter-killer antisubmarine exercises in the Atlantic, 271-272, 274-275; competition with other ships in her squadron, 272, 274, 276; port visit to Havana, 272-274; deployment to the Mediterranean, 275-276; problem with an inexperienced new executive officer, 276-278; training period at Guantanamo Bay, Cuba, 278-279; in early 1955

participated in an antisubmarine exercise, 279-280; during the exercise, collided with the submarine Jallao (SS-368), and an investigation followed, 280-282, 284; in mid-1955 visited New York City, 282-283; in 1955 earned the E for excellence in her squadron, 283; Burke declined to take the squadron commander's brother from Cuba to Jamaica because he didn't qualify, 323

Havana, Cuba
In the early 1950s the destroyer Harold J. Ellison (DD-864) made a port visit to this city, 272-274

Hazeltine, Lieutenant Colonel Charles B., Jr., USA (USMA, 1940)
In 1957-58, as a student at the Naval War College, was very impressive, aggressive, and knowledgeable but did not later become a general officer, 301-302, 305

Hearst, William R., Jr.
As publisher of the New York Journal-American in the mid-1950s demanded to know why a large number of U.S. Navy flag officers had stopped over in Ireland, 293

Heimark, Captain Jacob V., USN (USNA, 1940)
In the spring of 1964, while in the staff of CinCSouth at Naples, hosted a visit from Burke and his daughter, 397

Hensel, Commander Karl G., USN (USNA, 1923)
In 1943, while serving as a submarine division commander, had disagreements with Commander Glynn Donaho, skipper of the submarine Flying Fish (SS-229), 148-149

Hessel, Lieutenant Edward W., USN (USNA, 1937)
In his last year at the Naval Academy, 1936-37, was compassionate toward Burke, 15; in early 1943 returned to the United States on board a cargo ship after the carrier Wasp (CV-7) was sunk, 130

Hill, Rear Admiral Tom B., USN (USNA, 1922)
In 1941 became the first gunnery officer of the battleship North Carolina (BB-55) and was highly respected, 75, 86-87, 93-94, 97, 100, 118-119; later in World War II served as Pacific Fleet gunnery officer, 142; in 1953, as Commandant of Naval District Washington, presided over the decommissioning of the presidential yacht Williamsburg (AGC-369), 87

Holladay, Lieutenant Douglas S., Jr., USNR
Capable individual who served in the early 1970s as Burke's flag lieutenant, 527

Holland, USS (AS-3)
Submarine tender that in early 1945 was stationed at Guam as flagship for Vice Admiral Charles Lockwood, ComSubPac, 184-185

Holloway, Admiral James L. III, USN (USNA, 1943)
When Holloway was Chief of Naval Operations in the mid-1970s, Burke believed that people were taking action on Holloway's behalf that he would not countenance, 534-535; in 1977 asked Burke to be vice president of the Navy Relief Society, 540-541

Honolulu, Hawaii
Shortly before World War II the crew of the battleship West Virginia (BB-48) held a ship's party at the Young Hotel, 65-67

Hopley, Lieutenant (junior grade) Eric E., USN (USNA, 1942)
During the latter part of World War II, served in the submarine Flying Fish (SS-229), 159, 172, 181

Howard, Midshipman William C., Jr., USN (USNA, 1940)
Attended the Naval Academy in the late 1930s but was kicked out prior to graduation, 16-17, 33, 37, 40-41

Howard W. Gilmore, USS (AS-16)
Submarine tender that in late 1946 was stationed at Key West, Florida, interrupted by an overhaul at Philadelphia, 205-207

Hull, Commander Harry, USN (USNA, 1932)
In the summer of 1945, at Pearl Harbor, advised Burke not to leave submarines, 195

Hunters Point Navy Yard, San Francisco, California
In late 1944-early 1945 overhauled the submarine Flying Fish (SS-229), 175, 178-182

Hurst, Commander William J., USN (USNA, 1942)
In the early 1950s served as executive officer of the presidential yacht Williamsburg (AGC-369), 242

Hustvedt, Captain Olaf M., USN (USNA, 1909)
Distinguished individual who served in 1941 as the first commanding officer of the battleship North Carolina (BB-55), 78-79, 96

Hydeman, Commander Earl T., USN (USNA, 1932)
In the summer of 1945, as commanding officer of the submarine Sea Dog (SS-401), led a wolf pack in and out of the Sea of Japan, 186-192

Ingersoll, Vice Admiral Stuart H., USN (USNA, 1921)
As president of the Naval War College in the late 1950s complained about students having contact with the news media, 302-303

Inman, Commander Bobby R. Inman, USN
In early 1971, as a special intelligence officer for Commander Seventh Fleet, told Burke of a plan to homeport an aircraft carrier and her escorts in Yokosuka, Japan, 468

Indian Ocean
In the early 1970s Seabees were involved in construction projects to set up the island of Diego Garcia as a fleet support facility, 519-521

Inspection and Survey, Board of
From 1967 to 1988, Rear Admiral John Bulkeley served the Navy well as president of InSurv, 201-202, 505; early 1970s inspection of the fast combat support ship Seattle (AOE-3), 505-506; in the mid-1970s asked Burke if he would like to take over as head of InSurv, 202

Ireland
As publisher of the New York Journal-American in the mid-1950s, William R. Hearst, Jr., demanded to know why a large number of U.S. Navy flag officers had stopped over in Ireland, 293

Irvin, Captain William D., USN (USNA, 1927)
In the late 1940s headed the Service School Command at Great Lakes, Illinois, 215

Italy
In the early 1950s the destroyer Harold J. Ellison (DD-864) visited various ports in this country, 275-276; in the spring of 1964 the attack transport Fremont (APA-44) visited Naples, 396-397; in late 1964 Burke's family members visited various places in Italy, 407-408

Itaya, Admiral Takaichi, Japanese Maritime Self-Defense Force
In the early 1970s, as head of the Japanese Self-Defense Forces, has an excellent rapport with Burke, 478

J. Fred Talbott, USS (DD-150)
Old destroyer that made an East Coast cruise in the summer of 1938 to train midshipmen, 41-44, 48; living conditions on board, 43-44

Jackson, Rear Admiral Alexander, Jr., USN (Ret.) (USNA, 1925)
Retired officer who in the late 1960s and early 1970s headed the Navy section of the Reserve Officers Association and knew a great deal of legislative history, 446-447

Jallao, USS (SS-368)
In 1955 collided during an antisubmarine warfare exercise with the destroyer Harold J. Ellison (DD-864), and an investigation followed, 280-282, 284

Japan
Burke's contacts with foreign officers at the Naval War College in the late 1950s proved beneficial in later years, when he was in Japan, 305-306; in the summer of 1970, the U.S. Navy decided to withdraw its forces from Japan and then began implementing that decision by turning facilities over to the Japanese, 463, 467-468, 483-484; negotiations to return the facilities to U.S. control, 473-475, 485-486; role of the U.S. embassy in Tokyo in dealings with the Japanese Government, 463, 470-471, 474-476; hotsy baths as part of the culture, 465, 488-489; many U.S. visitors had to be entertained on their way through Japan, 465; in the early 1970s Burke discovered that the Japanese are slow to develop friendships, 412-413, 465-466, 477-478, 481; in 1971-72 the U.S. Navy, through Commander U.S. Naval Forces Japan, negotiated with the Japanese Government to homeport an aircraft carrier and her escorts in Yokosuka, 467-477; in the early 1970s the U.S. Navy would neither conform nor deny whether there were nuclear weapons on board warships that visited Japanese ports, 476; in the early 1970s there were a number of expatriate Americans working as businessmen in Japan, 479-480; Burke had a number of contacts with top Japanese business leaders, 479-481, 501; the Burkes enjoyed sightseeing in Japan, 482-483, 488-490, 499-501; in keeping with Japanese culture, Burke received a number of gifts because of his position, 490-492

Japanese Maritime Self-Defense Force
Formation of in the early 1950s was aided by strong support from Admiral Arleigh Burke, 462

Japanese Navy
On 15 September 1942, the Japanese submarine I-19 torpedoed the battleship North Carolina (BB-55) and the aircraft carrier Wasp (CV-7), 117-119; in the fall of 1943 a Japanese aircraft carrier escaped because the U.S. submarine Flying Fish (SS-229) had faulty torpedoes, 147; in June 1944 before and during the Battle of the Philippine Sea, 160-161; in 1943 Representative Andrew May revealed in an interview with the media that Japanese antisubmarine forces were not setting their depth charges deep enough, and casualties increased afterward, 174

Jarrett, Lieutenant Commander Harry B., USN (USNA, 1922)
As a company officer at the Naval Academy in the late 1930s, he displayed admirable leadership qualities, 23, 375

Johnson, Vice Admiral Felix L., USN (Ret.) (USNA, 1920)
In the late 1960s and early 1970s gave Burke useful advice on reorganizing the Naval Reserve, 451-452, 459

Johnson, James E.
In the early 1970s, while serving as Assistant Secretary of the Navy (Manpower and Reserve Affairs), visited Japan to assess the racial situation in U.S. Navy commands there, 495-496, 513

Johnston, Admiral Means, Jr., USN (USNA, 1939)
By retiring when he did in 1975, he was able to get substantially more in retired pay than if he had waited longer, 530-531

Juan Carlos, Prince/King
In 1962, shortly after his marriage, the Spanish prince visited the U.S. Naval Academy, 382-383

Kaine, Captain Francis R., USN
In the late 1960s, as Commander Naval Special War Group Pacific, at Coronado, California, was involved in training UDTs and SEALs for Vietnam, 430-431

Kelly, Captain James W., CHC, USN
Compassionate, helpful individual who served in the early 1960s as a chaplain at the Naval Academy, 343-344, 352-354, 366-367

Kennedy, President John F.
In January 1961 the Naval Academy participated in his inauguration in Washington, 357-358; as President emphasized physical fitness, 345; in June 1961 made the commencement address at the Naval Academy's graduation and noticed that there were few black midshipmen, 351, 363-364; during his term as President, students were given academic deferments from the draft, which led to discord later, 448-449; killed in November 1963, 385

Kent State University, Kent, Ohio
In May 1970 National Guardsmen shot and killed antiwar protesters at the university, 445-446

Key West, Florida
In late 1946 had an outbreak of polio among Navy families, 205; in 1952 the presidential yacht Williamsburg (AGC-369) went to Key West to provide support for President Harry S. Truman and his party, 239-240, 260-261

Kidd, Rear Admiral Isaac C., USN (USNA, 1906)
In 1940, as chief of staff to Commander Battleships, Battle Force, was friendly to Ensign Burke on board the battleship West Virginia (BB-48), 58-59, 62, 73

Kidd, Admiral Isaac C., Jr., USN (USNA, 1942)
Became friendly with Burke in the late 1930s when both were midshipmen at the Naval Academy, 58; connections later in life, 74, 540; presented Burke a Distinguished Service Medal in 1976 when he retired, 540

King, Commander Ernest J., Jr., USN (USNA, 1945)
In the mid-1960s this son of the World War II fleet commander in chief commanded an amphibious warfare ship, 408-409

King, Vice Admiral Jerome H., Jr., USN
In 1972, while serving as DCNO (Surface Warfare), asked about the identity of an officer who was writing top-notch messages for Burke, 493

Kirkpatrick, Rear Admiral Charles C., USN (USNA, 1931)
As a company officer at the Naval Academy in the late 1930s, he was an excellent role model of leadership for the midshipmen, 21-22, 29, 90; various duties over the years, 377; in the early 1960s served as superintendent of the academy, 344-345, 353, 373, 377-379, 383

Kirkpatrick, Lieutenant John E., USNR (USNA, 1931)
In World War II served in the battleship North Carolina (BB-55) and cruiser Oklahoma City (CL-91), later had a successful career in business, 85, 100

Koch, Lieutenant Colonel Robert J., USA (USMA, 1947
Army officer who served an exchange tour in the early 1960s at the Naval Academy, 337, 357

Korean War
While serving as the CNO's representative to General Douglas MacArthur in the early 1950s, Rear Admiral Arleigh Burke had a special set of code wheels to avoid going through the Army communications system, 462

Kossler, Captain Herman J., USN (USNA, 1934)
In the late 1940s served in the recruiting section of the Bureau of Naval Personnel, 213; in the early 1960s told Burke that the fitness reports given to officers serving at the Naval Academy were not likely to get them promoted, 360; after his retirement, he lived in Charleston and was a big help to Burke, 532

La Salle, USS (LPD-3)
In late 1964 served as flagship of Amphibious Squadron Six during a deployment to Europe, 404, 406, 410-413; load-out at Morehead City, North Carolina, 409-410; in the spring of 1965 deployed to the Caribbean, 414-415

Leave and Liberty
In 1937 Naval Academy midshipmen got liberty in Germany and England during a summer training cruise, 36-40; in 1939 midshipmen visited Canada, 48-49; in Hawaii shortly before World War II, 61, 65-67, in 1940 at Bremerton, Washington, 68; in 1940-41 in New Orleans, 73-74; in the autumn of 1941 near Annapolis, Maryland, 80-81; while on leave in San Francisco in 1943, several crew members of the submarine Flying Fish (SS-229) were drunk and disorderly, 145-146; in the spring of 1944 the crew of the Flying Fish enjoyed liberty at a rest camp on Majuro in the Marshall Islands, 156-157; in Australia in mid-1944, 161-162, 168; in the autumn of 1944 Burke went on 30 days' leave in New Orleans, 175-177; hospitality at Mom Chung's place in San Francisco in late 1944, 180-181; in New Orleans right after World War II, 200-201; in the early 1950s in Havana, Cuba, 272-274; in the

spring of 1964 the crew of the attack transport Fremont (APA-44) had port visits in Malta, Italy, and Spain, 395-398; while on liberty in Nice, France, in December 1964, two U.S. sailors raped a French woman, 410-411; in late 1964-early 1965, the amphibious transport dock La Salle (LPD-3) visited Spanish ports, 411-412

Lhamon, Midshipman George M., USN (USNA, 1939)
As a company commander at the Naval Academy in the late 1930s, discussed a disciplinary situation with Burke, 27

Lockwood, Vice Admiral Charles A., USN (USNA, 1912)
As Commander Submarine Force Pacific Fleet, was present at Pearl in 1943 when the skipper of the submarine Flying Fish (SS-229) was chewed out for misbehavior by his crew, 145-146; in early 1945 rode the Flying Fish as the crew trained for penetrating Japanese minefields, 182-183; in the summer of 1945 greeted submarines at Pearl Harbor after they returned from a venture through the minefields around the Sea of Japan, 191-194

Lovig, Lieutenant (junior grade) Lawrence, Jr., SC, USN (USNA, 1939)
Role on board the battleship North Carolina (BB-55) in August 1942, during the Battle of the Eastern Solomons, 115-116

Lyman, Rear Admiral Charles H. III, USN (USNA, 1926)
Warm individual who served as chief of staff in the late 1950s at the Naval War College, 302-303

Lyons, Commander James A., Jr., USN (USNA, 1952)
Aggressive, hard-working officer who in the mid-1960s had many high-level contacts within OpNav while working in the plans section, 417-418, 420; inadvertently left a classified material exposed when he left his office for a time, 417-418; in the early 1970s was administrative aide to OP-06, 503-504

MacArthur, General of the Army Douglas, USA (USMA, 1903)
While serving as the CNO's representative to MacArthur in the early 1950s, Rear Admiral Arleigh Burke had a special set of code wheels to avoid going through the Army communications system, 462

MacGregor, Commander Stephen H., Jr., USN (USNA, 1940)
In 1953, while commanding a destroyer, gave Burke useful tips on training, 270

Macondray, Lieutenant Commander Atherton, Jr., USN (USNA, 1921)
In 1941, while serving in the Bureau of Navigation, gave Burke an explanation for his transfer to the battleship North Carolina (BB-55), 75

Majuro, Marshall Islands
Fleet anchorage that the submarine Flying Fish (SS-229) visited in the spring of 1944 while between patrols, 156-159

Malta
    In the spring of 1964 the crew of the attack transport <u>Fremont</u> (APA-44) had a port visit in Malta, 395-396

Mare Island, California
    Used in the late 1960s for training boat crews for Vietnam operations because of the rivers in the area, 429-430, 433-434

Marine Corps, U.S.
    In the early 1960s assigned top-notch officers to the Naval Academy staff, 337-338, 359; in the mid-1960s a group of more than 450 Marines was on board the attack transport <u>Fremont</u> APA-44) before and during a deployment to the Mediterranean, 385, 387-395, 402-403; on board the amphibious transport dock <u>La Salle</u> (LPD-3) before a deployment in 1964 to the Mediterranean, 409-410; in the spring of 1965 tested the new CH-46 helicopter in the Caribbean and practiced amphibious landings, 414-415; in 1967 Marine units were stationed in the I Corps area of South Vietnam, and many were on Okinawa as well, 436-437; in the early 1970s an officer with the Marine detachment in Yokosuka, Japan, had a problem with alcohol abuse, 496-497

Markland, Captain Henry T., USN (USNA, (1908)
    In 1940-41 served as commanding officer of the battleship <u>West Virginia</u> (BB-48), 75-76

Marshall, Emmy
    Navy wife who served for many years as social director in the Naval Academy's Bancroft Hall, 32, 369-370

Martinez, Commander Lucian C., USN
    In the early 1970s served very effectively on the staff of Commander U.S. Naval Forces Japan, 466-467, 473, 477

Masuoka, Ichiro
    In the 1970s Masuoka was the unofficial ambassador to the U.S. Navy in Yokosuka, Japan, 465-466, 472, 484, 498-499; in 1971-72 served as a conduit to help negotiate the homeporting of an aircraft carrier and her escorts in Yokosuka, 471-472, 484

Maxwell, Lieutenant Commander William S., USN
    Immigrant, who had an unconventional approach to his job as assistant engineer officer of the battleship <u>North Carolina</u> (BB-55) during World War II, 88-89; post-Navy job in the city of New York, 88-89

McCain, Admiral John S., Jr., USN (USNA, 1931)
    As an instructor at the Naval Academy in the late 1930s, used salty language in teaching his classes, 26, 386-387; during World War II, while he was at sea, his

attractrive wife lived in New London, Connecticut, 133; son Joseph dropped out of the Naval Academy in 1961, 355-356; in the mid-1960s served as Commander Amphibious Force Atlantic Fleet, 385-386, 404-406; personality of, 386; in 1970, as Commander in Chief Pacific, briefed Burke on plans for U.S. naval forces in Japan, 464

McCain, Midshipman Joseph Pinckney, USN (USNA, 1964)
Despite being from a Navy family, didn't adapt well to Naval Academy discipline and dropped out at the end of his first year, 355-356; endeared himself to the McCain family, 356; in the mid-1960s, while living in Coronado, was a great help to the Burke family when their son had a brain tumor, 424

McCormack, Representative John W.
As Speaker of the House in the late 1960s and 1970s, demonstrated strong support for military reservists, 446

McCrory, Gunner Thomas S., USN
Colorful warrant officer who served in the crew of the battleship North Carolina (BB-55) during World War II, 93-94, 117-118

McCrory, Commander Woodrow Wilson, USN (USNA, 1938)
In the early 1950s, served a detail officer in the Bureau of Naval Personnel, 240, 264

McDaniel, Commander George T., Jr., USN (USNA, 1939)
Though he was non-reg as a Naval Academy midshipman in the late 1930s, he performed well in combat in World War II, 119-120; in the early 1950s, while in command of a destroyer, objected to submariners coming in for brief tours as destroyer skippers, 266

McFall, Commander Albert Dodge, USN (USNA, 1950)
First-class gentleman who in the mid-1950s served as flag lieutenant for Vice Admiral Robert Goldthwaite, 297; in the early 1960s was flag lieutenant to the superintendent of the Naval Academy, 335-336, 340-341; in early 1964 visited Burke on board the attack transport Fremont (APA-44) in the Mediterranean, 394; when he was commanding officer of Attack Squadron 74, he visited Burke's son Charly in Coronado in the fall of 1966 and then was killed in a carrier accident in December of that year, 427

McKee, Captain Fran, USN
In the early 1970s, while stationed in Washington, was involved in hearing a sexual harassment complaint and discussing it with the CNO, Admiral Elmo Zumwalt, 518

McMullen, Midshipman John J., USN (USNA, 1940)
Impressive individual who later became an engineering duty only specialist as an officer, 47

McNamara, Robert S.
As Secretary of Defense in the 1960s, wanted studies done on a wide variety of topics, 442-443; in the late 1960s was subject to opposition from Naval Reserve aviators, 455

McNitt, Captain Robert W., USN (USNA, 1938)
In the early 1960s did a great deal for the Naval Academy, including bringing in the first civilian academic dean, 350-351, 368

Medical Problems
In the spring of 1937, while he was a Naval Academy midshipman, Burke had a case of mumps, 20; Burke's eye problems, 45-47; in the 1930s and early 1940s the Naval Academy lost a number of high-quality midshipmen because they failed eye tests, 45-46; in 1944 a member of the crew of the submarine Flying Fish (SS-229) was treated for venereal disease with a new drug called penicillin, 169; in late 1944 some crew members of the Flying Fish requested transfers because they couldn't take the rigors of combat any longer, 178-179, 184; in late 1946 Key West, Florida, had an outbreak of polio among Navy families, 205; in December 1952 Captain Edwin Miller, commanding officer of the presidential yacht Williamsburg (AGC-369), had a heart attack and had to be hospitalized, 245, 250, 262; in the early 1960s Burke got run down from the demanding pace of serving as executive officer in the Naval Academy's Bancroft Hall, 374-376; in 1966 Burke's son Charly developed a brain tumor and died from it in June 1967, 423-424; in the early 1970s, Burke focused on cases of alcohol abuse among his subordinates, 496-497, 511-512

Melson, Rear Admiral Charles L., USN (USNA, 1927)
In the mid-1950s served as deputy chief of staff to Commander in Chief Atlantic Fleet, 289-292, 296, 325; in 1959, as superintendent of the Naval Academy, invited Burke to serve as executive officer in Bancroft Hall, 335-336

Merritt, Captain Robert G., USN (USNA, 1939)
In the mid-1960s, as an amphibious squadron commander, was embarked with his staff in the attack transport Fremont (APA-44), 387-388

Meyer, Armin H.
As U.S. ambassador to Japan in the early 1970s was involved in dealings with the Japanese Government on a plan to homeport an aircraft carrier and her escorts in Yokosuka, 470-471

Middle East
In the late 1950s, while at the Naval War College, Burke wrote a dissertation on the Middle East and Islam, 300-301

Midway, USS (CVA-41)
In October 1973 this aircraft carrier shifted her homeport to Yokosuka, Japan, as the result of U.S. negotiations accomplished in 1971-72, 467-477

Military Academy, West Point, New York
Comparison of its honor code in the early 1960s with the honor concept of the Naval Academy, 357; exchange weekends in the early 1960s with the Naval Academy, 380-301

Miller, Captain Edwin S., USN (USNA, 1933)
In the early 1950s served capably as the commanding officer of the presidential yacht Williamsburg (AGC-369), 241, 247-250, 254-255, 257, 259; in December 1952 had a heart attack and had to be hospitalized, 245, 250, 262

Mine Warfare
In 1945 U.S. submarines had FM sonar installed and used it to penetrate Japanese minefields, 182-183, 186-191; post-mission analysis by Vice Admiral Charles Lockwood, 192-193

Mini, Captain James H., USN (USNA, 1935)
Served as commandant of midshipmen, 1960-61, at the Naval Academy, 340, 362-363, 375

Minter, Rear Admiral Charles S., Jr., USN (USNA, 1937)
In the early 1960s served as commandant of the Naval Academy, 341, 344-346, 353, 375-378, 383

Missiles
In the late 1950s Submarine Division 63 operated in the Caribbean, principally in support of the Regulus missile program, 310-316, 323-325; precise navigation was important during the Regulus testing, 323-324; the Regulus program was slowed down and then canceled in the late 1950s because of the need to pay for the Polaris program, 318, 326

Moncure, Captain Samuel P., USN (USNA, 1932)
Capable officer who held a number of responsible assignments during his career but was not selected for flag rank, 215-216

Montgomery, Field Marshal Sir Bernard Law, British Army
Egotistical British officer who served as host in the mid-1950s for a NATO strategy conference near Paris, 293

Moore, Midshipman William Cabell, USN (USNA, 1943)
As a plebe at the Naval Academy in 1939, was treated with friendliness by upperclassman Burke, 53

Moorer, Admiral Thomas H., USN (USNA, 1933)
As Chief of Naval Operations in 1970, held off on implementing a plan to withdraw U.S. naval forces from Japan, 463

Morita, Akio
Co-founder of the Sony Corporation, he had a number of contacts with Burke in the early 1970s, 480

Morton, Lieutenant Commander William B., USN (USNA, 1940)
After standing low in his class at the Naval Academy, he served as a naval aviator in World War II and in the summer of 1945 was part of an aviation staff at Pearl Harbor, 194-195; in the spring of 1964, while in the staff of CinCSouth at Naples, hosted a visit from Burke and his daughter, 396-397

Mount Vernon, Virginia
The presidential yacht Margie made a cruise in 1952 to Mount Vernon with senior officials from Norway on board, 254-256

Murray, Captain Stuart S., USN (USNA, 1919)
In the summer of 1943 arranged for Burke to be transferred to the submarine Flying Fish (SS-229), even though he was destined for the ill-fated Wahoo (SS-238), 140-141

Muse, Rear Admiral George R., USN (USNA, 1938)
In the late 1960s served as Commander Naval Reserve Command, maintained frequent contact with the reserve office in OpNav, 456-458

Music
As Commandant of the Tenth Naval District in Puerto Rico in the late 1950s, Rear Admiral Dan Gallery was famous for his steel drum band, 312, 317

Mustin, Commander Henry C., USN (USNA, 1955)
Made a strong favorable impression on Burke in the late 1960s while serving in country in Vietnam, 428

National Guard, U.S.
In May 1970 National Guardsmen shot and killed antiwar protesters at Kent State University, 445-446

NATO
See: North Atlantic Treaty Organization (NATO)

Naval Academy, Annapolis, Maryland
Rigors of plebe year in 1936-37, 13-16; in the late 1930s the academy did not have a formalized honor system, 13, 26-27; mistreatment of juniors by those more senior, 13-16, 52-53; liberty for midshipmen in the late 1930s, 17-18; on 20 January 1937 midshipmen marched in a rain-soaked parade in Washington, D.C., to honor to second inauguration of President Franklin D. Roosevelt, 18-20; role in the late 1930s of duty officers, 18, 20-24, 82; academics in the late 1930s, 24-27; social activities in

the late 1930s for midshipmen, 30-34, 54, 369; summer cruises in the late 1930s provided both sightseeing and training, 34-44, 48-51; comparison of midshipman life style in the late 1930s with that of counterparts in civilian universities, 51-52; graduation of the class of 1940, 53-54; the Green Bowl Society was a secret group of Naval Academy graduates that looked out for each other in terms of assignments prior to and shortly after World War II, 208-209; in the early 1960s midshipmen stopped marching together to classes, 28, 349, 370-371; problems in the early 1960s with conversations in the administrative office in Bancroft Hall leaking to the midshipmen's magazine, 336-337; the Marine Corps assigned top-notch officers to the academy staff, 337-338, 359; enthusiasm of midshipmen's families at the end of plebe summer, 339; in the fall of 1960 the Naval Academy football team was involved in a ticket-scalping scandal that the superintendent, Rear Admiral John Davidson, decided to keep quiet, 339-341; in 1960 cadets from the Air Force Academy stole the goat mascot of the Naval Academy team, 361-363; midshipman leaders in the early 1960s, 341-342; disciplinary system and honor violations in the early 1960s, 15, 342-344, 354-356, 365-366, 374-375; value of chaplains in counseling midshipmen and staff members, 343-344, 352, 366-367; relationship of the Bancroft Hall organization to sports teams, 346-348; in the early 1960s restrictions on midshipmen kept them from maturing socially, 349-350; in the early 1960s the institution got its first academic dean and restructured the academic program, 350-351, 368, 371-372; in June 1961 President John Kennedy made the commencement address at the Naval Academy's graduation and noticed that there were few black midshipmen, 351, 363-364; in the early 1960s dozens of midshipmen were married, in violation of regulations, 352-353; comparison of the honor concept with that of West Point, 357; participation in January 1961 in President John Kennedy's inauguration, 357-358; Admiral Hyman Rickover interviewed midshipmen for the nuclear power program, 358-359; in the spring of 1961 Admiral Arleigh Burke spoke at the academy about the failed Bay of Pigs invasion in Cuba, 379-380; in 1962-64 Rear Admiral Charles Kirkpatrick served as superintendent of the academy, 344-345, 353, 373, 377-379, 383; in 1962 hosted a visit by Spain's Prince Juan Carlos and his bride, 382-383; in the early 1960s Captain Herman Kossler told Burke that the fitness reports given to officers serving at the Naval Academy were not likely to get them promoted, 360; Superintendent John Davidson shielded those below him in the chain of command from Admiral Hyman Rickover, 360-361; deaths of midshipmen, including suicides, 365-366; alumnus Pierre Bernard, a local banker, was a strong supporter of the academy, 367-368; dress parades in the early 1960s, 369-370; in the early 1960s few of the officers on staff had much postgraduate education, 371; increase in postgraduate opportunities for newly commissioned officers, 372-273; exchange weekends with West Point, 380-301

Naval Reserve, U.S.

In the period shortly before World War II, reserve officers on board the battleship West Virginia (BB-48) were not treated with the respect they deserved, 69-70, 442, 451; reserve officers made a valuable contribution on board the battleship North Carolina (BB-55) during World War II, 98; in the summer of 1967, Burke met with

Naval Reserve public affairs officers in Los Angeles to get advice on working with the news media, 431-432; in the late 1960s several flag officers declined the OpNav job of overseeing the reserves because they were looked upon with scorn, 441-442; only symbolic call-ups of reservists in the late 1960s, 442; in the 1968-70 period Burke ran a study that led to the reorganization of the Naval Reserve into functional components, 442-444, 450-455, 459; political influence on the structure of the Naval Reserve, 443-445; in the late 1960s and early 1970s, many universities dropped their ROTC units because of unrest related to the Vietnam War, 448-450; relationship between the OpNav reserve office and the component commanders for the air and surface reserves, 456-458; in the early 1970s a number of expatriate U.S. Naval Reservists lived and worked in Japan, 479; in the mid-1970s, as commandant of the Sixth Naval District, Burke visited many reserve units, 536

Naval War College, Newport, Rhode Island
In the late 1950 the student body was divided into committees, and Burke wrote a dissertation on the Middle East and Islam, 300-301; in 1957-58 Army Lieutenant Colonel Charles B. Hazeltine was a top-notch student at the college, 301-302; focus of course work included writing of plans and opportunities to read, 302; assessment of the college's leadership in the late 1950s, 302-303; submarine officers Eugene P. Wilkinson and James B. Osborn were students in the late 1950s, 304-305; war games, 305; Burke's contacts with foreign officers in the late 1950s proved beneficial in later years, when he was in Japan, 305-306; public speaking class in the late 1950s was beneficial, 308-309

Navigation
In the early 1950s the pilot on board the presidential yacht Williamsburg (AGC-369) often used seaman's eye when navigating on the Potomac River, 242-244, 253-254; precise navigation was important in the late 1950s during the testing of Regulus missiles in the Caribbean, 323-324

Navy Relief Society
Activities in the late 1970s and early 1980s on behalf of Navy and Marine Corps personnel who needed financial assistance, 540-554

New London, Connecticut
Burke was a student at the Submarine School from April to July of 1943, 131-137; in the early 1950s a number of submarine families lived in the area, 236-237, 285

New Orleans, Louisiana
Port visit right after World War II by the submarine Guardfish (SS-217), 199-200

News Media
Heavy coverage in 1941 of the new fast battleship North Carolina (BB-55), 93-94; in a 1952 news conference President Harry Truman did an impressive job in talking to reporters, but they weren't accurate in their reports, 240-241; as publisher of the New York Journal-American in the mid-1950s, William R. Hearst, Jr., demanded to know

why a large number of U.S. Navy flag officers had stopped over in Ireland, 293; as president of the Naval War College in the late 1950s, Vice Admiral Stuart Ingersoll complained about students having contact with the news media, 302-303; in the summer of 1967, Burke met with Naval Reserve public affairs officers in Los Angeles to get advice on working with the news media, 431-432

New York, USS (BB-34)
In the summer of 1939 made a summer training cruise on the East Coast for Naval Academy midshipmen, 48-51

New York City
In 1955 a number of ships of Destroyer Flotilla Four made a port call to the city, 282-283

New York Navy Yard, Brooklyn, New York
In the summer of 1941 installed radar and other equipment on board the battleship North Carolina (BB-55), 78; repair in 1941 of damaged British warships, 97-98

Nimitz, Admiral Chester W., USN (USNA, 1905)
In 1943, as Commander in Chief Pacific Fleet, observed tests of faulty submarine torpedoes at Pearl Harbor, 142; present at Pearl in 1943 when the skipper of the submarine Flying Fish (SS-229) was chewed out for misbehavior by his crew, 145-146

Nitze, Paul H.
As Secretary of the Navy in early 1964, visited the attack transport Fremont (APA-44) near Italy, 390-391

Norfolk Naval Shipyard, Portsmouth, Virginia
In the summer and fall of 1963 overhauled the attack transport Fremont (APA-44), 384-385

North Atlantic Treaty Organization (NATO)
In the mid-1950s a group of more than a dozen flag officers on the SACLant staff in Norfolk went to Paris for a NATO conference, 292-293; in early 1964 the attack transport Fremont (APA-44) participated in a NATO exercise in the Mediterranean, 397-398; amphibious exercises in the Mediterranean in the mid-1960s, 408; in the mid-1960s was involved in NATO negotiations concerning the Standing Naval Force Atlantic, 418-419

North Carolina, USS (BB-55)
In 1941, as the ship was preparing to go into commission, she had well-qualified officers assigned, 75-78, 83-84; festive commissioning ceremony in April 1941, 92-93, 95; in 1941 received lots of public attention and became known as "The Showboat," 78, 93-94; public thefts of silverware, 94-95; gunnery trials and practice in 1941-42, 93-94, 97, 99-101, 105-106; off-ship training for the crew in 1941, 97;

installation of radar in the summer of 1941, 78; in the autumn of 1941 was involved in shakedown training, 79-81, 86, 99; the ship was at the New York Navy Yard in December 1941 when Pearl Harbor was attacked and went to Norfolk soon afterward, 107-111; in late 1941 Captain Oscar Badger lost confidence in his navigator and replaced him, 82-83; role of the gunnery department, 84-87, 93-94; engineering department, 88-89; wardroom seating arrangements, 89; operation of the communications department, 95-96; operations around Maine in early 1942, 100-102; in the spring of 1942 entered the Pacific for the first time and received a warm welcome at Pearl Harbor, 103-105, 111-114; operations in the Pacific in the summer of 1942, including the Battle of the Eastern Solomons, 114-117; on 15 September 1942 the ship was torpedoed while in the Guadalcanal campaign, 46, 117-119; subsequent repairs at Pearl Harbor, 119, return to the South Pacific following repairs, 121, 123-126; the ship is now a memorial in Wilmington, North Carolina, 77-78, 112

Norway
The auxiliary presidential yacht Margie made a cruise in 1952 from Washington, D.C., to Mount Vernon, Virginia, with senior officials from Norway on board, 254-256

Nuclear Power Program
In September 1953 Rear Admiral Hyman Rickover had a hand in laying the keel for the Navy's second nuclear submarine, Seawolf (SSN-575) at Electric Boat, 228; in the early 1960s Naval Academy midshipmen were interviewed for entry into the nuclear power program, 358-359

Nuclear Weapons
In the 1950s the Martin Company developed the P6M jet-powered seaplane for nuclear weapons delivery, but it never went into production, 287-288; in the early 1970s the U.S. Navy would neither conform nor deny whether there were nuclear weapons on board warships that visited Japanese ports, 476

O'Connor, Rear Admiral John J., CHC, USN
As Chief of Chaplains in the late 1970s had contacts with the Navy Relief Society about funding for abortions, 550-551

Owens, Lieutenant (junior grade) Harley G., USN
During World War II served as engineer officer of the submarine Flying Fish (SS-229), 143, 154, 158-159

P6M Seamaster
Jet-powered seaplane that was developed by the Martin Company in the 1950s for nuclear weapons delivery but never went into production, 287-288

Packard, David
  As Deputy Secretary of Defense from 1969 to 1971, made a strong, favorable impression during reserve policy meetings, 458-459

Panama Canal
  In the summer of 1945, right after World War II, several submarines were passing through the canal, and one crew member fell overboard and drowned, 198-199

Paris, France
  In the mid-1950s a large group of NATO's senior officers gathered near Paris for a strategy meeting, 293; sights and sounds of the city, 293-294

Parlett, Ensign Roger V., Jr., USN (USNA, 1940)
  Naval Academy classmate who served with Burke in the battleship West Virginia (BB-48) after graduation, 56-57, 62, 73

Pay and Allowances
  In early 1943 a Navy commander found that his pay was less than that of the lowest paid able-bodied seaman on board the merchant ship in which he was traveling, 130; in the late 1960s Congress instituted cost of living allowance raises for retired military personnel, 530-531

Pearl Harbor, Hawaii
  In 1940-41 served as an operating base for ships of the Battle Force, 56-59, 61, 63-65; in June 1942 the new battleship North Carolina (BB-55) received a warm welcome when she arrived for the first time, 112; in the fall of 1942 the Pearl Harbor Navy Yard repaired the damaged battleship North Carolina (BB-55), 119-120; in 1943 was the site of tests of faulty submarine torpedoes, 142; in 1943, Eleanor Roosevelt, the President's wife, visited Pearl Harbor and talked with Commander Glynn Donaho, skipper of the submarine Flying Fish (SS-229), 144; visit by the Flying Fish to Pearl in the autumn of 1944, 174-175; in the summer of 1945 Vice Admiral Charles Lockwood greeted submarines at Pearl Harbor after they returned from a venture through the minefields around the Sea of Japan, 191-194; reaction on Ford Island when the war with Japan ended in August 1945, 195

Peniston, Captain Robert C, USN (Ret.) (USNA, 1947)
  In the early 1950s served as navigator of the presidential yacht Williamsburg (AGC-369), 243-245; activities after retirement, 245

Peterson, Commander Richard W., USN (USNA, 1931)
  Hard-to-please individual who in June 1944 became the first commanding officer of the submarine Icefish (SS-367), 153

Philippines
  In 1967 member nations of the Southeast Asia Treaty Organization held a conference in Manila, where conditions were dangerous, 440; that same year a congressional

subcommittee held a hearing in Baguio on the subject of the Vietnam War, 440-441; in early 1971 the U.S. Seventh Fleet held a quarterly scheduling conference at Baguio, 468

Philippine Sea, Battle of
Role of U.S. submarines in the June 1944 battle near the Mariana Islands, 160-161

Photography
In the summer of 1941 a news photographer got a dramatic shot of the battleship North Carolina (BB-55) firing at night, 93-94

Pinkston, Earl Roland (USNA, 1932)
In the 1930s taught at the Bullis prep school in Washington, D.C., later taught for many years on the faculty of the Naval Academy, 8

Pirie, Rear Admiral Robert B., USN (USNA, 1926)
In the mid-1950s served as chief of staff to Commander in Chief Atlantic Fleet, 285-286, 288-289; in 1956 tried to get Burke to smuggle some whiskey into the United States for him, 294; in 1956 went nightclubbing in Paris while there for a NATO conference, 294

Pittard, Captain George F., USN (USNA, 1934)
In the mid-1950s did a superb job while serving in the strategic plans section of the Atlantic Fleet staff, 285-286

Planning
In the mid-1950s the staff of Commander in Chief Atlantic Fleet was involved in planning in a variety of areas, 285-286; in the mid-1960s the OP-06 section of OpNav was doing planning in a variety of areas, including Vietnam, 417

Plusch, Chief Signalman William E., USN
In the early 1940s did an excellent job running the signal bridge of the new battleship North Carolina (BB-55), 81-82, 94, 96, 127

Potomac River
In the early 1950s Lieutenant Walter Slye served as pilot whenever the presidential yacht Williamsburg (AGC-369) steamed on the river, 242-244, 253-254

Preston, Lieutenant Commander James Tate, USN (USNA, 1945)
Was Burke's roommate at the Naval Academy, 18, 32, 55; served in a cruiser after being commissioned, 63; later killed when a kamikaze hit his ship in April 1945, 157

Prisoners of War
In the summer of 1945 the submarine Flying Fish (SS-229) captured a Japanese prisoner, 189-190

Promotion of Officers
 In the autumn of 1944 Burke passed a physical exam and was promoted to lieutenant commander, 177

Propulsion Plants
 On board the battleship Arkansas (BB-33) in 1937 the engineering spaces were uncomfortably hot, 36

Prostitution
 In the autumn of 1944, while the submarine Flying Fish (SS-229) was in overhaul in San Francisco, Burke and his wife stayed in an apartment building that apparently had once housed prostitutes, 177-178

Public Relations
 In the summer of 1967, Burke met with Naval Reserve public affairs officers in Los Angeles and got useful advice on working with the news media, 431-433

Puller, Lieutenant General Lewis B., USMC (Ret.)
 In the late 1960s Burke learned that Puller was well thought of by the news media, with the result that negative stories about him were squelched, 432

Puerto Rico
 In the late 1950s Submarine Division 63 operated out of Puerto Rico, principally in support of the Regulus missile program, 310-316, 323-324; in the late 1950s there was a strong Navy League chapter there, 313; social contacts during the late 1950s in San Juan for the Burke family, 316-320; in the late 1950s liquor was available at cheap prices in Puerto Rico, leading to temptations to smuggle it into the United States, 322

Puget Sound Navy Yard, Bremerton, Washington
 In the autumn of 1940 did repair and modernization work on several of the Pacific Fleet battleships, 68-69

Purdy, Lieutenant Commander George I., USNR (USNA, 1931)
 Expatriate American who lived and worked in Japan in the early 1970s, 479-480

Racial Issues
 In the late 1930s there was contention on whether to honor a black servant in the Burke plot of an Alexandria, Virginia, cemetery, 3; in June 1961 President John Kennedy made the commencement address at the Naval Academy's graduation and noticed that there were few black midshipmen, 351, 363-364, in the early 1970s, while serving as Commander U.S. Naval Forces Japan, Burke maintained an open-door policy and had a race-relations committee, 494-496; Burke felt that in the early 1970s the naval headquarters in Washington sent out people to various commands as spies to report on the racial situation, 509-515; in the early 1970s Navy flag officers attended black-white seminars, 513-514

Radar
    In the summer of 1941 the battleship North Carolina (BB-55) received a CXAM search radar and later got fire-control radar, 78; role of fire control radar in the shooting by the North Carolina, 99-100, 105; use of in 1944 by the submarine Flying Fish (SS-229) for night surface attacks, 154-155; in the late 1950s was used for terminal guidance of Regulus missiles launched from submarines, 310-311

Radio
    Use of for communications by the battleship West Virginia (BB-48) in the early 1940s when she was flagship for Commander Battleships, Battle Force, 59-61, 64; use of voice radio in 1953 by destroyers for tactical communications, 269-270

Ramage, Rear Admiral Lawson P., USN (USNA, 1931)
    In the late 1950s, as a cruiser division commander, advised Burke to seek duty in OpNav rather than the Naval Academy, 336

Ramey Air Force Base, Puerto Rico
    In the late 1950s was used to support Submarine Division 63 in its Regulus missile tests, 314-315

Ramsbotham, Captain Robert S., USN (USNA, 1929)
    In the late 1950s served as chief of staff for the Tenth Naval District in Puerto Rico, 312

Rauch, Rear Admiral Charles F., Jr., USN (USNA, 1948)
    In the early 1970s, as Assistant Chief of Personnel for Personal Affairs, sent representatives to various commands to assess the personnel situation, 509-513, 519

Recruiting/Retention
    Efforts in the mid-1950s to improve reenlistment rates in the Atlantic Fleet were hampered by heavy operating schedules, 295-296

Refo, Midshipman John F., USN (USNA, 1940)
    Fellow Virginian who became a friend of Burke when they were at the Naval Academy, 49

Religion
    Over the years Burke has had strong connections with the Episcopal Church and during his youth attended Episcopal High School in Alexandria, Virginia, 4-6, 8, 10-11, 15; in the late 1950s, while at the Naval War College, Burke wrote a dissertation on the Middle East and Islam, 300-301; energetic Christmas celebration in Puerto Rico in the late 1950s, 317-320; value of chaplains in counseling midshipmen and staff members in the early 1960s at the Naval Academy, 343-344, 352-354, 366-367

Regulus Missiles
   In the late 1950s Submarine Division 63 operated in the Caribbean, principally in support of the Regulus missile program, 310-316; precise navigation was important during the testing, 323-324; the program was slowed down and then canceled in the late 1950s because of the need to pay for the Polaris program, 318, 326

<u>Requin</u>, USS (SS-481)
   Submarine that was in Pearl Harbor at the end of war in August 1945, then returned to the East Coast, 196-197; a lookout was inadvertently left topside when the boat submerged, 197-198

Reserve Officers Association
   Well-organized group that in the late 1960s and early 1970s strongly represented the interests of its members in dealings with Congress, 444, 446-447, 453

Reserve Officers Training Corps (ROTC)
   In the late 1960s and early 1970s, many universities dropped their ROTC units because of unrest related to the Vietnam War, 448-450

Reuther, Lieutenant (junior grade) Roland A., USN
   Mustang officer who served in the submarines <u>Seahorse</u> (SS-304) and <u>Flying Fish</u> (SS-229) during World War II, 166-167, 183

Ricketts, Lieutenant Claude V., USN (USNA, 1929)
   Was highly respected while serving as first lieutenant of the battleship <u>West Virginia</u> (BB-48) in the early 1940s, 70-71

Rickover, Rear Admiral Hyman G., USN (USNA, 1922)
   In September 1953 had a hand in laying the keel for the Navy's second nuclear submarine, <u>Seawolf</u> (SSN-575) at Electric Boat, 228; in the early 1960s interviewed Naval Academy midshipmen for entry into the nuclear power program, 358-359; in the early 1960s Naval Academy Superintendent John Davidson shielded those below him in the chain of command from Admiral Rickover, 360-361

Risser, Lieutenant Commander Robert D., USN (USNA, 1934)
   In 1943-44 served as commanding officer of the submarine <u>Flying Fish</u> (SS-229), 148, 150-151, 159, 164-166, 170, 172, 180-181, 184, 186-189, 193-194; marriage of in 1945, 193

Robertson, Midshipman Alexander Stuart, Jr., USN (USNA, 1940)
   Attended Bullis prep school with Burke in the 1930s and later entered the Naval Academy in 1936 but later dropped out, 7-8, 19

Robertson, Lieutenant General Donn J., USMC (Ret.)
   In the mid-1970s served as president of the Navy Relief Society, 541, 544-545

Roosevelt, Eleanor
   In 1943 the President's wife visited Pearl Harbor and talked with Commander Glynn Donaho, skipper of the submarine Flying Fish (SS-229), 144

Roosevelt, President Franklin D.
   On 20 January 1937 Naval Academy midshipmen marched in a rain-soaked parade in Washington, D.C., to honor to second inauguration of President Roosevelt, 18-20; in the summer of 1939 hosted the King and Queen of England, 48

Roosevelt Roads Naval Air Station, Puerto Rico
   In the late 1950s served as a base for Submarine Division 63, which was testing Regulus missiles, 311-314, 316; quarters for submarine staff officers, 312-313, 316, 324

ROTC
   See: Reserve Officers Training Corps (ROTC)

Royal Navy
   In the summer of 1941 the New York Navy Yard repaired damaged British warships, 97-98; in December 1941 the battleship Duke of York was at Norfolk after having brought Prime Minister Winston Churchill to the United States, 110-111; in the summer of 1942 a British liaison officer served on board the battleship North Carolina (BB-55), 114-115; in the spring of 1964, Burke met several British naval officers when the attack transport Fremont (APA-44) visited Malta, 395; by that time British power in the Mediterranean had faded, 398

Runner, USS (SS-476)
   Submarine that was based at San Juan, Puerto Rico, in the late 1950s during missile tests, 313

Sabin, Lieutenant Commander Lorenzo S., Jr., USN (USNA, 1921)
   Fine man who served shortly before World War II as gunnery officer of the battleship West Virginia (BB-48), 75

Sablefish, USS (SS-303)
   In 1950 got a snorkel installed during a yard period, 229; in the early 1950s operated out of New London, Connecticut and did well in competition with other boats in her squadron, 230-238, 240; in late 1950 was involved in ASW exercises against other submarines, 233; the only black personnel in the crew were stewards, 235; gave rides to Submarine School students in an effort to get the good ones to join the crew, 238-239, 285

Salzer, Vice Admiral Robert S., USN (Ret.)
   Served very capably from 1978 to 1982 as president of the Navy Relief Society, 541, 544-545, 550-551; his wife Jane was very helpful in a volunteer role, 545, 552

Sanctuary, USS (AH-17)
In the early 1970s was converted to a dependent support ship and also served as a test ship for mixed crews of men and women, 515-519

San Francisco, California
While on leave in San Francisco in 1943, several crew members of the submarine Flying Fish (SS-229) were drunk and disorderly, 145-146; in late 1944-early 1945 the Flying Fish had an overhaul at Hunters Point Navy Yard, 175, 178-182; while the ship was in overhaul Burke and his wife stayed in an apartment building that apparently had once housed prostitutes, 177-178; hospitality at Mom Chung's place in San Francisco in late 1944, 180-181

San Juan, Puerto Rico
In the late 1950s was a base for U.S. submarines, 313; social contacts in the late 1950s for the Burke family, 316-320; in that period Felisa Rincon de Gautier was the popular, energetic mayor of San Juan, 317-320

Sasebo, Japan
In the early 1970s the U.S. Fleet Activities complex at Sasebo was returned to the Japanese and then had to be retrieved, 476; Burke made an interesting visit to the area, 500-501

Schacht, Commander Kenneth G., USN (USNA, 1935)
Submarine division commander with whom Burke had a squabble in 1952 while Burke was commanding the Sablefish (SS-303), 230, 240

Scheu, Lieutenant Donald T., USN (USNA, 1940)
Was killed in February 1944 when the submarine Scorpion (SS-278) was lost, 157

Schmidt, Captain John Sneed, USN (USNA, 1937)
In the early 1960s served as academic aide to the superintendent of the Naval Academy, 340, 351, 356, 363

Schumm, Captain Brooke, USN (USNA, 1927)
In the late 1940s headed distribution of enlisted personnel while serving in the Bureau of Naval Personnel, 210

Seabees
In the early 1970s were involved in construction projects to set up the island of Diego Garcia in the Indian Ocean as a fleet support facility, 519-521

Seahorse, USS (SS-304)
Exploits during World War II while under the command of Commander Slade Cutter, 166-167

SEALs
In the fall of 1964 a group of SEALS got in trouble in Spain and had to be disciplined, 405-406; in Vietnam in 1966 the same SEALs were commended for their actions, 406, 429

SEATO
See: Southeast Asia Treaty Organization

Seattle, USS (AOE-3)
Fast combat support ship that in the early 1970s was being loosely run, lost the top of her radar mast to a bridge, and the captain was relieved for cause, 505-506, 515

Seawolf, USS (SSN-575)
The keel for the Navy's second nuclear submarine was laid in September 1953 at Electric Boat, 228

Security Problems
While working in the plans section of OpNav in the mid-1960s, Lieutenant Commander Ace Lyons inadvertently left classified material exposed when he left his office for a time, 417-418

Semmes, Vice Admiral Benedict, J., Jr., USN (USNA, 1934)
In 1953, while serving in the Bureau of Naval Personnel, told Burke he could have essentially whatever he wanted for his next assignment because he hadn't embarrassed the Navy while serving in the presidential yacht Williamsburg (AGC-369), 264-266; in 1954, while on the ComDesLant staff, supported Burke in being able to retain command of the destroyer Harold J. Ellison (DD-864), 283; advised Burke on the path to flag rank, 284-285; in 1966, as Chief of Naval Personnel, transferred Burke soon after his selection to flag rank, 422

Service Force Atlantic Fleet
In the mid-1970s had control of several naval stations on the East Coast, some of which were closed down, 504, 506-507; operated underway replenishment ships, 505-508, 515, 524-527; Burke was impressed by the aviators sent to command Service Force ships, 507-508; the Service Force didn't get the quality of people that other parts of the Navy did, 508; Burke resented what he considered spying on his people by representatives from Washington, 509-510; alcohol abuse problems in the early 1970s among force personnel, 511-512; in the early 1970s the dependent support ship Sanctuary (AH-17) was used as a test ship for mixed crews of men and women, 515-519; among the subordinate commands were Seabees, who were involved in construction projects on the island of Diego Garcia, 519-521; in January 1975 was merged with other commands to form the new Naval Surface Force, Atlantic Fleet, 522

Seventh Fleet, U.S.
In early 1971 the fleet held a quarterly scheduling conference at Baguio in the Philippines, 468-469; role of Commander U.S. Naval Forces Japan in supporting the Seventh Fleet in the early 1970s, 470

Sexual Harassment
In the early 1970s, the Navy investigated a complaint of sexual harassment that involved officers from the dependent support ship Sanctuary (AH-17), 517-519

Shangri-La
Presidential retreat in the Maryland mountains that was operated in the early 1950s by Navy stewards, 242, 247, 259, 261-262

Shannon, Captain Edgar F., USNR
Naval Reserve officer who served in the late 1960s and early 1970s as president of the University of Virginia, 447-450; led campus protests during the Vietnam war, which probably prevented him from making admiral, 449-450

Shaw, Captain Claude B., USN (USNA, 1942)
In the early 1970s, as Commander Fleet Activities Sasebo, Japan, invited Burke for a visit to the area, 500-501

Shear, Ensign Harold E., USN (USNA, 1942)
In the summer of 1939 met his future wife in Maine while on a Naval Academy training cruise, 50; was married in Maine in April 1942 after restrictions were removed on marriages of academy graduates, 102

Shepard, Lieutenant Commander Alan B., USN (USNA, 1945)
In the mid-1950s lived near Burke in Virginia Beach, 299; in the late 1950s was a student at the Naval War College until leaving class early to take part in the space program, 306-307

Shepard, Commander Andrew G., USN (USNA, 1917)
Individual who did a fine job as first executive officer of the battleship North Carolina (BB-55) when she was commissioned in 1941, 77, 87, 97, 108, 110

Shepherd, Lieutenant Commander John E., USN (USNA, 1939)
Attended Submarine School in 1943, 135; died when the submarine Trigger (SS-237) was lost in March 1945, 113

Sieglaff, Commander William Bernard, USN (USNA, 1931)
In early 1945 was project officer for the program to equip submarines with FM sonar to prepare them to penetrate Japanese minefields, 182-184, 192; in the late 1940s had tours of duty as the submarine detail officer in the Bureau of Naval Personnel and as a submarine division commander, 213

Simmons, Ensign Kenneth G., USN (USNA, 1940)
During World War II served as division officer for a 5-inch gun battery on board the battleship North Carolina (BB-55), 85

Sixth Fleet, U.S.
In early 1964 the attack transport Fremont (APA-44) visited a number of ports and participated in various exercises while in the Mediterranean, 390-394; Vice Admiral William Gentner, Commander Sixth Fleet, visited the ship, 394-395

Sixth Naval District
As district commandant of the in the mid-1970s, Burke had many contacts with the people and institutions of the Charleston, South Carolina, 529-530; he was double-hatted as commander of the Charleston Naval Base, 531-532

Slye, Lieutenant Walter C., USNR
In the early 1950s served as first lieutenant and Potomac River pilot on board the presidential yacht Williamsburg (AGC-369), 242-244, 253-254

Small, Rear Admiral Walter L., Jr., USN (USNA, 1938)
During World War II served as executive officer of the submarine Flying Fish (SS-229), 140, 143-144, 147-148, 150, 153; in the mid-1950s served in the operational planning section of the staff of Commander in Chief Atlantic Fleet, 286; in the mid-1960s was involved in NATO negotiations concerning the Standing Naval Force Atlantic, 418-419; in the early 1970s attended a race-relations session, 513

Smedberg, Vice Admiral William R. III, USN (USNA, 1926)
As Chief of Naval Personnel in the early 1960s had frequent conversations with the superintendents of the Naval Academy on how programs were going, 373

Smith, Rear Admiral Daniel F., Jr., USN (USNA, 1932)
In August 1970 turned over command of U.S. Naval Forces Japan to Burke, 464-465

Smith, Captain James C., USNR (USNA, 1940)
Expatriate American who lived and worked in Japan in the early 1970s, 479

Smith, Rear Admiral Jerome F., Jr., USN, (USNA, 1961)
In the early 1960s was a fine midshipman at the Naval Academy, later served as commandant of the Industrial College of the Armed Forces, 341-342

Smith, USS (DD-378)
Destroyer that was heavily damaged by the Japanese in October 1942 during the Battle of Santa Cruz Islands, 119-121

Snyder, Ensign Joseph C., USN (USNA, 1940)
In 1941 served as a detail officer in the Bureau of Navigation, 75

Snyder, Richard
    As Foreign Service officer in the early 1970s was only partially cooperative in the Navy's dealings with the Japanese Government on a plan to homeport an aircraft carrier and her escorts in Yokosuka, 470-471, 474-476

Sonar
    Installation of FM sonar in the submarine Flying Fish (SS-229) in early 1945 to prepare the submarine for Japanese minefields, 182-183

Southeast Asia Treaty Organization
    In 1967 representatives from member nations held a conference at Manila in the Philippines, 440

Soviet Navy
    In the mid-1950s Admiral Jerauld Wright offered a case of whiskey to the first skipper who forced a Soviet submarine to surface, 296

Spain
    In 1962, shortly after his marriage, the Prince Juan Carlos visited the U.S. Naval Academy, 382-383; in early 1964 the attack transport Fremont (APA-44) made a port visit to Barcelona, 397-398; Spanish desire to reclaim Gibraltar, 398; in the fall of 1964 U.S. amphibious forces staged the large-scale Exercise Steel Pike near Rota, 405-406; in late 1964-early 1965 the amphibious transport dock La Salle (LPD-3) visited Barcelona and Valencia, 398, 406, 411-412

Spruance, USS (DD-963)
    Commissioning ceremony in September 1975 at Pascagoula, Mississippi, 535-536

Standing Naval Force Atlantic
    In the mid-1960s Rear Admiral Walt Small was involved in NATO negotiations concerning the Standing Naval Force Atlantic, 418-419

State Department, U.S.
    In 1971-72 U.S. diplomatic officials in Tokyo did not really embrace a program to homeport an aircraft carrier and her escorts in Yokosuka, so U.S. naval officials in Japan had to work around the embassy, 463, 470-476

Staubach, Midshipman Roger T., USN (USNA, 1965)
    Top-notch football player who starred for the Naval Academy in the early 1960s, 348

Stennis, Senator John C.
    In the late 1960s was involved in getting cost of living allowance raises for retired military personnel, 530-531; in 1975 attended the commissioning of the destroyer Spruance (DD-963) at Pascagoula, Mississippi, 535

Stevens, Commander Wynne A., USN
Destroyerman and attorney who represented Burke during an investigation in the mid-1950s into a collision between the destroyer Harold J. Ellison (DD-864) and the submarine Jallao (SS-368), 281-282

Stonington, Connecticut
Pleasant community where several Navy people lived in the mid-1940s, 202-203

Street, Ensign Abbot P., USN (USNA, 1940)
One of several Virginians in the Naval Academy class of 1940, 39-40, 52; as an ensign served in the light cruiser Milwaukee (CL-5).

Stryker, Lieutenant Commander Joe W., USN (USNA, 1925)
In the late 1930s served as a duty officer at the Naval Academy, 82; in early 1942 became navigator of the battleship North Carolina (BB-55) and served several skippers in that role, 82-83, 92, 115, 128, 385; impressed on Burke the importance of the amphibious force, 385

Styer, Rear Admiral Charles W., USN (USNA, 1918)
As Commander Submarine Force Atlantic Fleet in 1945, visited Pearl Harbor to arrange for the transfer of submarines from the Pacific to the Atlantic, 196-197; around the end of World II a domineering nurse controlled when Styer could see his grandchild, 206

Styer, Commander Charles W., Jr., USN (USNA, 1941)
During World War II served in the submarine Flying Fish (SS-229), 140, 143; he and his wife had a child around the end of World War II and had to put up with a domineering nurse, 205; in the late 1950s commanded Submarine Division 63 in the Atlantic and was involved in Regulus missile testing, 310

Submarine Division 63
In the late 1950s operated in the Caribbean, principally in support of the Regulus missile program, 310-316, 323-325; officers in the division had some problems in the late 1950s so that Burke got one skipper and one exec relieved of duty, 320-321; Burke had a practice of giving individual submarines a free practice operational readiness inspection that helped prepare them for the real thing, 322, 328-329; the Regulus program was slowed down and then canceled in the late 1950s because of the need to pay for the Polaris program, 318, 326; after the missile mission ceased, the boats were involved in antisubmarine missions, 329-331

Submarine School, New London, Connecticut
In 1939 was visited by Naval Academy midshipmen on cruise, 44; when he arrived at the school in the spring of 1943, Burke found people were more relaxed than those in the two battleships in which he had served, 131; rundown on Burke's classmates, 132-133; living accommodations for students, 133; instructors and curriculum in early 1943, 134-137; in the early 1950s the submarine Sablefish (SS-303) gave rides

to Submarine School students in an effort to get the good ones to join the boat's crew, 238-239

Submarine Warfare
War patrols in the Pacific in 1943-45 by the submarine <u>Flying Fish</u> (SS-229), 147-148, 151-152, 154-156, 160-161, 169-171; in 1943 Representative Andrew May revealed in an interview with the media that Japanese antisubmarine forces were not setting their depth charges deep enough, and casualties increased afterward, 174; in 1945 U.S. submarines had FM sonar installed and used it to penetrate Japanese minefields, 182-183, 186-189

Surface Force Atlantic Fleet, Naval
Was created in January 1975 by combining several commands that had previously been separate, 522-523

Surface Warfare
In the mid-1970s a new surface warfare designator was created in the U.S. Navy, 523-524

Temple, Rear Admiral Harry B., USN (USNA, 1924)
In 1953 commanded a hunter-killer task group built around an escort carrier, 271-272

Thebaud, Commander Leo H., USN (USNA, 1913)
As executive officer at the Naval Academy in the late 1930s and early 1940s provided an excellent example of leadership, 23-24

<u>Theodore Roosevelt</u>, USS (CVN-71)
In 1990 Burke visited this aircraft carrier and was very much impressed by the professionalism of her enlisted crew, 234-235

Torpedoes
On 15 September 1942, the Japanese submarine <u>I-19</u> torpedoed the battleship <u>North Carolina</u> (BB-55) and the aircraft carrier <u>Wasp</u> (CV-7), 117-119; problems during World War II with the Mark XIV torpedo, 135, 141-142; in late 1943 a torpedo fired by the submarine <u>Flying Fish</u> (SS-229) made a circular run, 147; successful attacks in 1943-44 by the <u>Flying Fish</u>, 152, 155-156; in 1944 the submarine <u>Tullibee</u> (SS-284) was sunk by the circular run of a torpedo, 157

Training
Naval Academy summer cruises in the late 1930s provided both sightseeing and training, 34-42, 50-51; in the summer of 1941, members of the crew of the battleship <u>North Carolina</u> (BB-55) received off-ship training at various sites, 97; in 1941-42 the <u>North Carolina</u> was involved in underway shakedown training and gunnery training, 79-81, 86, 99-101, 105-106; in 1943 at the Submarine School in New London, 135-136; training of the crew of the submarine <u>Flying Fish</u> (SS-229) in early 1945 in

preparation for entering Japanese minefields, 182-183, 185-186; by the summer of 1945 the submarine Guardfish (SS-217) had been taken off war patrols and was serving at Pearl Harbor as a training boat for prospective commanding officers and as a target for training ASW forces, 194-195; in the late 1940s the Dale Carnegie course proved very helpful to Burke in enabling him to master public speaking, 211-212; in the early 1950s the fleet training group at Guantanamo Bay, Cuba, was perceived as merciless by skippers of ships that went there, 266; in mid-1953 prospective skippers of destroyers received training at Key West, 267; need for training in the early 1950s of inexperienced officers on board the destroyer Harold J. Ellison (DD-864), 269-271, 276-278; refresher training in 1955 at Guantanamo Bay, Cuba, for the crew of the Harold J. Ellison, 278-279; in the late 1950s the boats of Submarine Division 63 were involved in antisubmarine training missions, 329-331; in 1966-67 Amphibious Group Three in California oversaw the training of Navy boat personnel near Mare Island, California, to prepare them for operations in and around Vietnam, 426, 429-430, 433-434

Triebel, Captain Charles O., USN (USNA, 1929)
As Commander Submarine Squadron Eight in 1950, complained about the difficulty learning the thoughts of his submarine skippers, 400

Truman, President Harry S.
In 1952 stood low in public opinion polls, 232; in a 1952 news conference did an impressive job in talking to reporters, 240-241; shortly before Christmas in 1952 he and his family entertained the crew of the presidential yacht Williamsburg (AGC-369) at the White House, 245-246; was occasionally on board the Williamsburg himself, 251, 257-257; Burke assessed Truman's inner circle people as being less impressive than those of his successor, Dwight Eisenhower, 251-252

Tullibee, USS (SS-284)
In 1944 was sunk by the circular run of one of her own torpedoes, 39, 157

Twelfth Naval District, San Francisco, California
While on leave in San Francisco in 1943, several crew members of the submarine Flying Fish (SS-229) were drunk and disorderly, leading to chewing out for those in their chain of command, 145-146

Twisdale, Lieutenant Colonel Robert H., USMC (USNA, 1943)
In the early 1960s did a fine job as the senior Marine stationed at the Naval Academy, 337-338, 359

Tyree, Vice Admiral John A., Jr., USN (USNA, 1933)
In 1950, as a submarine division commander, took Burke and the Sablefish (SS-303) to sea without giving Burke a chance to become familiar with the boat, 230; valuable advice to Burke regarding a missing publication, 230-231; in 1952, while in BuPers, told Burke he would be going to command the presidential yacht Williamsburg (AGC-369), 231-232; in 1953 discussed Burke's next assignment, 264; in 1970, as

Naval Inspector General, directed Burke to attend a briefing at the Pentagon, despite the fact that Burke had other plans, 462-463

Uchida, Admiral K., Japanese Maritime Self-Defense Force
In the early 1970s held discussions with U.S. naval officers about homeporting an aircraft carrier and her escorts in Yokosuka and supported the program, 473-474; comments on a Japanese writer's suicide in 1970, 487; other contacts with Burke, 499-500

Ultra
Limited distribution of Ultra messages on board the submarine Flying Fish (SS-229) during World War II, 174

Vaughn, Major General Harry H., USAR
In the early 1950s served as military aide to President Harry S. Truman, 246-247

Venereal Disease
In 1944 a member of the crew of the submarine Flying Fish (SS-229) was treated for venereal disease with a new drug called penicillin, 169

Vieques
Site of Marine Corps practice amphibious landings in the spring of 1965, 415

Vietnam War
During the mid-1960s the OP-06 organization in OpNav was involved with current plans for Vietnam, 417; in late 1966, Burke went on a fact-finding tour to South Vietnam, 406, 426-429, 439; in 1966-67 Amphibious Group Three in California oversaw the training of Navy boat personnel near Mare Island, California, to prepare them for operations in and around Vietnam, 426, 429-430, 433-434; in 1967 the Amphibious Force Seventh Fleet commanded landing operations in Vietnam, 436-437; that same year a congressional subcommittee held a hearing in the Philippines on the subject of the Vietnam War, 440-441; in the late 1960s and early 1970s, many universities dropped their ROTC units because of unrest related to the Vietnam War, 448-450

Wada, Doug
Japanese-American who in the early 1970s served as a go-between from Commander U.S. Naval Forces Japan to the Japanese Government concerning a program to homeport an aircraft carrier and her escorts in Yokosuka, 471-472, 484

Ward, Lieutenant Alfred G., USN (USNA, 1932)
Top-notch individual who was the first fire control officer when the battleship North Carolina (BB-55) was commissioned in 1941, 76-77, 84, 127; had a knack for dealing with the ship's difficult commanding officer, Captain Oscar Badger, 82-83

Ward, Rear Admiral Norvell G., USN (USNA, 1935)
In 1966-67, as Commander U.S. Naval Forces Vietnam, hosted Burke and explained the war situation, 428, 438-439

Warden, Captain Horace D., MC, USN
Navy doctor who served in the early 1950s as personal physician to President Harry S. Truman, 240-241, 246, 249; in 1966, as commanding officer of the San Diego Naval Hospital, was able to advise Burke about his son's brain tumor, 423

Warder, Rear Admiral Frederick B., USN (USNA, 1925)
In early 1960, as Commander Submarine Force Atlantic Fleet, visited Puerto Rico to observe operations during Exercise Springboard, 314-315, 325; in the late 1950s invited Burke to serve as officer in charge of the Submarine School, but Burke declined, 335-336

Warner, Lieutenant Commander Arthur H., Jr., USN (USNA, 1942)
In 1950, following a tour of duty in the Bureau of Naval Personnel, became executive officer of the submarine Sablefish (SS-303), 229, 231, 237-238

Washington, D.C.
On 20 January 1937 Naval Academy midshipmen marched in a rain-soaked parade on Pennsylvania Avenue to honor to second inauguration of President Franklin D. Roosevelt, 18-20

Washington, USS (BB-56)
Battleship that was commissioned in 1941 but received far less public attention than her sister, North Carolina (BB-55), 78; gunnery training, 106; in early 1942 operated around Maine, then left in March for Britain, and the embarked flag officer, Rear Admiral John Wilcox, was lost overboard, 101

Wasp, USS (CV-7)
Operations with the battleship North Carolina (BB-55) in 1942, 101, 112, 114, 117-118; torpedoed and sunk on 15 September 1942, 117-118

Watkins, Commander Frank T., USN (USNA, 1922)
During World War II served as a submarine division commander and was given brief command of the Flying Fish (SS-229) for combat experience, 139, 148-149

Watkins, Commander James D., USN (USNA, 1949)
In the late 1950s was an outstanding young executive officer of the submarine Barbero (SSG-317), 321, 326; in the mid-1960s, while living in San Diego, he and his sons were kind to the Burkes at a time when their son had a brain tumor, 424

Weather
On 20 January 1937 Naval Academy midshipmen marched in a rain-soaked parade in Washington, D.C., to honor to second inauguration of President Franklin D.

Roosevelt, 18-20; in late 1943 the submarine <u>Flying Fish</u> (SS-229) encountered such heavy seas near Hong Kong that a crew member was nearly washed overboard, 152-153

Weisner, Vice Admiral Maurice F., USN (USNA, 1941)
In 1971, as Commander Seventh Fleet, gave orders to implement the homeporting of an aircraft carrier and her escorts in Yokosuka, Japan, 467-470

Weems, Captain Philip Van Horn, USN (Ret.) (USNA, 1912)
In the early 1960s was still wrestling at the Naval Academy, 50 years after he had graduated, 344

Wells, Lieutenant Commander Heyden F., USN (USNA, 1938)
Shortly after World War II served in the Bureau of Naval Personnel, 208-209

Wentworth, Rear Admiral Ralph S., Jr., USN (USNA, 1944)
In the early 1970s, as Commander Cruiser-Destroyer Flotilla Two, commented on Burke's penchant for complaining about things he objected to, 512

<u>West Virginia</u>, USS (BB-48)
In 1940-41 was based with other fleet ships at Pearl Harbor, 56-59, 61, 63-65; Commander Boyd Alexander was a difficult executive officer, 57-58, 70, 73; in 1941 Burke encountered a new staff officer with whom he'd previously had an unpleasant experience at the Naval Academy, 27-28; in the early 1940s junior officers went on liberty in Southern California, 46; shipboard communications, 59-61, 64, 76; equator-crossing ceremony, 161-162; Vice Admiral William Pye was embarked as Commander Battleships, Battle Force, 58-59, 61; life in the junior officers' mess, 61-62; in the autumn of 1940 the ship returned to the West Coast for modernization and for crew recreation, 67-69, 73; Naval Reserve officers in the crew were not treated with the respect they deserved, 69-70, 442, 451; antiquated antiaircraft guns, 69, 77; the ship had some quality officers, such as Lieutenant Claude Rickets, 70-71; assessment of the enlisted crew members, 71-72; disciplinary problems, 72; in June 1942 the ship was still at Pearl Harbor, 112-113; an enlisted man from the crew in the early 1940s subsequently attended the Naval Academy and became a submariner, 321

Wilcox, Rear Admiral John W., Jr., USN (USNA, 1905)
In 1941 had his Battleship Division Six flag briefly in the <u>North Carolina</u> (BB-55), 126; in March 1942, while his flagship <u>Washington</u> (BB-56) was en route Britain, Wilcox was lost overboard, 101

Wilkinson, Rear Admiral Eugene P., USN
In the late 1940s, while working in the nuclear power program at Westinghouse, put on an act that gave the impression to fellow submariners that he was dumb, 226-227; later gave the same impression while at the Naval War College in the late 1950s,

227, 304-305; in 1970, after serving as chief of staff to Commander U.S. Forces Japan, gave Burke good reasons for being commander U.S. Naval Forces Japan, 461

Williamsburg, USS (AGC-369)
In 1952 went to Key West, Florida, to provide support for President Harry S. Truman and his party, 239-240, 260-261; in the early 1950s, many of the enlisted crew members had been on board for many years until Burke began making changes, 241-242, 244; the crew also ran the mess at the White House and the presidential retreat Shangri-La, 242, 247, 259, 261-262; because of the presidential spotlight, the crew was allowed zero tolerance for mistakes, 247-250; various trips on the Potomac, 242-244, 253-254, 254-258, 263; in 1952 the auxiliary yacht Margie made a cruise to Mount Vernon with senior officials from Norway on board, 254-256; in 1953 underwent overhaul at the Norfolk Naval Shipyard, 253; President Dwight Eisenhower had a conference on board with representatives from France, 253; serving of alcohol on board, 259-260; protocol was observed, 261; in early 1953 the ship went to Norfolk for a meeting between Admiral Lynde McCormick and President Dwight Eisenhower, 234; handling characteristics, 256-257; the ship was decommissioned in June 1953 because of a recommendation to Eisenhower that he not keep it, 87, 264; service in the ship gave Burke a wide range of choices for his next assignment, 264-266

Wilson, Lieutenant Commander David Spencer (USNA, 1940)
In 1937, as a midshipman, went sightseeing in England, 39-40; personality, 40; as an ensign served in the battleship Pennsylvania (BB-38), 62, 68, 131; in mid-1943 entered Submarine School, 131-132, 138; lost with the submarine Tullibee (SS-284) in 1944, 39, 157

Wilson, Major General Winston P., USAFR
In 1970, as head of the National Guard Bureau, testified to Congress in the wake of the incident that year in which National Guardsmen shot and killed antiwar protesters at Kent State University, 445-446

Winslow, Captain Edward H., USN (USNA, 1942)
In the mid-1960s commanded the amphibious transport dock La Salle (LPD-3) after having served on board a number of other ships previously, 408

Wisconsin, SS (Commercial Cargo Ship)
In early 1943 transported Burke and other servicemen from Noumea, New Caledonia, to the United States, 129-131; a Navy commander traveling on board found that his pay was less than that of the lowest paid able-bodied seaman in the crew of the Wisconsin, 130

Women in Service
In the early 1970s the dependent support ship Sanctuary (AH-17) was used as a test ship for mixed crews of men and women, 515-518

Wood, Captain Chester C. Wood, USN (USNA, 1924)
In late 1941 was the first commanding officer of the destroyer Bristol (DD-453), 109; in the mid-1940s rented a house to the Burkes, 202

Woods, Rear Admiral Edgar L., MC, USN
In the late 1930s commanded the naval hospital at Annapolis, Maryland, 20, 43, 56; in late 1941 was commanding officer of the naval hospital at Portsmouth, Virginia, 109, 111; during World War II served as an inspector for Navy medical activities on the West Coast, 104, 175-176

Wright, Admiral Jerauld, USN (USNA, 1918)
Was tough while serving as a Naval Academy duty officer in the late 1930s, 290; very sharp while serving in the mid-1950s as Commander in Chief Atlantic Fleet, 289-291; spent a good deal of time on his NATO job as Supreme Allied Commander Atlantic, 292; in the mid-1950s offered a case of whiskey to the first skipper who forced a Soviet submarine to surface, 296; in the late 1950s was an outstanding guest speaker at the Naval War College, 308; received witty messages from Vice Admiral Cat Brown, 413

Wylie, Lieutenant Joseph C., Jr., USN (USNA, 1932)
As a company officer at the Naval Academy in the late 1930s, he displayed admirable leadership qualities, 22; in late 1941 was executive officer of the destroyer Bristol (DD-453), 109

Yokosuka, Japan
In the summer of 1970 Burke and his wife Betty had a hotsy bath in this city that had the headquarters of U.S. Naval Forces Japan, 465; in the 1970s Ichiro Masuoka was the city's unofficial ambassador to the U.S. Navy, 465-466, 472, 484, 498-499; under a plan that went into effect for a time in 1970, the presence of the U.S. Navy in Yokosuka was substantially reduced and then reinstated, 467, 473-475; in early 1971 Commander Seventh Fleet gave orders to implement the homeporting of an aircraft carrier and her escorts in Yokosuka, and the issue was subsequently negotiated, 467-476; in the early 1970s the U.S. base at Yokosuka reported to Commander Service Force Seventh Fleet, 470; in the early 1970s the mayor was a practical Socialist, 476-477, 491; a local tailor made clothes for Burke at bargain prices, 491-492

Yorktown (Virginia) Naval Weapons Station
In the early 1970s provided weapons replenishment to Atlantic Fleet ships, 506-507

Young, Commander Charles M., USN (USNA, 1942)
In the mid-1950s served in the operational planning section of the staff of Commander in Chief Atlantic Fleet, 286-288

Zemmer, Lieutenant Commander Harold M., USN (USNA, 1927)
   Unsociable officer who served during World War II in the gunnery department of the battleship North Carolina (BB-55), 86-87, 100

Zumwalt, Admiral Elmo R., Jr., USN (USNA, 1943)
   As aide to Secretary of the Navy Paul Nitze in early 1964, visited the attack transport Fremont (APA-44) near Italy, 390-391; soon after he became Chief of Naval Operations in 1970, the decision was made to withdraw U.S. naval forces from Japan, 463; later he had discussions with the Japanese about homeporting a U.S. aircraft carrier and her escorts in Yokosuka, Japan, 473; in the summer of 1971 he and his wife visited Japan, and he talked with U.S. Navy enlisted men there, 493-494, 497-498, 511; Burke's assessment of Zumwalt's tenure as CNO, 496, 509-512, 518, 525; changed previous rules on how long admirals could serve, 538

www.ingramcontent.com/pod-product-compliance
Lightning Source LLC
Chambersburg PA
CBHW082147070526
44585CB00020B/2125